Pretty Guardian ★

Sailor Moon

1

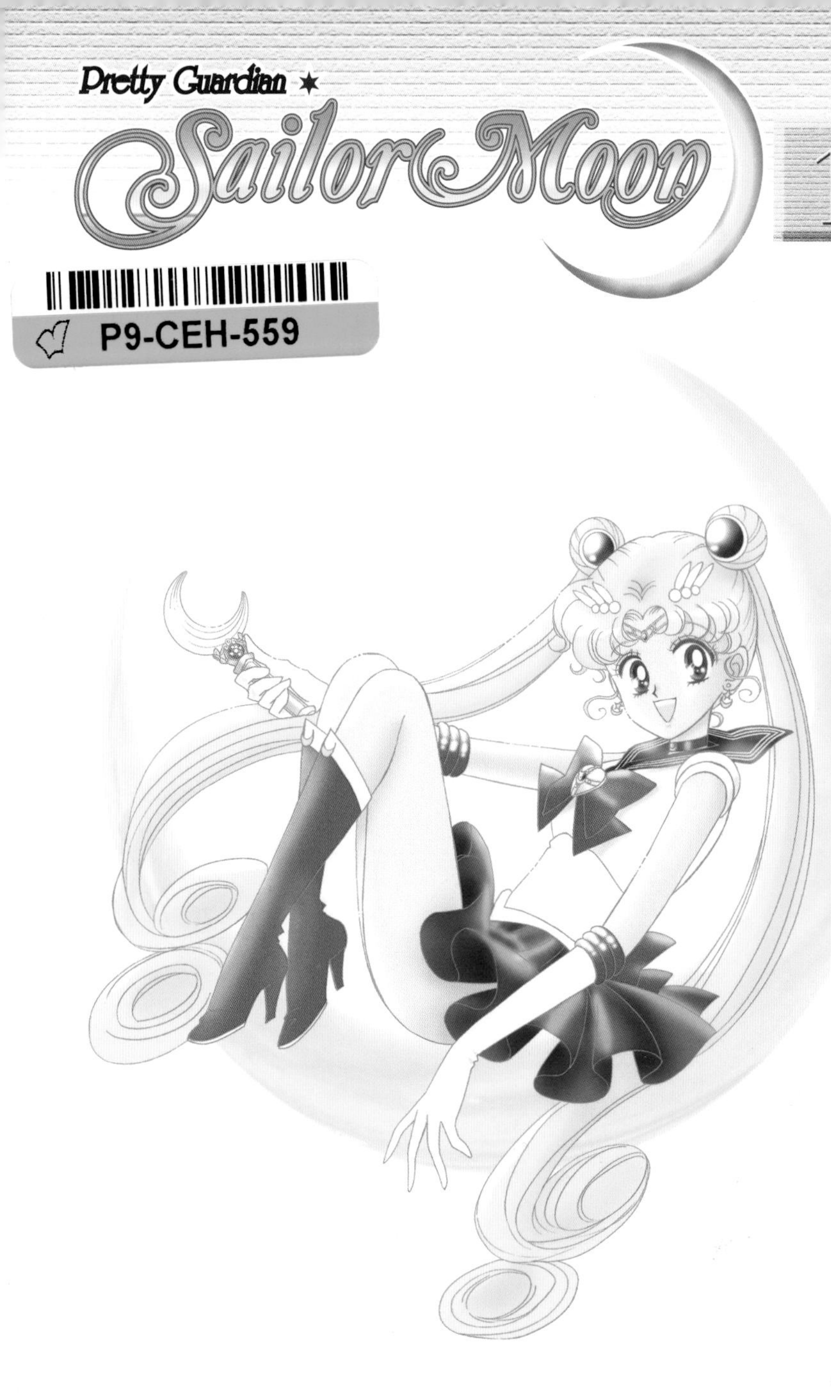

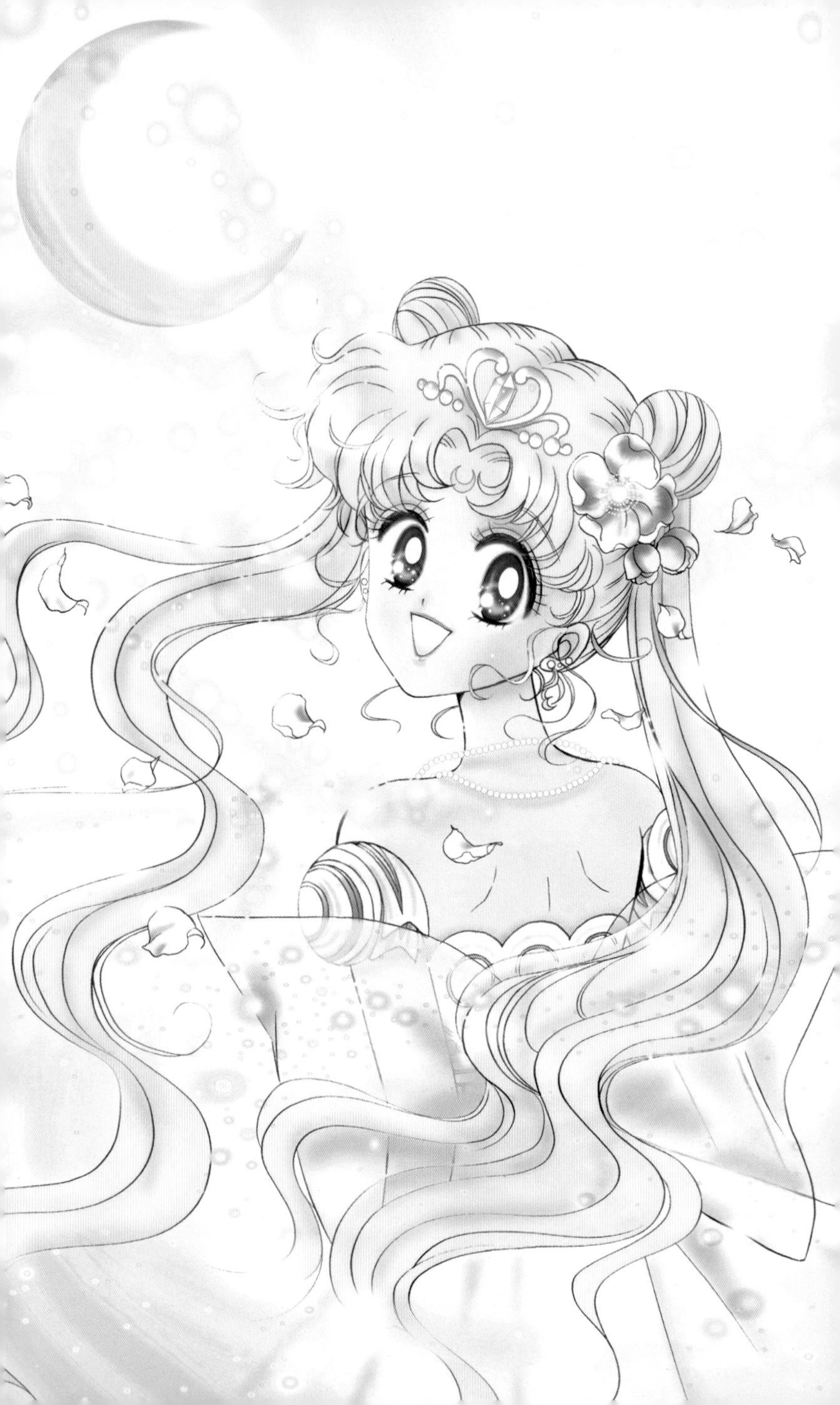

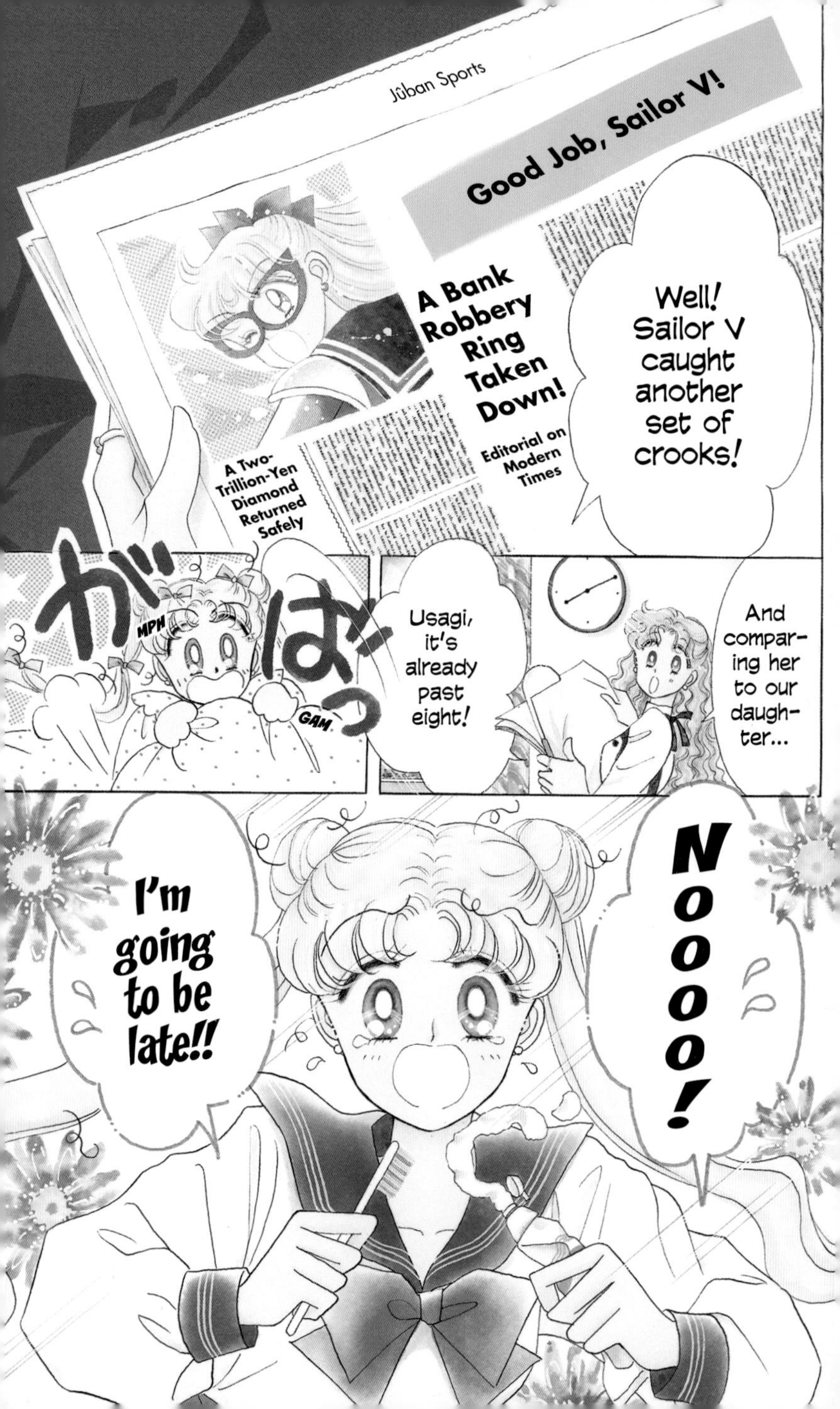
Jûban Sports
Good Job, Sailor V!
A Bank Robbery Ring Taken Down!
Editorial on Modern Times
A Two-Trillion-Yen Diamond Returned Safely
Well! Sailor V caught another set of crooks!
And comparing her to our daughter...
Usagi, it's already past eight!
がばっ
MPH
GAM
Noooo!
I'm going to be late!!

Act 1
Usagi, Sailor Moon

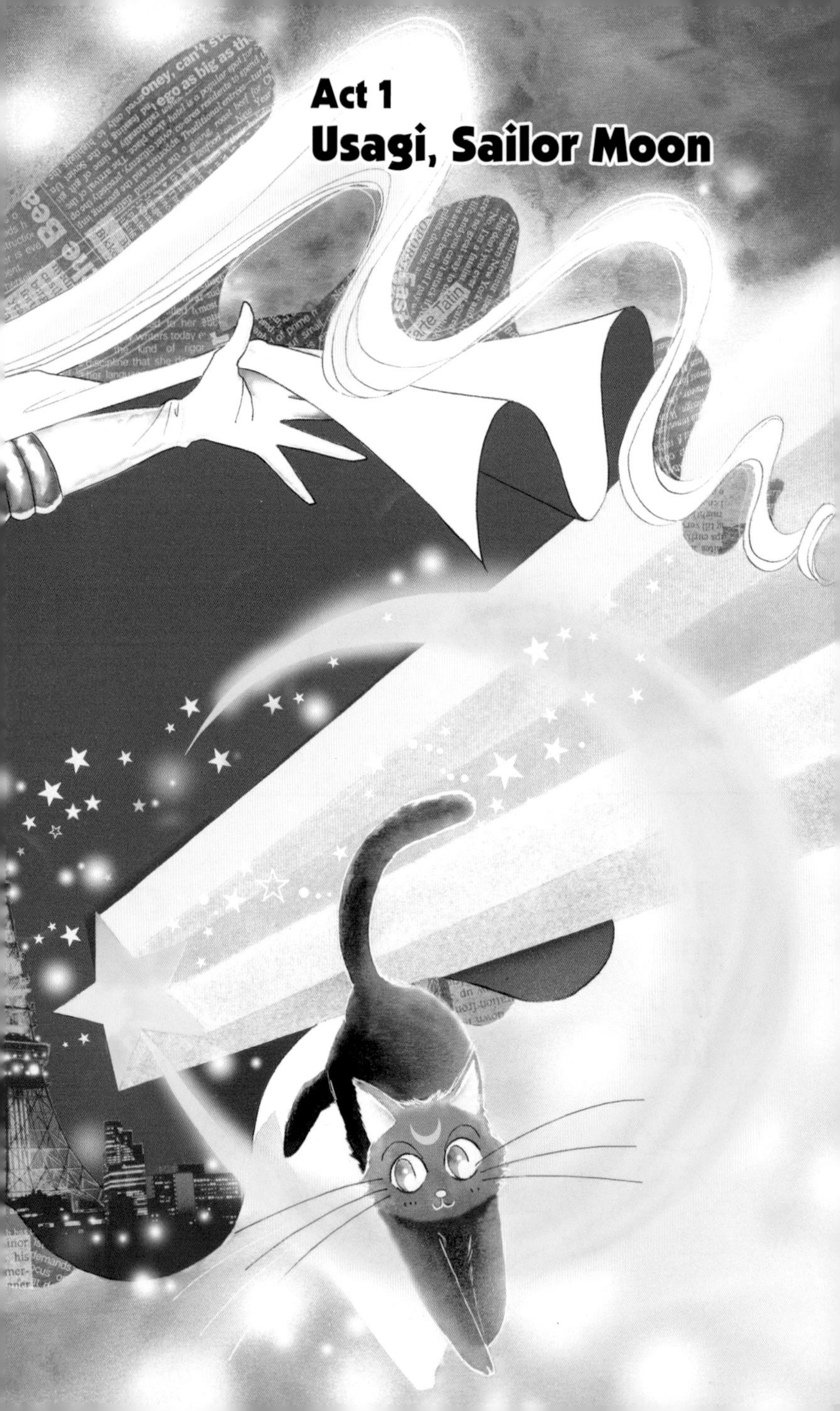

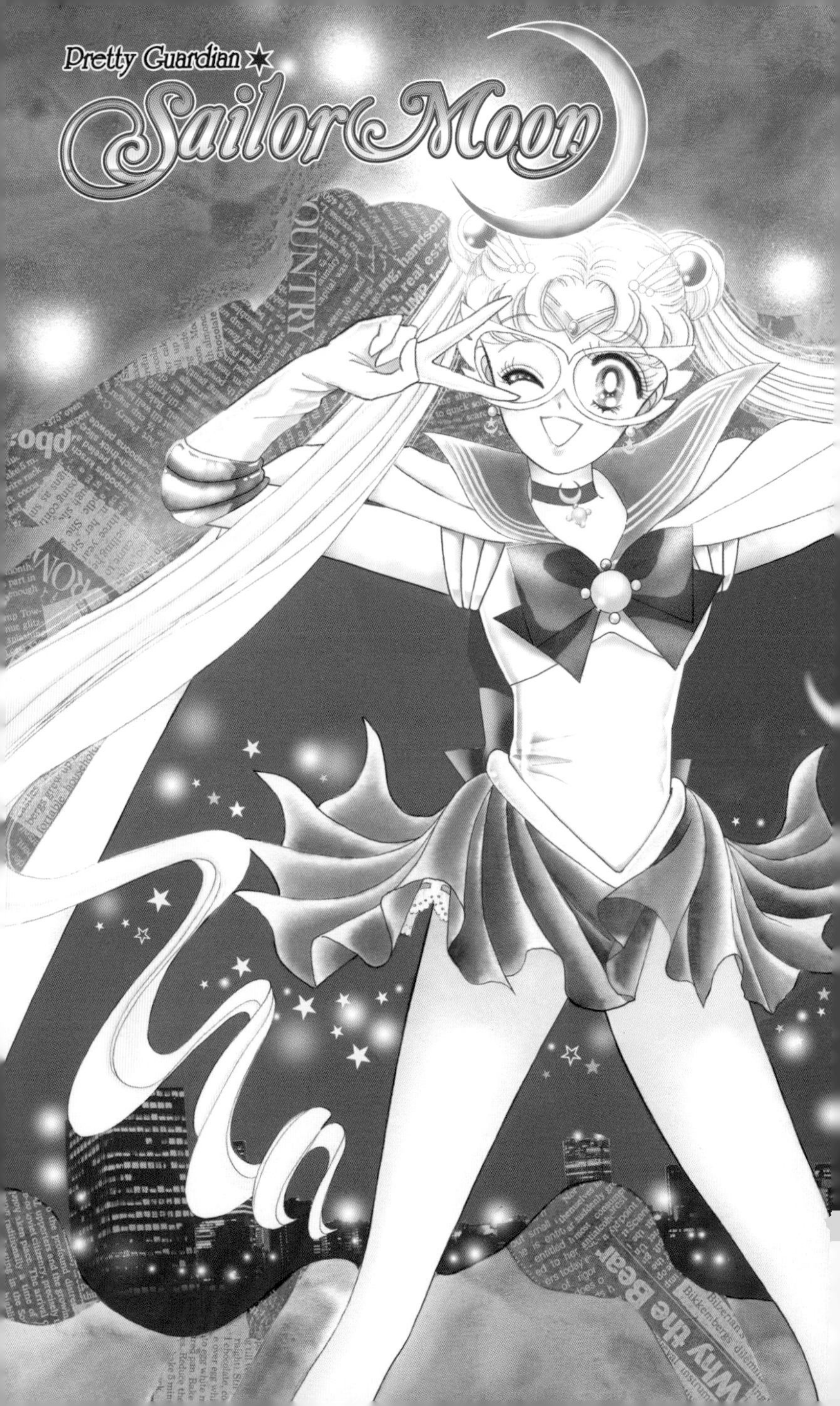
Pretty Guardian
Sailor Moon

CONTENTS

Pretty Guardian SAILORMOON

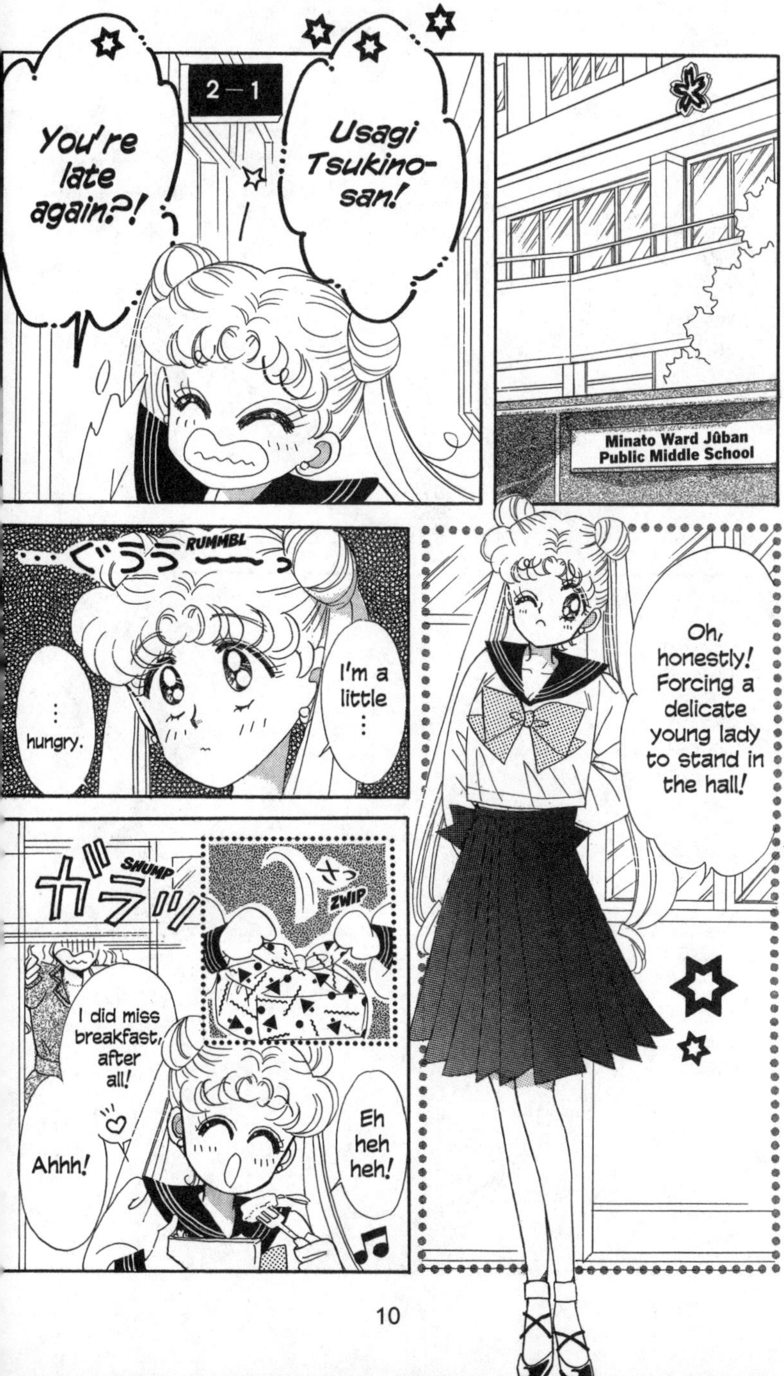

Minato Ward Jûban Public Middle School
2—1
Usagi Tsukino-san!
You're late again?!
Oh, honestly! Forcing a delicate young lady to stand in the hall!
ぐううーーっ
RUMMBL
I'm a little …
… hungry.
さっ
ZWIP
ガラッ
SHUMP
Eh heh heh!
I did miss breakfast, after all!
Ahhh!

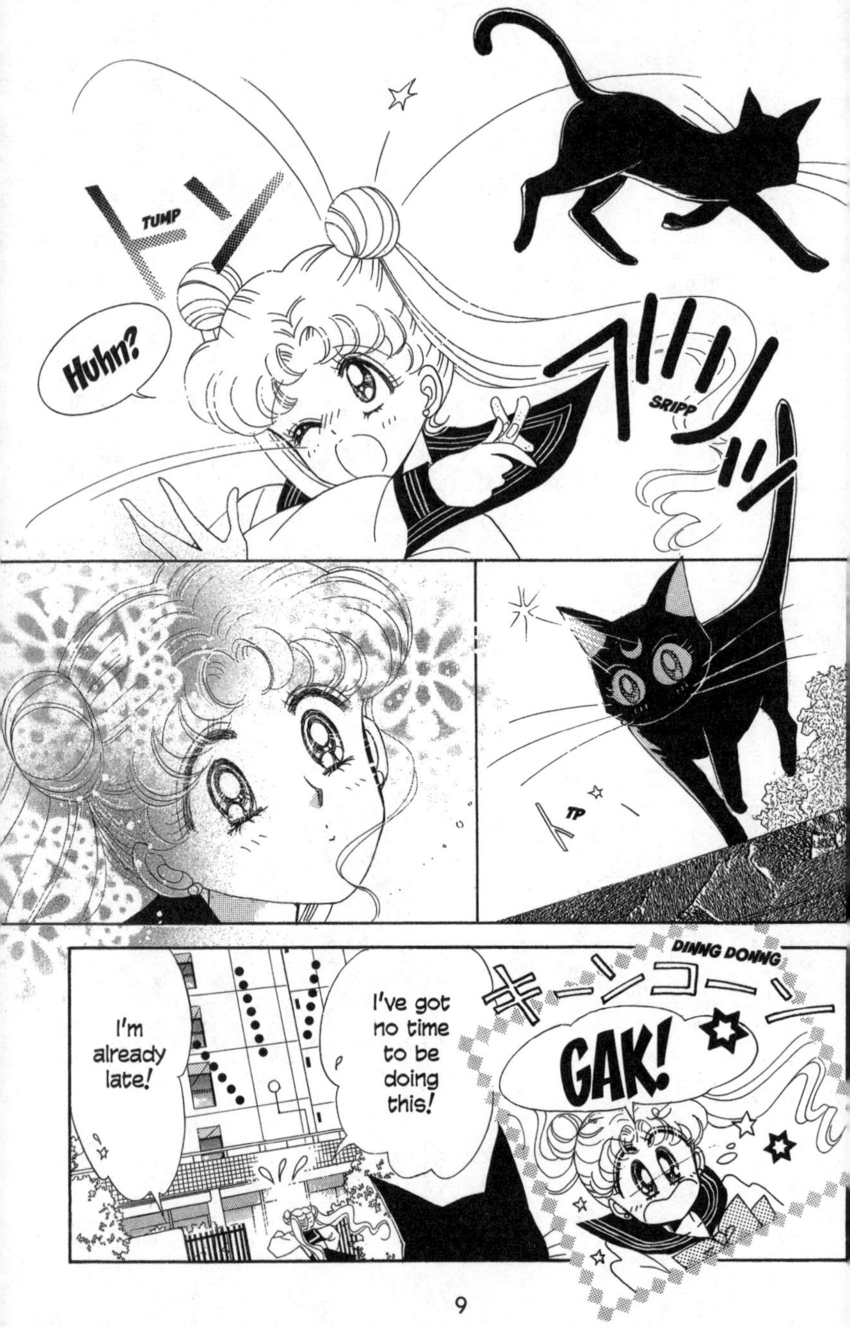
TUMP
Huhn?
SRIPP
TP
DINNG DONNG
GAK!
I've got no time to be doing this!
I'm already late!

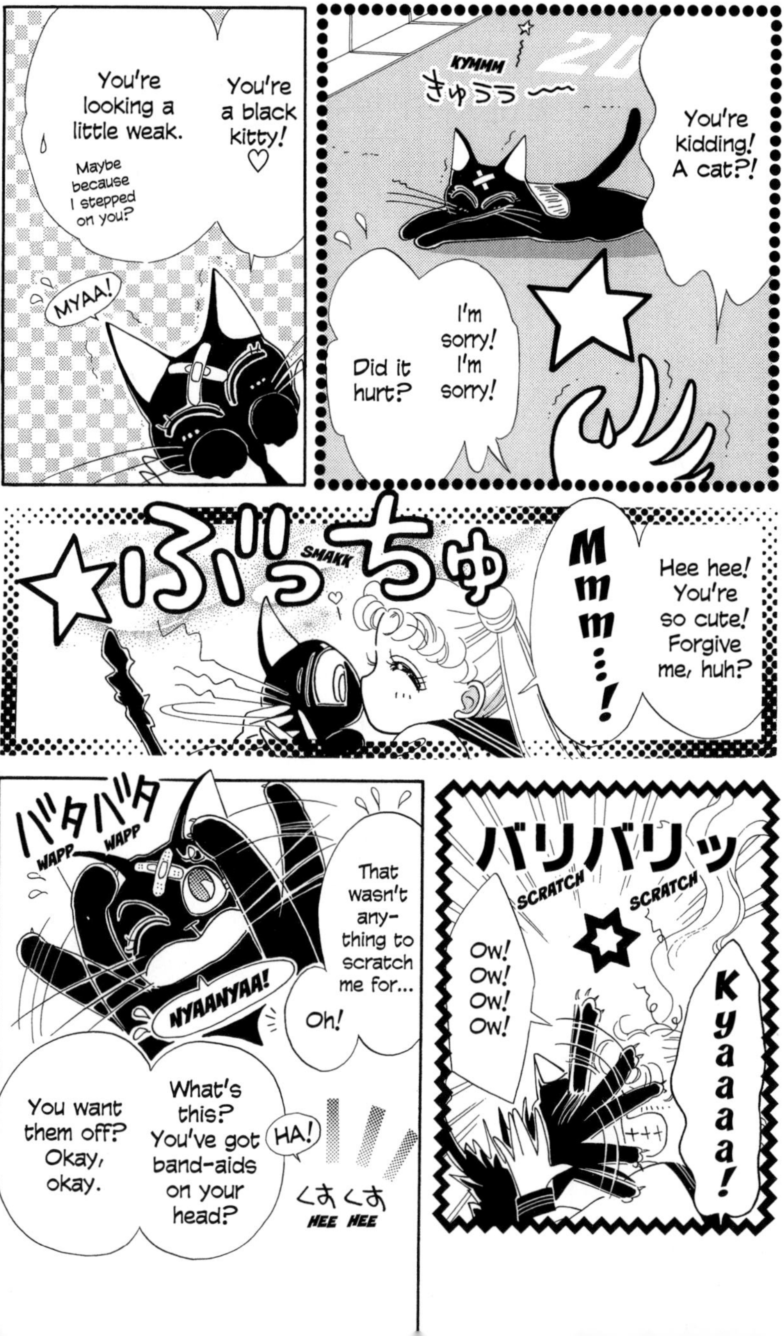
You're kidding! A cat?!
KYMMM
きゅうう〜
I'm sorry! I'm sorry!
Did it hurt?
You're a black kitty! ♡
You're looking a little weak.
Maybe because I stepped on you?
MYAA!
Hee hee! You're so cute! Forgive me, huh?
Mmm...!
ぶっちゅ
SMAKK
バリバリッ
SCRATCH SCRATCH
Kyaaaaa!
Ow! Ow! Ow! Ow!
That wasn't anything to scratch me for...
Oh!
バタバタ
WAPP WAPP
NYAANYAA!
What's this? You've got band-aids on your head?
HA!
くすくす
HEE HEE
You want them off? Okay, okay.

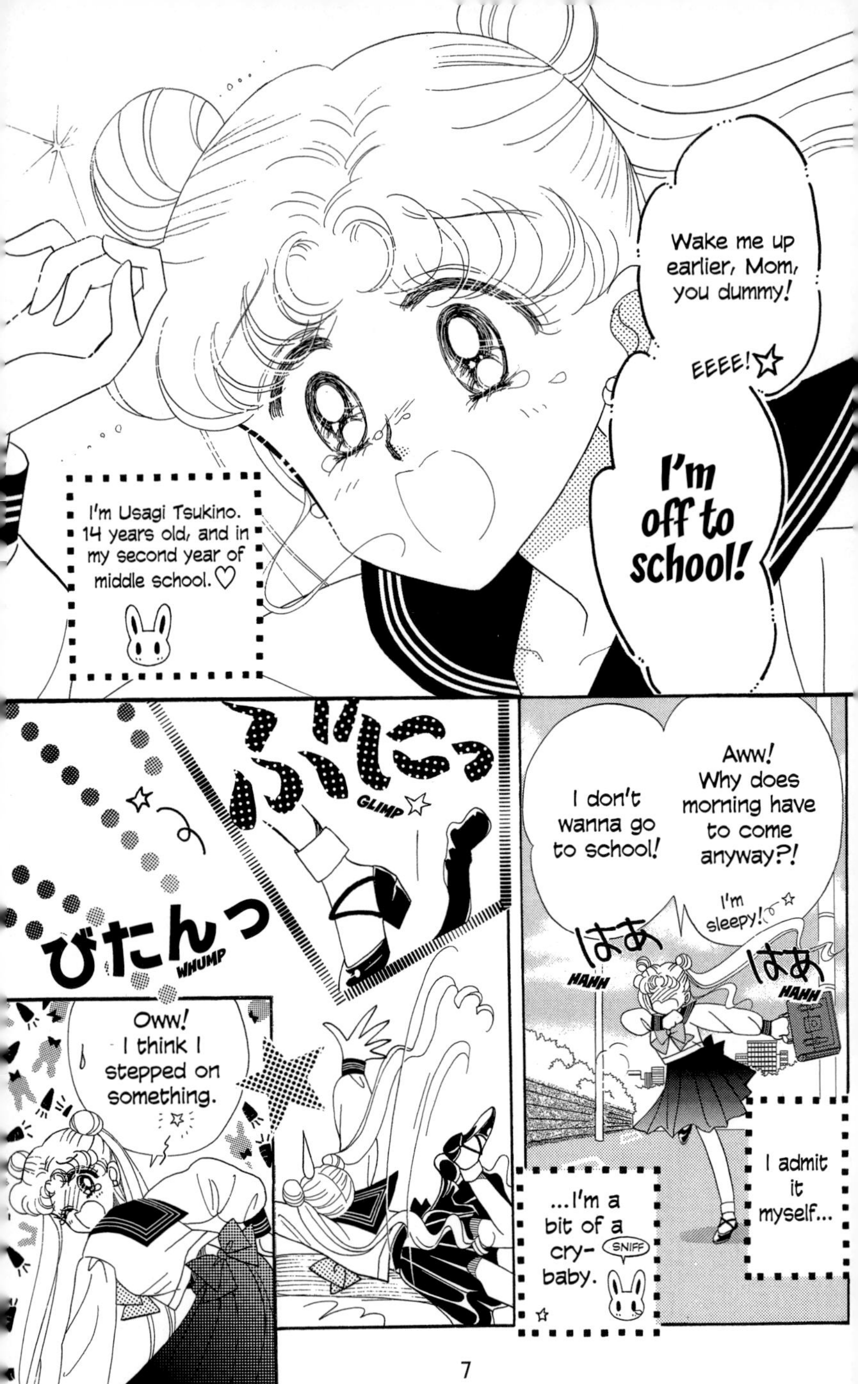

Wake me up earlier, Mom, you dummy!
EEEE!☆
I'm off to school!
I'm Usagi Tsukino. 14 years old, and in my second year of middle school.♡
Aww! Why does morning have to come anyway?!
I don't wanna go to school!
I'm sleepy!
はあ
HAHN
はあ
HAHN
I admit it myself...
...I'm a bit of a cry-baby.
SNIFF
ぷにっ
GLIMP
びたんっ
WHUMP
Oww! I think I stepped on something.

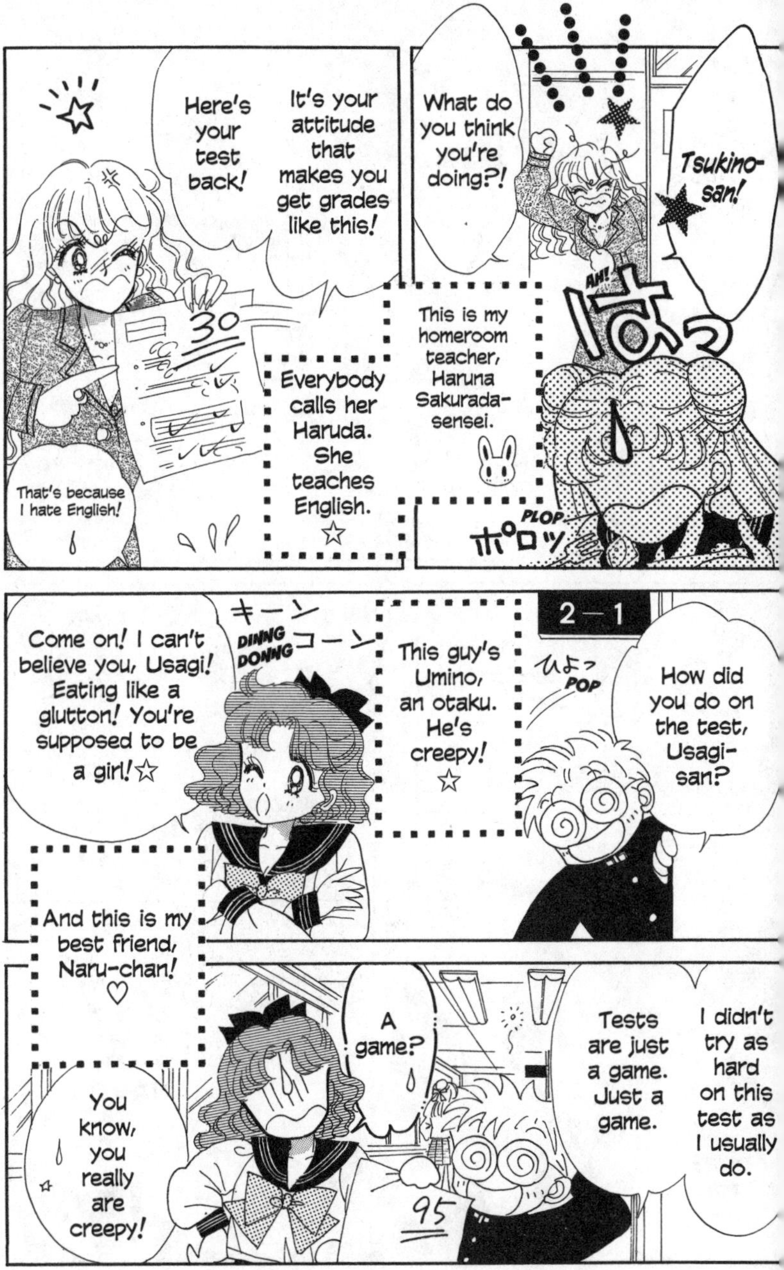
Tsukino-san!
AH! はっ
What do you think you're doing?!
PLOP ポロッ
This is my homeroom teacher, Haruna Sakurada-sensei.
It's your attitude that makes you get grades like this!
Here's your test back!
30
Everybody calls her Haruda. She teaches English. ☆
That's because I hate English!
How did you do on the test, Usagi-san?
ひよっ POP
2—1
This guy's Umino, an otaku. He's creepy! ☆
キーン DINNG
コーン DONNG
Come on! I can't believe you, Usagi! Eating like a glutton! You're supposed to be a girl!☆
And this is my best friend, Naru-chan! ♡
I didn't try as hard on this test as I usually do.
Tests are just a game. Just a game.
A game?
95
You know, you really are creepy!

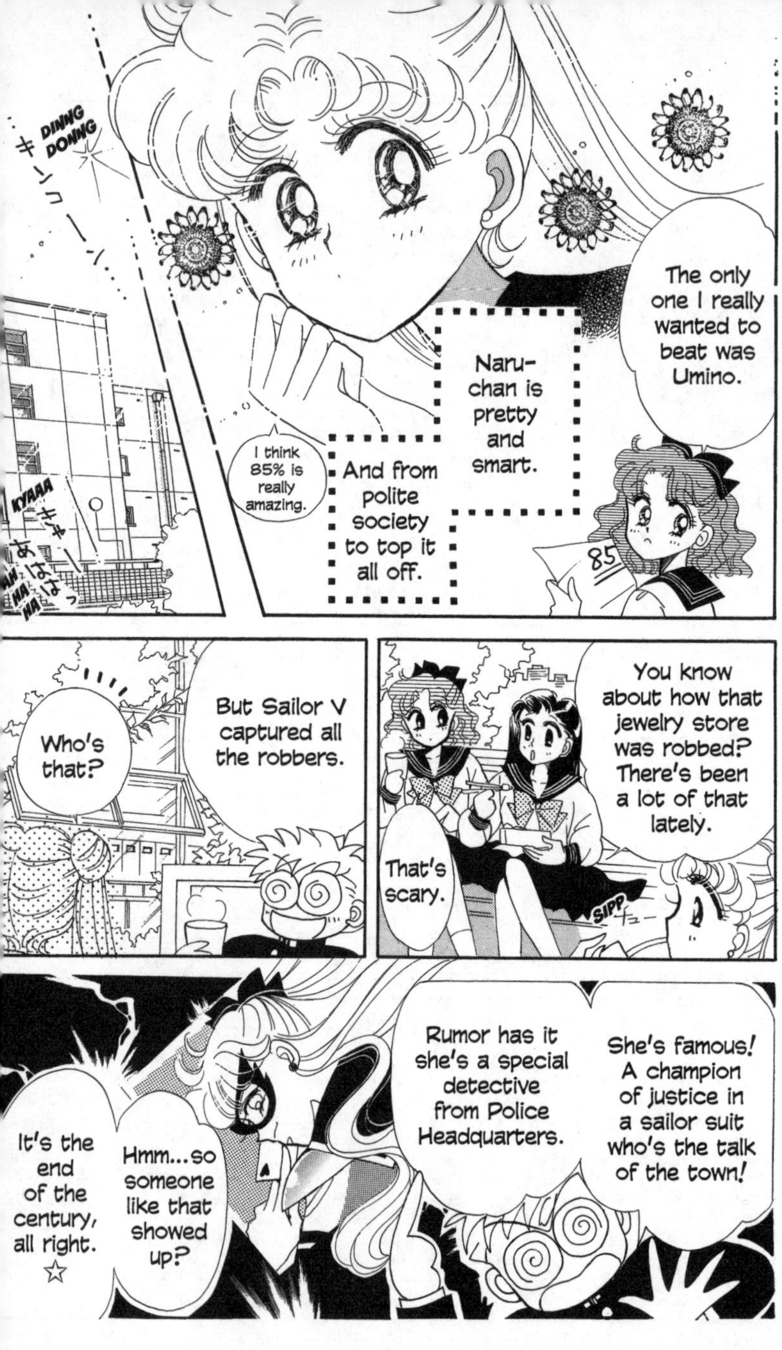
DINNG DONNG
The only one I really wanted to beat was Umino.
Naru-chan is pretty and smart.
And from polite society to top it all off.
I think 85% is really amazing.
85
KYAAA
AH HA HA
You know about how that jewelry store was robbed? There's been a lot of that lately.
That's scary.
SIPP
But Sailor V captured all the robbers.
Who's that?
She's famous! A champion of justice in a sailor suit who's the talk of the town!
Rumor has it she's a special detective from Police Headquarters.
Hmm...so someone like that showed up?
It's the end of the century, all right. ☆

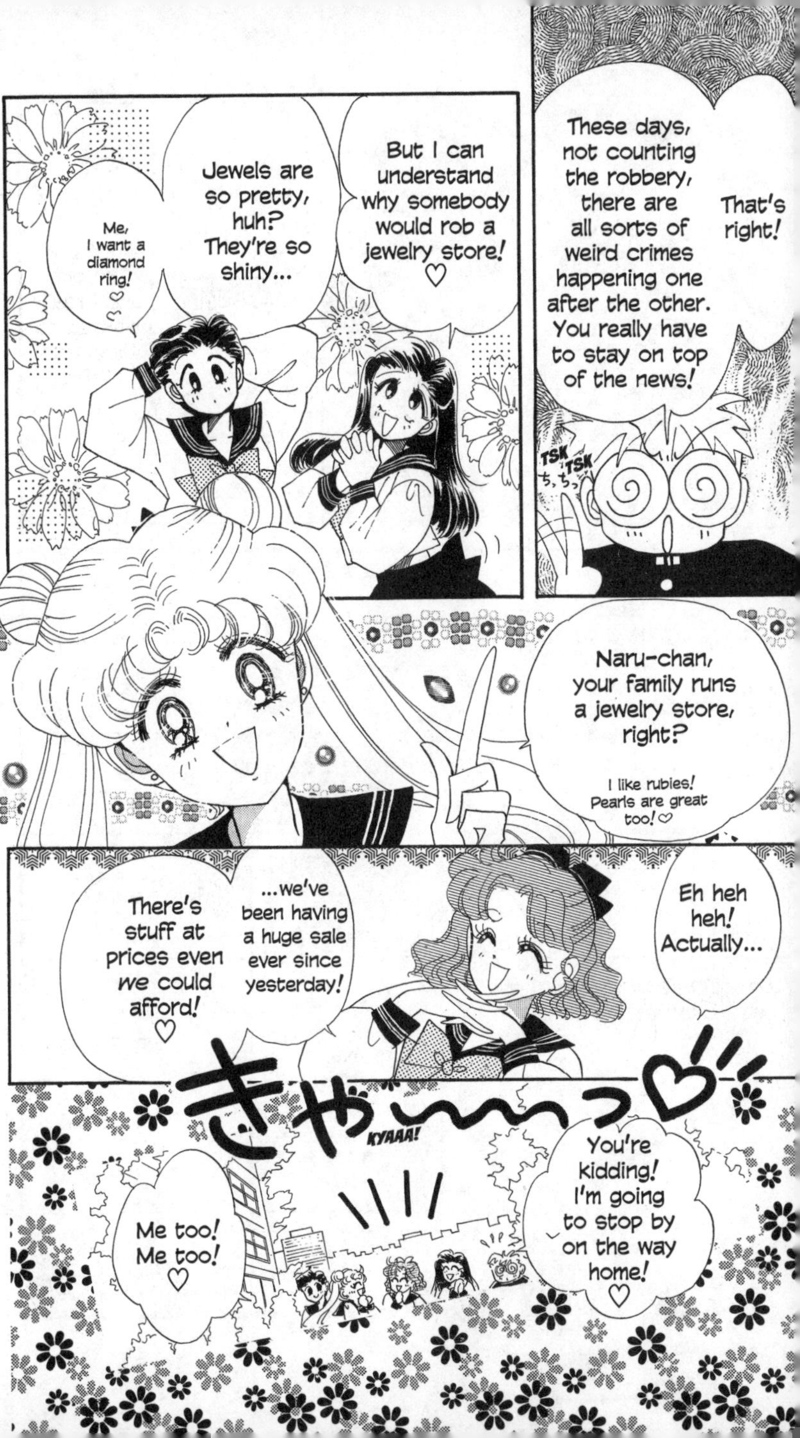

That's right!
These days, not counting the robbery, there are all sorts of weird crimes happening one after the other. You really have to stay on top of the news!
TSK TSK
ちっちっ
But I can understand why somebody would rob a jewelry store! ♡
Jewels are so pretty, huh? They're so shiny...
Me, I want a diamond ring! ♡
Naru-chan, your family runs a jewelry store, right?
I like rubies! Pearls are great too! ♡
Eh heh heh! Actually...
...we've been having a huge sale ever since yesterday!
There's stuff at prices even we could afford! ♡
きゃ〜〜っ♡
KYAAA!
You're kidding! I'm going to stop by on the way home! ♡
Me too! Me too! ♡

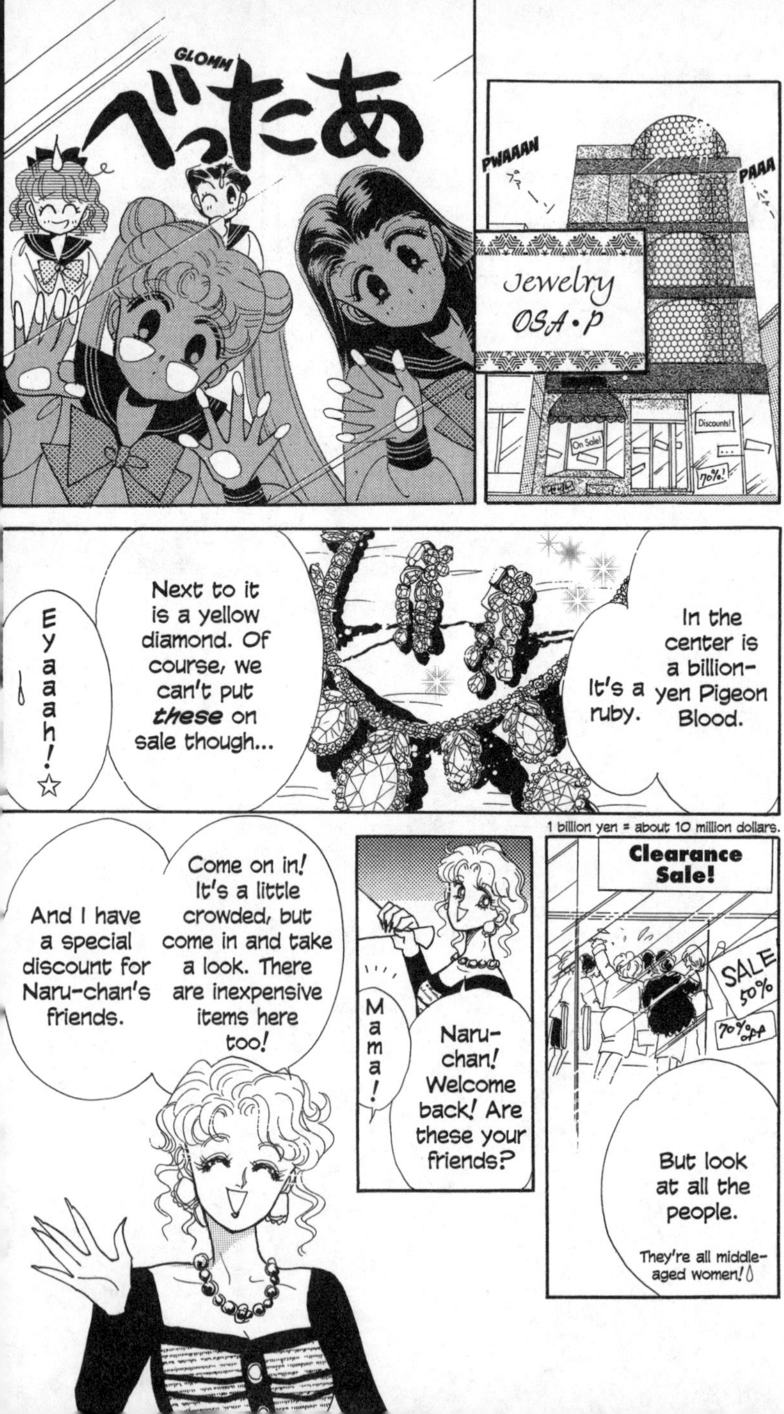

PWAAAN
PAAA
Jewelry OSA・P
On Sale!
Discounts!
70%!
GLOMM
べったあ
In the center is a billion-yen Pigeon Blood.
It's a ruby.
Next to it is a yellow diamond. Of course, we can't put *these* on sale though...
Eyaaaah!☆
Clearance Sale!
SALE 50%
70% off
But look at all the people.
They're all middle-aged women!
Naru-chan! Welcome back! Are these your friends?
Mama!
Come on in! It's a little crowded, but come in and take a look. There are inexpensive items here too!
And I have a special discount for Naru-chan's friends.

1 billion yen = about 10 million dollars.

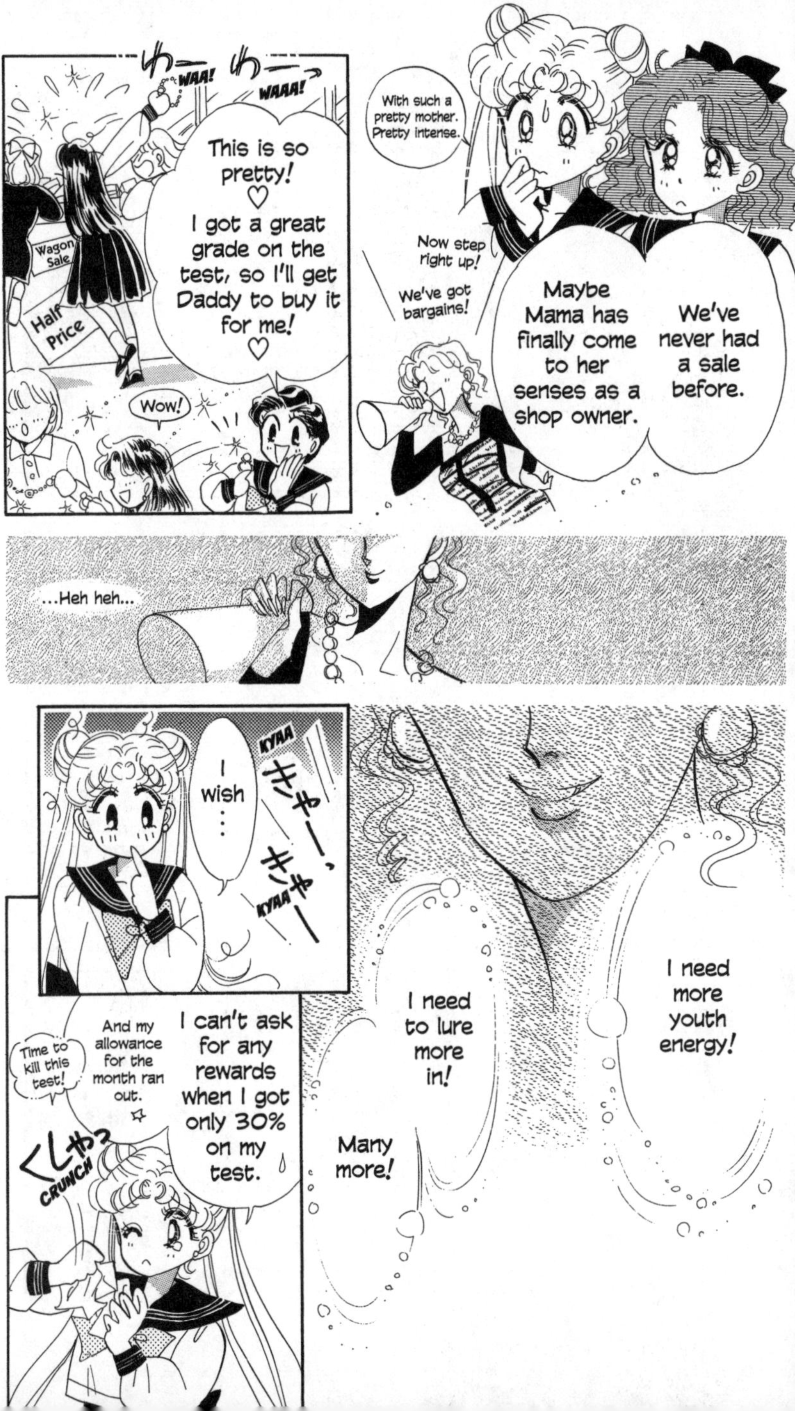
With such a pretty mother. Pretty intense.
We've never had a sale before.
Maybe Mama has finally come to her senses as a shop owner.
Now step right up!
We've got bargains!
わー WAA! わー WAAA!
This is so pretty! ♡ I got a great grade on the test, so I'll get Daddy to buy it for me! ♡
Wagon Sale
Half Price
Wow!
...Heh heh...
I need more youth energy!
I need to lure more in!
Many more!
I wish...
きゃー KYAA
きゃー KYAA
I can't ask for any rewards when I got only 30% on my test.
And my allowance for the month ran out.
Time to kill this test!
くしゃっ CRUNCH

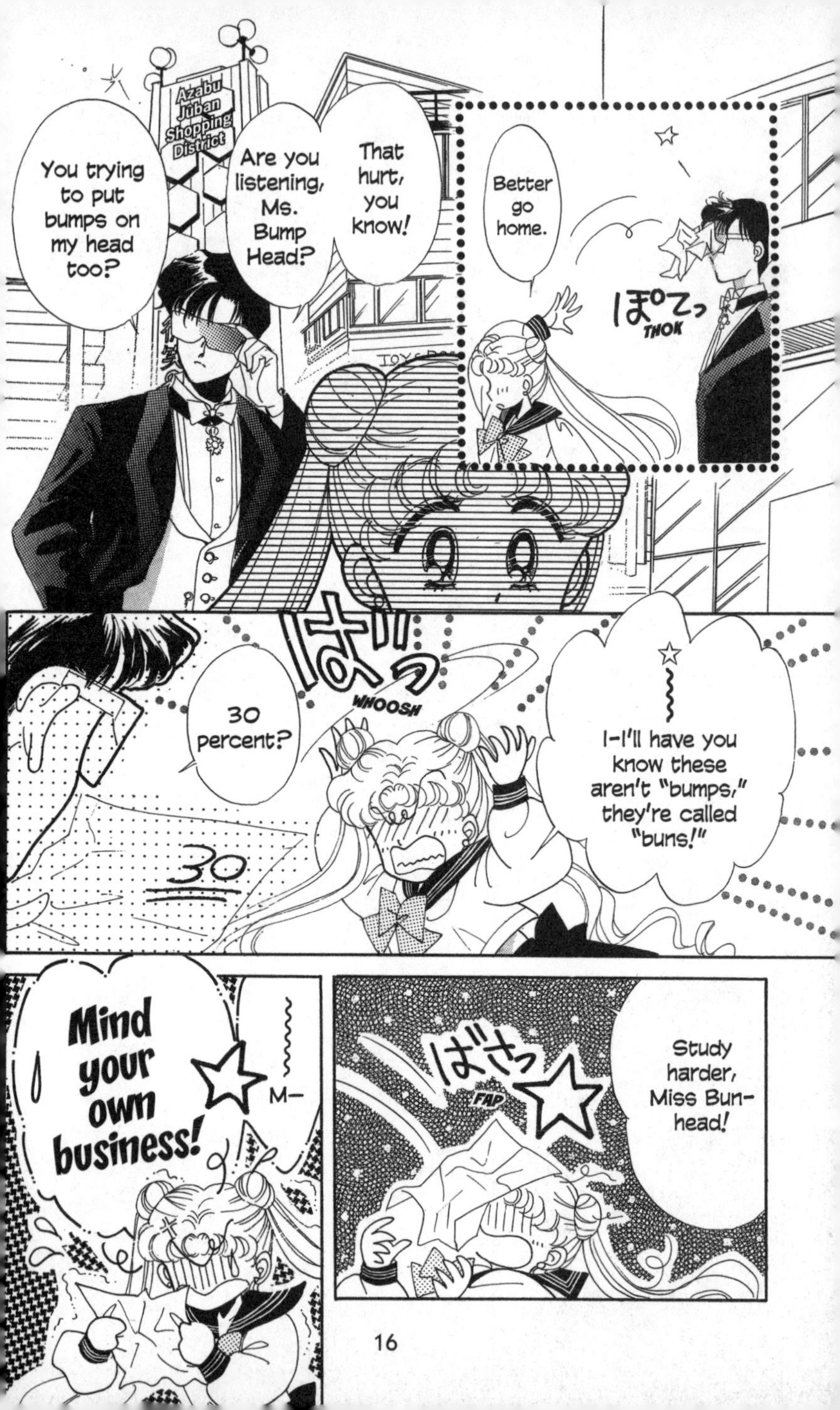
Better go home.
ぽてっ
THOK
That hurt, you know!
Are you listening, Ms. Bump Head?
Azabu Jūban Shopping District
You trying to put bumps on my head too?
I-I'll have you know these aren't "bumps," they're called "buns!"
はっ
WHOOSH
30 percent?
30
Study harder, Miss Bun-head!
ばさっ
FAP
M—
Mind your own business!

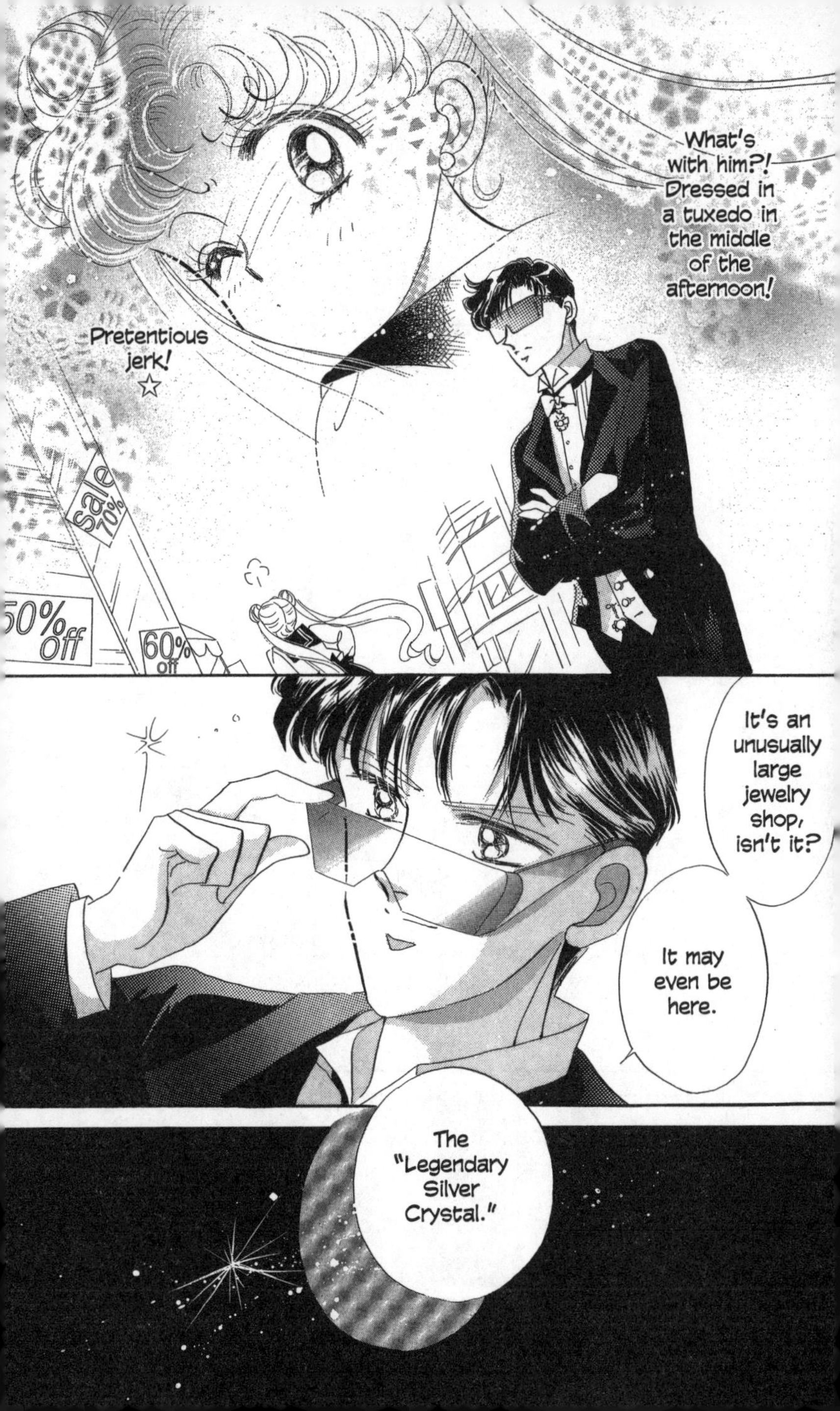
What's with him?! Dressed in a tuxedo in the middle of the afternoon!
Pretentious jerk! ☆
Sale 70%
50% off
60% off
It's an unusually large jewelry shop, isn't it?
It may even be here.
The "Legendary Silver Crystal."

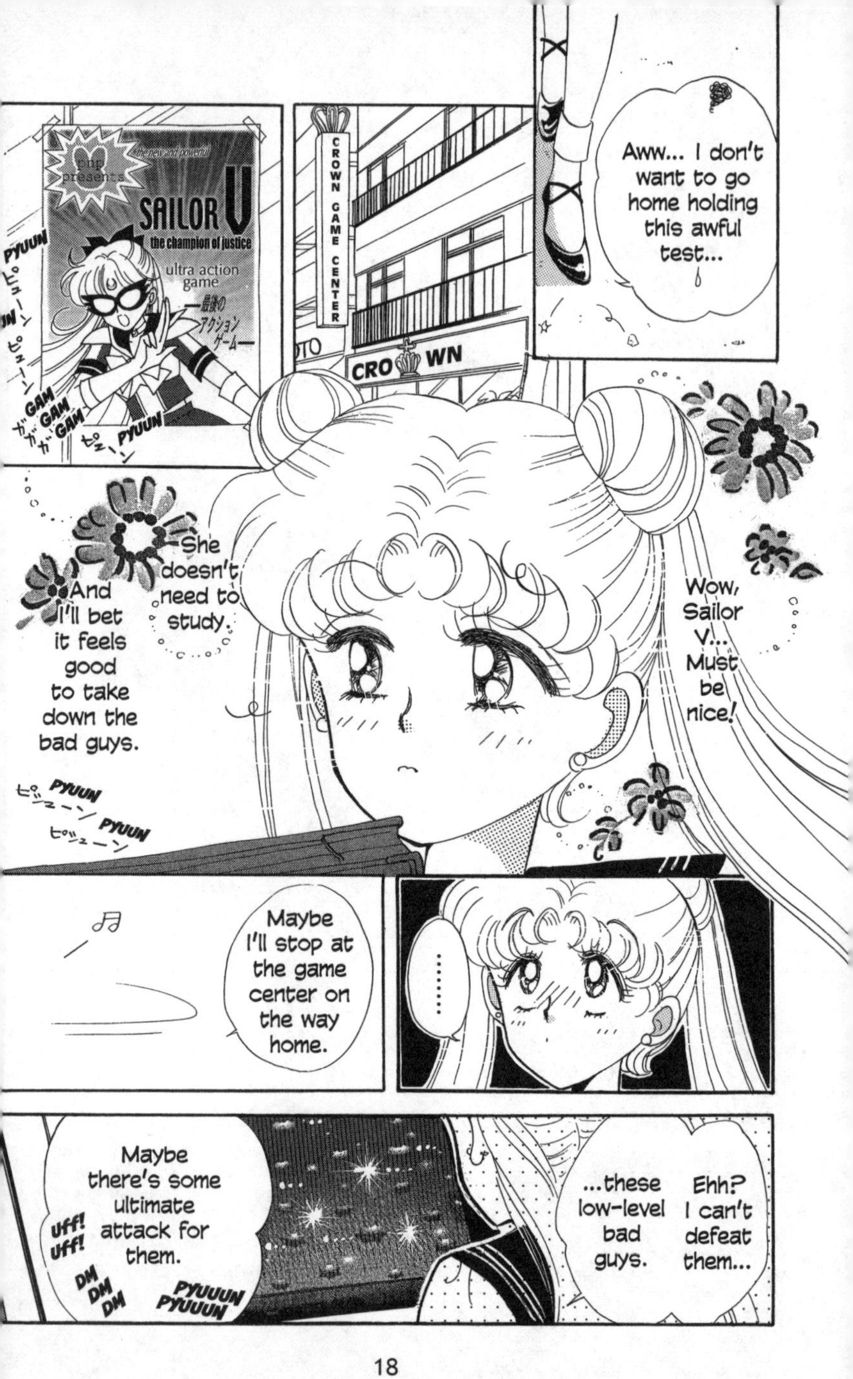
Aww... I don't want to go home holding this awful test...
CROWN GAME CENTER
CROWN
pnp presents
the new and powerful
SAILOR V
the champion of justice
ultra action game
最後のアクションゲーム
PYUUN
GAM GAM GAM
PYUUN
Wow, Sailor V... Must be nice!
She doesn't need to study.
And I'll bet it feels good to take down the bad guys.
PYUUN
PYUUN
......
Maybe I'll stop at the game center on the way home.
Ehh? I can't defeat them...
...these low-level bad guys.
Maybe there's some ultimate attack for them.
Uff! Uff!
DM DM DM
PYUUUN PYUUUN

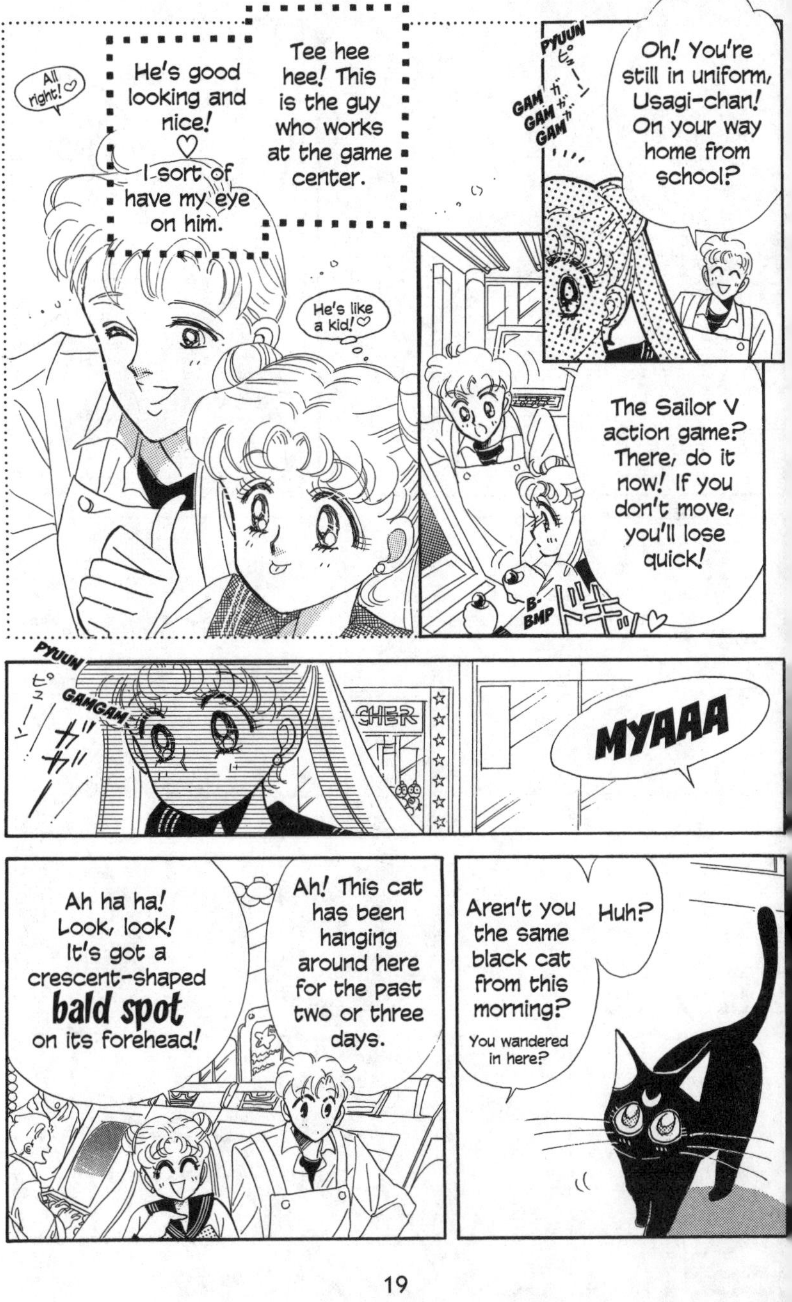

PYUUN
GAM GAM GAM
Oh! You're still in uniform, Usagi-chan! On your way home from school?
The Sailor V action game? There, do it now! If you don't move, you'll lose quick!
B-BMP
Tee hee hee! This is the guy who works at the game center.
He's good looking and nice! ♡ I sort of have my eye on him.
All right! ♡
He's like a kid! ♡
MYAAA
PYUUN
GAMGAM
Huh?
Aren't you the same black cat from this morning?
You wandered in here?
Ah! This cat has been hanging around here for the past two or three days.
Ah ha ha! Look, look! It's got a crescent-shaped **bald spot** on its forehead!

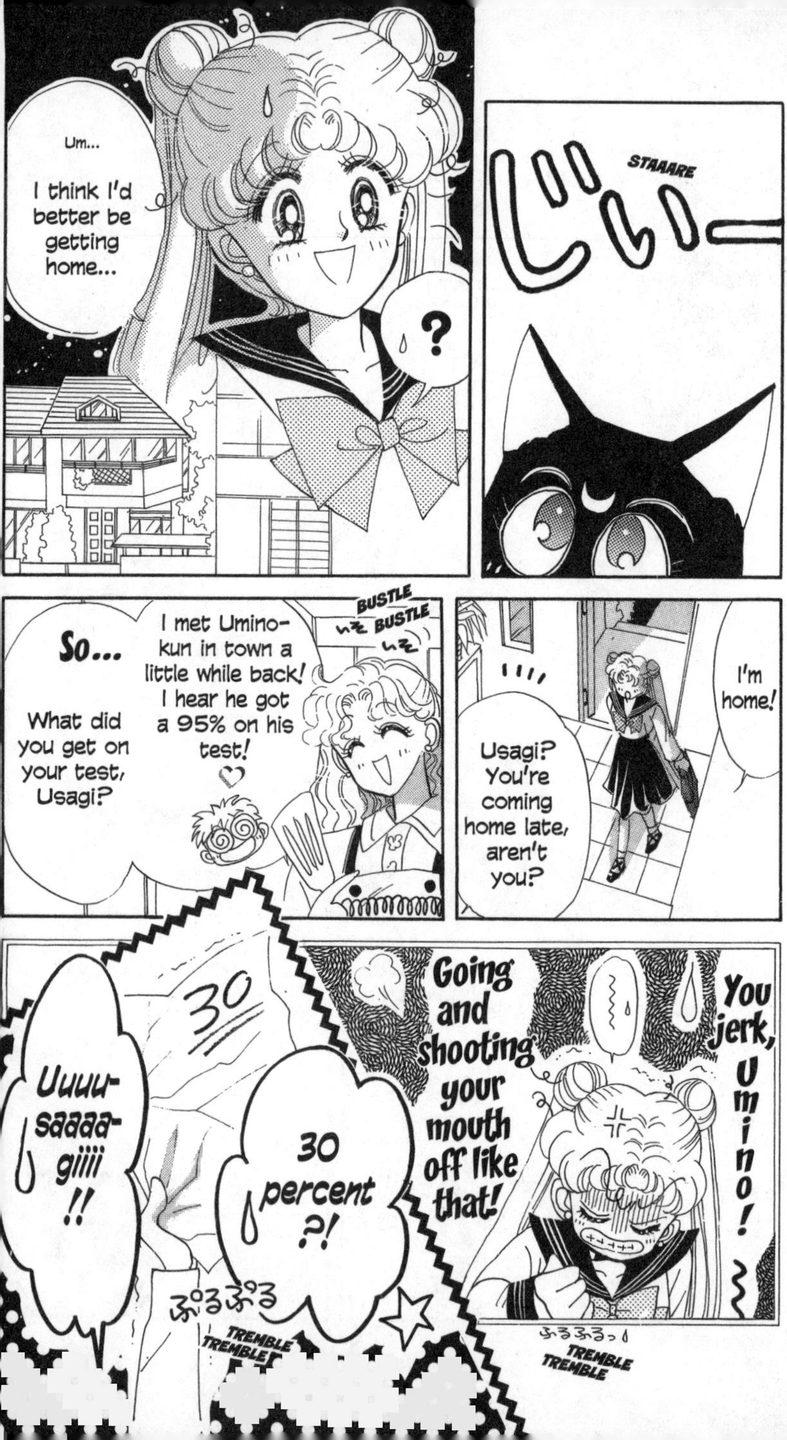

じぃー
STAARE
Um...
I think I'd better be getting home...
?
I'm home!
Usagi? You're coming home late, aren't you?
いそ いそ
BUSTLE BUSTLE
I met Umino-kun in town a little while back! I hear he got a 95% on his test! ♡
So...
What did you get on your test, Usagi?
You jerk, Umino!
Going and shooting your mouth off like that!
ぷるぷるっ
TREMBLE TREMBLE
30 percent ?!
30
Uuuu-saaaa-giiii !!
ぷるぷる
TREMBLE TREMBLE

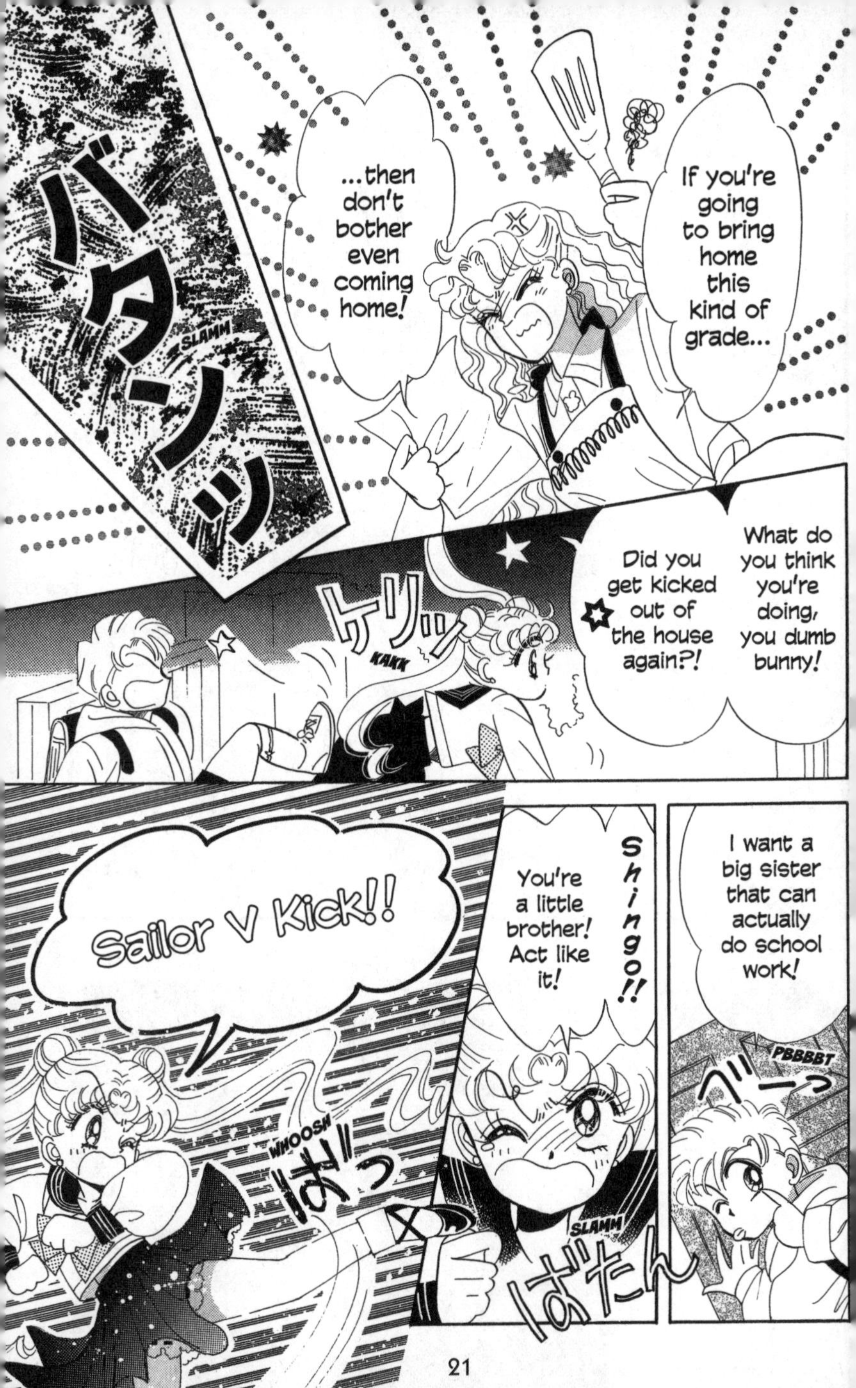

If you're going to bring home this kind of grade...
...then don't bother even coming home!
バターンッ
SLAMM
What do you think you're doing, you dumb bunny!
Did you get kicked out of the house again?!
ケリッ
KAKK
I want a big sister that can actually do school work!
べーっ
PBBBBT
Shingo!!
You're a little brother! Act like it!
ばたん
SLAMM
Sailor V Kick!!
ばっ
WHOOSH

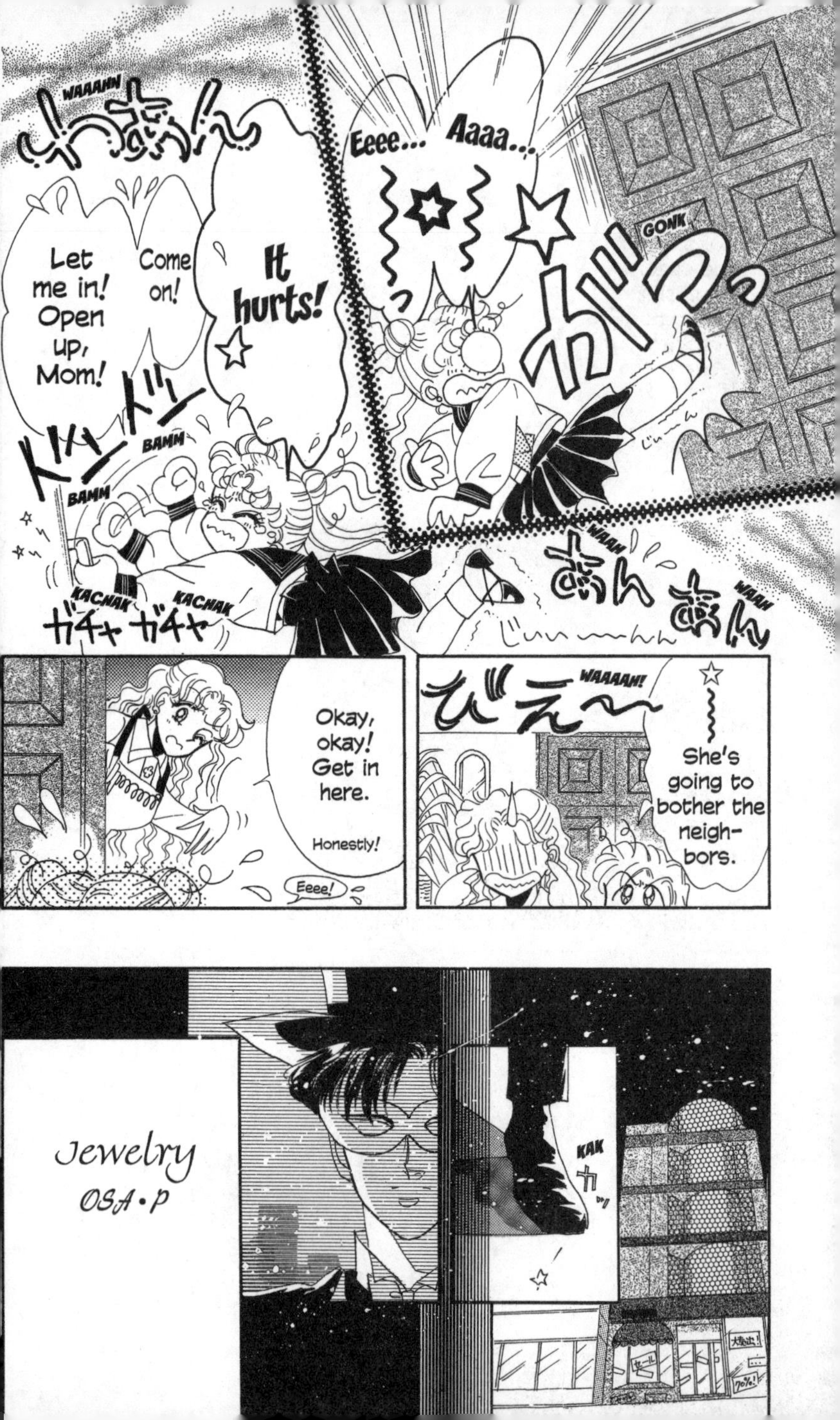

Eeee... Aaaa...
GONK
WAAAHN
It hurts!
Come on!
Let me in! Open up, Mom!
BAMM
BAMM
KACHAK KACHAK
WAAH
WAAH
WAAAAH!
She's going to bother the neighbors.
Okay, okay! Get in here.
Honestly!
Eeee!
KAK
Jewelry OSA•P

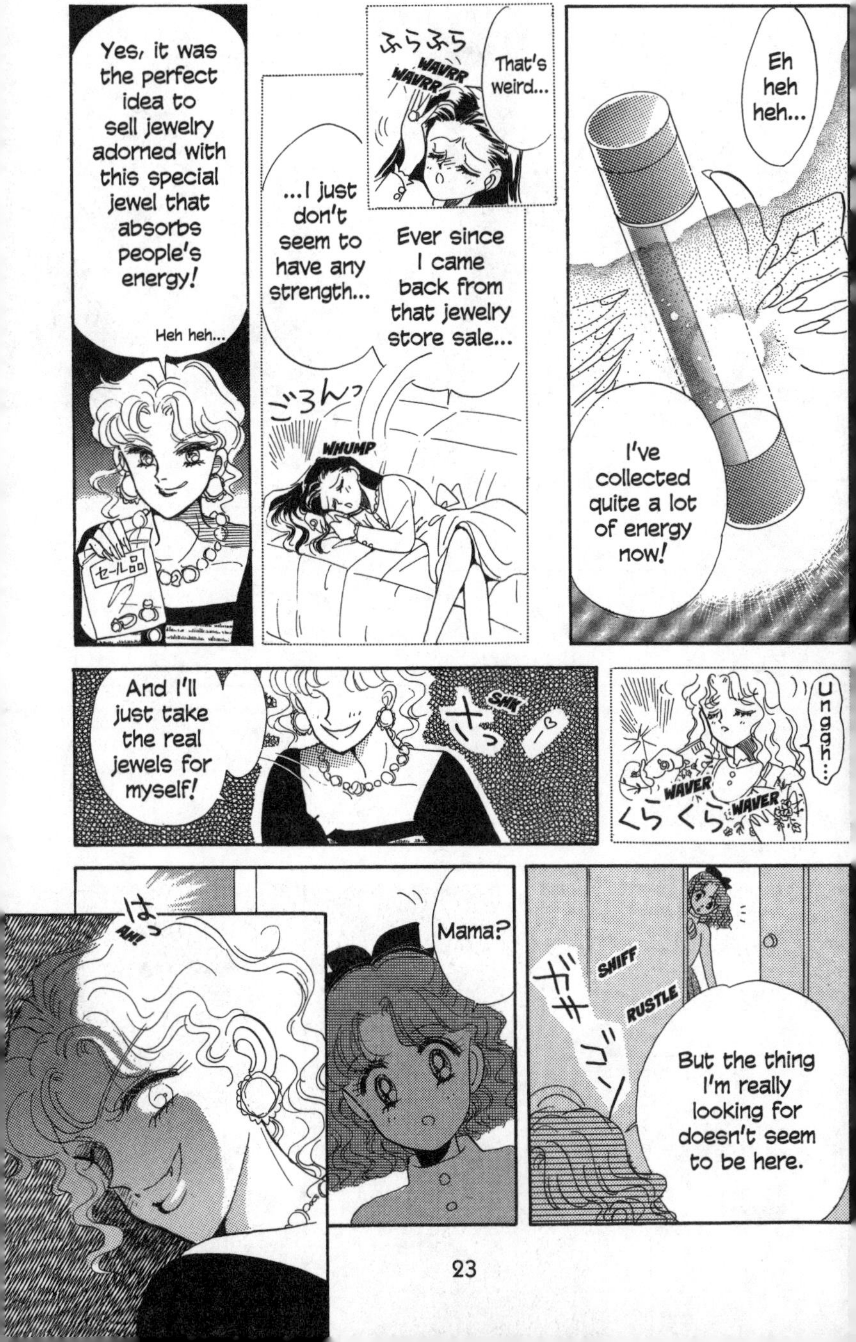
Eh heh heh...
I've collected quite a lot of energy now!
ふらふら
WAVRR WAVRR
That's weird...
Ever since I came back from that jewelry store sale...
...I just don't seem to have any strength...
ごろんっ
WHUMP
Yes, it was the perfect idea to sell jewelry adorned with this special jewel that absorbs people's energy!
Heh heh...
セール品
Unggh...
くらくら
WAVER WAVER
And I'll just take the real jewels for myself!
SNK
さっ
SHIFF
RUSTLE
But the thing I'm really looking for doesn't seem to be here.
Mama?
はっ
AH!

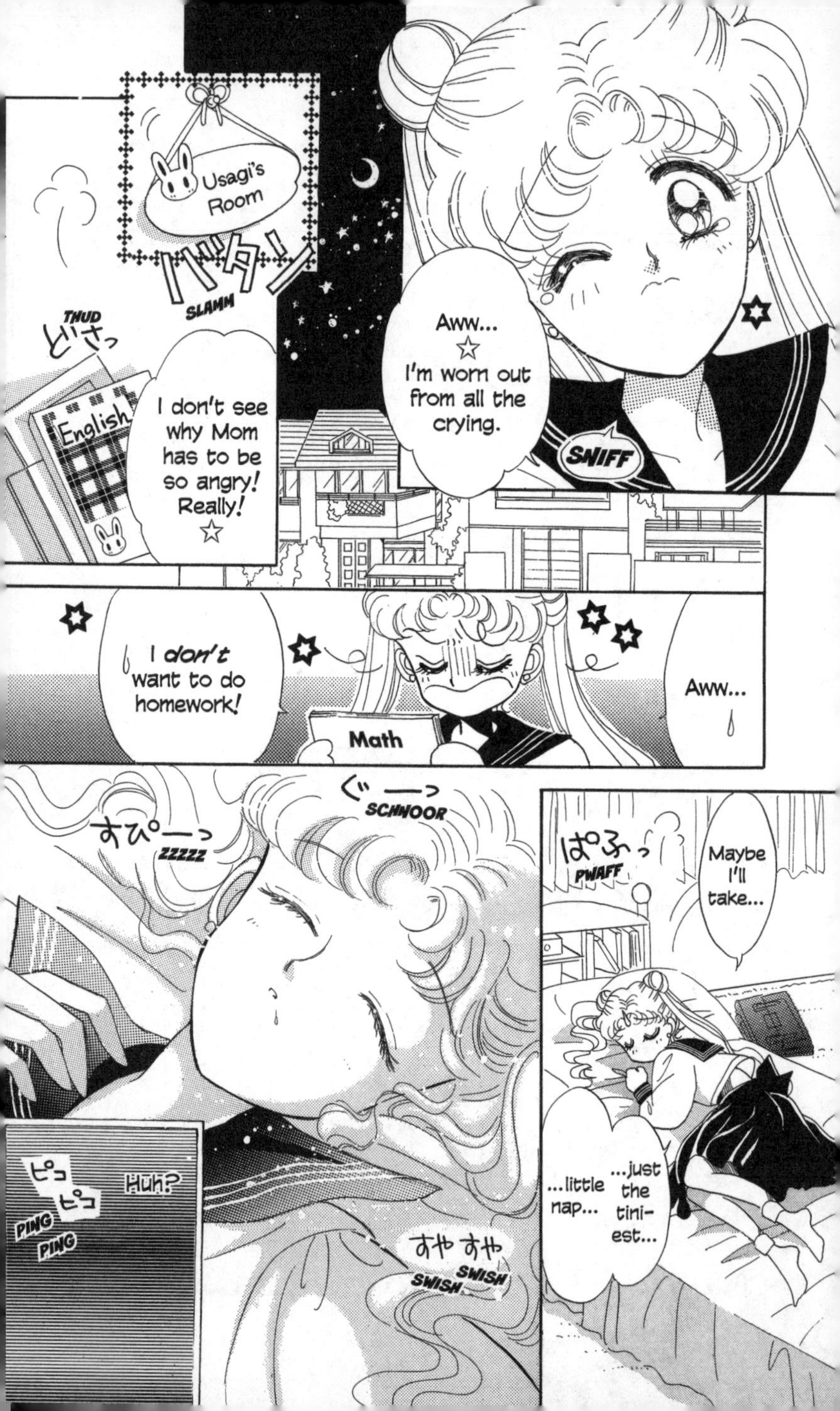

Aww... ☆ I'm worn out from all the crying.
SNIFF
Usagi's Room
バタン
SLAMM
どさっ
THUD
English
I don't see why Mom has to be so angry! Really! ☆
Aww...
I don't want to do homework!
Math
ぱふっ
PWAFF
Maybe I'll take...
...just the tini-est...
...little nap...
ぐーっ
SCHNOOR
すぴーっ
ZZZZZ
すやすや
SWISH SWISH
ピコピコ
PING PING
Huh?

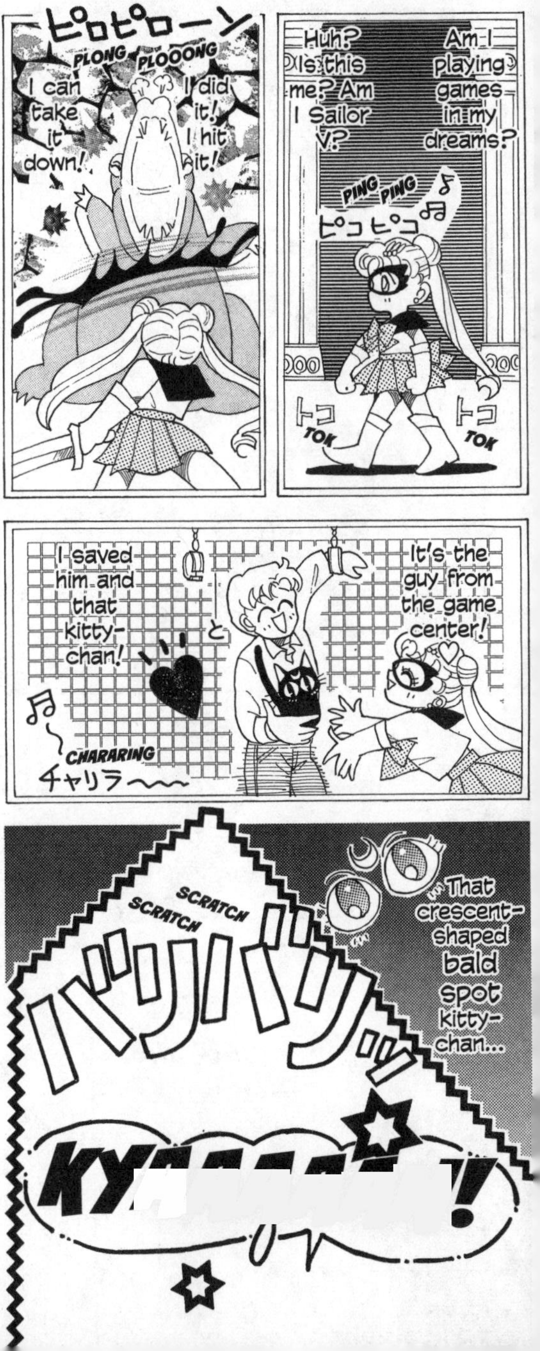
Am I playing games in my dreams?
Huh? Is this me? Am I Sailor V?
PING PING
ピコピコ
トコ
TOK
トコ
TOK
ピロピローン
PLOOONG
PLONG
I did it! I hit it!
I can take it down!
It's the guy from the game center!
と
I saved him and that kitty-chan!
CHARARING
チャリラ〜〜〜
That crescent-shaped bald spot kitty-chan...
SCRATCH
SCRATCH
バリバリッ
KY !

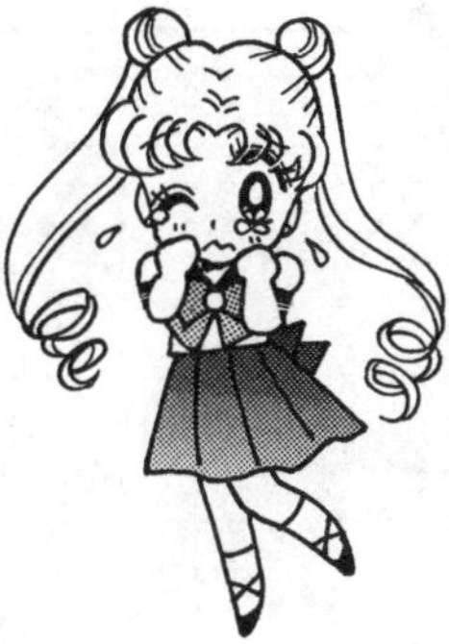

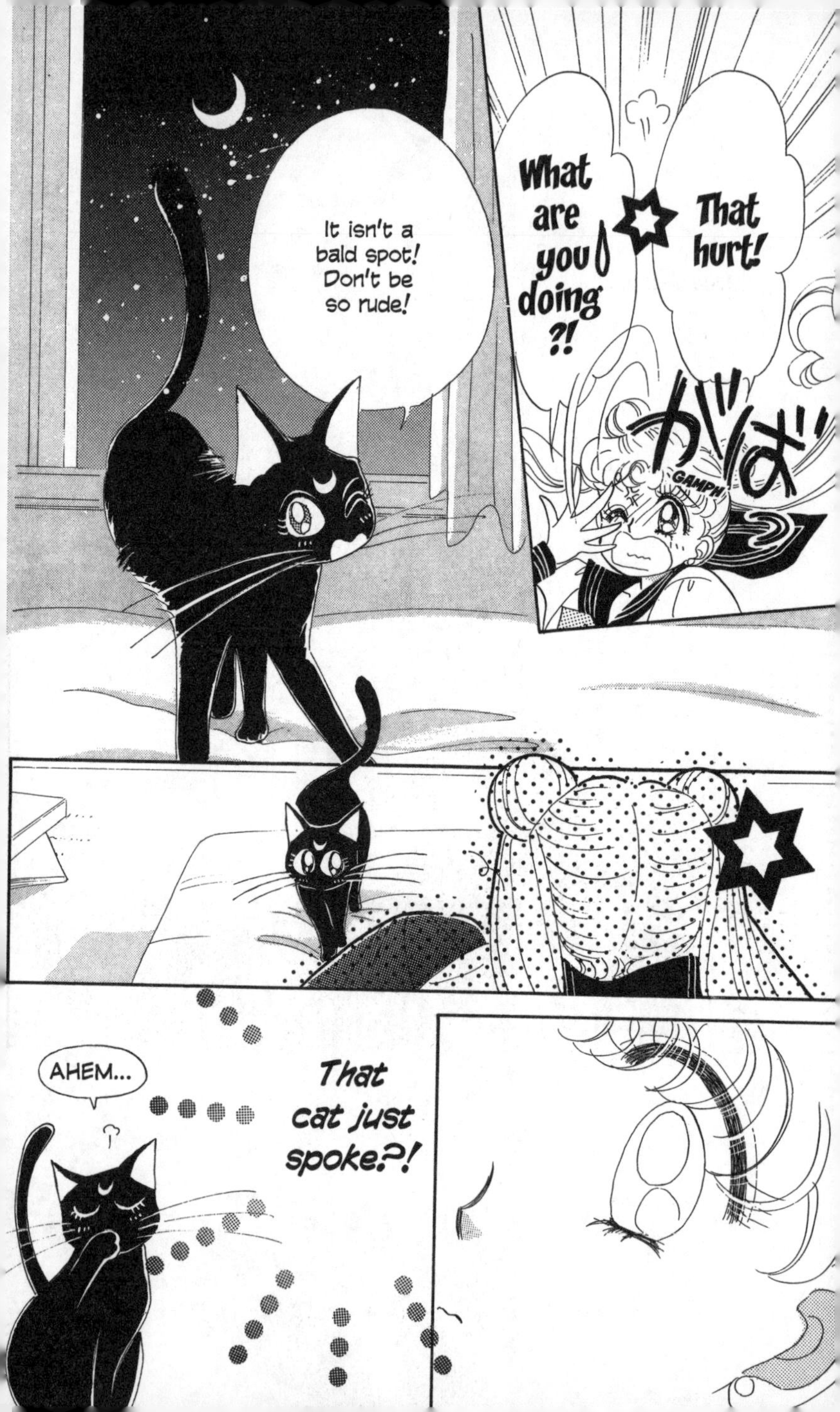
That hurt!
What are you doing?!
GAMPH
It isn't a bald spot! Don't be so rude!
That cat just spoke?!
AHEM...

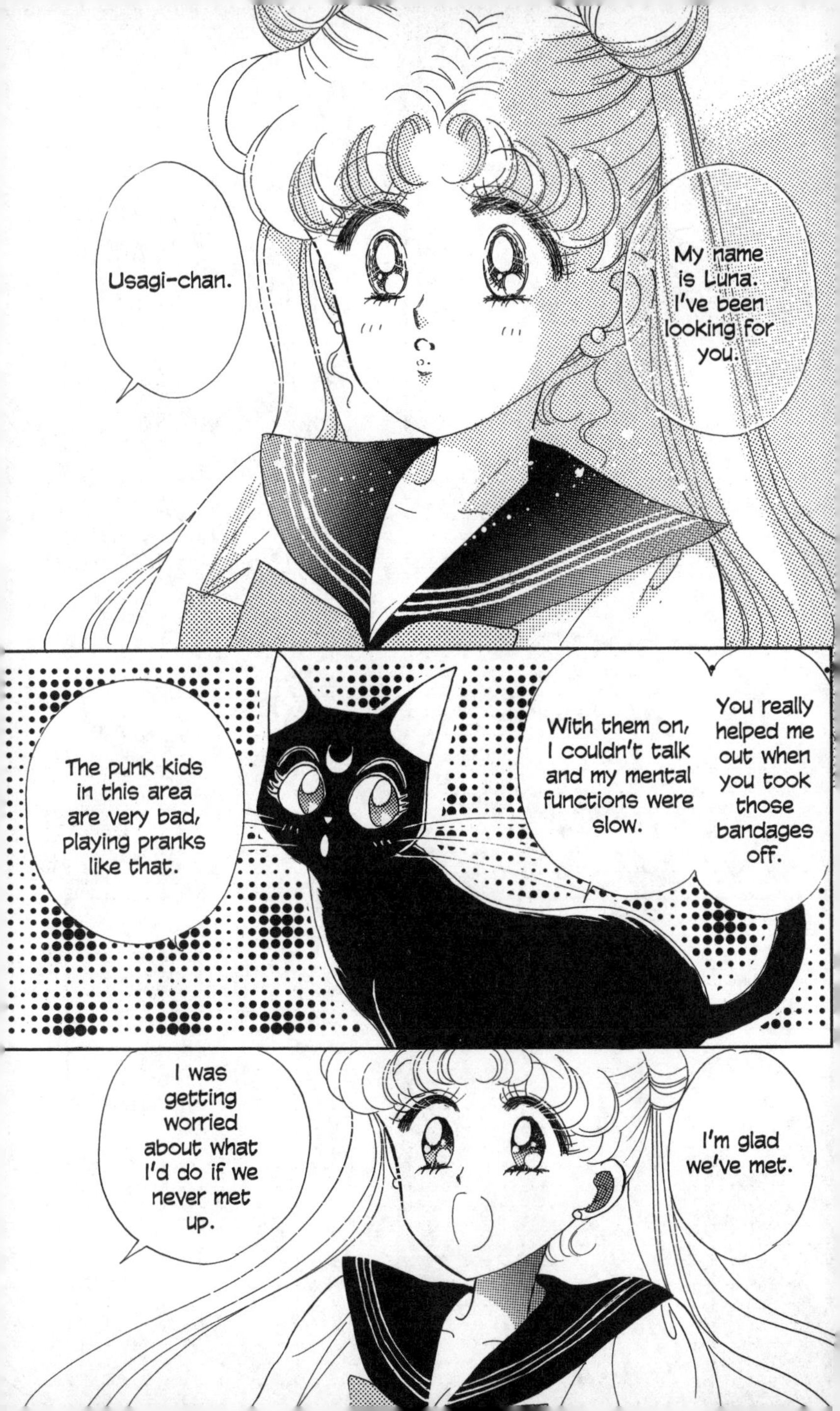
My name is Luna. I've been looking for you.
Usagi-chan.
You really helped me out when you took those bandages off.
With them on, I couldn't talk and my mental functions were slow.
The punk kids in this area are very bad, playing pranks like that.
I'm glad we've met.
I was getting worried about what I'd do if we never met up.

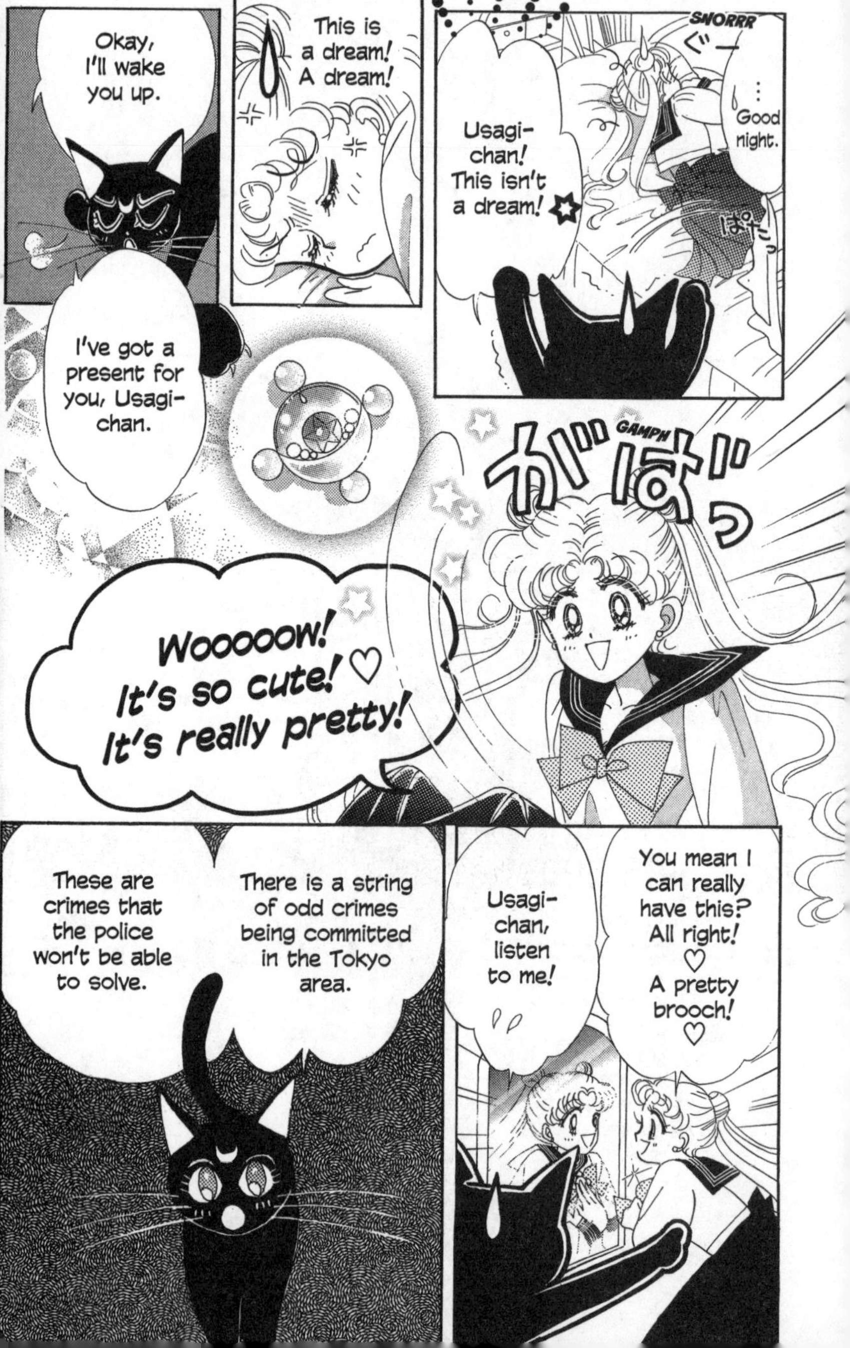
SNORRR
ぐー
... Good night.
ぱたっ
Usagi-chan! This isn't a dream!
This is a dream! A dream!
Okay, I'll wake you up.
I've got a present for you, Usagi-chan.
GAMPH
がばっ
Woooow! It's so cute! ♡ It's really pretty!
You mean I can really have this? All right! ♡ A pretty brooch! ♡
Usagi-chan, listen to me!
There is a string of odd crimes being committed in the Tokyo area.
These are crimes that the police won't be able to solve.

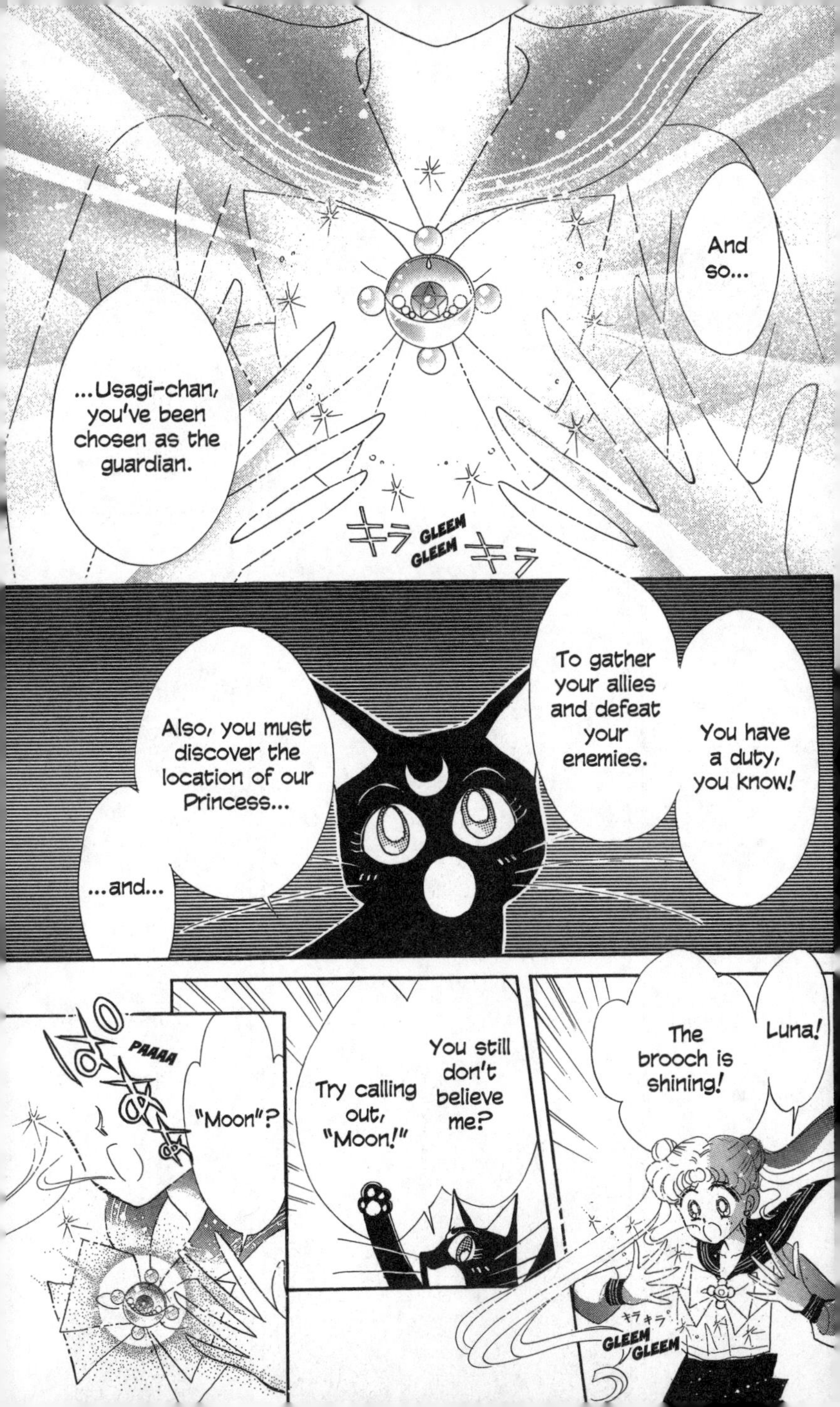
And so...
...Usagi-chan, you've been chosen as the guardian.
キラ GLEEM GLEEM キラ
You have a duty, you know!
To gather your allies and defeat your enemies.
Also, you must discover the location of our Princess...
...and...
Luna!
The brooch is shining!
キラキラ
GLEEM GLEEM
You still don't believe me?
Try calling out, "Moon!"
"Moon"?
PAAAA

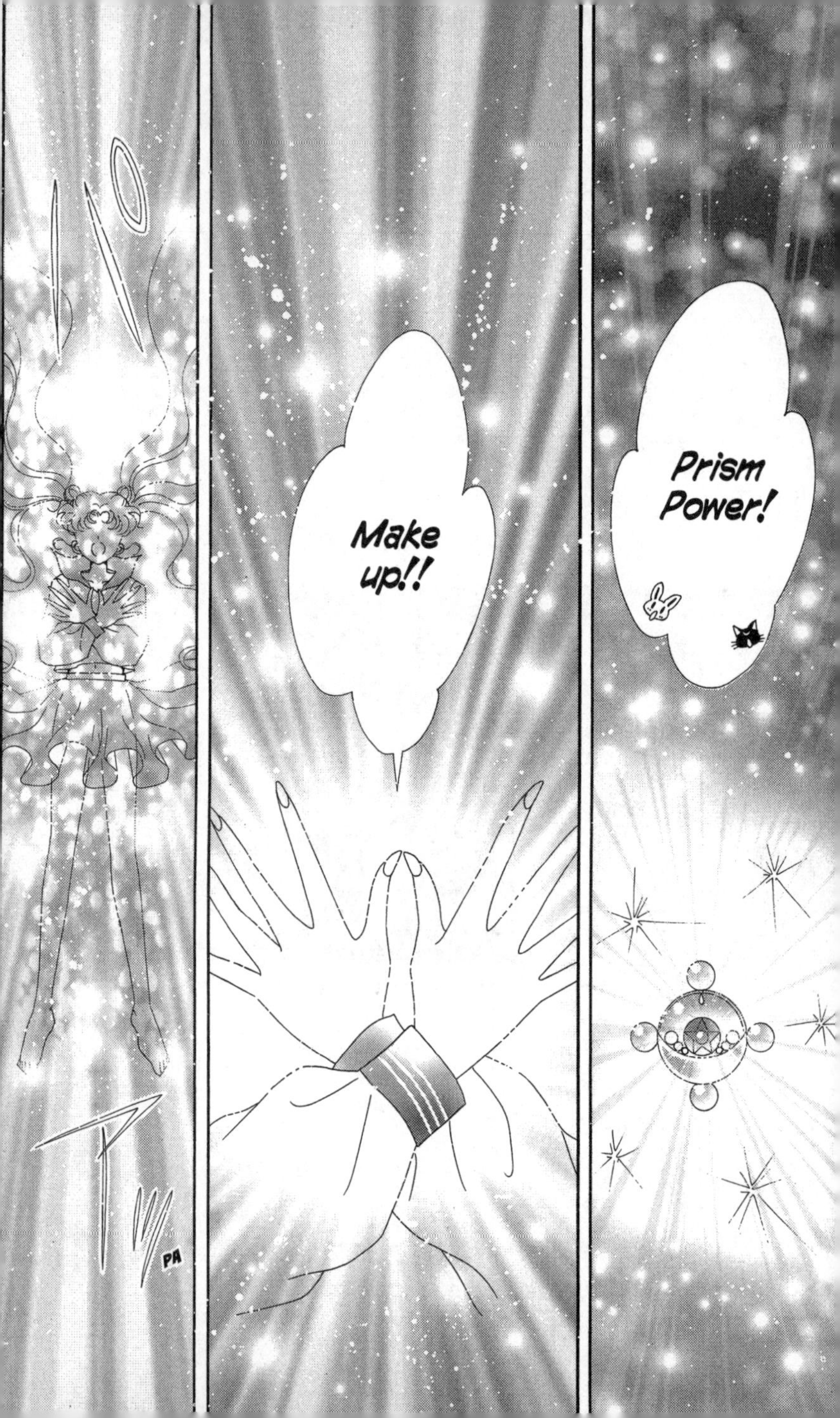
Prism Power!
Make up!!
PA

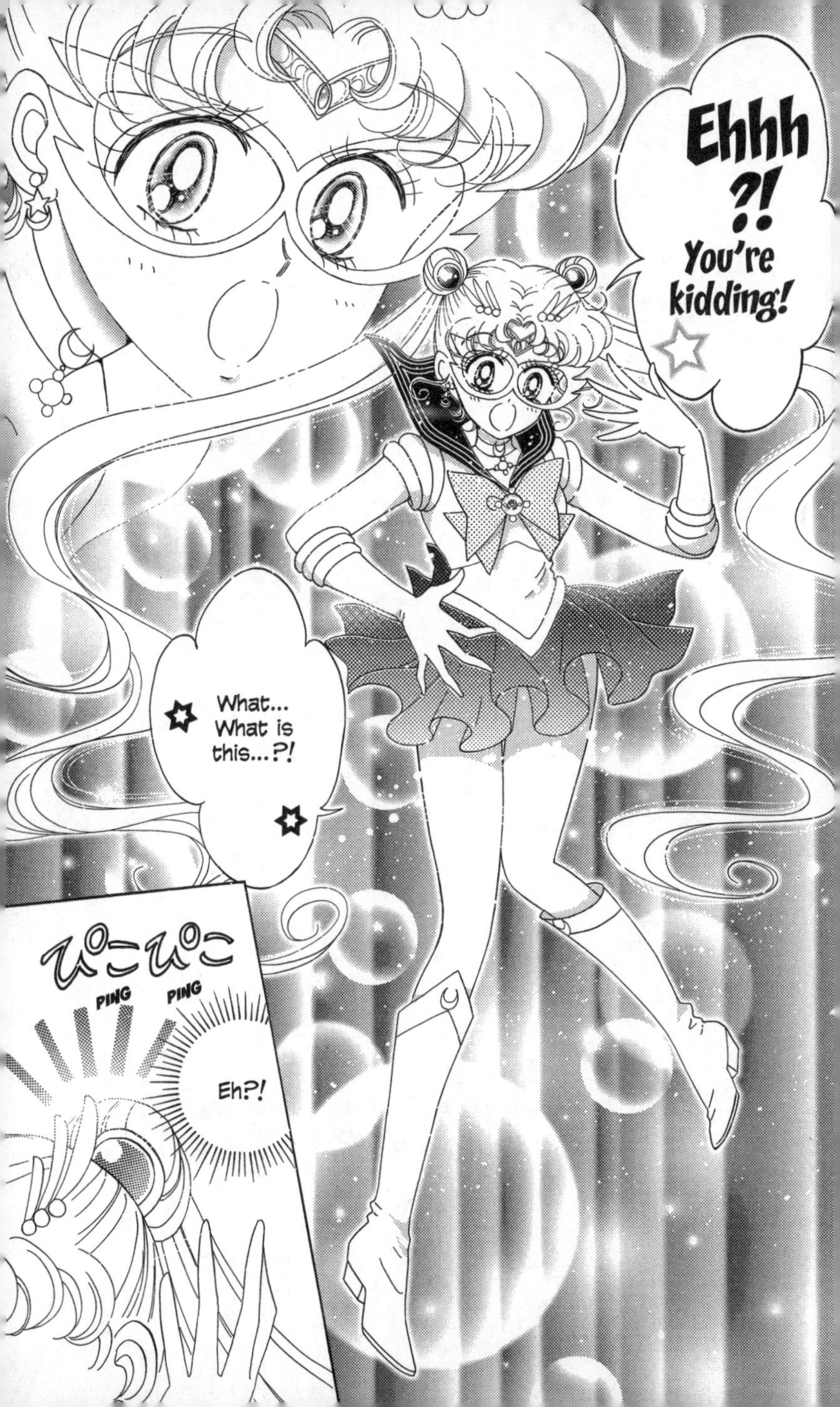
Ehhh ?! You're kidding!
What... What is this...?!
ぴこぴこ
PING PING
Eh?!

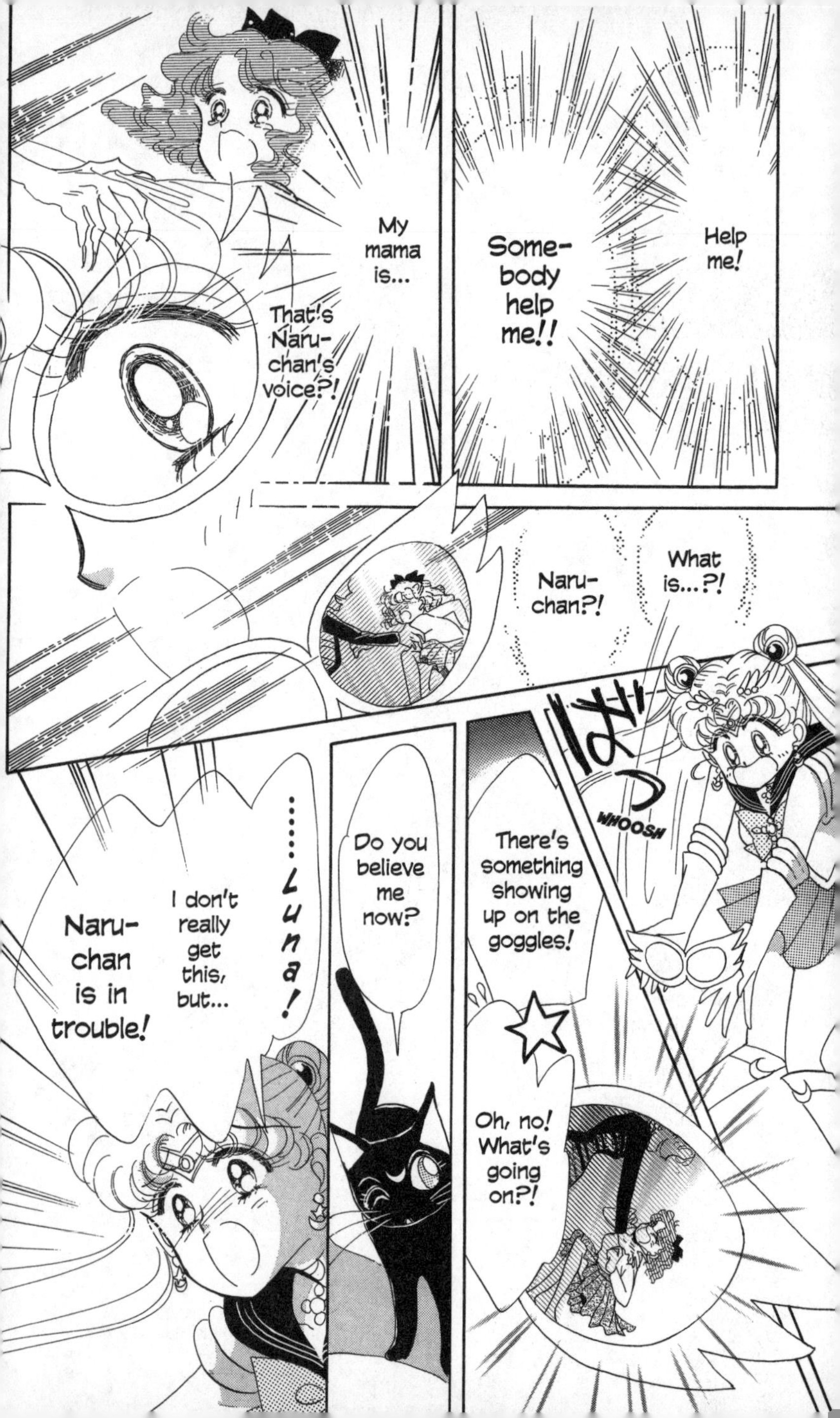
Help me!
Some-body help me!!
My mama is...
That's Naru-chan's voice?!
What is...?!
Naru-chan?!
はっ
WHOOSH
There's something showing up on the goggles!
Oh, no! What's going on?!
Do you believe me now?
......Luna!
I don't really get this, but...
Naru-chan is in trouble!

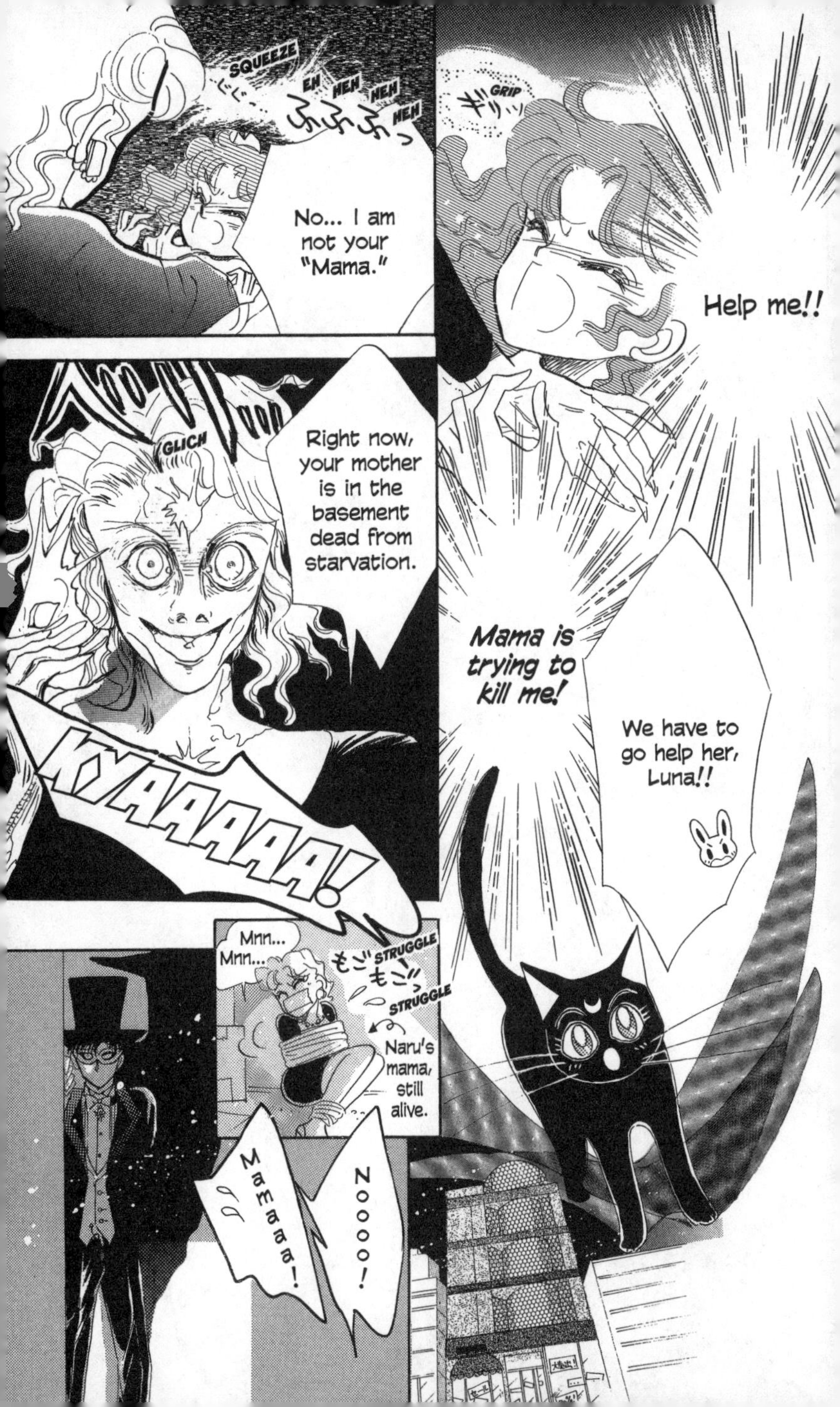
GRIP
Help me!!
Mama is trying to kill me!
We have to go help her, Luna!!
SQUEEZE
EH HEH HEH HEH
No... I am not your "Mama."
GLICH
Right now, your mother is in the basement dead from starvation.
KYAAAAAA!
Mnn... Mnn...
STRUGGLE
STRUGGLE
Naru's mama, still alive.
Noooo!
Mamaaa!

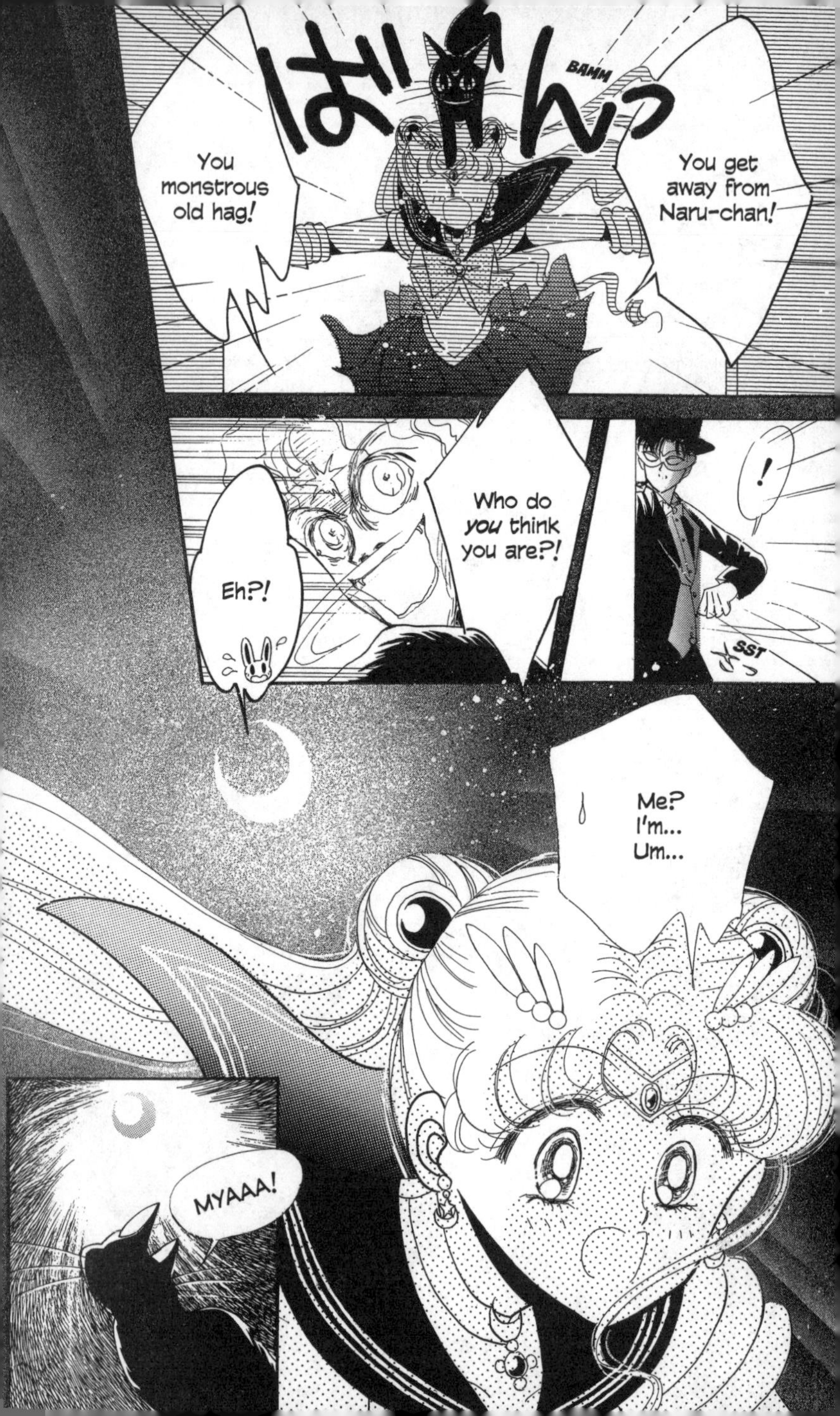

BAMM
You get away from Naru-chan!
You monstrous old hag!
!
SST
Who do *you* think you are?!
Eh?!
Me? I'm... Um...
MYAAA!

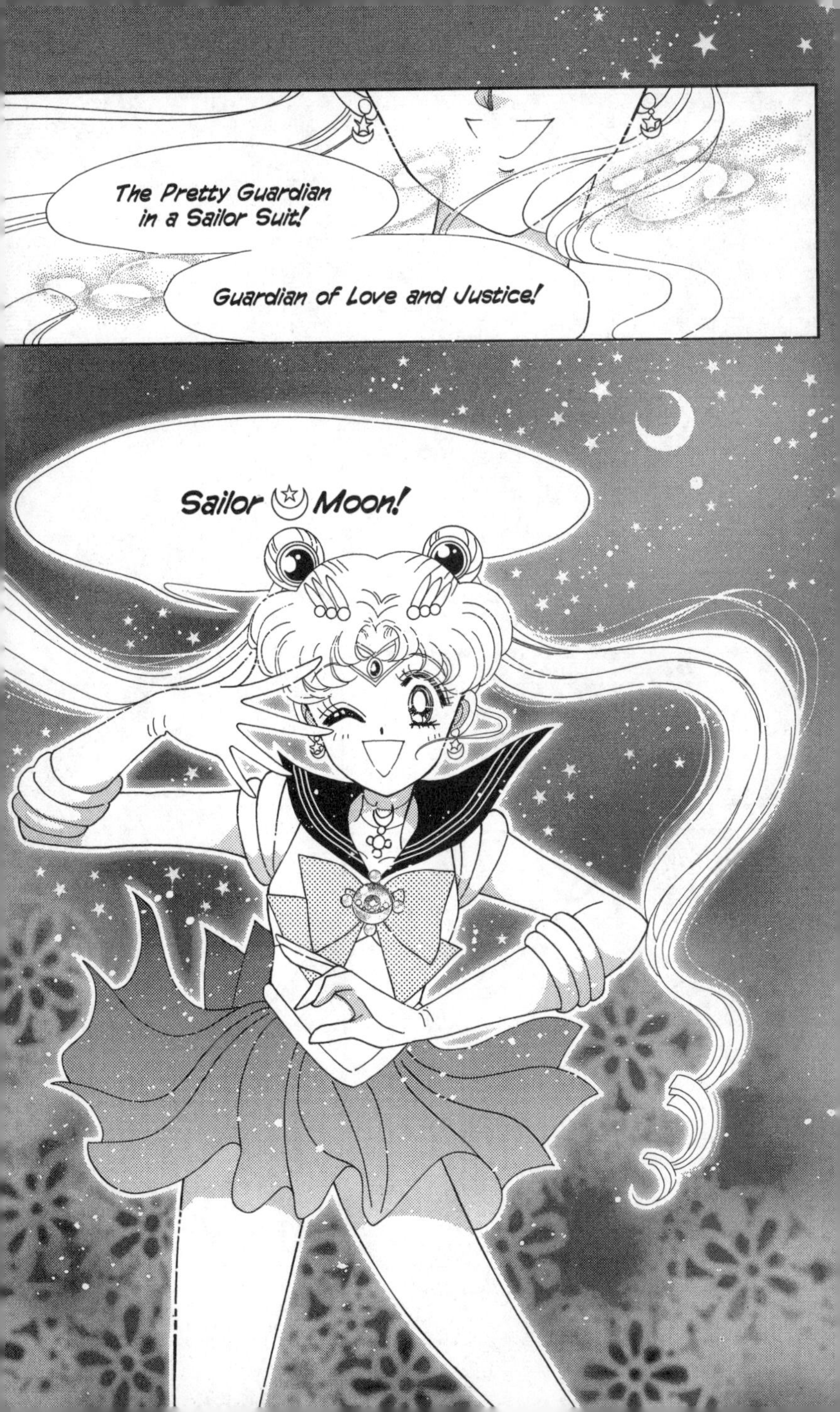
The Pretty Guardian in a Sailor Suit!
Guardian of Love and Justice!
Sailor Moon!

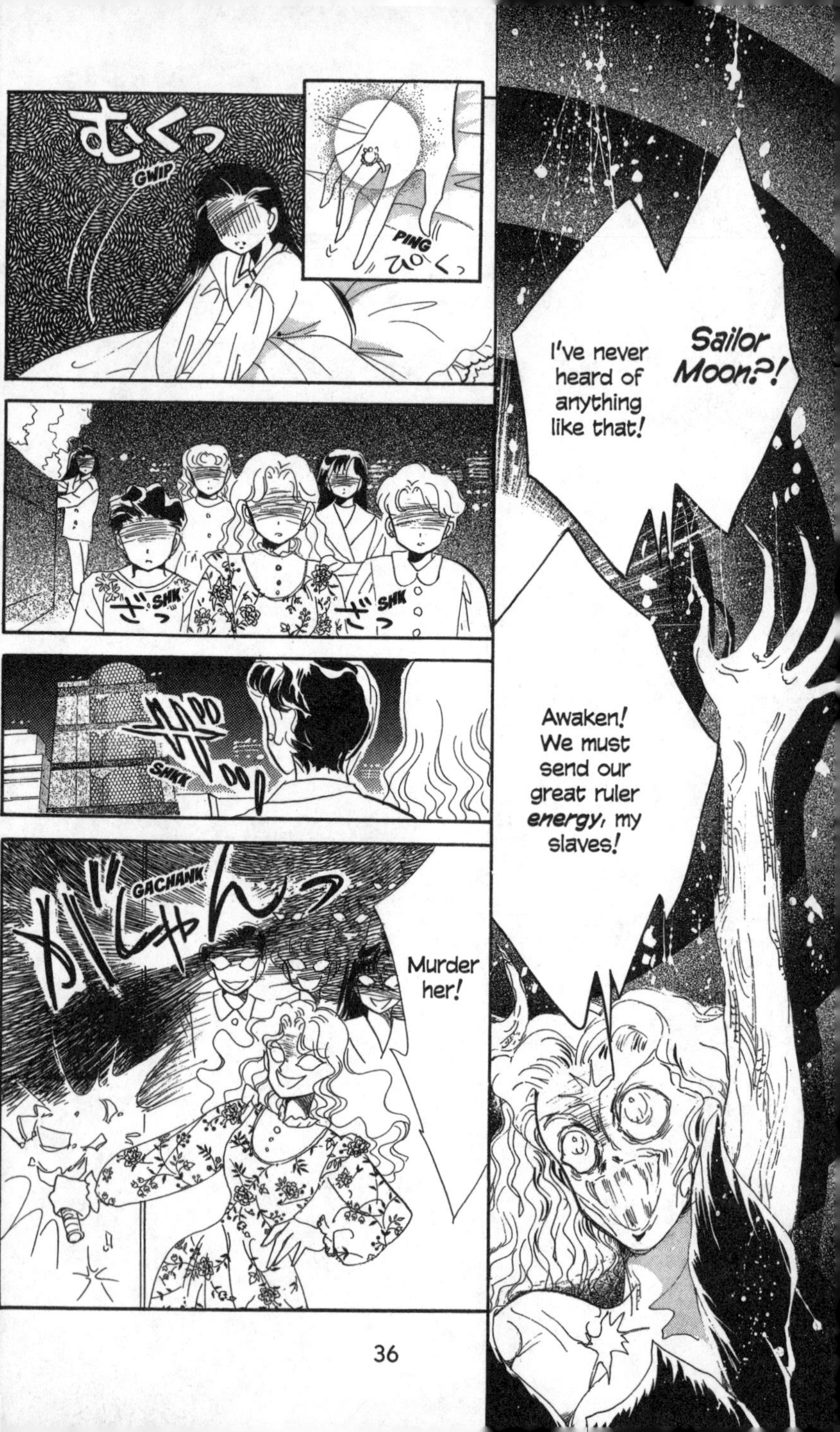
Sailor Moon?!
I've never heard of anything like that!
Awaken! We must send our great ruler *energy*, my slaves!
PING
ぴくっ
むくっ
GWIP
ざっ
SHK
ざっ
SHK
ザッ
PD
SHKK
DO
がしゃんっ
GACHANK
Murder her!

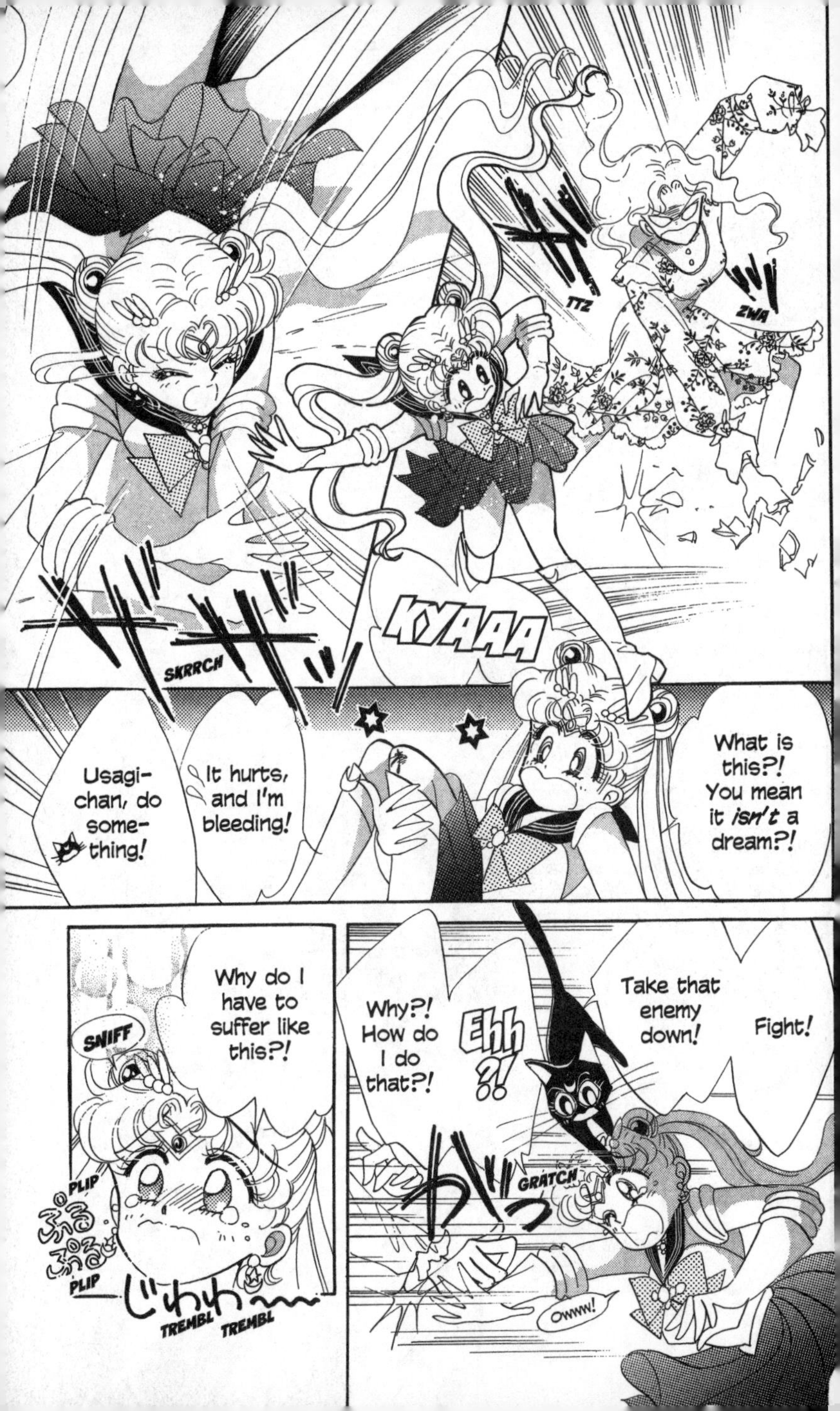
ZWA
TTZ
KYAAA
SKRRCH
What is this?! You mean it *isn't* a dream?!
It hurts, and I'm bleeding!
Usagi-chan, do something!
Fight!
Take that enemy down!
Ehh ?!
Why?! How do I do that?!
GRATCH
OWWW!
Why do I have to suffer like this?!
SNIFF
PLIP
PLIP
TREMBL
TREMBL

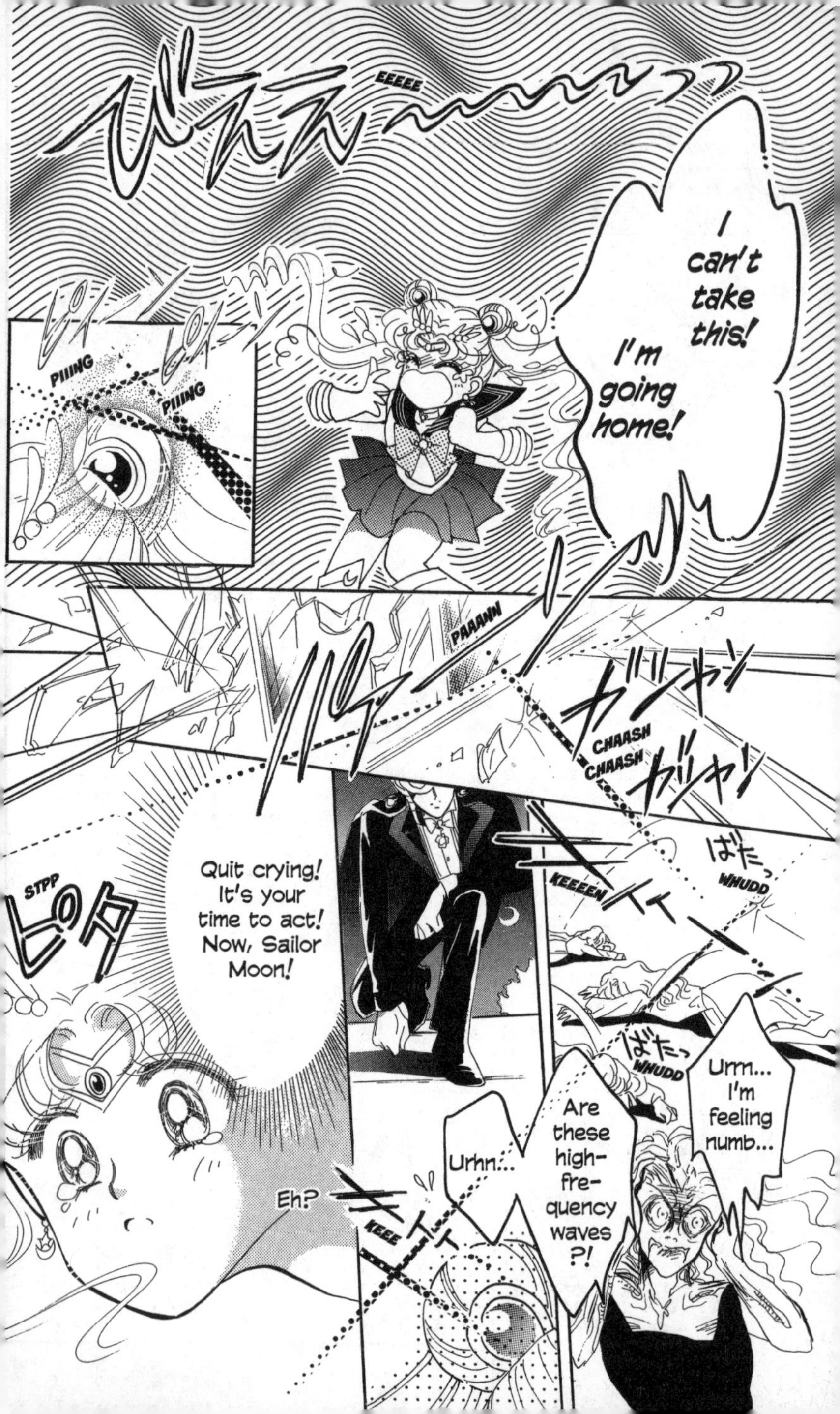
EEEEE
I can't take this!
I'm going home!
PIIING
PIIING
PAAANN
CHAASH
CHAASH
KEEEEN
WHUDD
WHUDD
Urrn... I'm feeling numb...
Are these high-fre-quency waves?!
Urhn...
Quit crying! It's your time to act! Now, Sailor Moon!
STPP
Eh?
KEEE

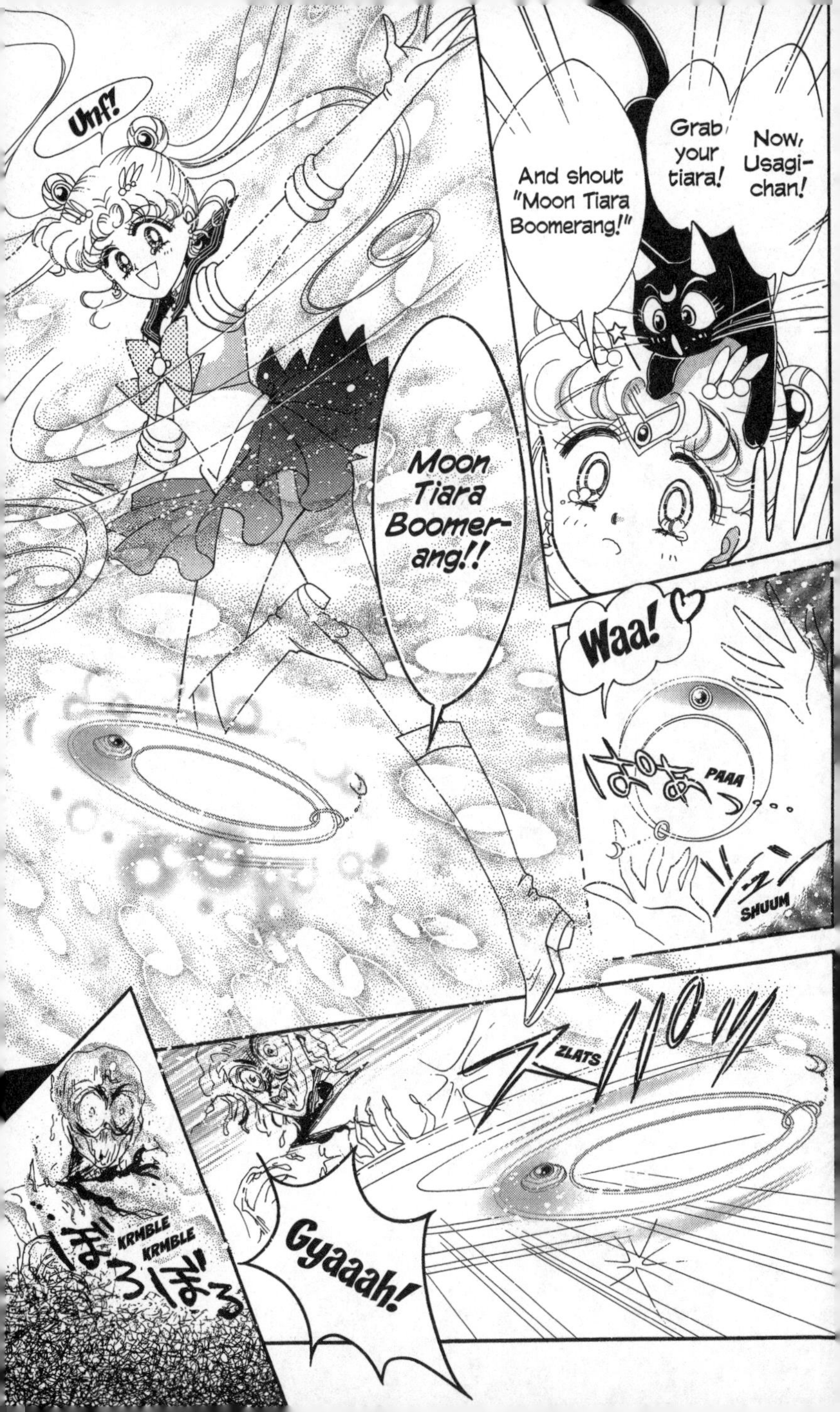

Now, Usagi-chan!
Grab your tiara!
And shout "Moon Tiara Boomerang!"
Waa!
PAAA
SHUUM
Unf!
Moon Tiara Boomer-ang!!
ZLATS
Gyaaah!
KRMBLE KRMBLE

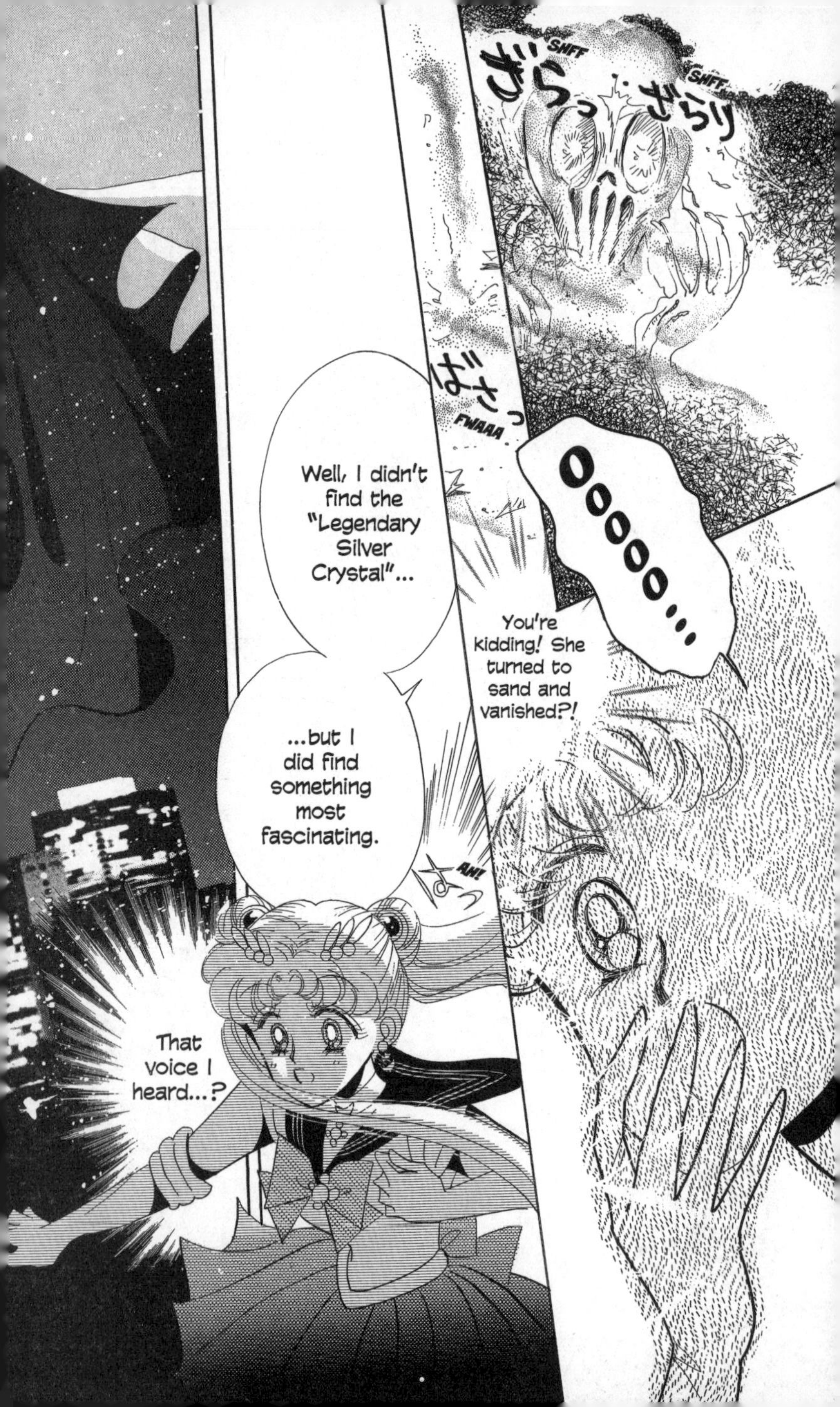

ざらっ
SHFF
ざらり
SHFF
ばさっ
FWAAA
Ooooo...
You're kidding! She turned to sand and vanished?!
Well, I didn't find the "Legendary Silver Crystal"...
...but I did find something most fascinating.
あっ
AH!
That voice I heard...?

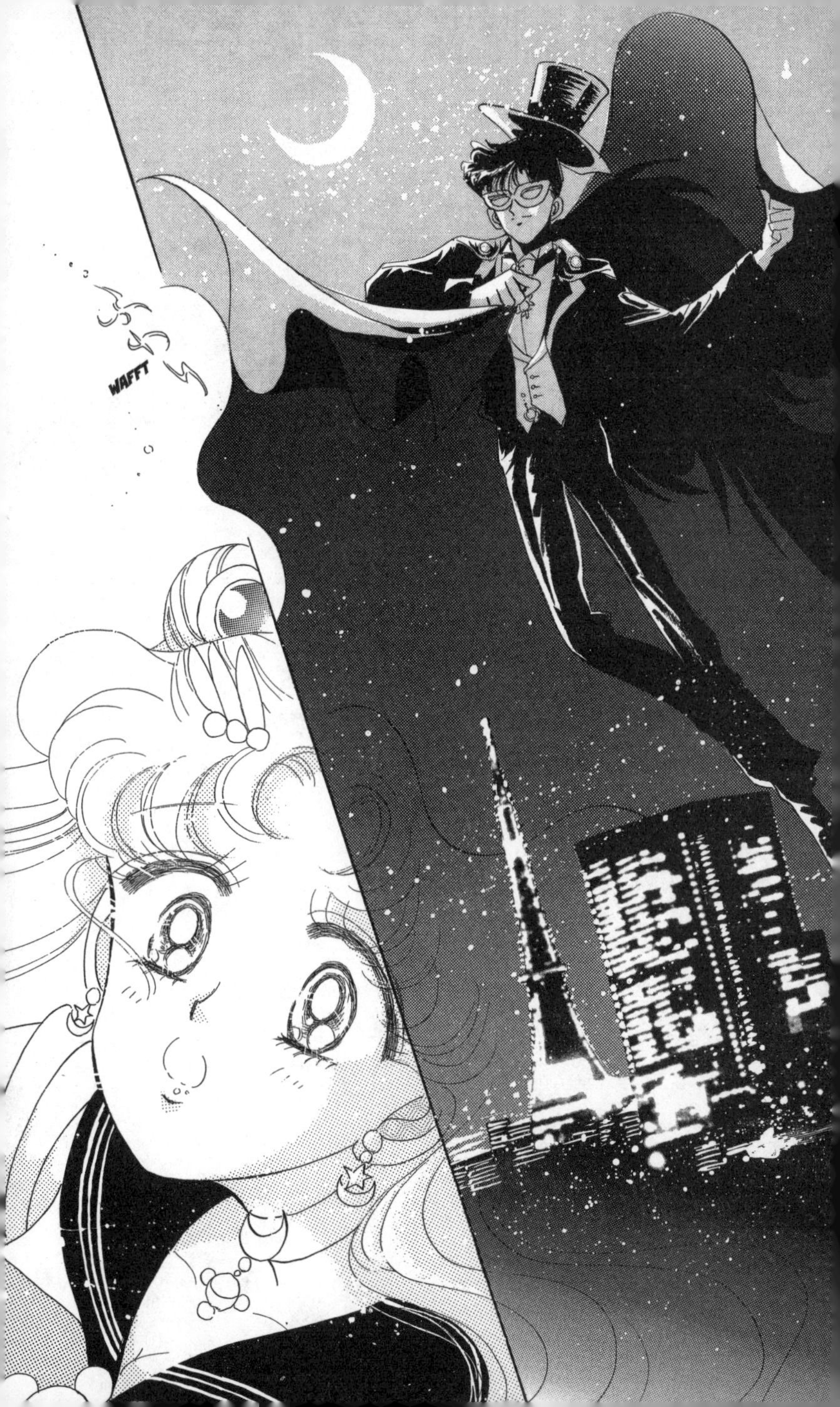
WAFFT

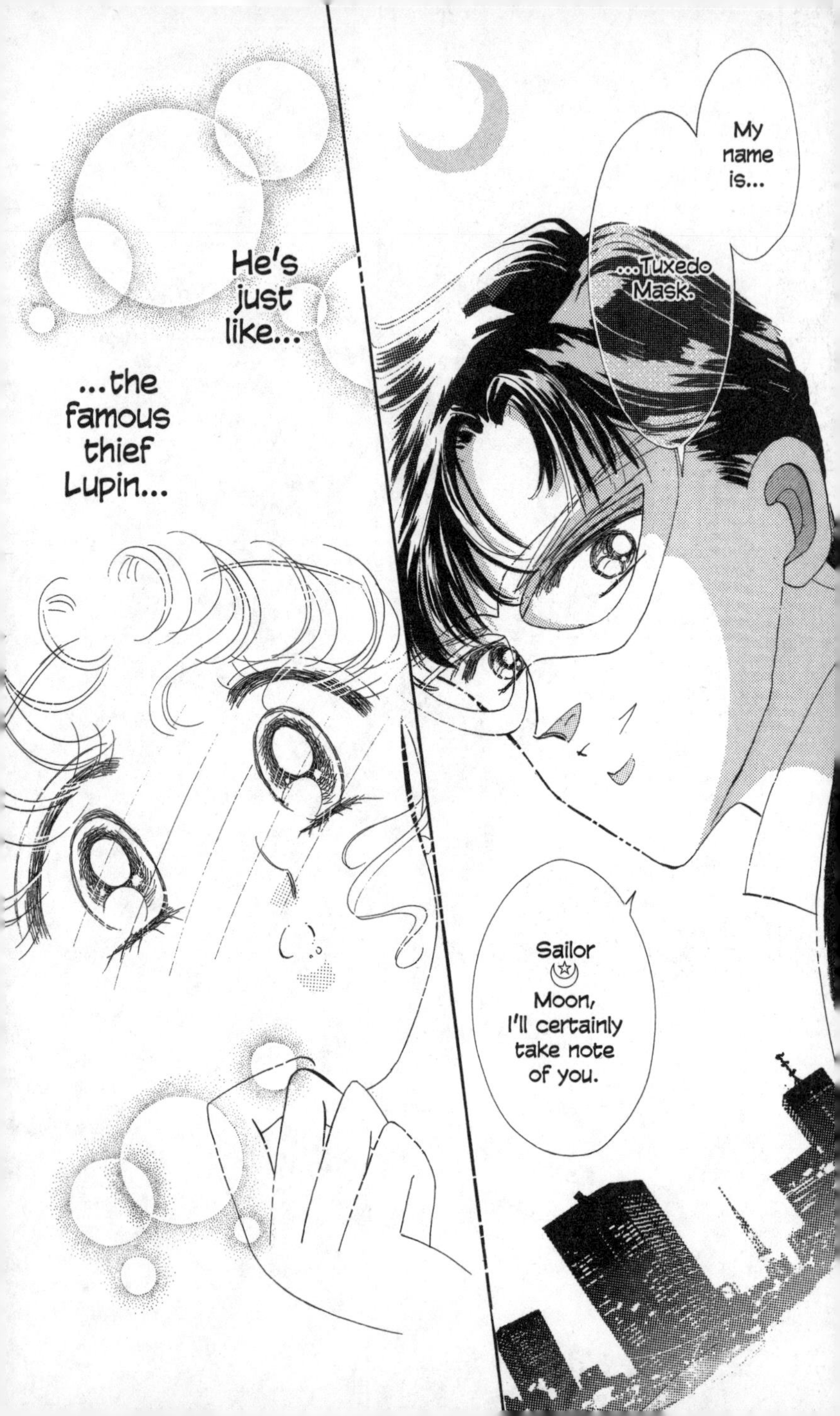
My name is...
...Tuxedo Mask.
Sailor Moon, I'll certainly take note of you.
He's just like...
...the famous thief Lupin...

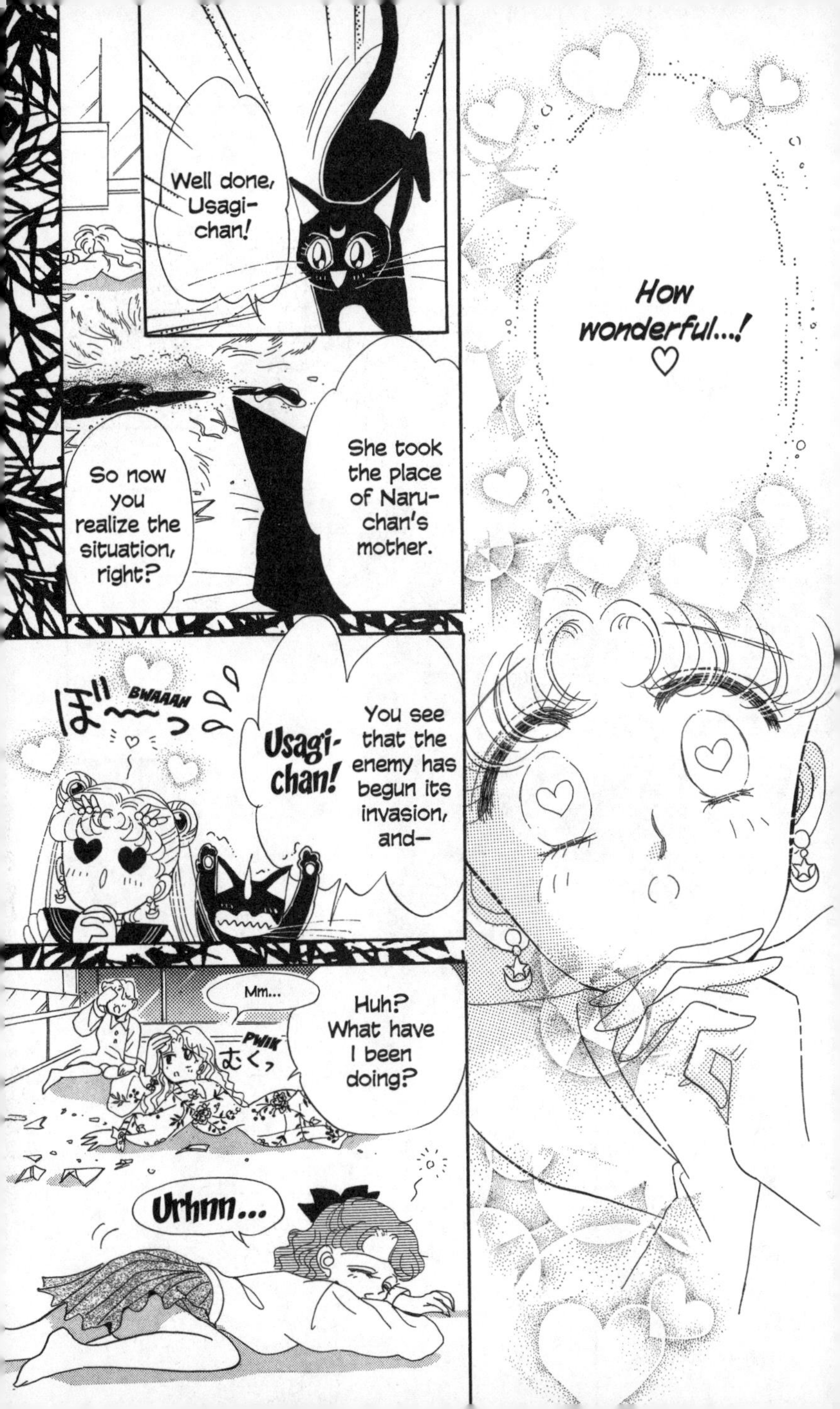

How wonderful...! ♡
Well done, Usagi-chan!
She took the place of Naru-chan's mother.
So now you realize the situation, right?
Usagi-chan!
You see that the enemy has begun its invasion, and—
ぼ~~っ
BWAAAH
Huh? What have I been doing?
Mm...
むくっ
PWIK
Urhnn...

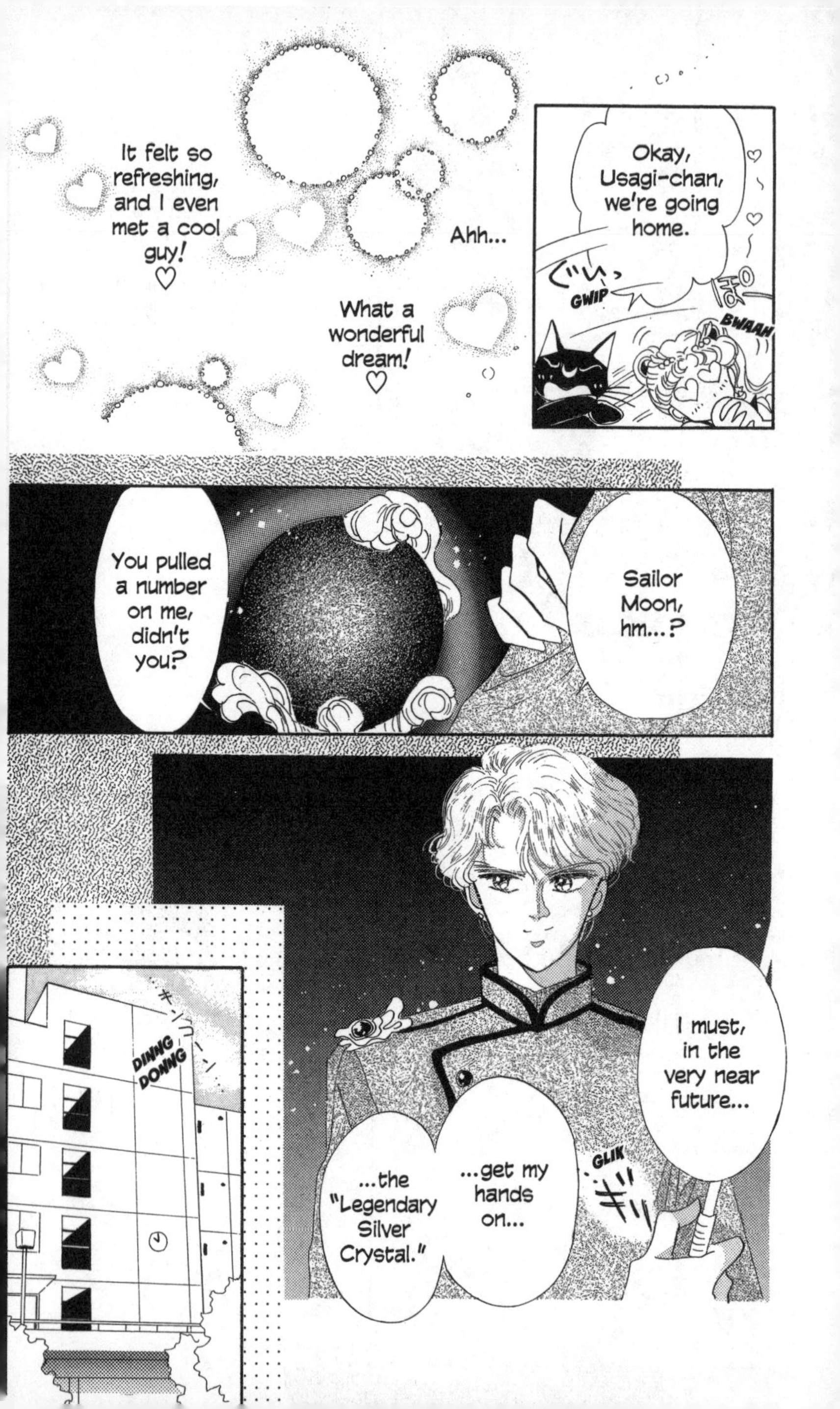

Okay, Usagi-chan, we're going home.
ぐいっ
GWIP
ぽー
BWAAH
Ahh...
What a wonderful dream! ♡
It felt so refreshing, and I even met a cool guy! ♡
Sailor Moon, hm...?
You pulled a number on me, didn't you?
I must, in the very near future...
GLIK
ギッ
...get my hands on...
...the "Legendary Silver Crystal."
キンコーン
DING DONG

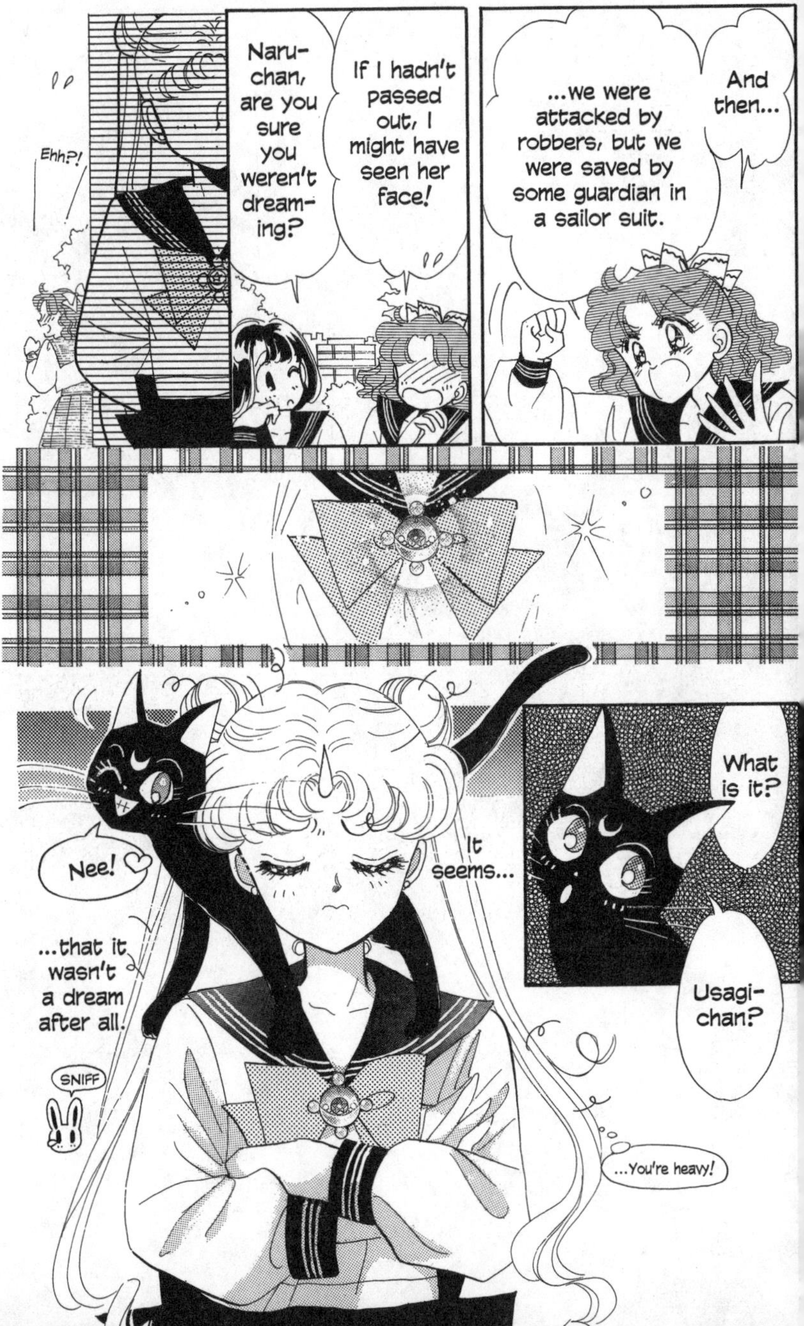
And then...
...we were attacked by robbers, but we were saved by some guardian in a sailor suit.
If I hadn't passed out, I might have seen her face!
Naru-chan, are you sure you weren't dreaming?
Ehh?!
What is it?
Usagi-chan?
It seems...
Nee! ♡
...that it wasn't a dream after all.
SNIFF
...You're heavy!

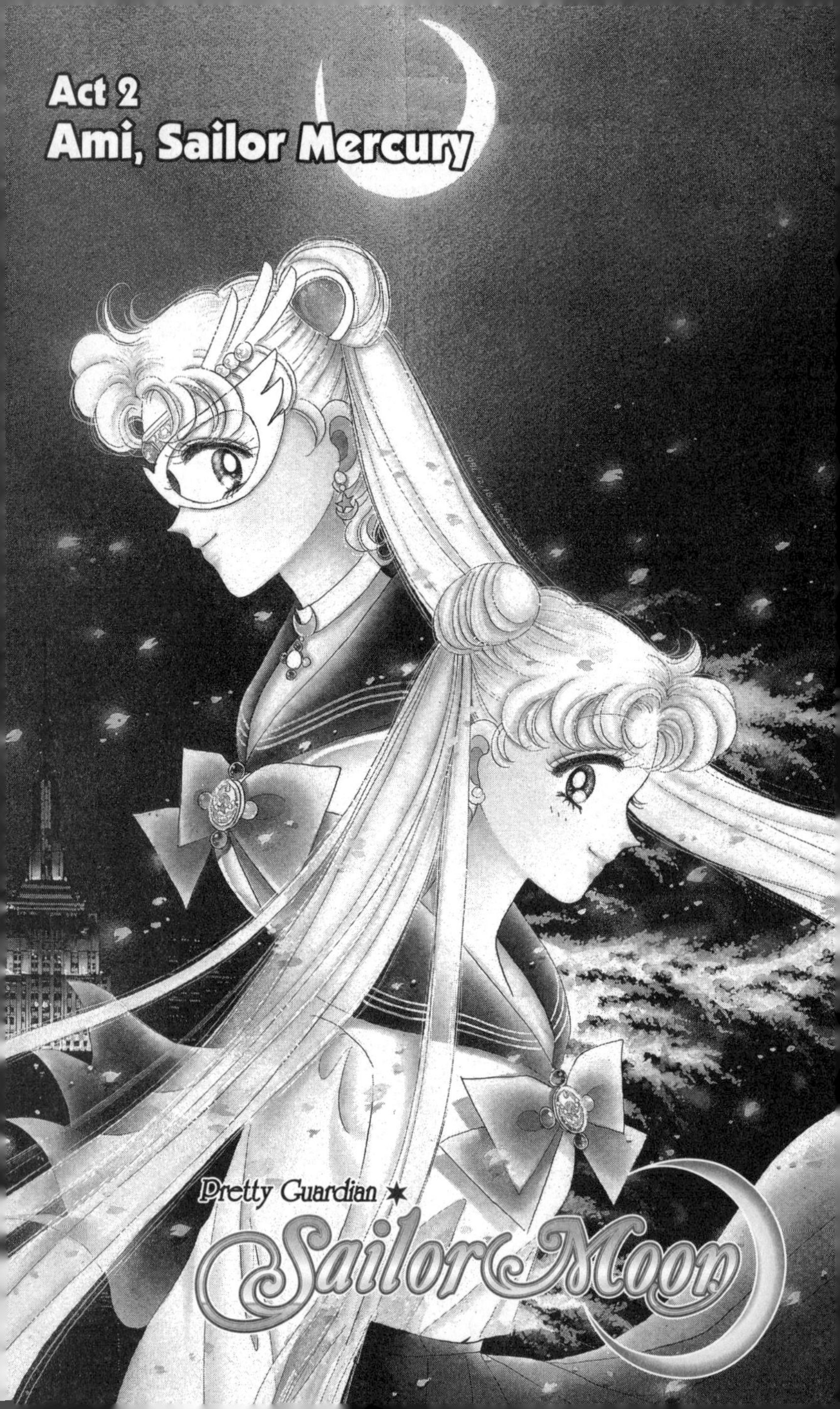
Act 2
Ami, Sailor Mercury
Pretty Guardian ★
Sailor Moon

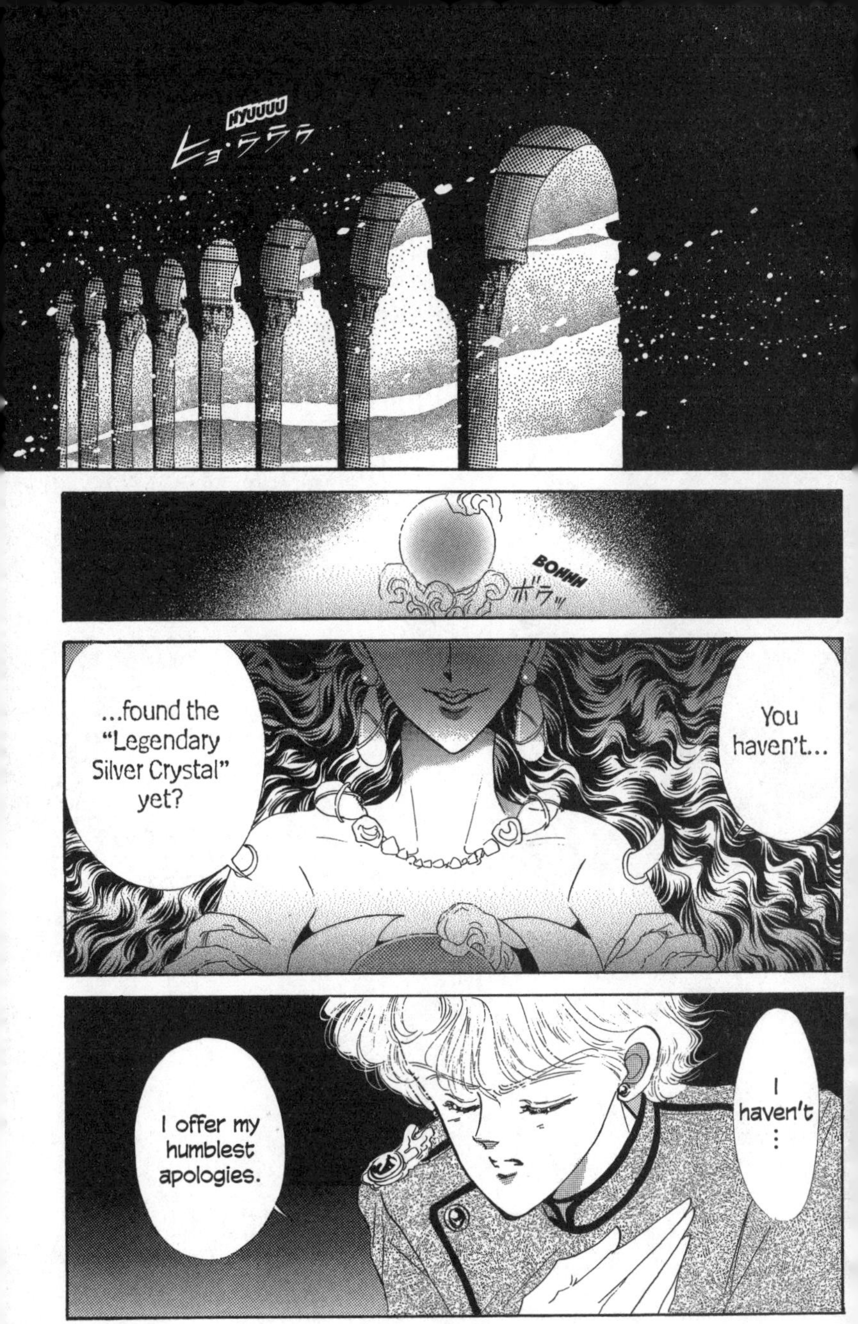
HYUUUU
ヒョ・ラララ
BOHHH
ボウッ
You haven't...
...found the "Legendary Silver Crystal" yet?
I haven't ...
I offer my humblest apologies.

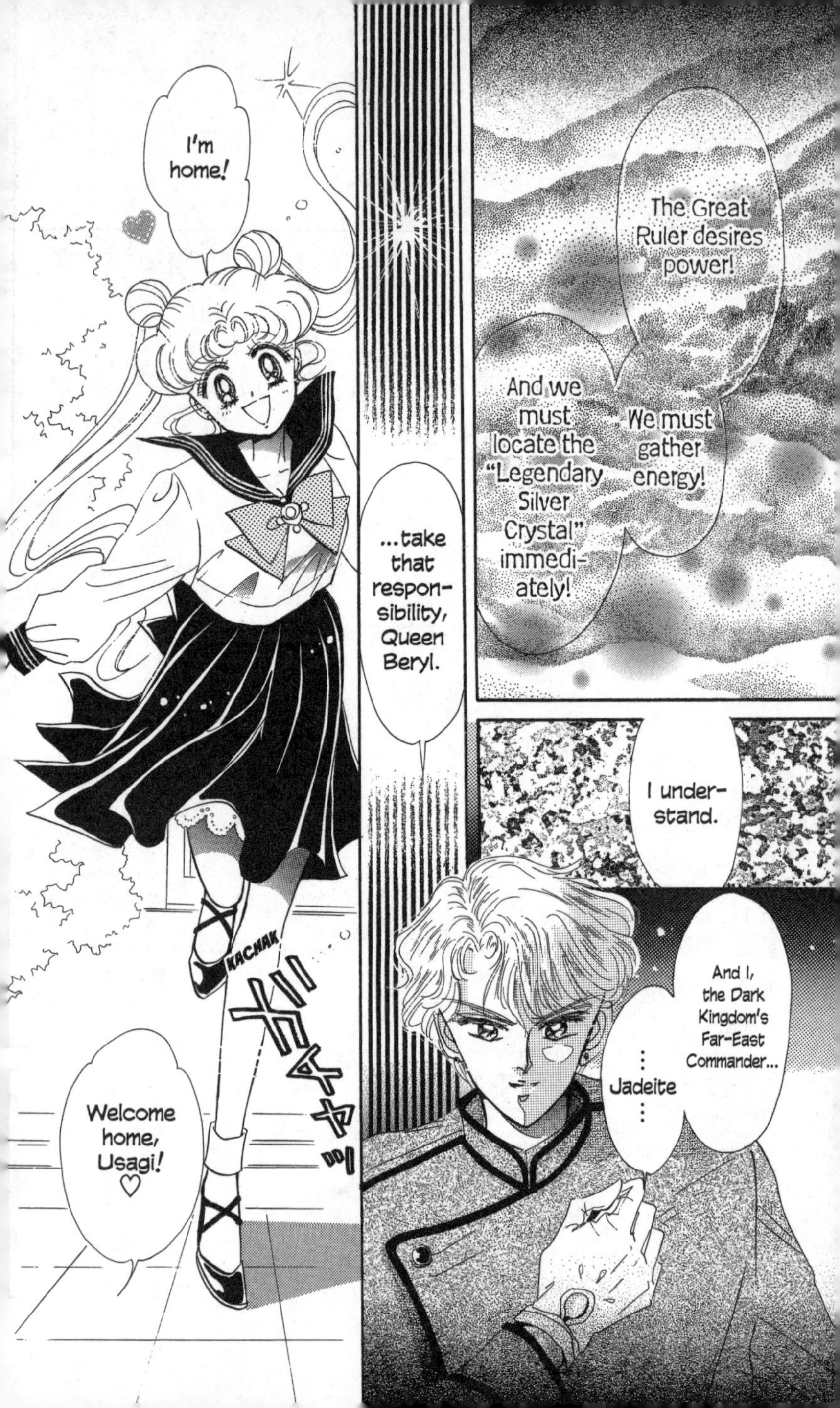
The Great Ruler desires power!
We must gather energy!
And we must locate the "Legendary Silver Crystal" immedi-ately!
I under-stand.
And I, the Dark Kingdom's Far-East Commander...
...Jadeite...
...take that respon-sibility, Queen Beryl.
I'm home!
KACHAK
Welcome home, Usagi! ♡

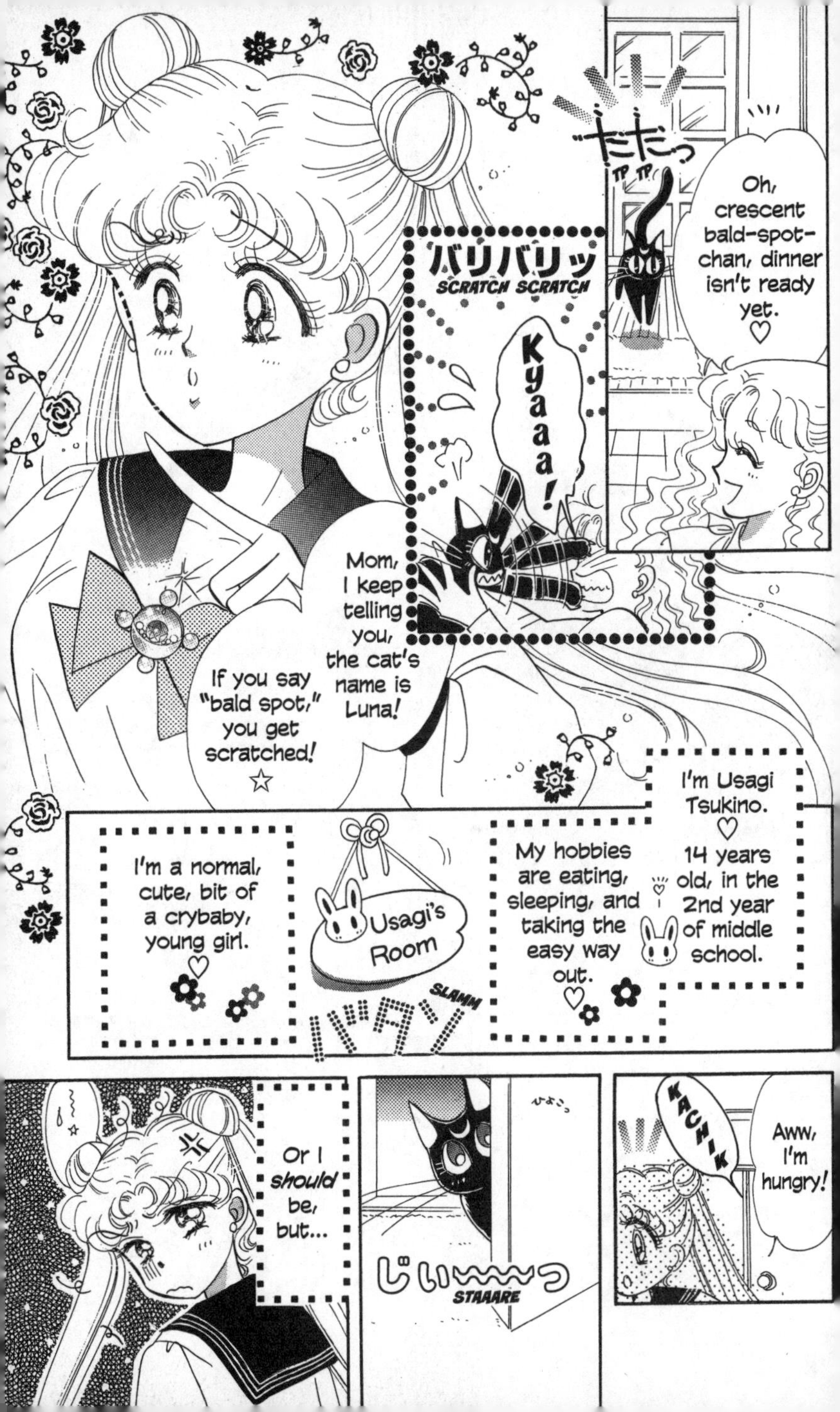
ただっ
TP TP
Oh, crescent bald-spot-chan, dinner isn't ready yet. ♡
バリバリッ
SCRATCH SCRATCH
Kyaaa!
Mom, I keep telling you, the cat's name is Luna!
If you say "bald spot," you get scratched! ☆
I'm Usagi Tsukino. ♡ 14 years old, in the 2nd year of middle school.
My hobbies are eating, sleeping, and taking the easy way out. ♡
Usagi's Room
SLAMM
I'm a normal, cute, bit of a crybaby, young girl. ♡
KACHIK
Aww, I'm hungry!
STAAARE
Or I *should* be, but...

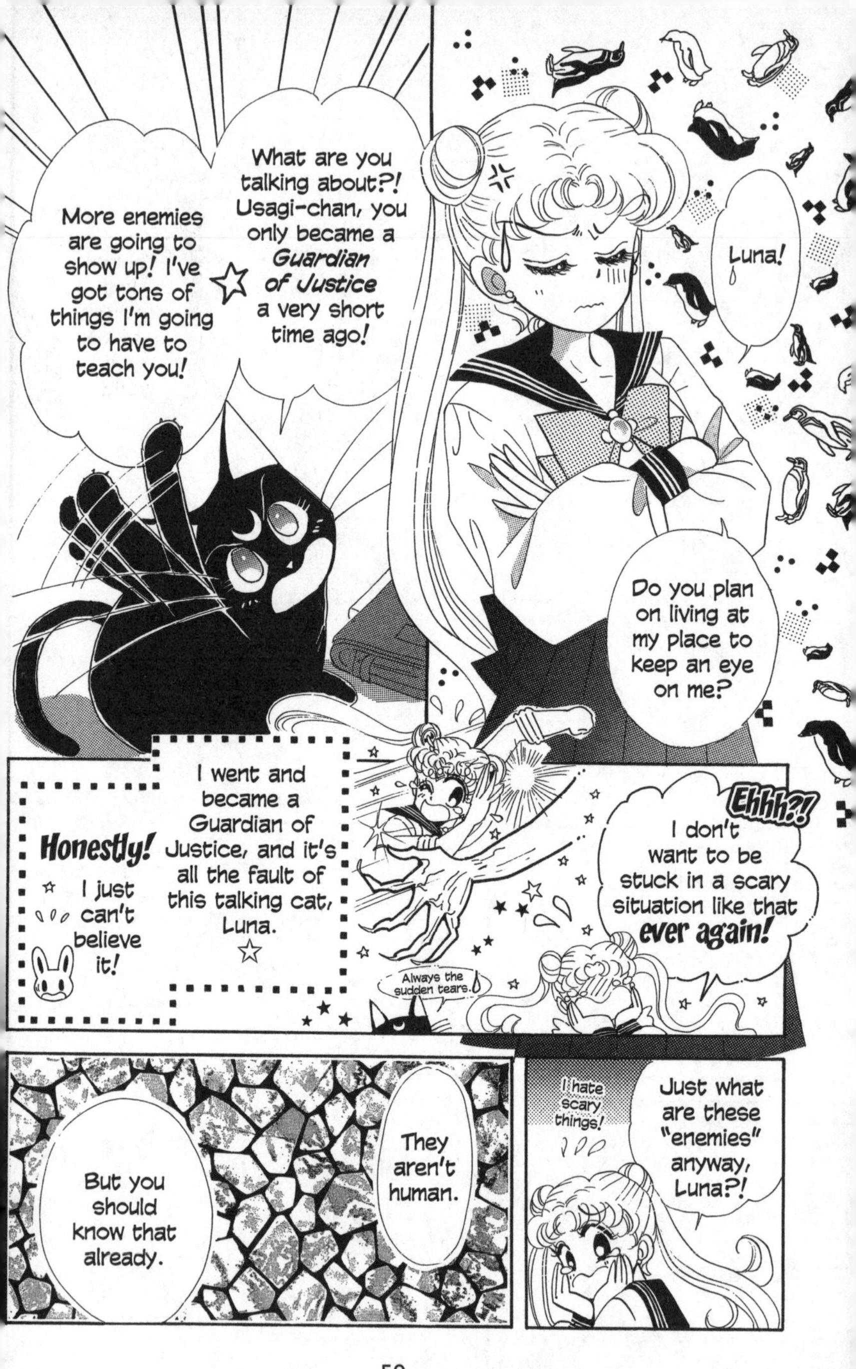
Luna!
Do you plan on living at my place to keep an eye on me?
What are you talking about?! Usagi-chan, you only became a *Guardian of Justice* a very short time ago!
More enemies are going to show up! I've got tons of things I'm going to have to teach you!
Ehhh?!
I don't want to be stuck in a scary situation like that **ever again!**
Always the sudden tears.
I went and became a Guardian of Justice, and it's all the fault of this talking cat, Luna.
Honestly! I just can't believe it!
Just what are these "enemies" anyway, Luna?!
I hate scary things!
They aren't human.
But you should know that already.

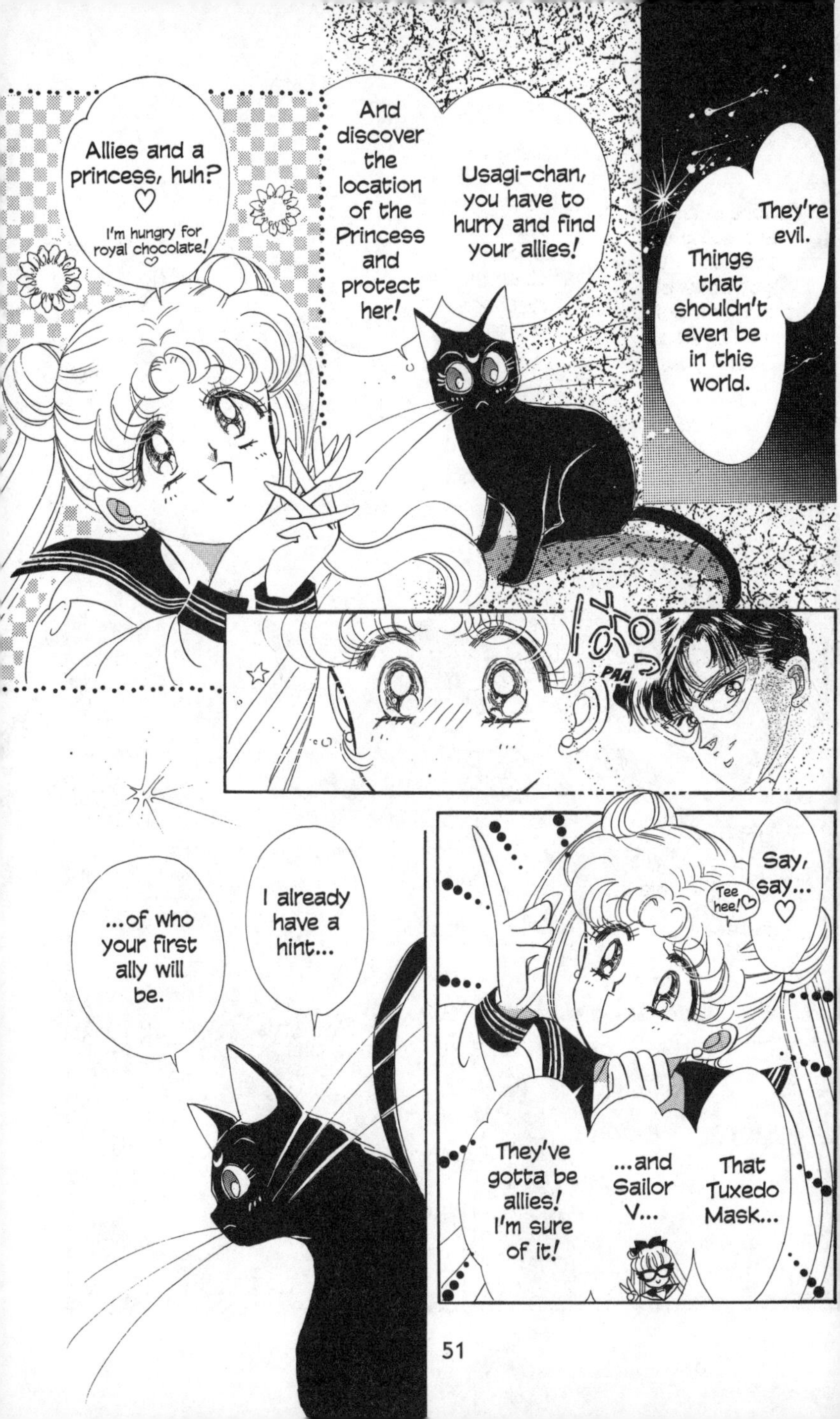

They're evil.
Things that shouldn't even be in this world.
Usagi-chan, you have to hurry and find your allies!
And discover the location of the Princess and protect her!
Allies and a princess, huh? ♡
I'm hungry for royal chocolate! ♡
PAA
Say, say... ♡
Tee hee! ♡
That Tuxedo Mask...
...and Sailor V...
They've gotta be allies! I'm sure of it!
I already have a hint...
...of who your first ally will be.

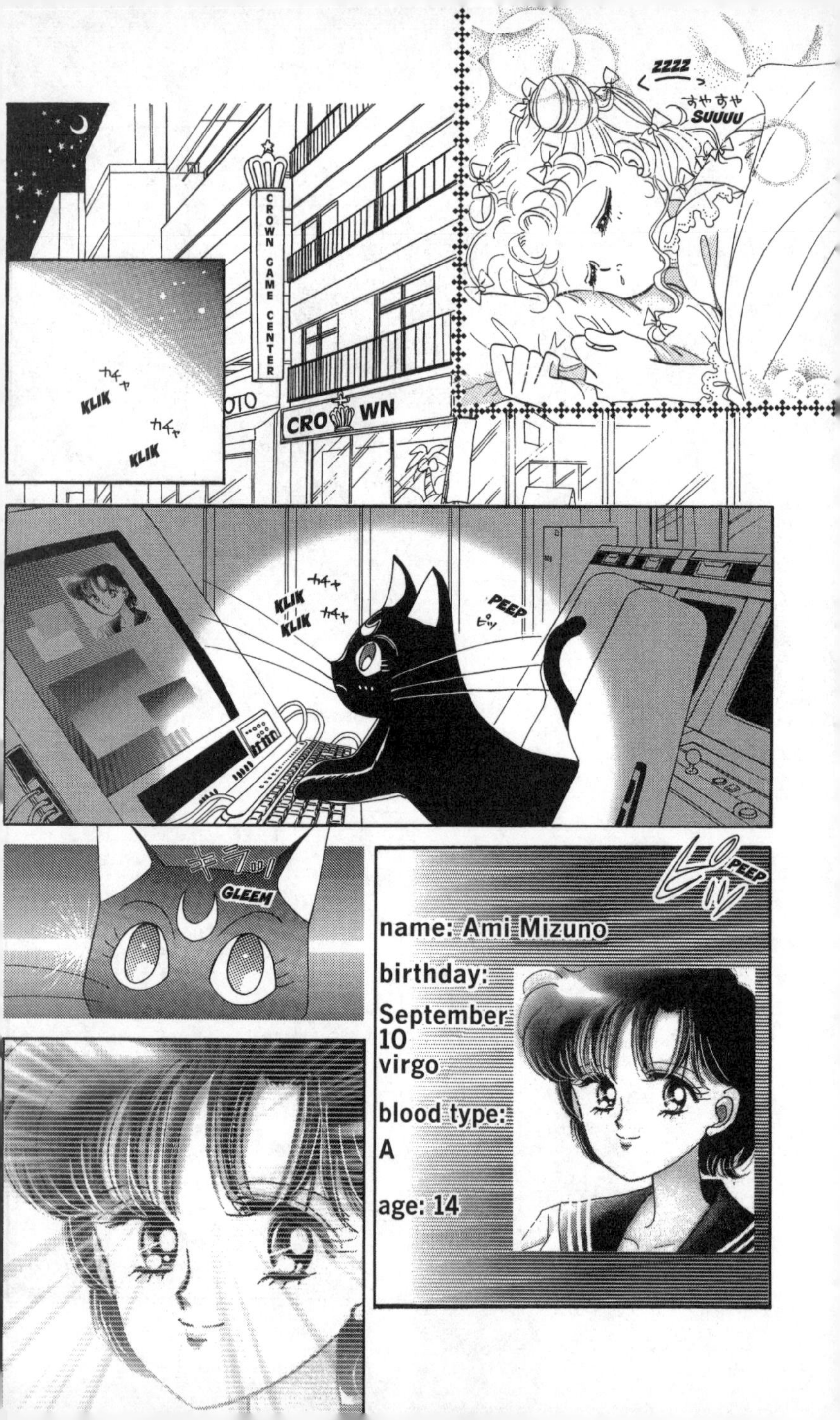
ZZZZ
すやすや
SUUUU
CROWN GAME CENTER
CROWN
カチャ
KLIK
カチャ
KLIK
KLIK KLIK
カチャ カチャ
PEEP
ピッ
ピッ
PEEP
name: Ami Mizuno
birthday:
September 10
virgo
blood type:
A
age: 14
キラッ
GLEEM

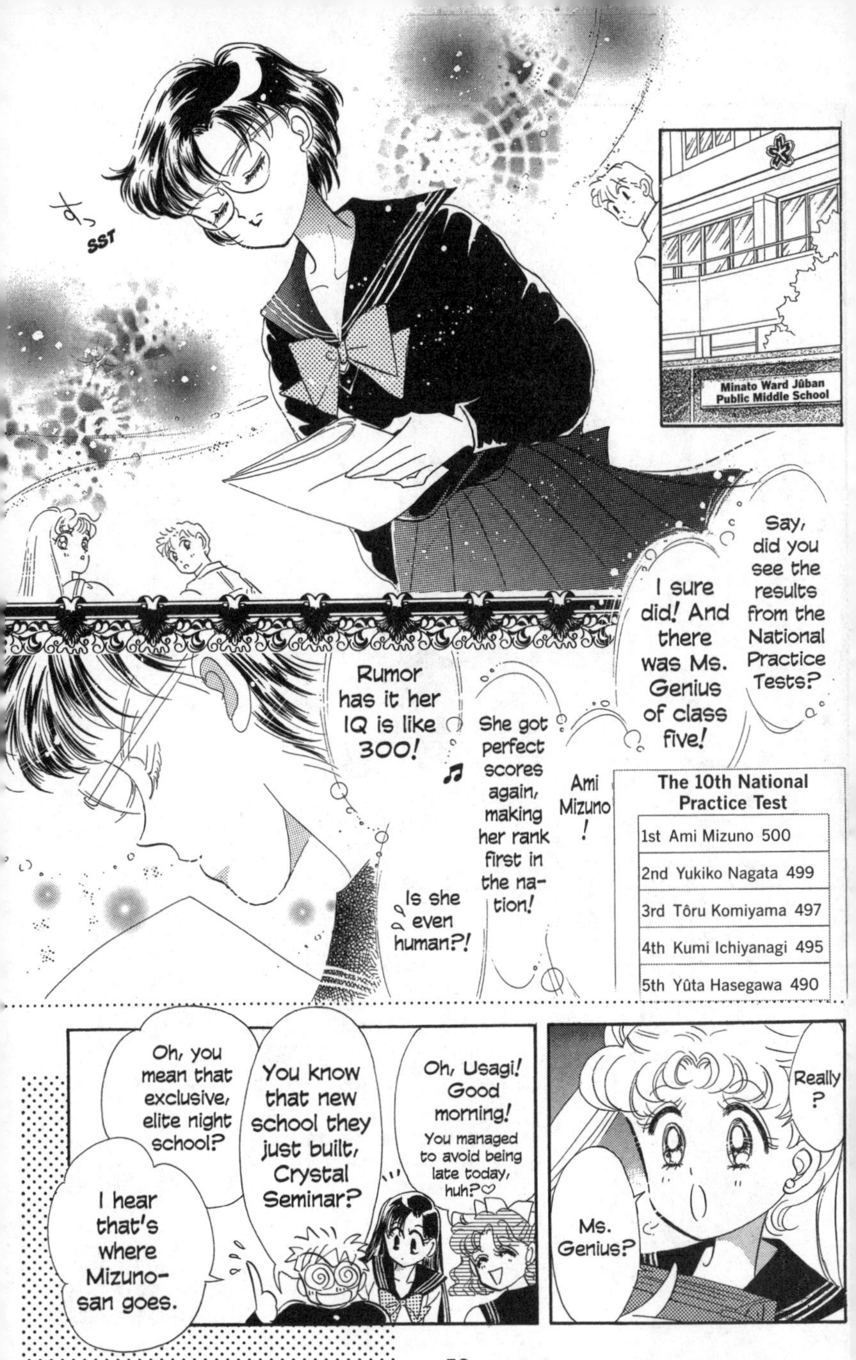

Minato Ward Jûban Public Middle School
すっ
SST
Say, did you see the results from the National Practice Tests?
I sure did! And there was Ms. Genius of class five!
The 10th National Practice Test
1st Ami Mizuno 500
2nd Yukiko Nagata 499
3rd Tôru Komiyama 497
4th Kumi Ichiyanagi 495
5th Yûta Hasegawa 490
Ami Mizuno!
She got perfect scores again, making her rank first in the nation!
Rumor has it her IQ is like 300!
Is she even human?!
Really?
Ms. Genius?
Oh, Usagi! Good morning!
You managed to avoid being late today, huh?♡
You know that new school they just built, Crystal Seminar?
Oh, you mean that exclusive, elite night school?
I hear that's where Mizuno-san goes.

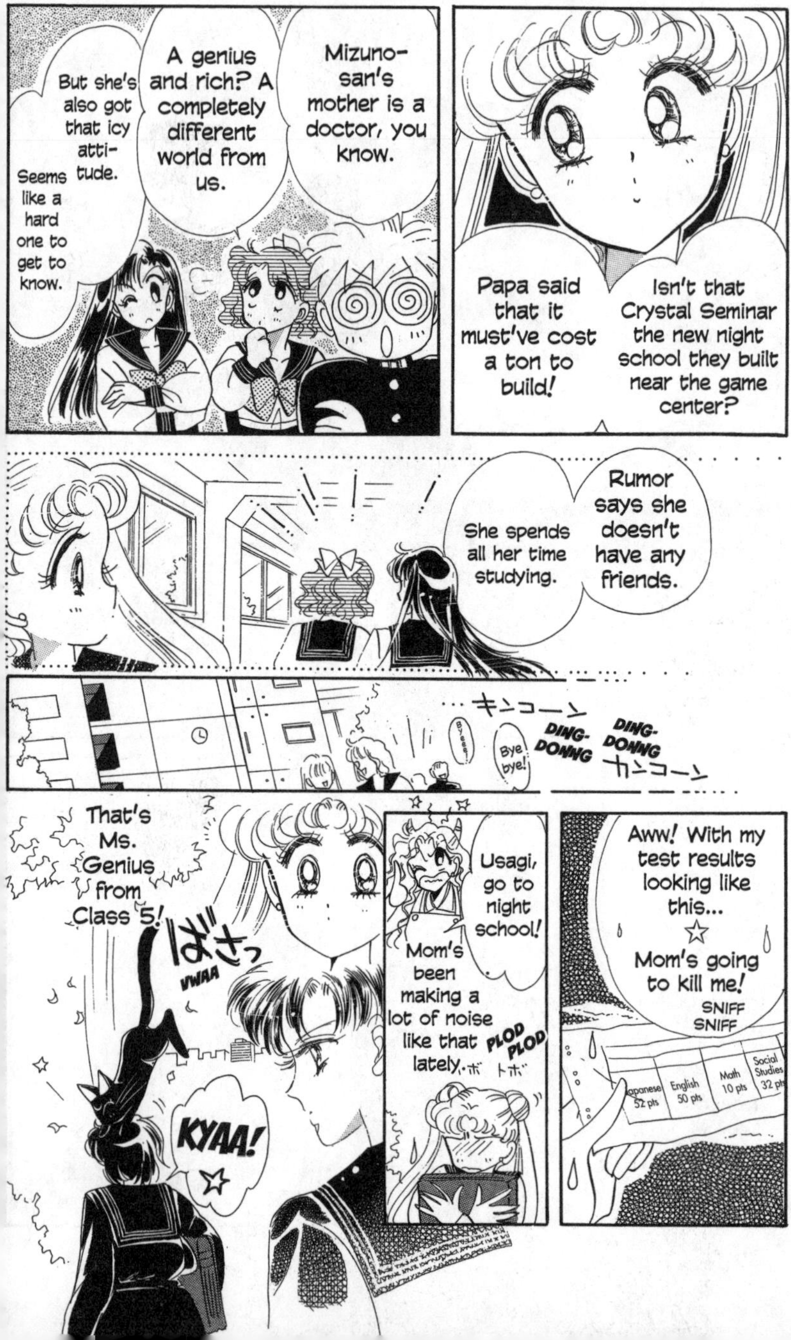
Isn't that Crystal Seminar the new night school they built near the game center?
Papa said that it must've cost a ton to build!
Mizuno-san's mother is a doctor, you know.
A genius and rich? A completely different world from us.
But she's also got that icy atti- tude.
Seems like a hard one to get to know.
Rumor says she doesn't have any friends.
She spends all her time studying.
DING-DONNG
カンコーン
キンコーン
DING-DONNG
Bye bye!
Byeee!
Aww! With my test results looking like this... ☆ Mom's going to kill me!
SNIFF SNIFF
Japanese 52 pts
English 50 pts
Math 10 pts
Social Studies 32 pts
Usagi, go to night school!
Mom's been making a lot of noise like that lately.
PLOD PLOD
ボトボ
That's Ms. Genius from Class 5!
ばきっ
VWAA
KYAA!

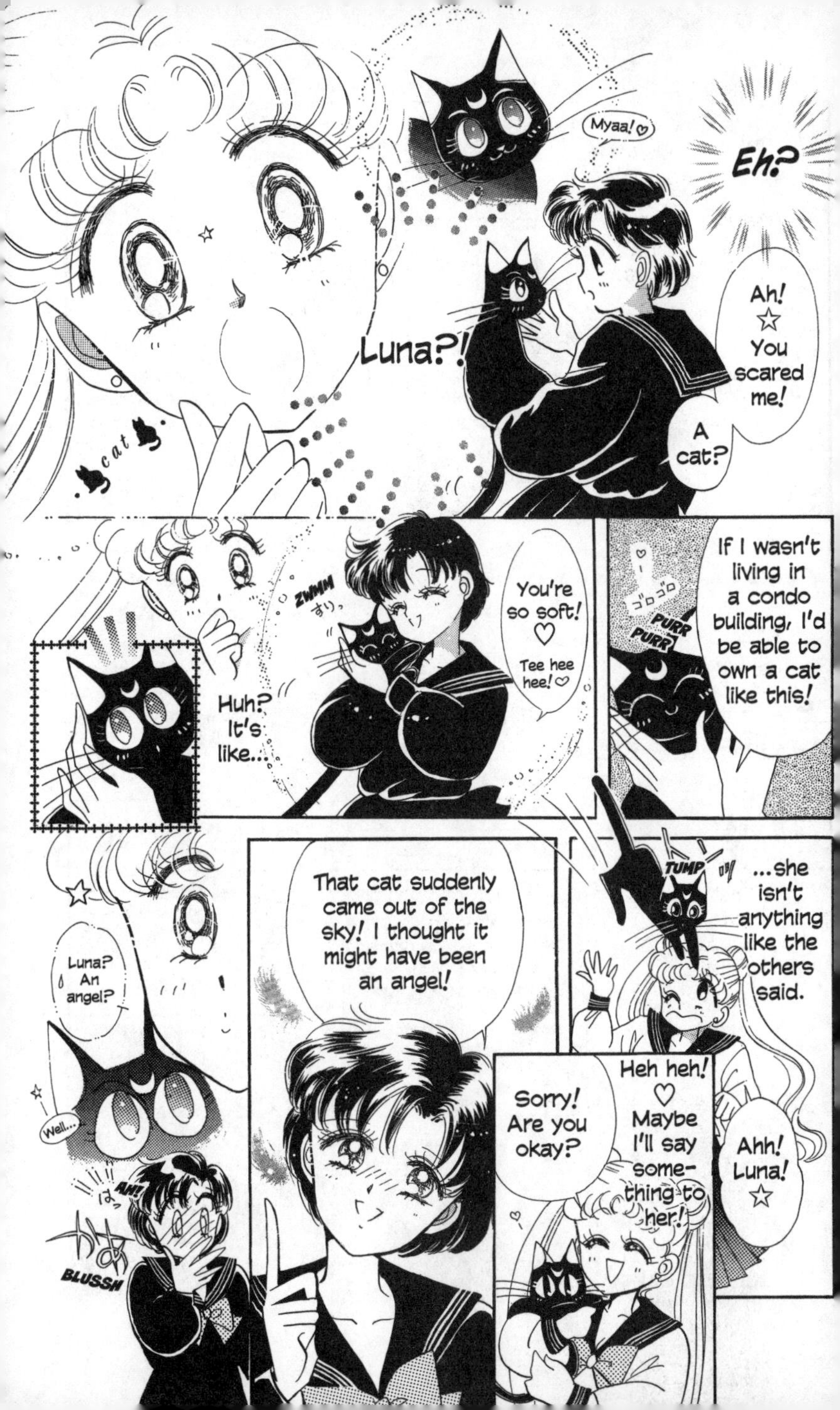

Eh?
Myaa! ♡
Ah! ☆ You scared me!
A cat?
Luna?!
cat
ゴロゴロ
PURR PURR
If I wasn't living in a condo building, I'd be able to own a cat like this!
You're so soft! ♡
Tee hee hee! ♡
ZWMM すりっ
Huh? It's like...
TUMP
...she isn't anything like the others said.
Ahh! Luna! ☆
Heh heh! ♡ Maybe I'll say some-thing to her!
Sorry! Are you okay?
That cat suddenly came out of the sky! I thought it might have been an angel!
Luna? An angel?
Well...
AH! はっ
BLUSSH

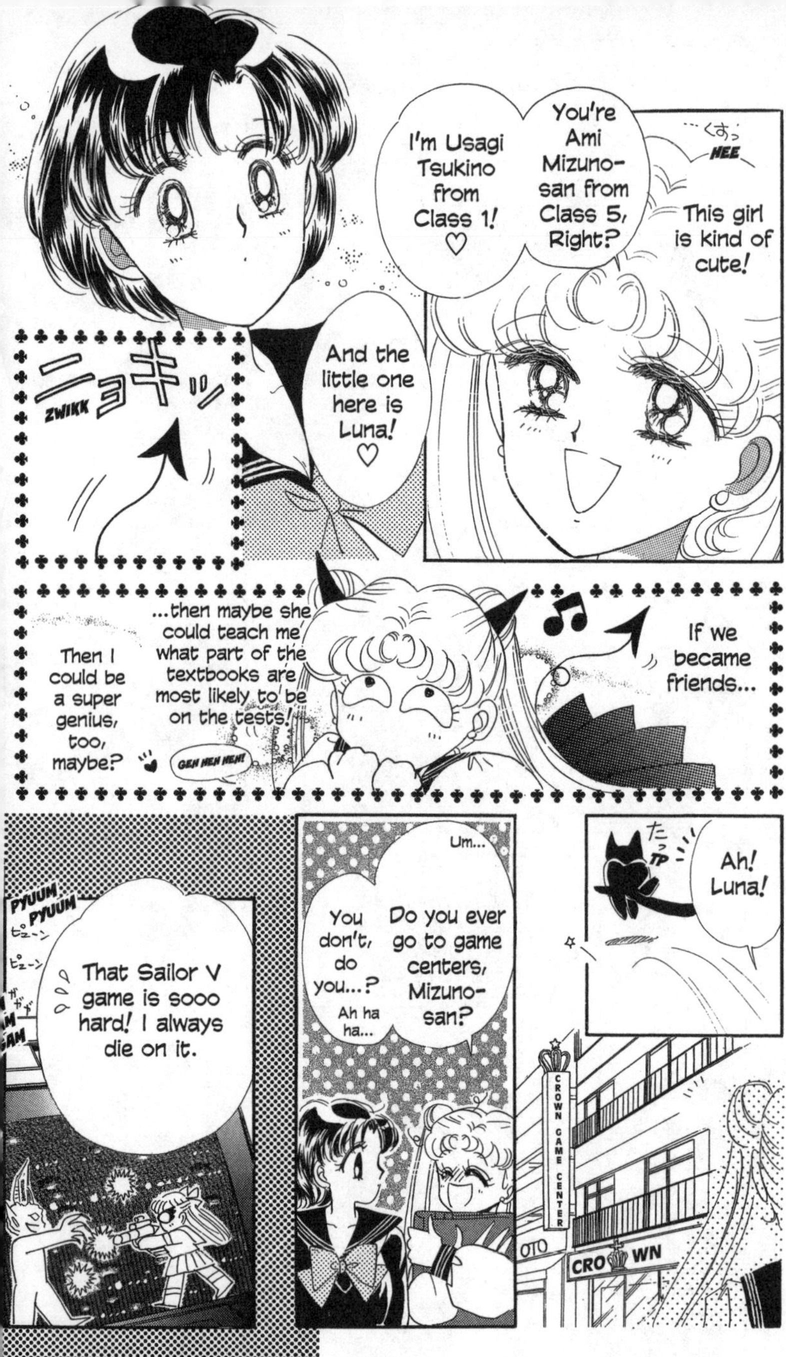
…くすっ
HEE
This girl is kind of cute!
You're Ami Mizuno-san from Class 5, Right?
I'm Usagi Tsukino from Class 1! ♡
And the little one here is Luna! ♡
ニョキッ
ZWIKK
If we became friends...
...then maybe she could teach me what part of the textbooks are most likely to be on the tests!
Then I could be a super genius, too, maybe?
GEH HEH HEH!
たっ
TP
Ah! Luna!
CROWN GAME CENTER
CRO WN
Um...
Do you ever go to game centers, Mizuno-san?
You don't, do you...?
Ah ha ha...
PYUUM PYUUM
That Sailor V game is sooo hard! I always die on it.

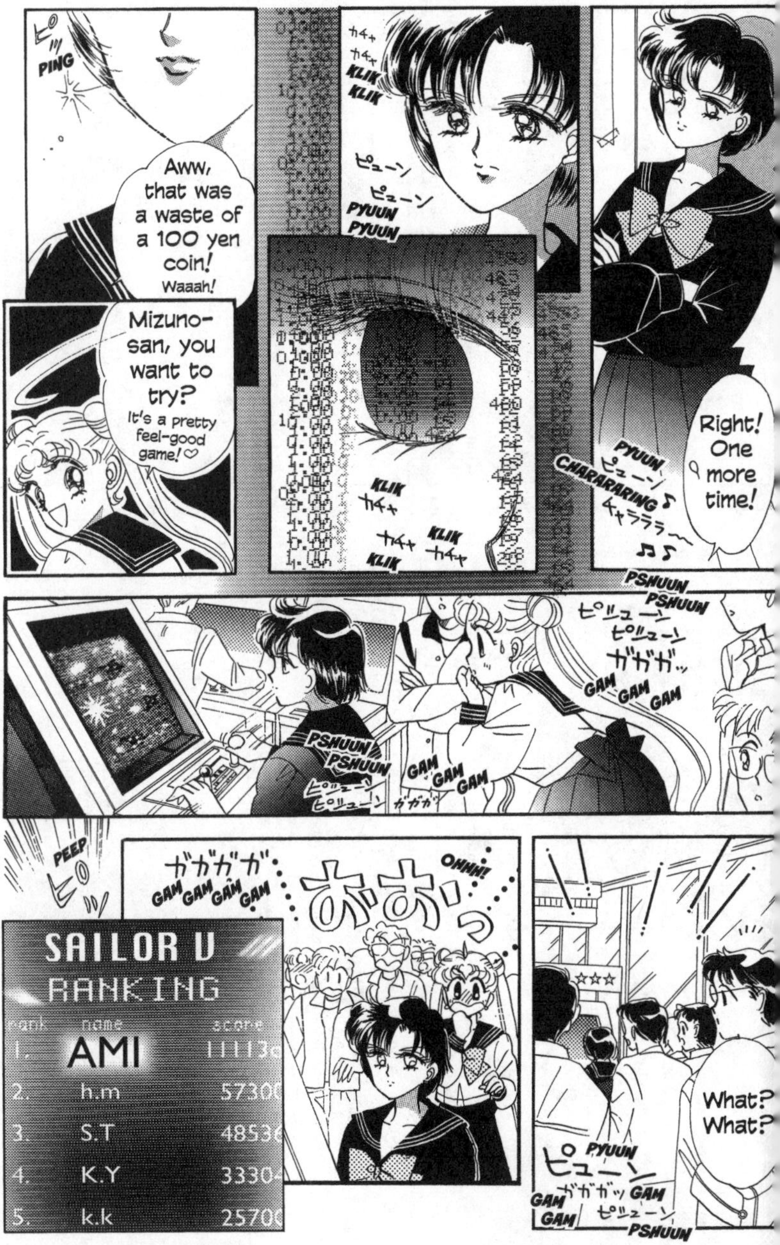
Right! One more time!
PYUUN
ピューン
CHARARARING
チャララララ~
カチャ カチャ
KLIK KLIK
ピューン ピューン
PYUUN PYUUN
KLIK
カチャ
カチャ
KLIK
KLIK
カチャ
ピッ
PING
Aww, that was a waste of a 100 yen coin! Waaah!
Mizuno-san, you want to try? It's a pretty feel-good game!♡
PSHUUN PSHUUN
ピシューン ピシューン
ガガガッ
GAM GAM GAM
PSHUUN PSHUUN
GAM GAM GAM
ピシューン ピシューン ガガガッ
What? What?
ピューン PYUUN
ガガガッ GAM
GAM GAM
ピシューン
PSHUUN
ガガガガ
GAM GAM GAM GAM
おおっ
OHHH!
PEEP
ピッ
SAILOR V
RANKING
rank name score
1. AMI 11113
2. h.m 57300
3. S.T 48536
4. K.Y 3330
5. k.k 25700

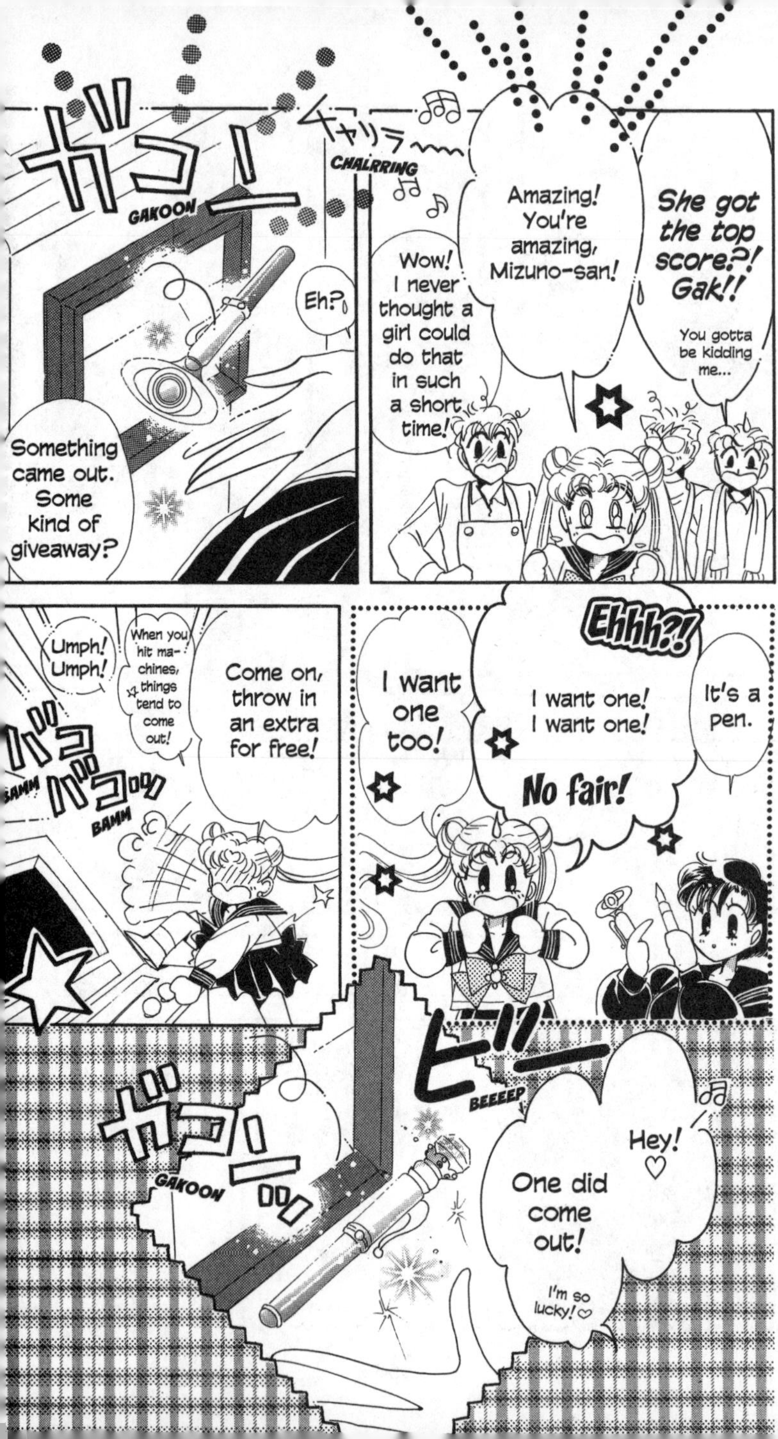
キャリラ
CHALRRING
She got the top score?! Gak!!
You gotta be kidding me...
Amazing! You're amazing, Mizuno-san!
Wow! I never thought a girl could do that in such a short time!
ガコー
GAKOON
Eh?
Something came out. Some kind of giveaway?
It's a pen.
Ehhh?!
I want one! I want one!
No fair!
I want one too!
Come on, throw in an extra for free!
When you hit machines, things tend to come out!
Umph! Umph!
BAMM
BAMM
ビー
BEEEEP
Hey! ♡
One did come out!
I'm so lucky! ♡
GAKOON

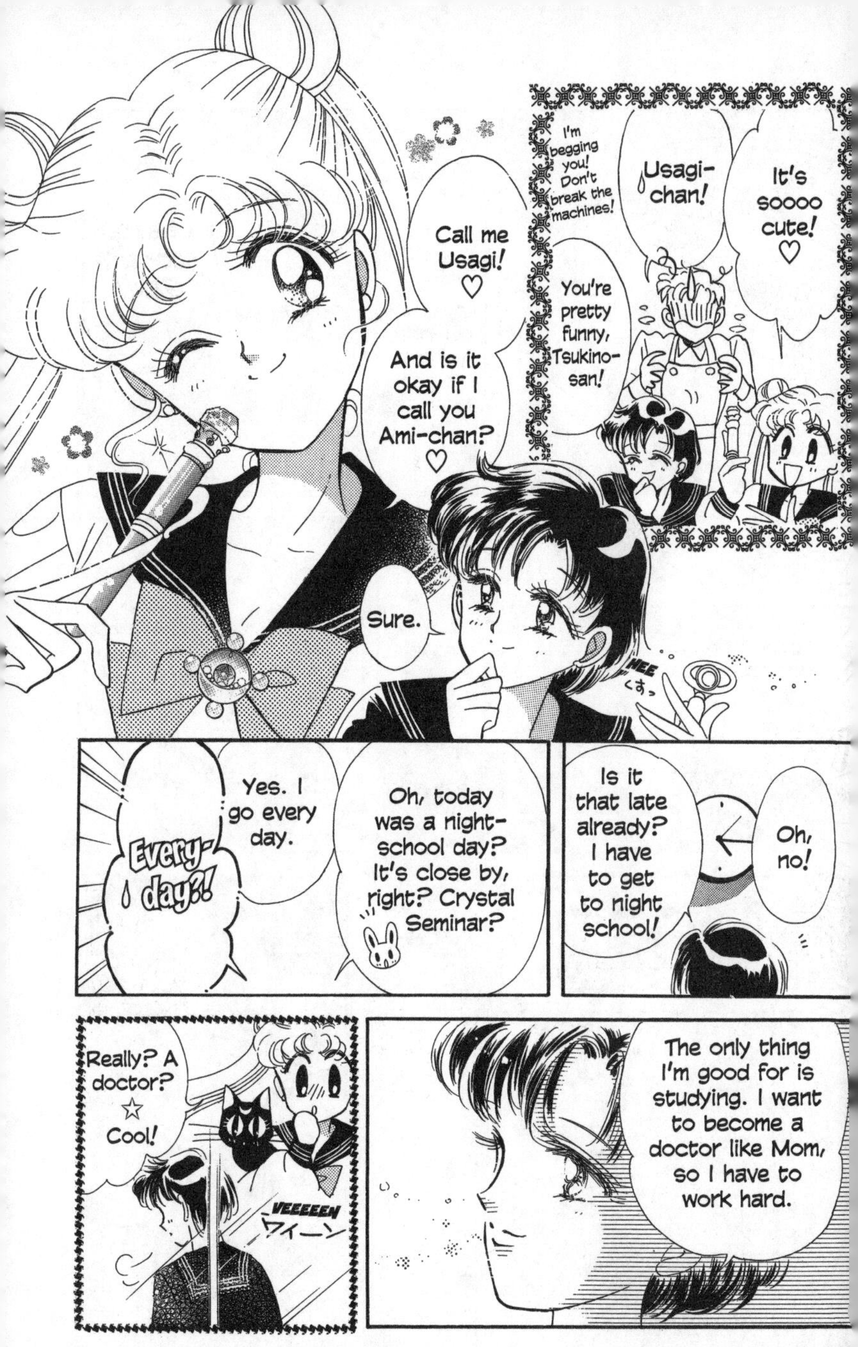

It's soooo cute! ♡
Usagi-chan!
I'm begging you! Don't break the machines!
You're pretty funny, Tsukino-san!
Call me Usagi! ♡
And is it okay if I call you Ami-chan? ♡
Sure.
HEE
くすっ
Oh, no!
Is it that late already? I have to get to night school!
Oh, today was a night-school day? It's close by, right? Crystal Seminar?
Yes. I go every day.
Every-day?!
The only thing I'm good for is studying. I want to become a doctor like Mom, so I have to work hard.
Really? A doctor? ☆ Cool!
VEEEEEN
ワイーン

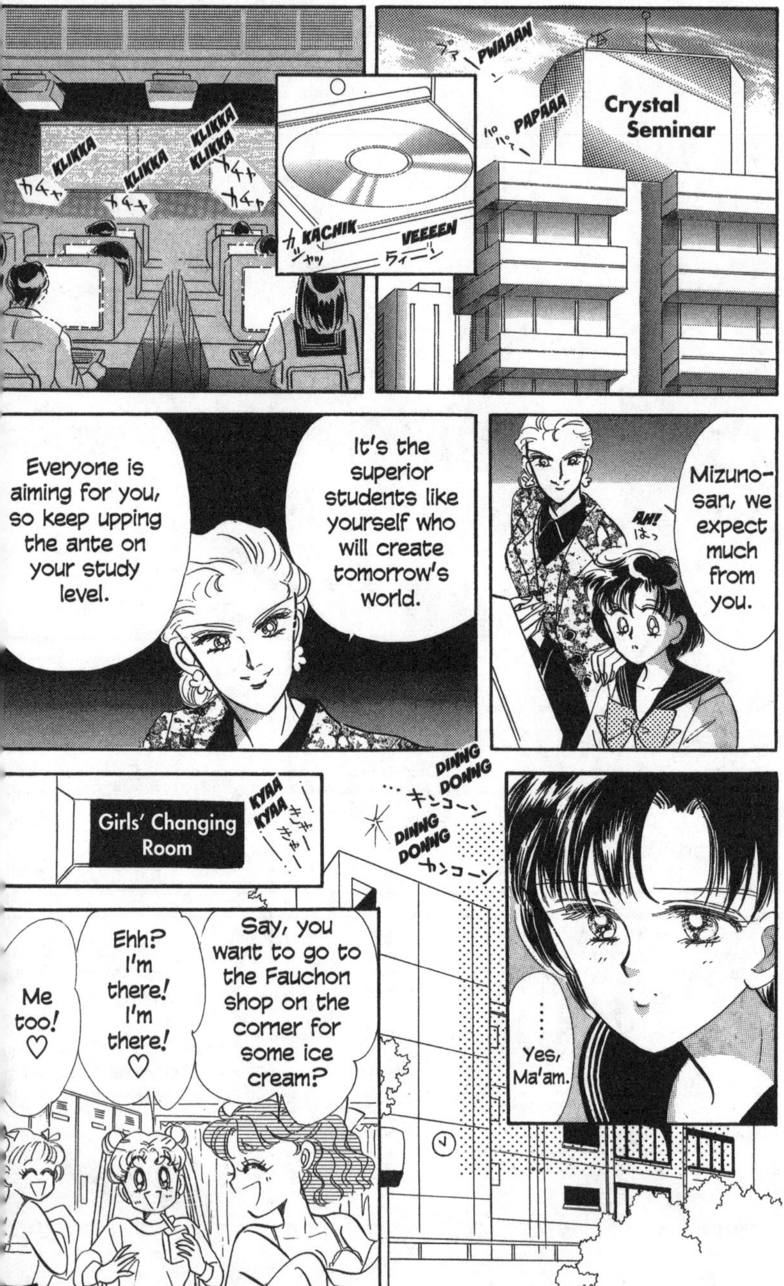
PWAAAN
PAPAAA
Crystal Seminar
KACHIK
VEEEEN
KLIKKA
KLIKKA
KLIKKA KLIKKA
AH!
Mizuno-san, we expect much from you.
It's the superior students like yourself who will create tomorrow's world.
Everyone is aiming for you, so keep upping the ante on your study level.
...... Yes, Ma'am.
DINNG DONNG
DINNG DONNG
Girls' Changing Room
KYAA KYAA
Say, you want to go to the Fauchon shop on the corner for some ice cream?
Ehh? I'm there! I'm there! ♡
Me too! ♡

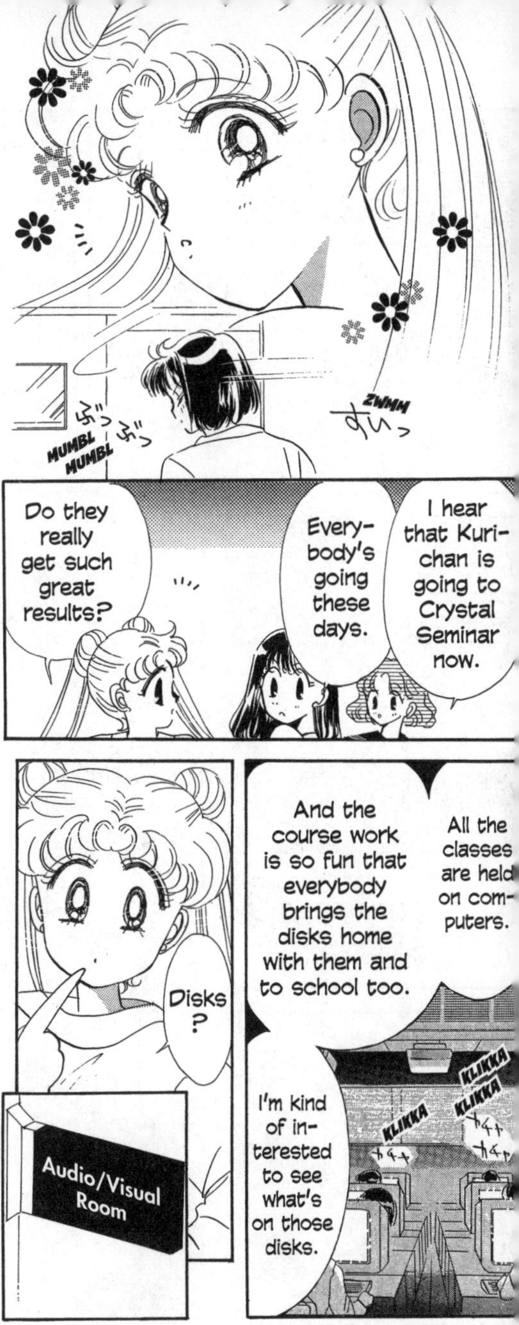
ZWMM
MUMBL MUMBL
I hear that Kuri-chan is going to Crystal Seminar now.
Every-body's going these days.
Do they really get such great results?
All the classes are held on com-puters.
And the course work is so fun that everybody brings the disks home with them and to school too.
I'm kind of in-terested to see what's on those disks.
KLIKKA
KLIKKA KLIKKA
Disks?
Audio/Visual Room

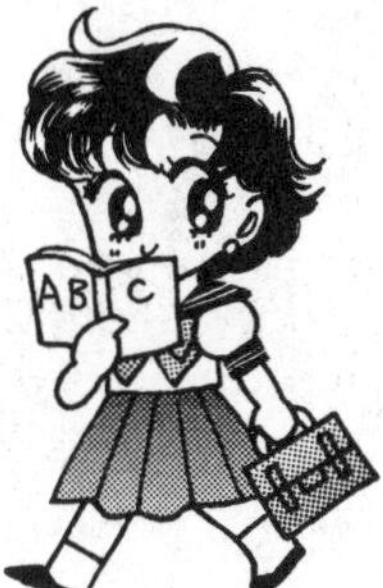
AB C

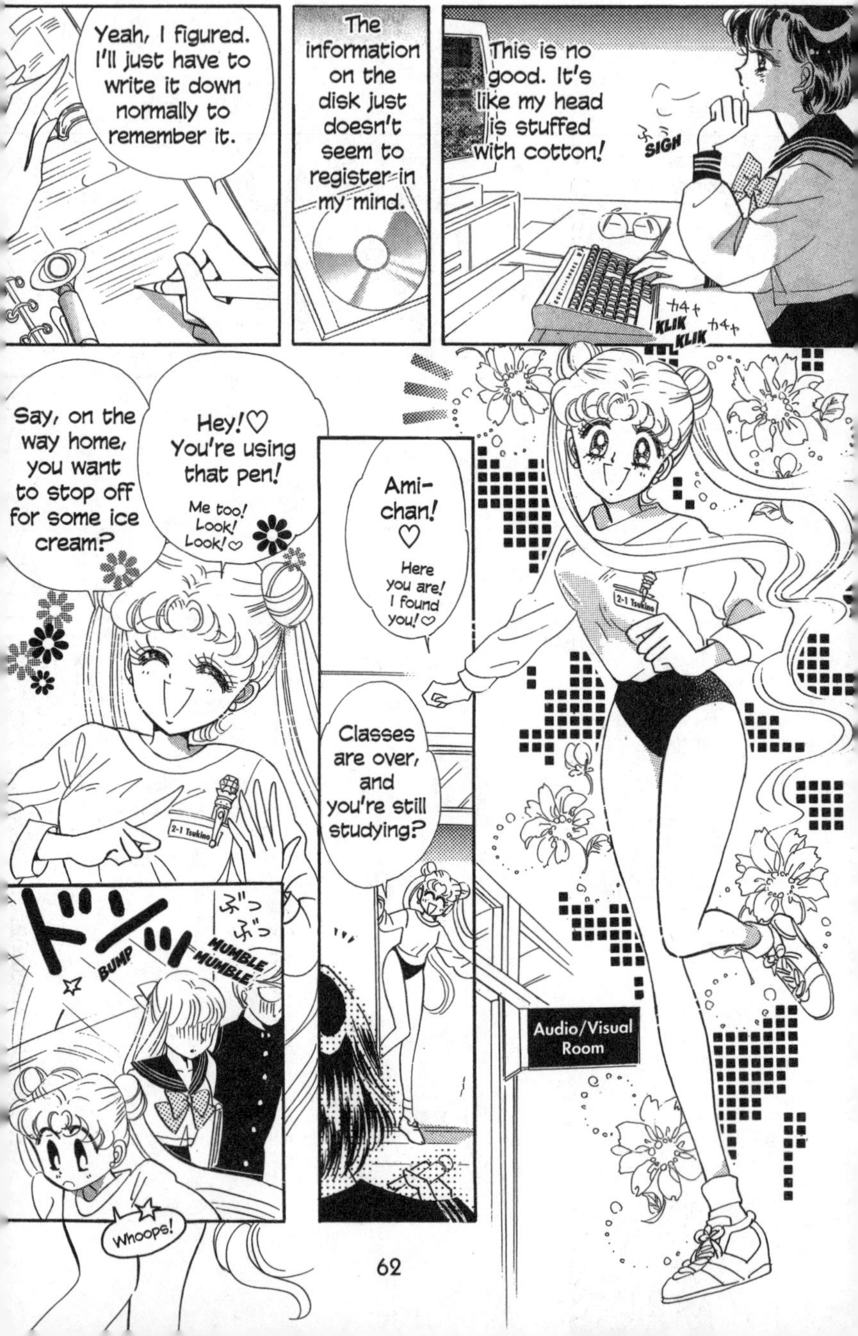
This is no good. It's like my head is stuffed with cotton!
SIGH
KLIK KLIK
The information on the disk just doesn't seem to register in my mind.
Yeah, I figured. I'll just have to write it down normally to remember it.
2-1 Tsukino
Audio/Visual Room
Ami-chan! ♡
Here you are! I found you! ♡
Classes are over, and you're still studying?
Hey! ♡ You're using that pen!
Me too! Look! Look! ♡
Say, on the way home, you want to stop off for some ice cream?
2-1 Tsukino
BUMP
ぶつぶつ
MUMBLE MUMBLE
Whoops!

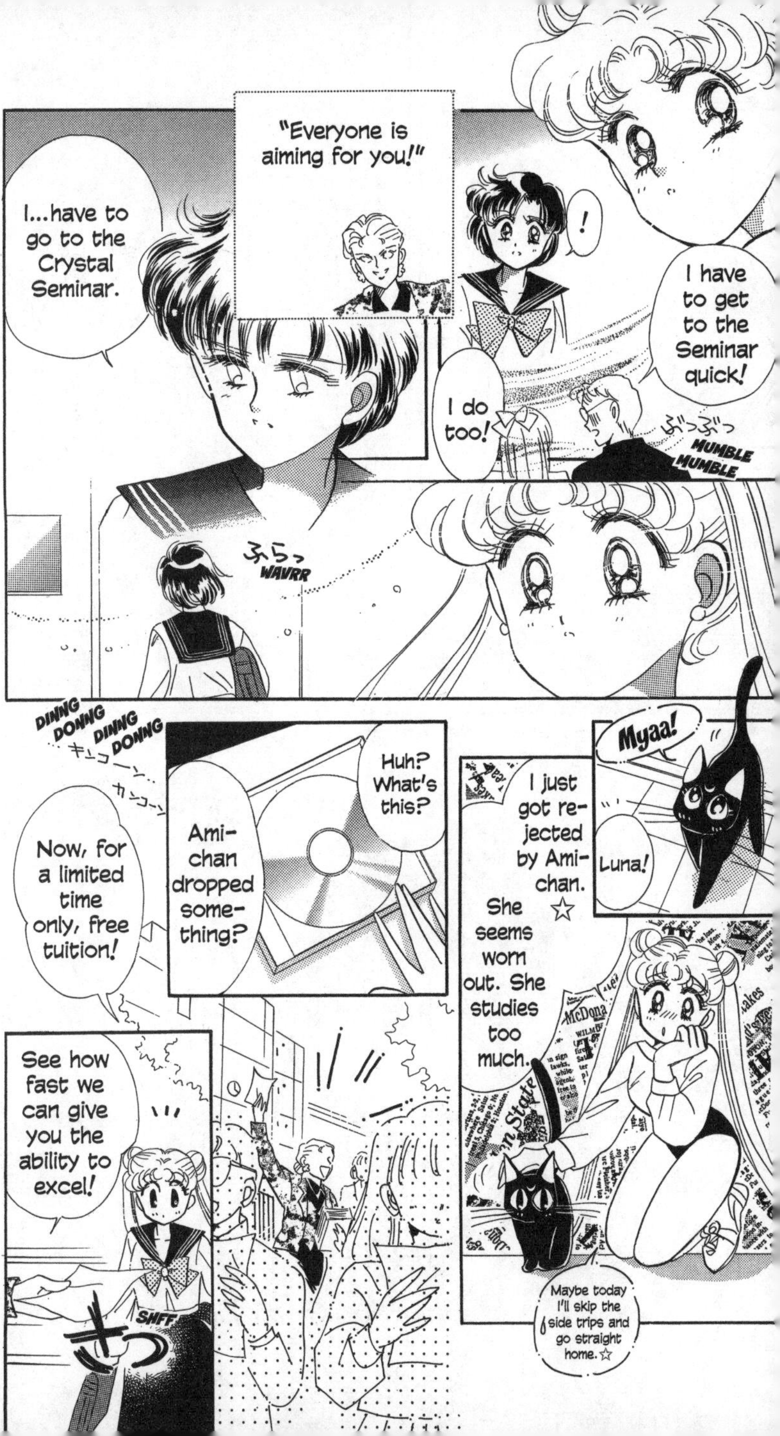

!
I have to get to the Seminar quick!
I do too!
ぶつぶつ
MUMBLE MUMBLE
"Everyone is aiming for you!"
I...have to go to the Crystal Seminar.
ふらっ
WAVRR
Myaa!
Luna!
I just got rejected by Ami-chan. ☆
She seems worn out. She studies too much.
Maybe today I'll skip the side trips and go straight home. ☆
Huh? What's this?
Ami-chan dropped something?
DINNG DONNG DINNG DONNG
キンコーン カンコーン
Now, for a limited time only, free tuition!
See how fast we can give you the ability to excel!
SHFF

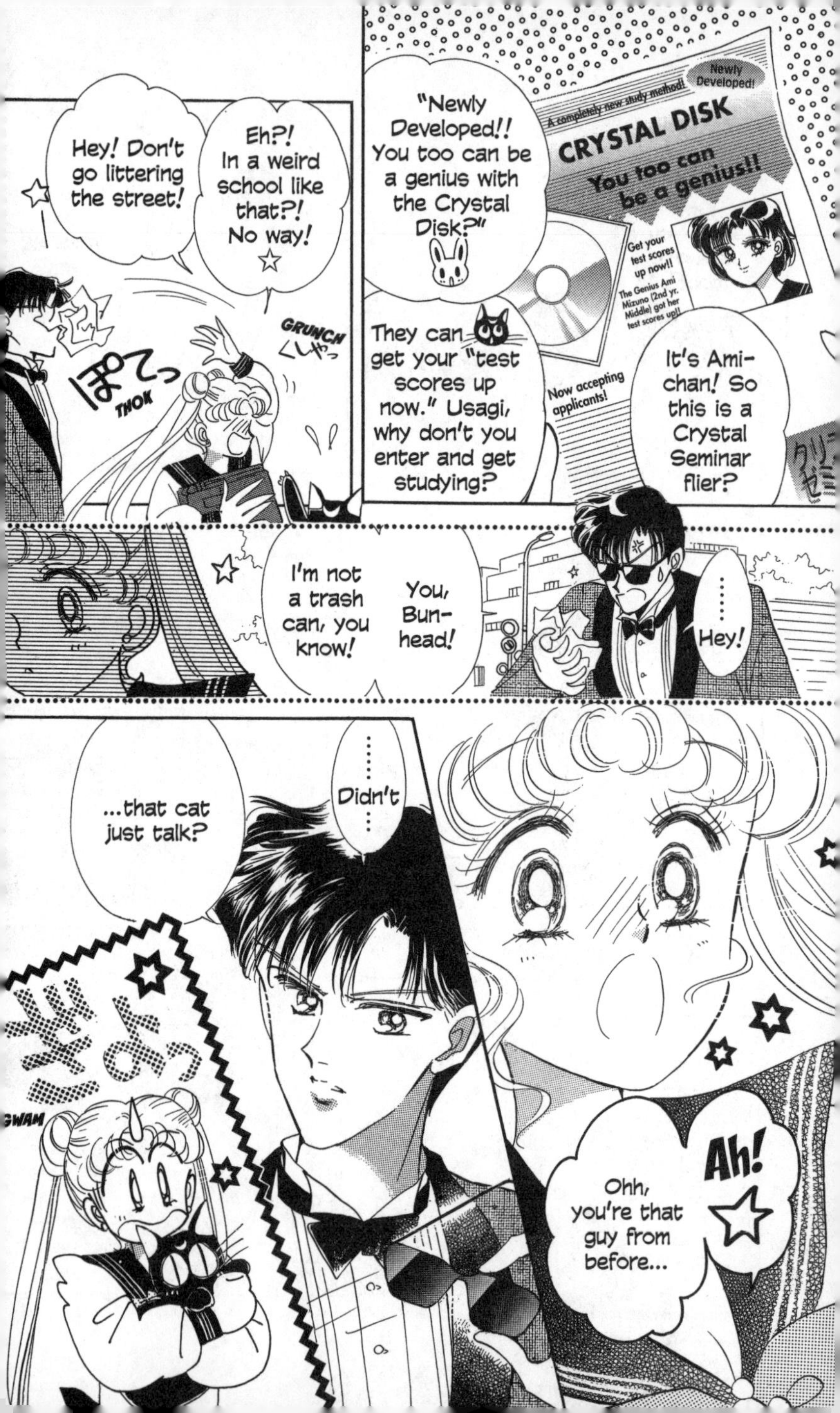
Newly Developed!
A completely new study method!
CRYSTAL DISK
You too can be a genius!!
Get your test scores up now!!
The Genius Ami Mizuno (2nd yr. Middle) got her test scores up!!
Now accepting applicants!
"Newly Developed!! You too can be a genius with the Crystal Disk?"
It's Ami-chan! So this is a Crystal Seminar flier?
They can get your "test scores up now." Usagi, why don't you enter and get studying?
Eh?! In a weird school like that?! No way!
Hey! Don't go littering the street!
GRUNCH
くしゃっ
ぽてっ
THOK
......Hey!
You, Bun-head!
I'm not a trash can, you know!
Ah!
Ohh, you're that guy from before...
......Didn't
...that cat just talk?
GWAM

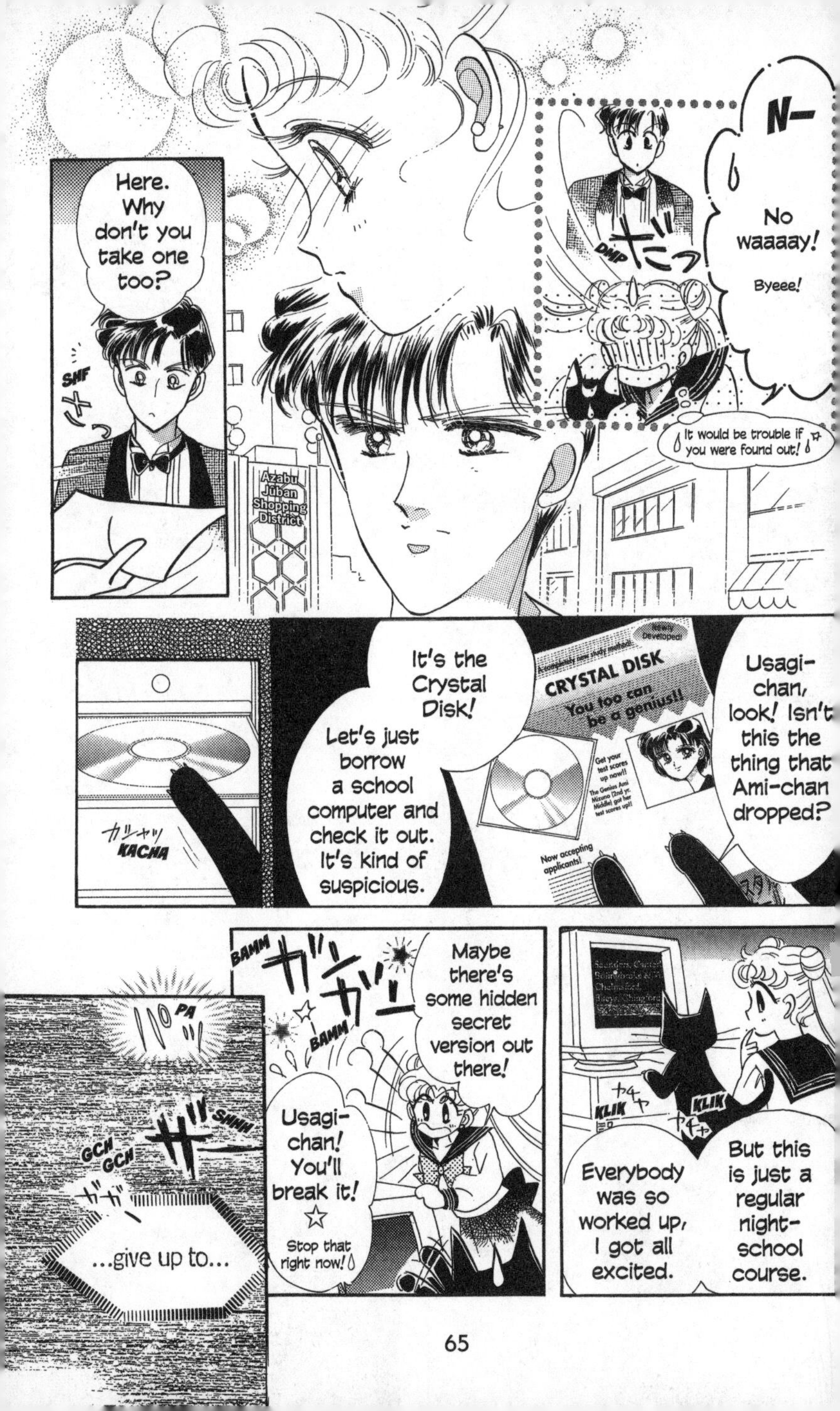
N—
No waaaay!
Byeee!
DMP
It would be trouble if you were found out!
Azabu Jûban Shopping District
Here. Why don't you take one too?
SNF
Usagi-chan, look! Isn't this the thing that Ami-chan dropped?
Newly Developed!
A completely new study method!
CRYSTAL DISK
You too can be a genius!!
Get your test scores up now!!
The Genius Ami Mizuno (2nd yr. Middle) got her test scores up!!
Now accepting applicants!
It's the Crystal Disk!
Let's just borrow a school computer and check it out. It's kind of suspicious.
KACHA
KLIK
KLIK
But this is just a regular night-school course.
Everybody was so worked up, I got all excited.
BAMM
BAMM
Maybe there's some hidden secret version out there!
Usagi-chan! You'll break it! ☆
Stop that right now!
PA
SHHH
GCH GCH
...give up to...

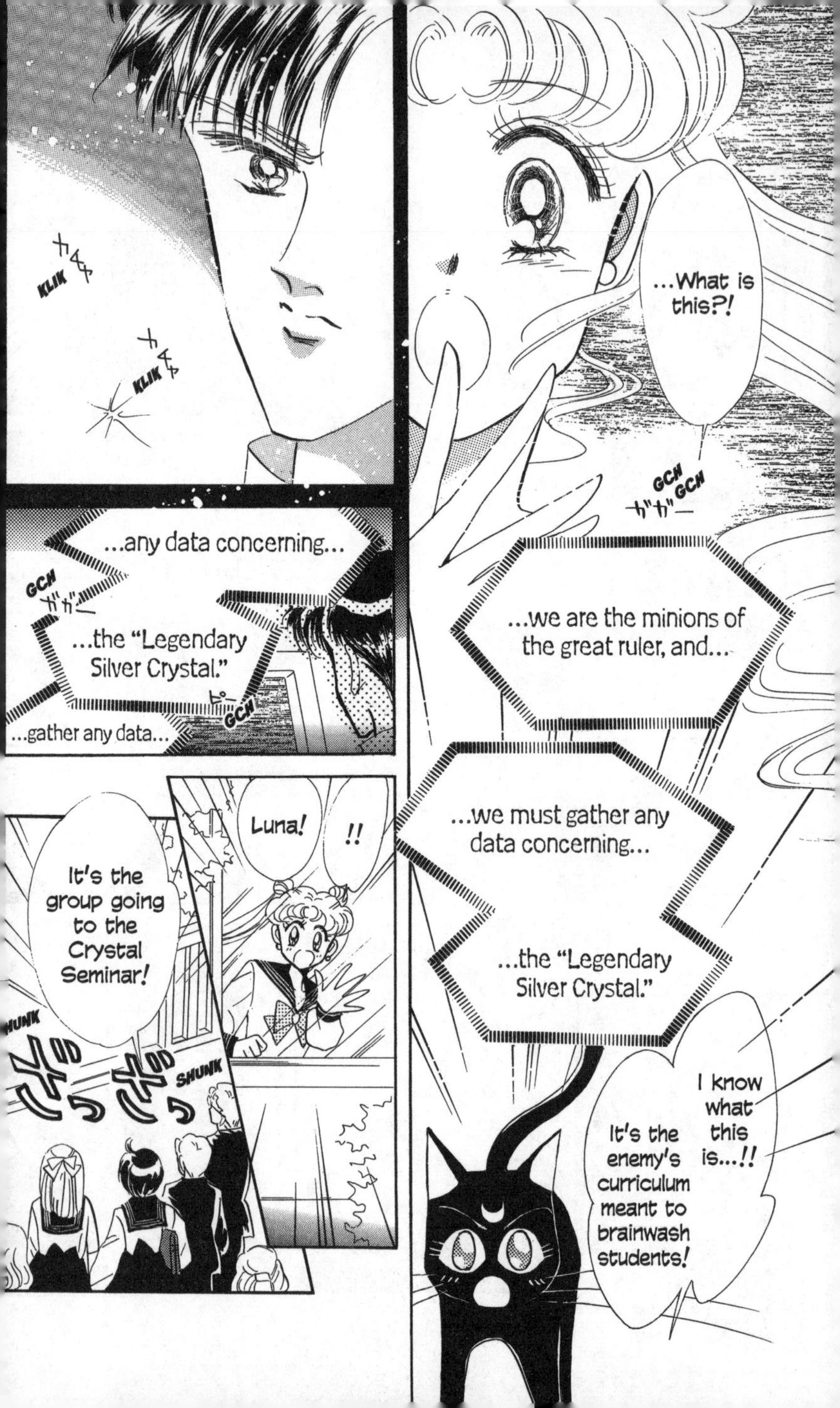

...What is this?!
GCH GCH
...we are the minions of the great ruler, and...
...we must gather any data concerning...
...the "Legendary Silver Crystal."
I know what this is...!!
It's the enemy's curriculum meant to brainwash students!
KLIK
KLIK
...any data concerning...
GCH
...the "Legendary Silver Crystal."
GCH
...gather any data...
Luna!
!!
It's the group going to the Crystal Seminar!
SHUNK
SHUNK

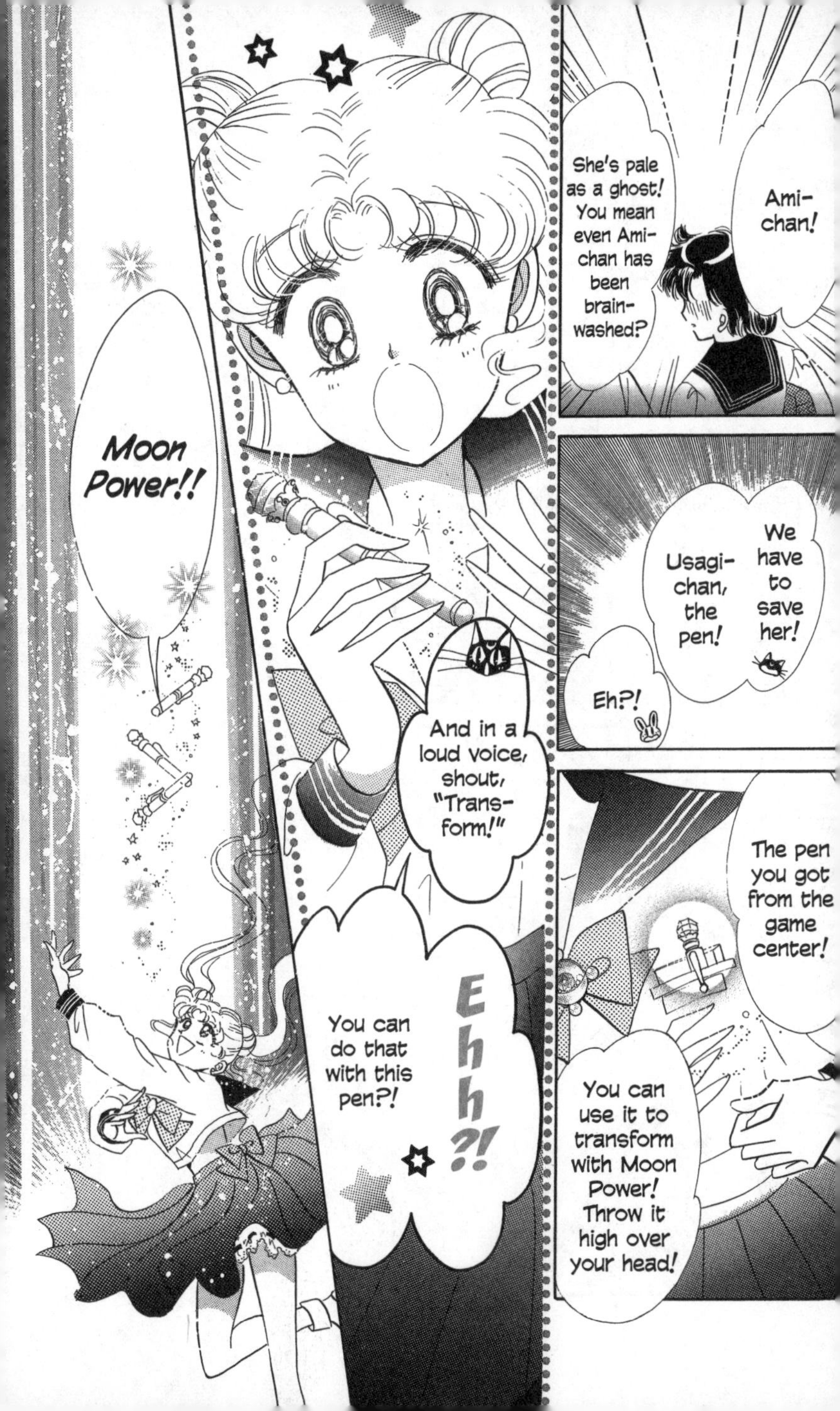
Ami-chan!
She's pale as a ghost! You mean even Ami-chan has been brain-washed?
We have to save her!
Usagi-chan, the pen!
Eh?!
The pen you got from the game center!
You can use it to transform with Moon Power! Throw it high over your head!
And in a loud voice, shout, "Transform!"
Ehh?!
You can do that with this pen?!
Moon Power!!

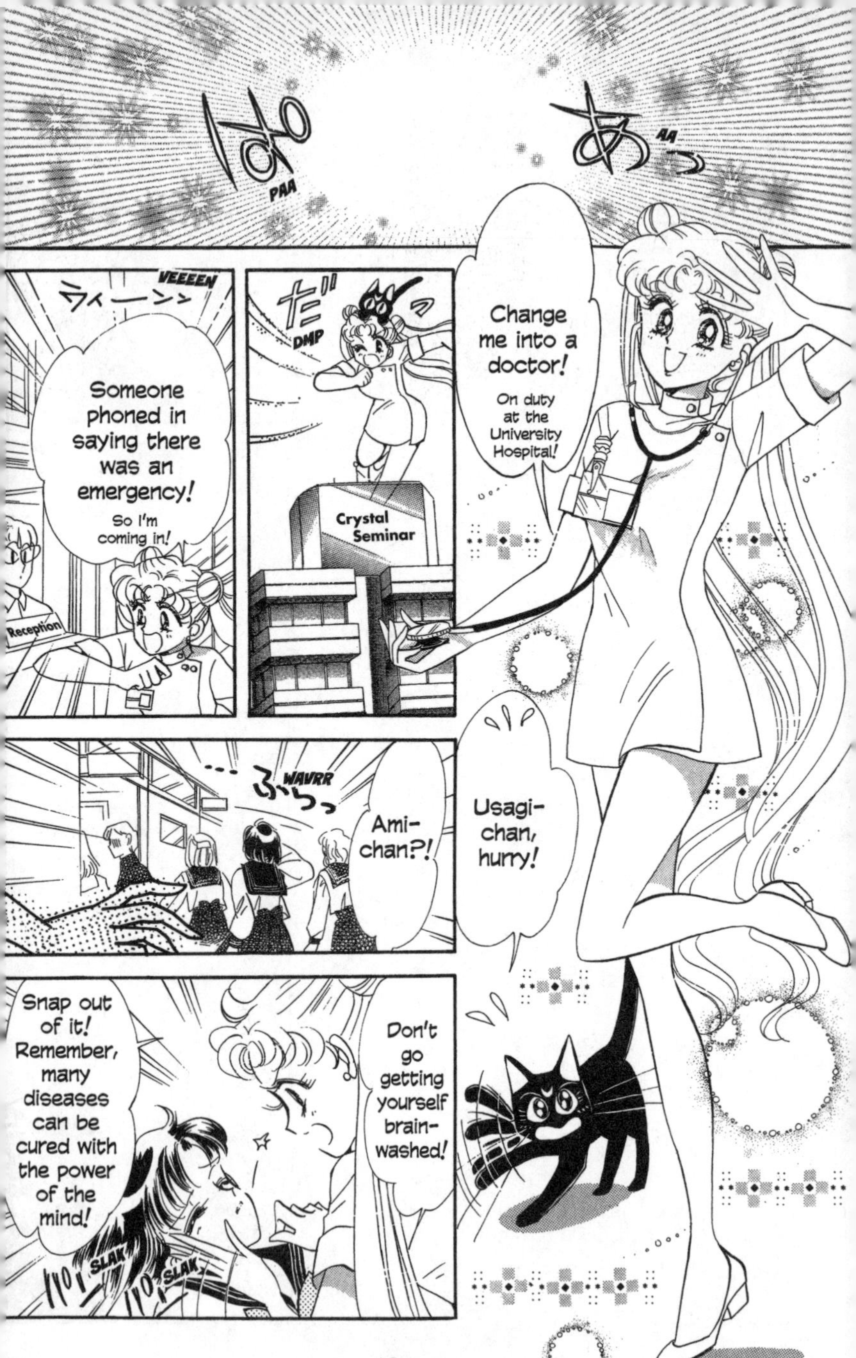
AA
PAA
Change me into a doctor!
On duty at the University Hospital!
Usagi-chan, hurry!
DMP
Crystal Seminar
VEEEEN
Someone phoned in saying there was an emergency!
So I'm coming in!
Reception
Ami-chan?!
WAVRR
...
Don't go getting yourself brain-washed!
Snap out of it! Remember, many diseases can be cured with the power of the mind!
SLAK
SLAK

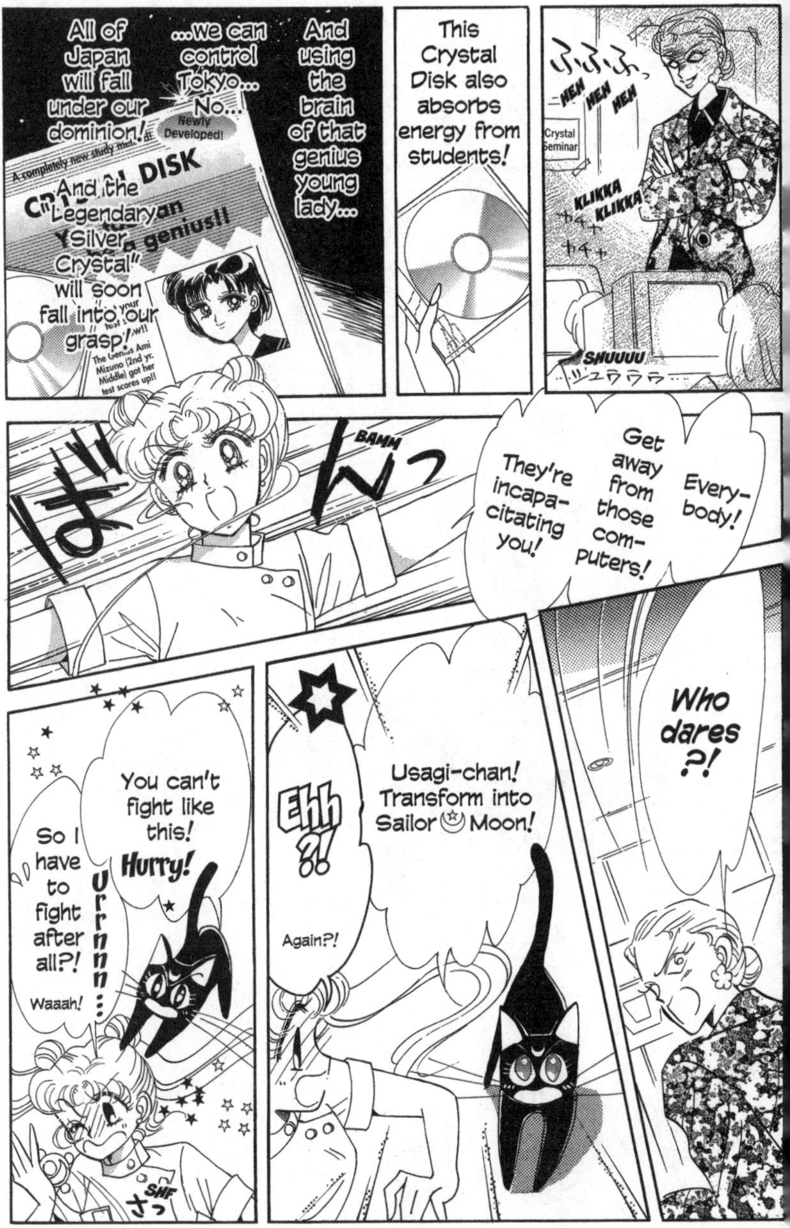
ふふふっ
HEH HEH HEH
Crystal Seminar
KLIKKA KLIKKA
カチャカチャ
SHUUUU
シュラララ…
This Crystal Disk also absorbs energy from students!
And using the brain of that genius young lady...
...we can control Tokyo... No...
All of Japan will fall under our dominion!
Newly Developed!
DISK
The Genius Ami Mizuno (2nd yr. Middle) got her test scores up!!
And the Legendary "Silver Crystal" will soon fall into our grasp!
Every-body!
Get away from those com-puters!
They're incapa-citating you!
BAMM
ばんっ
Who dares ?!
Usagi-chan! Transform into Sailor Moon!
Ehh ?!
Again?!
You can't fight like this! Hurry!
So I have to fight after all?!
Urrnnn...
Waaah!
SHF
さっ

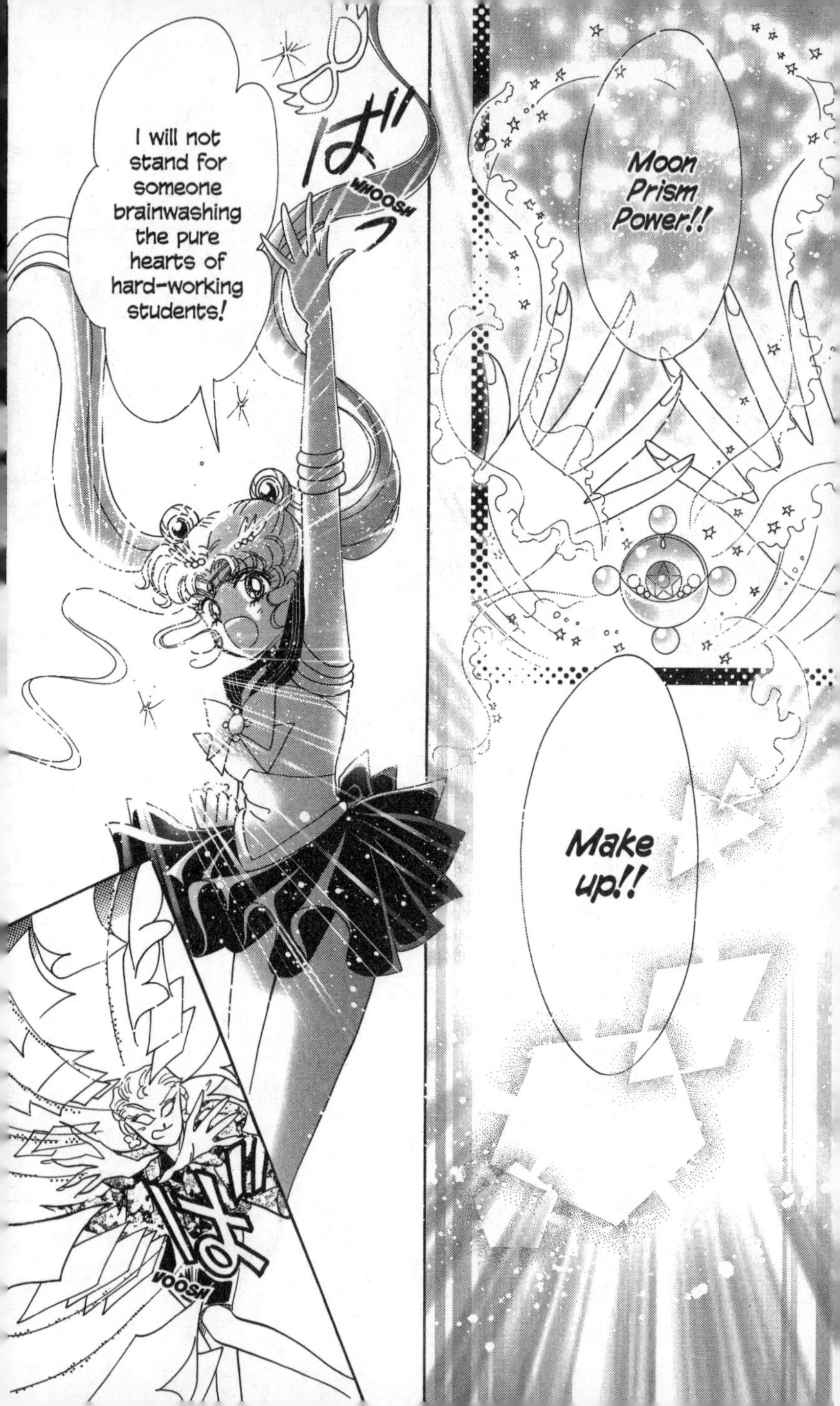
Moon Prism Power!!
Make up!!
I will not stand for someone brainwashing the pure hearts of hard-working students!
ばっ
WHOOSH
VOOSH

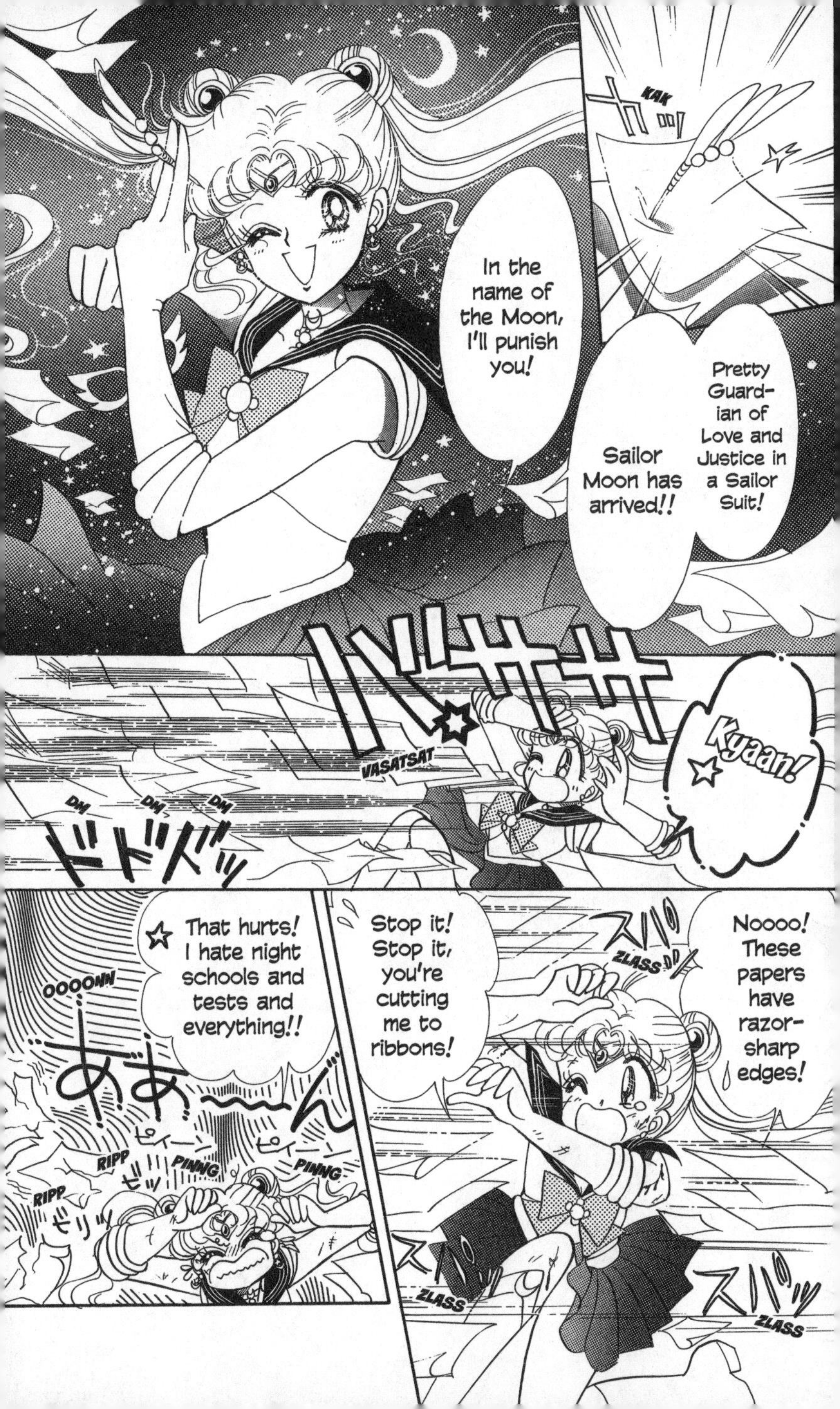

KAK
Pretty Guardian of Love and Justice in a Sailor Suit!
Sailor Moon has arrived!!
In the name of the Moon, I'll punish you!
Kyaan!
VASATSAT
DM DM DM
ZLASS
Noooo! These papers have razor-sharp edges!
ZLASS
ZLASS
Stop it! Stop it, you're cutting me to ribbons!
That hurts! I hate night schools and tests and everything!!
OOOONN
PINNG
PINNG
RIPP
RIPP

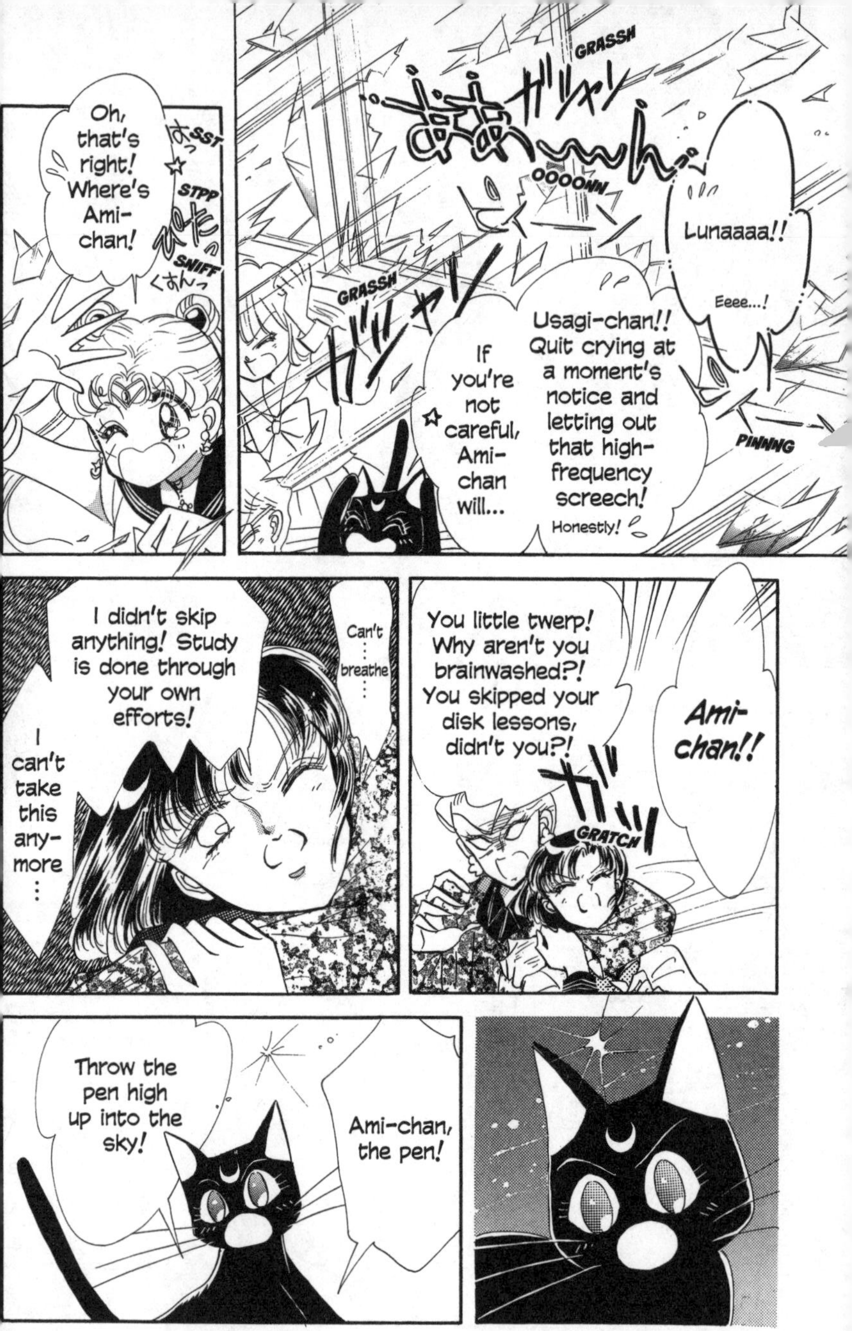

GRASSH
OOOONN
Lunaaaa!!
Eeee...!
PINNNG
Usagi-chan!! Quit crying at a moment's notice and letting out that high-frequency screech! Honestly!
If you're not careful, Ami-chan will...
GRASSH
Oh, that's right! Where's Ami-chan!
SST
STPP
SNIFF
Ami-chan!!
You little twerp! Why aren't you brainwashed?! You skipped your disk lessons, didn't you?!
GRATCH
Can't... breathe...
I didn't skip anything! Study is done through your own efforts!
I can't take this anymore...
Ami-chan, the pen!
Throw the pen high up into the sky!

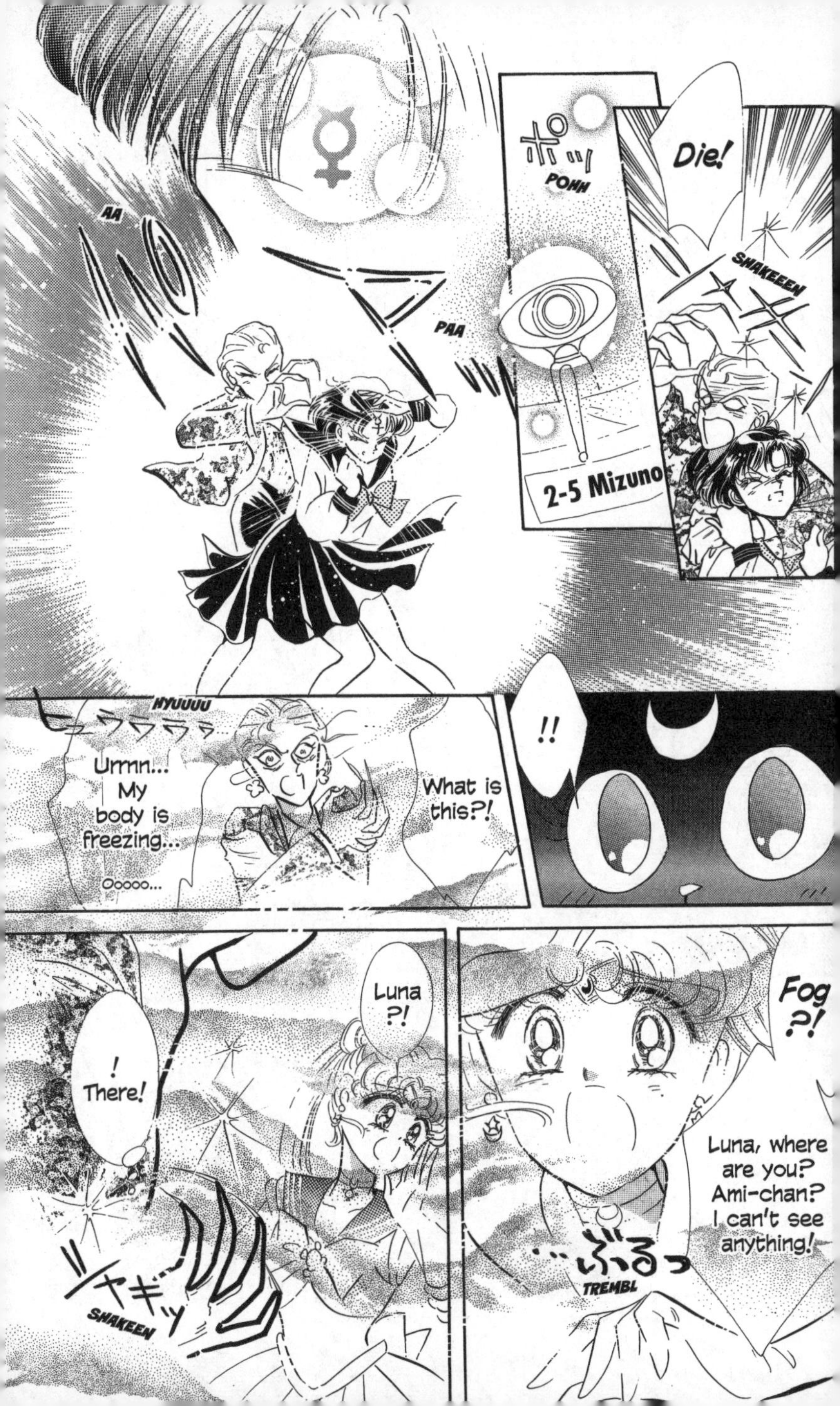

Die!
SHAKEEEN
ポッ
POHH
2-5 Mizuno
AA
PAA
HYUUUU
What is this?!
Urmn... My body is freezing...
Ooooo...
!!
Fog ?!
Luna, where are you? Ami-chan? I can't see anything!
ぶるっ
TREMBL
Luna ?!
! There!
SHAKEEN

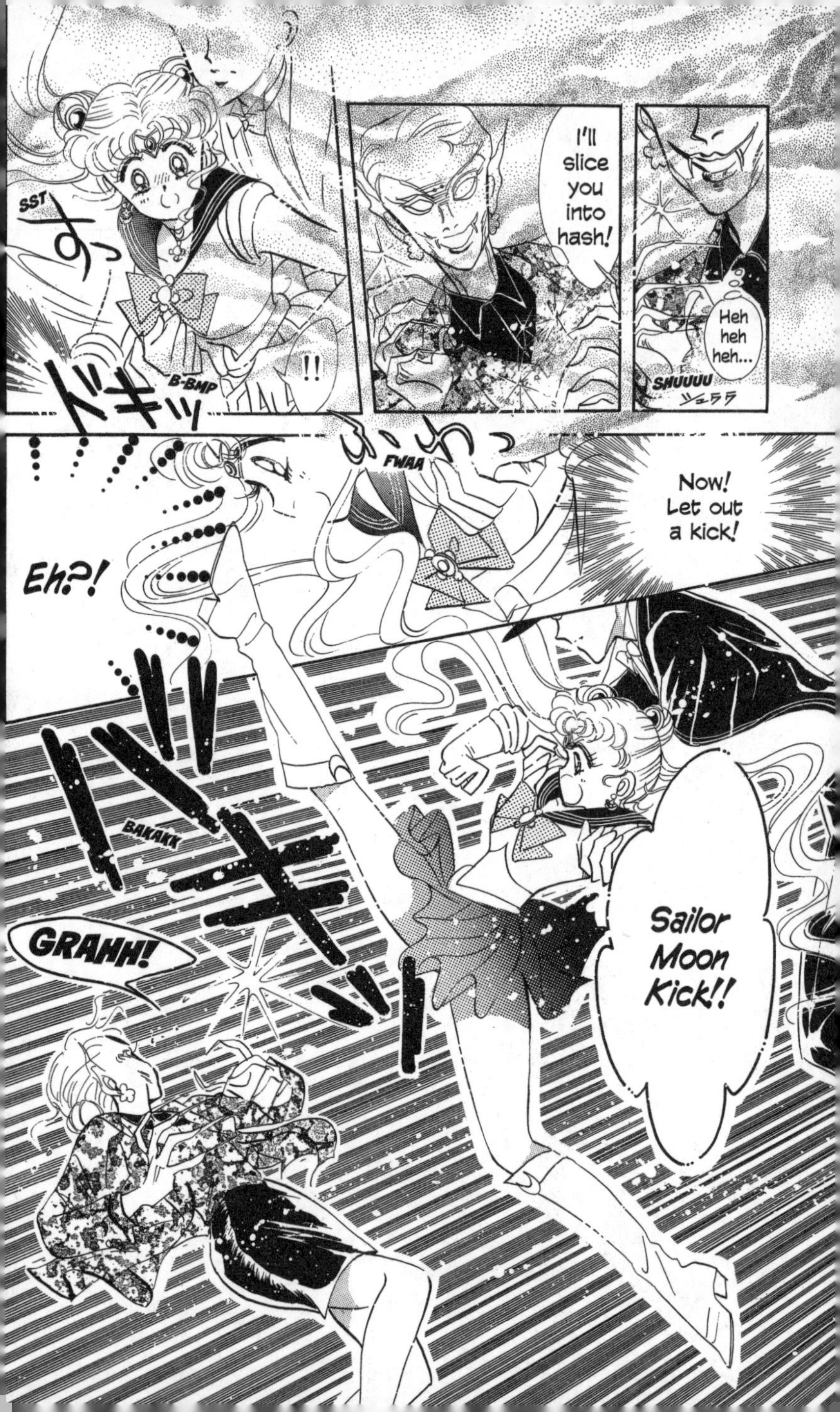

Heh heh heh...
SHUUUU
I'll slice you into hash!
SST
B-BMP
!!
Now! Let out a kick!
FWAA
Eh?!
Sailor Moon Kick!!
BAKAKK
GRAHH!

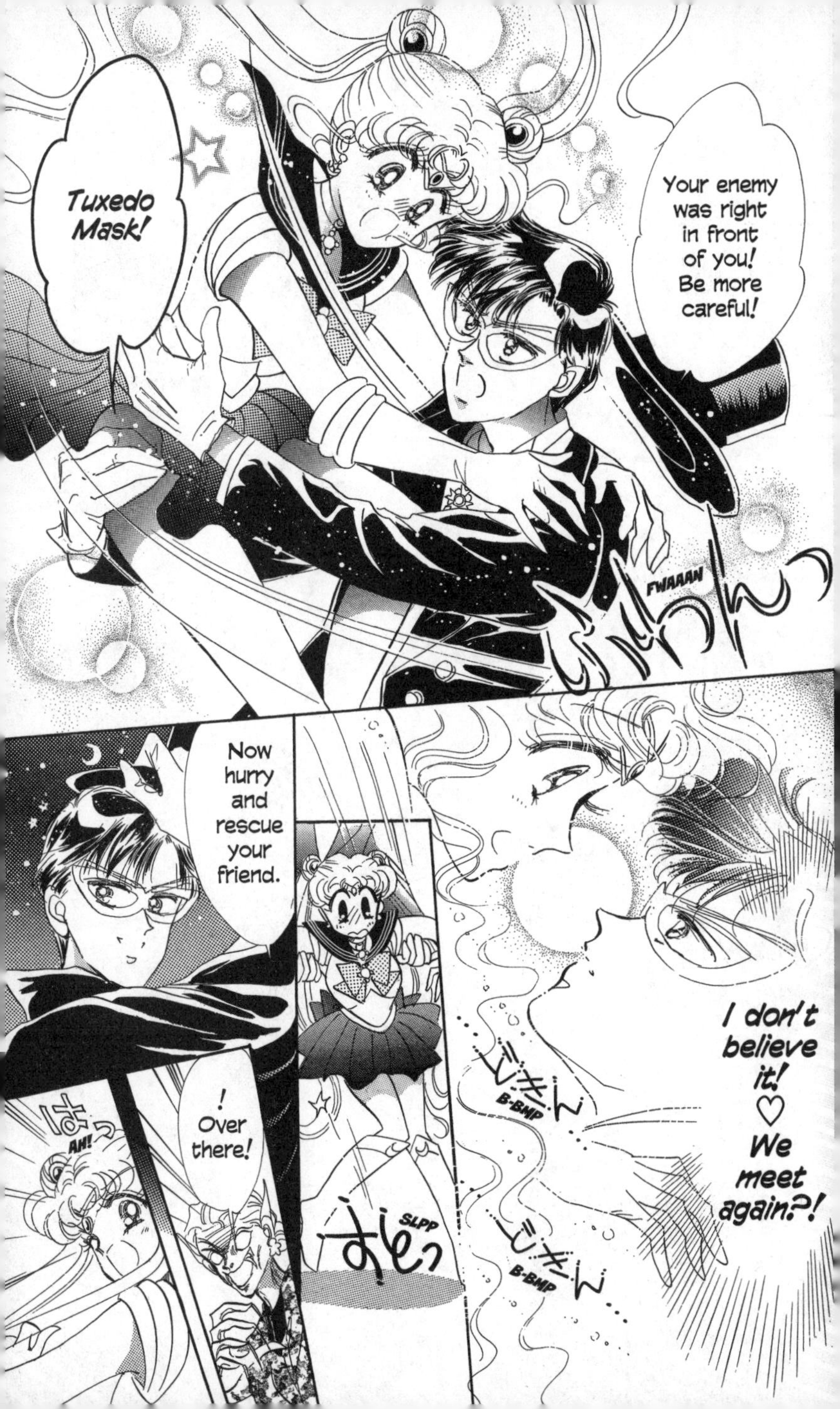
Your enemy was right in front of you! Be more careful!
Tuxedo Mask!
FWAAAN
I don't believe it! ♡ We meet again?!
B-BMP
B-BMP
Now hurry and rescue your friend.
SLPP
! Over there!
AH!

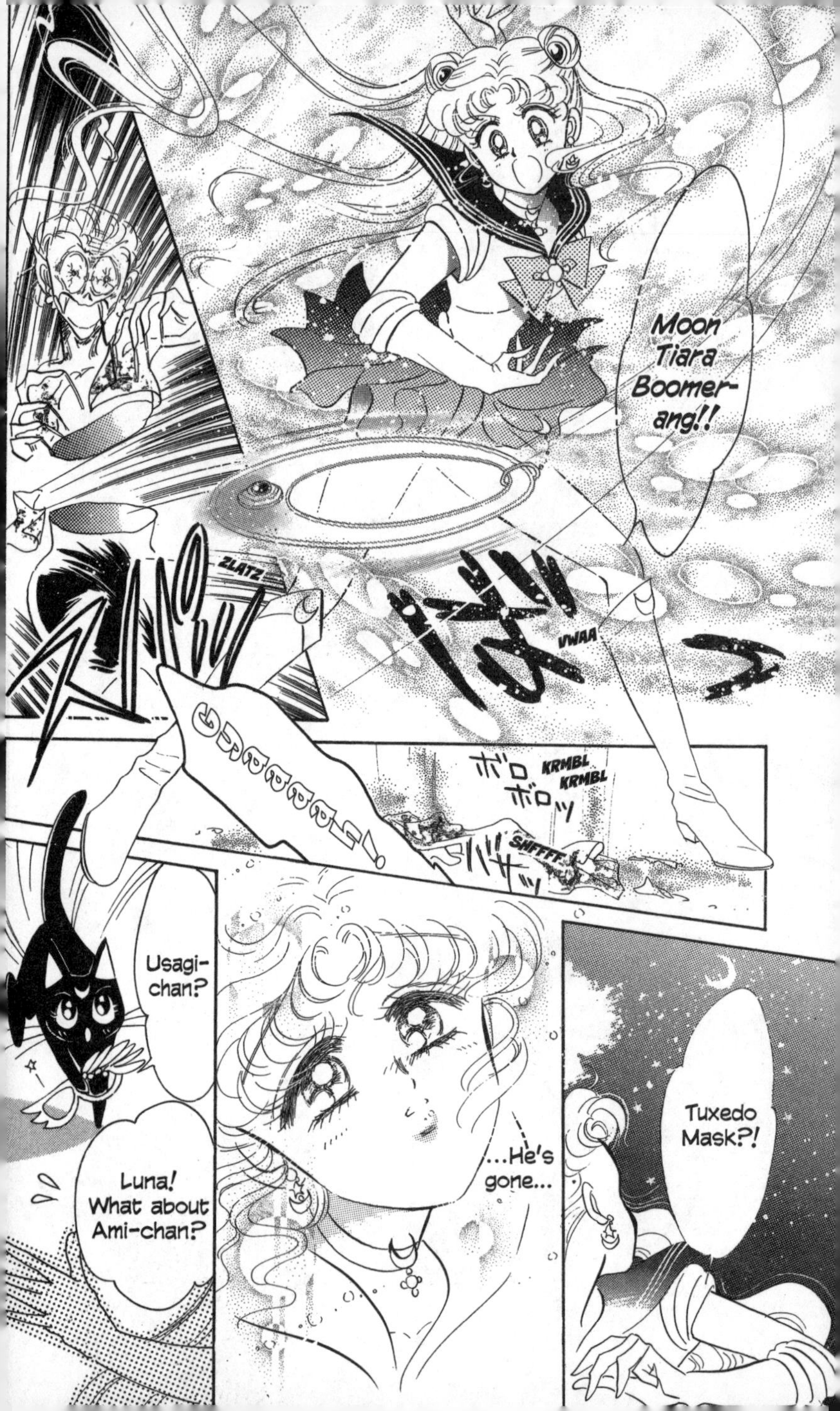
Moon Tiara Boomerang!!
VWAA
ZLATZ
GYAAAAH!
ボロ ボロッ
KRMBL KRMBL
バザッ
SHFFFF
Tuxedo Mask?!
...He's gone...
Usagi-chan?
Luna! What about Ami-chan?

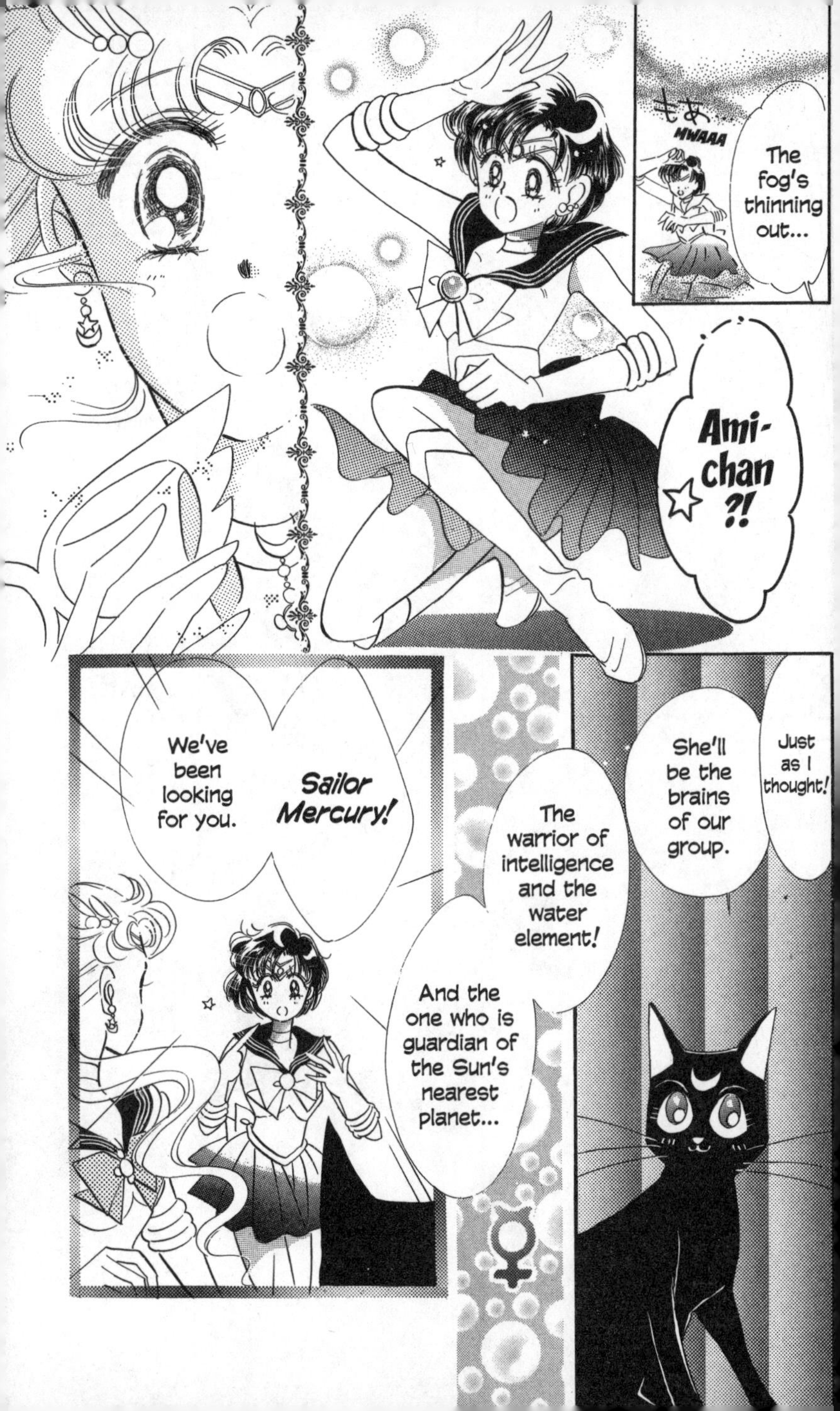

もあ
HWAAA
The fog's thinning out...
Ami-chan?!
Just as I thought!
She'll be the brains of our group.
The warrior of intelligence and the water element!
And the one who is guardian of the Sun's nearest planet...
Sailor Mercury!
We've been looking for you.

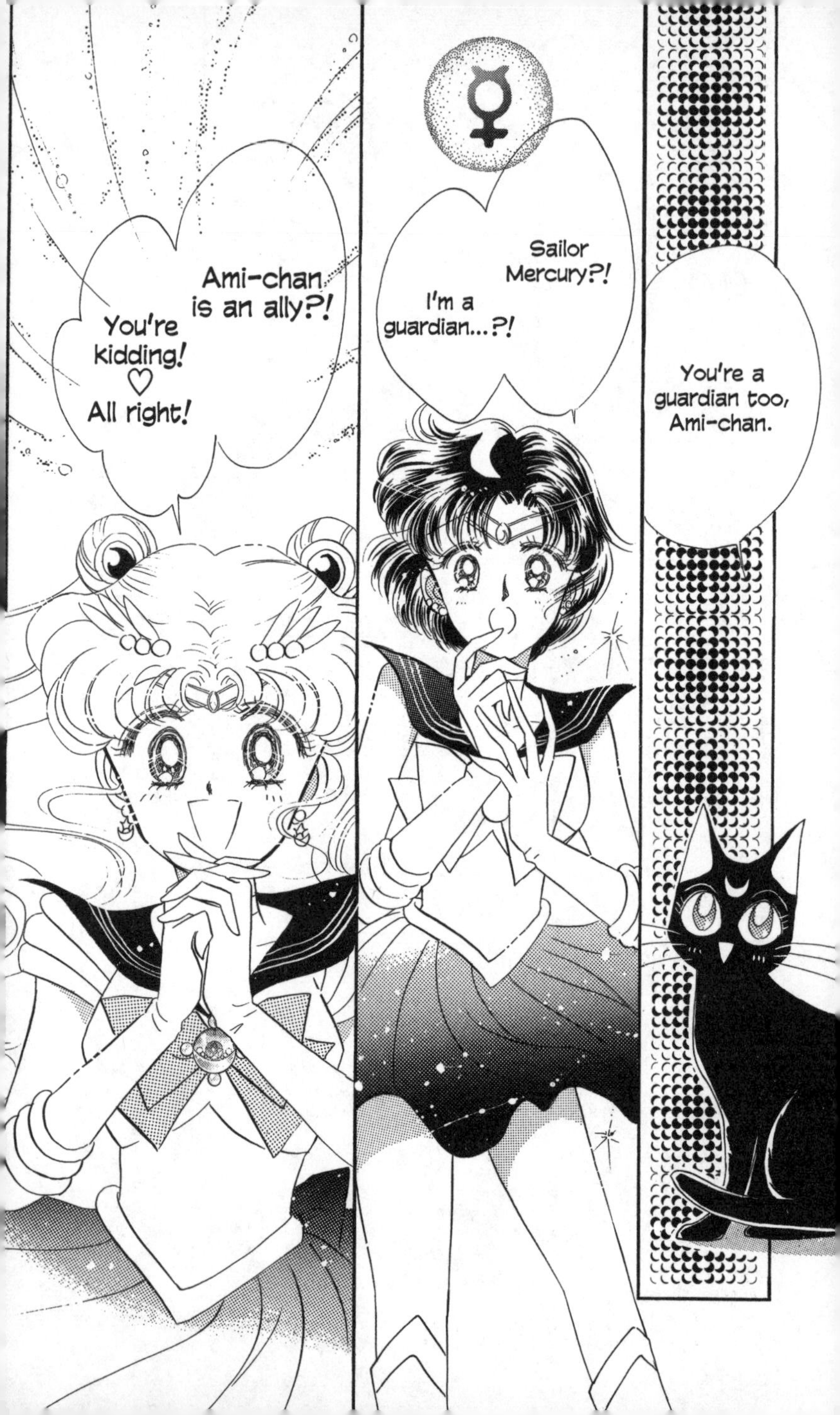
You're a guardian too, Ami-chan.
Sailor Mercury?! I'm a guardian...?!
Ami-chan is an ally?! You're kidding! ♡ All right!

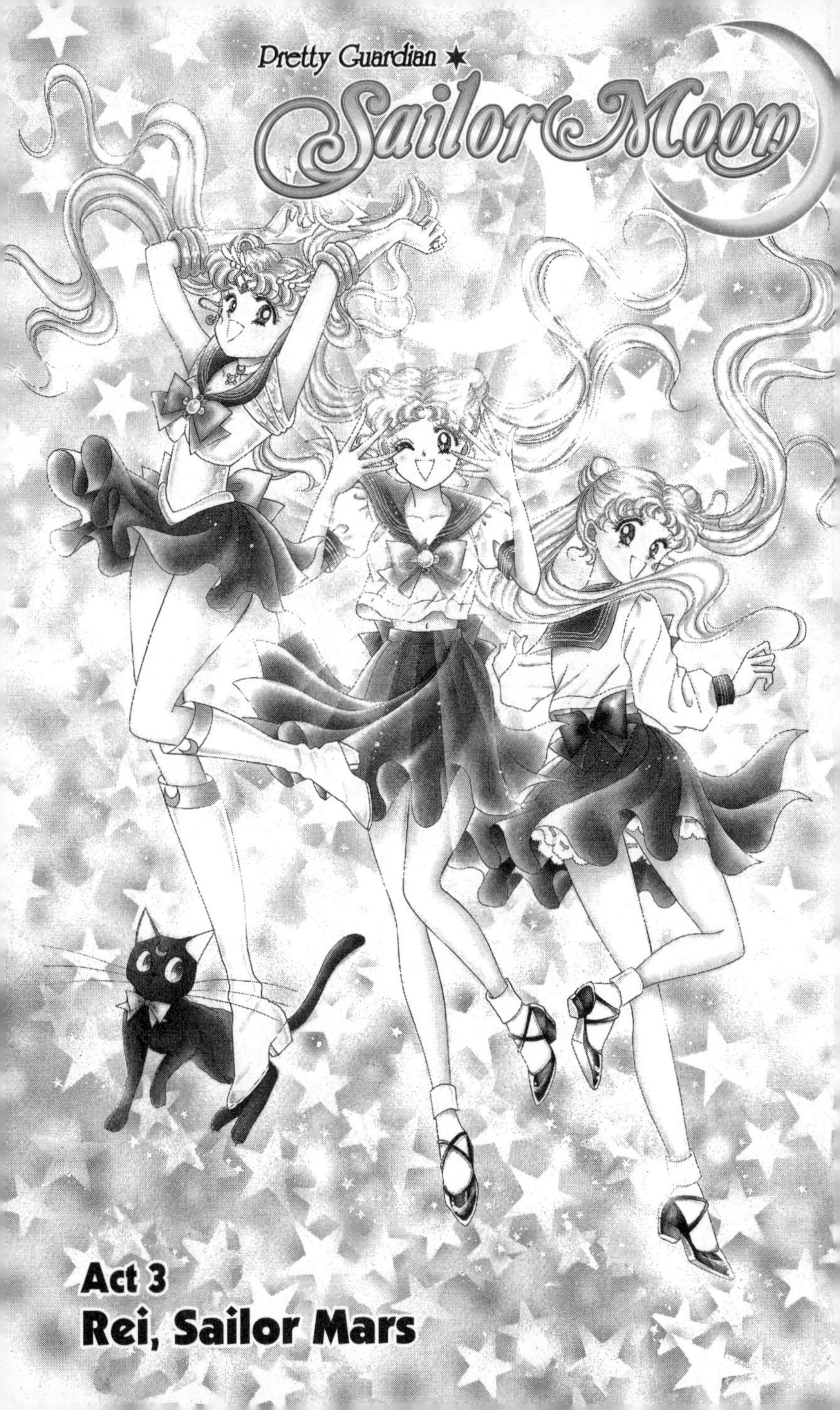
Pretty Guardian ★
Sailor Moon
Act 3
Rei, Sailor Mars

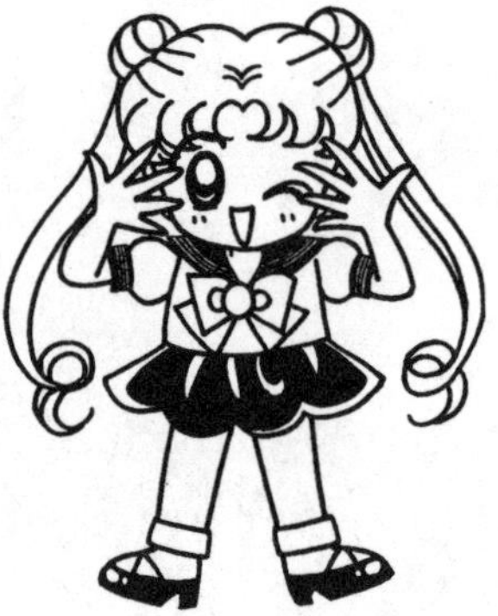
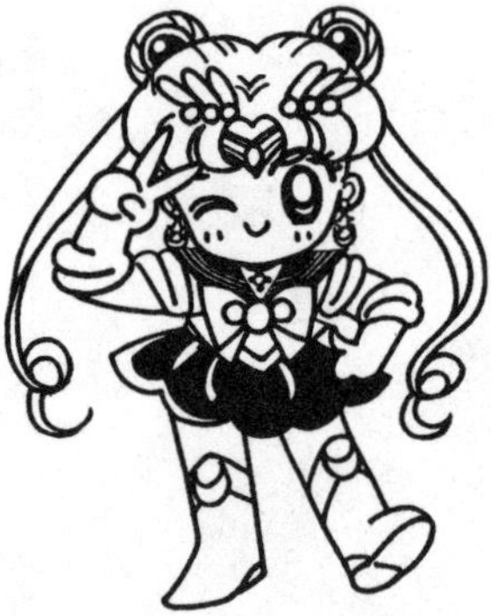
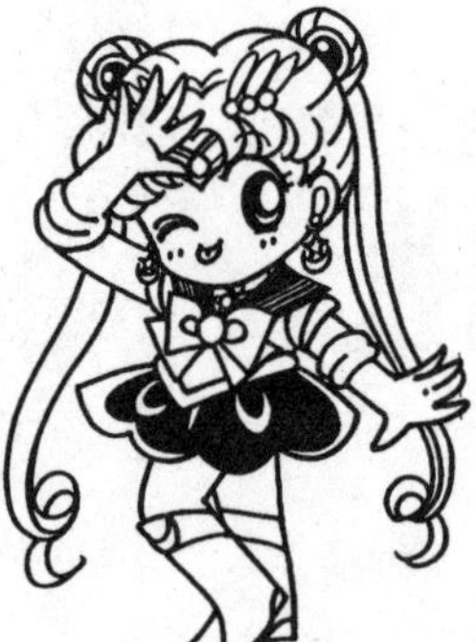
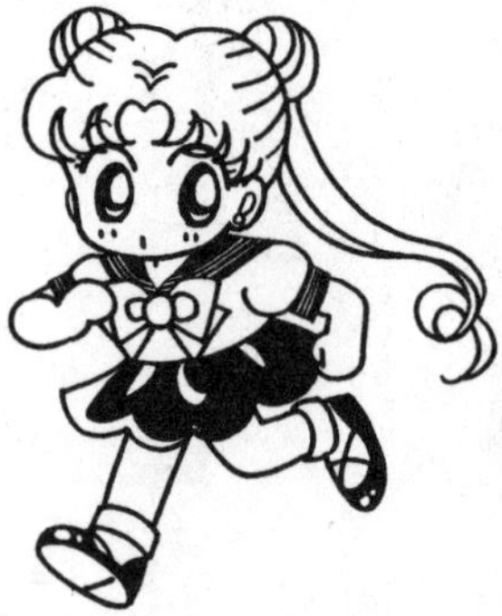

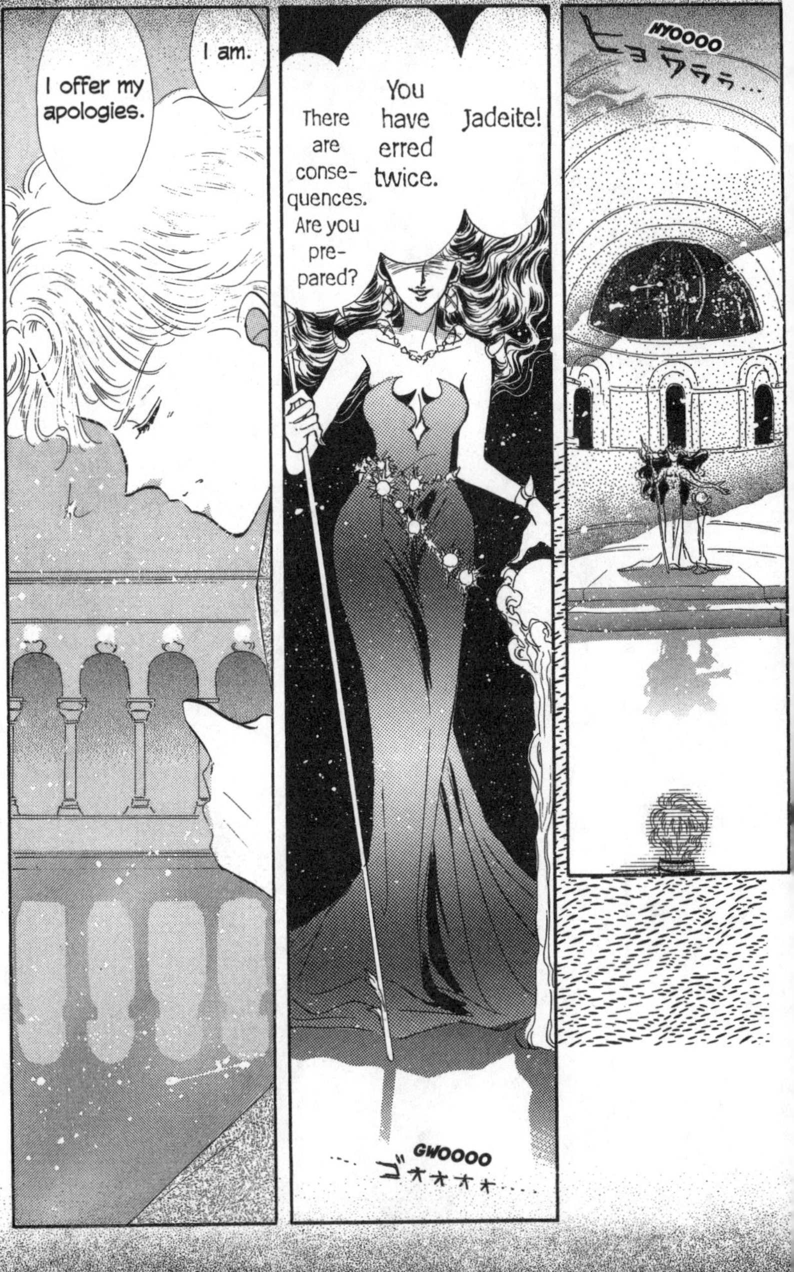
HYOOOO
Jadeite!
You have erred twice.
There are consequences. Are you prepared?
GWOOOO
I am.
I offer my apologies.

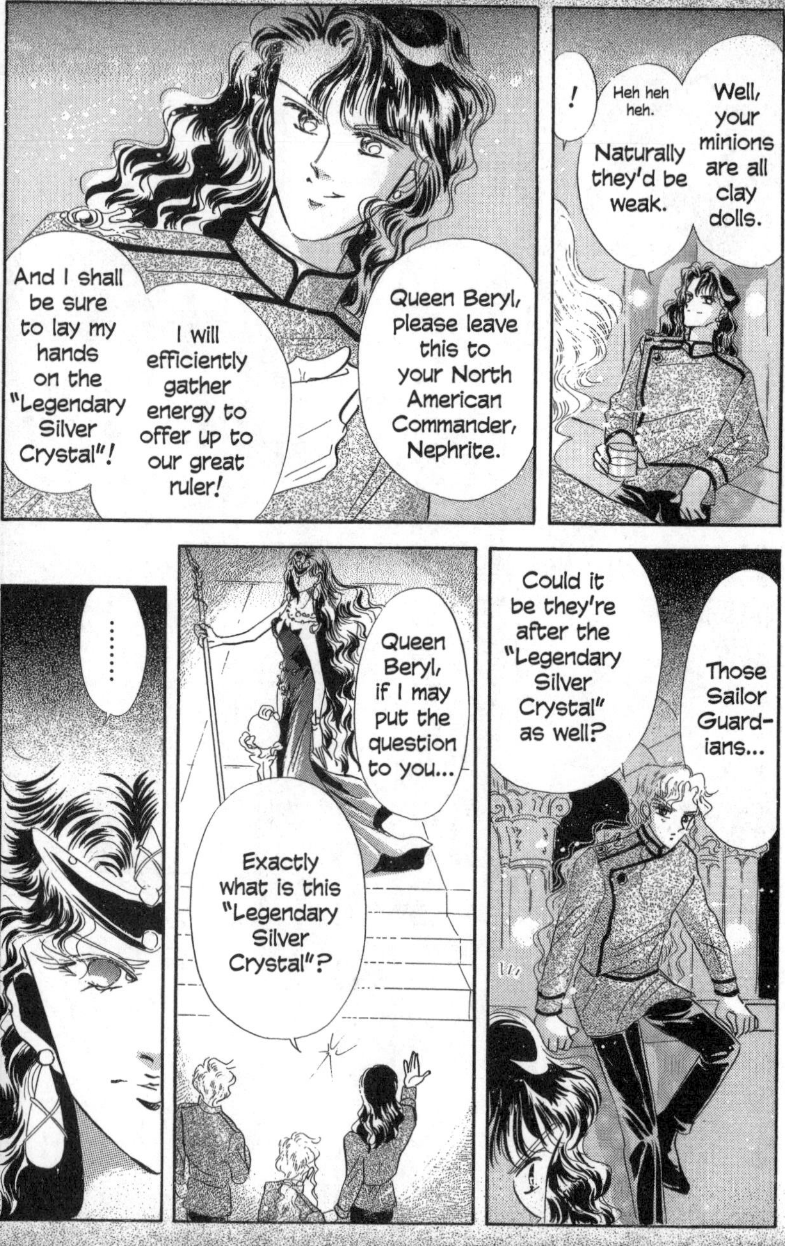
Well, your minions are all clay dolls.
Heh heh heh.
Naturally they'd be weak.
!
Queen Beryl, please leave this to your North American Commander, Nephrite.
I will efficiently gather energy to offer up to our great ruler!
And I shall be sure to lay my hands on the "Legendary Silver Crystal"!
Those Sailor Guard-ians...
Could it be they're after the "Legendary Silver Crystal" as well?
Queen Beryl, if I may put the question to you...
Exactly what is this "Legendary Silver Crystal"?
……

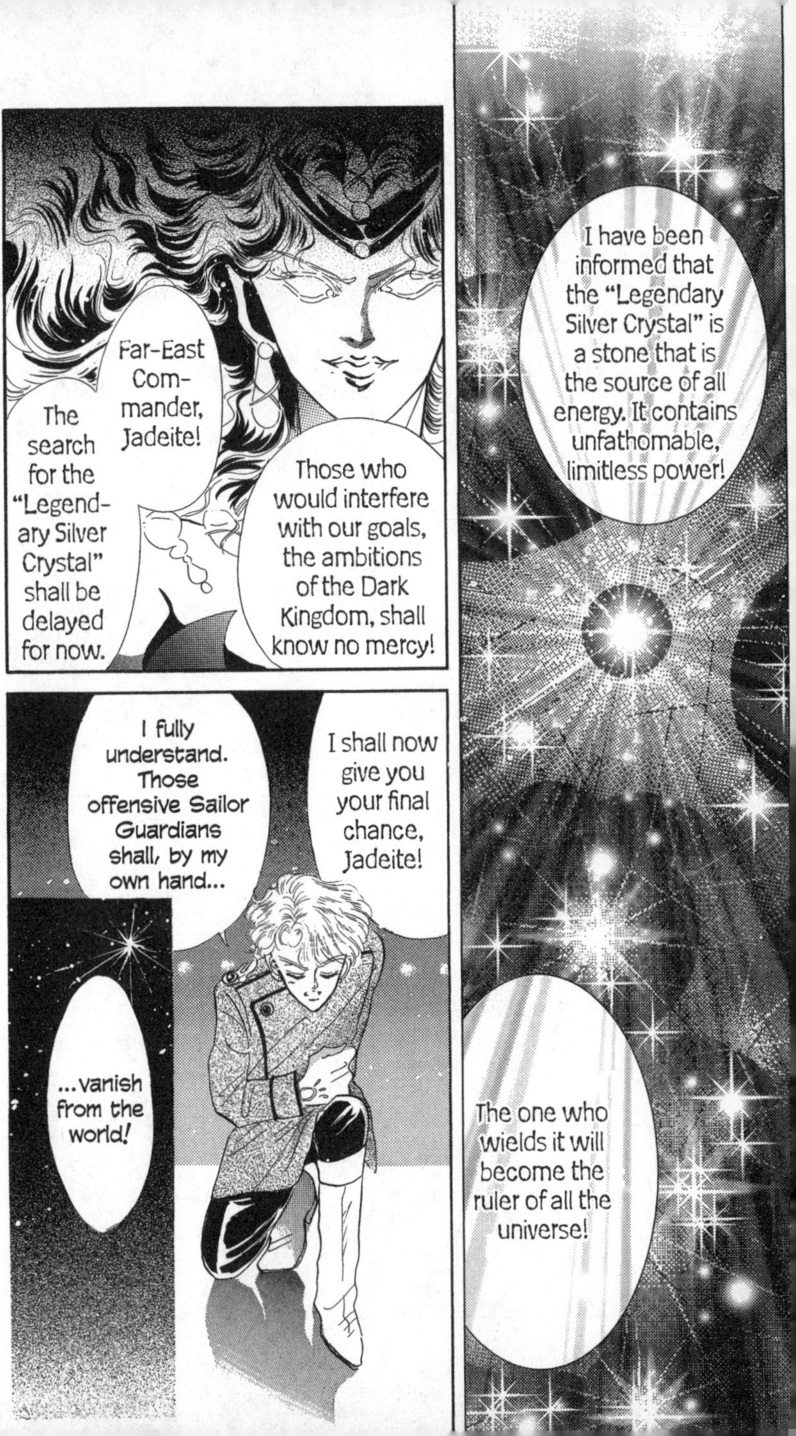
I have been informed that the "Legendary Silver Crystal" is a stone that is the source of all energy. It contains unfathomable, limitless power!
The one who wields it will become the ruler of all the universe!
Far-East Commander, Jadeite!
The search for the "Legendary Silver Crystal" shall be delayed for now.
Those who would interfere with our goals, the ambitions of the Dark Kingdom, shall know no mercy!
I shall now give you your final chance, Jadeite!
I fully understand. Those offensive Sailor Guardians shall, by my own hand...
...vanish from the world!

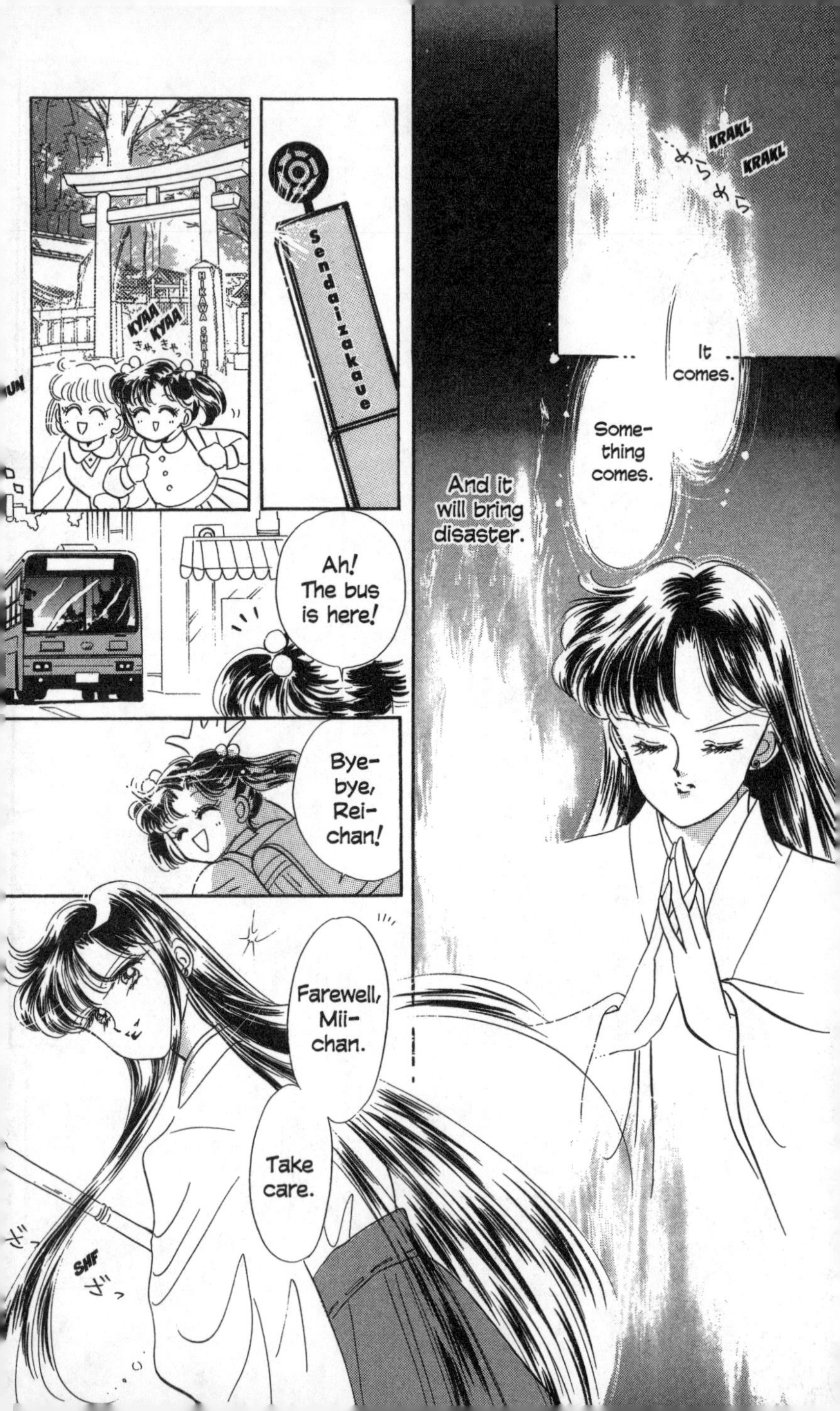
KRAKL
KRAKL
めらめら
It comes.
Something comes.
And it will bring disaster.
Sendaizakaue
HIKAWA SHRINE
KYAA KYAA
きゃっきゃっ
Ah! The bus is here!
Bye-bye, Rei-chan!
Farewell, Mii-chan.
Take care.
SHF
ざっ

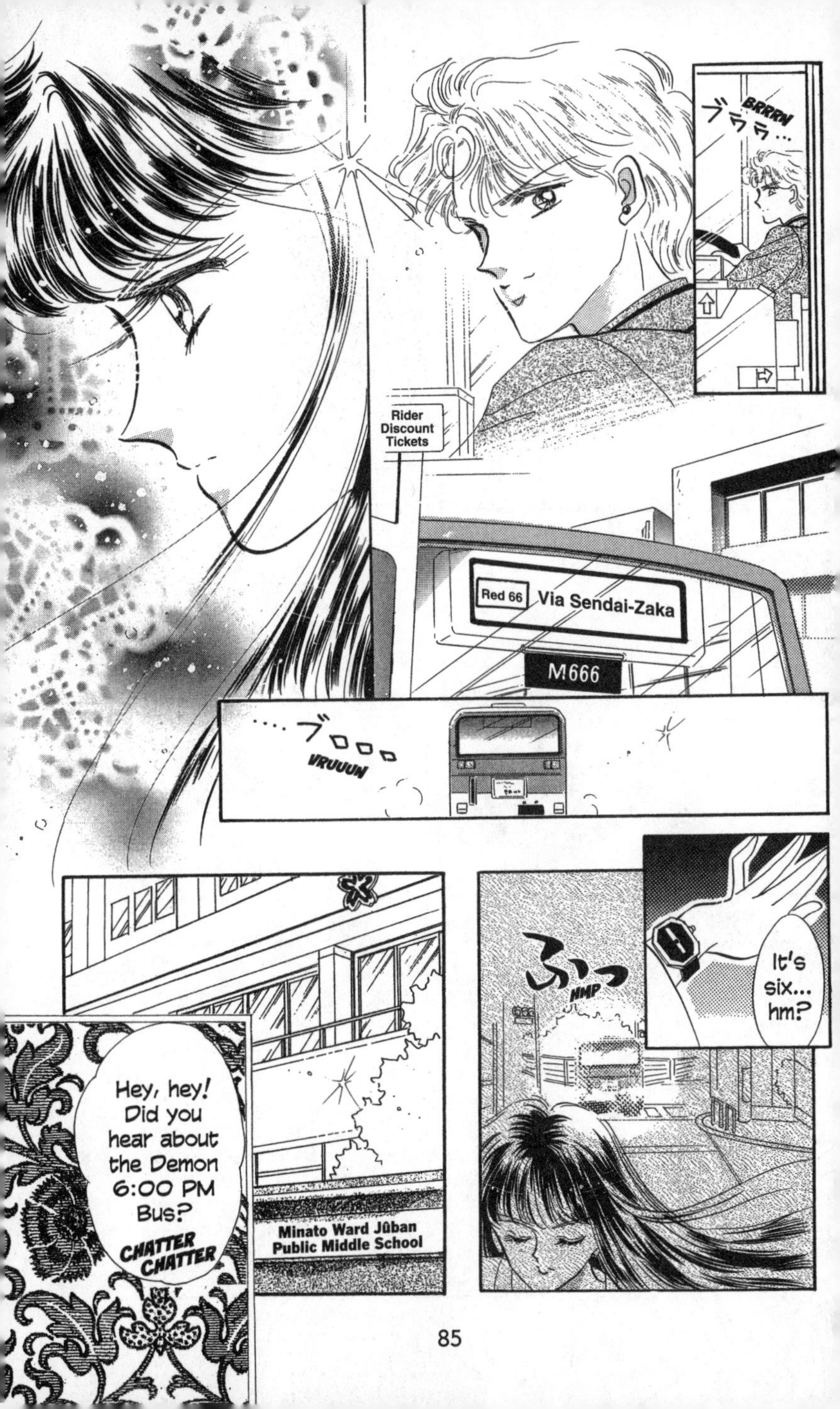

ブララ…
BRRRN
Rider Discount Tickets
Red 66
Via Sendai-Zaka
M666
…ブロロロ
VRUUUN
It's six... hm?
ふっ
HMP
Minato Ward Jûban Public Middle School
Hey, hey! Did you hear about the Demon 6:00 PM Bus?
CHATTER CHATTER

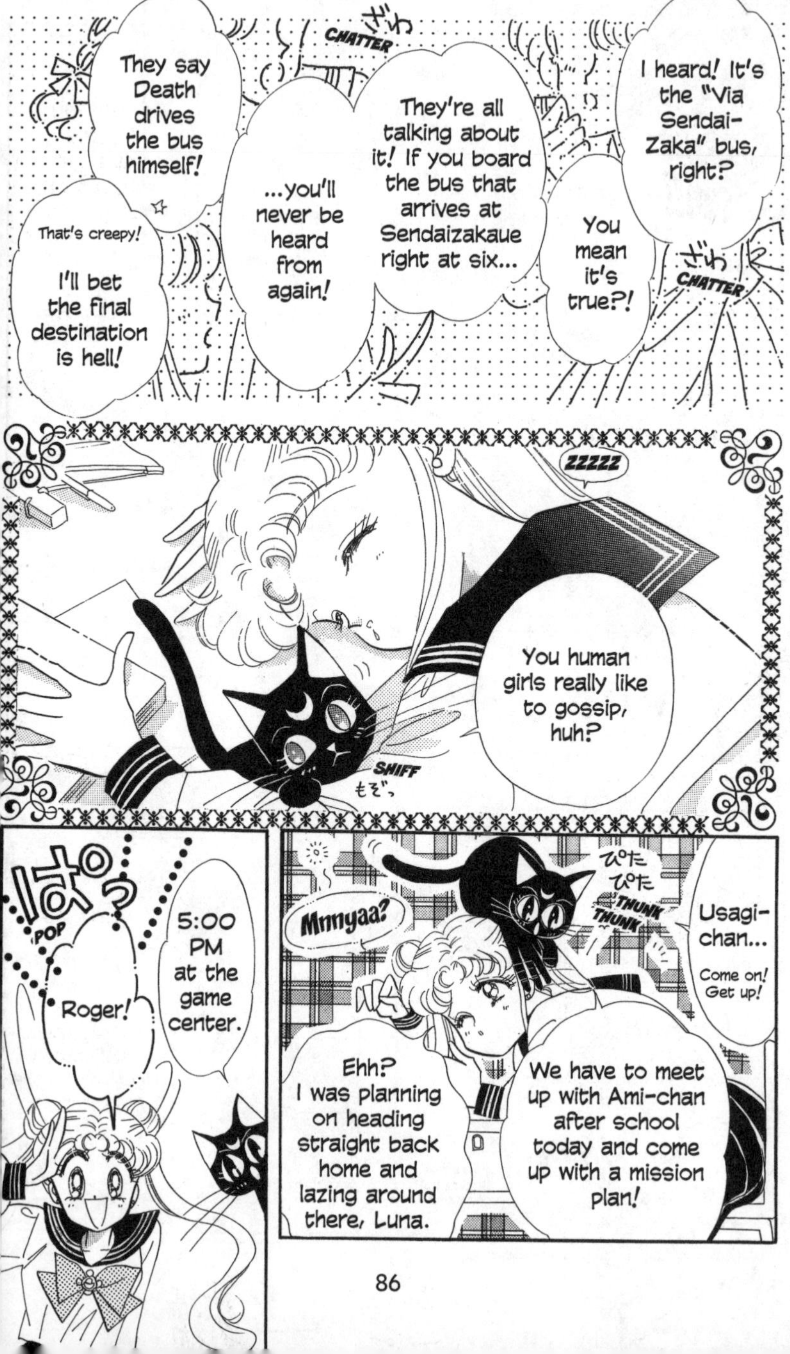
ざわ
CHATTER
I heard! It's the "Via Sendai-Zaka" bus, right?
You mean it's true?!
ざわ
CHATTER
They're all talking about it! If you board the bus that arrives at Sendaizakaue right at six...
...you'll never be heard from again!
They say Death drives the bus himself!
That's creepy!
I'll bet the final destination is hell!
ZZZZZ
You human girls really like to gossip, huh?
SNIFF
もぞっ
ぴた ぴた
THUNK THUNK
Usagi-chan...
Come on! Get up!
Mnnyaa?
We have to meet up with Ami-chan after school today and come up with a mission plan!
Ehh? I was planning on heading straight back home and lazing around there, Luna.
はっ
POP
5:00 PM at the game center.
Roger!

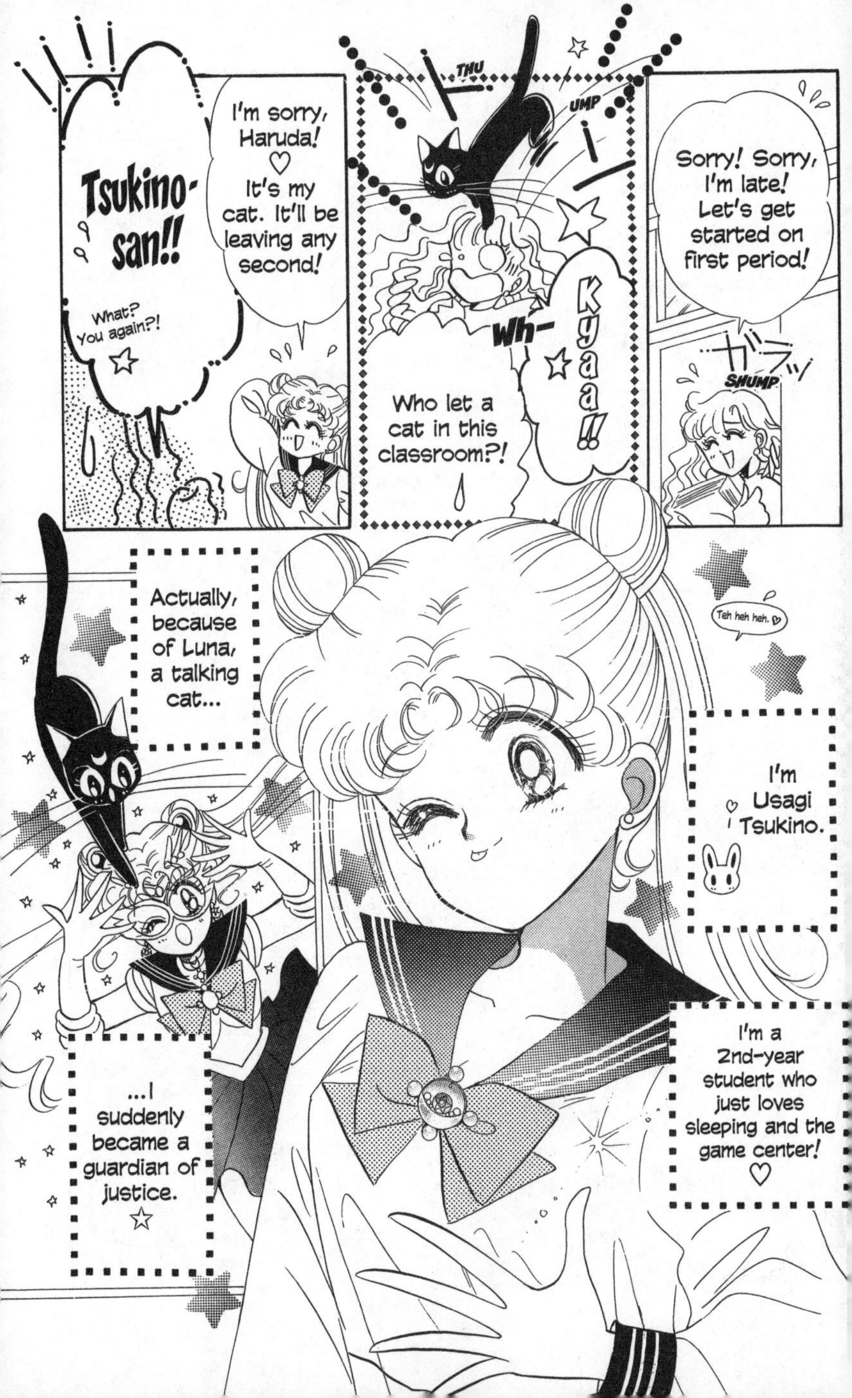

Sorry! Sorry, I'm late! Let's get started on first period!
SHUMP
THUMP
Wh-
Kyaa!!
Who let a cat in this classroom?!
Tsukino-san!!
What? You again?!
I'm sorry, Haruda! ♡ It's my cat. It'll be leaving any second!
Teh heh heh. ♡
I'm Usagi Tsukino.
I'm a 2nd-year student who just loves sleeping and the game center! ♡
Actually, because of Luna, a talking cat...
...I suddenly became a guardian of justice. ☆

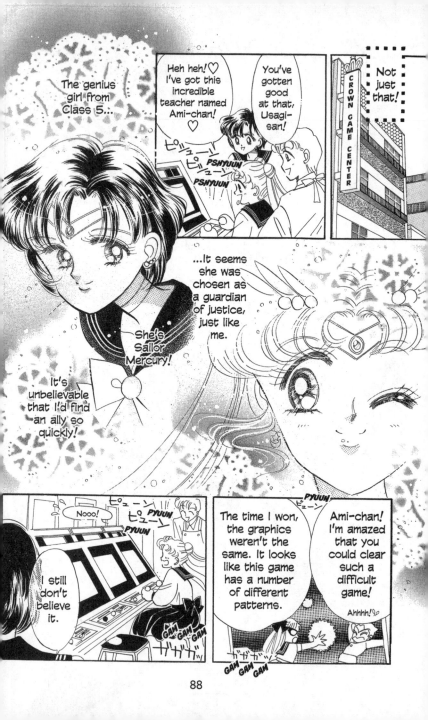

Not just that!
CROWN GAME CENTER
You've gotten good at that, Usagi-san!
Heh heh! ♡ I've got this incredible teacher named Ami-chan! ♡
PSHYUUN
PSHYUUN
The genius girl from Class 5...
She's Sailor Mercury!
...It seems she was chosen as a guardian of justice, just like me.
It's unbelievable that I'd find an ally so quickly!
PYUUN
Ami-chan! I'm amazed that you could clear such a difficult game!
The time I won, the graphics weren't the same. It looks like this game has a number of different patterns.
Ahhhh!
GAM GAM GAM
Nooo!
PYUUN
PYUUN
I still don't believe it.
GAM GAM GAM

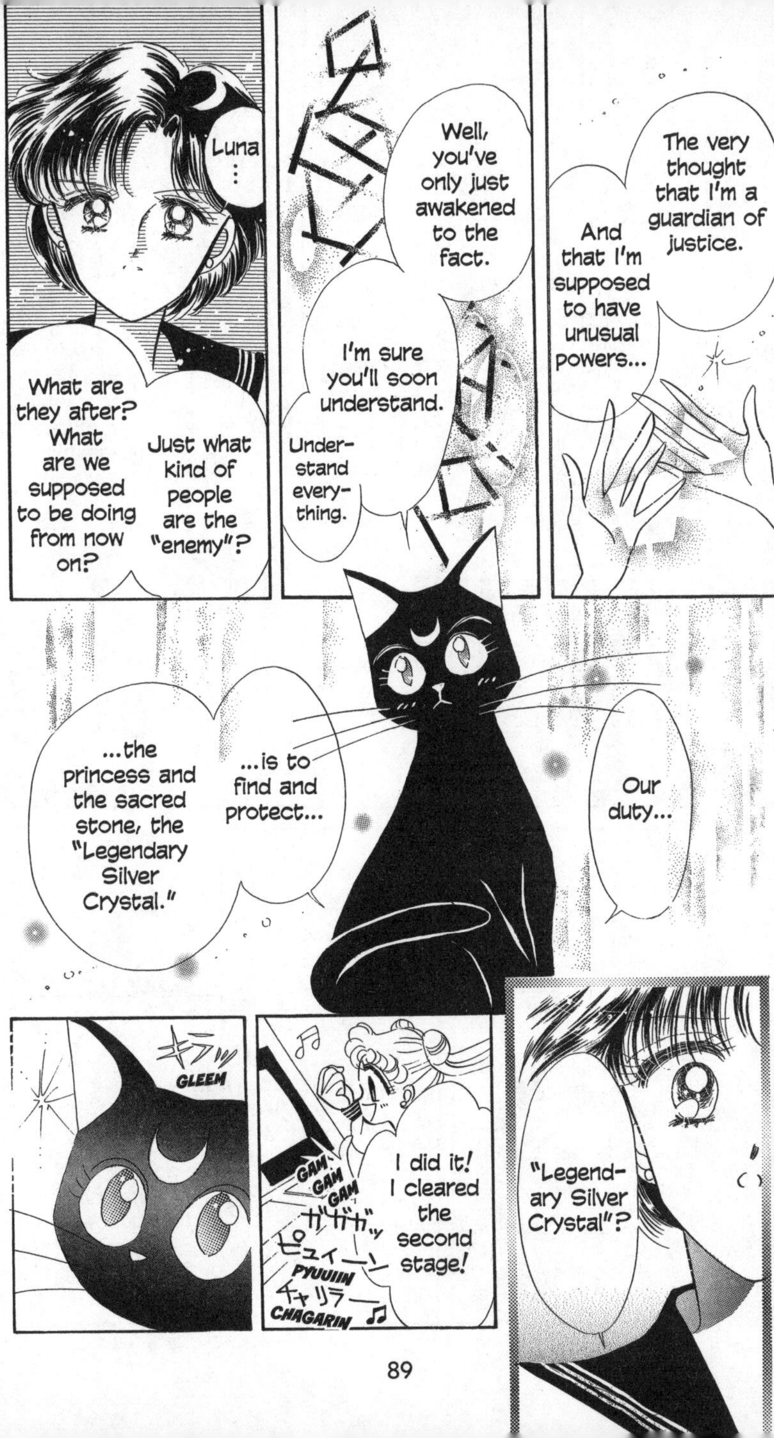
The very thought that I'm a guardian of justice.
And that I'm supposed to have unusual powers...
Well, you've only just awakened to the fact.
I'm sure you'll soon understand.
Under-stand every-thing.
Luna...
Just what kind of people are the "enemy"?
What are they after? What are we supposed to be doing from now on?
Our duty...
...is to find and protect...
...the princess and the sacred stone, the "Legendary Silver Crystal."
"Legend-ary Silver Crystal"?
I did it! I cleared the second stage!
GAM GAM GAM
ガガガッ
ピュイーン
PYUUIIN
チャリラー
CHAGARIN
キラッ
GLEEM

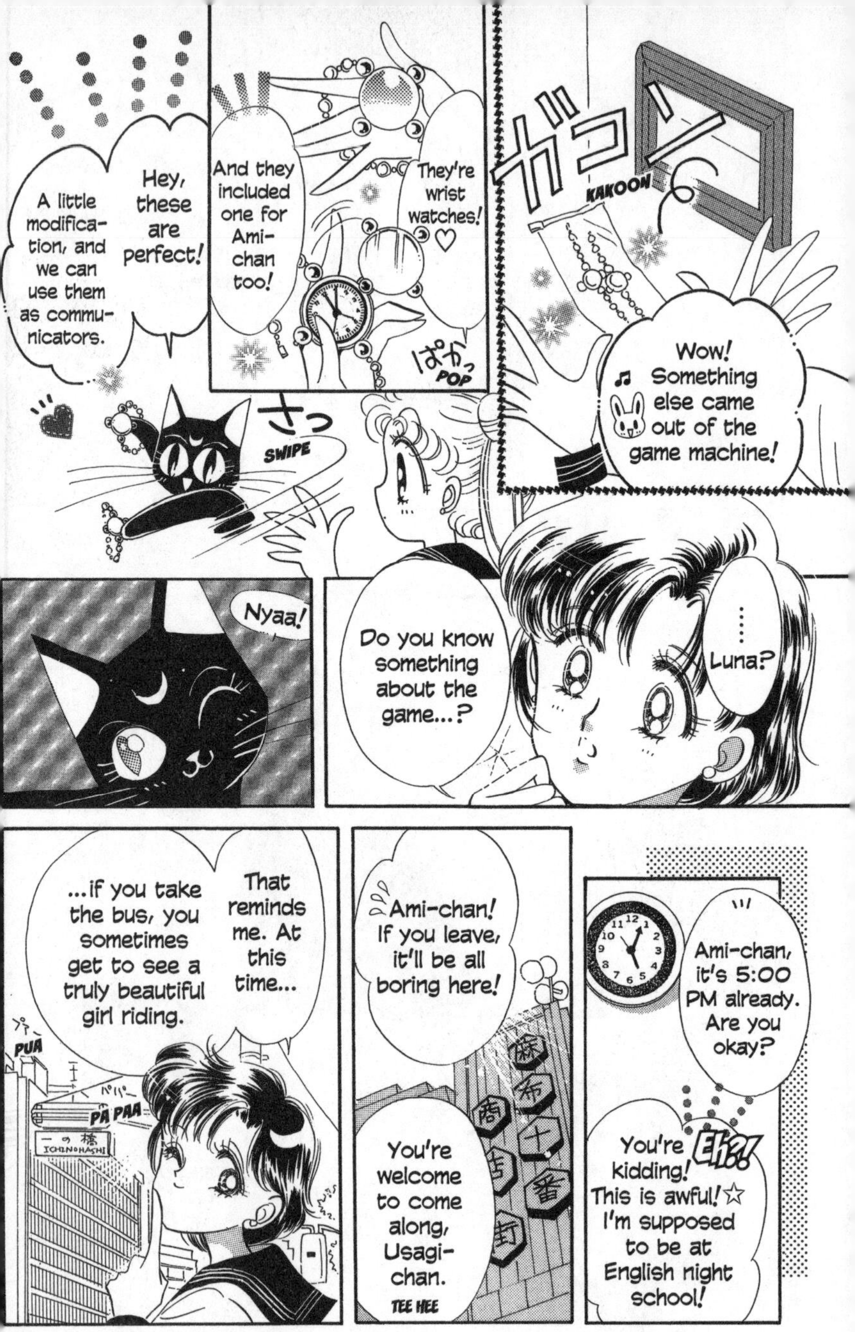

KAKOON
Wow! ♫ Something else came out of the game machine!
They're wrist watches! ♡
And they included one for Ami-chan too!
POP
Hey, these are perfect!
A little modification, and we can use them as communicators.
SWIPE
......Luna?
Do you know something about the game...?
Nyaa!
Ami-chan, it's 5:00 PM already. Are you okay?
Eh?!
You're kidding! This is awful!☆ I'm supposed to be at English night school!
Ami-chan! If you leave, it'll be all boring here!
You're welcome to come along, Usagi-chan.
TEE HEE
That reminds me. At this time...
...if you take the bus, you sometimes get to see a truly beautiful girl riding.
PUA
PA PAA
ICHINOHASHI

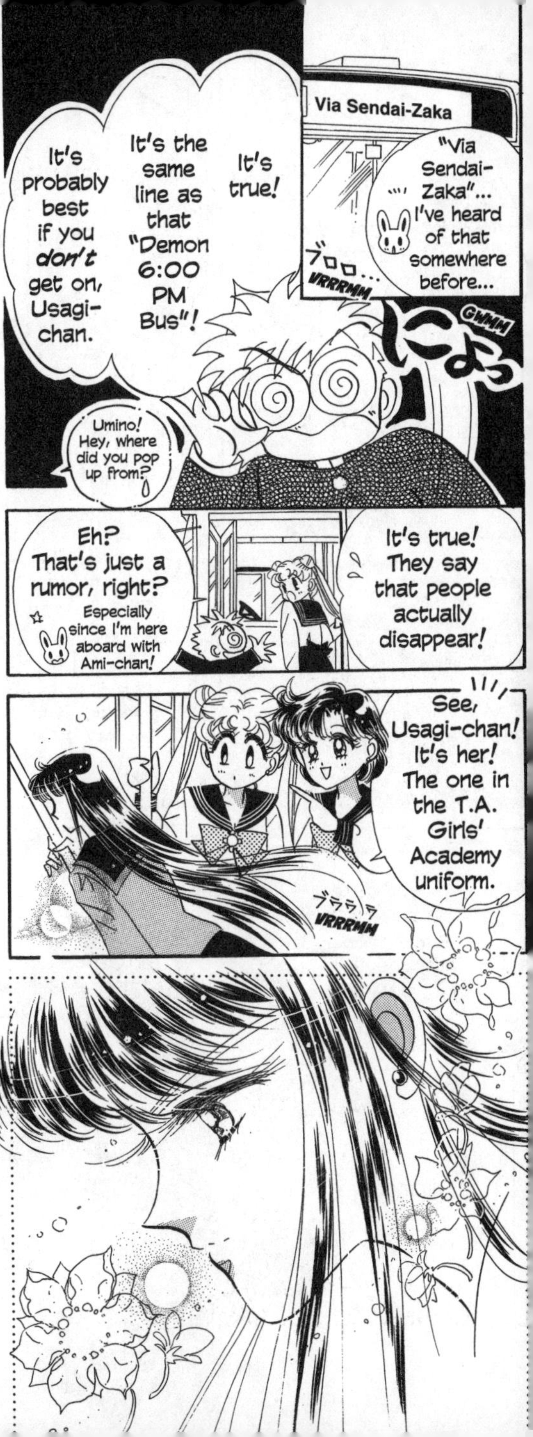

Via Sendai-Zaka
"Via Sendai-Zaka"... I've heard of that somewhere before...
ブロロ... VRRRMM
にょっ GWMM
It's true!
It's the same line as that "Demon 6:00 PM Bus"!
It's probably best if you *don't* get on, Usagi-chan.
Umino! Hey, where did you pop up from?
It's true! They say that people actually disappear!
Eh? That's just a rumor, right?
Especially since I'm here aboard with Ami-chan!
See, Usagi-chan! It's her! The one in the T.A. Girls' Academy uniform.
ブララ VRRRMM

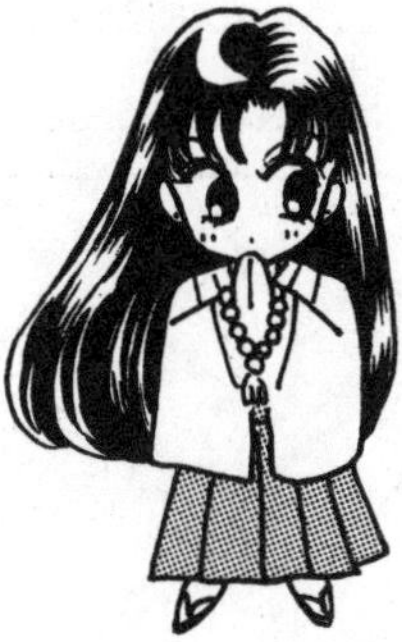

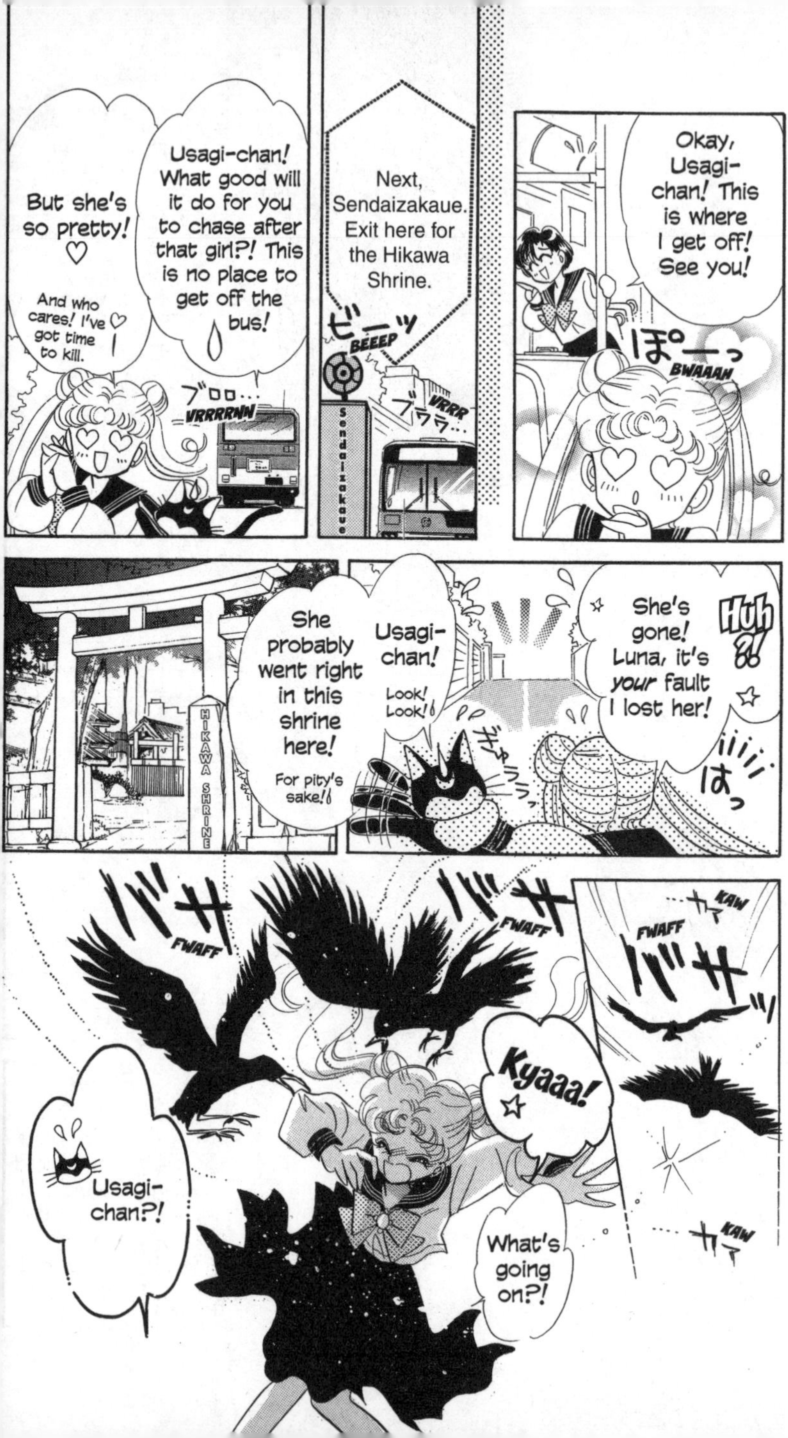
Okay, Usagi-chan! This is where I get off! See you!
ぽーっ
BWAAAN
Next, Sendaizakaue. Exit here for the Hikawa Shrine.
ビーッ
BEEEP
Sendaizakaue
ブララ…
VRRR
Usagi-chan! What good will it do for you to chase after that girl?! This is no place to get off the bus!
But she's so pretty! ♡
And who cares! I've ♡ got time to kill.
ブロロ…
VRRRRNN
Huh?!
She's gone! Luna, it's your fault I lost her!
はっ
Usagi-chan!
Look! Look!
ギュララ
She probably went right in this shrine here!
For pity's sake!
HIKAWA SHRINE
カァ
KAW
FWAFF
バサ
Kyaaa!
What's going on?!
カァ
KAW
バサ
FWAFF
バサ
FWAFF
Usagi-chan?!

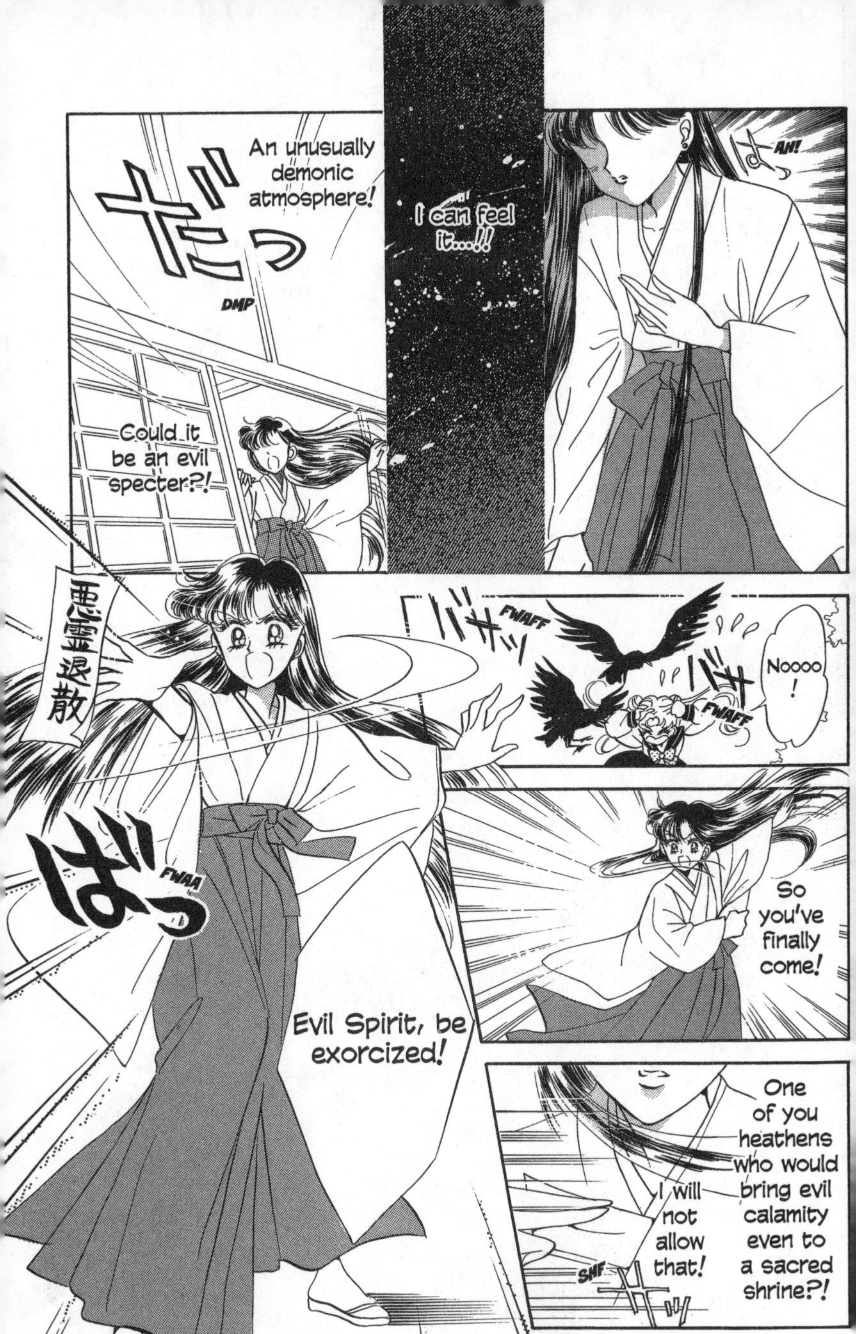
AH!
I can feel it...!!
An unusually demonic atmosphere!
DMP
Could it be an evil specter?!
FWAFF
FWAFF
Noooo!
So you've finally come!
One of you heathens who would bring evil calamity even to a sacred shrine?!
I will not allow that!
SHF
悪霊退散
FWAA
Evil Spirit, be exorcized!

Ward: Evil Spirit Be Exorcized.

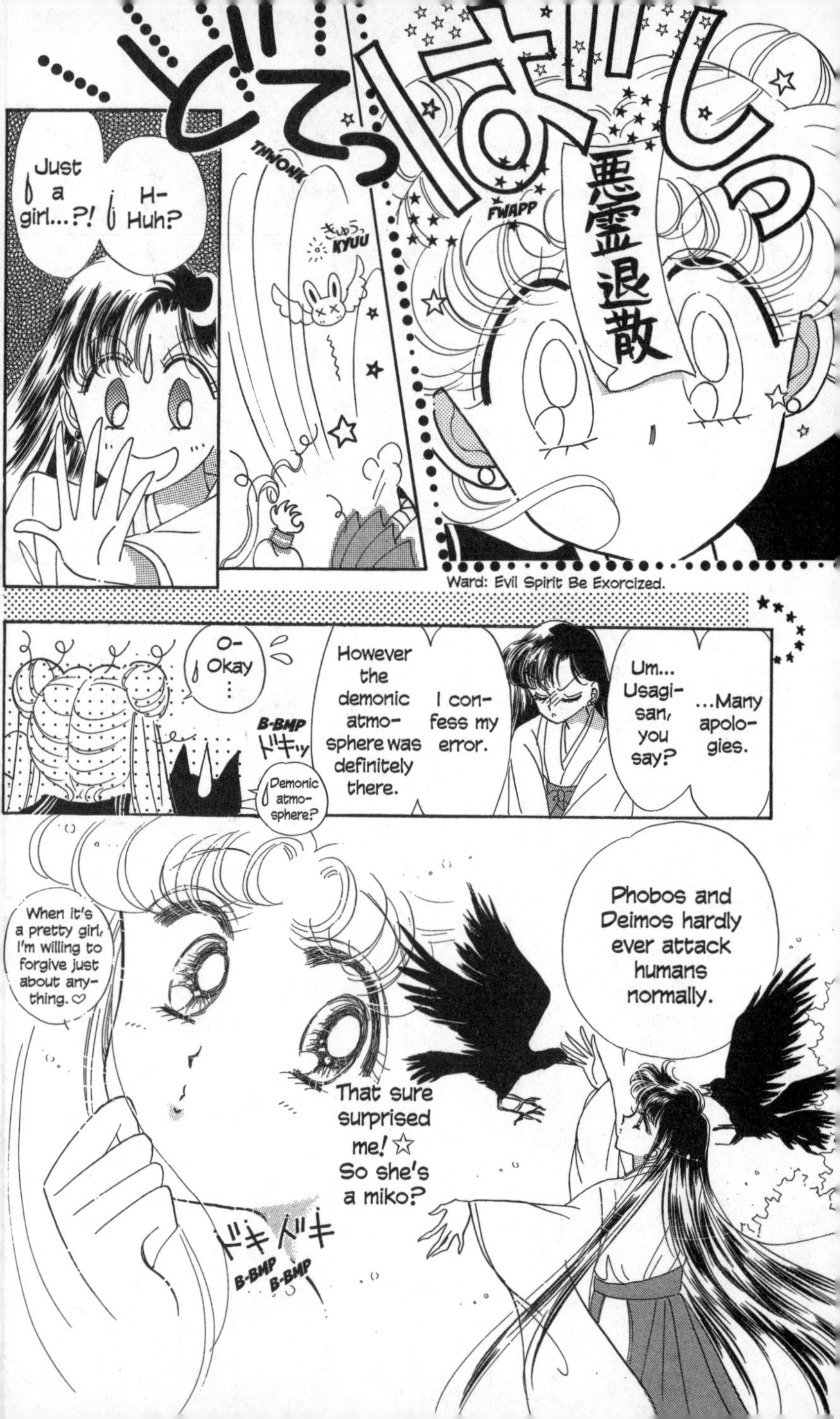

……どてっ
はりっ
FWAPP
悪霊退散
Ward: Evil Spirit Be Exorcized.
THWONK
きゅうっ KYUU
H- Huh?
Just a girl...?!
...Many apologies.
Um... Usagi-san, you say?
I confess my error.
However the demonic atmosphere was definitely there.
Demonic atmosphere?
B-BMP ドキッ
O-Okay...
Phobos and Deimos hardly ever attack humans normally.
That sure surprised me! ☆ So she's a miko?
ドキドキ
B-BMP B-BMP
When it's a pretty girl, I'm willing to forgive just about anything. ♡

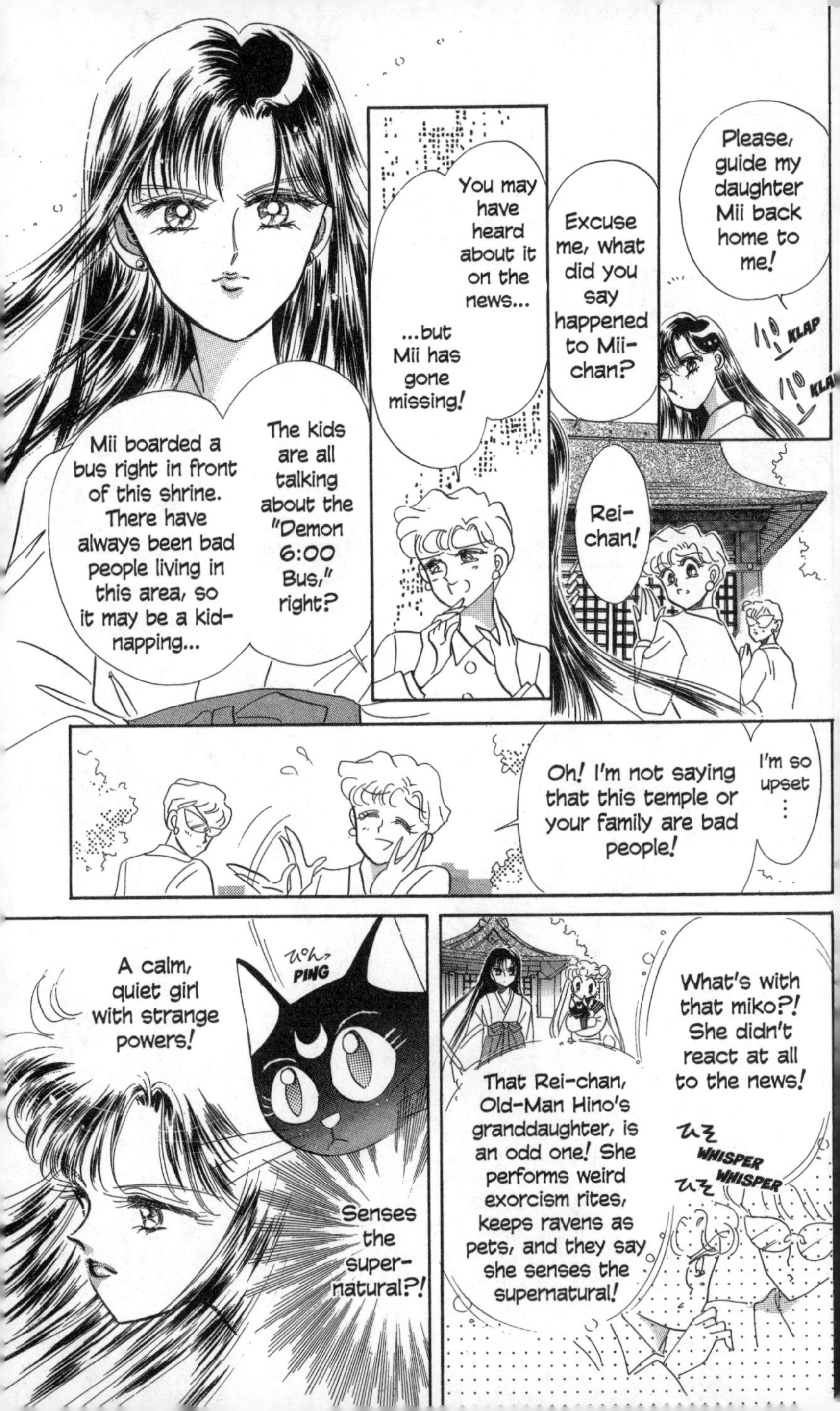
Please, guide my daughter Mii back home to me!
KLAP
KLAP
Excuse me, what did you say happened to Mii-chan?
Rei-chan!
You may have heard about it on the news...
...but Mii has gone missing!
The kids are all talking about the "Demon 6:00 Bus," right?
Mii boarded a bus right in front of this shrine. There have always been bad people living in this area, so it may be a kid-napping...
I'm so upset...
Oh! I'm not saying that this temple or your family are bad people!
What's with that miko?! She didn't react at all to the news!
That Rei-chan, Old-Man Hino's granddaughter, is an odd one! She performs weird exorcism rites, keeps ravens as pets, and they say she senses the supernatural!
ひそ
WHISPER
ひそ
WHISPER
ぴん
PING
A calm, quiet girl with strange powers!
Senses the super-natural?!

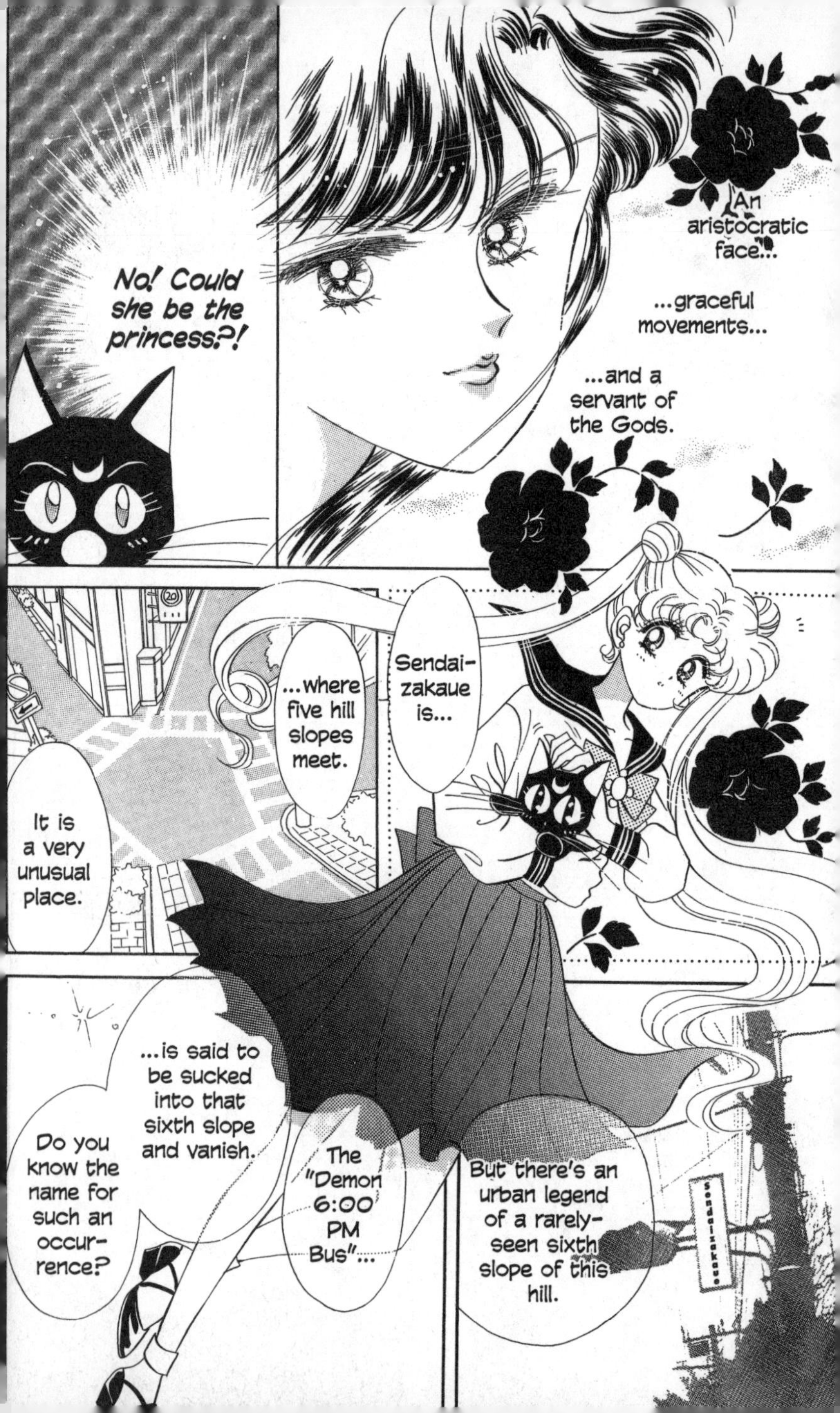
An aristocratic face...
...graceful movements...
...and a servant of the Gods.
No! Could she be the princess?!
Sendai-zakaue is...
...where five hill slopes meet.
It is a very unusual place.
But there's an urban legend of a rarely-seen sixth slope of this hill.
Sendaizakaue
The "Demon 6:00 PM Bus"...
...is said to be sucked into that sixth slope and vanish.
Do you know the name for such an occurrence?

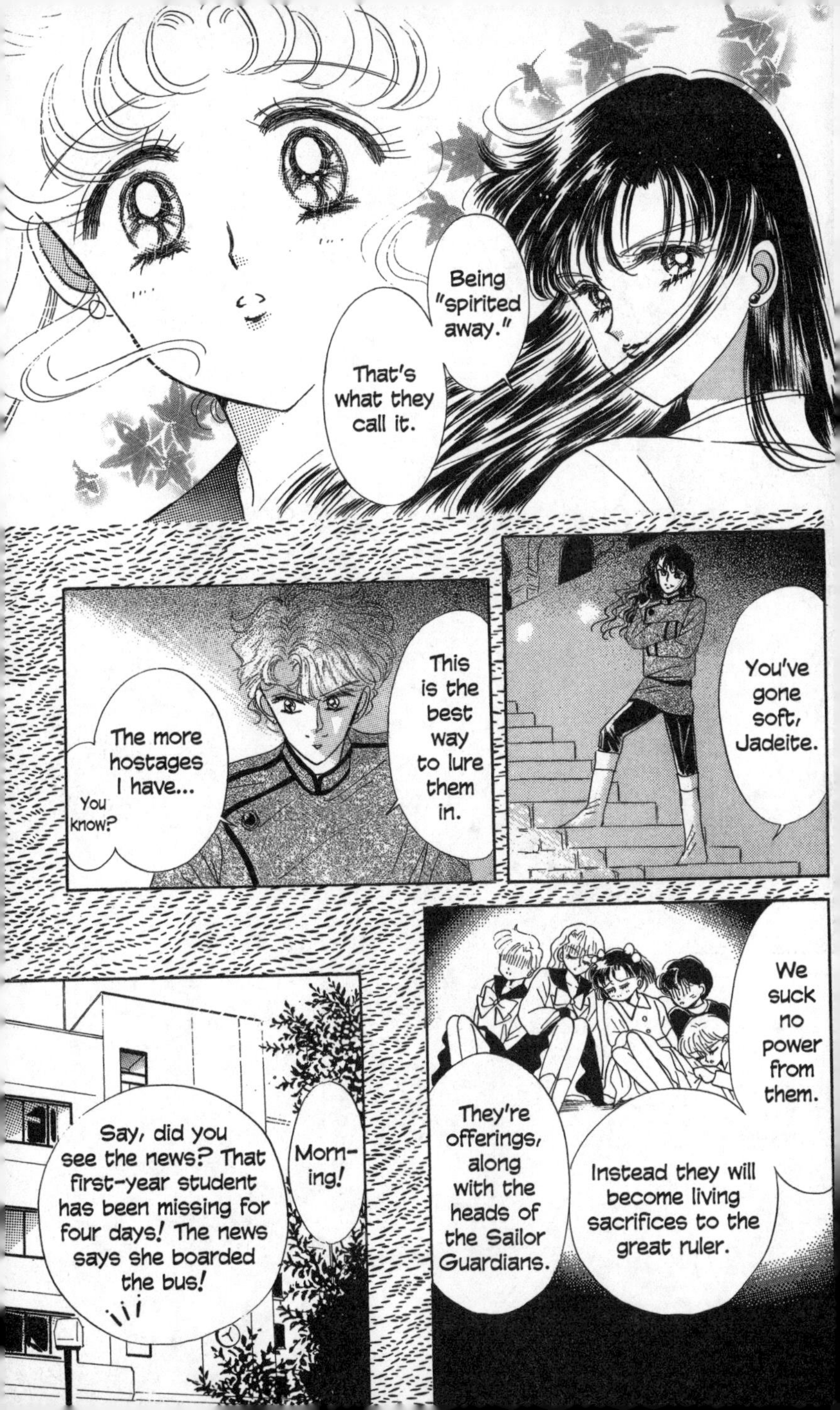
Being "spirited away."
That's what they call it.
You've gone soft, Jadeite.
This is the best way to lure them in.
The more hostages I have...
You know?
We suck no power from them.
Instead they will become living sacrifices to the great ruler.
They're offerings, along with the heads of the Sailor Guardians.
Morn-ing!
Say, did you see the news? That first-year student has been missing for four days! The news says she boarded the bus!

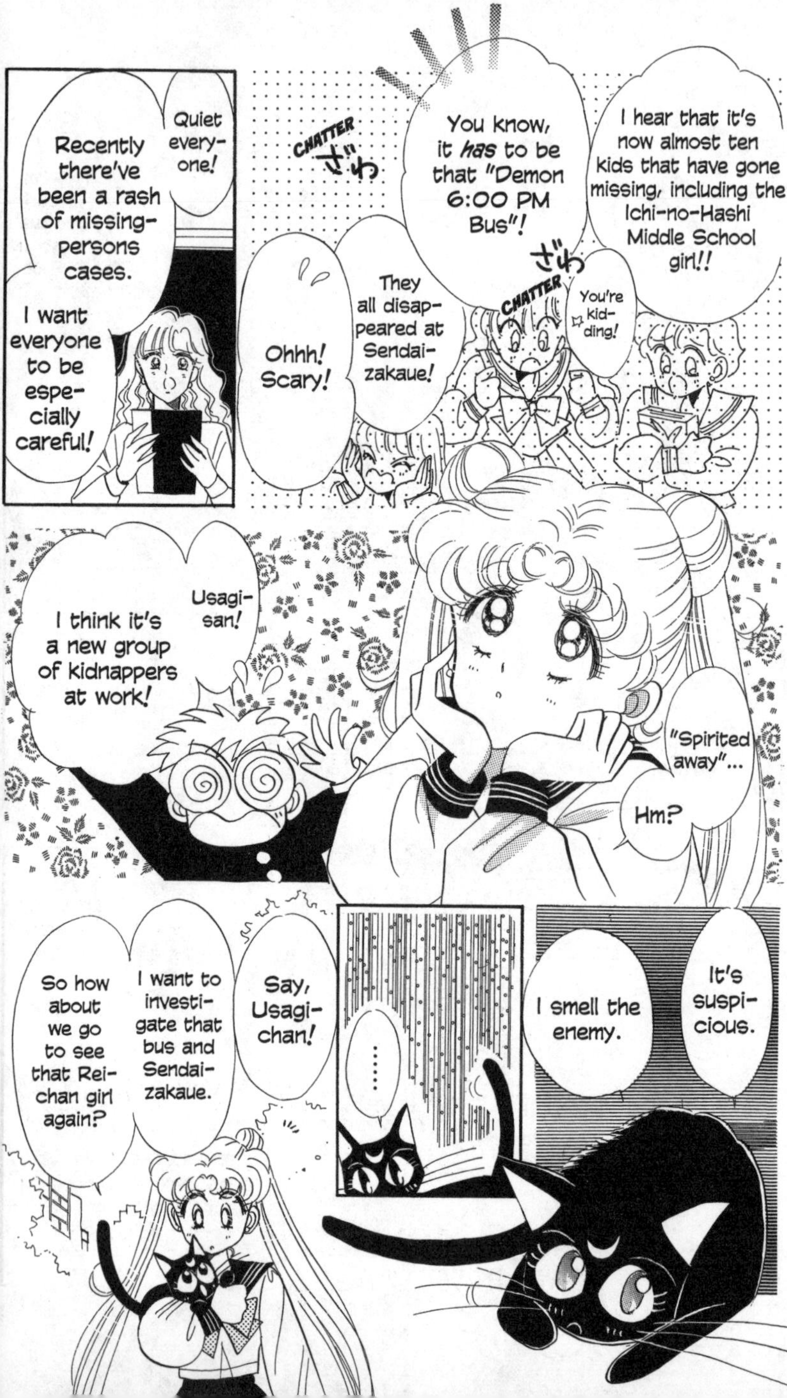
I hear that it's now almost ten kids that have gone missing, including the Ichi-no-Hashi Middle School girl!!
You know, it *has* to be that "Demon 6:00 PM Bus"!
CHATTER
ざわ
CHATTER
ざわ
You're kid-ding!
They all disap-peared at Sendai-zakaue!
Ohhh! Scary!
Quiet every-one!
Recently there've been a rash of missing-persons cases.
I want everyone to be espe-cially careful!
"Spirited away"...
Hm?
Usagi-san!
I think it's a new group of kidnappers at work!
It's suspi-cious.
I smell the enemy.
......
Say, Usagi-chan!
I want to investi-gate that bus and Sendai-zakaue.
So how about we go to see that Rei-chan girl again?

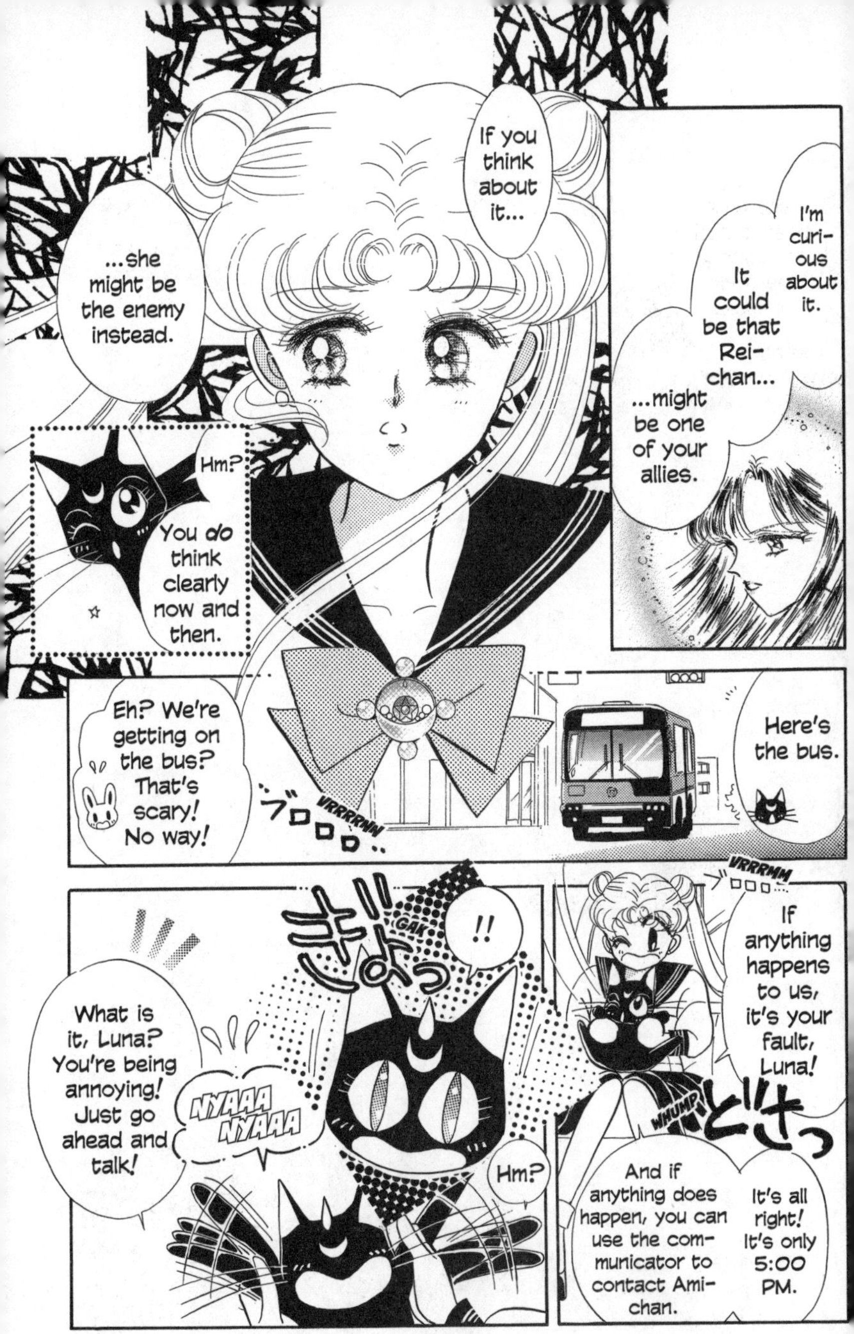
I'm curious about it.
It could be that Rei-chan...
...might be one of your allies.
If you think about it...
...she might be the enemy instead.
Hm?
You *do* think clearly now and then.
Here's the bus.
VRRRRMM
ブロロロ..
Eh? We're getting on the bus? That's scary! No way!
VRRRMM
ロロロ...
If anything happens to us, it's your fault, Luna!
WHUMP
どさっ
It's all right! It's only 5:00 PM.
And if anything does happen, you can use the communicator to contact Ami-chan.
!!
GAK
ぎょっ
What is it, Luna? You're being annoying! Just go ahead and talk!
NYAAA NYAAA
Hm?

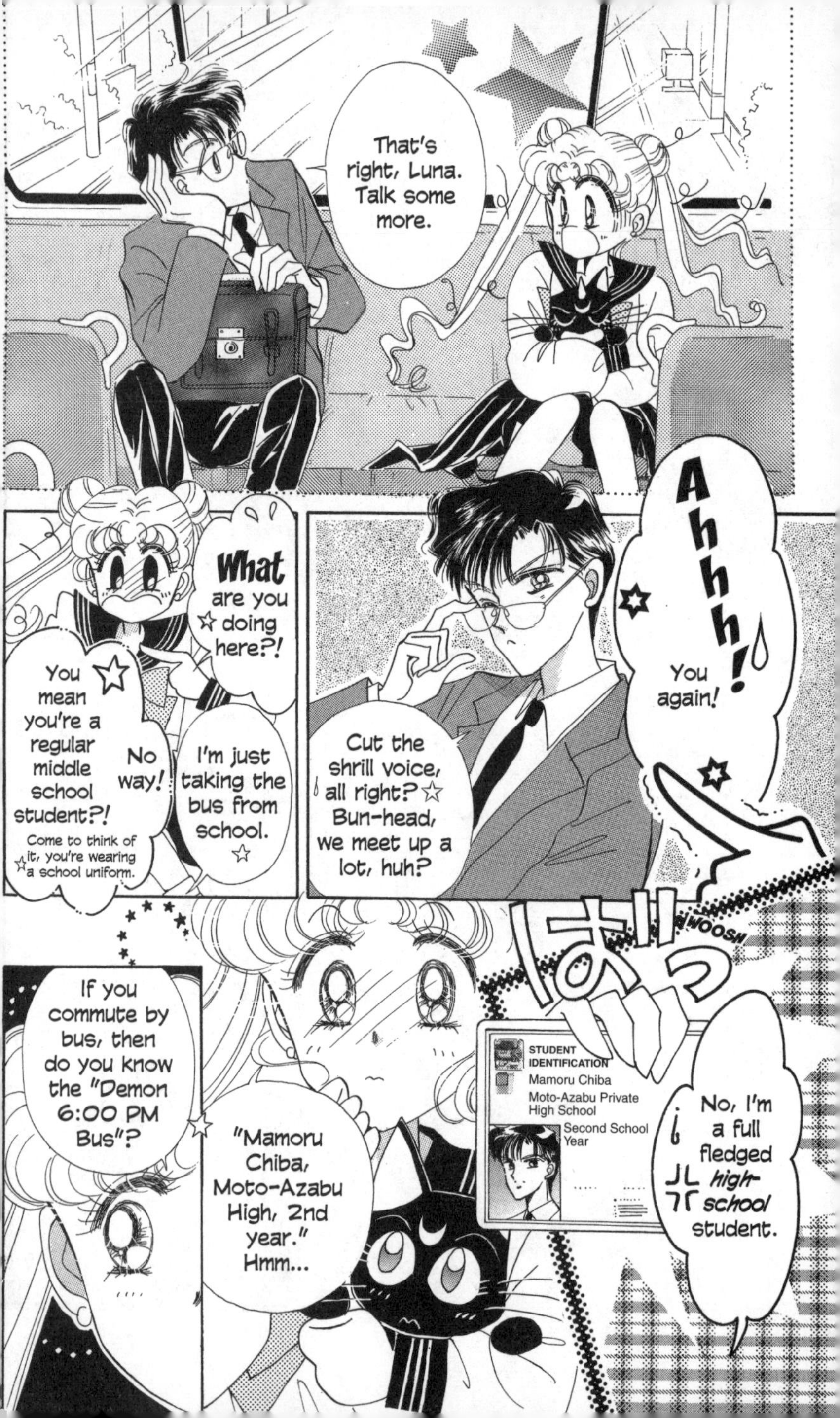
That's right, Luna. Talk some more.
Ahhh! You again!
Cut the shrill voice, all right? Bun-head, we meet up a lot, huh?
What are you doing here?!
I'm just taking the bus from school.
No way!
You mean you're a regular middle school student?!
Come to think of it, you're wearing a school uniform.
はっ
WOOSH
STUDENT IDENTIFICATION
Mamoru Chiba
Moto-Azabu Private High School
Second School Year
No, I'm a full fledged high school student.
"Mamoru Chiba, Moto-Azabu High, 2nd year." Hmm...
If you commute by bus, then do you know the "Demon 6:00 PM Bus"?

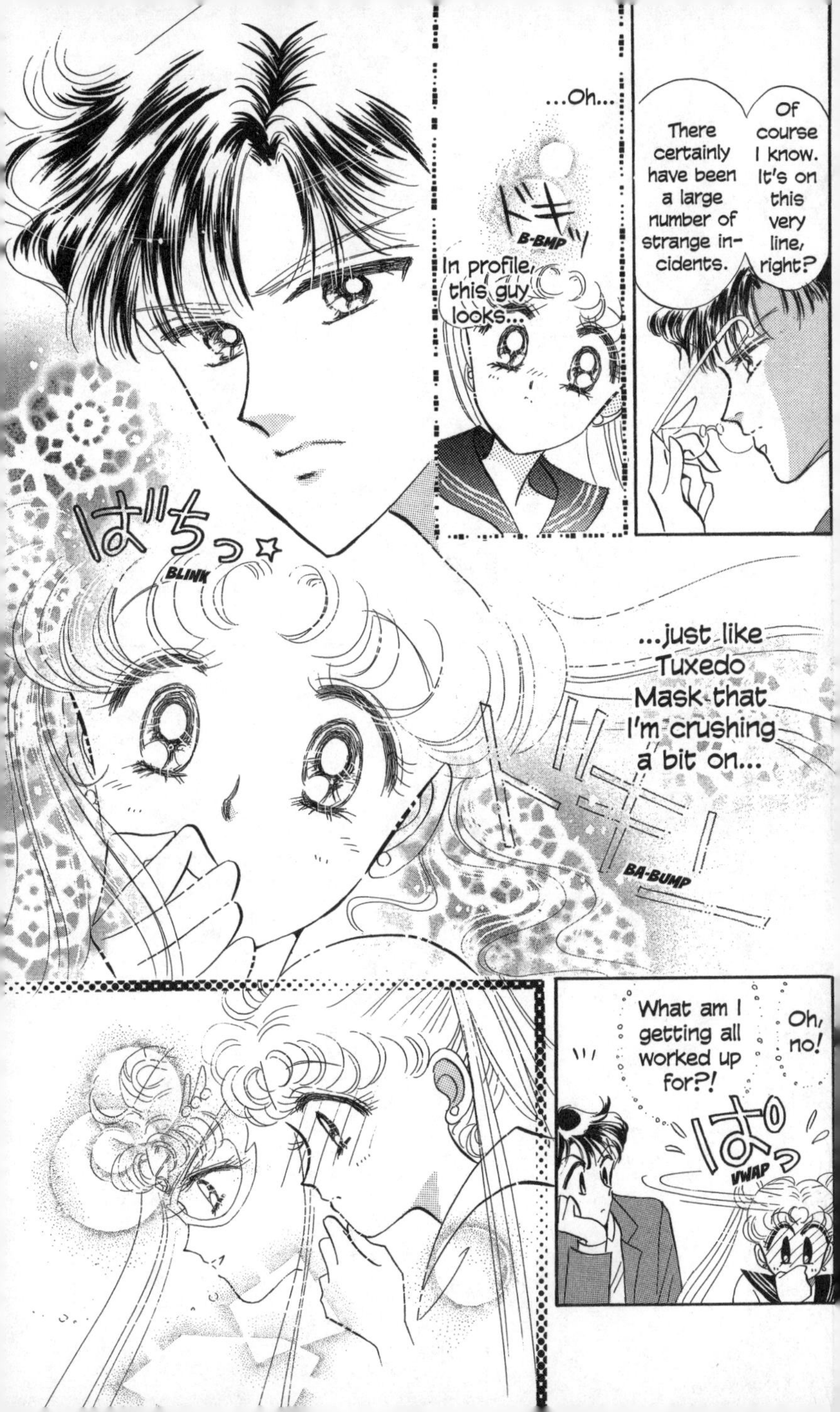
Of course I know. It's on this very line, right?
There certainly have been a large number of strange incidents.
...Oh...
ドキッ
B-BMP
In profile, this guy looks...
ぱちっ☆
BLINK
...just like Tuxedo Mask that I'm crushing a bit on...
BA-BUMP
Oh, no!
What am I getting all worked up for?!
ぱっ
VWAP

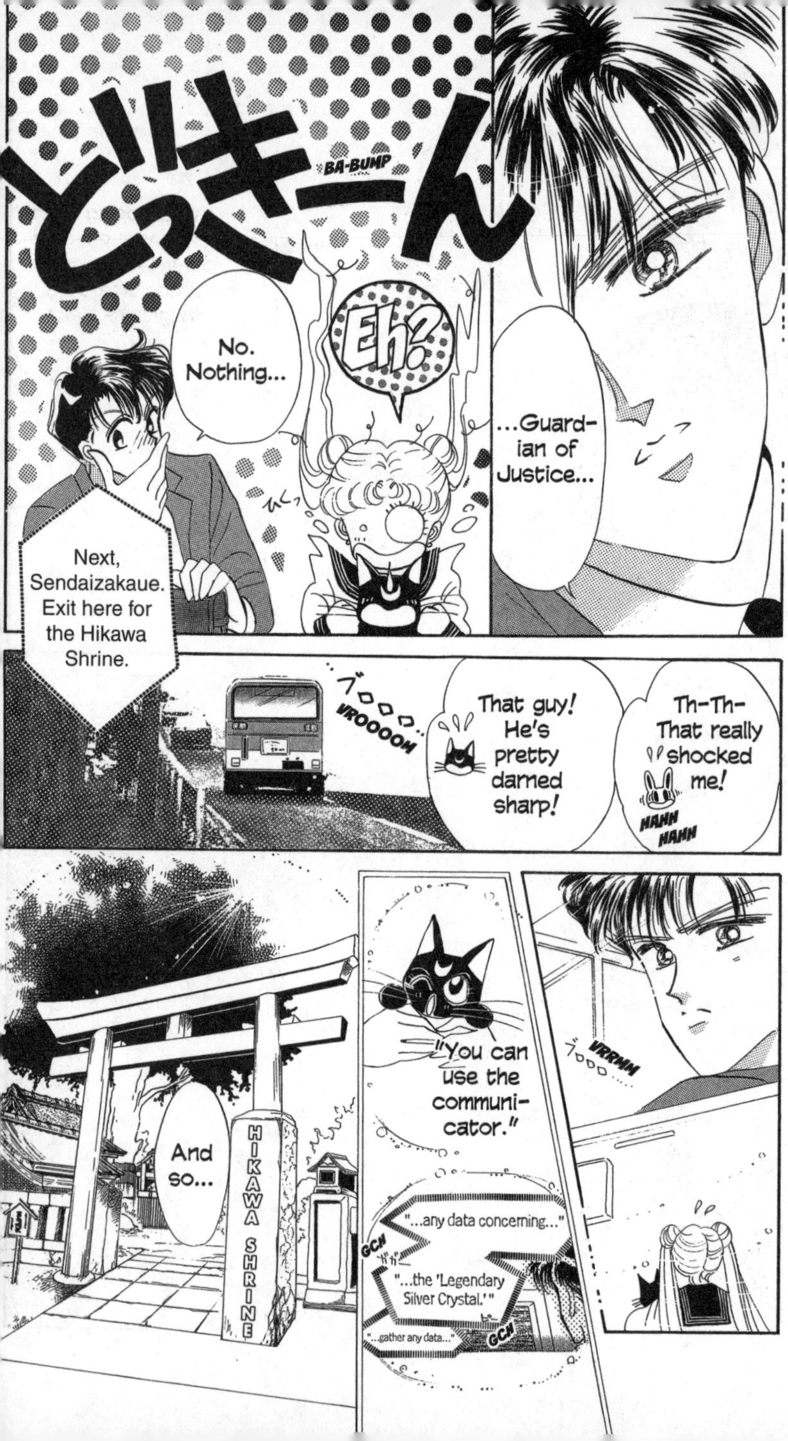
...Guard-ian of Justice...
どっきーん
BA-BUMP
Eh?
No. Nothing...
Next, Sendaizakaue. Exit here for the Hikawa Shrine.
Th-Th-That really shocked me!
HAHH HAHH
That guy! He's pretty darned sharp!
VROOOOM
VRRMM
"You can use the communicator."
"...any data concerning..."
GCH
"...the 'Legendary Silver Crystal.'"
"...gather any data..."
GCH
And so...
HIKAWA SHRINE

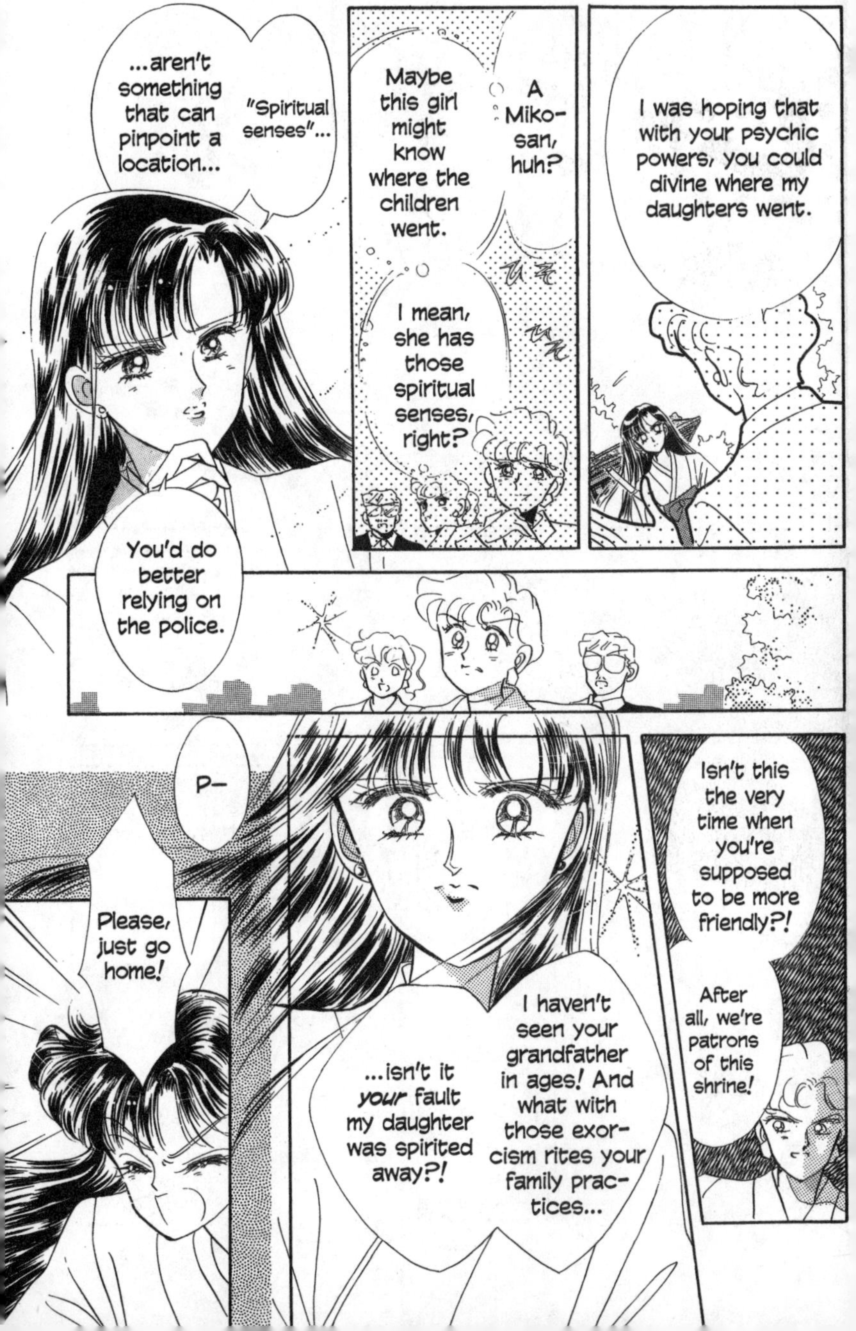
I was hoping that with your psychic powers, you could divine where my daughters went.
A Miko-san, huh?
Maybe this girl might know where the children went.
I mean, she has those spiritual senses, right?
"Spiritual senses"...
...aren't something that can pinpoint a location...
You'd do better relying on the police.
Isn't this the very time when you're supposed to be more friendly?!
After all, we're patrons of this shrine!
I haven't seen your grandfather in ages! And what with those exorcism rites your family practices...
...isn't it *your* fault my daughter was spirited away?!
P–
Please, just go home!

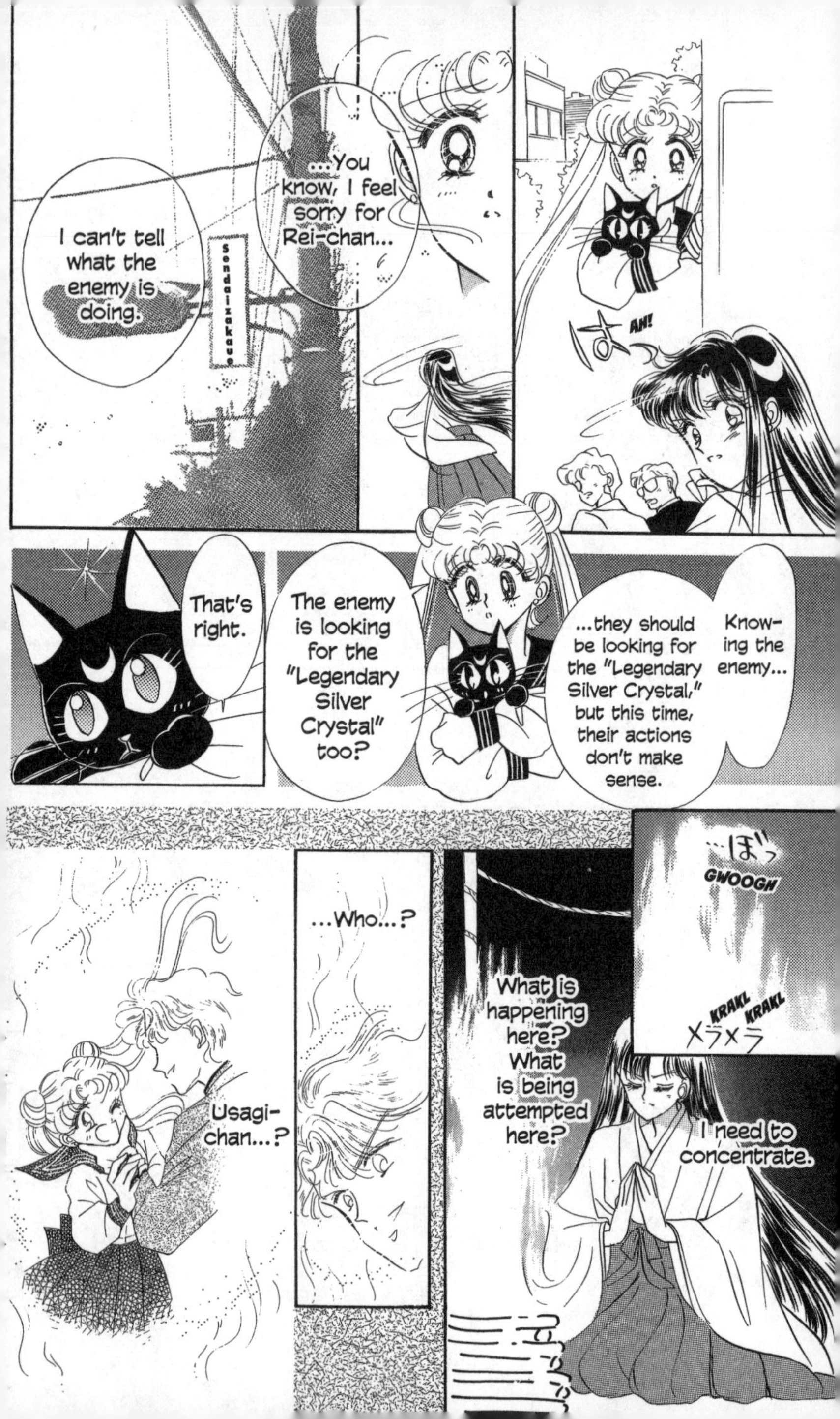

は AH!
...You know, I feel sorry for Rei-chan...
I can't tell what the enemy is doing.
Sendaizakaue
Know-ing the enemy...
...they should be looking for the "Legendary Silver Crystal," but this time, their actions don't make sense.
The enemy is looking for the "Legendary Silver Crystal" too?
That's right.
…ぼっ GWOOGH
KRAKL KRAKL メラメラ
I need to concentrate.
What is happening here? What is being attempted here?
...Who...?
Usagi-chan...?

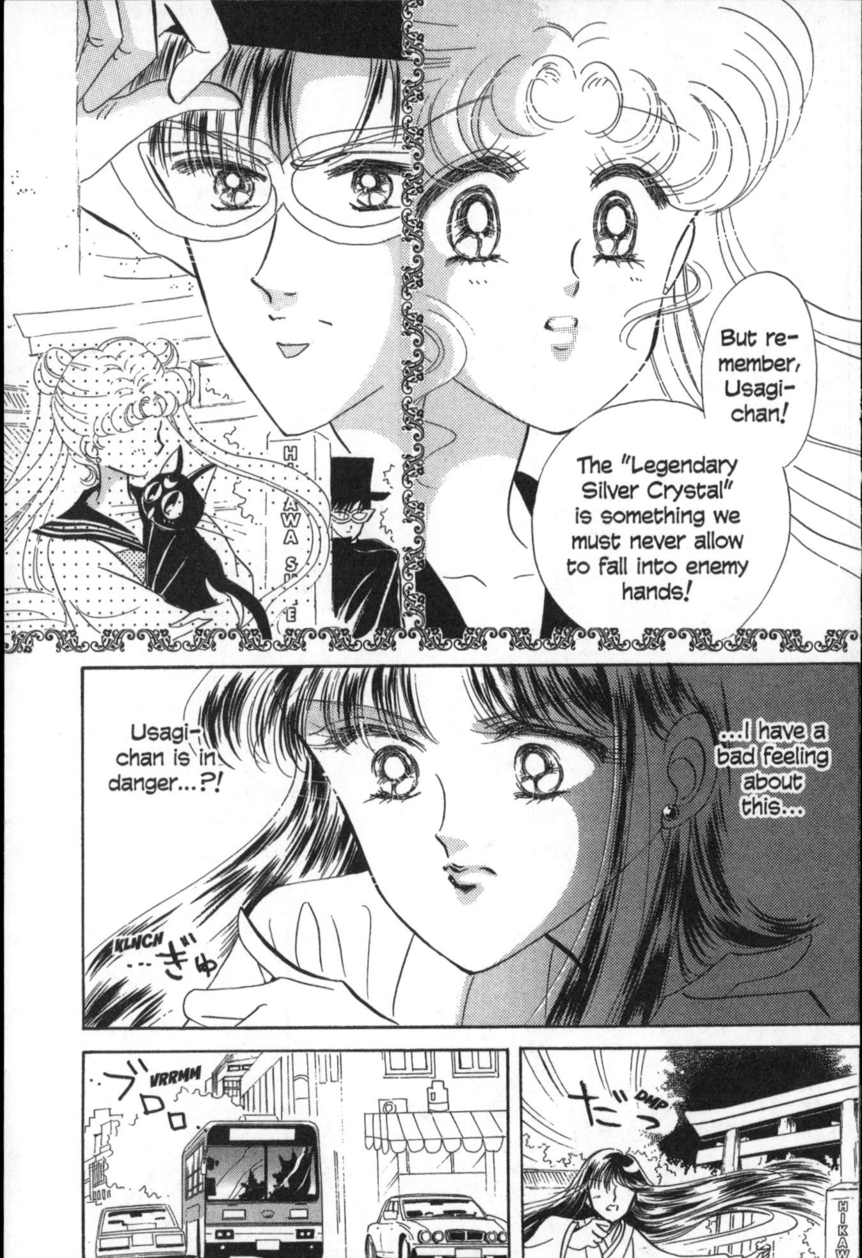
But re-member, Usagi-chan!
The "Legendary Silver Crystal" is something we must never allow to fall into enemy hands!
...I have a bad feeling about this...
Usagi-chan is in danger...?!
KLNCH
...ぎゅ
たっ
DMP
HIKAWA SHR
ブロロ
VRRMM

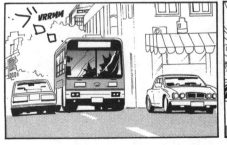

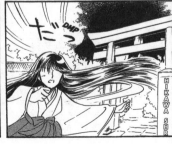

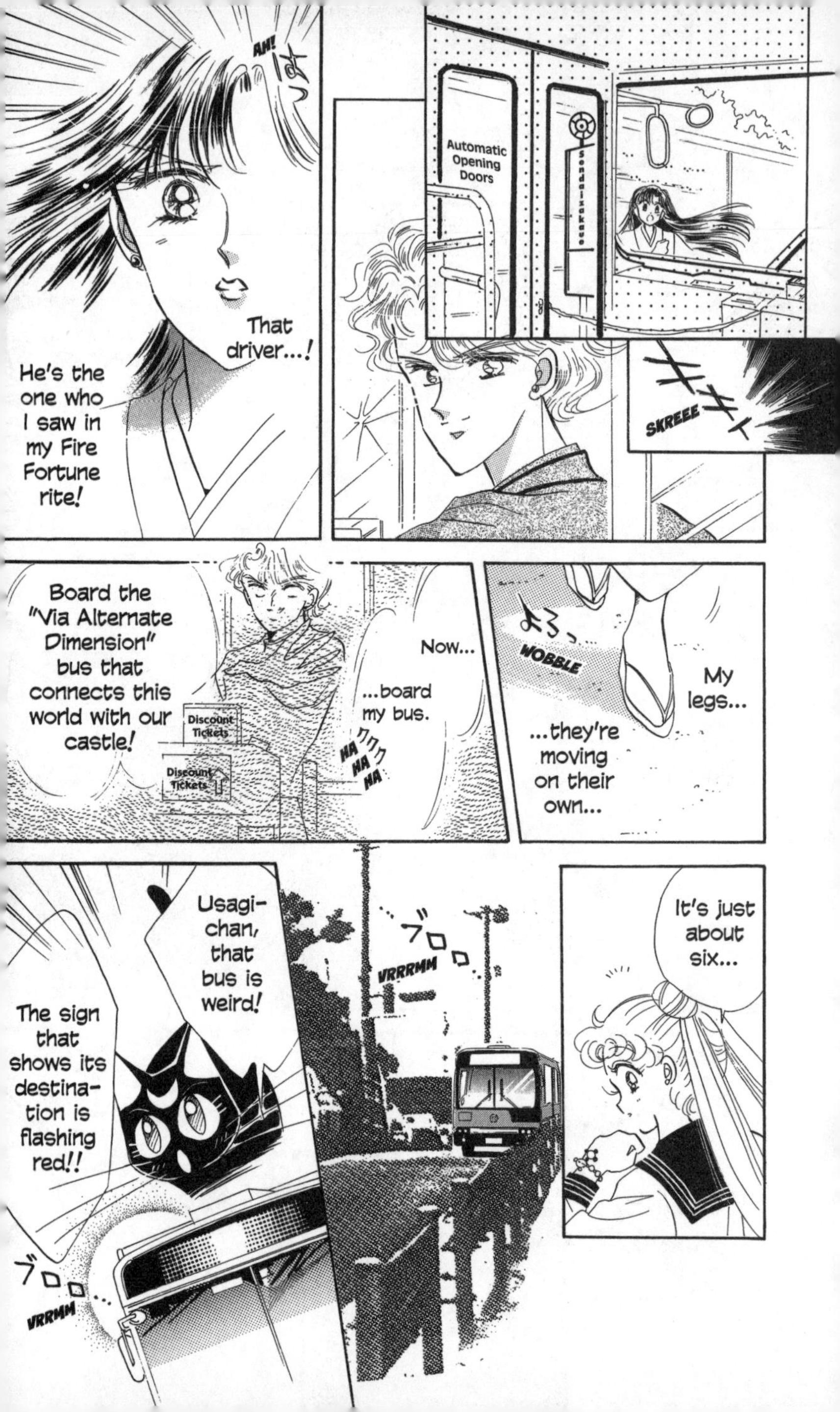
Automatic Opening Doors
SKREEE
AH!
That driver...!
He's the one who I saw in my Fire Fortune rite!
My legs...
WOBBLE
...they're moving on their own...
Now...
...board my bus.
HA HA HA
Board the "Via Alternate Dimension" bus that connects this world with our castle!
Discount Tickets
Discount Tickets
It's just about six...
VRRRMM
Usagi-chan, that bus is weird!
The sign that shows its destination is flashing red!!
VRRMM

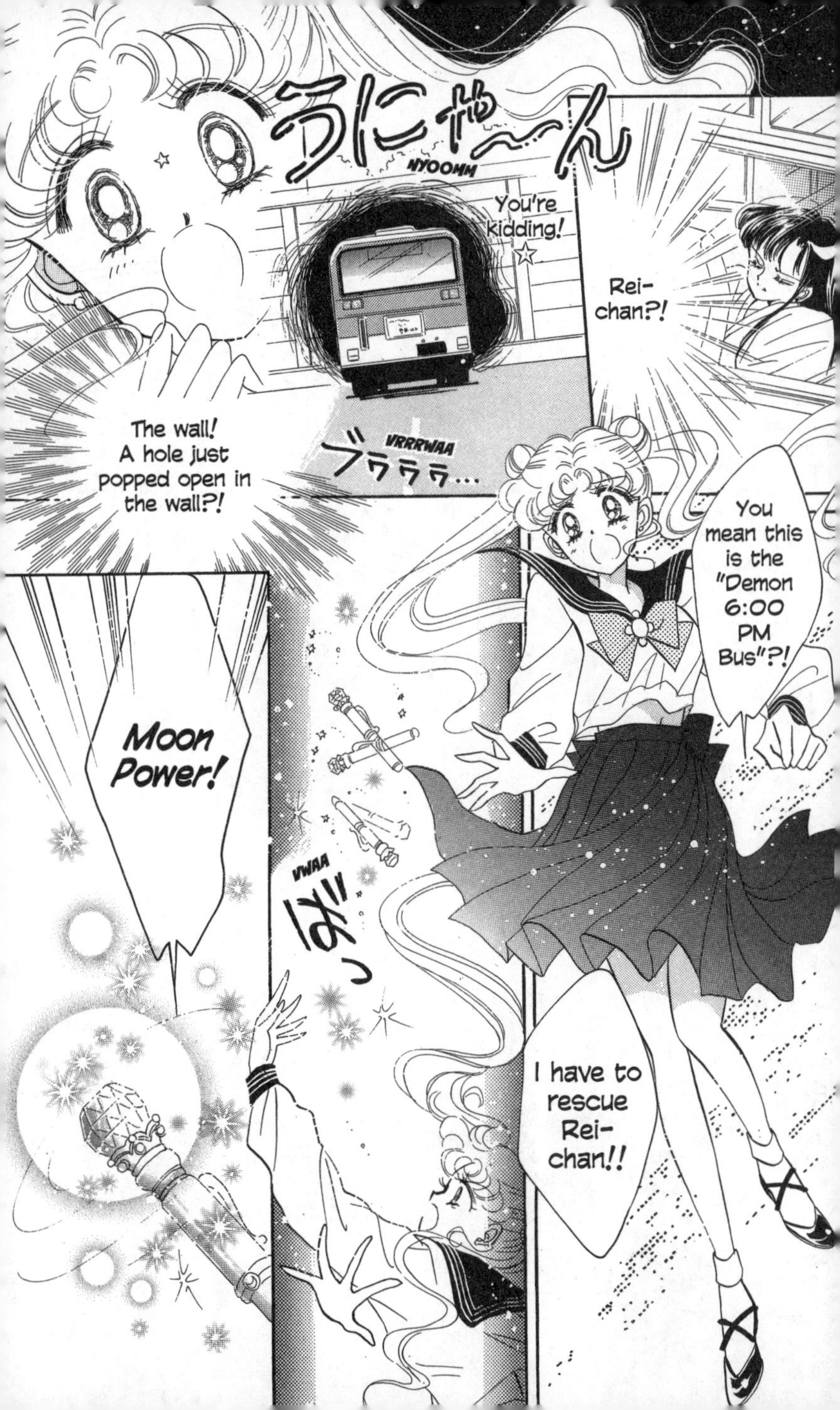
Rei-chan?!
うにゃ〜ん
NYOOMM
You're kidding!
The wall! A hole just popped open in the wall?!
ブヮララ…
VRRRWAA
You mean this is the "Demon 6:00 PM Bus"?!
I have to rescue Rei-chan!!
ばっ
VWAA
Moon Power!

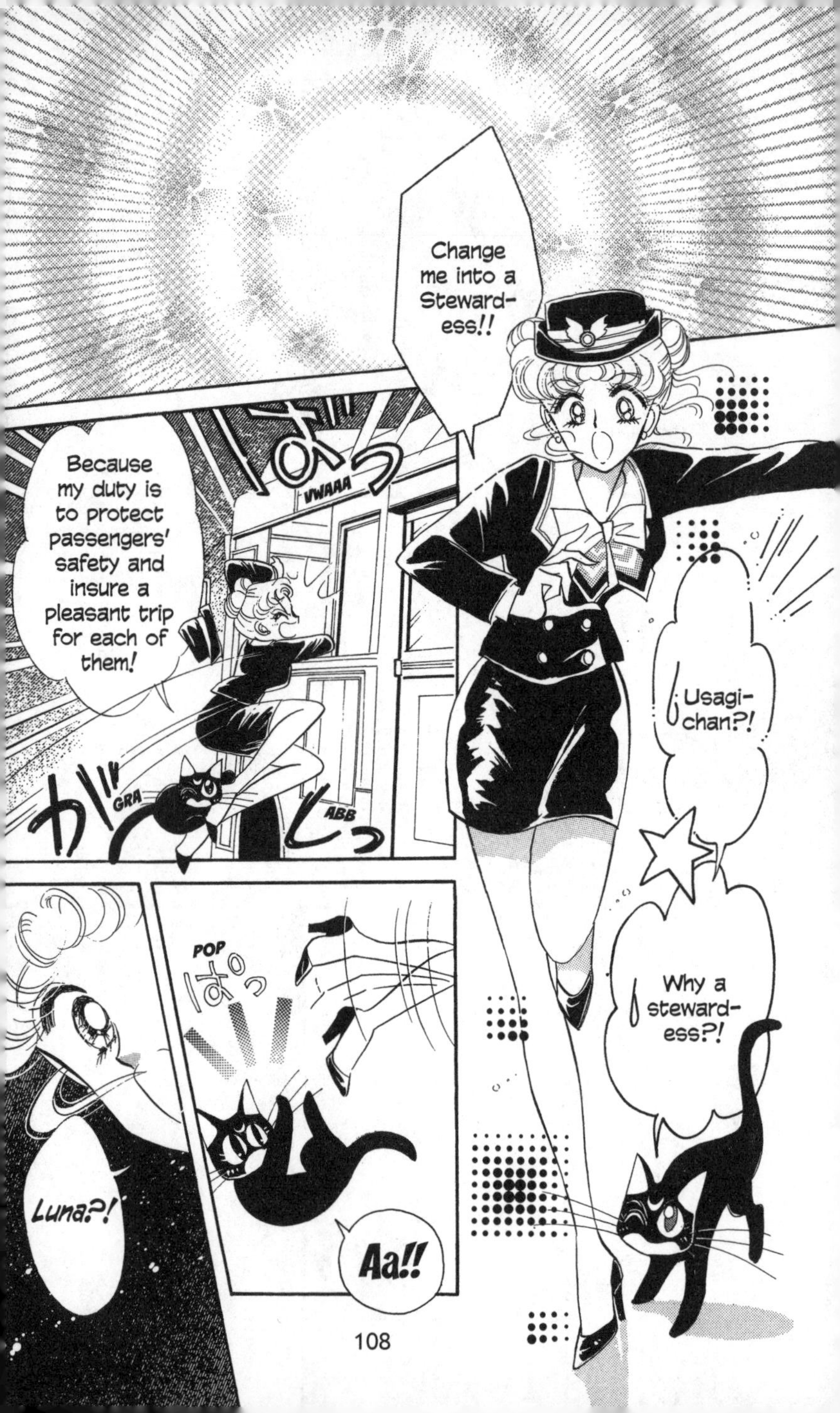
Change me into a Steward-ess!!
Usagi-chan?!
Why a steward-ess?!
VWAAA
Because my duty is to protect passengers' safety and insure a pleasant trip for each of them!
GRA
ABB
POP
Aa!!
Luna?!

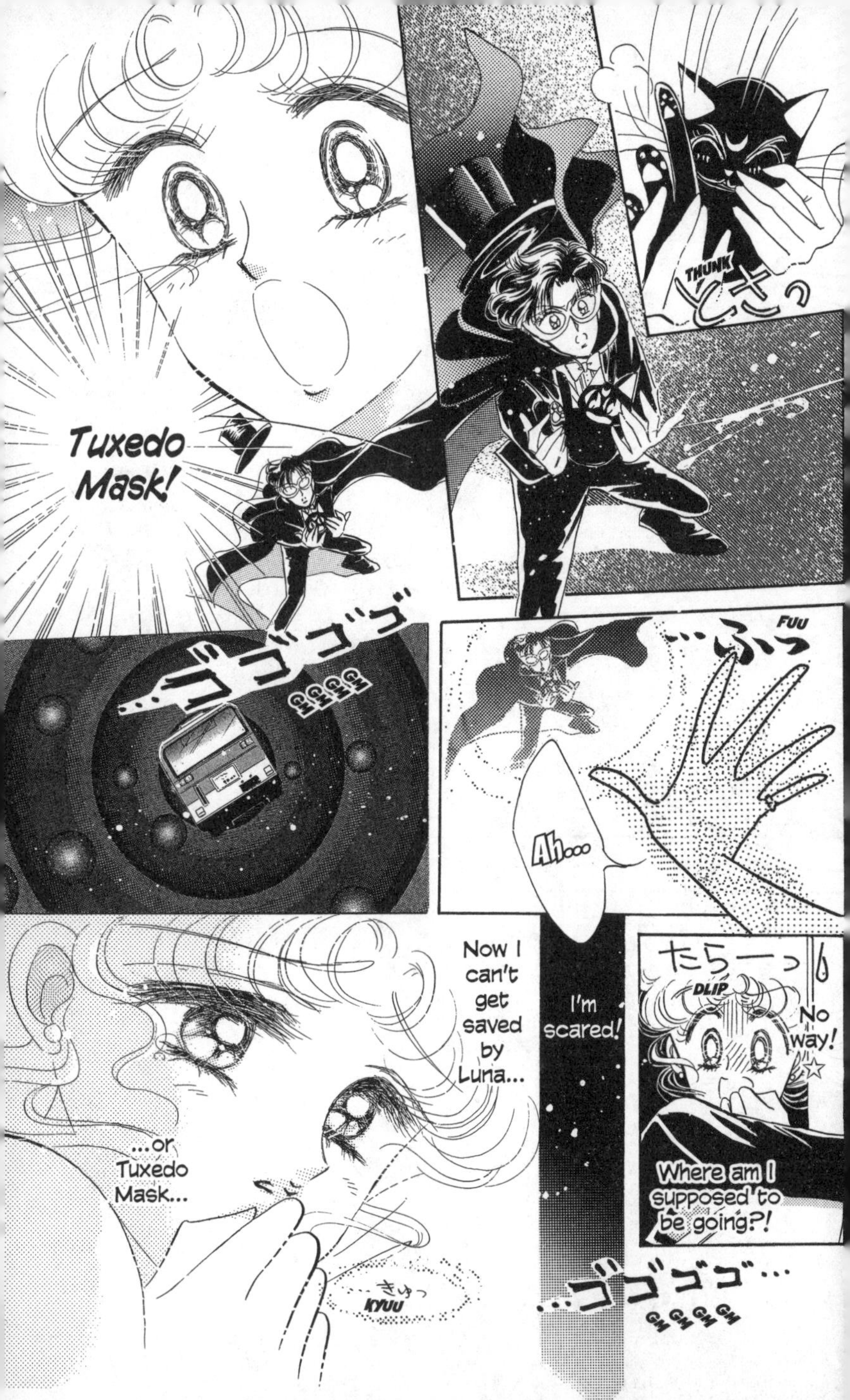
THUNK
とさっ
Tuxedo Mask!
...ふっ
FUU
Ah...
ゴゴゴゴ
GM GM GM GM
たらーっ
DLIP
No way!
Where am I supposed to be going?!
I'm scared!
Now I can't get saved by Luna...
...or Tuxedo Mask...
...きゅっ
KYUU
...ゴゴゴゴ...
GM GM GM GM

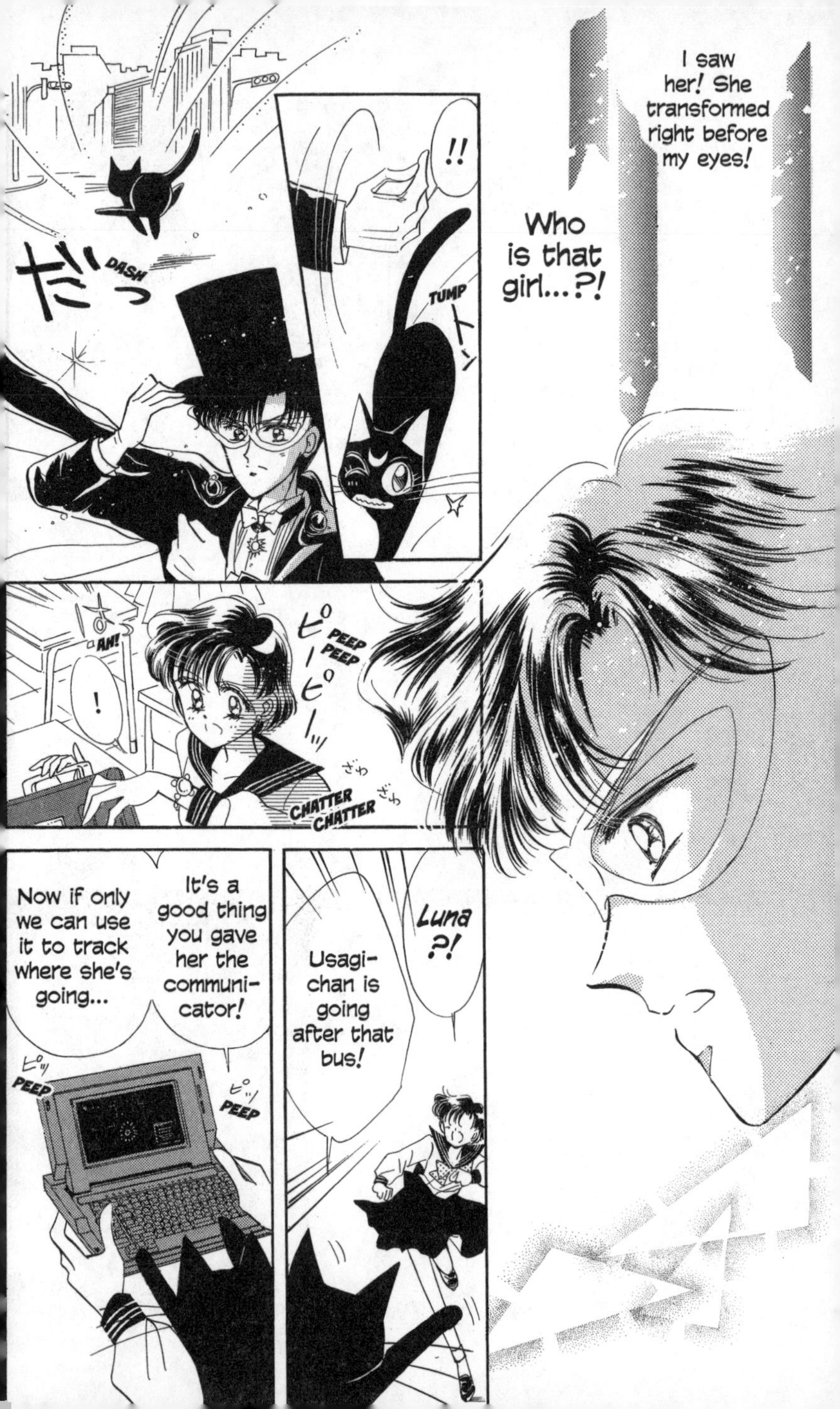

I saw her! She transformed right before my eyes!
Who is that girl...?!
!!
TUMP
DASH
PEEP PEEP
AH!
!
CHATTER CHATTER
Luna ?!
Usagi-chan is going after that bus!
It's a good thing you gave her the communicator!
Now if only we can use it to track where she's going...
PEEP
PEEP

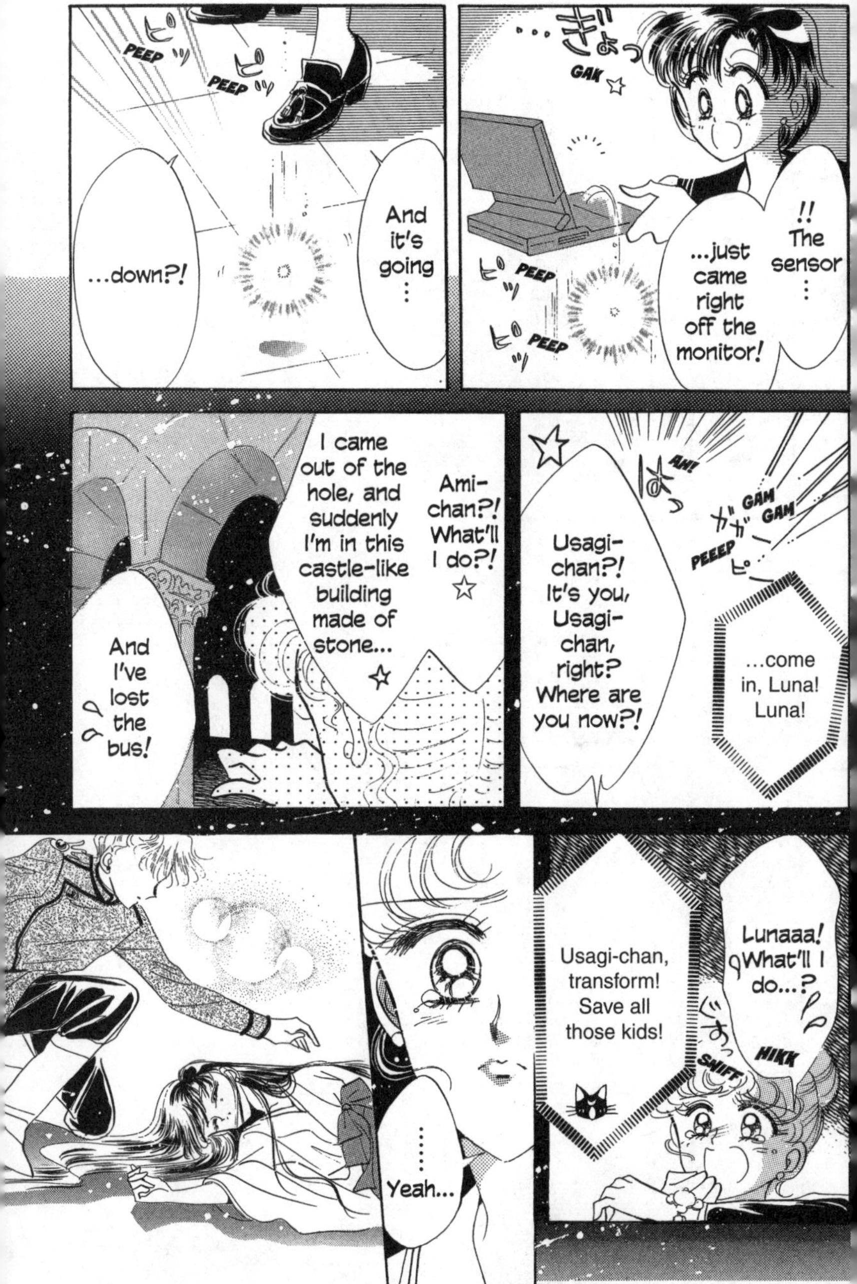

GAK
!! The sensor...
...just came right off the monitor!
PEEP
PEEP
PEEP
PEEP
And it's going...
...down?!
AH!
GAM GAM
PEEEP
...come in, Luna! Luna!
Usagi-chan?! It's you, Usagi-chan, right? Where are you now?!
Ami-chan?! What'll I do?!
I came out of the hole, and suddenly I'm in this castle-like building made of stone...
And I've lost the bus!
Lunaaa! What'll I do...?
HIKK
SNIFF
Usagi-chan, transform! Save all those kids!
......Yeah...

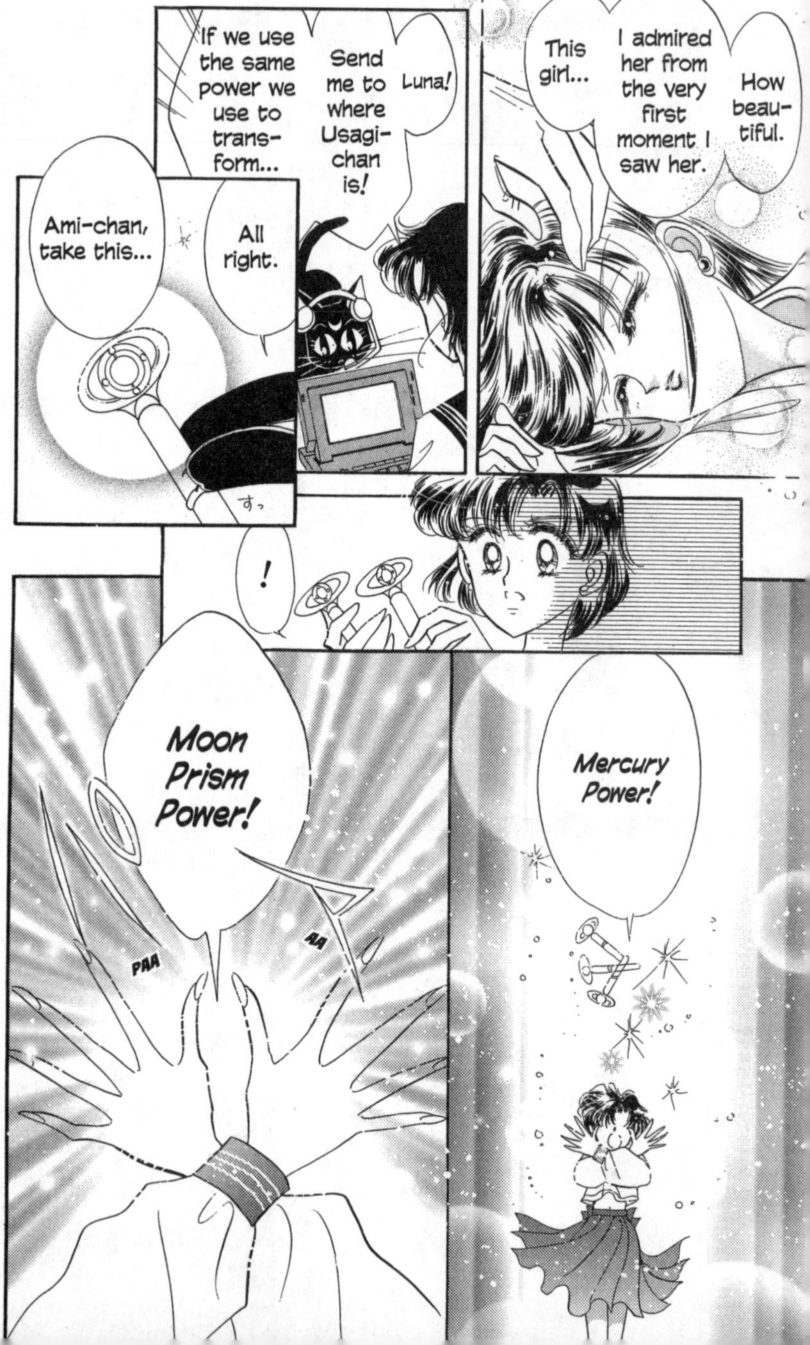
How beautiful.
I admired her from the very first moment I saw her.
This girl...
Luna!
Send me to where Usagi-chan is!
If we use the same power we use to transform...
All right.
Ami-chan, take this...
すっ
!
Mercury Power!
Moon Prism Power!
AA
PAA

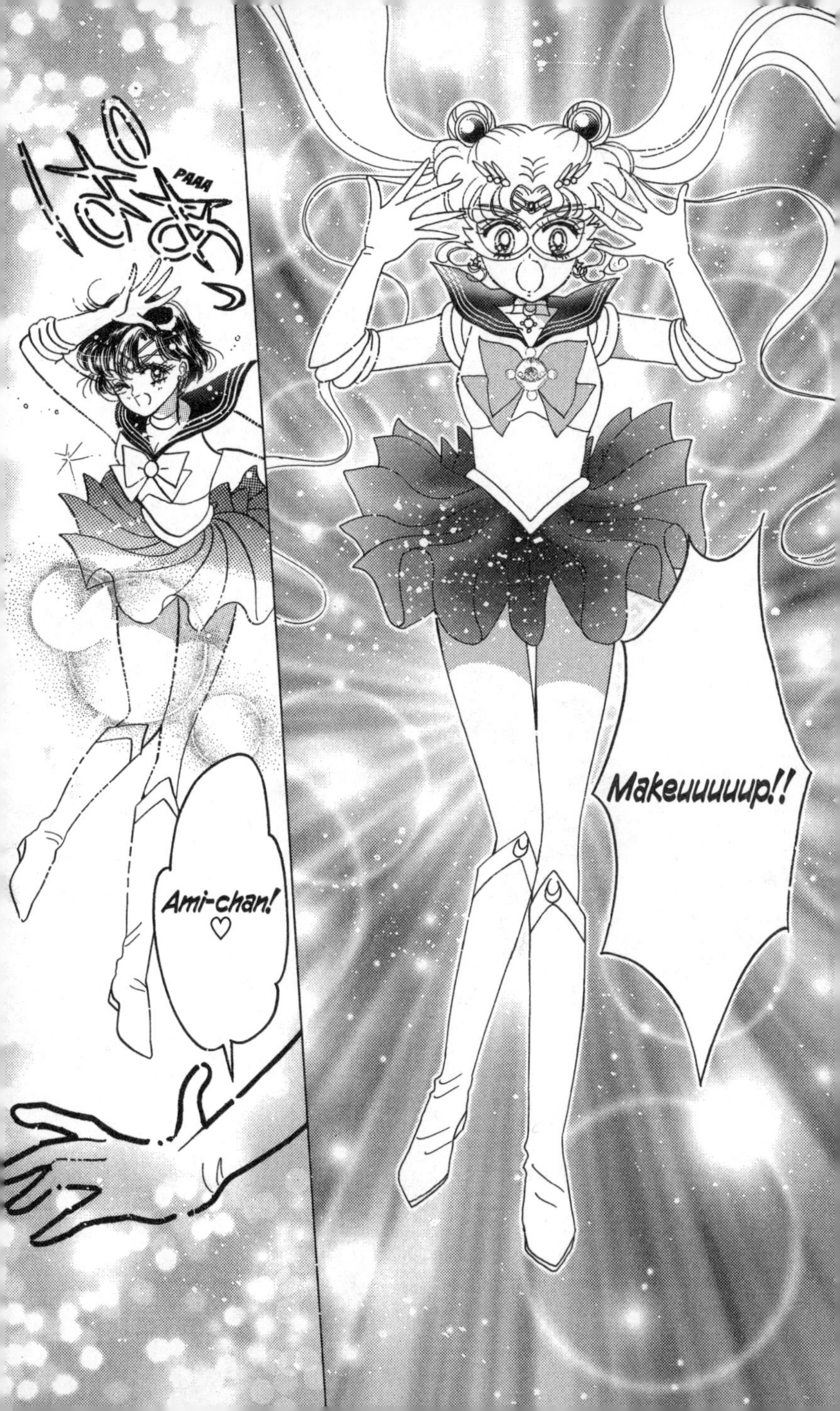
Makeuuuuup!!
PAAA
Ami-chan! ♡

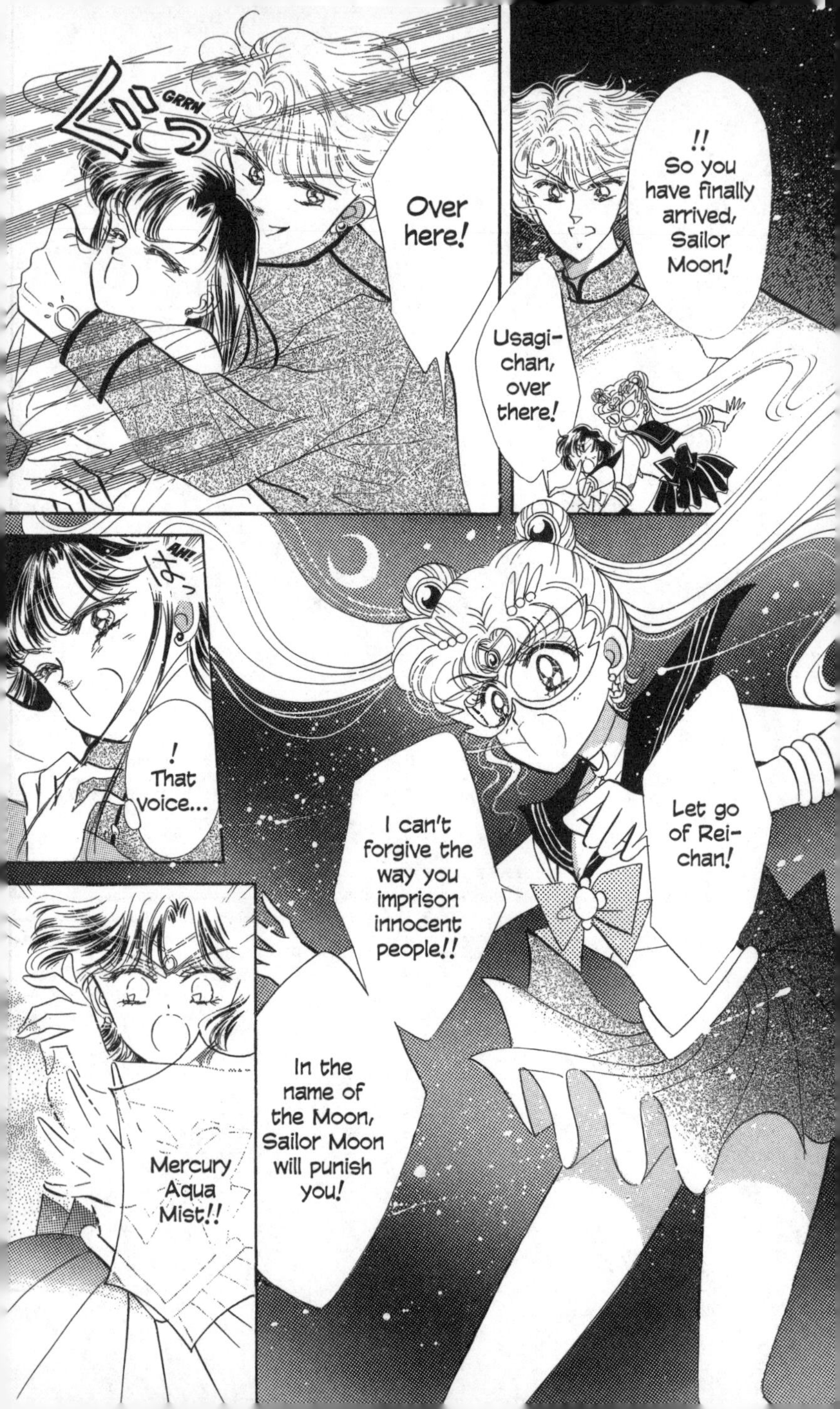
!! So you have finally arrived, Sailor Moon!
Usagi-chan, over there!
GRRN
Over here!
Let go of Rei-chan!
I can't forgive the way you imprison innocent people!!
In the name of the Moon, Sailor Moon will punish you!
AH!
! That voice...
Mercury Aqua Mist!!

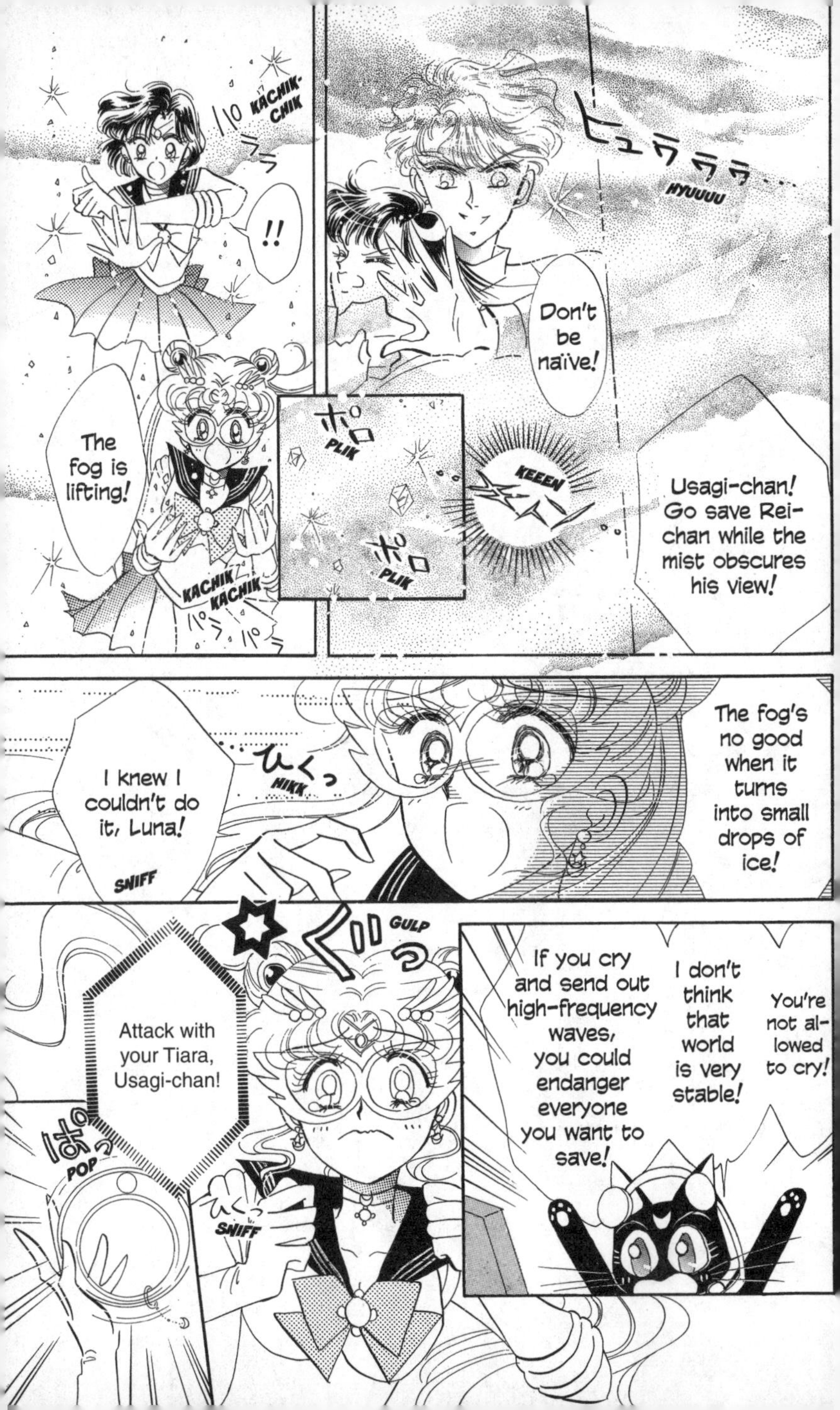

ヒュラララ…
HYUUUU
Usagi-chan! Go save Rei-chan while the mist obscures his view!
Don't be naïve!
ポロ
PLIK
ポロ
PLIK
KEEEN
KACHIK-CHIK
!!
The fog is lifting!
KACHIK KACHIK
The fog's no good when it turns into small drops of ice!
ひくっ
HIKK
I knew I couldn't do it, Luna!
SNIFF
You're not al-lowed to cry!
I don't think that world is very stable!
If you cry and send out high-frequency waves, you could endanger everyone you want to save!
GULP
Attack with your Tiara, Usagi-chan!
ひくっ
SNIFF
はっ
POP

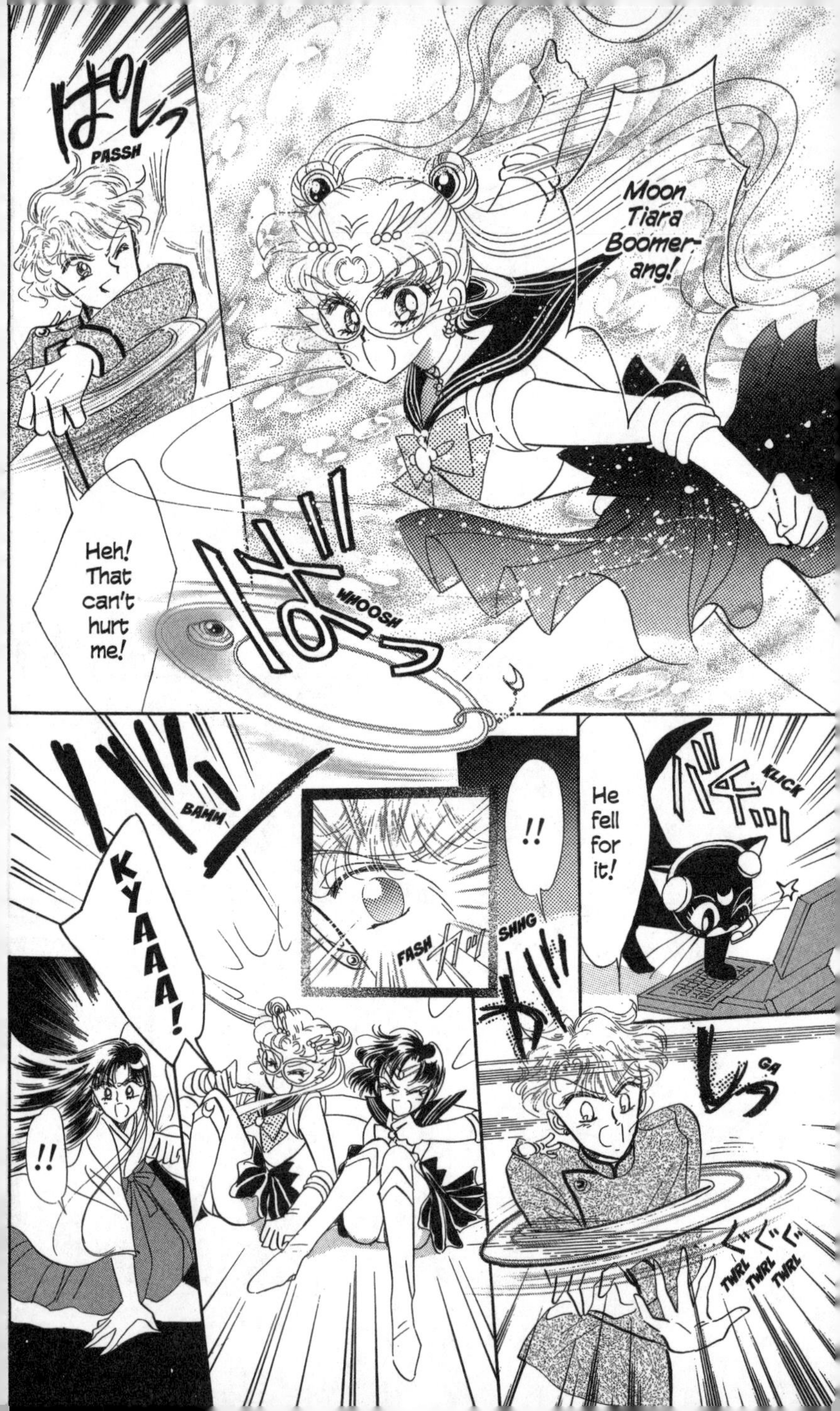
Moon Tiara Boomer-ang!
WHOOSH
PASSH
Heh! That can't hurt me!
He fell for it!
KLICK
!!
FASH
SHHG
GA
TWRL TWRL TWRL
BAMM
KYAAA!
!!

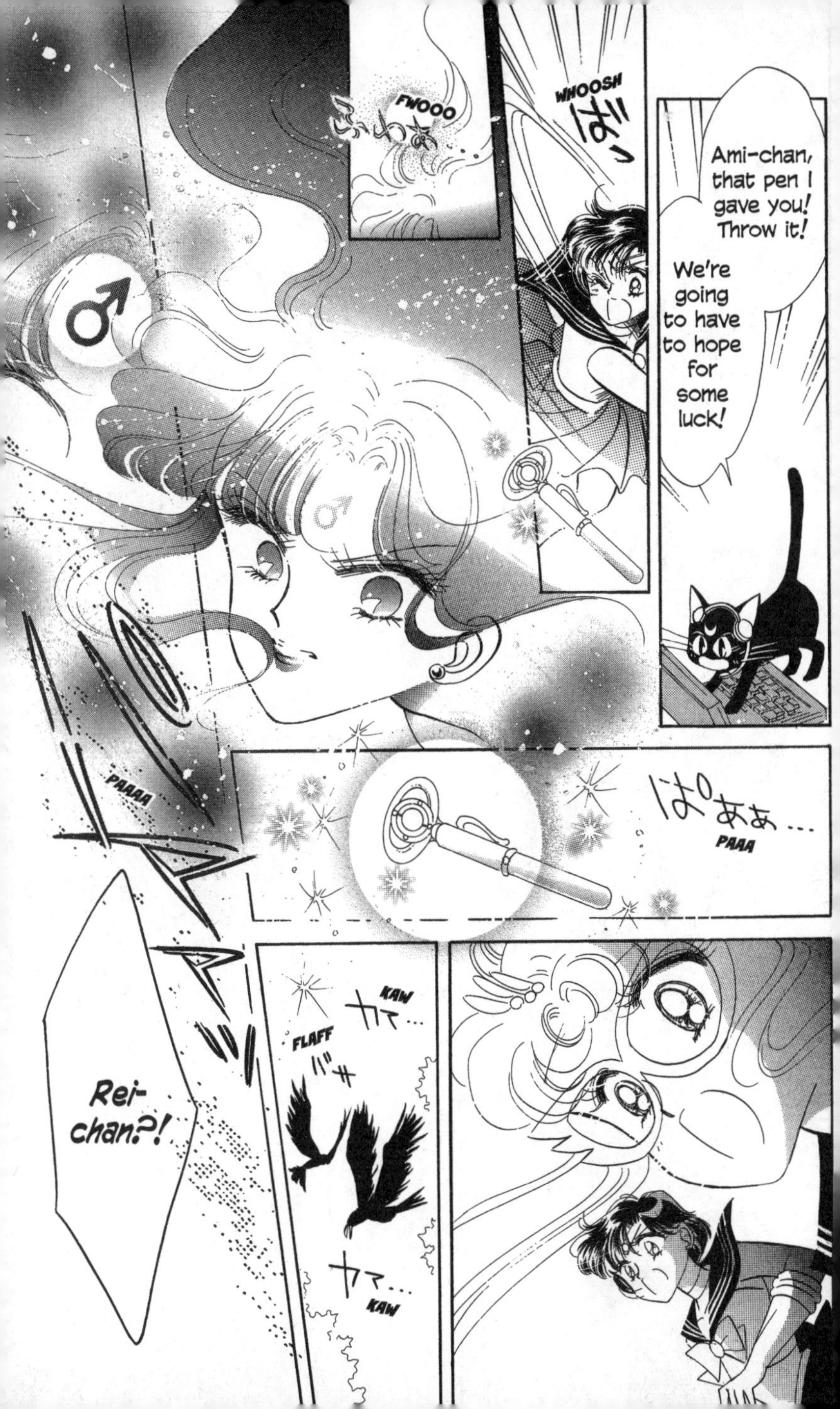
Ami-chan, that pen I gave you! Throw it!
We're going to have to hope for some luck!
WHOOSH
ぼっ
FWOOO
PAAAA
ぱあぁ…
PAAA
KAW
カァ…
FLAFF
バサ
カァ…
KAW
Rei-chan?!

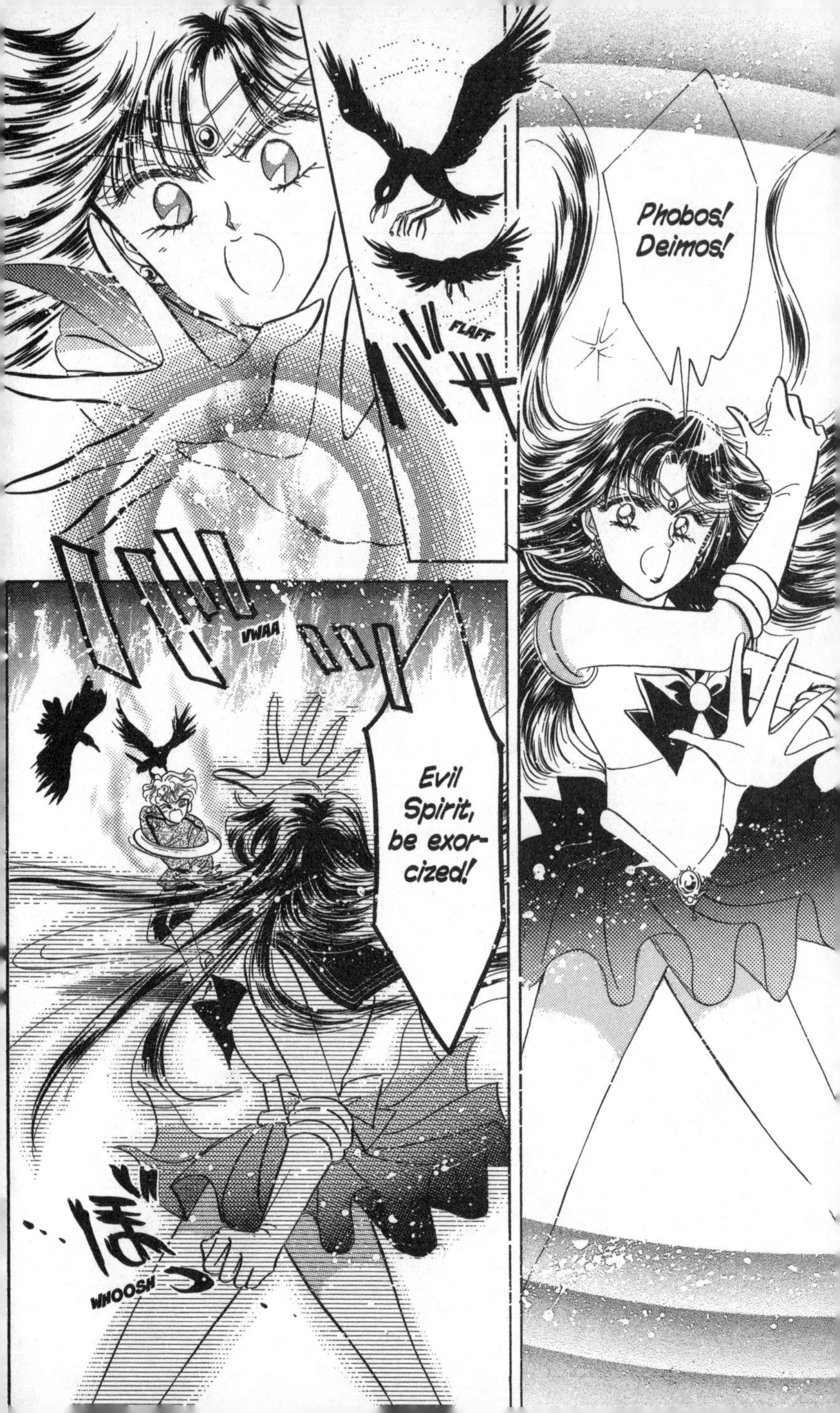

Phobos! Deimos!
FLAFF
VWAA
Evil Spirit, be exorcized!
WHOOSH

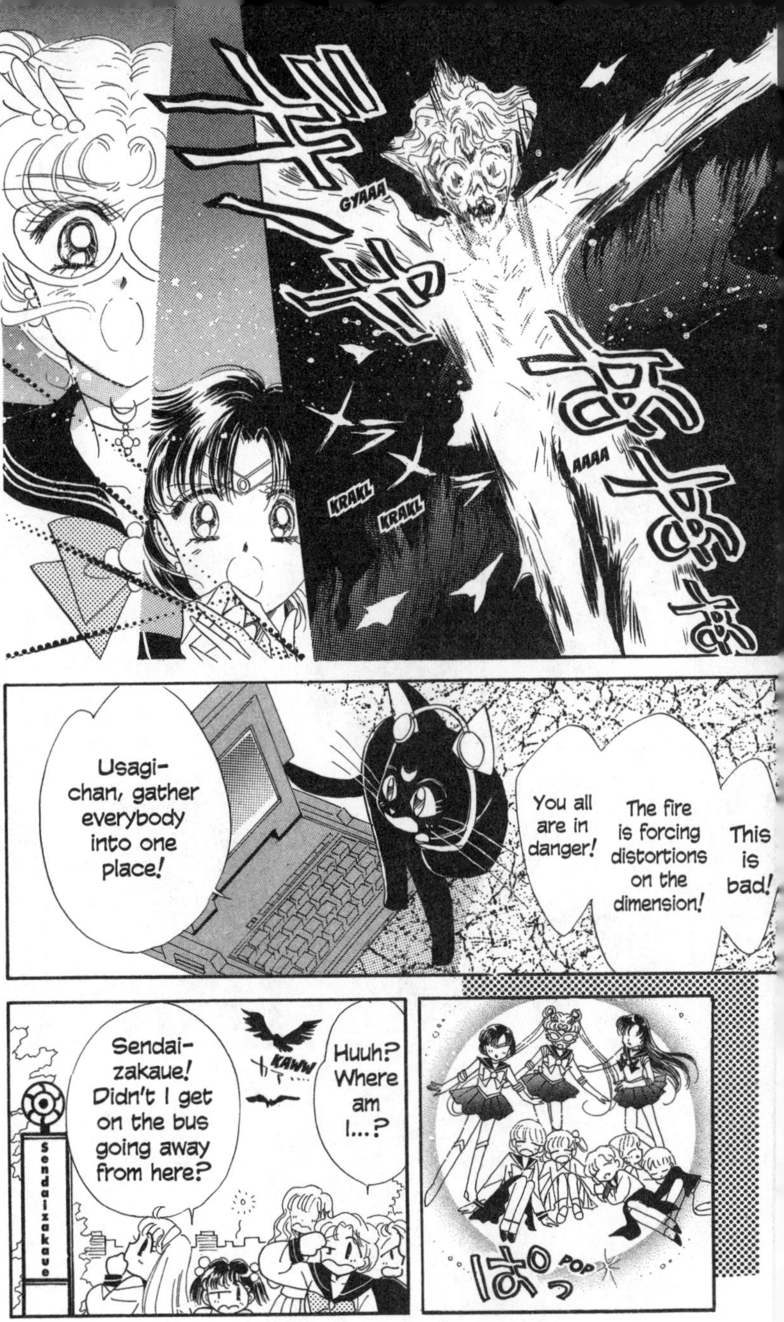

GYAAA
KRAKL
KRAKL
AAAA
This is bad!
The fire is forcing distortions on the dimension!
You all are in danger!
Usagi-chan, gather everybody into one place!
POP
Huuh? Where am I...?
KAWW
Sendai-zakaue! Didn't I get on the bus going away from here?
Sendaizakaue

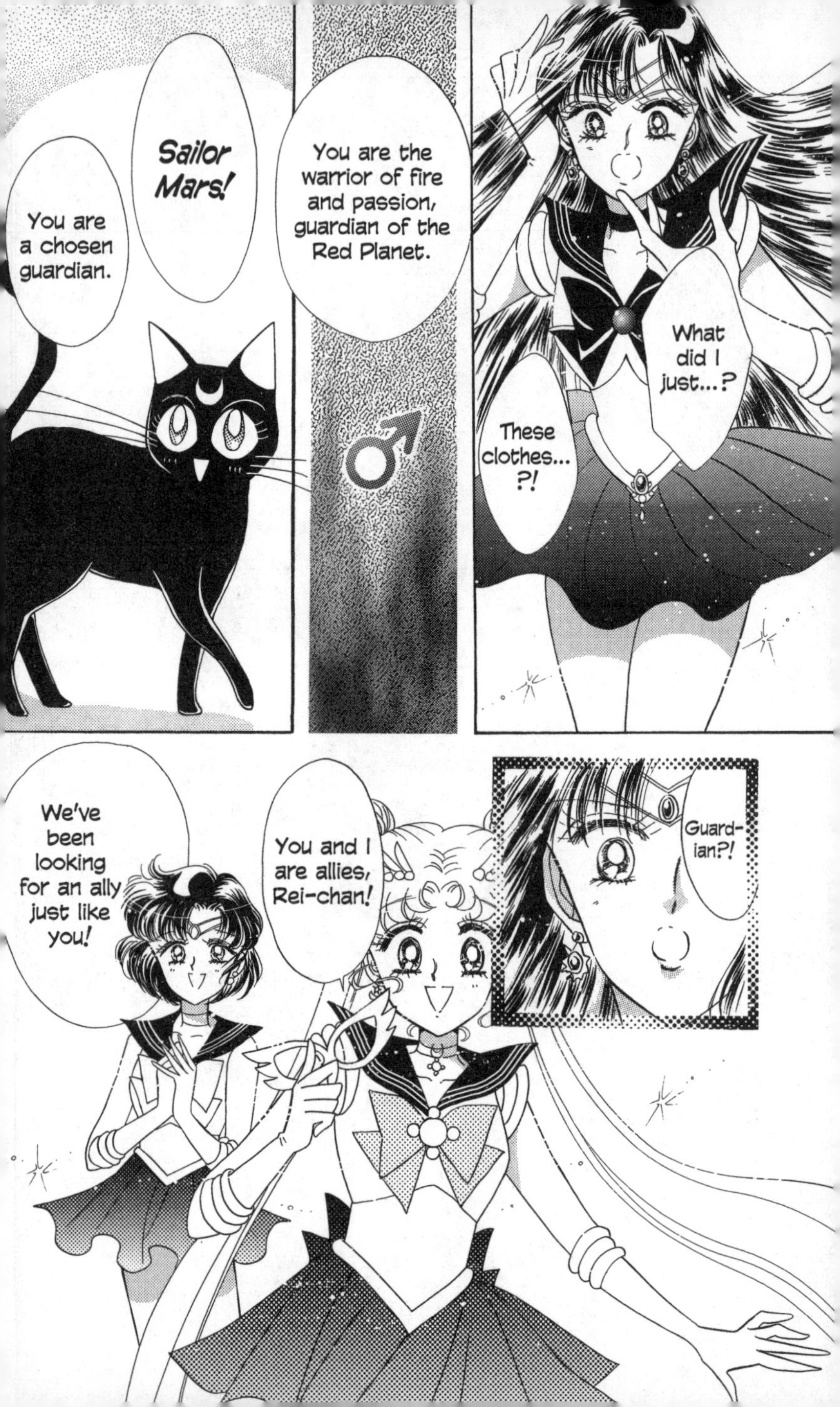
What did I just...?
These clothes...?!
You are the warrior of fire and passion, guardian of the Red Planet.
Sailor Mars!
You are a chosen guardian.
Guardian?!
You and I are allies, Rei-chan!
We've been looking for an ally just like you!

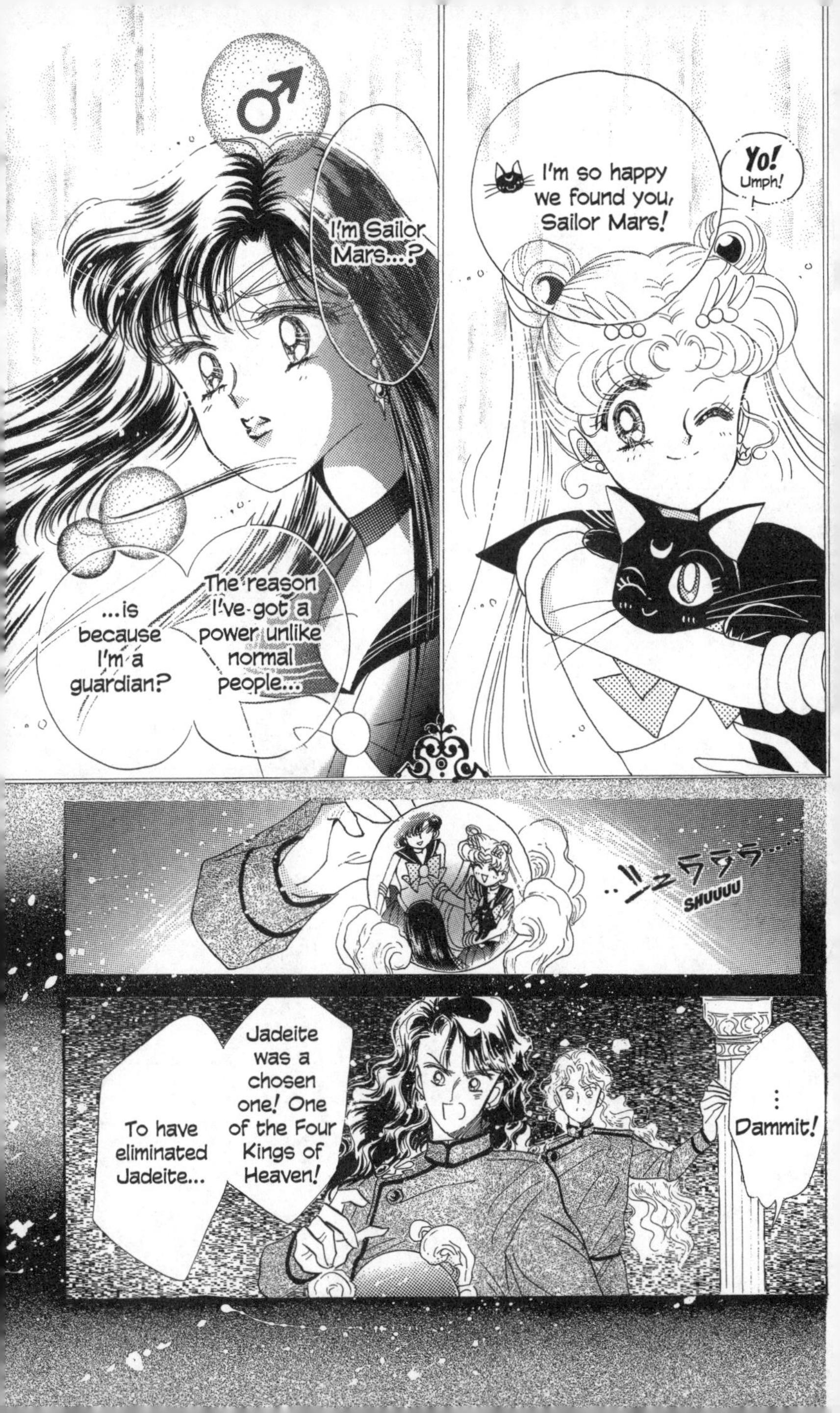
Yo! Umph!
I'm so happy we found you, Sailor Mars!
I'm Sailor Mars...?
The reason I've got a power unlike normal people...
...is because I'm a guardian?
SHUUUU
...Dammit!
Jadeite was a chosen one! One of the Four Kings of Heaven!
To have eliminated Jadeite...

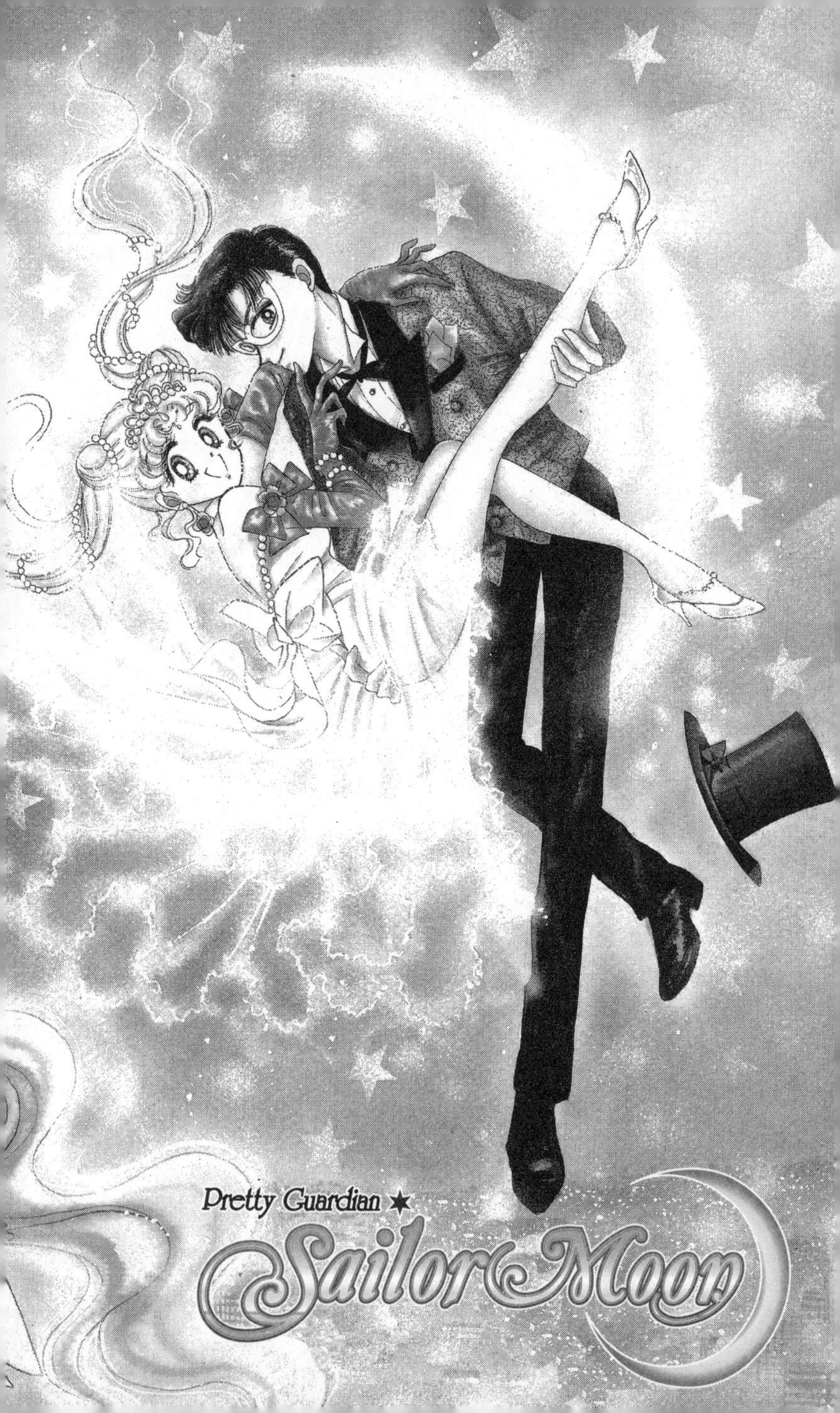
Pretty Guardian ★
Sailor Moon

Act 4
Masquerade Dance Party

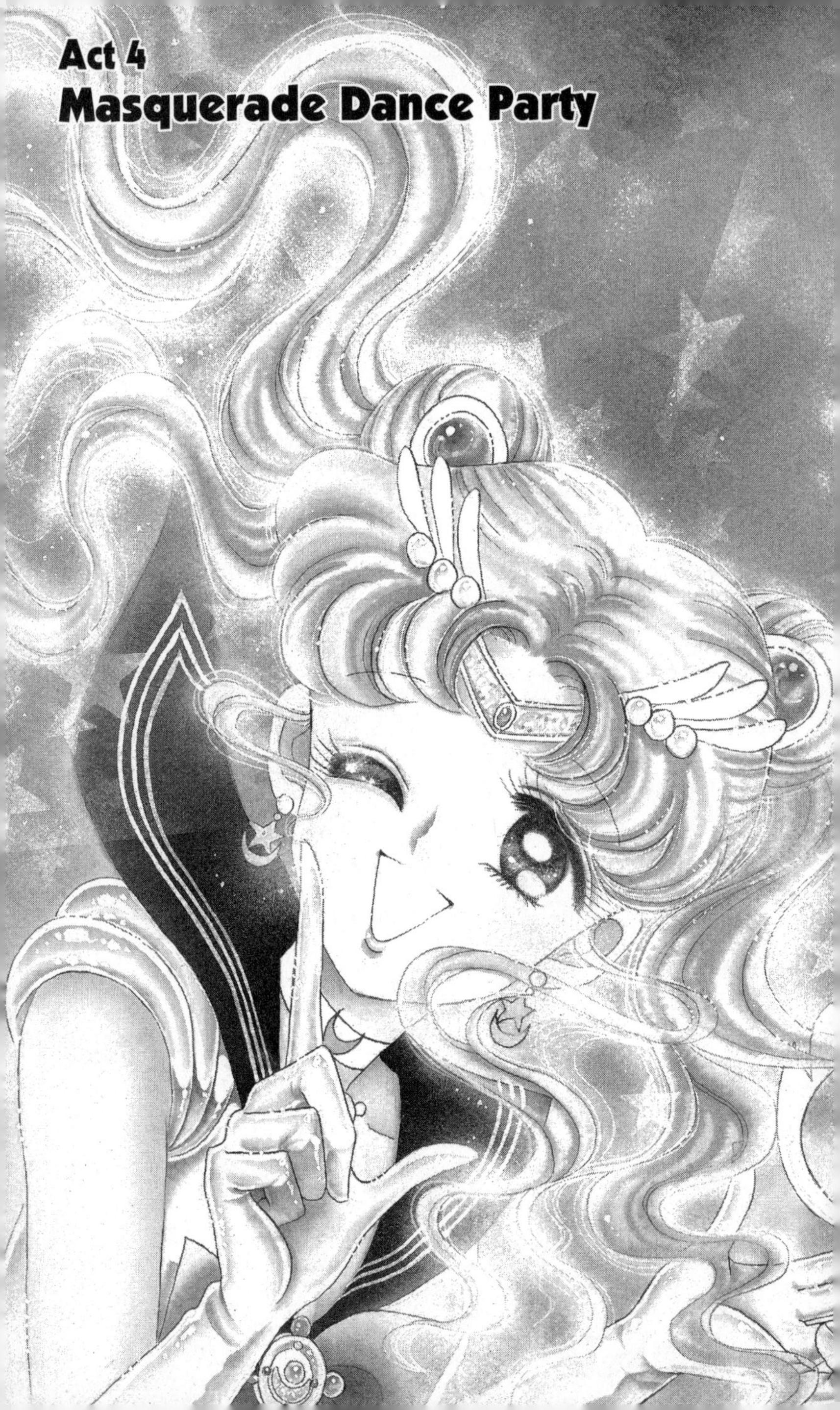

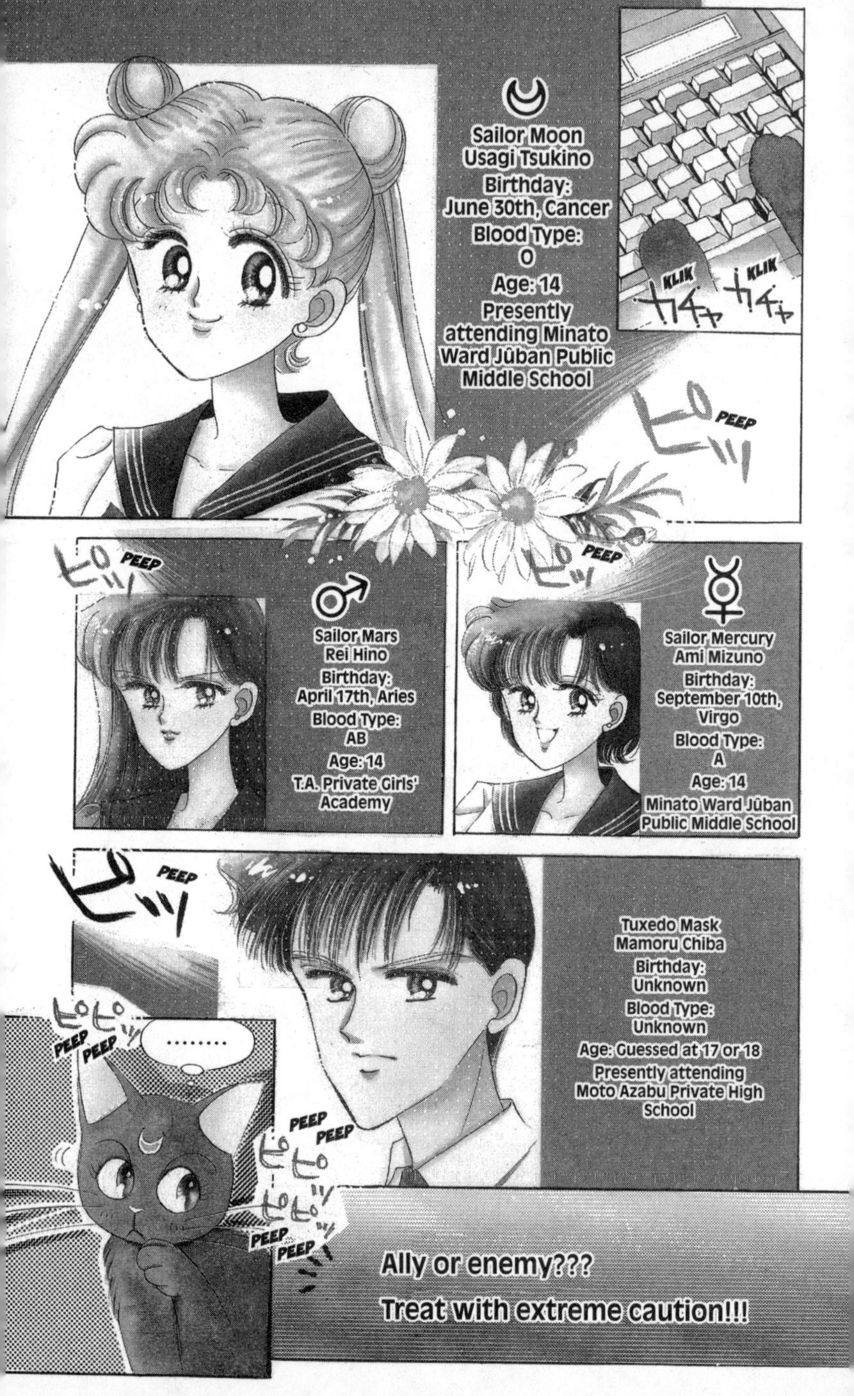
KLIK
KLIK
Sailor Moon
Usagi Tsukino
Birthday:
June 30th, Cancer
Blood Type:
O
Age: 14
Presently attending Minato Ward Jûban Public Middle School
PEEP
PEEP
Sailor Mercury
Ami Mizuno
Birthday:
September 10th, Virgo
Blood Type:
A
Age: 14
Minato Ward Jûban Public Middle School
PEEP
Sailor Mars
Rei Hino
Birthday:
April 17th, Aries
Blood Type:
AB
Age: 14
T.A. Private Girls' Academy
Tuxedo Mask
Mamoru Chiba
Birthday:
Unknown
Blood Type:
Unknown
Age: Guessed at 17 or 18
Presently attending Moto Azabu Private High School
PEEP
PEEP
PEEP
PEEP PEEP
....
PEEP PEEP
Ally or enemy???
Treat with extreme caution!!!

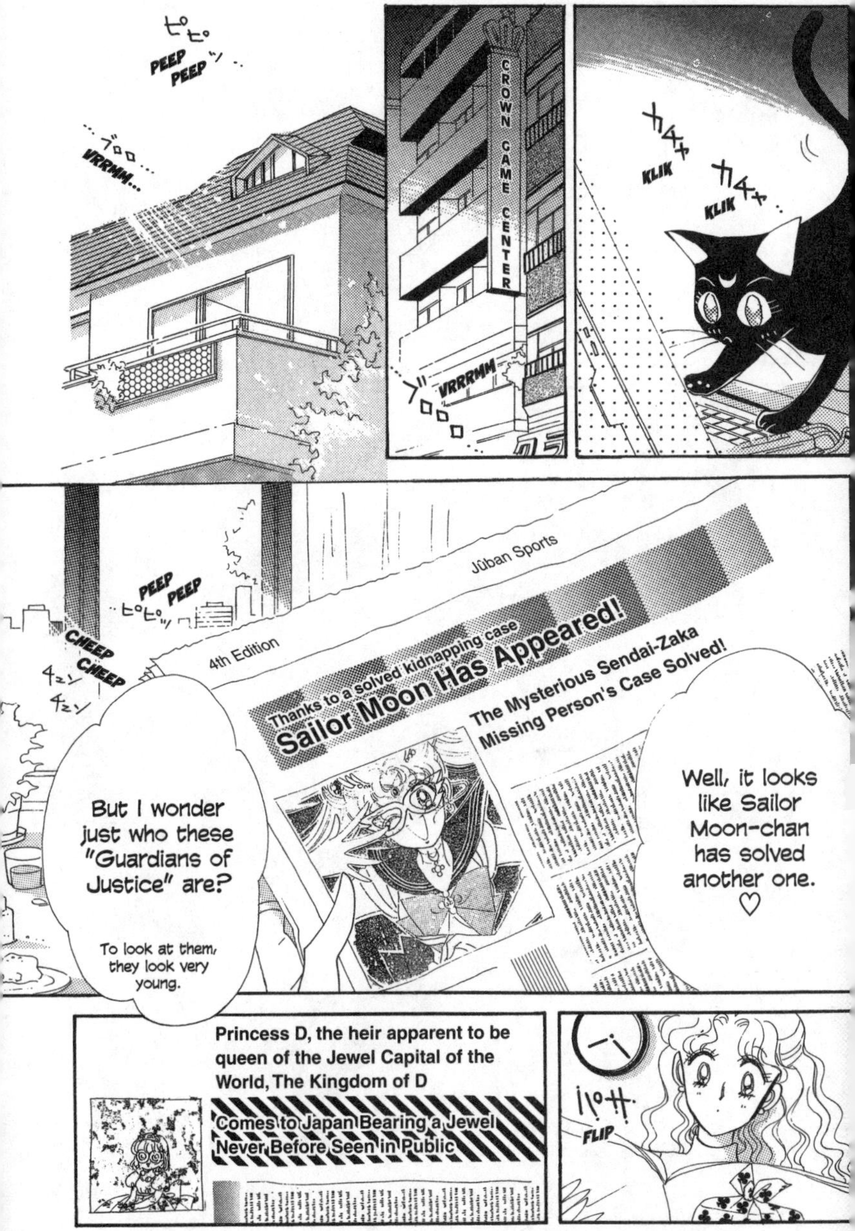
KLIK
KLIK
CROWN GAME CENTER
VRRRMM
PEEP
PEEP
VRRMM...
PEEP
PEEP
CHEEP
CHEEP
Jûban Sports
4th Edition
Thanks to a solved kidnapping case
Sailor Moon Has Appeared!
The Mysterious Sendai-Zaka Missing Person's Case Solved!
Well, it looks like Sailor Moon-chan has solved another one. ♡
But I wonder just who these "Guardians of Justice" are?
To look at them, they look very young.
FLIP
Princess D, the heir apparent to be queen of the Jewel Capital of the World, The Kingdom of D
Comes to Japan Bearing a Jewel Never Before Seen in Public

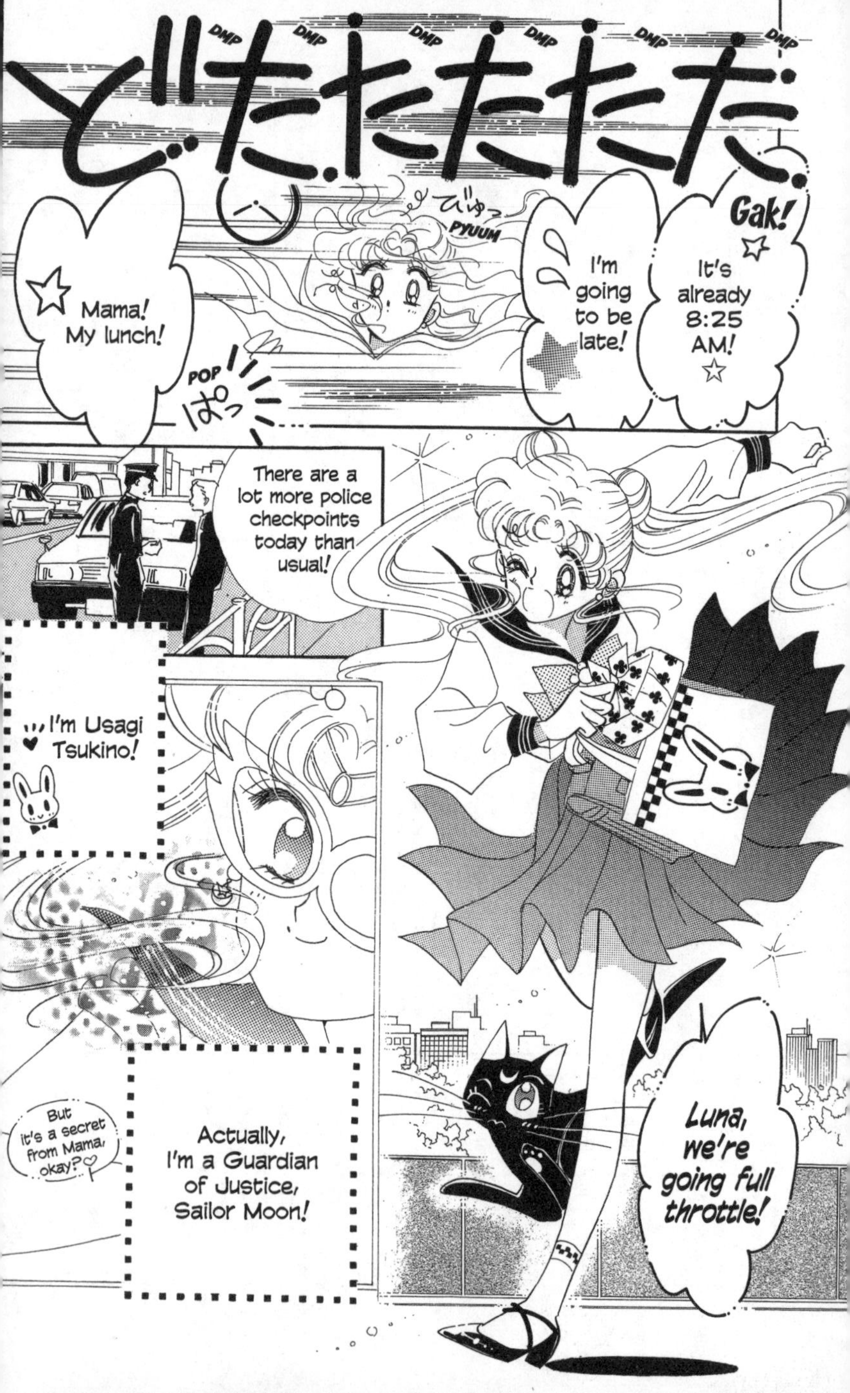

どたたたた
DMP DMP DMP DMP DMP DMP
Gak!
It's already 8:25 AM!
I'm going to be late!
ひゅっ
PYUUM
Mama! My lunch!
POP
ぱっ
Luna, we're going full throttle!
There are a lot more police checkpoints today than usual!
I'm Usagi Tsukino!
Actually, I'm a Guardian of Justice, Sailor Moon!
But it's a secret from Mama, okay?

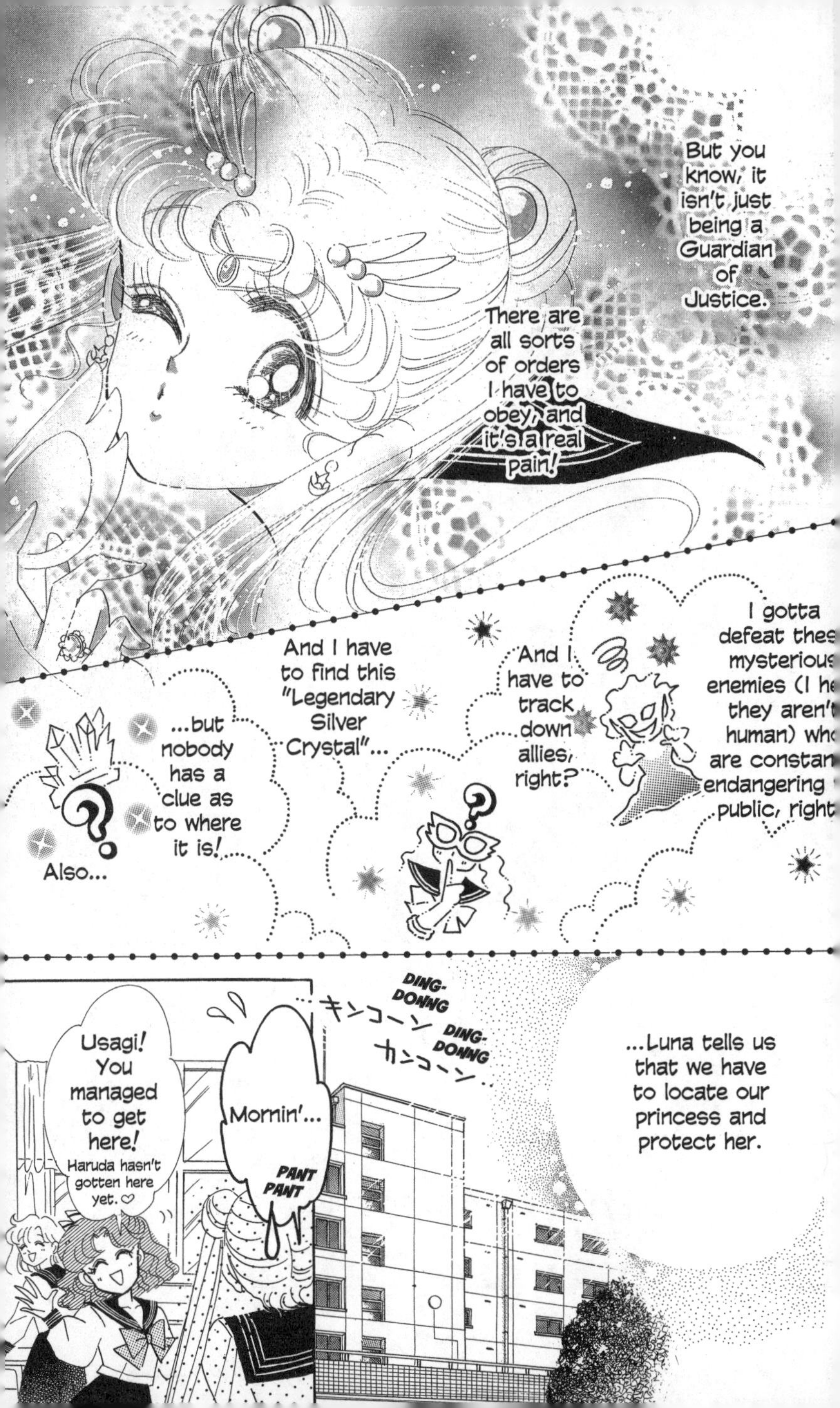

But you know, it isn't just being a Guardian of Justice.
There are all sorts of orders I have to obey, and it's a real pain!
I gotta defeat thes mysterious enemies (I he they aren't human) who are constan endangering public, right
And I have to track down allies, right?
And I have to find this "Legendary Silver Crystal"...
...but nobody has a clue as to where it is!
Also...
...Luna tells us that we have to locate our princess and protect her.
DING-DONNG
キンコーン
DING-DONNG
カンコーン
Mornin'...
PANT PANT
Usagi! You managed to get here!
Haruda hasn't gotten here yet. ♡

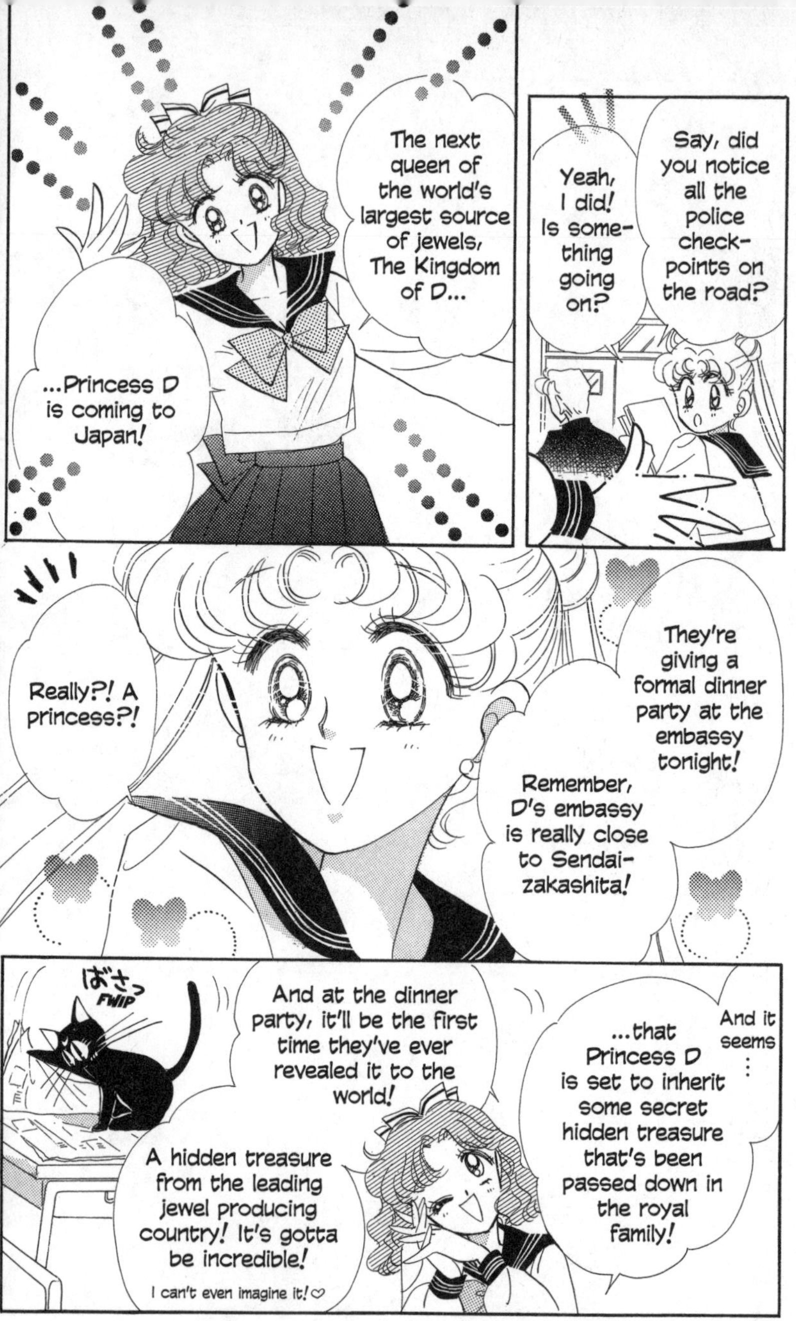
Say, did you notice all the police check-points on the road?
Yeah, I did! Is some-thing going on?
The next queen of the world's largest source of jewels, The Kingdom of D...
...Princess D is coming to Japan!
They're giving a formal dinner party at the embassy tonight!
Remember, D's embassy is really close to Sendai-zakashita!
Really?! A princess?!
And it seems :
...that Princess D is set to inherit some secret hidden treasure that's been passed down in the royal family!
And at the dinner party, it'll be the first time they've ever revealed it to the world!
ばさっ
FWIP
A hidden treasure from the leading jewel producing country! It's gotta be incredible!
I can't even imagine it! ♡

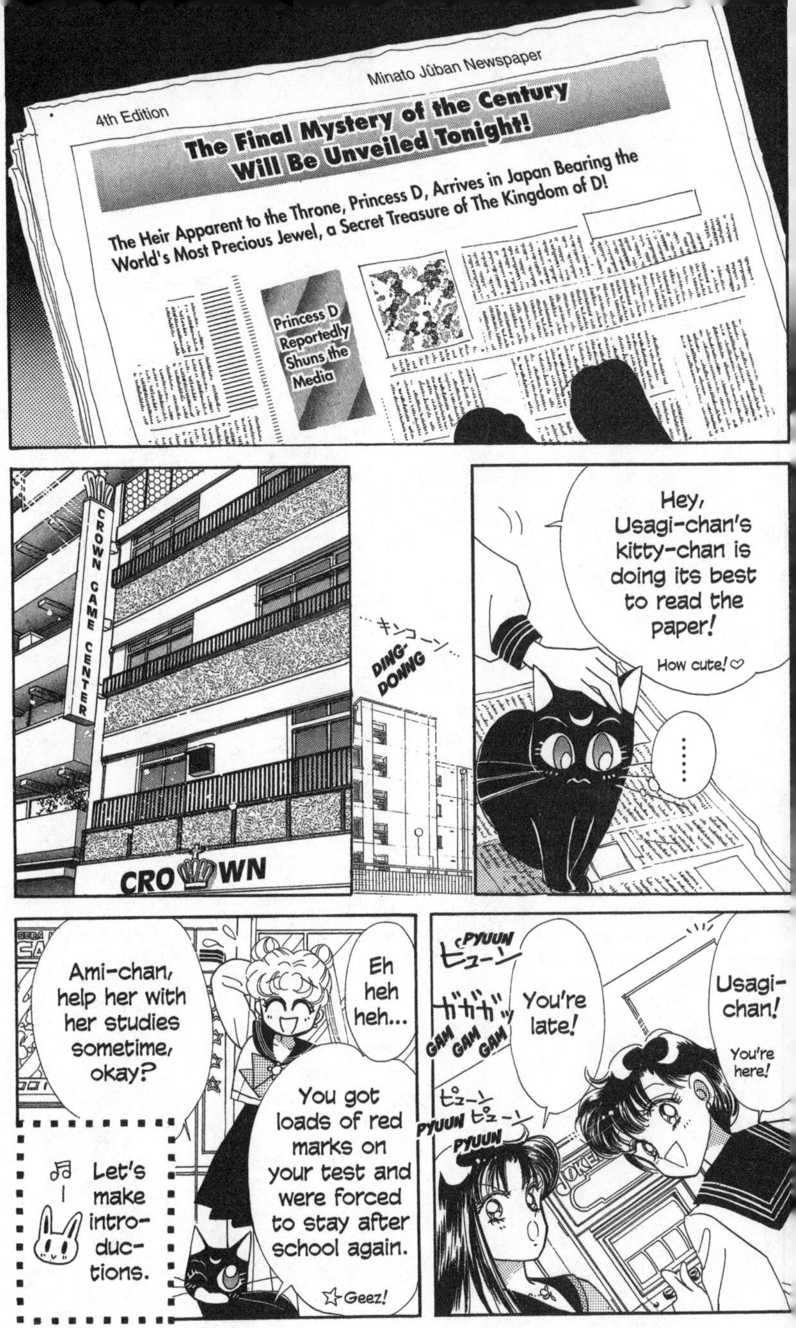
Minato Jûban Newspaper
4th Edition
The Final Mystery of the Century Will Be Unveiled Tonight!
The Heir Apparent to the Throne, Princess D, Arrives in Japan Bearing the World's Most Precious Jewel, a Secret Treasure of The Kingdom of D!
Princess D Reportedly Shuns the Media
Hey, Usagi-chan's kitty-chan is doing its best to read the paper!
How cute! ♡
......
キンコーン
DING-DONNG
CROWN GAME CENTER
CROWN
Usagi-chan!
You're here!
ピューン
PYUUN
You're late!
ガガガッ
GAM GAM GAM
ピューン ピューン
PYUUN PYUUN
Eh heh heh...
Ami-chan, help her with her studies sometime, okay?
You got loads of red marks on your test and were forced to stay after school again.
☆Geez!
Let's make intro-duc-tions.

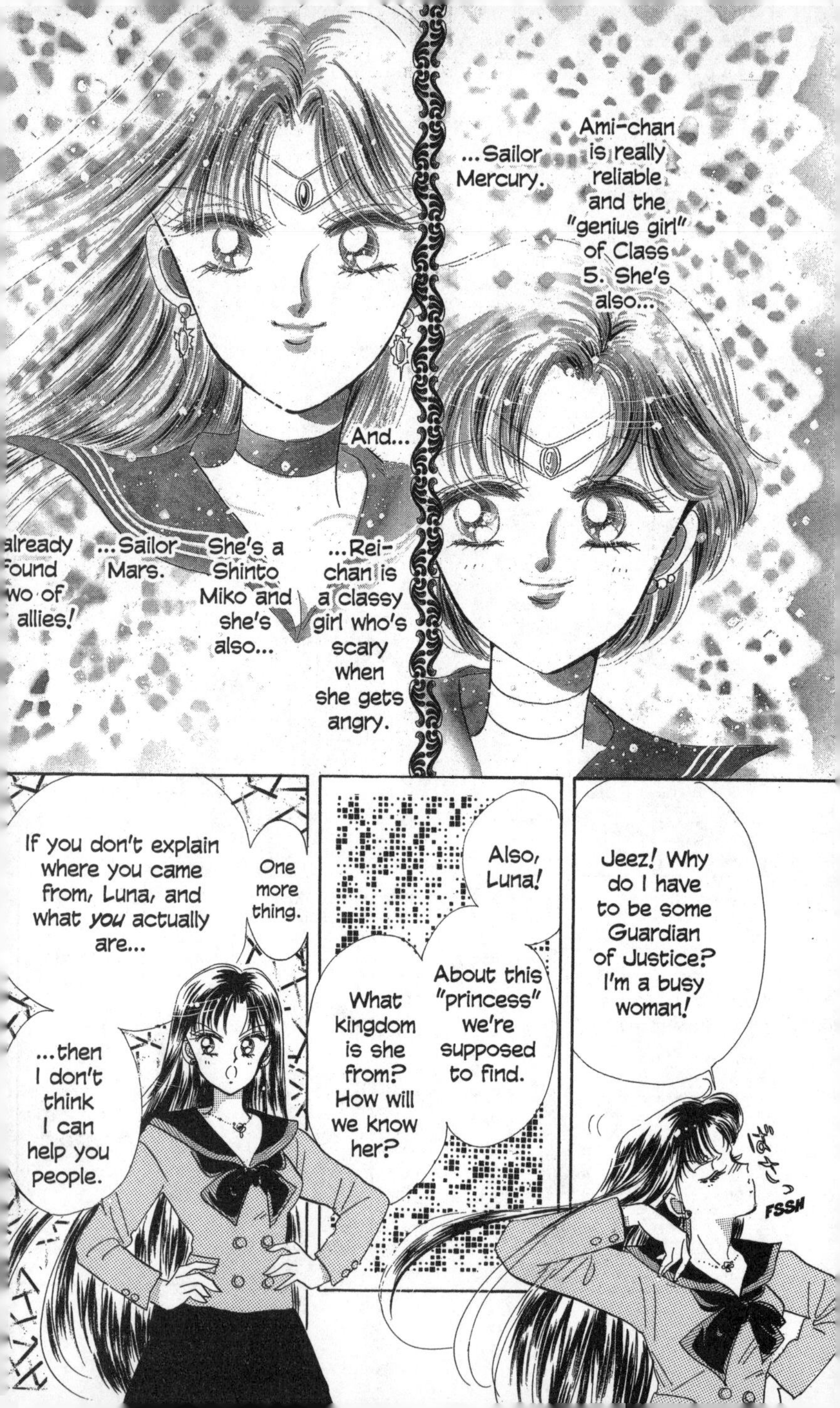

Ami-chan is really reliable and the "genius girl" of Class 5. She's also...
...Sailor Mercury.
And...
...Rei-chan is a classy girl who's scary when she gets angry.
She's a Shinto Miko and she's also...
...Sailor Mars.
already ound wo of allies!
Jeez! Why do I have to be some Guardian of Justice? I'm a busy woman!
FSSH
Also, Luna!
About this "princess" we're supposed to find.
What kingdom is she from? How will we know her?
One more thing.
If you don't explain where you came from, Luna, and what *you* actually are...
...then I don't think I can help you people.

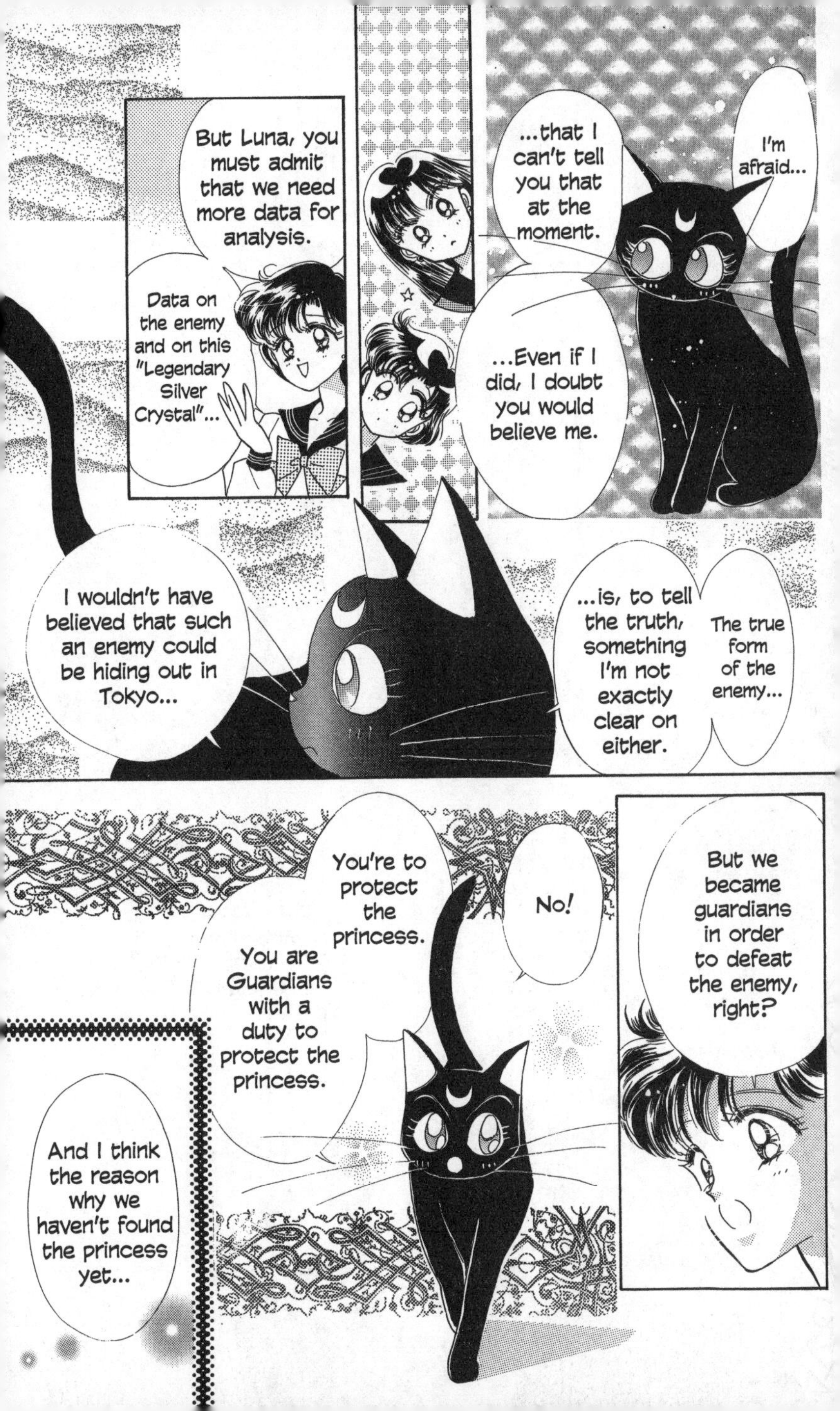
I'm afraid...
...that I can't tell you that at the moment.
...Even if I did, I doubt you would believe me.
But Luna, you must admit that we need more data for analysis.
Data on the enemy and on this "Legendary Silver Crystal"...
The true form of the enemy...
...is, to tell the truth, something I'm not exactly clear on either.
I wouldn't have believed that such an enemy could be hiding out in Tokyo...
But we became guardians in order to defeat the enemy, right?
No!
You're to protect the princess.
You are Guardians with a duty to protect the princess.
And I think the reason why we haven't found the princess yet...

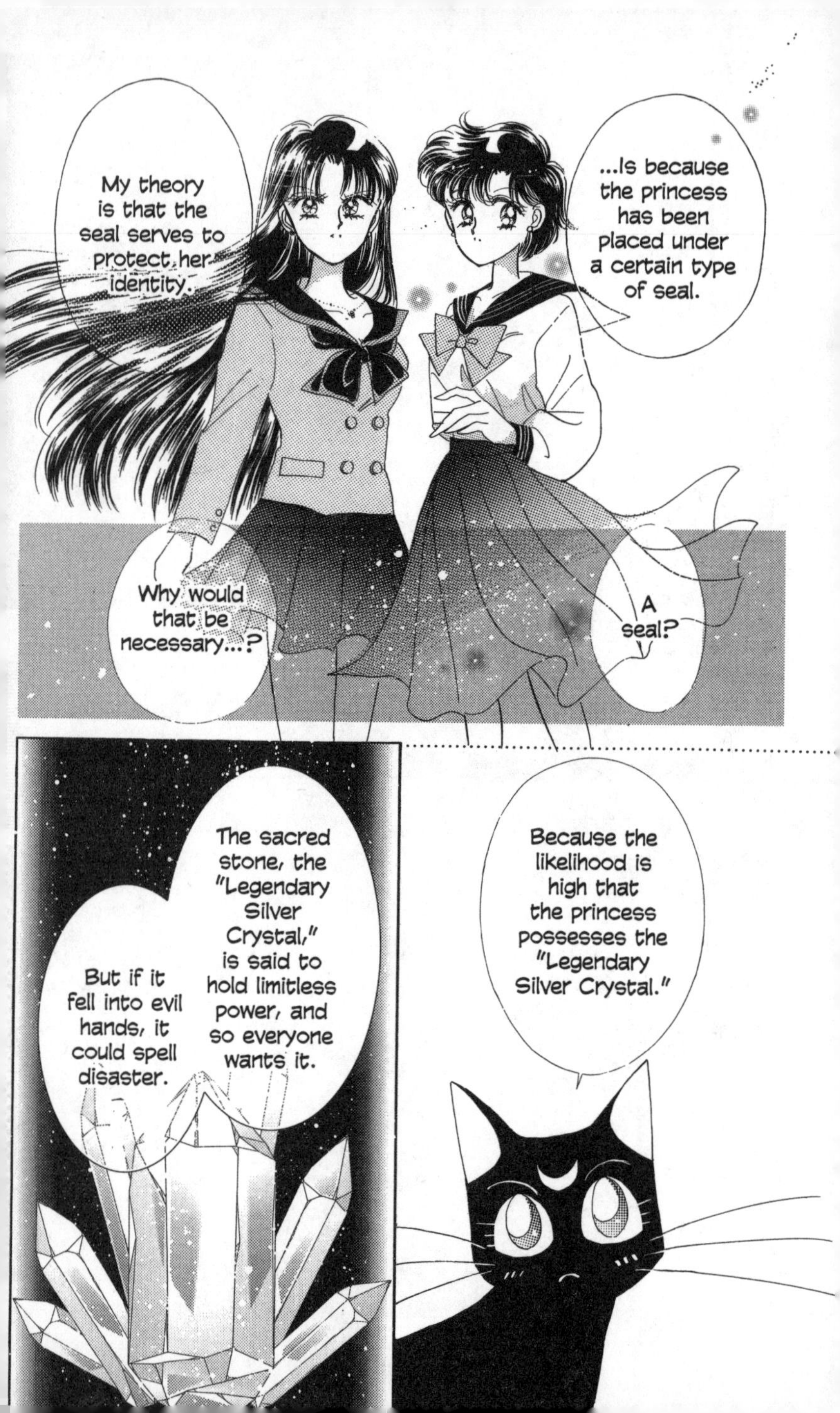
...Is because the princess has been placed under a certain type of seal.
My theory is that the seal serves to protect her identity.
A seal?
Why would that be necessary...?
Because the likelihood is high that the princess possesses the "Legendary Silver Crystal."
The sacred stone, the "Legendary Silver Crystal," is said to hold limitless power, and so everyone wants it.
But if it fell into evil hands, it could spell disaster.

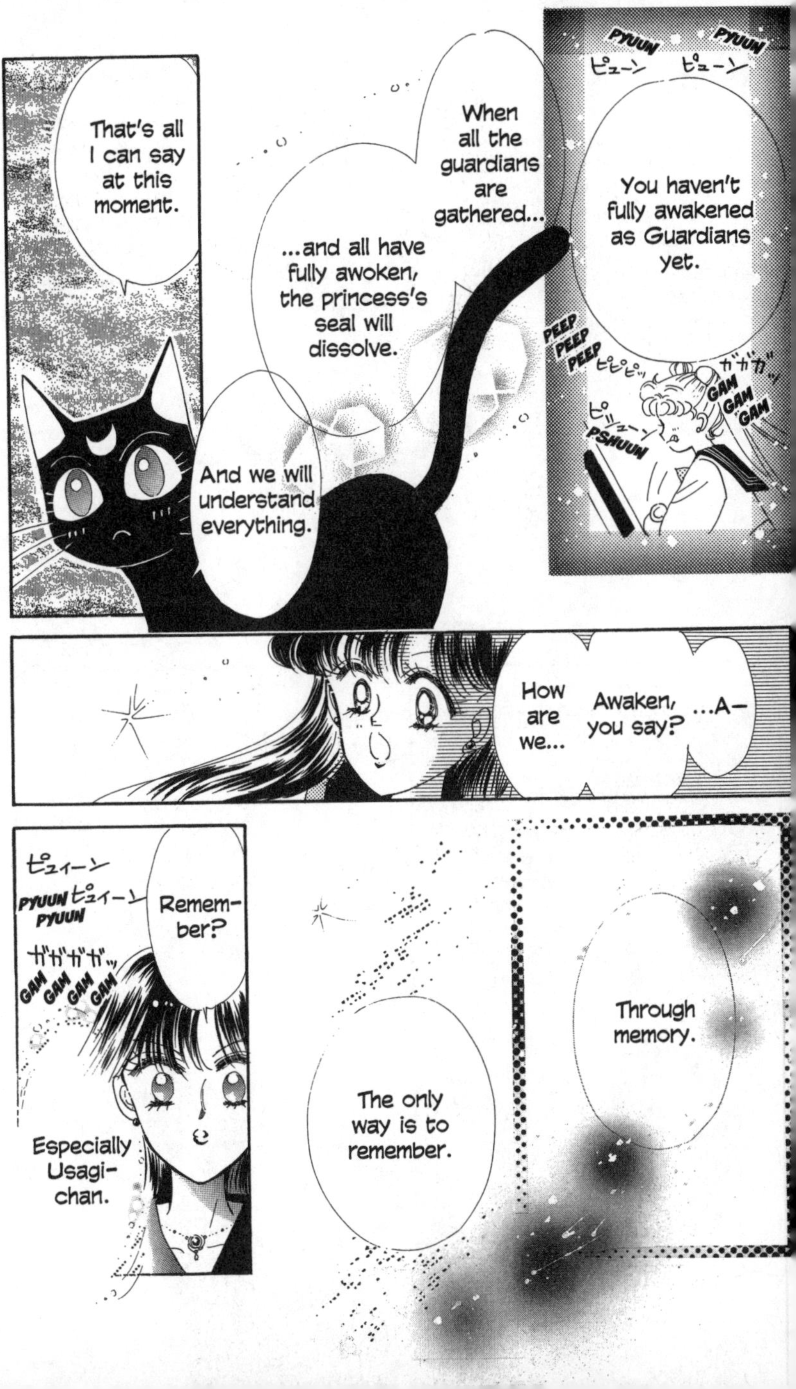
PYUUN PYUUN
ピューン ピューン
You haven't fully awakened as Guardians yet.
PEEP PEEP PEEP
ピピピッ
ガガガッ
GAM GAM GAM
ピシューン
PSHUUN
When all the guardians are gathered...
...and all have fully awoken, the princess's seal will dissolve.
And we will understand everything.
That's all I can say at this moment.
...A—
Awaken, you say?
How are we...
Through memory.
The only way is to remember.
ピュイーン
PYUUN
ピュイーン
PYUUN
Remember?
ガガガガッ
GAM GAM GAM GAM
Especially Usagi-chan.

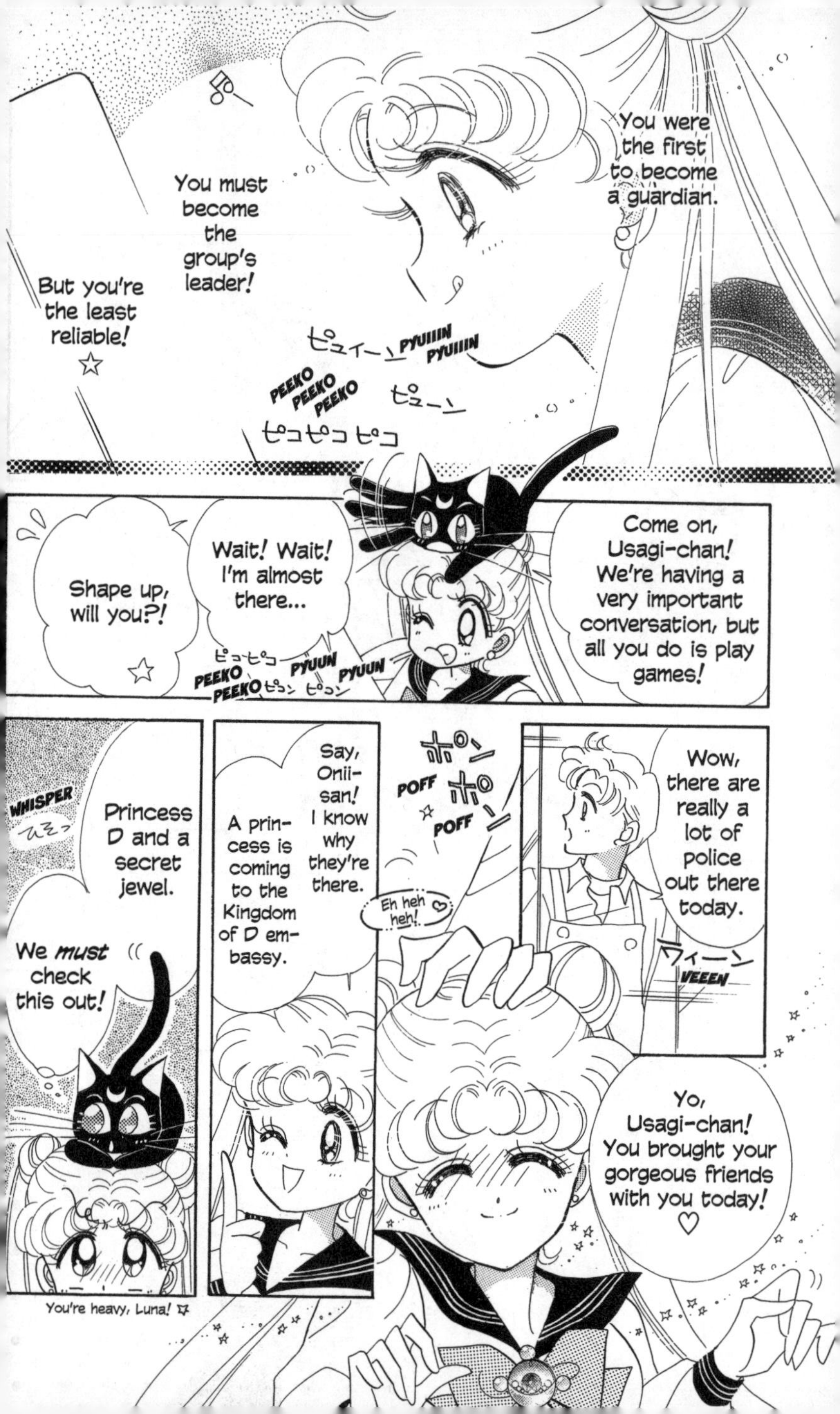

You were the first to become a guardian.
You must become the group's leader!
But you're the least reliable! ☆
ピュイーン PYUIIIN PYUIIIN ピューン
PEEKO PEEKO PEEKO ピコピコピコ
Come on, Usagi-chan! We're having a very important conversation, but all you do is play games!
Wait! Wait! I'm almost there...
Shape up, will you?! ☆
ピコピコ PEEKO PEEKO ピコン ピコン PYUUN PYUUN
Wow, there are really a lot of police out there today.
ヴィーン VEEEN
Yo, Usagi-chan! You brought your gorgeous friends with you today! ♡
ポン POFF ポン POFF
Eh heh heh! ♡
Say, Onii-san! I know why they're there.
A prin-cess is coming to the Kingdom of D em-bassy.
WHISPER ひそっ
Princess D and a secret jewel.
We *must* check this out!
You're heavy, Luna! ☆

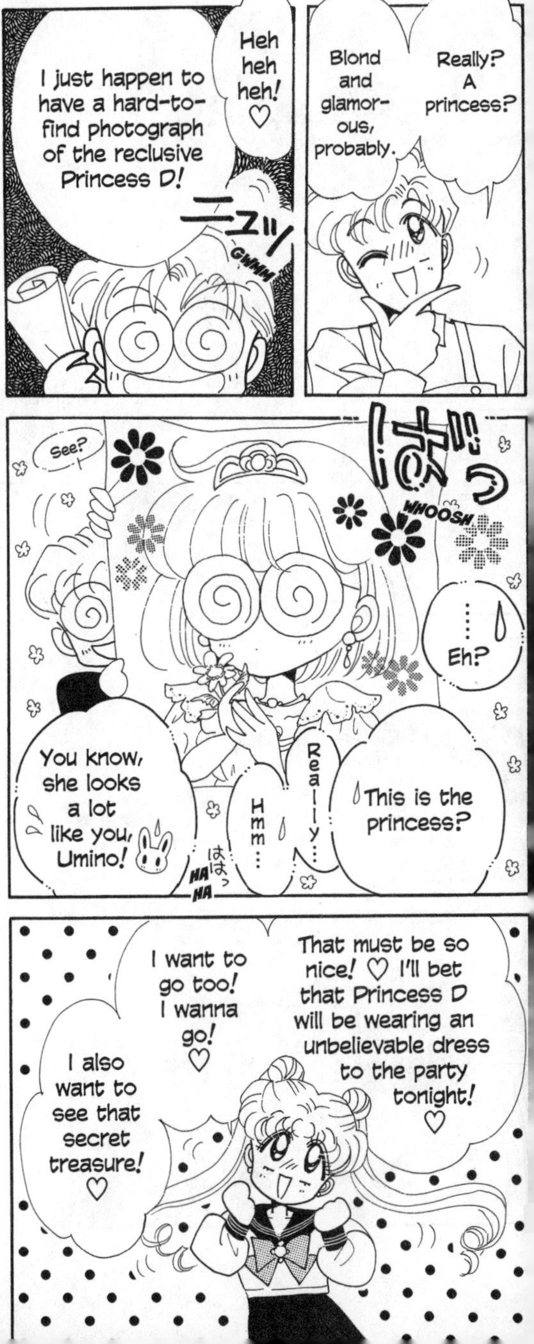
Really? A princess?
Blond and glamorous, probably.
Heh heh heh! ♡
I just happen to have a hard-to-find photograph of the reclusive Princess D!
ニュッ
GWMMM
ぱっ
WHOOSH
...Eh?
See?
This is the princess?
Really...
Hmm...
You know, she looks a lot like you, Umino!
ははっ
HA HA
That must be so nice! ♡ I'll bet that Princess D will be wearing an unbelievable dress to the party tonight! ♡
I want to go too! I wanna go! ♡
I also want to see that secret treasure! ♡

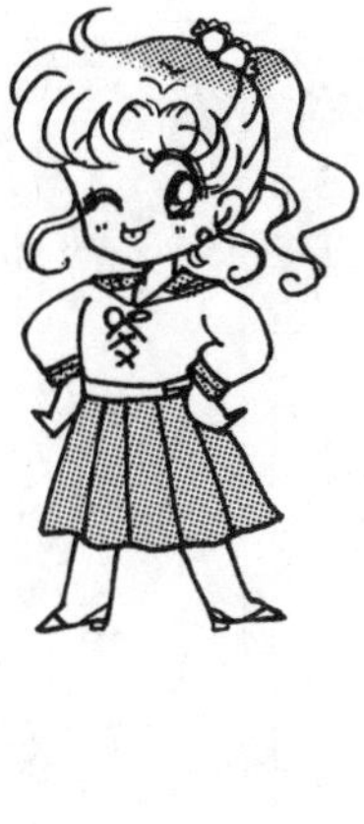

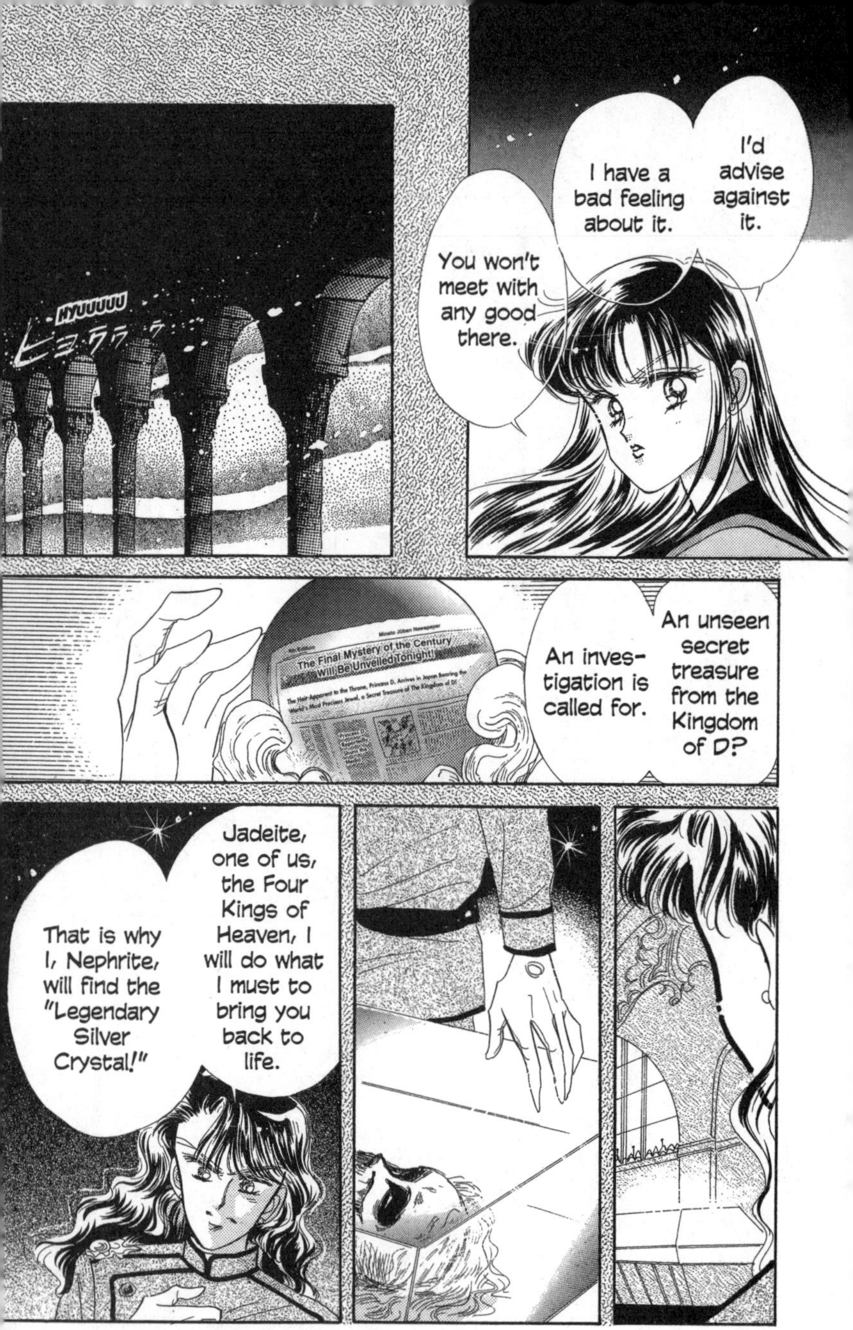
I'd advise against it.
I have a bad feeling about it.
You won't meet with any good there.
HYUUUUU
An unseen secret treasure from the Kingdom of D?
An investigation is called for.
The Final Mystery of the Century Will Be Unveiled Tonight!
Jadeite, one of us, the Four Kings of Heaven, I will do what I must to bring you back to life.
That is why I, Nephrite, will find the "Legendary Silver Crystal!"

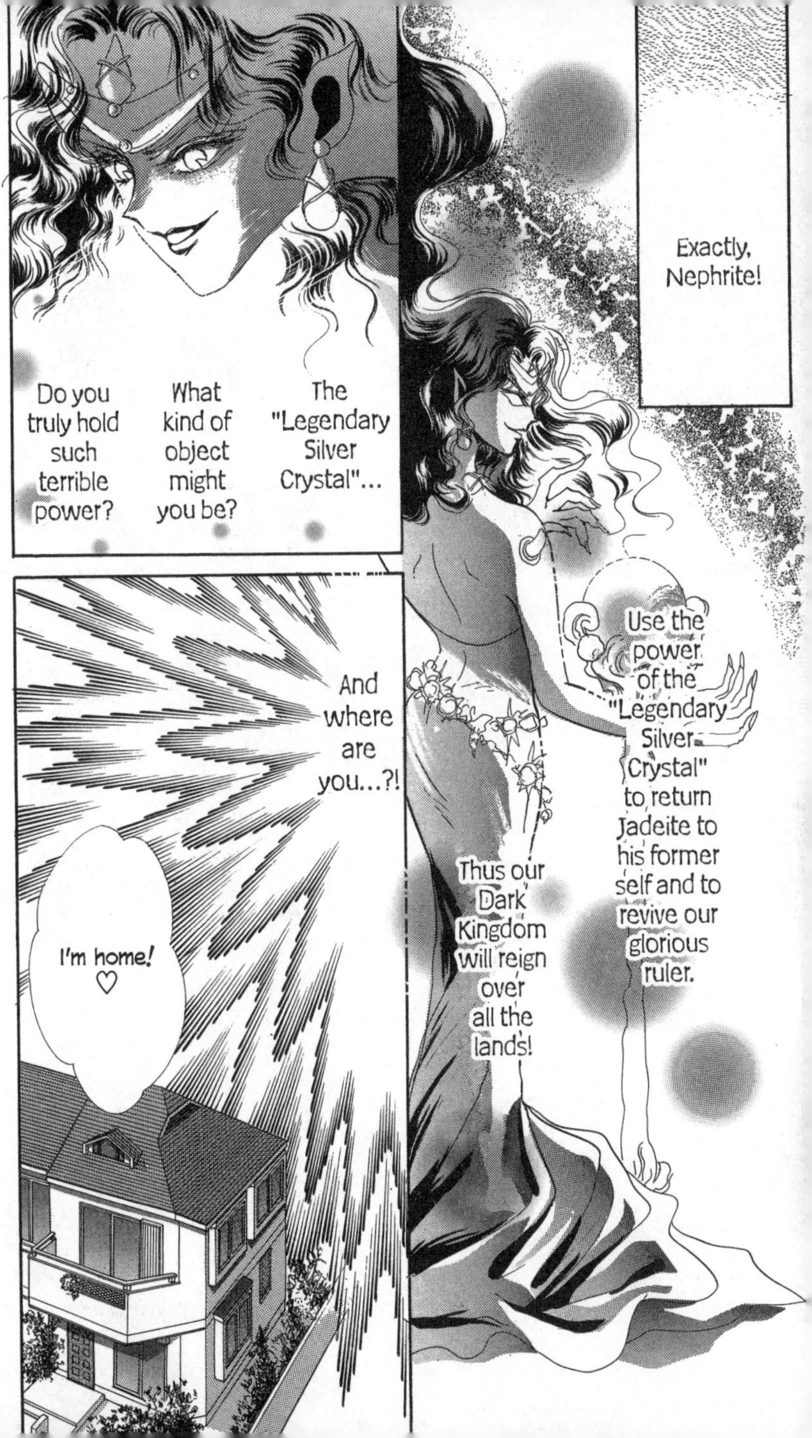
Exactly, Nephrite!
Use the power of the "Legendary Silver Crystal" to return Jadeite to his former self and to revive our glorious ruler.
Thus our Dark Kingdom will reign over all the lands!
The "Legendary Silver Crystal"...
What kind of object might you be?
Do you truly hold such terrible power?
And where are you...?!
I'm home! ♡

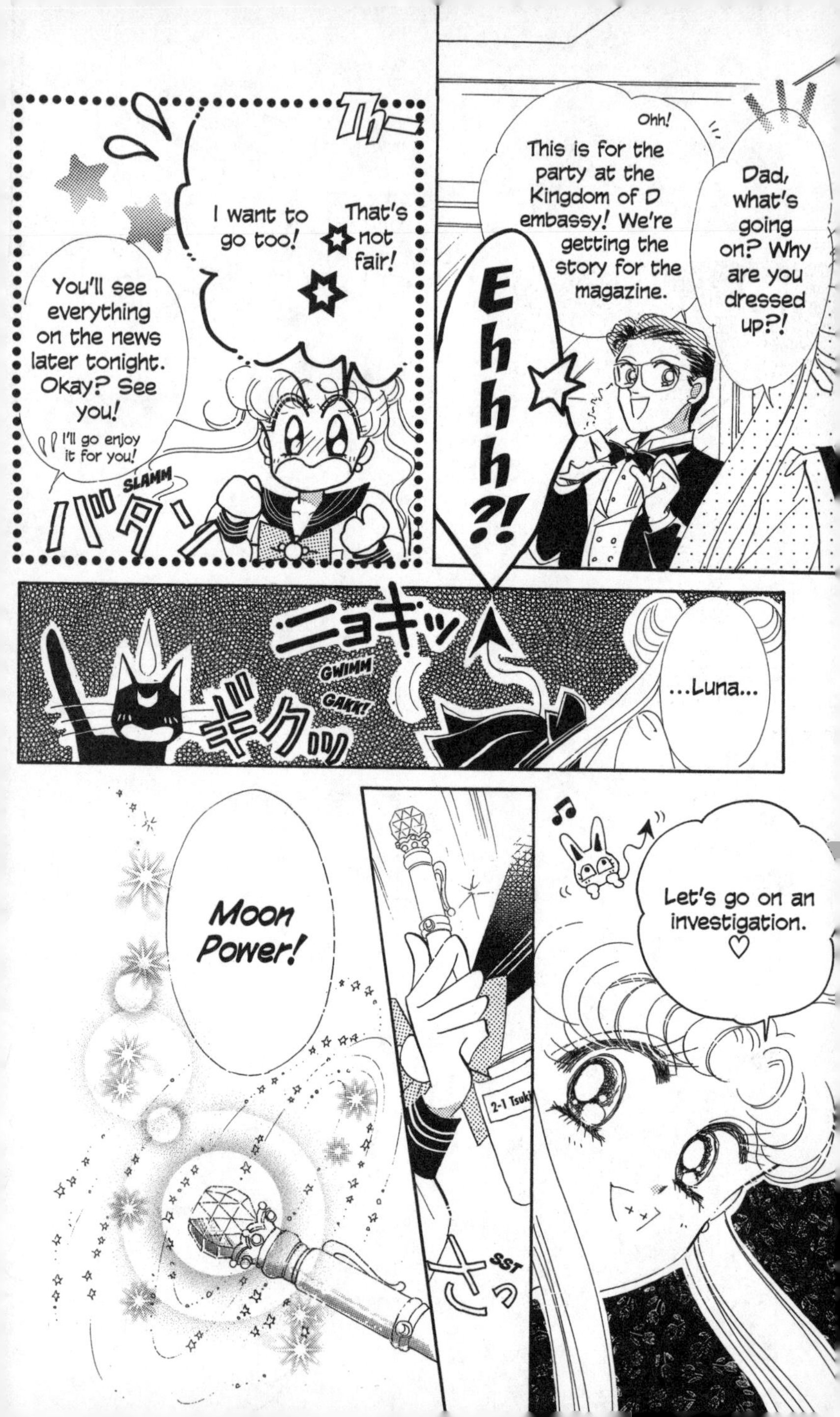

Dad, what's going on? Why are you dressed up?!
Ohh! This is for the party at the Kingdom of D embassy! We're getting the story for the magazine.
Ehhh?!
That's not fair!
I want to go too!
You'll see everything on the news later tonight. Okay? See you!
I'll go enjoy it for you!
SLAMM
バタン
...Luna...
ニョキッ
GWIMM
ギクッ
GAKK!
Let's go on an investigation. ♡
SST
さっ
Moon Power!

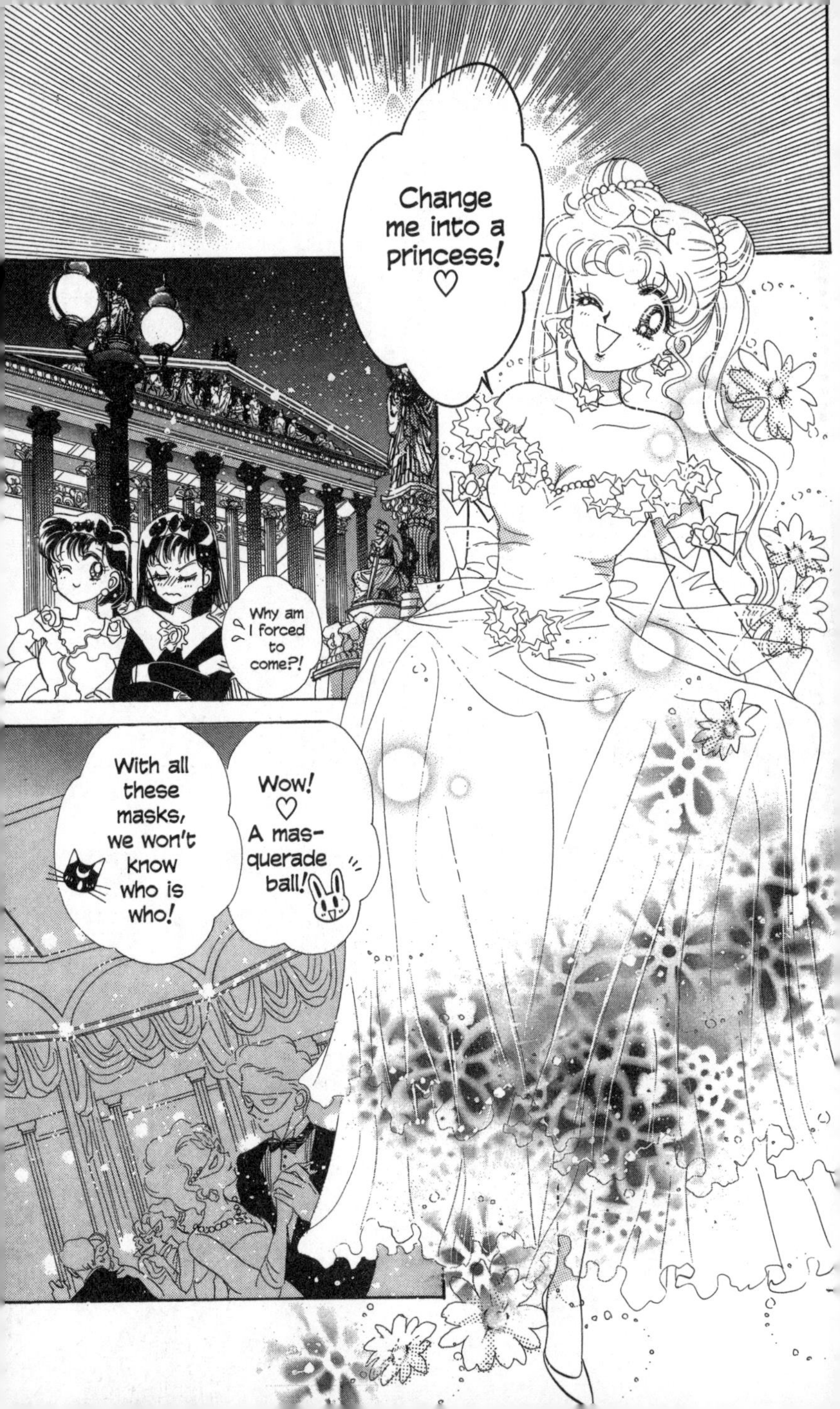
Change me into a princess! ♡
Why am I forced to come?!
Wow! ♡ A mas-querade ball!
With all these masks, we won't know who is who!

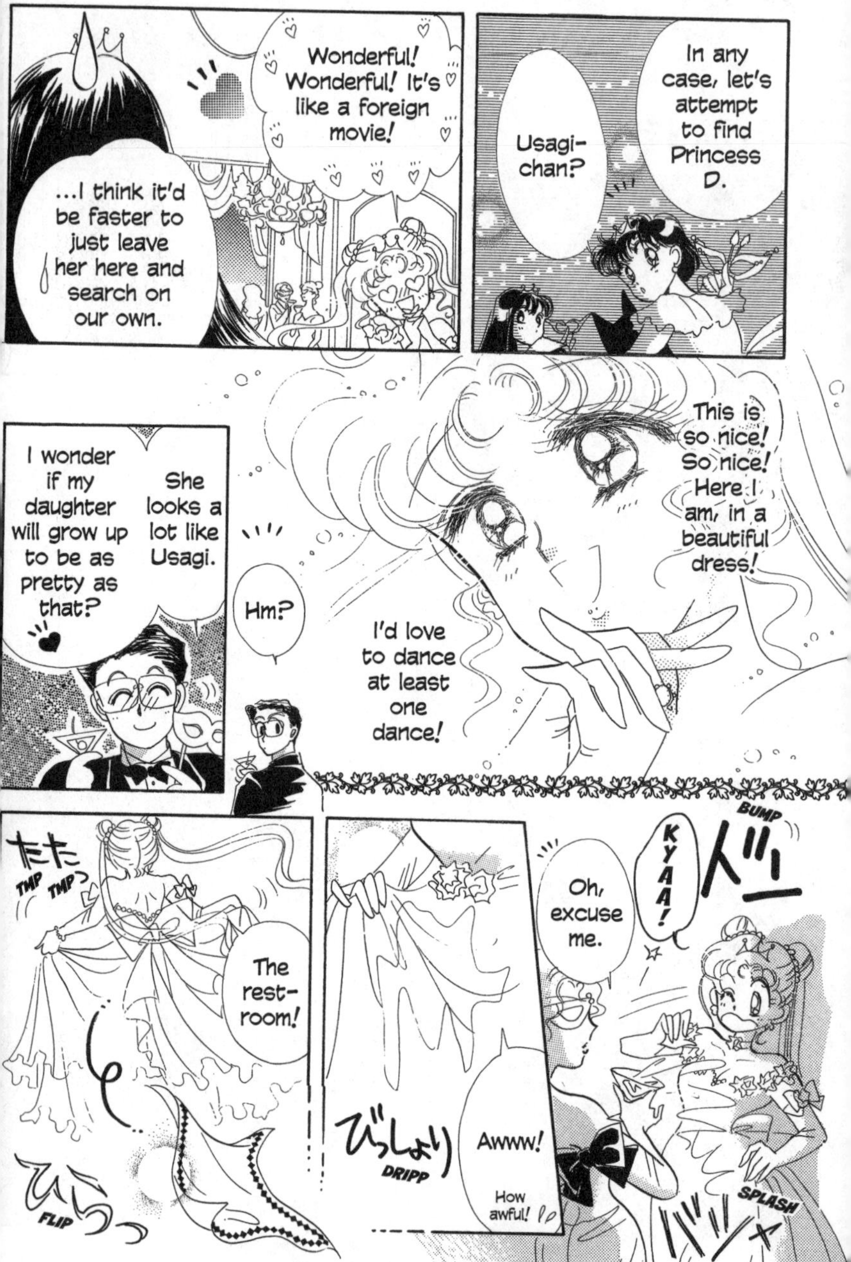

In any case, let's attempt to find Princess D.
Usagi-chan?
Wonderful! Wonderful! It's like a foreign movie!
...I think it'd be faster to just leave her here and search on our own.
This is so nice! So nice! Here I am, in a beautiful dress!
I'd love to dance at least one dance!
She looks a lot like Usagi.
Hm?
I wonder if my daughter will grow up to be as pretty as that?
BUMP
KYAA!
Oh, excuse me.
SPLASH
Awww!
How awful!
びっしょり
DRIPP
The rest-room!
たたた
TMP TMP
ひらっ
FLIP

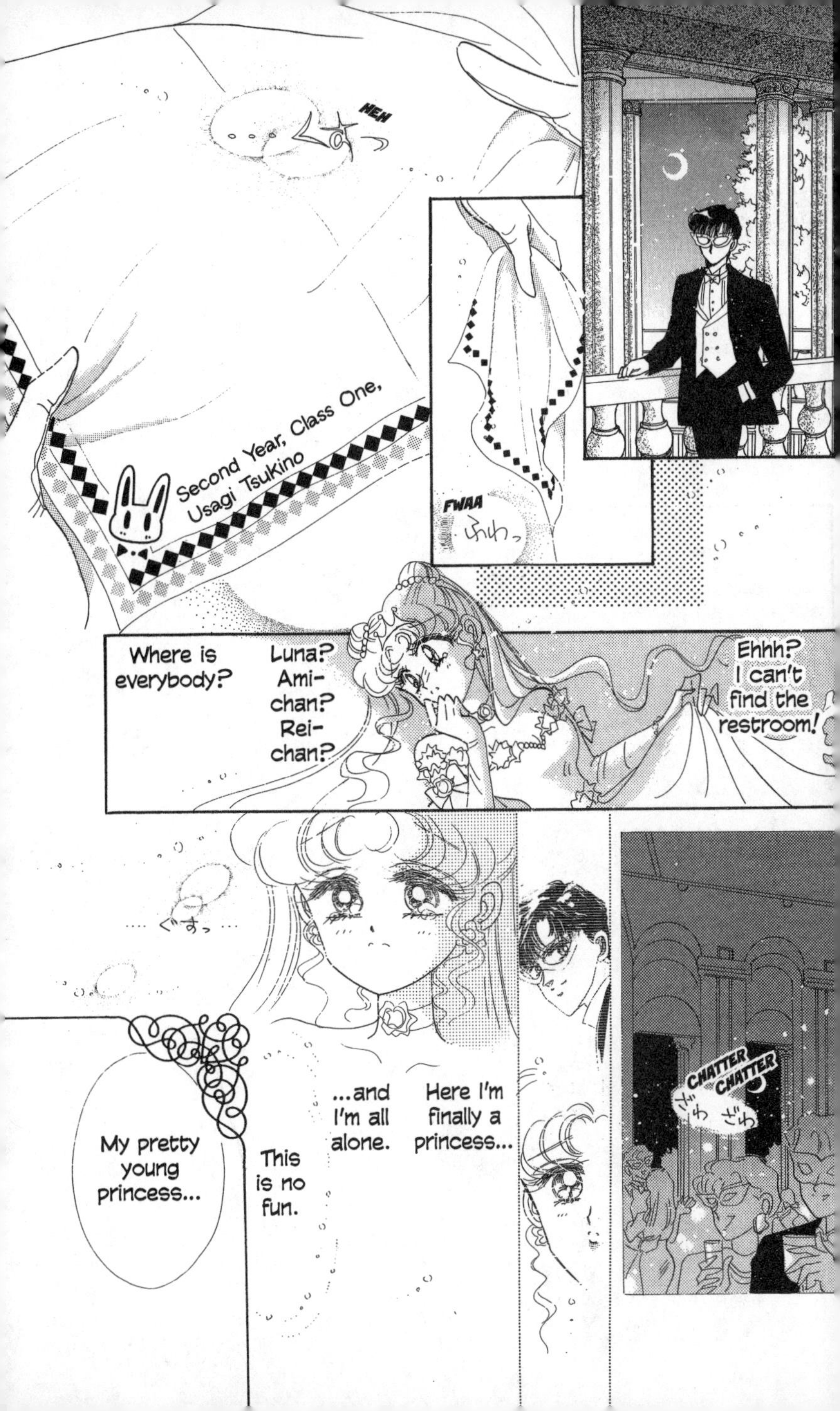

FWAA
ふわっ
HEH
くすっ
Second Year, Class One,
Usagi Tsukino
Ehhh? I can't find the restroom!
Luna? Ami-chan? Rei-chan?
Where is everybody?
CHATTER CHATTER
ざわ ざわ
Here I'm finally a princess...
...and I'm all alone.
This is no fun.
…ぐすっ…
My pretty young princess...

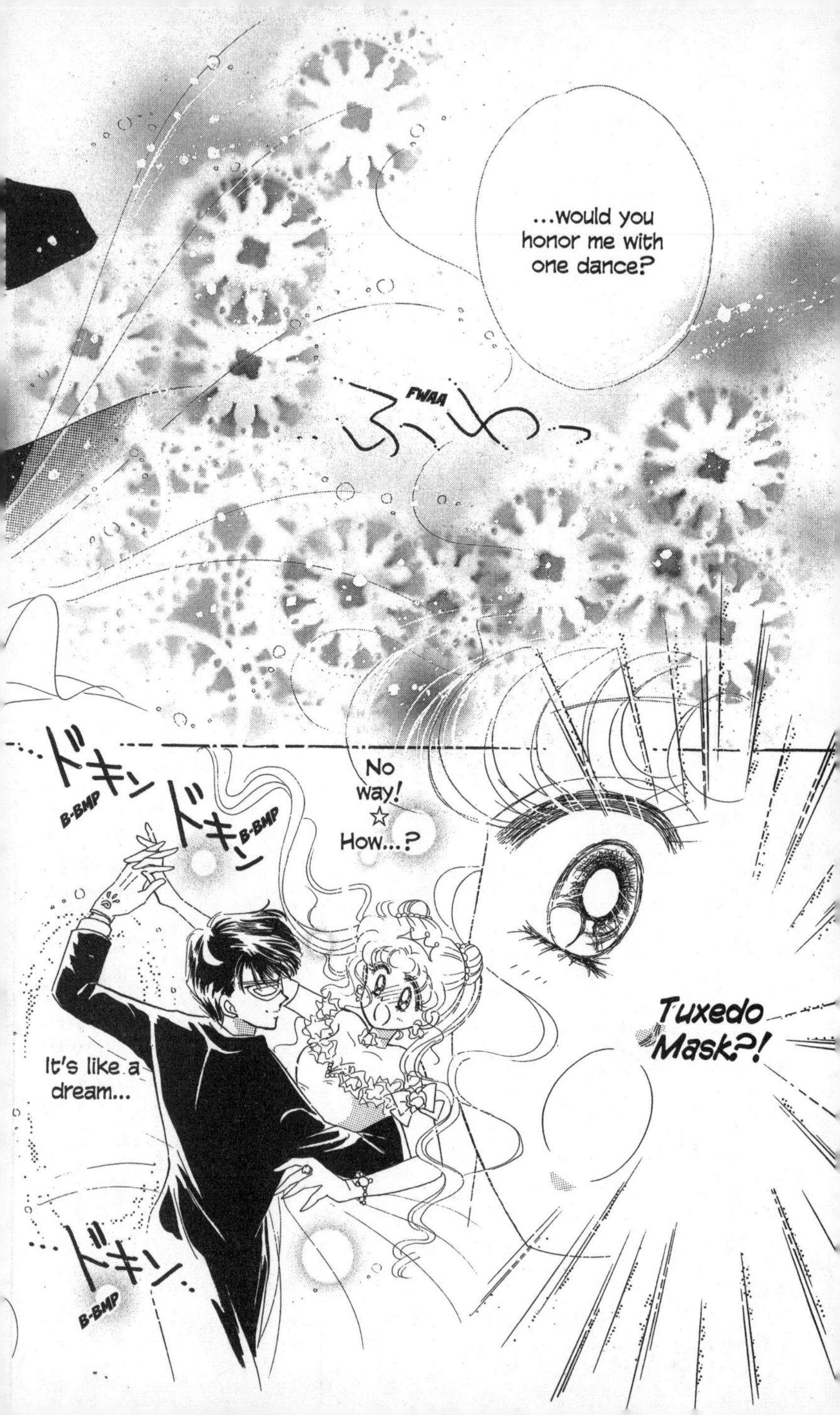
...would you honor me with one dance?
ふわっ
FWAA
Tuxedo Mask?!
No way! ☆ How...?
ドキン
B-BMP
ドキン
B-BMP
It's like a dream...
ドキン
B-BMP

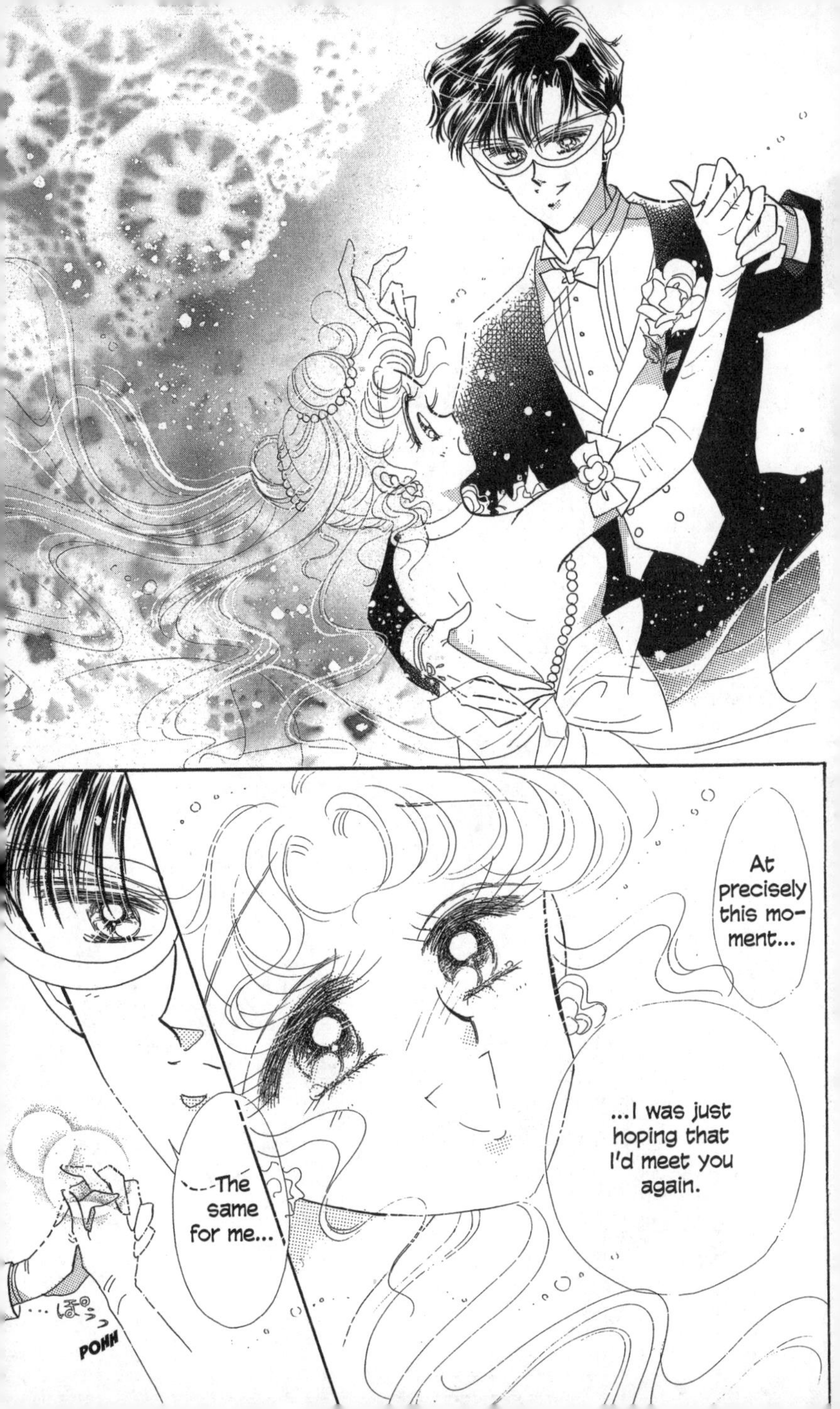
At precisely this moment...
...I was just hoping that I'd meet you again.
The same for me...
POHH

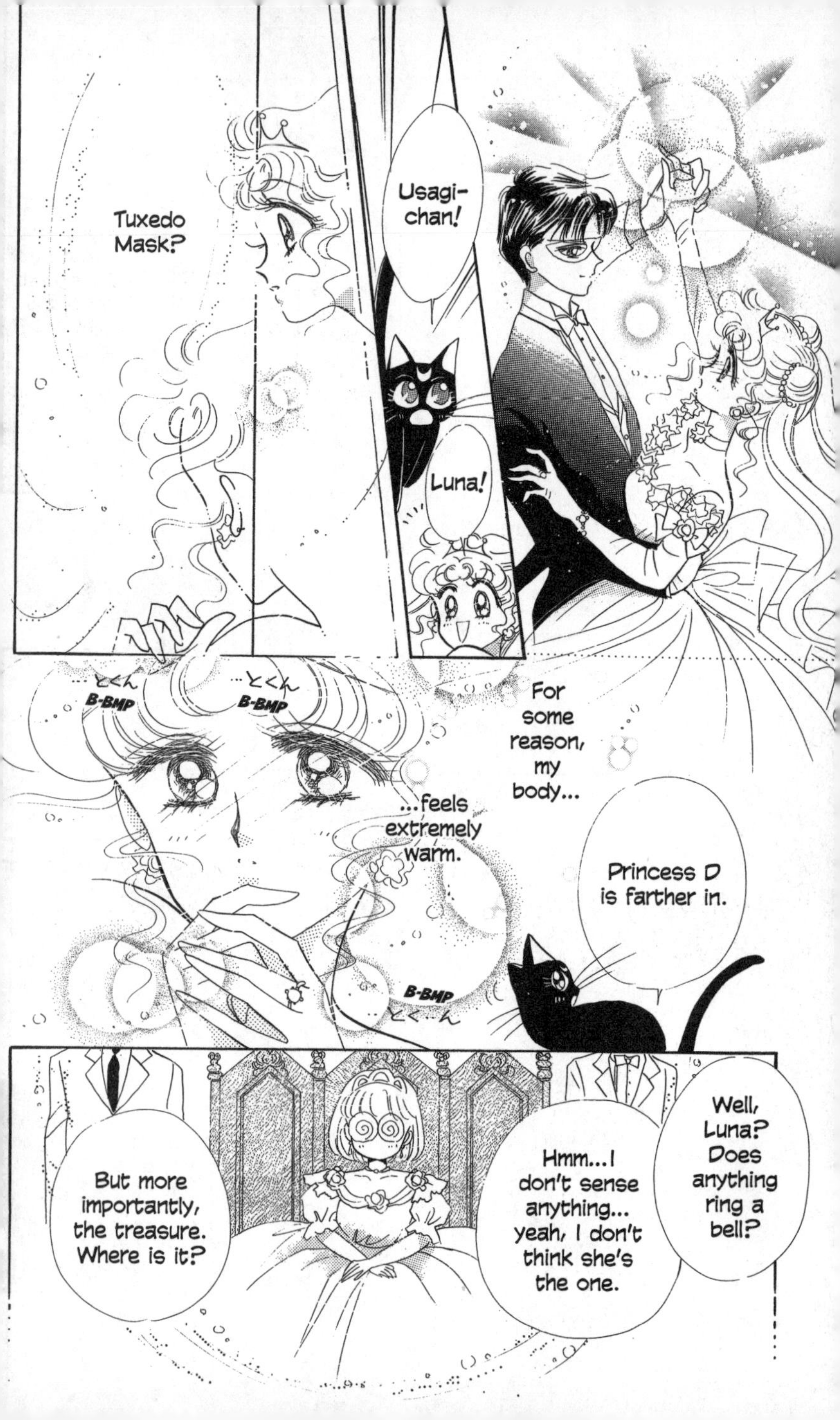
Usagi-chan!
Luna!
Tuxedo Mask?
For some reason, my body...
...feels extremely warm.
...とくん B-BMP
...とくん B-BMP
B-BMP とく…ん
Princess D is farther in.
Well, Luna? Does anything ring a bell?
Hmm...I don't sense anything... yeah, I don't think she's the one.
But more importantly, the treasure. Where is it?

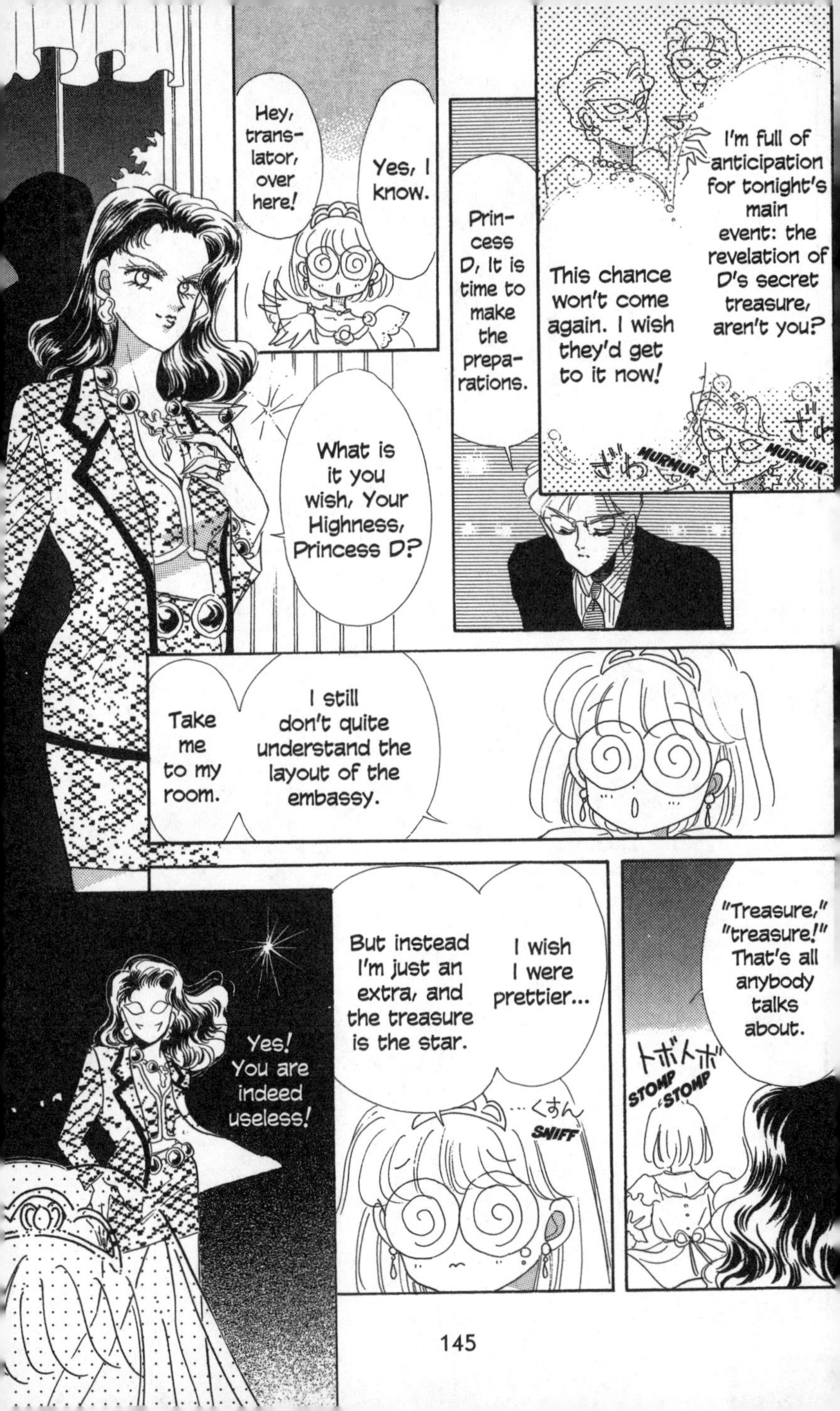

I'm full of anticipation for tonight's main event: the revelation of D's secret treasure, aren't you?
This chance won't come again. I wish they'd get to it now!
ざわ MURMUR
ざわ MURMUR
Princess D, It is time to make the preparations.
Yes, I know.
Hey, translator, over here!
What is it you wish, Your Highness, Princess D?
I still don't quite understand the layout of the embassy.
Take me to my room.
"Treasure," "treasure!" That's all anybody talks about.
トボトボ STOMP STOMP
I wish I were prettier...
But instead I'm just an extra, and the treasure is the star.
…くすん SNIFF
Yes! You are indeed useless!

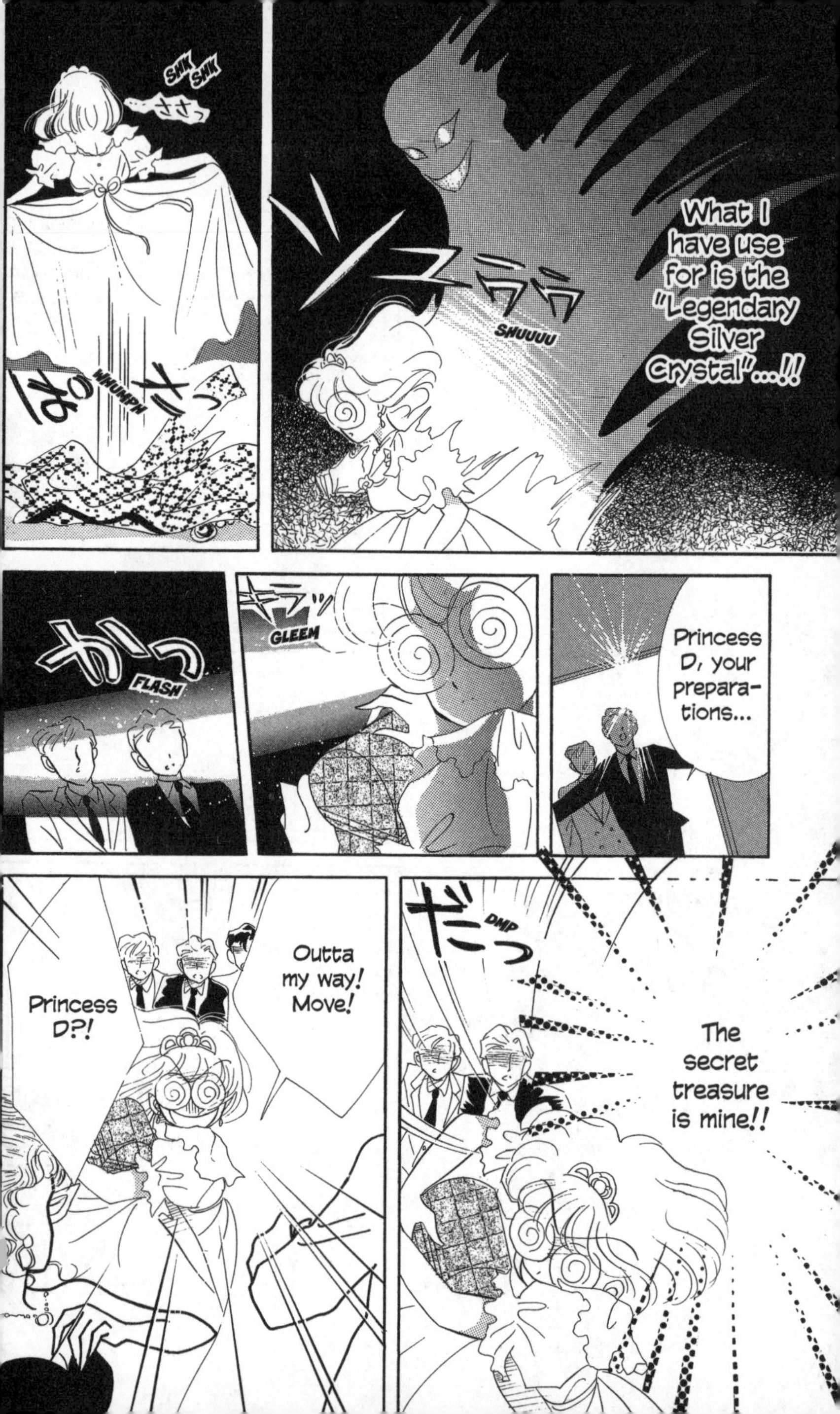

SHUUUU
What I have use for is the "Legendary Silver Crystal"...!!
SHK SHK
ささっ
WHUMPH
Princess D, your preparations...
GLEEM
FLASH
かっ
だっ
DMP
The secret treasure is mine!!
Outta my way! Move!
Princess D?!

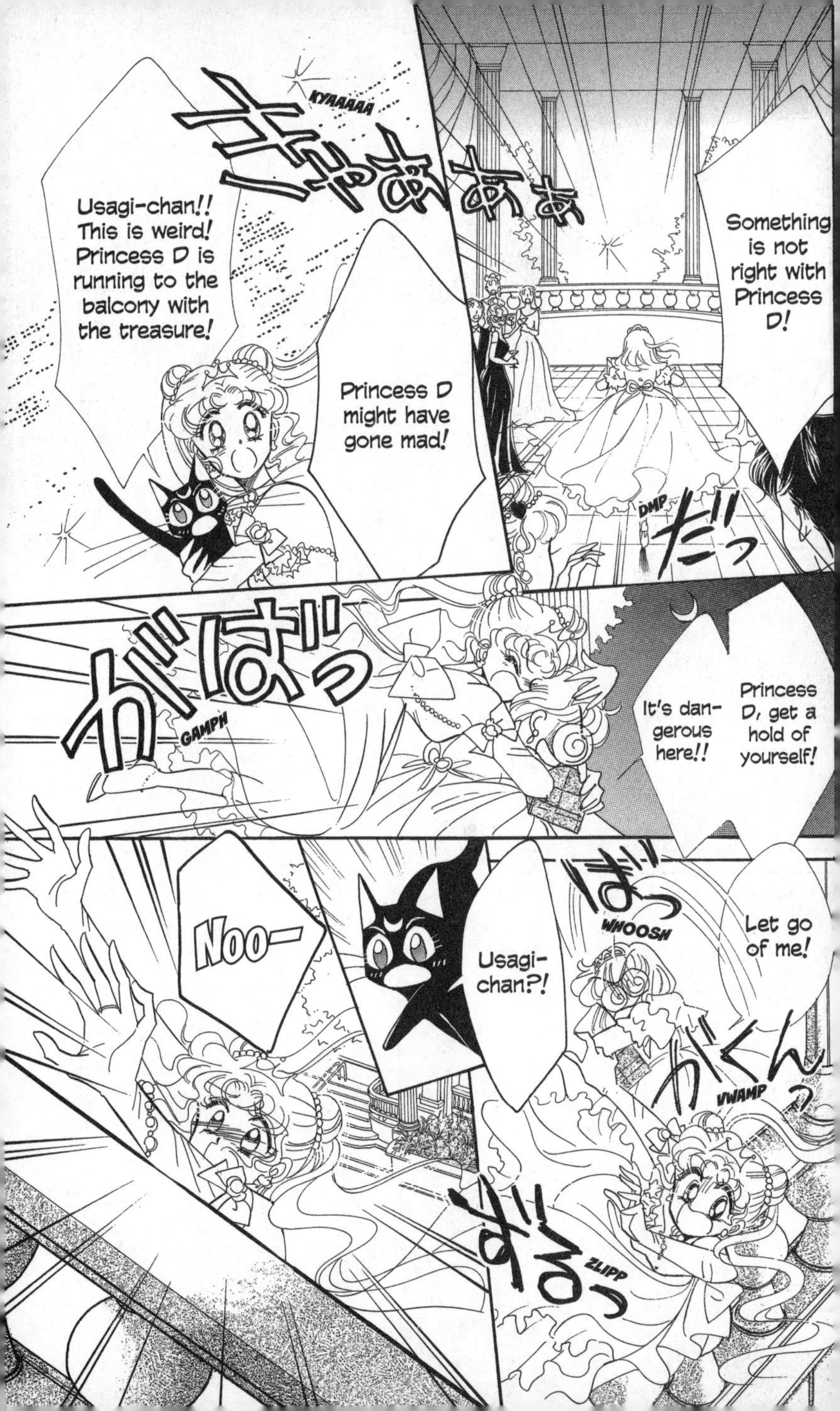
Something is not right with Princess D!
DMP
だっ
KYAAAAA
きゃあああ
Usagi-chan!! This is weird! Princess D is running to the balcony with the treasure!
Princess D might have gone mad!
Princess D, get a hold of yourself!
It's dangerous here!!
がばっ
GAMPH
Let go of me!
ばっ
WHOOSH
がくんっ
VWAMP
ずるっ
ZLIPP
Usagi-chan?!
Noo-

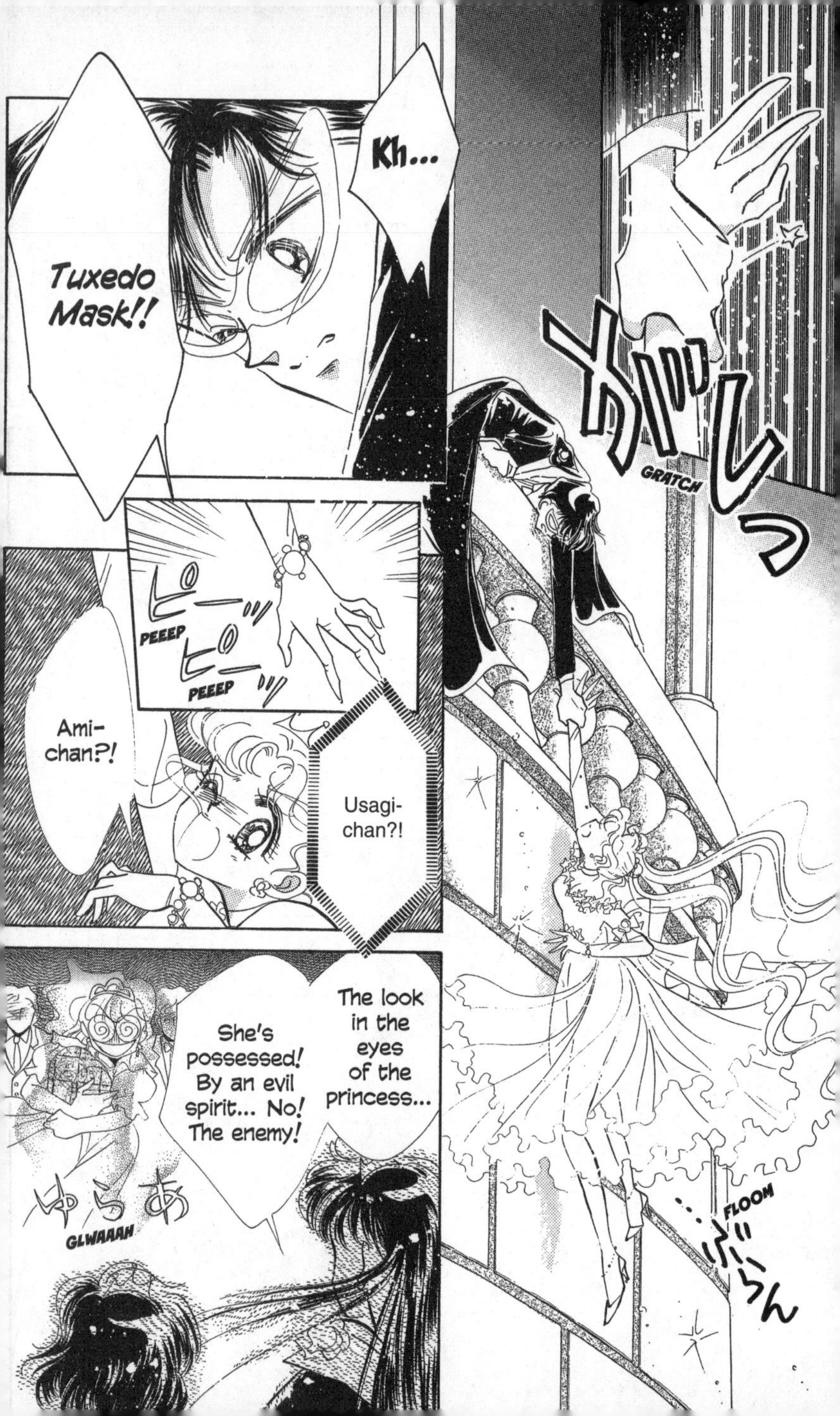
GRATCH
FLOOM
Kh...
Tuxedo Mask!!
PEEEP
PEEEP
Usagi-chan?!
Ami-chan?!
The look in the eyes of the princess...
She's possessed! By an evil spirit... No! The enemy!
GLWAAAH

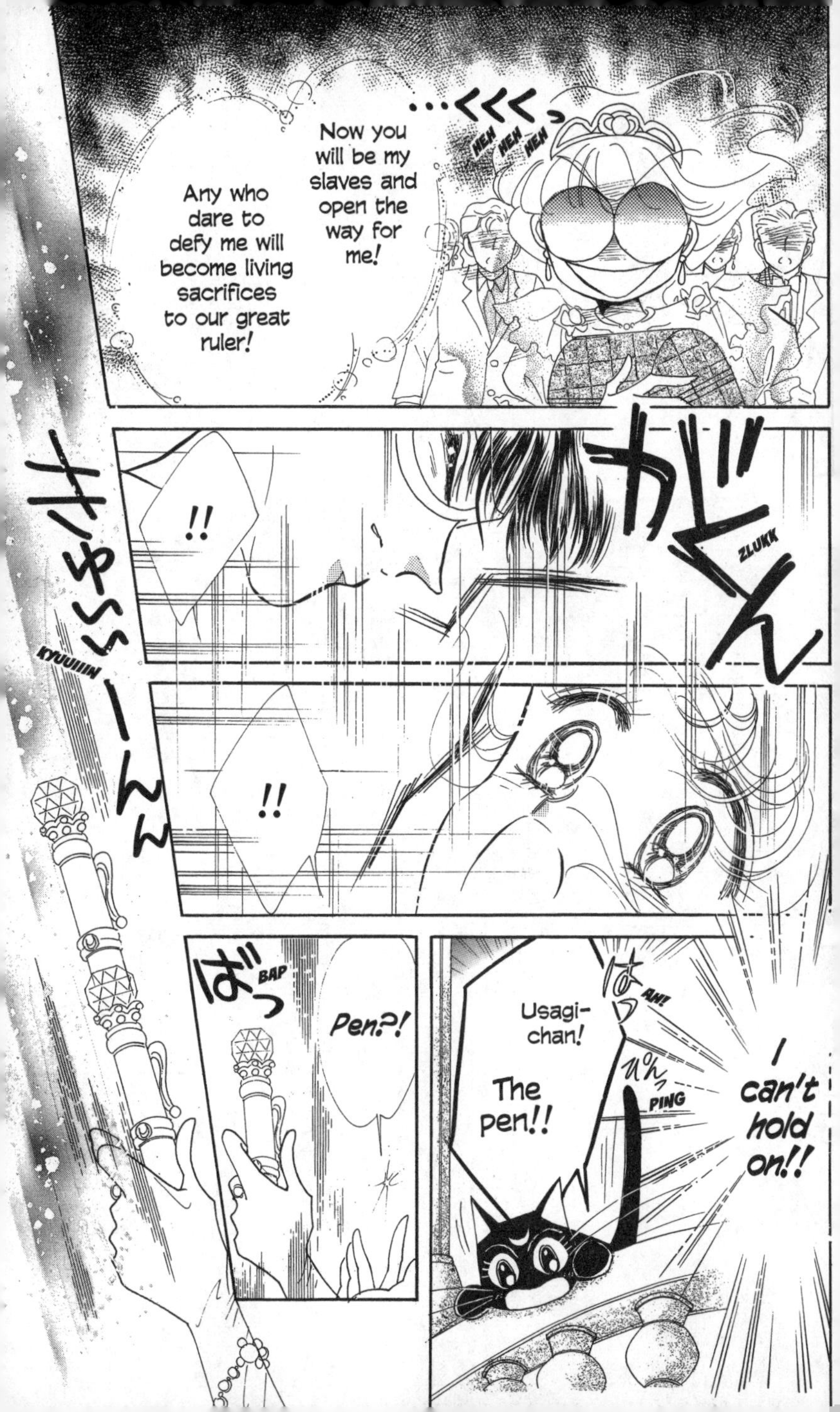
…くくく
HEH HEH HEH
Now you will be my slaves and open the way for me!
Any who dare to defy me will become living sacrifices to our great ruler!
がごん
ZLUKK
!!
!!
きゅいいーんん
KYUUIIIN
はっ
AH!
Usagi-chan!
The pen!!
ぴん
PING
I can't hold on!!
ばっ
BAP
Pen?!

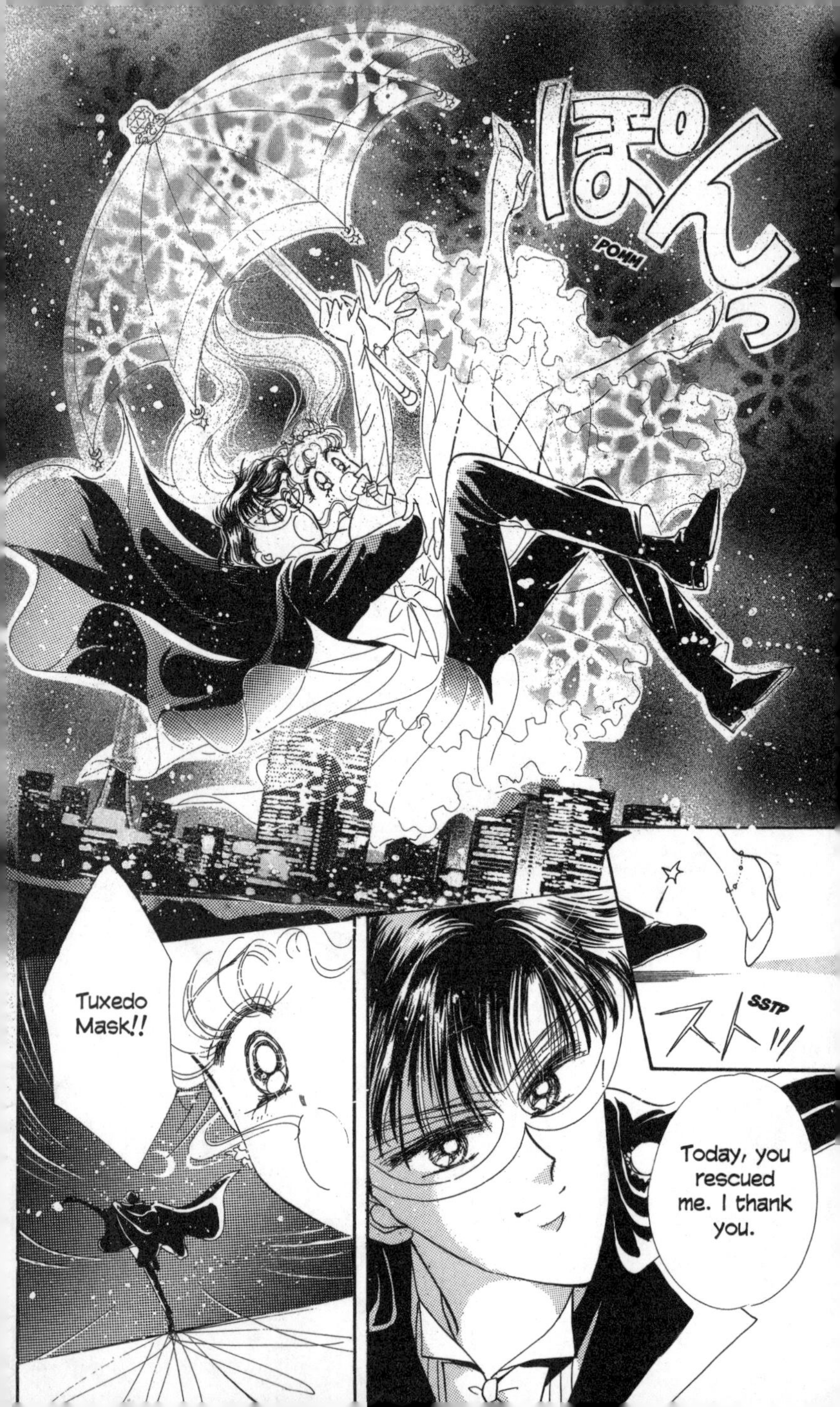

ぽんっ
POMM
ストッ
SSTP
Today, you rescued me. I thank you.
Tuxedo Mask!!

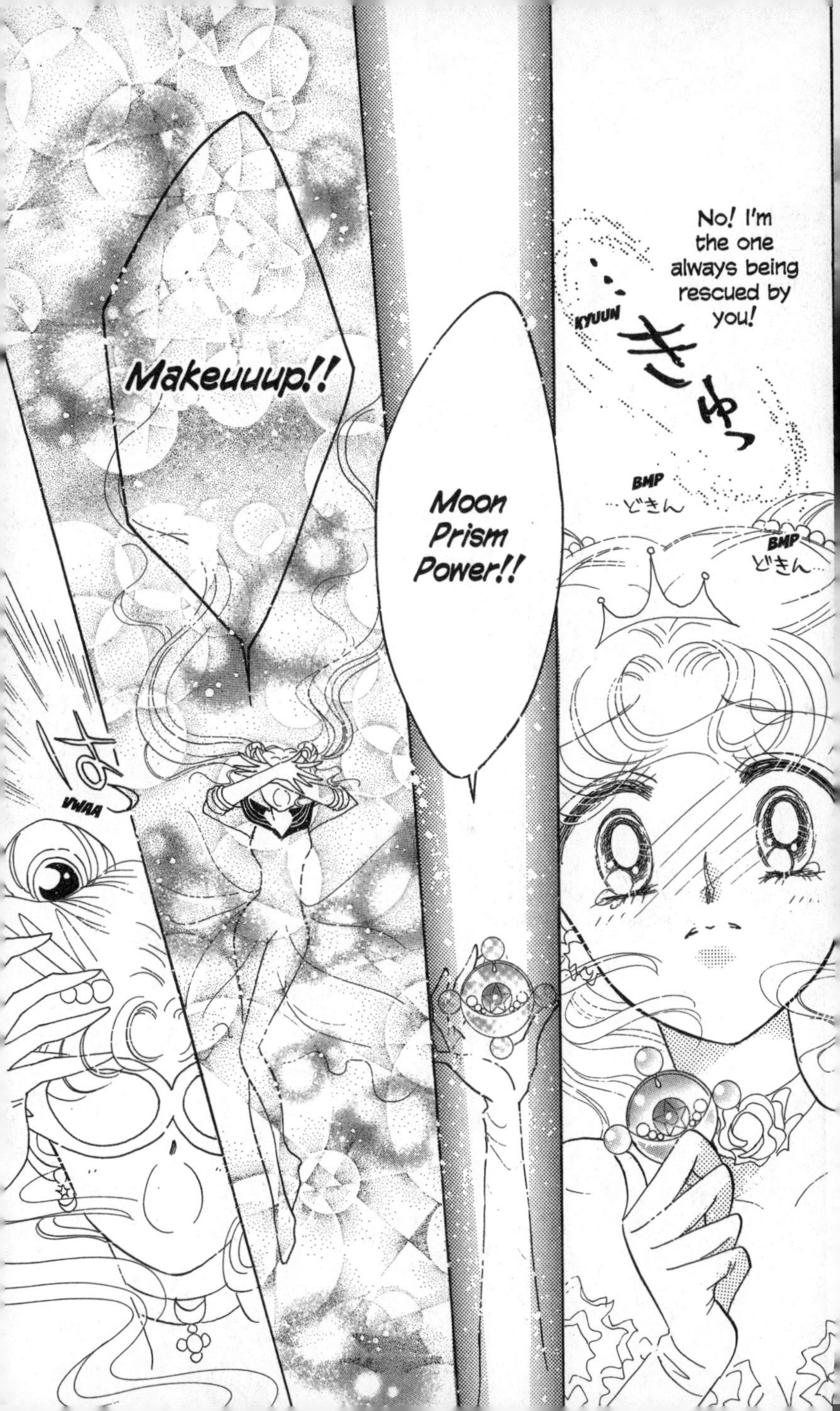
No! I'm the one always being rescued by you!
KYUUN
きゅっ
BMP
…どきん
BMP
どきん…
Moon Prism Power!!
Makeuuup!!
VWAA
はっ

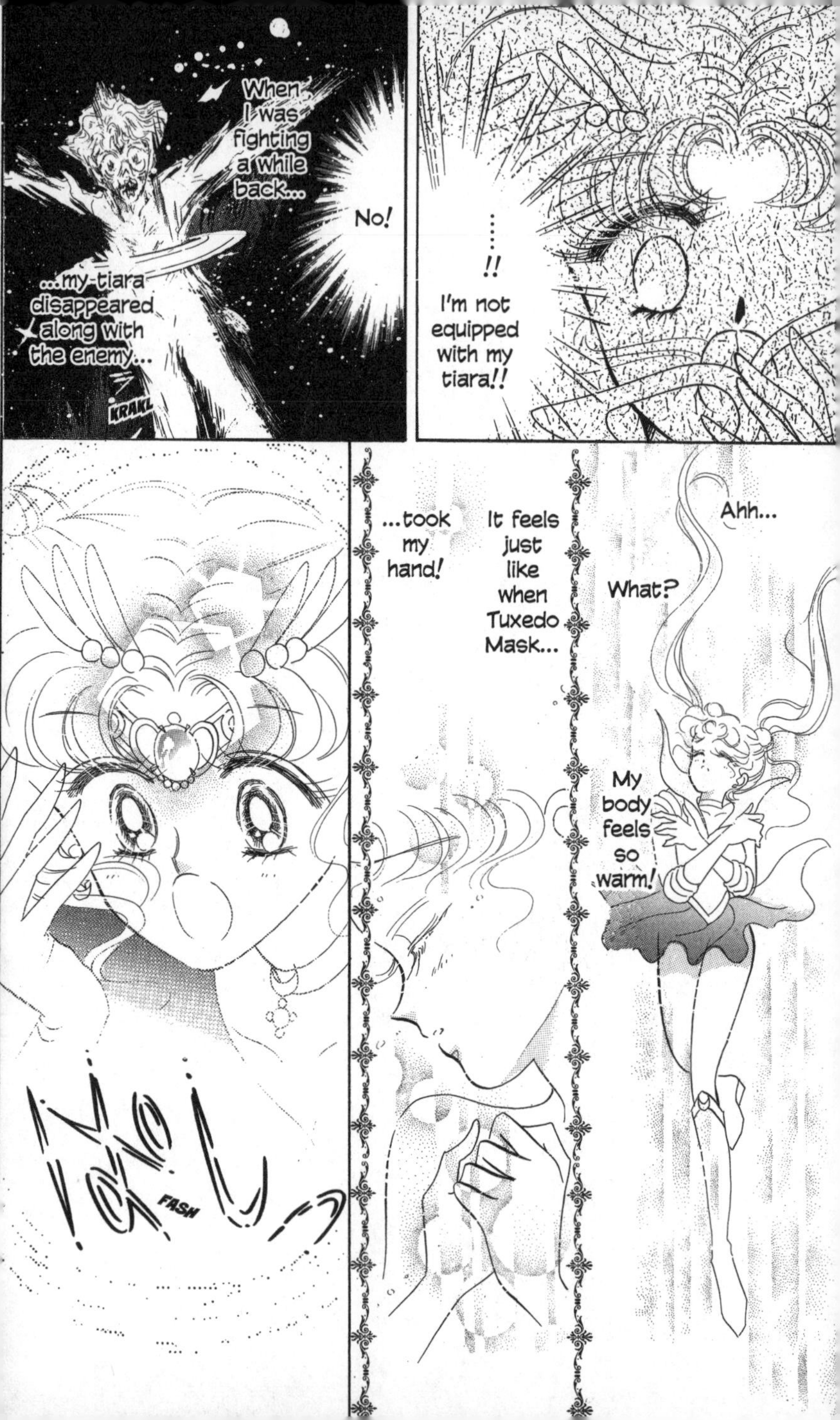

......
!!
I'm not equipped with my tiara!!
When I was fighting a while back...
No!
...my tiara disappeared along with the enemy...
KRAKL
Ahh...
What?
My body feels so warm!
It feels just like when Tuxedo Mask...
...took my hand!
FASH

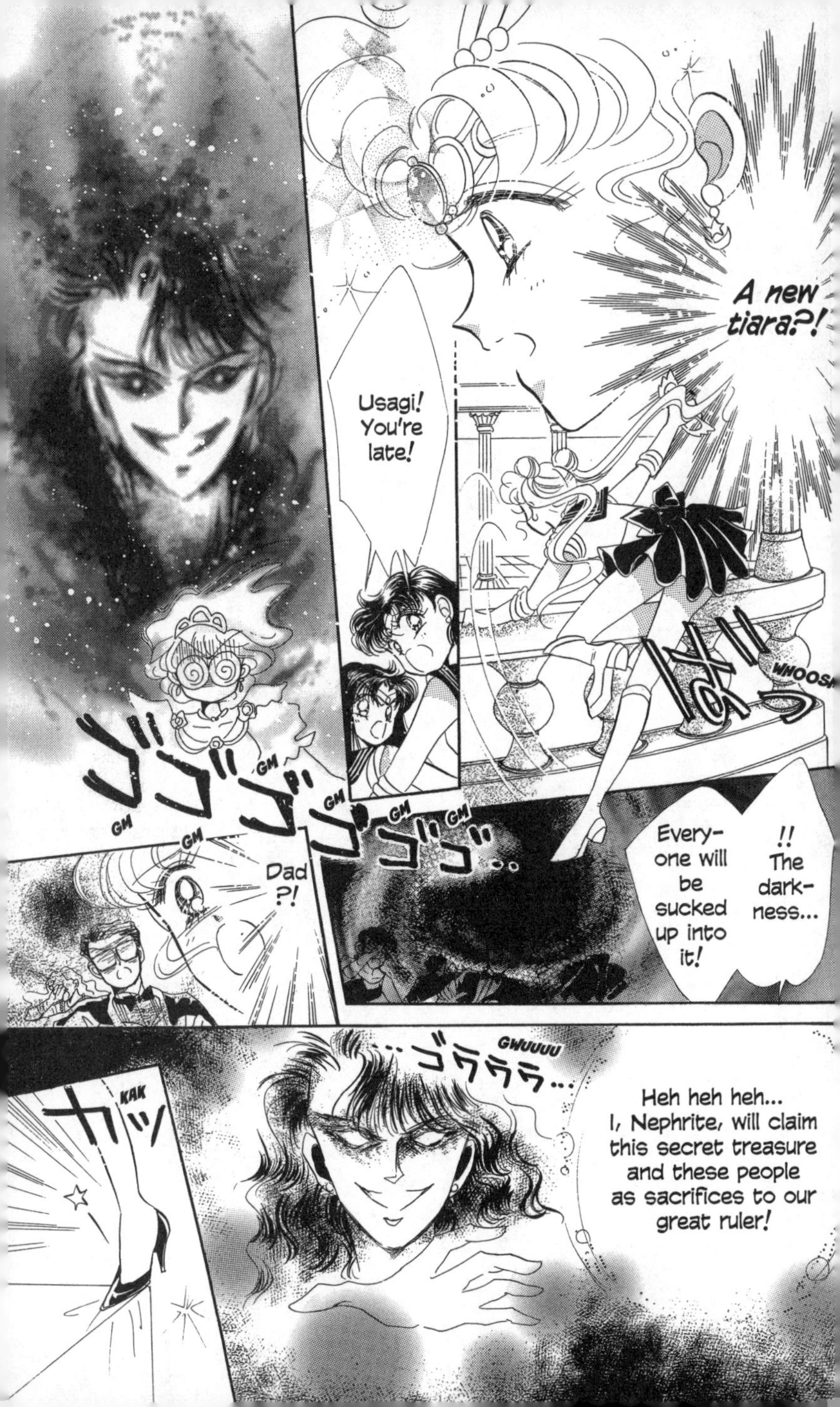
A new tiara?!
WHOOSH
Usagi! You're late!
GM
GM
GM
GM
GM
GM
!! The darkness...
Every-one will be sucked up into it!
Dad?!
GWUUUU
Heh heh heh... I, Nephrite, will claim this secret treasure and these people as sacrifices to our great ruler!
KAK

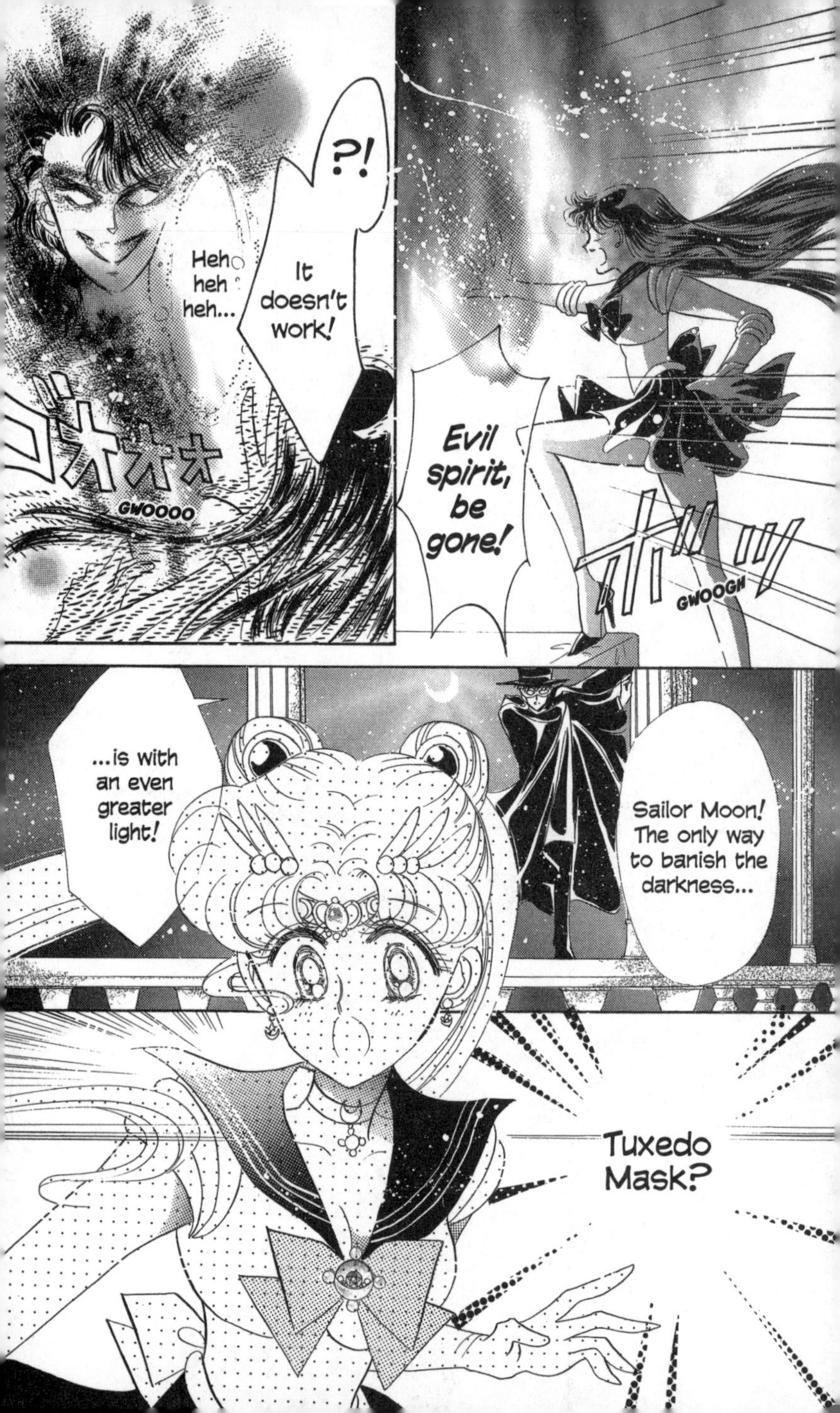
Evil spirit, be gone!
GWOOGH
?!
It doesn't work!
Heh heh heh...
GWOOOO
Sailor Moon! The only way to banish the darkness...
...is with an even greater light!
Tuxedo Mask?

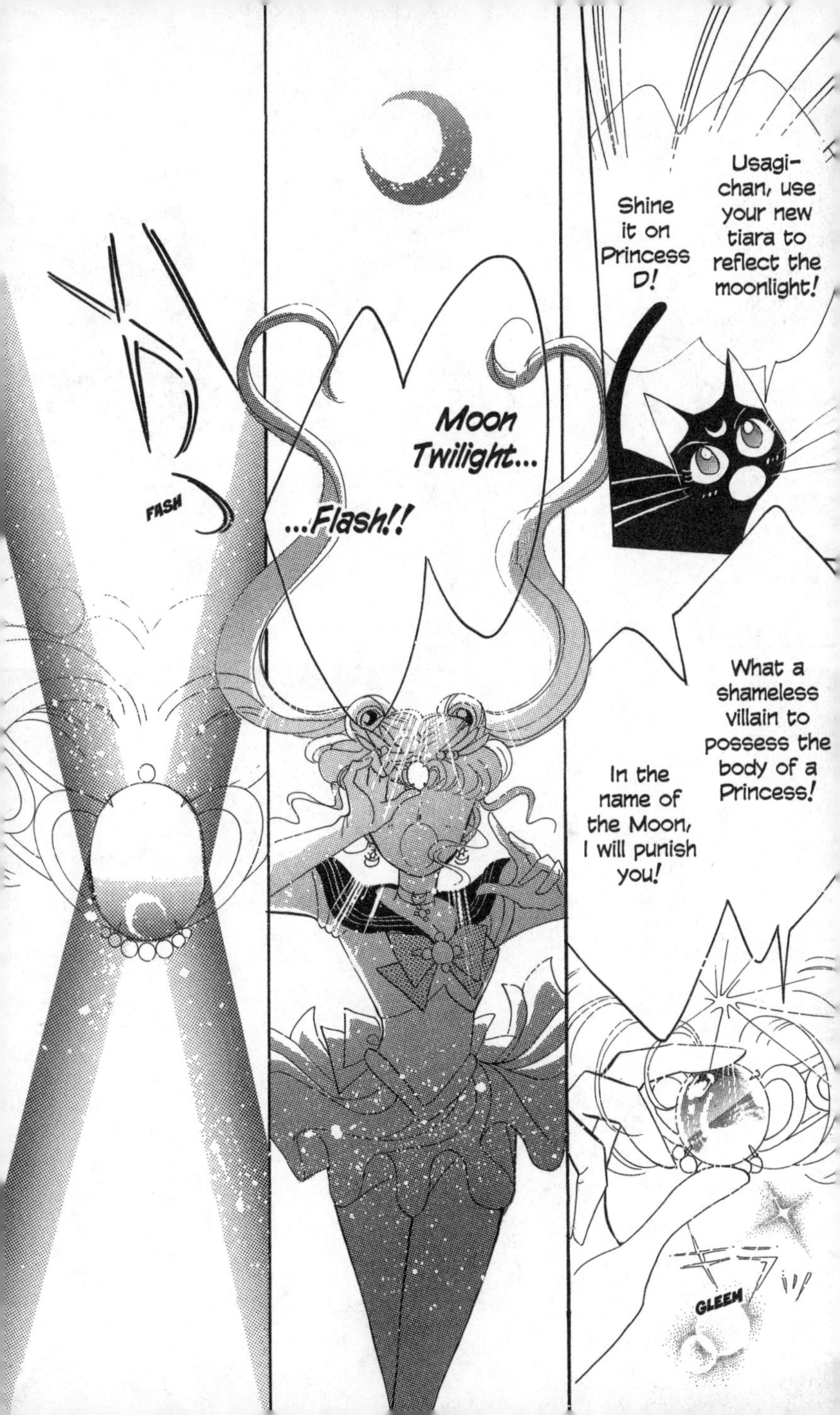

Usagi-chan, use your new tiara to reflect the moonlight!
Shine it on Princess D!
What a shameless villain to possess the body of a Princess!
In the name of the Moon, I will punish you!
GLEEM
Moon Twilight...
...Flash!!
FASH

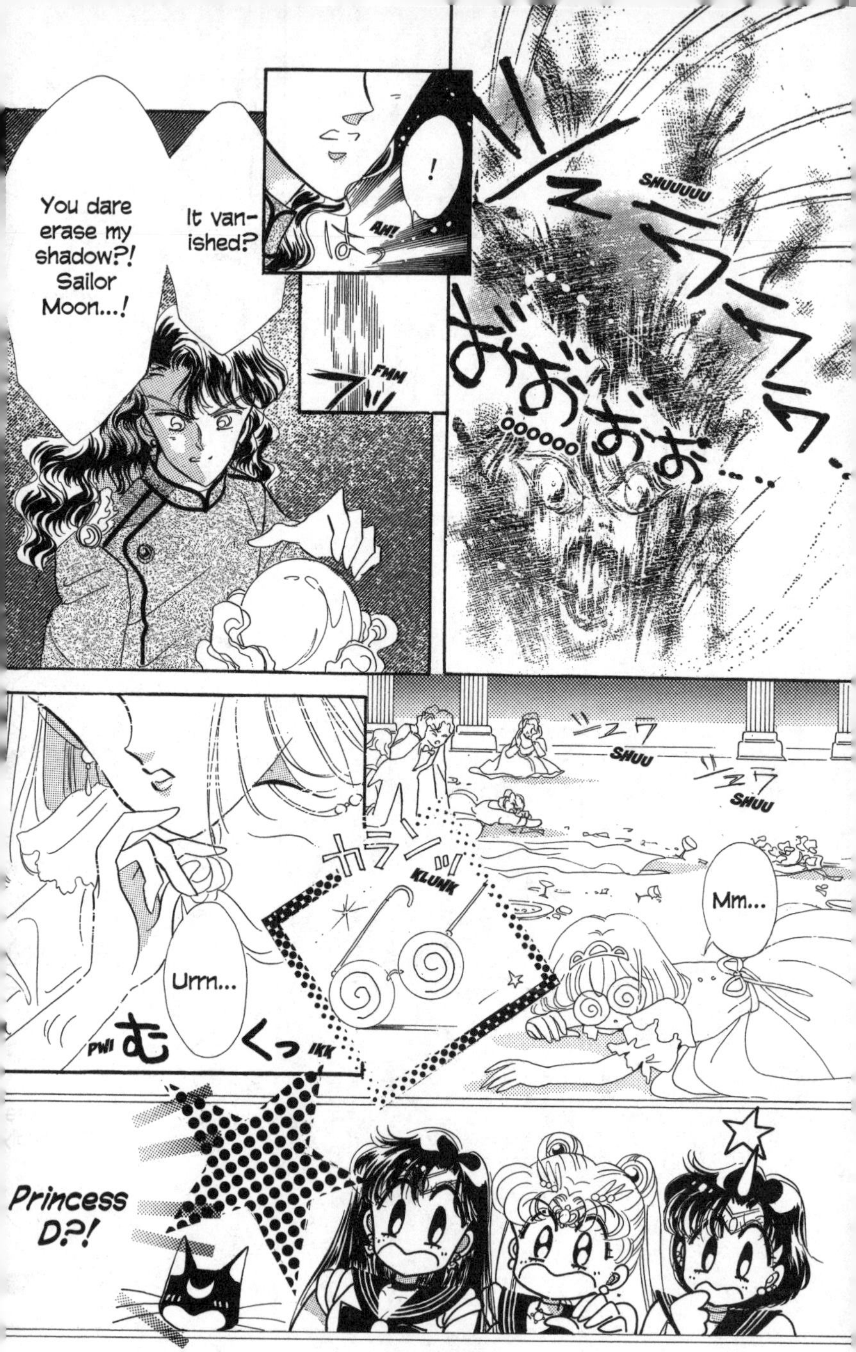
SHUUUUU
OOOOOOO
!
AH!
FMM
It van-
ished?
You dare
erase my
shadow?!
Sailor
Moon...!
SHUU
SHUU
KLUNK
Mm...
Urrn...
IKK
PWI
Princess
D?!

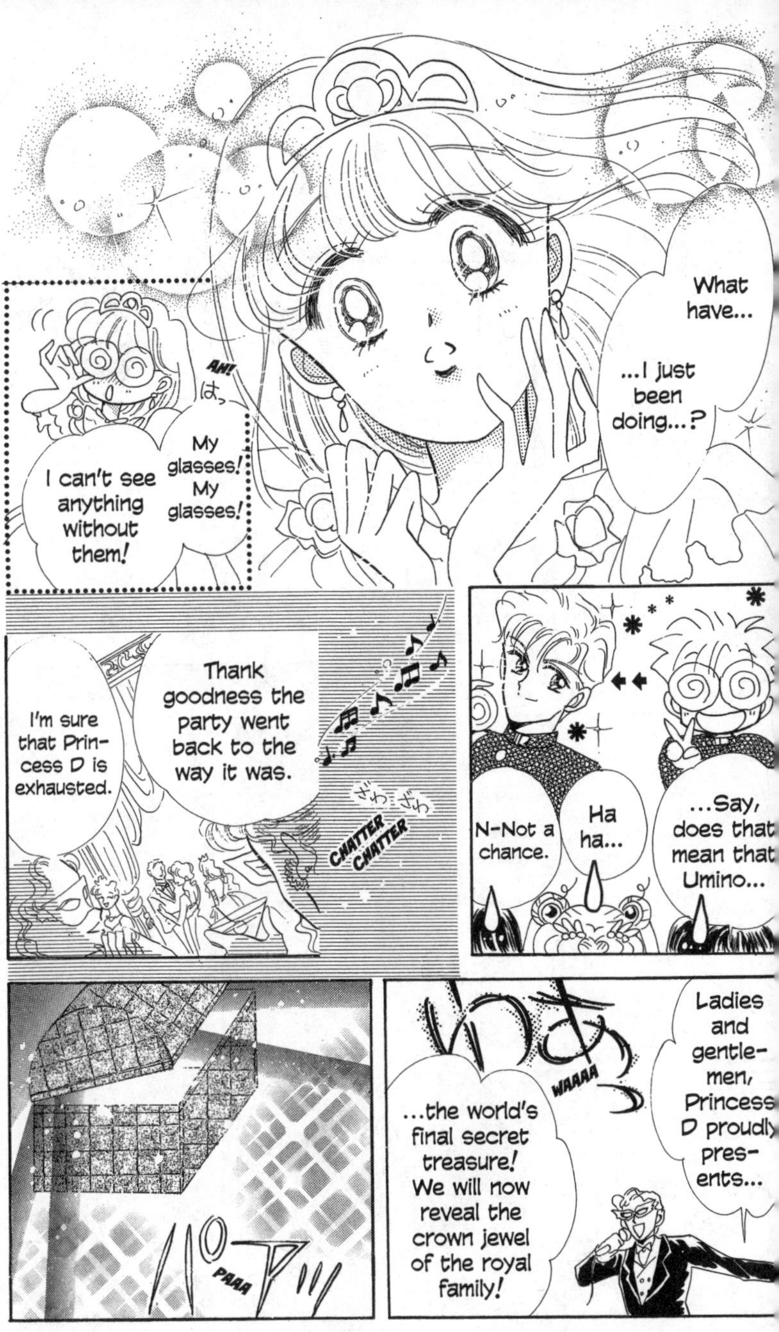
What have...
...I just been doing...?
AH!
はっ
My glasses! My glasses!
I can't see anything without them!
...Say, does that mean that Umino...
Ha ha...
N-Not a chance.
Thank goodness the party went back to the way it was.
I'm sure that Princess D is exhausted.
ざわ ざわ
CHATTER CHATTER
Ladies and gentlemen, Princess D proudly presents...
わあっ
WAAAA
...the world's final secret treasure! We will now reveal the crown jewel of the royal family!
パーッ
PAAA

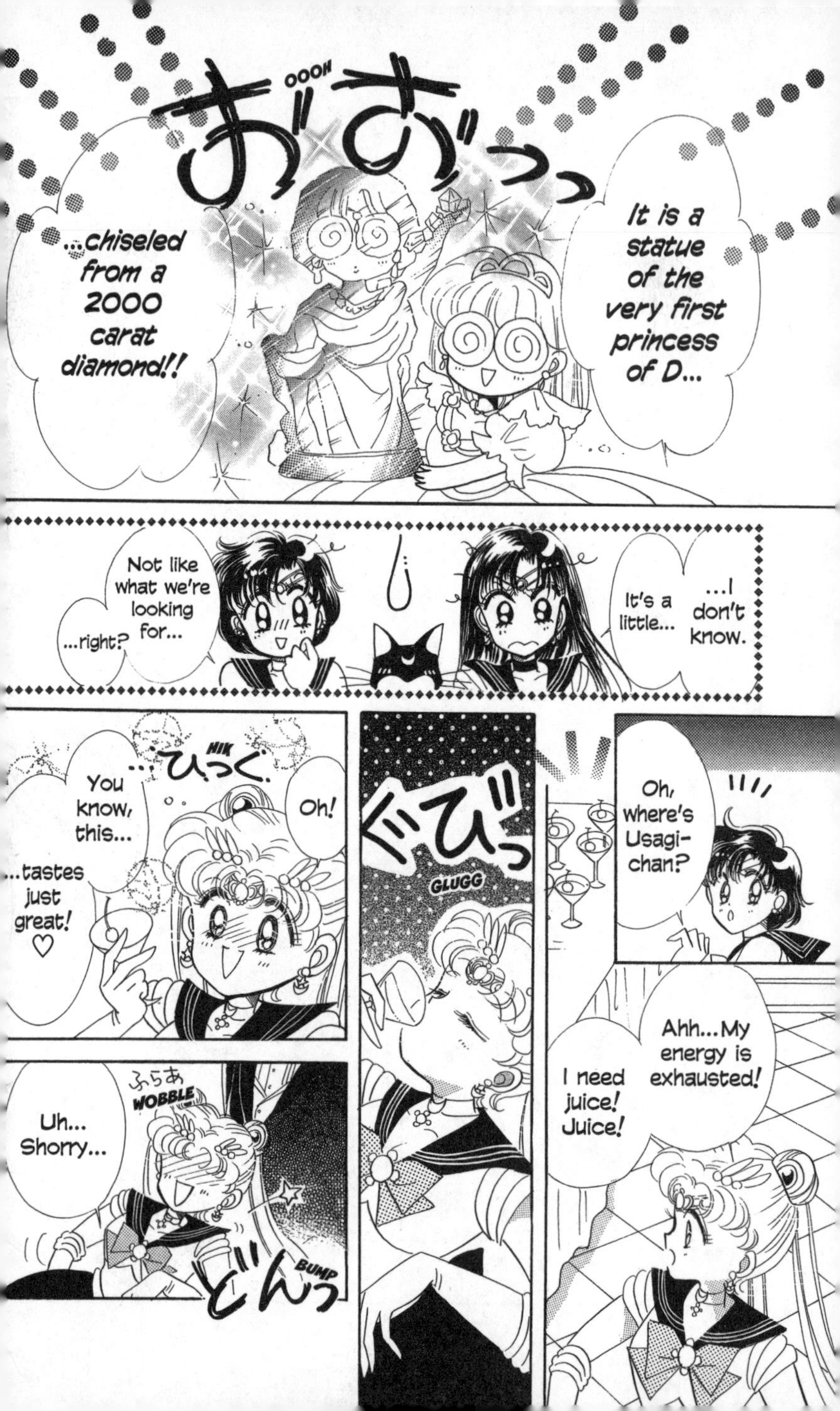
おおっっ
OOOH
It is a statue of the very first princess of D...
...chiseled from a 2000 carat diamond!!
It's a little...
...I don't know.
Not like what we're looking for...
...right?
Oh, where's Usagi-chan?
Ahh...My energy is exhausted!
I need juice! Juice!
ぐびっ
GLUGG
ひっく
HIK
Oh!
You know, this...
...tastes just great! ♡
ふらあ
WOBBLE
Uh... Shorry...
どんっ
BUMP

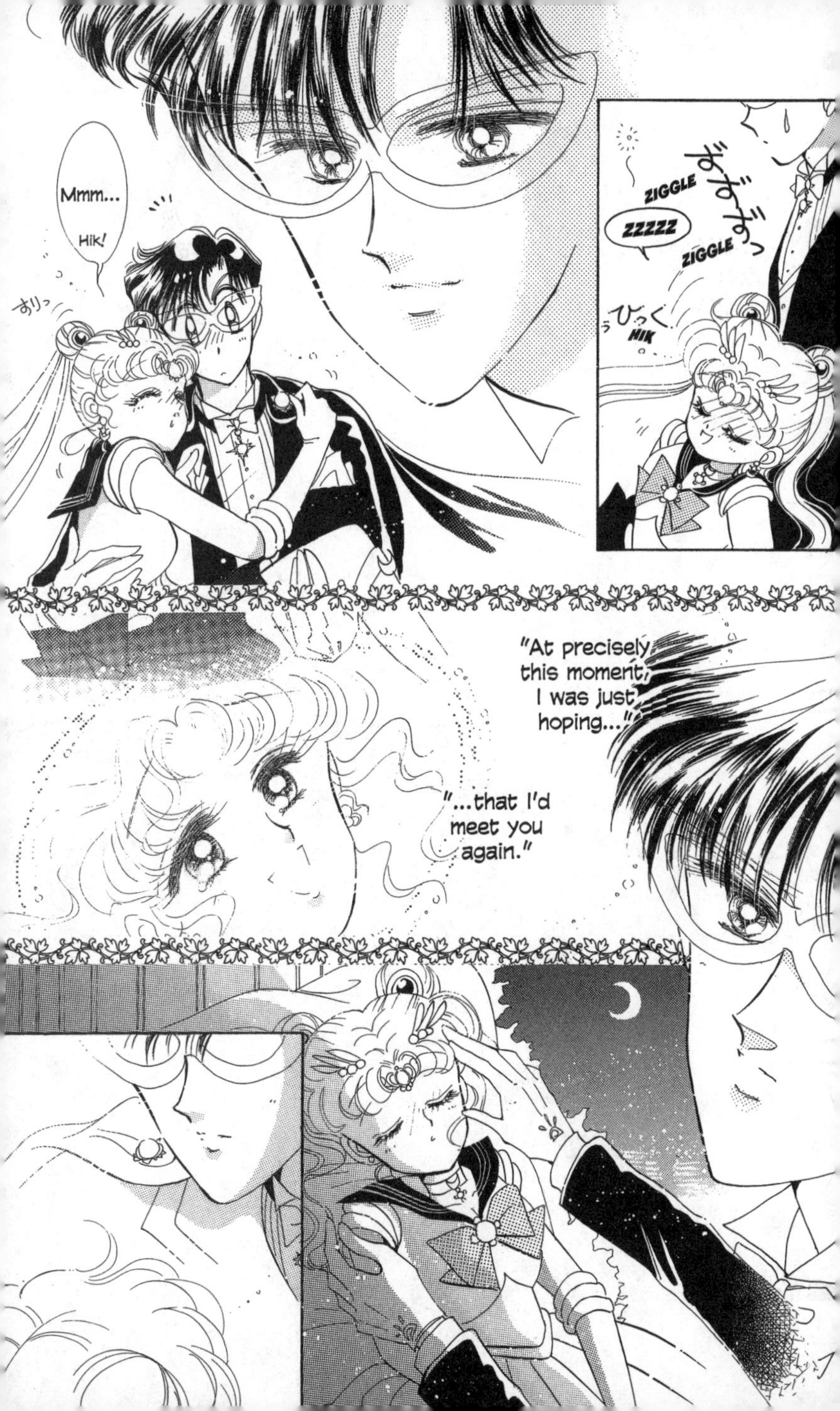

ずずずっ
ZIGGLE
ZZZZZ
ZIGGLE
ひっく
HIK
Mmm...
Hik!
すりっ
"At precisely this moment, I was just hoping..."
"...that I'd meet you again."

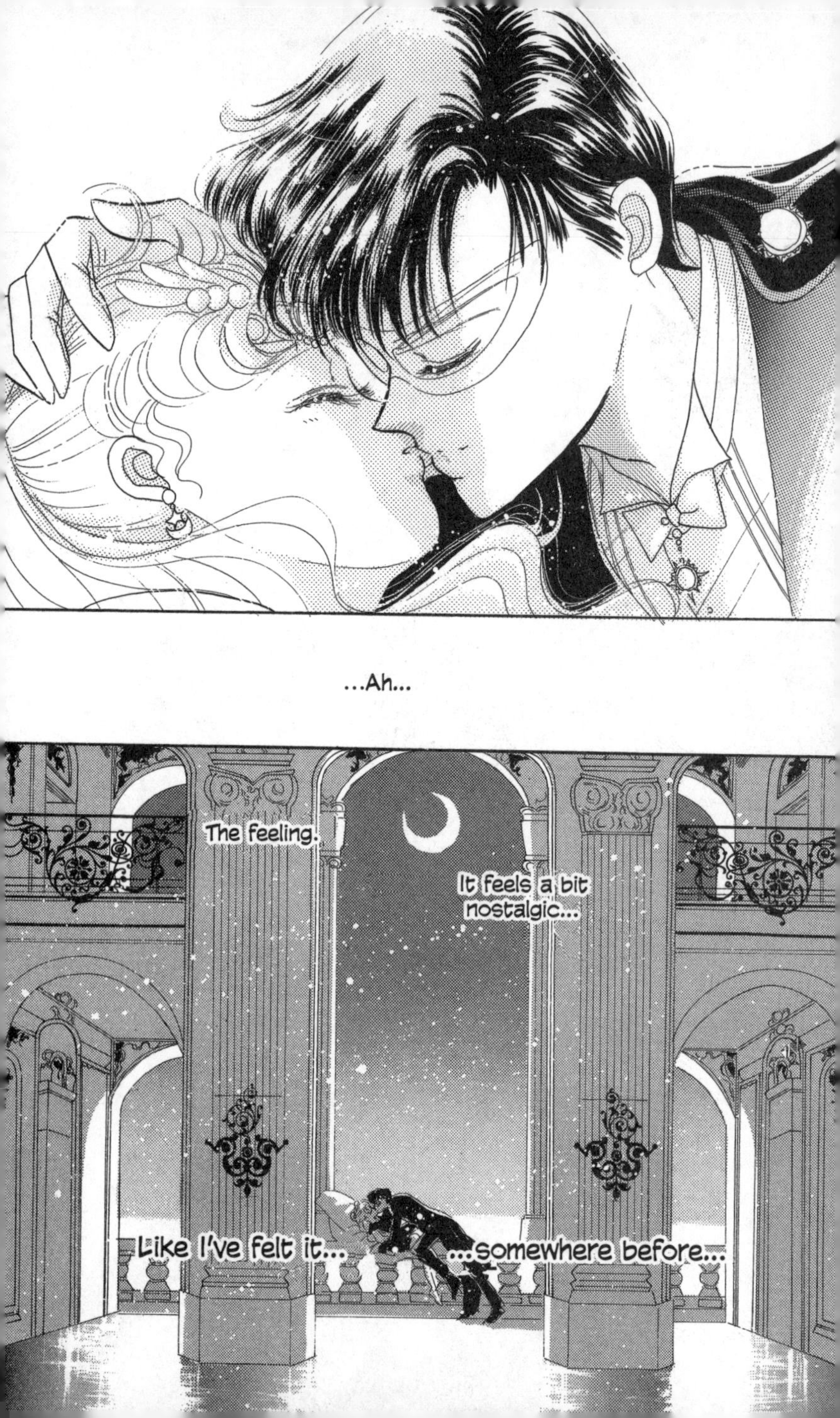
...Ah...
The feeling.
It feels a bit nostalgic...
Like I've felt it...
...somewhere before...

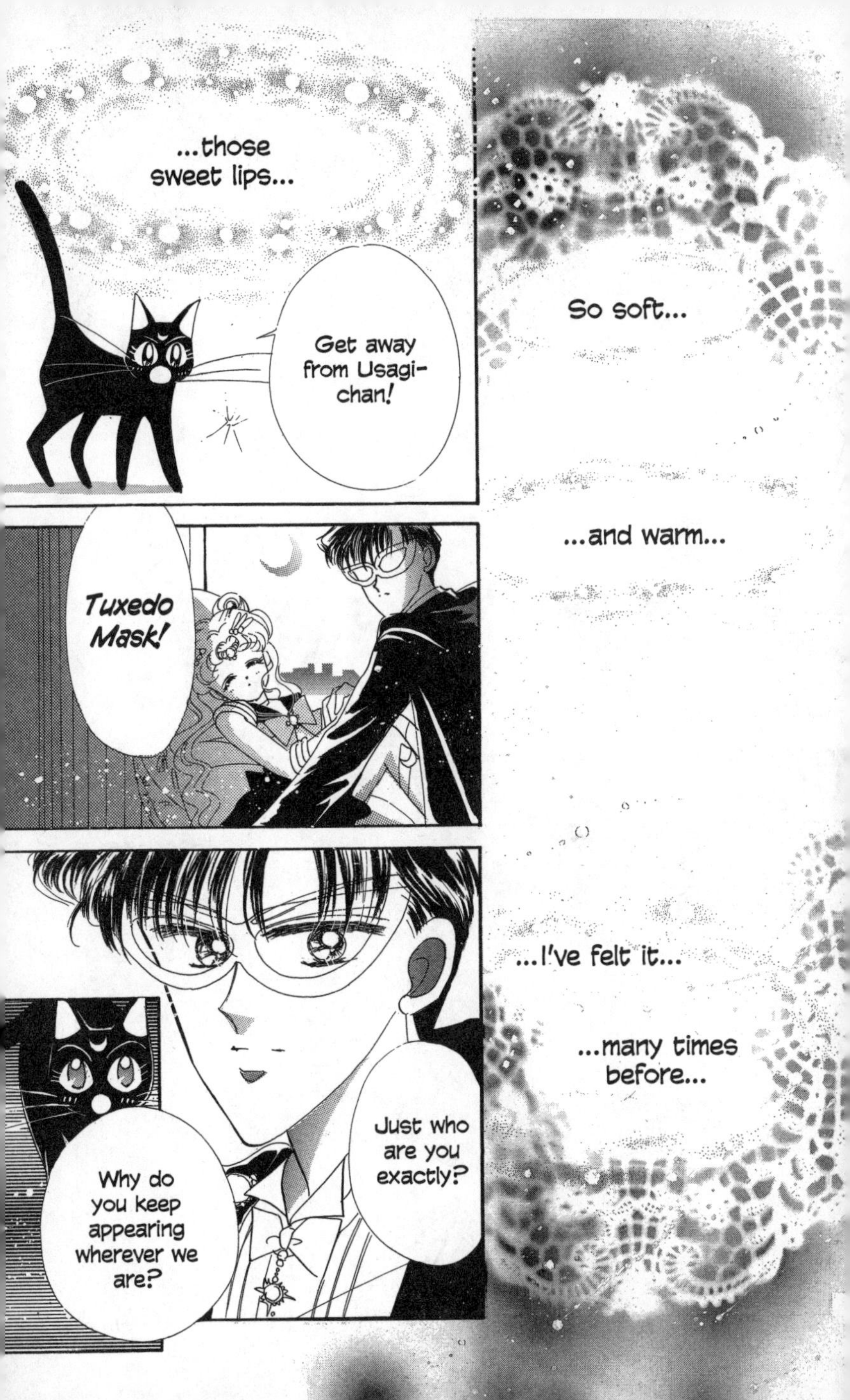
So soft...
...and warm...
...I've felt it...
...many times before...
...those sweet lips...
Get away from Usagi-chan!
Tuxedo Mask!
Just who are you exactly?
Why do you keep appearing wherever we are?

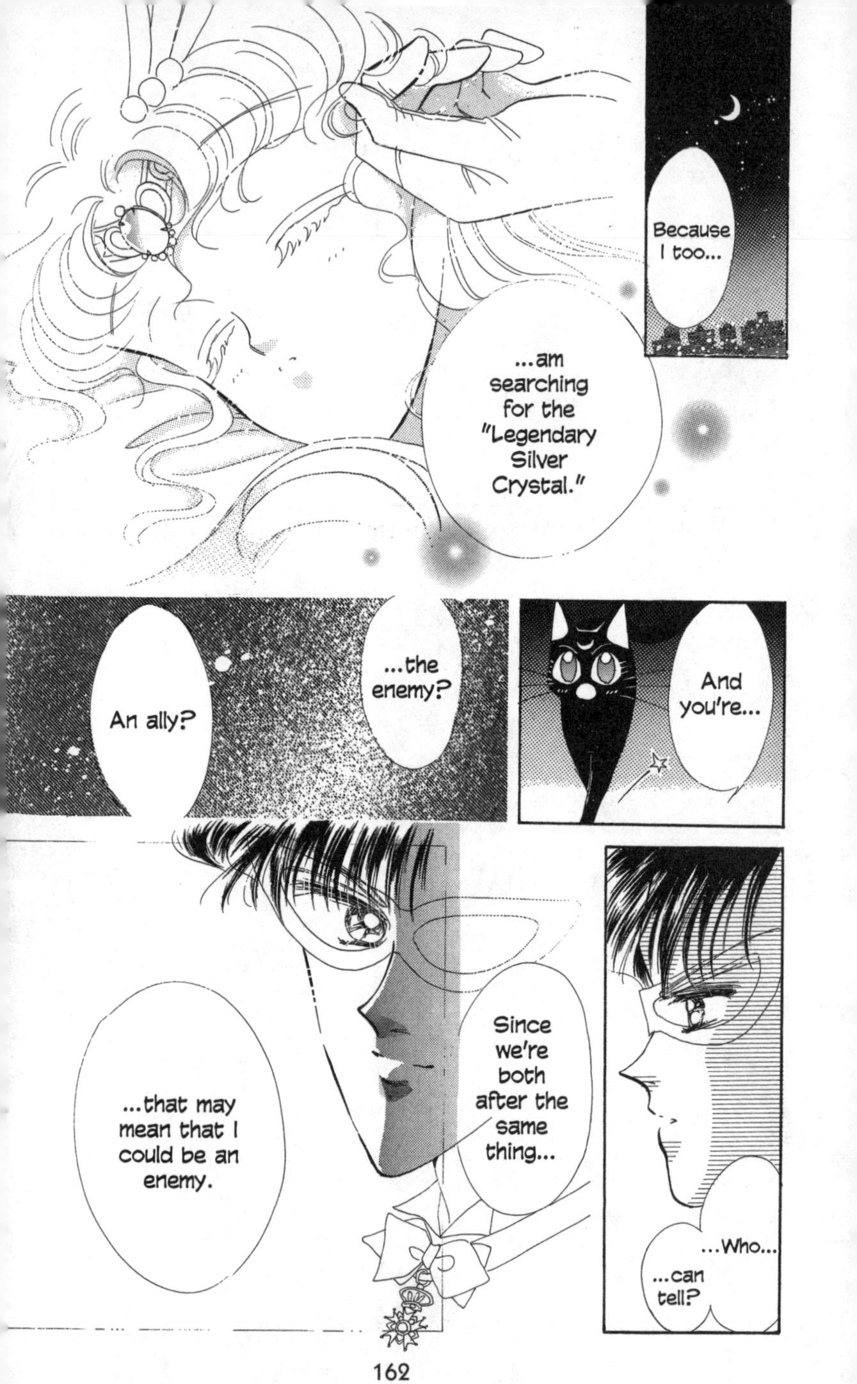
Because I too...
...am searching for the "Legendary Silver Crystal."
And you're...
...the enemy?
An ally?
...Who...
...can tell?
Since we're both after the same thing...
...that may mean that I could be an enemy.

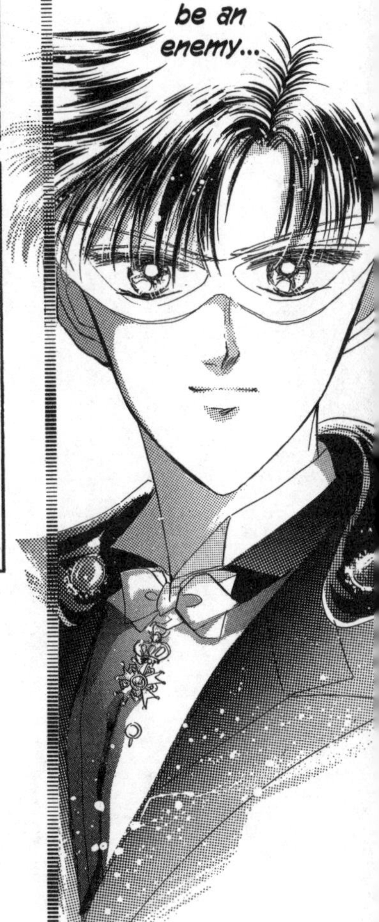

Could be an enemy...

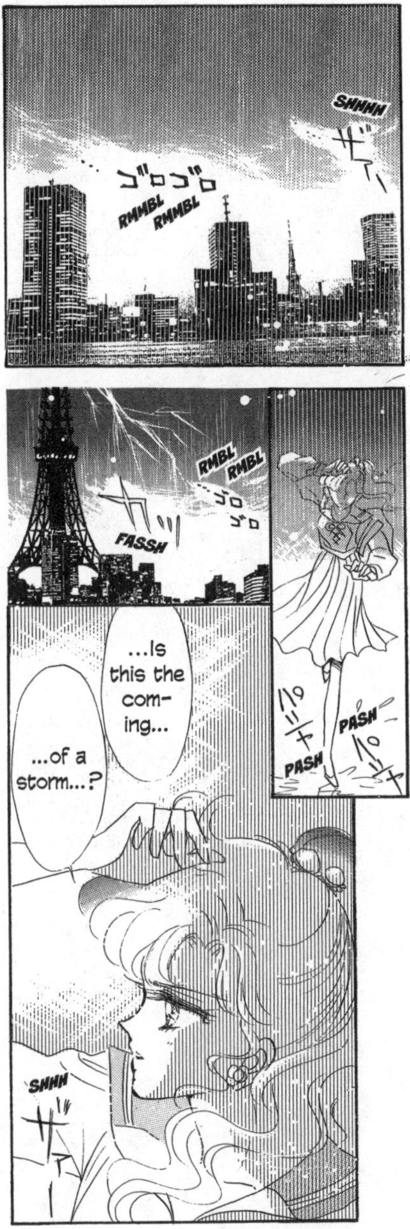

SHHHHH
ザァ
ゴロゴロ
RMMBL RMMBL
PASH
パシャ
PASH
パシャ
RMBL RMBL
ゴロゴロ
FASSH
カッ
...Is this the coming...
...of a storm...?
SHHH
ザァ

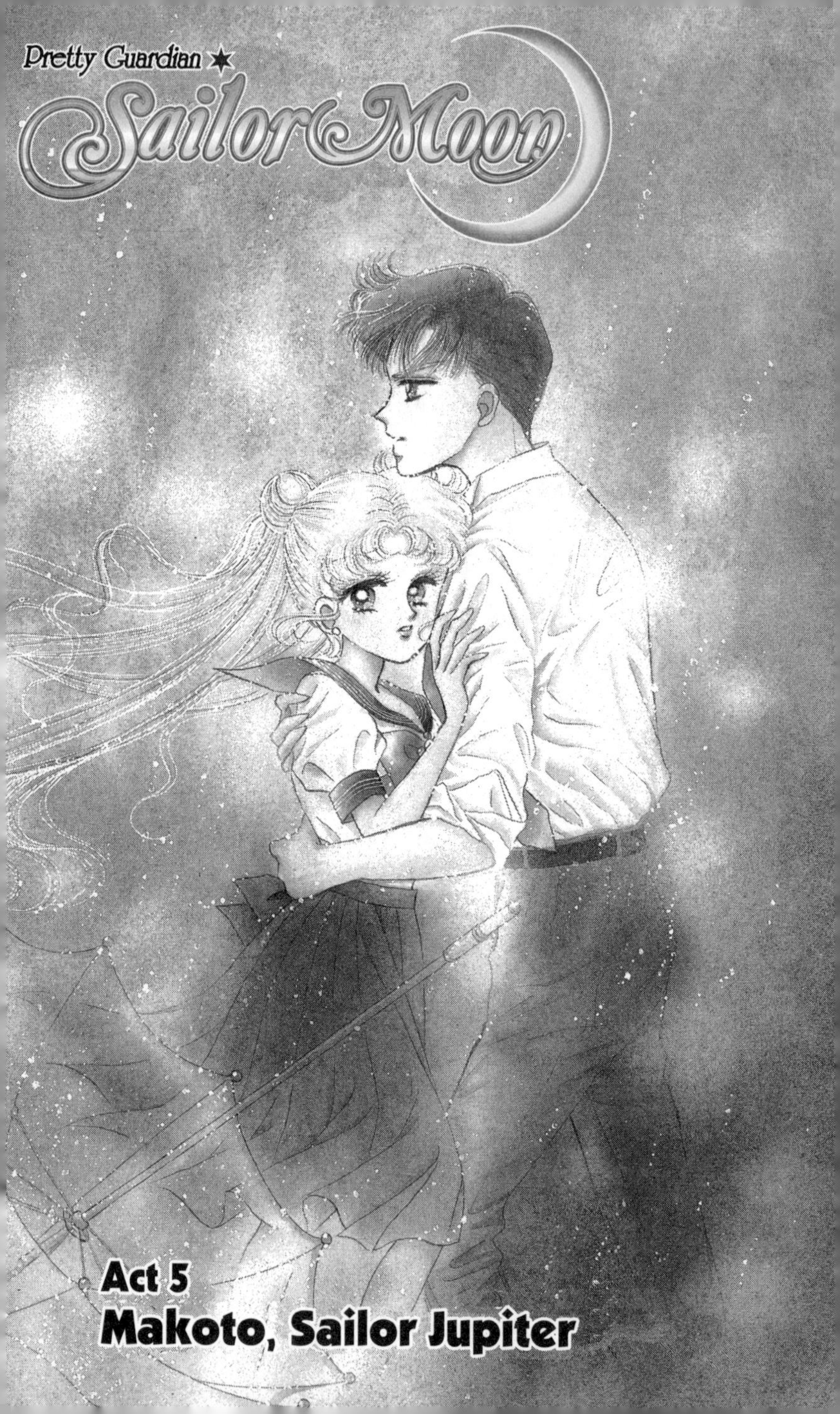
Pretty Guardian
Sailor Moon
Act 5
Makoto, Sailor Jupiter

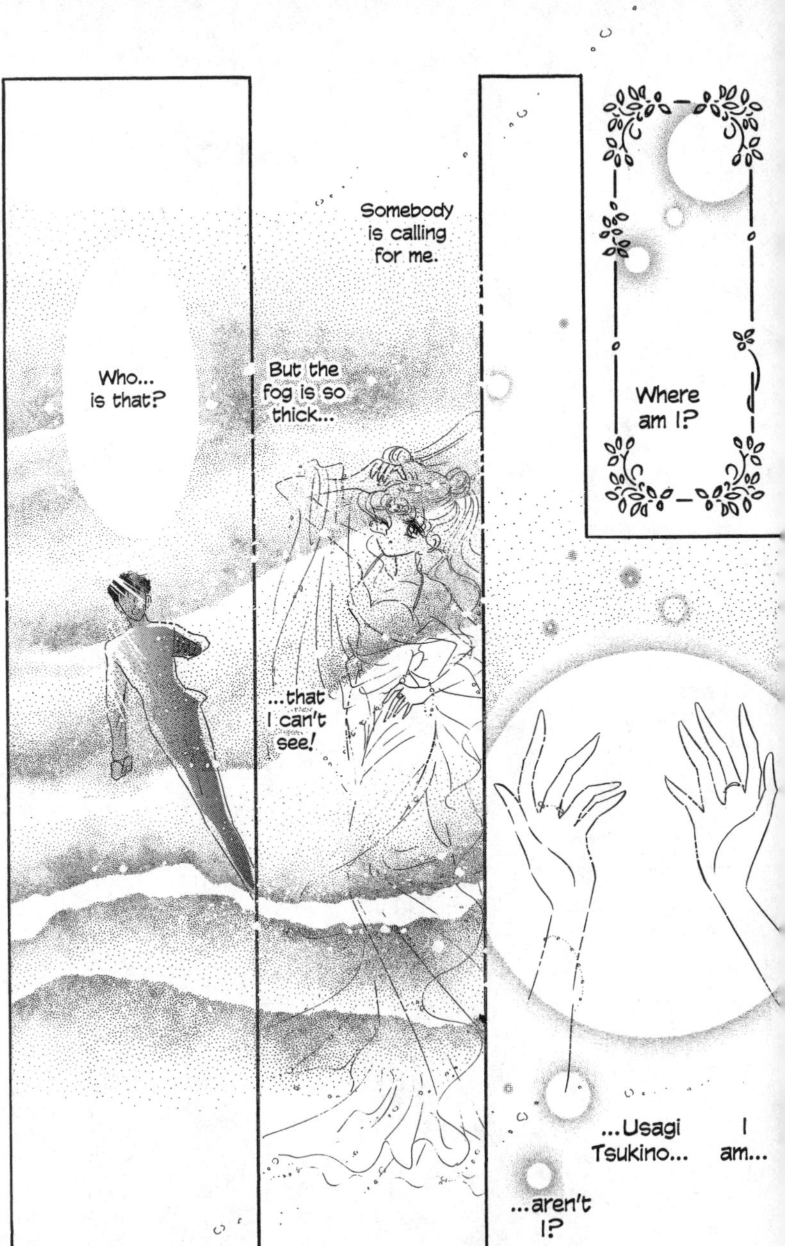
Where am I?
I am...
...Usagi Tsukino...
...aren't I?
Somebody is calling for me.
But the fog is so thick...
...that I can't see!
Who... is that?

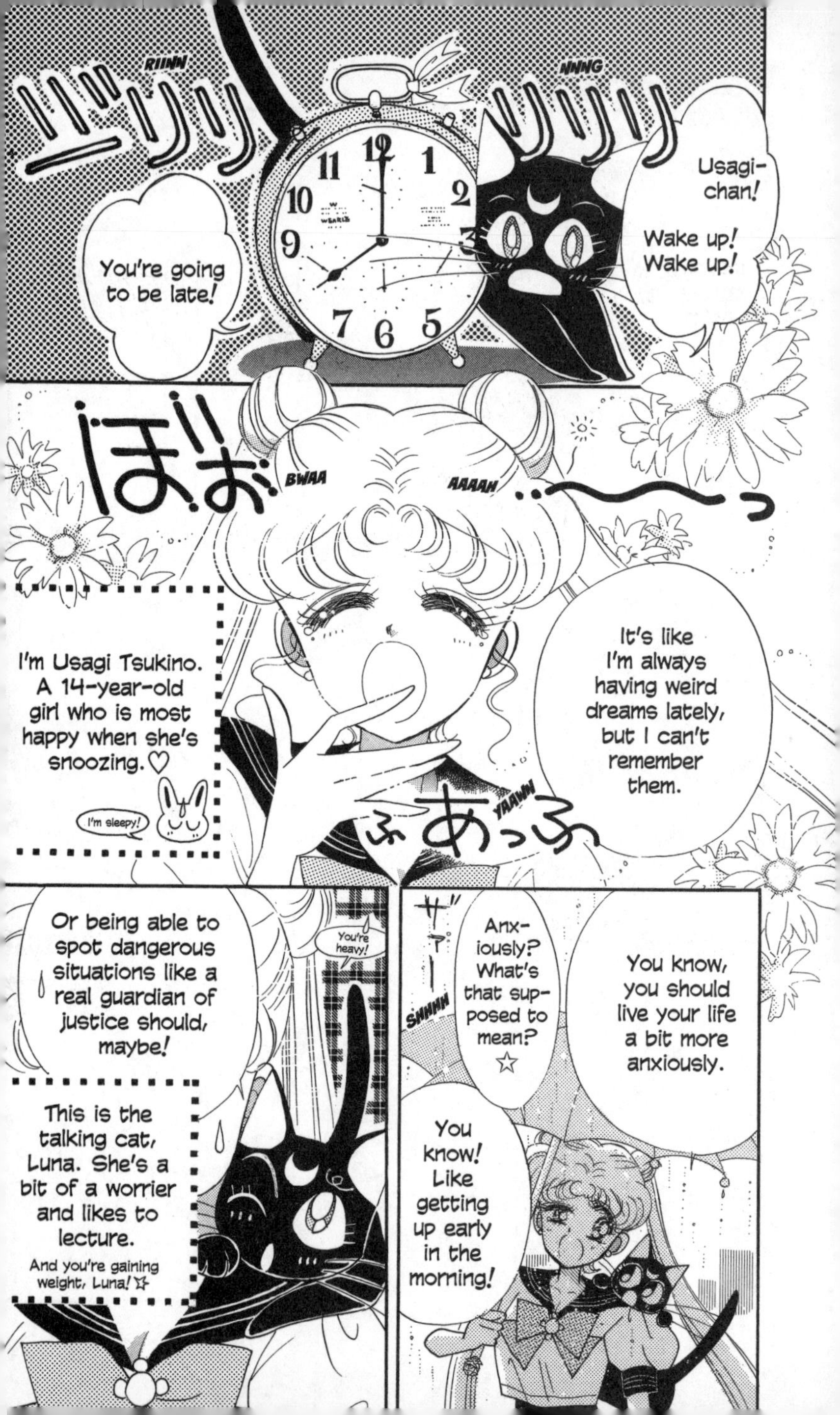
RIINN
NNNG
Usagi-chan!
Wake up! Wake up!
You're going to be late!
BWAA
AAAAH
It's like I'm always having weird dreams lately, but I can't remember them.
YAAWN
I'm Usagi Tsukino. A 14-year-old girl who is most happy when she's snoozing.♡
I'm sleepy!
You know, you should live your life a bit more anxiously.
Anxiously? What's that supposed to mean? ☆
SHHHH
You know! Like getting up early in the morning!
Or being able to spot dangerous situations like a real guardian of justice should, maybe!
You're heavy!
This is the talking cat, Luna. She's a bit of a worrier and likes to lecture.
And you're gaining weight, Luna! ☆

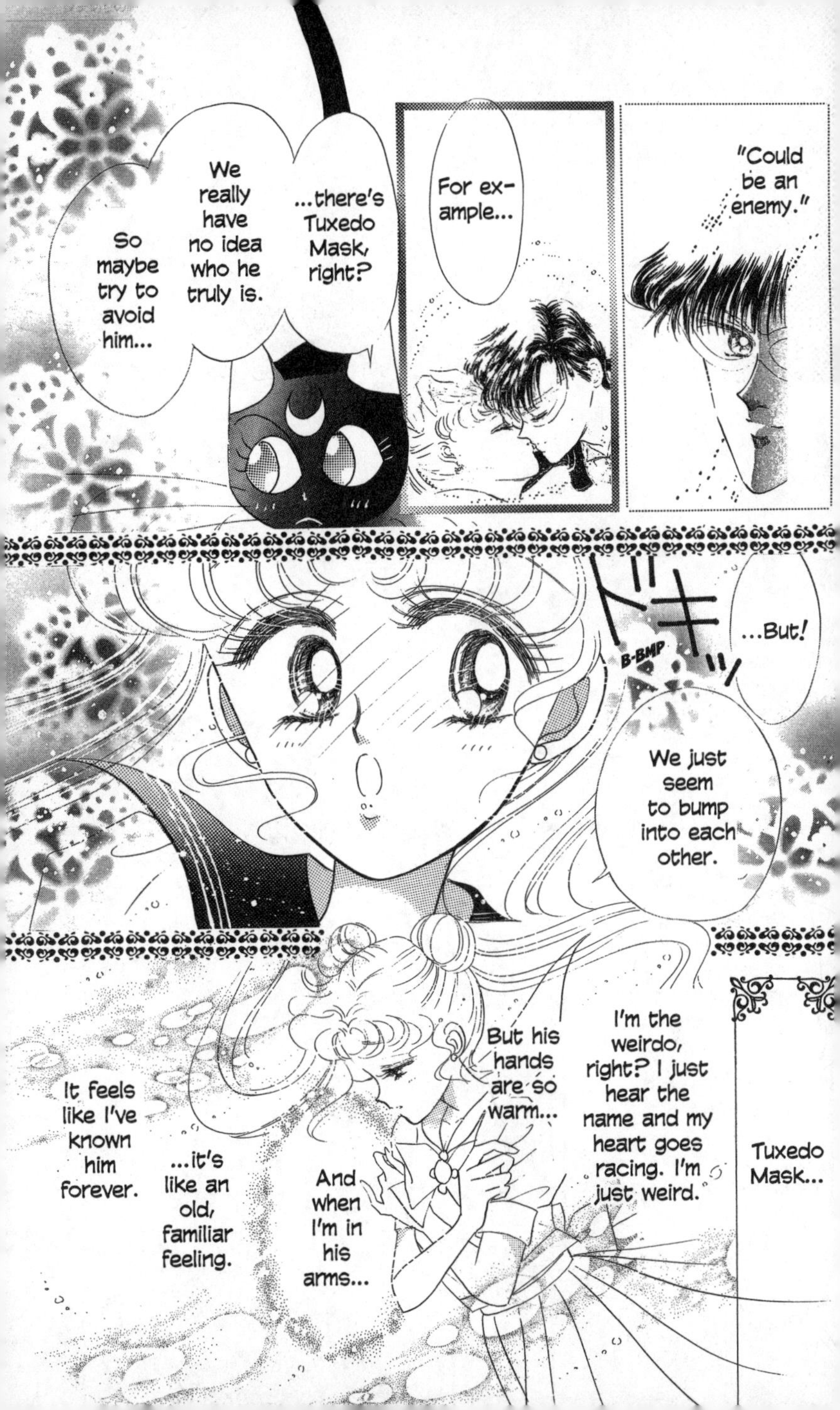
"Could be an enemy."
For ex-ample...
...there's Tuxedo Mask, right?
We really have no idea who he truly is.
So maybe try to avoid him...
...But!
ドキッ
B-BMP
We just seem to bump into each other.
Tuxedo Mask...
I'm the weirdo, right? I just hear the name and my heart goes racing. I'm just weird.
But his hands are so warm...
And when I'm in his arms...
...it's like an old, familiar feeling.
It feels like I've known him forever.

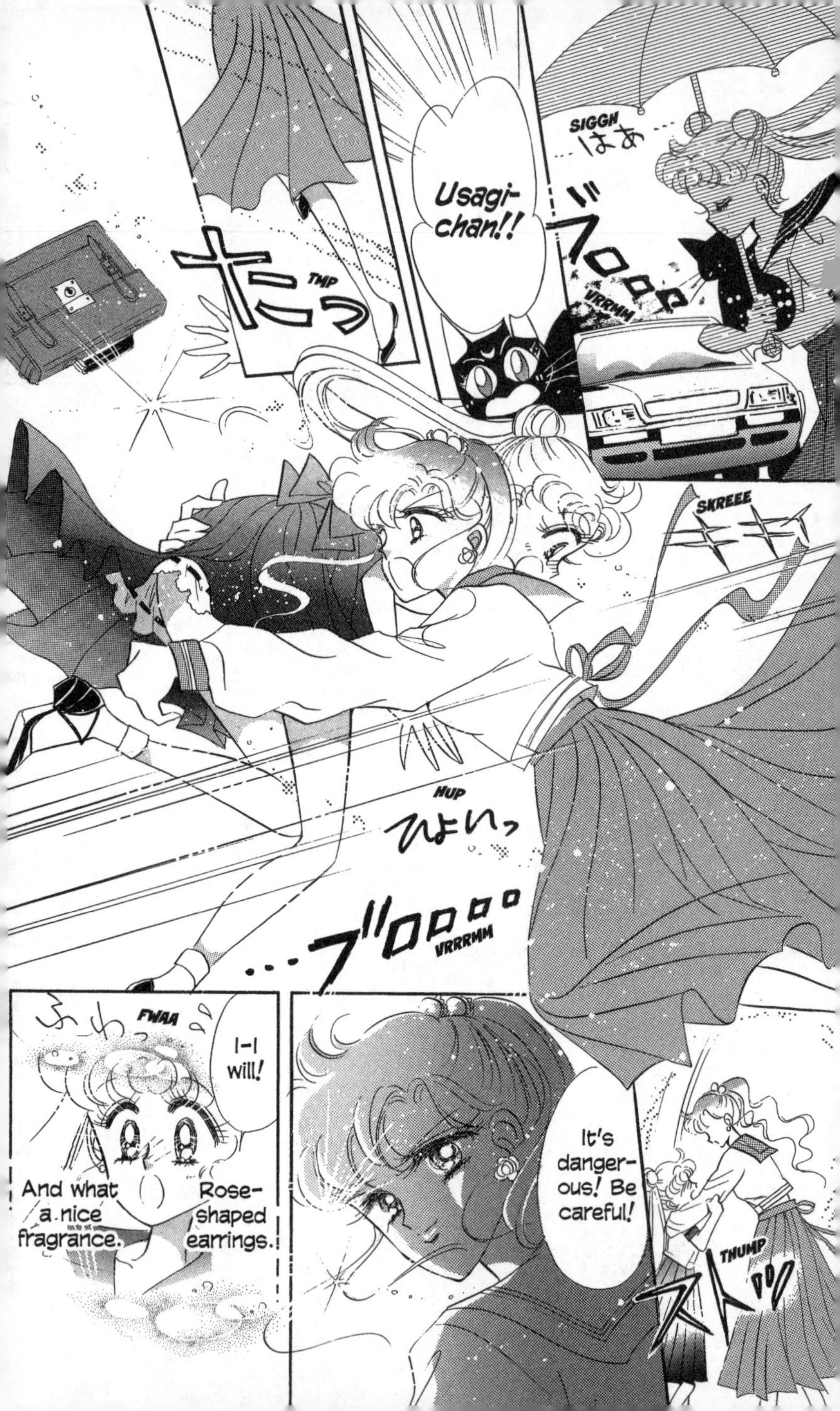
SIGGH
はあ
ブロロロ
VRRRMM
Usagi-chan!!
たっ
TMP
SKREEE
キキキ
HUP
ひょいっ
…ブロロロロ
VRRRMM
It's danger-ous! Be careful!
THUMP
ふわっ
FWAA
I-I will!
Rose-shaped earrings.
And what a nice fragrance.

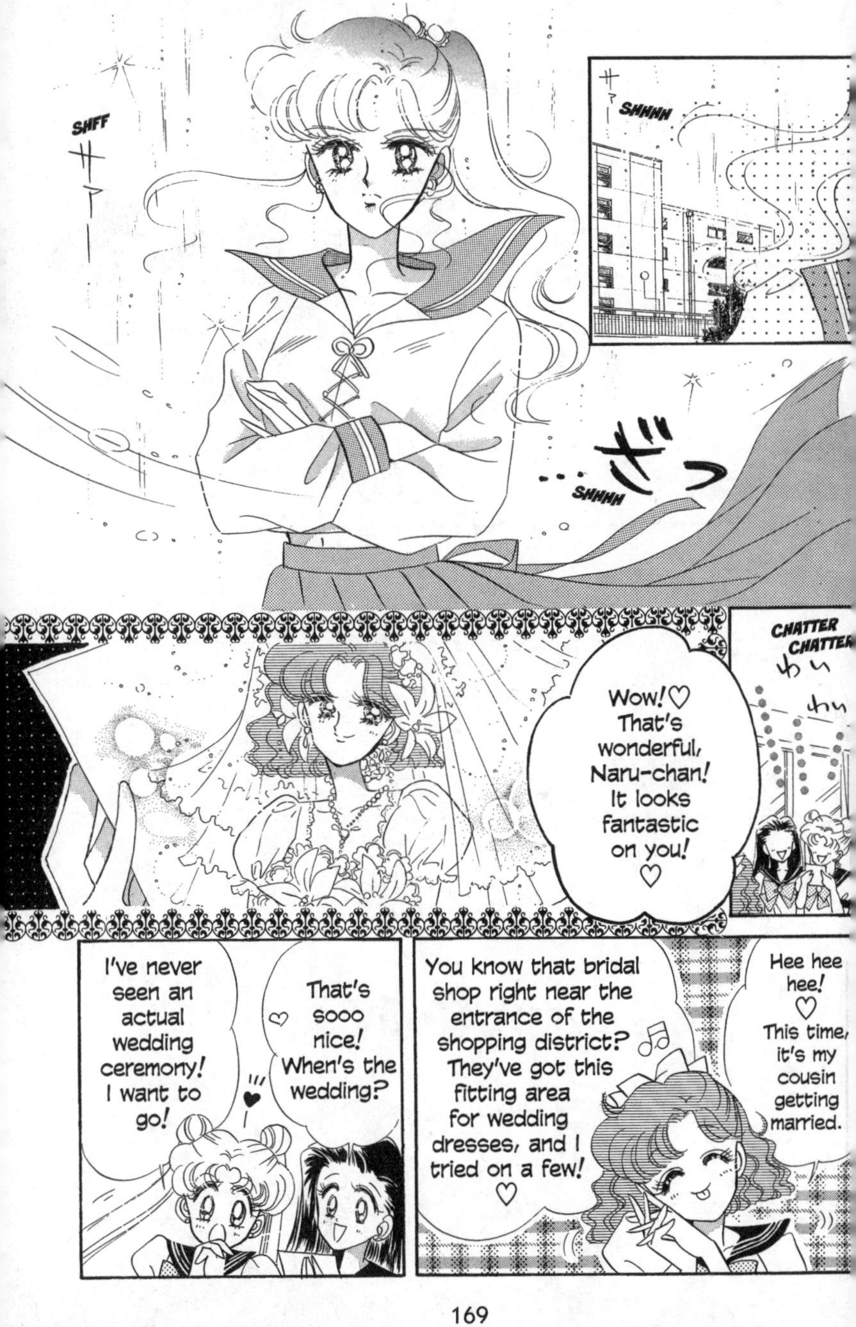
SHHHH
サァー
SHFF
サァー
...ざっ
SHHHH
CHATTER CHATTER
わいわい
Wow!♡ That's wonderful, Naru-chan! It looks fantastic on you! ♡
Hee hee hee! ♡ This time, it's my cousin getting married.
You know that bridal shop right near the entrance of the shopping district? They've got this fitting area for wedding dresses, and I tried on a few! ♡
That's sooo nice! When's the wedding?
I've never seen an actual wedding ceremony! I want to go!

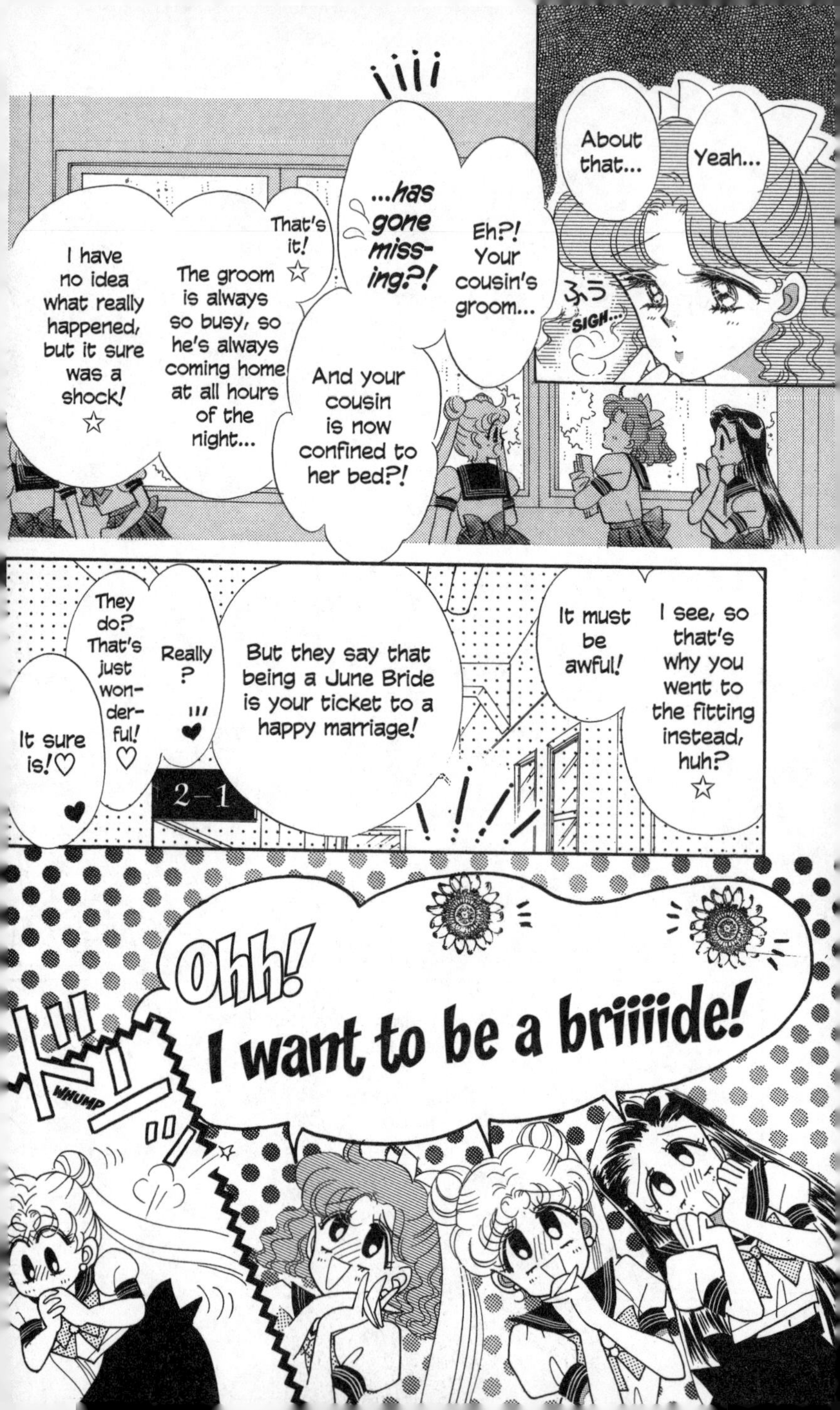

Yeah...
About that...
ふう
SIGH...
Eh?! Your cousin's groom...
...has gone missing?!
And your cousin is now confined to her bed?!
That's it! ☆
The groom is always so busy, so he's always coming home at all hours of the night...
I have no idea what really happened, but it sure was a shock! ☆
I see, so that's why you went to the fitting instead, huh? ☆
It must be awful!
But they say that being a June Bride is your ticket to a happy marriage!
Really?
They do? That's just wonderful! ♡
It sure is! ♡
2-1
Ohh! I want to be a briiiide!
WHUMP

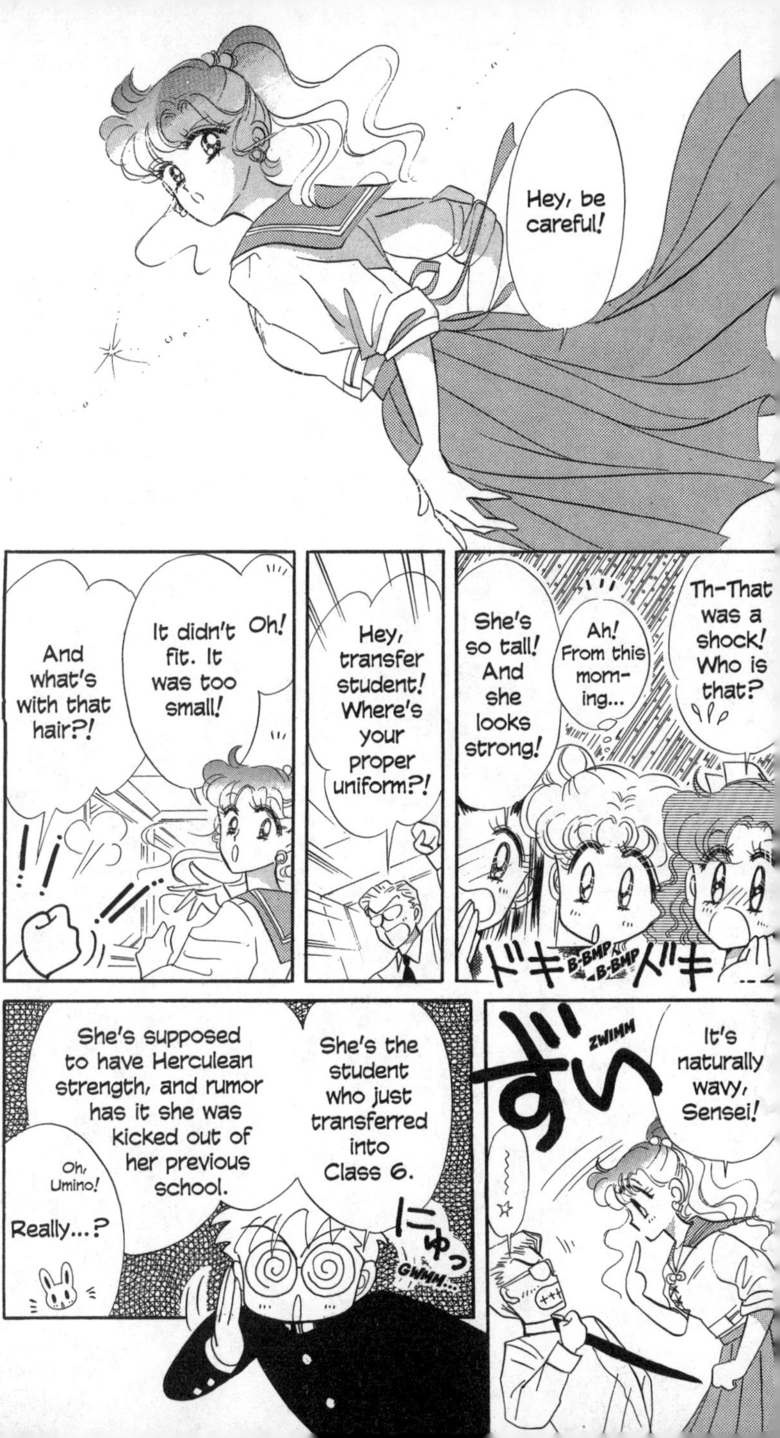
Hey, be careful!
Th-That was a shock! Who is that?
Ah! From this morning...
She's so tall! And she looks strong!
ドキ B-BMP ドキ B-BMP
Hey, transfer student! Where's your proper uniform?!
Oh!
It didn't fit. It was too small!
And what's with that hair?!
ずい ZWIMM
It's naturally wavy, Sensei!
She's the student who just transferred into Class 6.
She's supposed to have Herculean strength, and rumor has it she was kicked out of her previous school.
Oh, Umino!
Really...?
にゅっ GWMM...

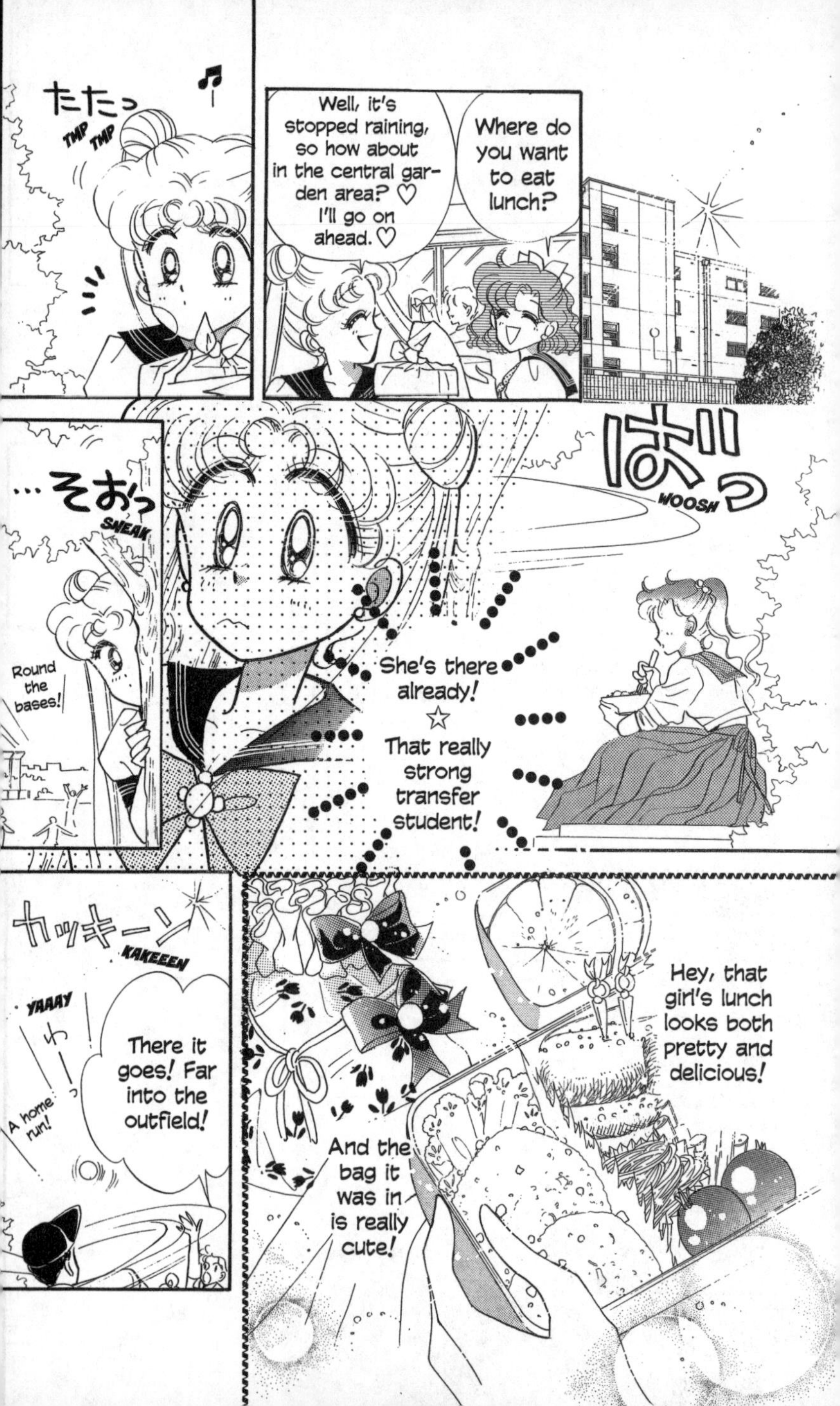
Where do you want to eat lunch?
Well, it's stopped raining, so how about in the central garden area? ♡ I'll go on ahead. ♡
たたっ
TMP TMP
はっ
WOOSH
She's there already! ☆ That really strong transfer student!
…そおっ
SNEAK
Round the bases!
Hey, that girl's lunch looks both pretty and delicious!
And the bag it was in is really cute!
カッキーン
KAKEEEN
There it goes! Far into the outfield!
YAAAY
わー
A home run!

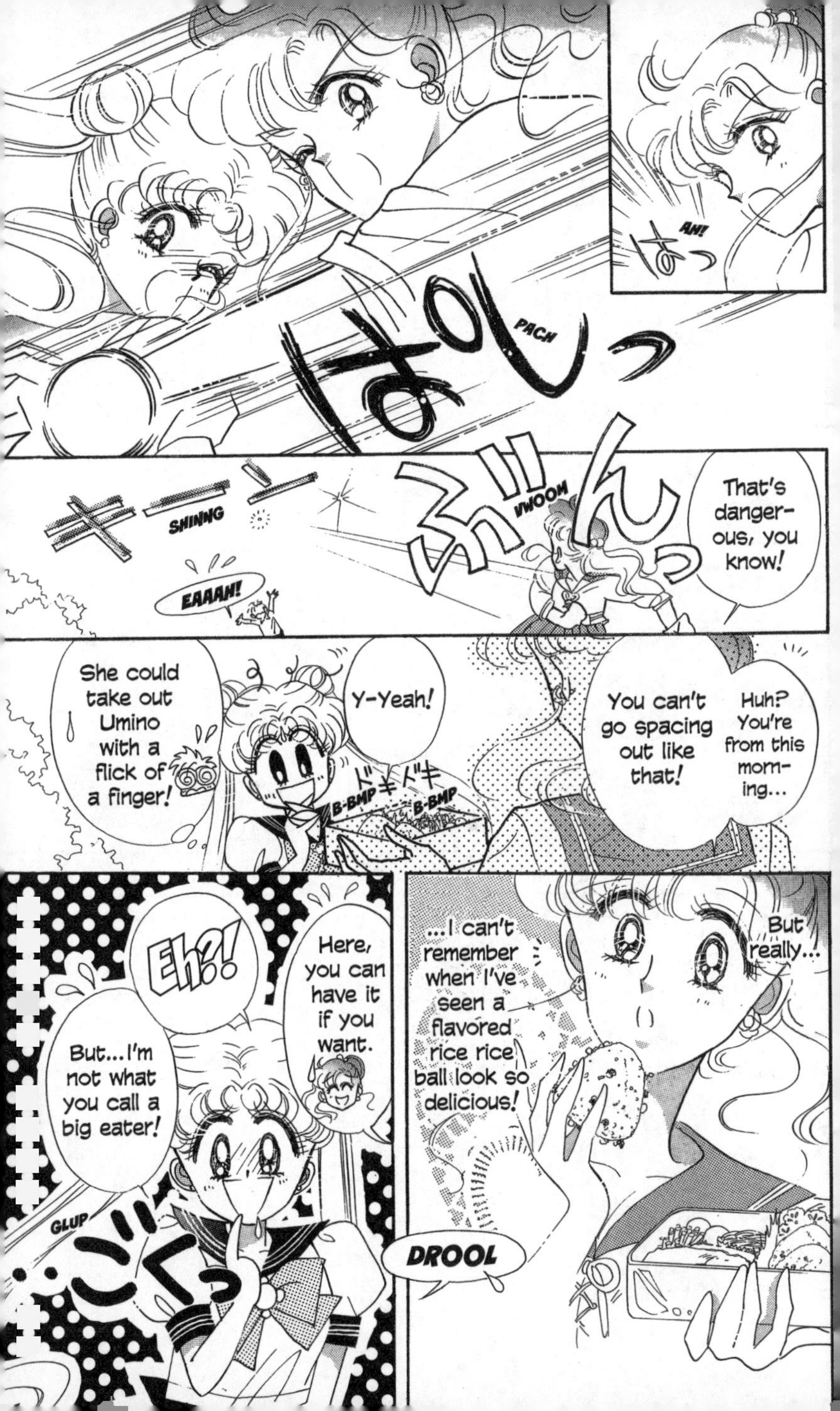
AH!
あっ
ぱしっ
PACH
That's danger-ous, you know!
ぶんっ
VWOOM
キーン
SHINNG
EAAAH!
Huh? You're from this morn-ing...
You can't go spacing out like that!
Y-Yeah!
ドキドキ
B-BMP B-BMP
She could take out Umino with a flick of a finger!
But really...
...I can't remember when I've seen a flavored rice rice ball look so delicious!
DROOL
Here, you can have it if you want.
Eh?!
But...I'm not what you call a big eater!
GLUP
ごくっ

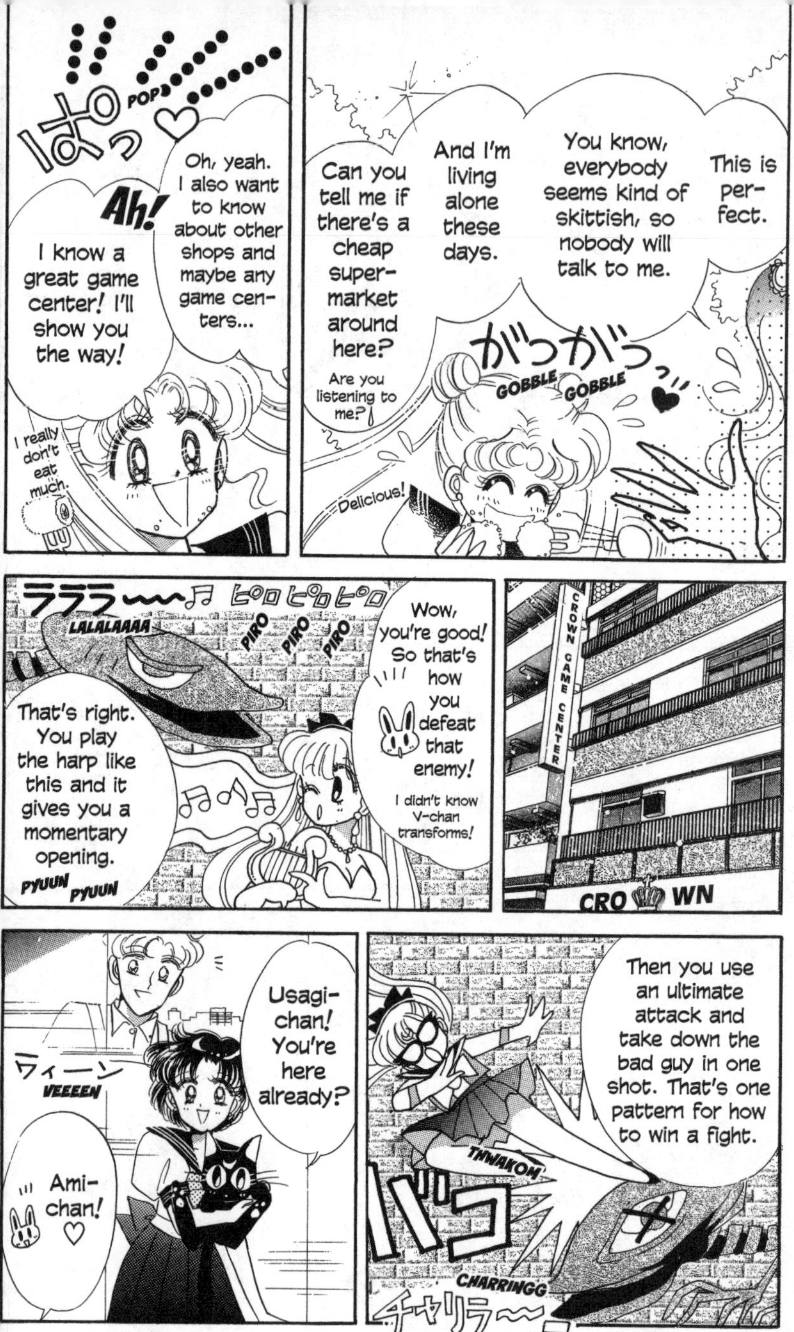
This is per-fect.
You know, everybody seems kind of skittish, so nobody will talk to me.
And I'm living alone these days.
Can you tell me if there's a cheap super-market around here?
Are you listening to me?
がつがつっ
GOBBLE GOBBLE
Delicious!
ぱっ
POP
Oh, yeah. I also want to know about other shops and maybe any game cen-ters...
Ah!
I know a great game center! I'll show you the way!
I really don't eat much.
CROWN GAME CENTER
CRO WN
Wow, you're good! So that's how you defeat that enemy!
I didn't know V-chan transforms!
ピロピロピロ
PIRO PIRO PIRO
ラララ〜
LALALAAAA
That's right. You play the harp like this and it gives you a momentary opening.
PYUUN PYUUN
Then you use an ultimate attack and take down the bad guy in one shot. That's one pattern for how to win a fight.
バコ
THWAKOM
チャリラ〜
CHARRINGG
Usagi-chan! You're here already?
ウィーン
VEEEEN
Ami-chan! ♡

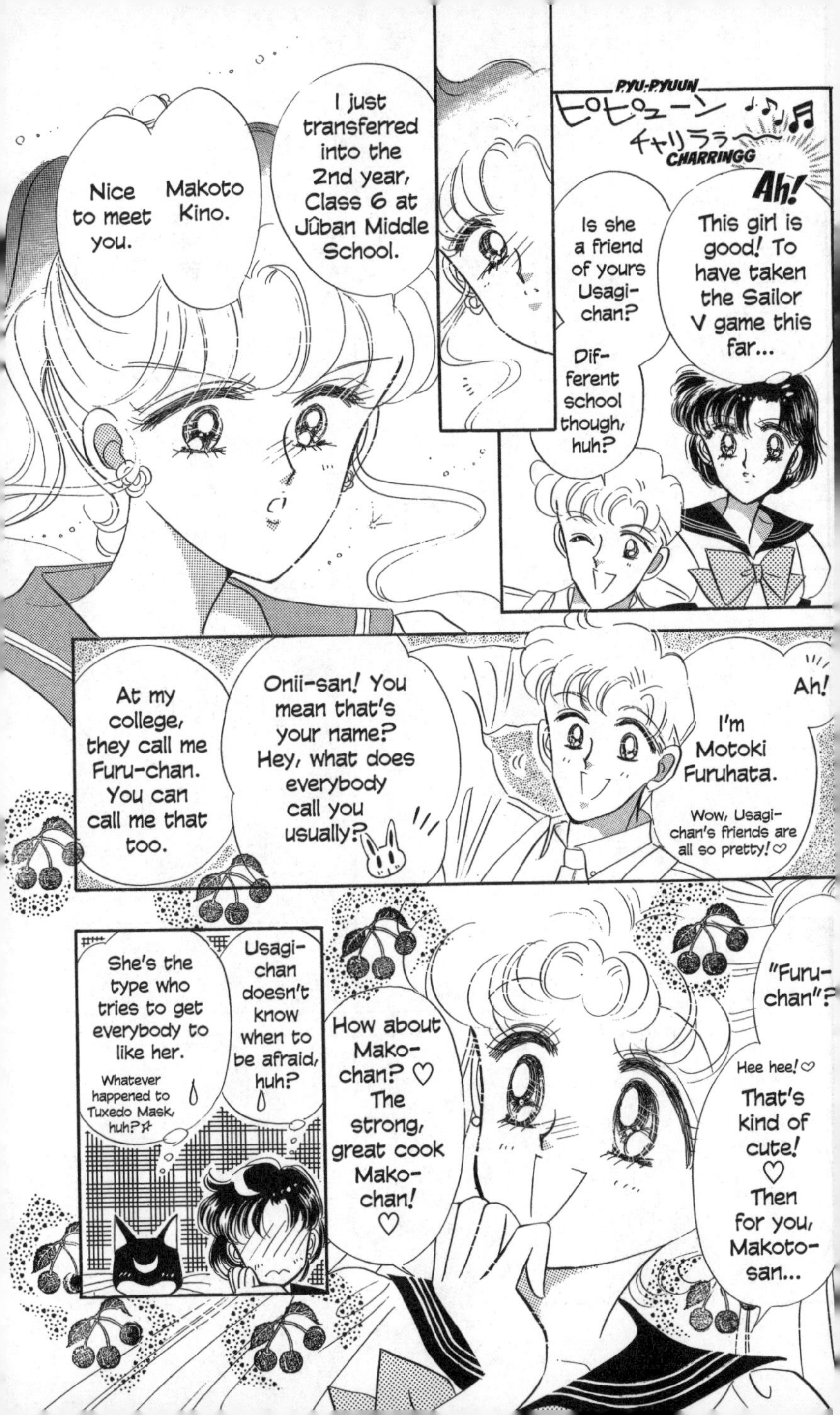
PYU-PYUUN
ピピューン
チャリララ〜
CHARRINGG
Ah! This girl is good! To have taken the Sailor V game this far...
Is she a friend of yours Usagi-chan?
Different school though, huh?
I just transferred into the 2nd year, Class 6 at Jûban Middle School.
Makoto Kino.
Nice to meet you.
Ah!
I'm Motoki Furuhata.
Wow, Usagi-chan's friends are all so pretty! ♡
Onii-san! You mean that's your name? Hey, what does everybody call you usually?
At my college, they call me Furu-chan. You can call me that too.
"Furu-chan"?
Hee hee! ♡
That's kind of cute! ♡ Then for you, Makoto-san...
How about Mako-chan? ♡ The strong, great cook Mako-chan! ♡
Usagi-chan doesn't know when to be afraid, huh?
She's the type who tries to get everybody to like her.
Whatever happened to Tuxedo Mask, huh?☆

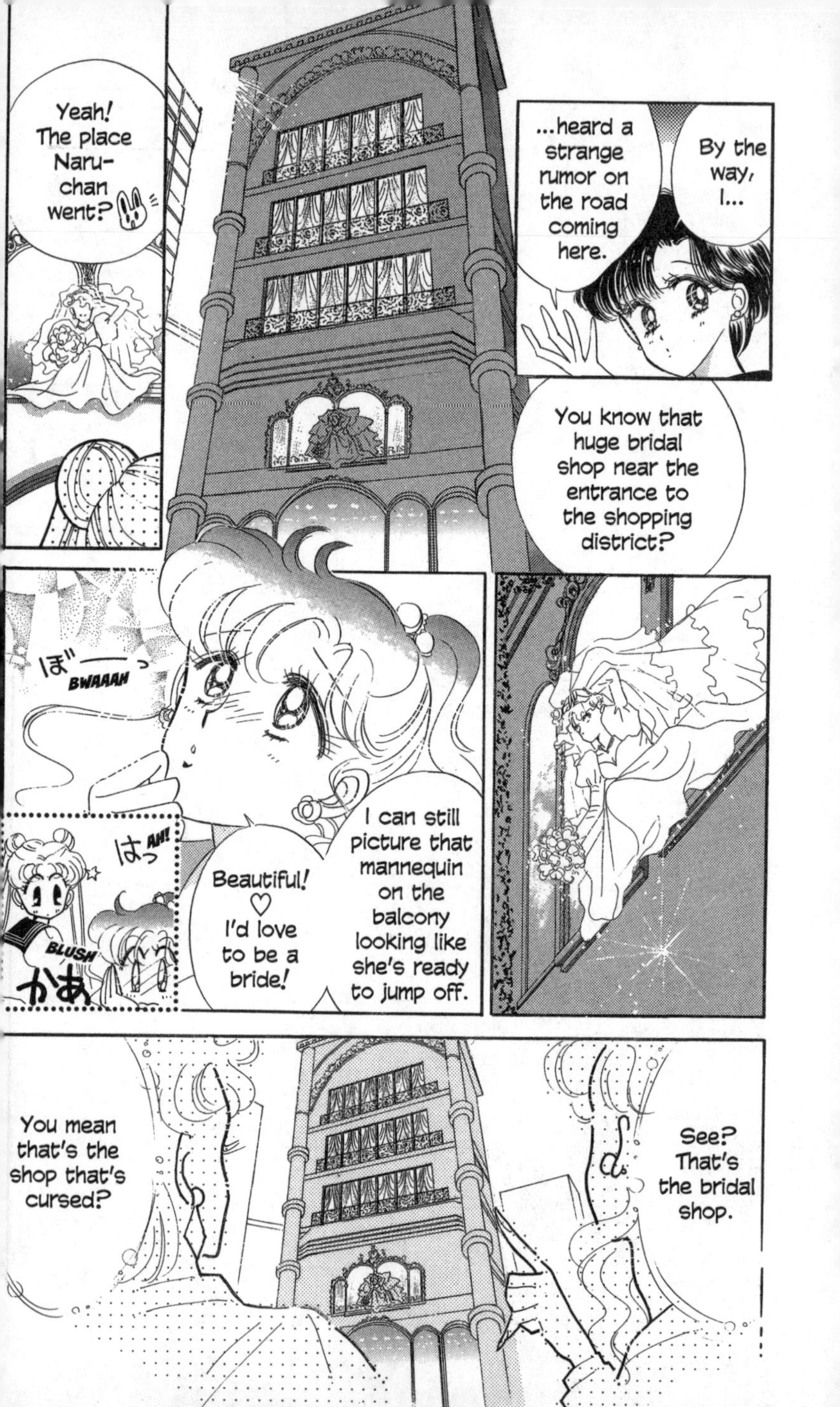
By the way, I...
...heard a strange rumor on the road coming here.
You know that huge bridal shop near the entrance to the shopping district?
Yeah! The place Naru-chan went?
I can still picture that mannequin on the balcony looking like she's ready to jump off.
Beautiful! ♡ I'd love to be a bride!
ぼーっ BWAAAH
はっ AH!
かあ BLUSH
See? That's the bridal shop.
You mean that's the shop that's cursed?

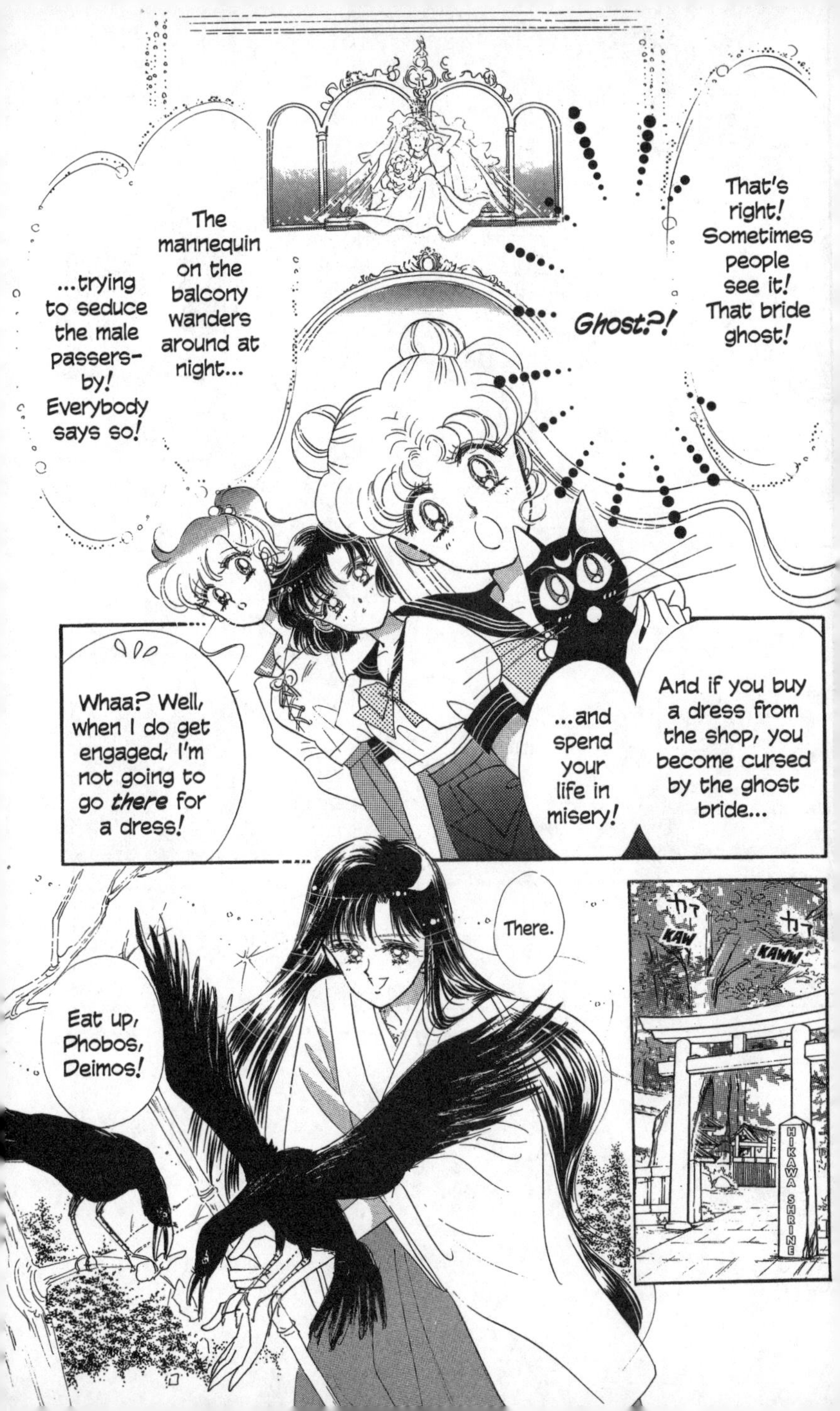
That's right! Sometimes people see it! That bride ghost!
Ghost?!
The mannequin on the balcony wanders around at night...
...trying to seduce the male passers-by! Everybody says so!
And if you buy a dress from the shop, you become cursed by the ghost bride...
...and spend your life in misery!
Whaa? Well, when I do get engaged, I'm not going to go there for a dress!
KAW
KAWW
HIKAWA SHRINE
There.
Eat up, Phobos, Deimos!

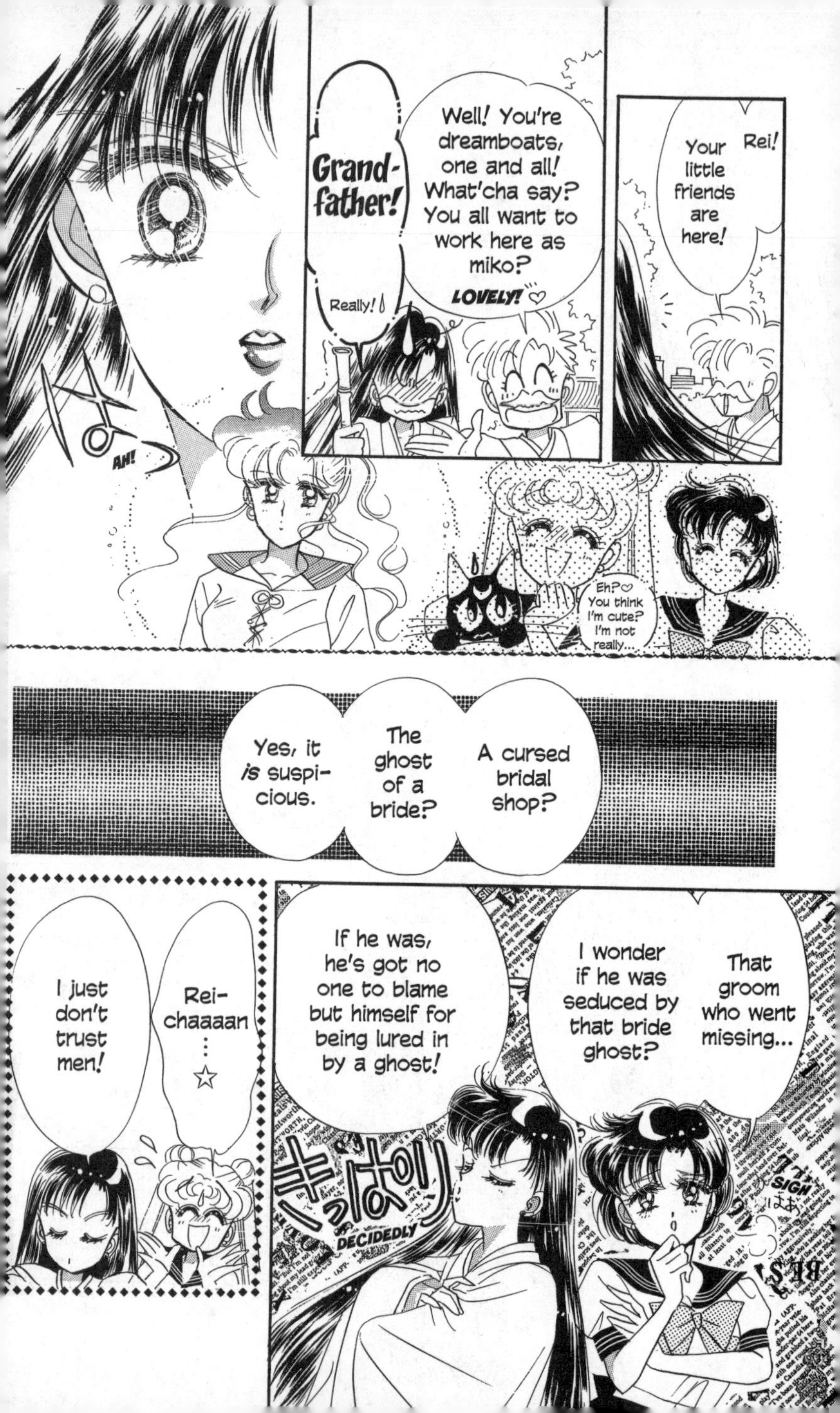

Rei!
Your little friends are here!
Well! You're dreamboats, one and all! What'cha say? You all want to work here as miko?
LOVELY! ♡
Grand-father!
Really!
AH!
Eh? ♡ You think I'm cute? I'm not really...
A cursed bridal shop?
The ghost of a bride?
Yes, it *is* suspicious.
That groom who went missing...
I wonder if he was seduced by that bride ghost?
SIGH
If he was, he's got no one to blame but himself for being lured in by a ghost!
キッパリ
DECIDEDLY
Rei-chaaaan ...☆
I just don't trust men!

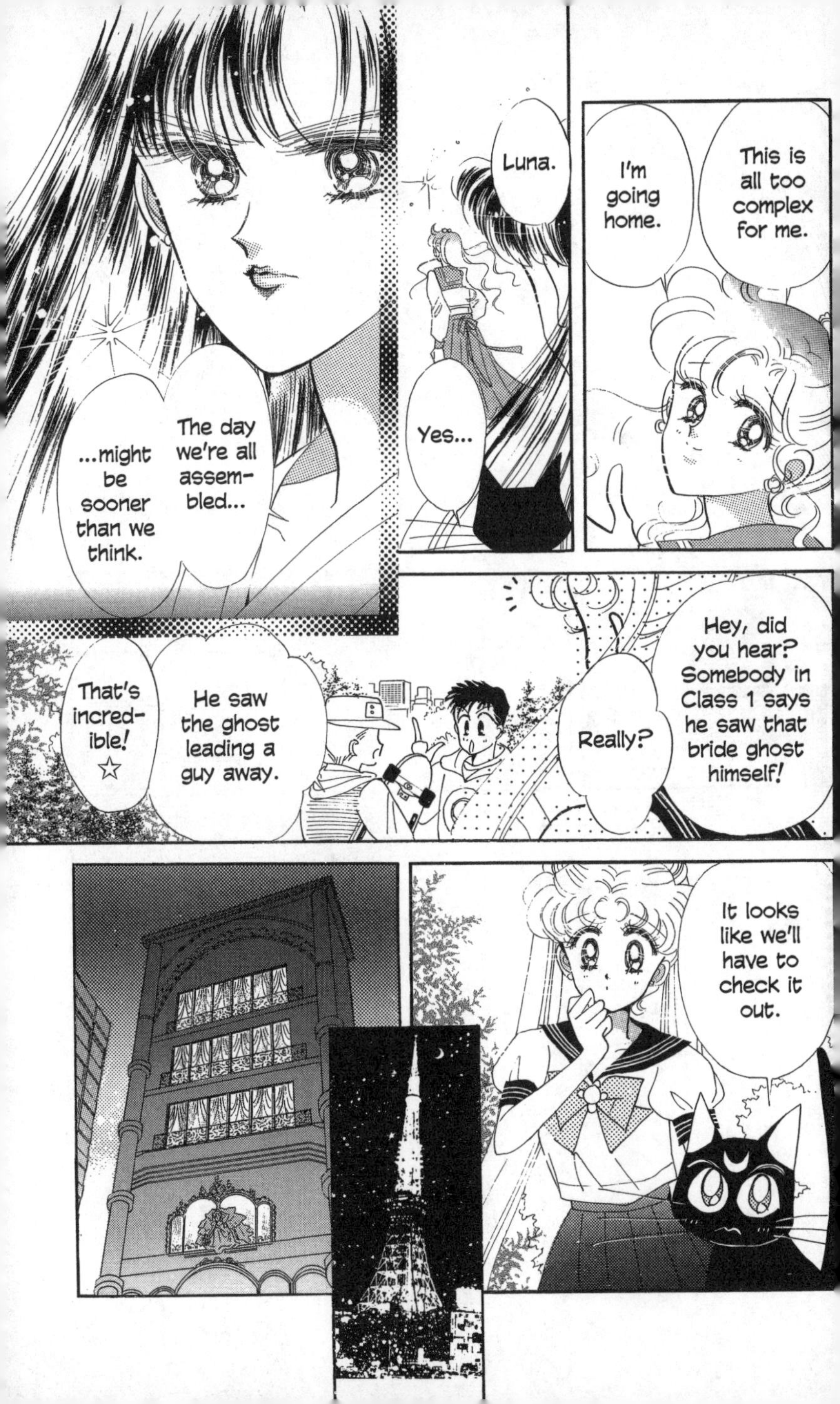
This is all too complex for me.
I'm going home.
Luna.
Yes...
The day we're all assembled...
...might be sooner than we think.
Hey, did you hear? Somebody in Class 1 says he saw that bride ghost himself!
Really?
He saw the ghost leading a guy away.
That's incredible! ☆
It looks like we'll have to check it out.

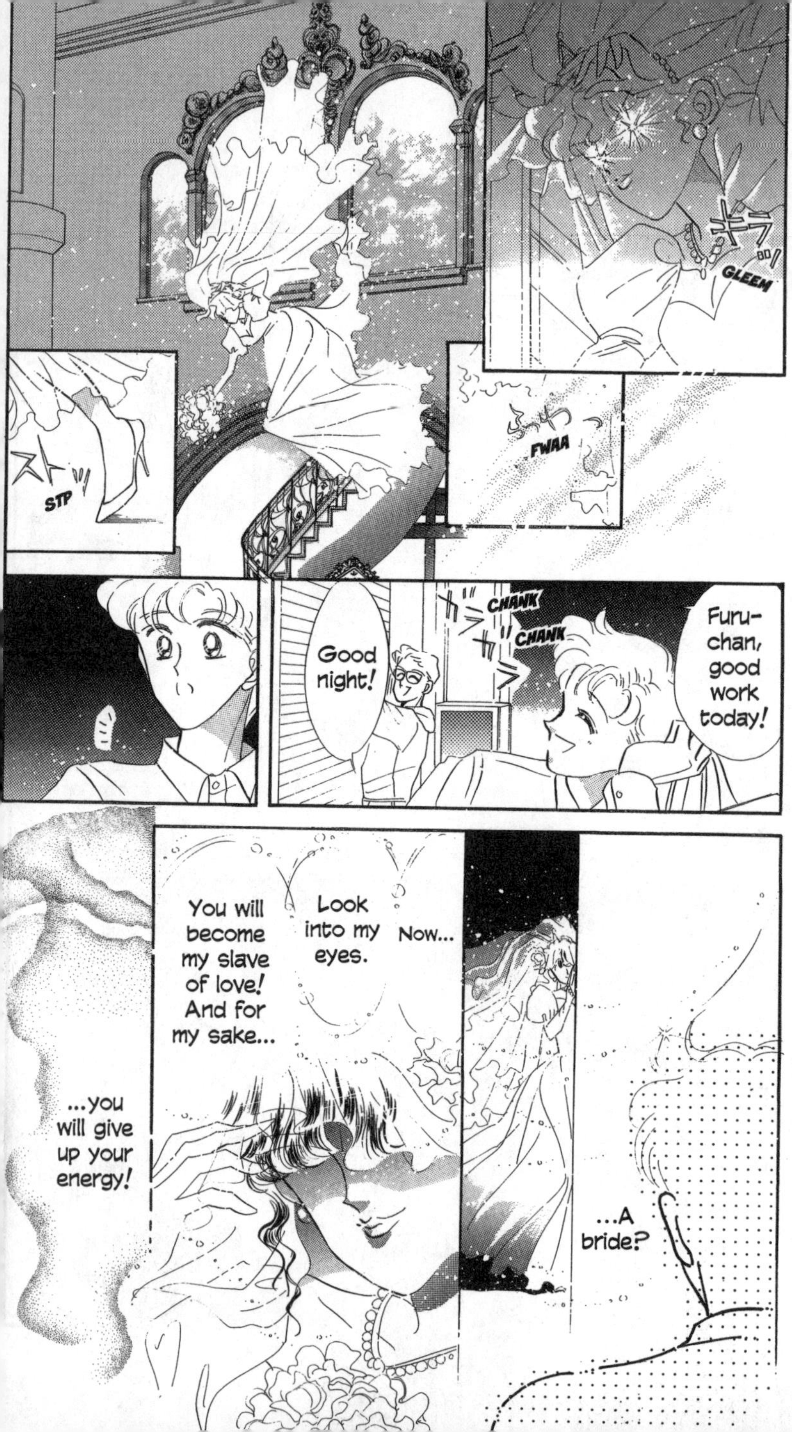
GLEEM
FWAA
STP
Furu-chan, good work today!
CHANK
CHANK
Good night!
...A bride?
Now...
Look into my eyes.
You will become my slave of love! And for my sake...
...you will give up your energy!

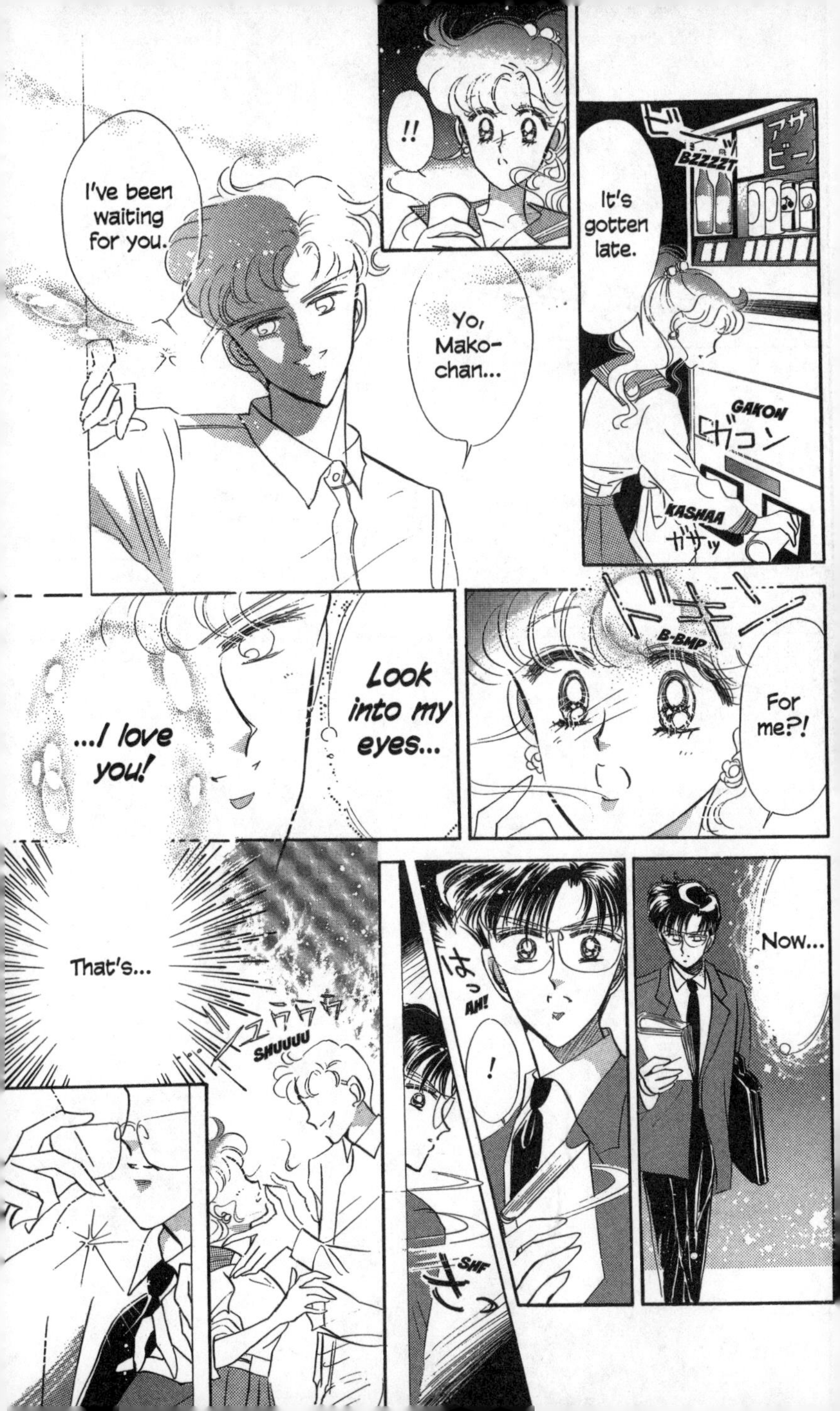
BZZZZT
It's gotten late.
GAKON
ガコン
KASHAA
ガサッ
!!
Yo, Mako-chan...
I've been waiting for you.
B-BMP
For me?!
Look into my eyes...
...I love you!
Now...
はっ
AH!
!
SHF
That's...
SHUUUU

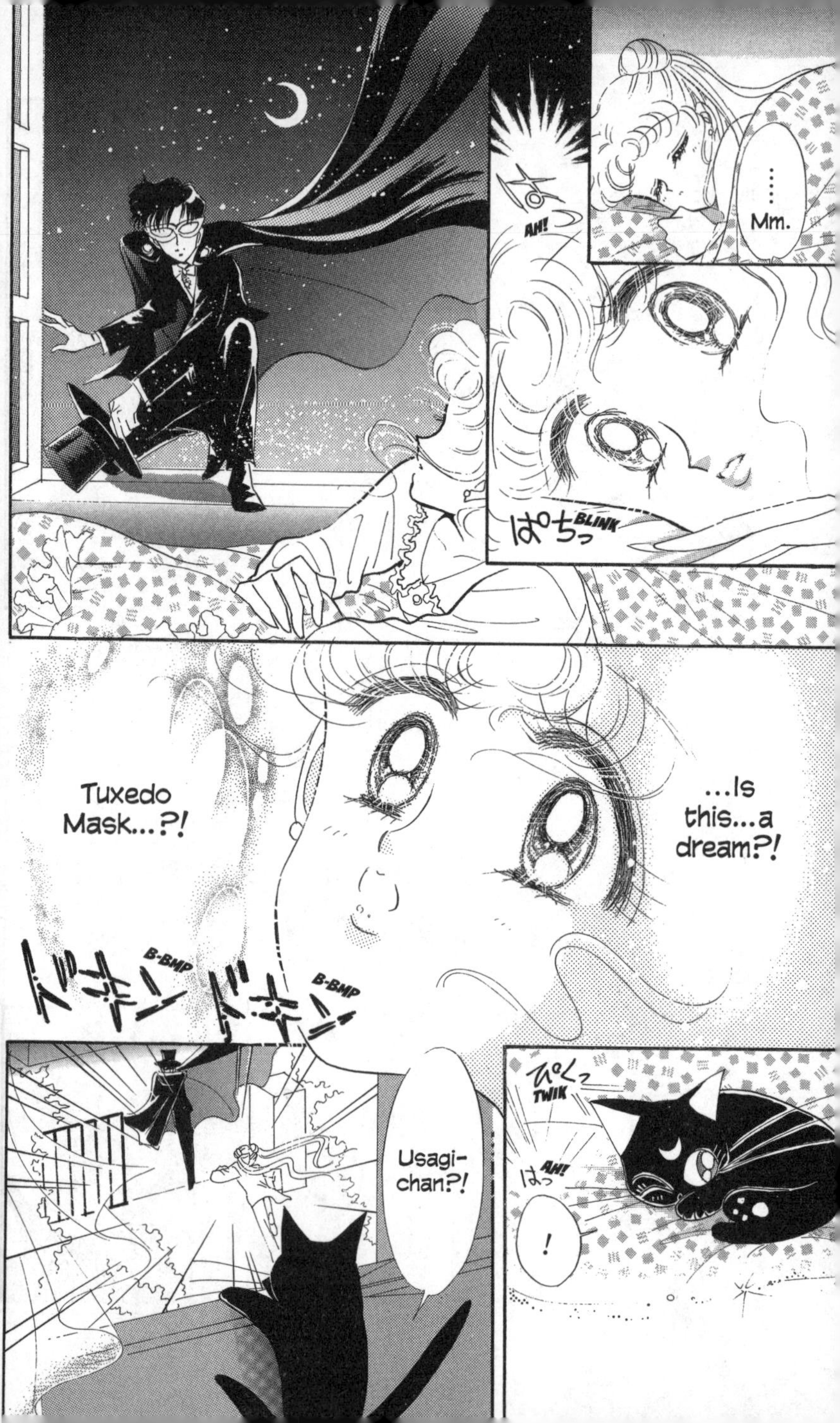
……
Mm.
AH!
ぱちっ BLINK
...Is this...a dream?!
Tuxedo Mask...?!
B-BMP
B-BMP
ぴくっ TWIK
はっ AH!
!
Usagi-chan?!

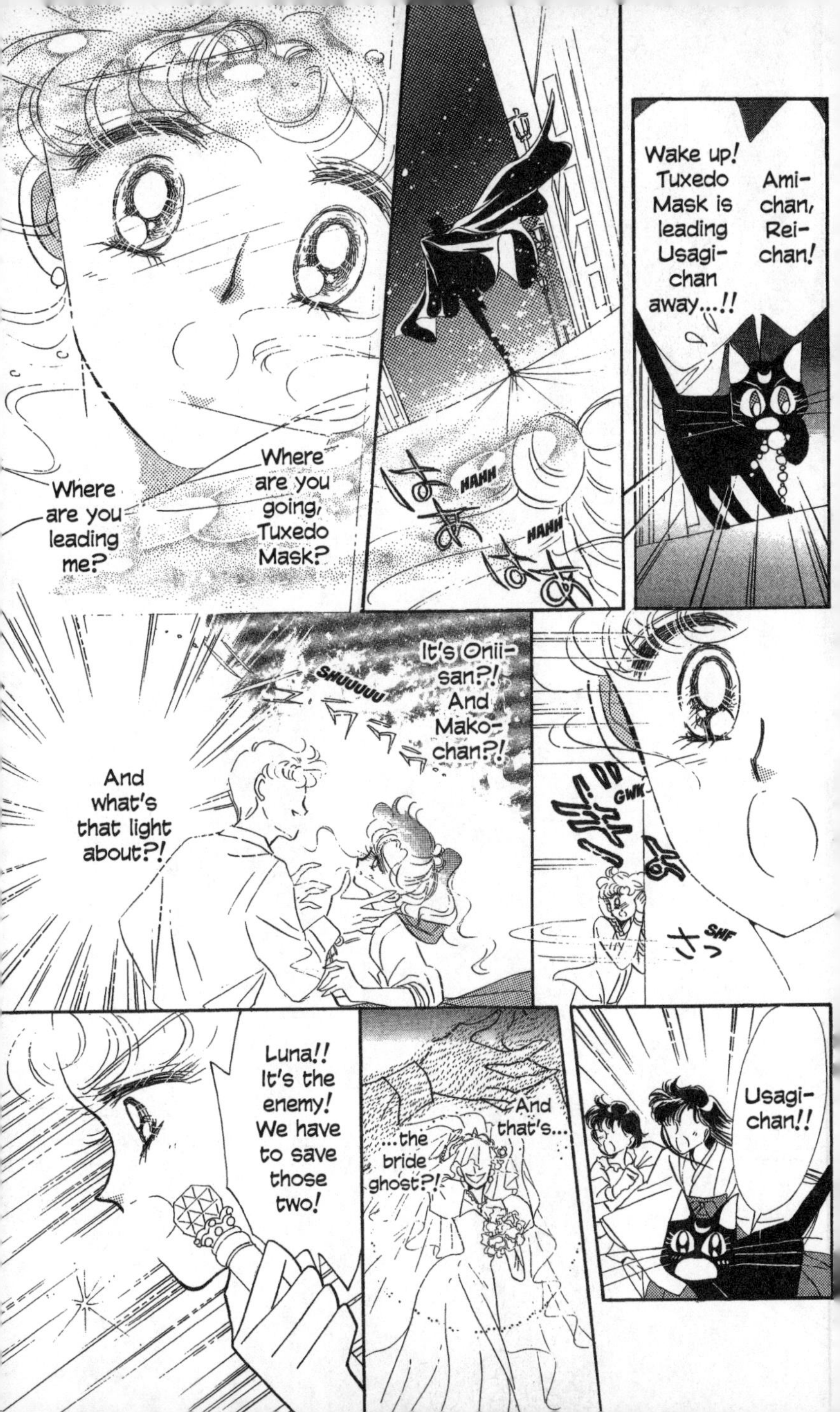
Ami-chan, Rei-chan!
Wake up! Tuxedo Mask is leading Usagi-chan away...!!
HAHH
HAHH
Where are you going, Tuxedo Mask?
Where are you leading me?
GWK
SHF
SHUUUUU
It's Onii-san?! And Mako-chan?!
And what's that light about?!
Usagi-chan!!
And that's...
...the bride ghost?!
Luna!! It's the enemy! We have to save those two!

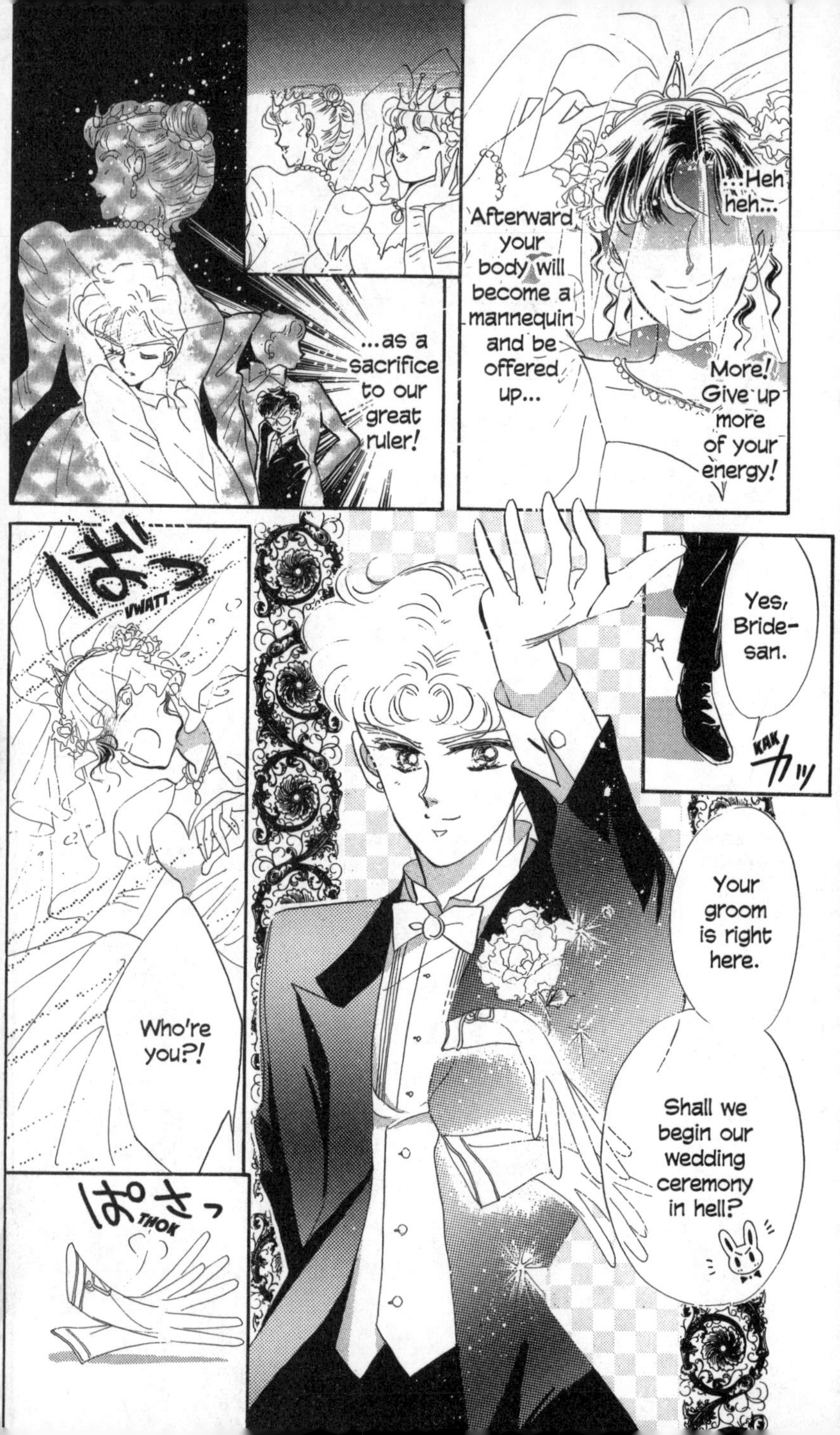

...Heh heh...
Afterward your body will become a mannequin and be offered up...
More! Give up more of your energy!
...as a sacrifice to our great ruler!
Yes, Bride-san.
KAK
カッ
Your groom is right here.
Shall we begin our wedding ceremony in hell?
ばっ
VWATT
Who're you?!
ぱさっ
THOK

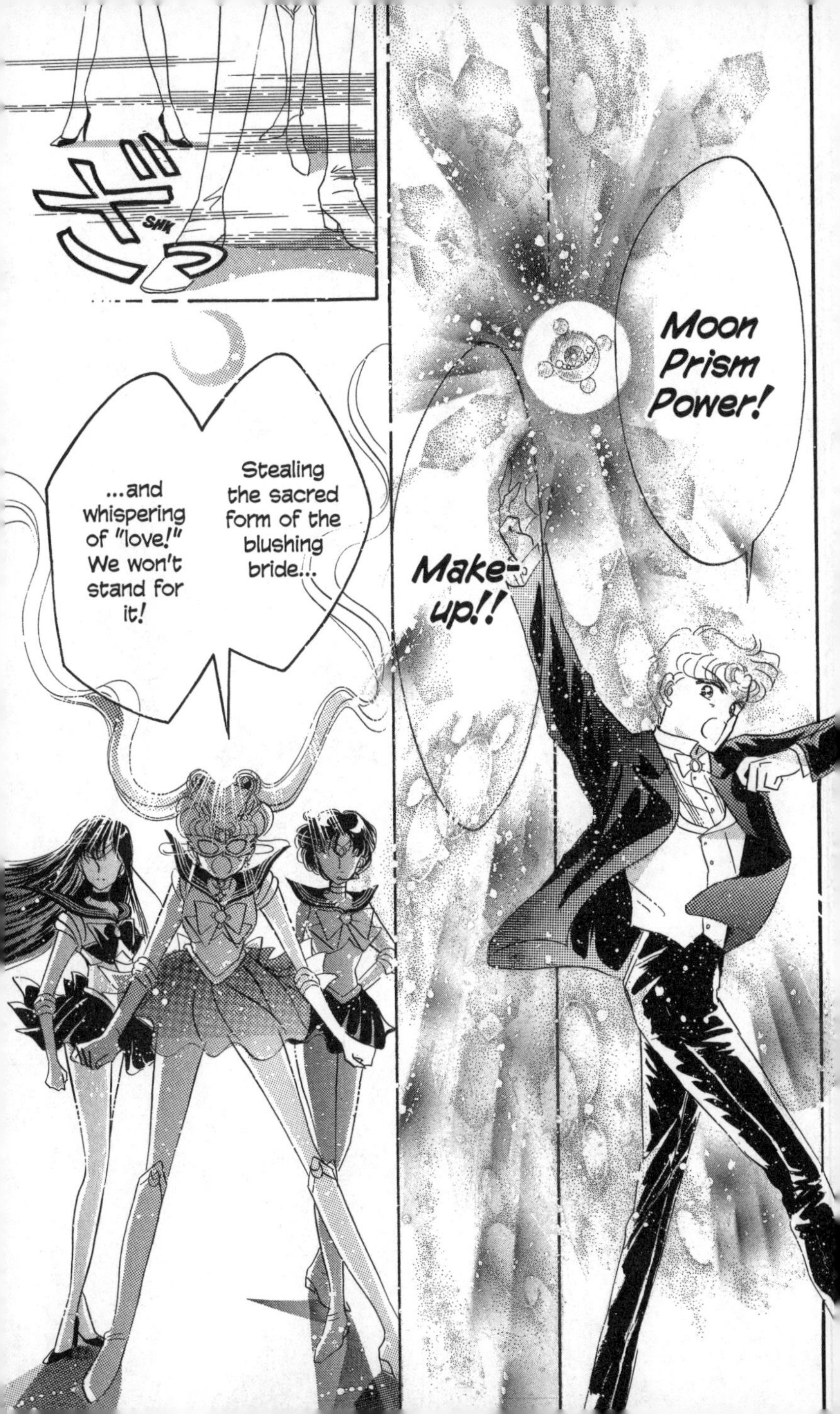
Moon Prism Power!
Make-up!!
SHK
Stealing the sacred form of the blushing bride...
...and whispering of "love!" We won't stand for it!

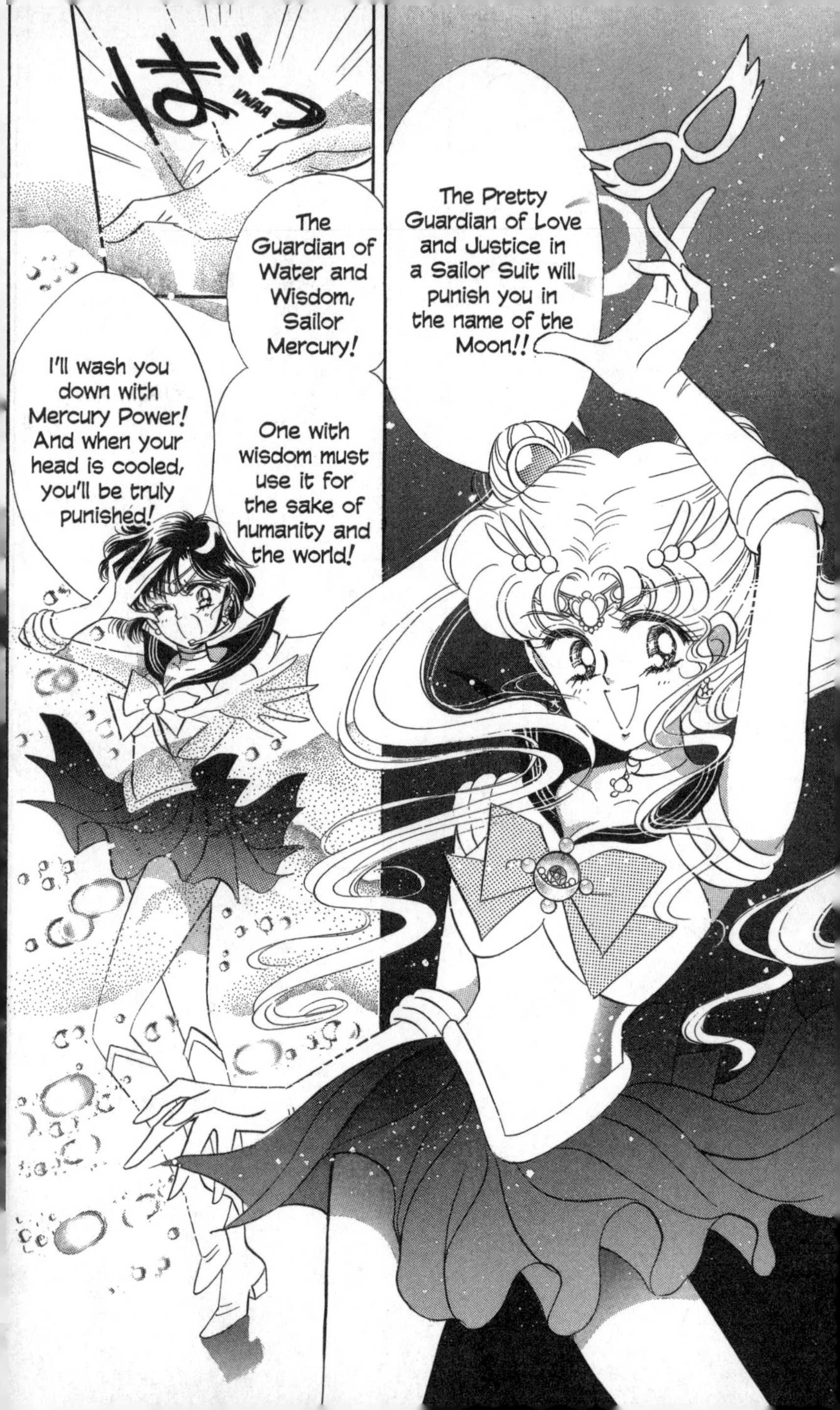
The Pretty Guardian of Love and Justice in a Sailor Suit will punish you in the name of the Moon!!
ばっ
VWAA
The Guardian of Water and Wisdom, Sailor Mercury!
One with wisdom must use it for the sake of humanity and the world!
I'll wash you down with Mercury Power! And when your head is cooled, you'll be truly punished!

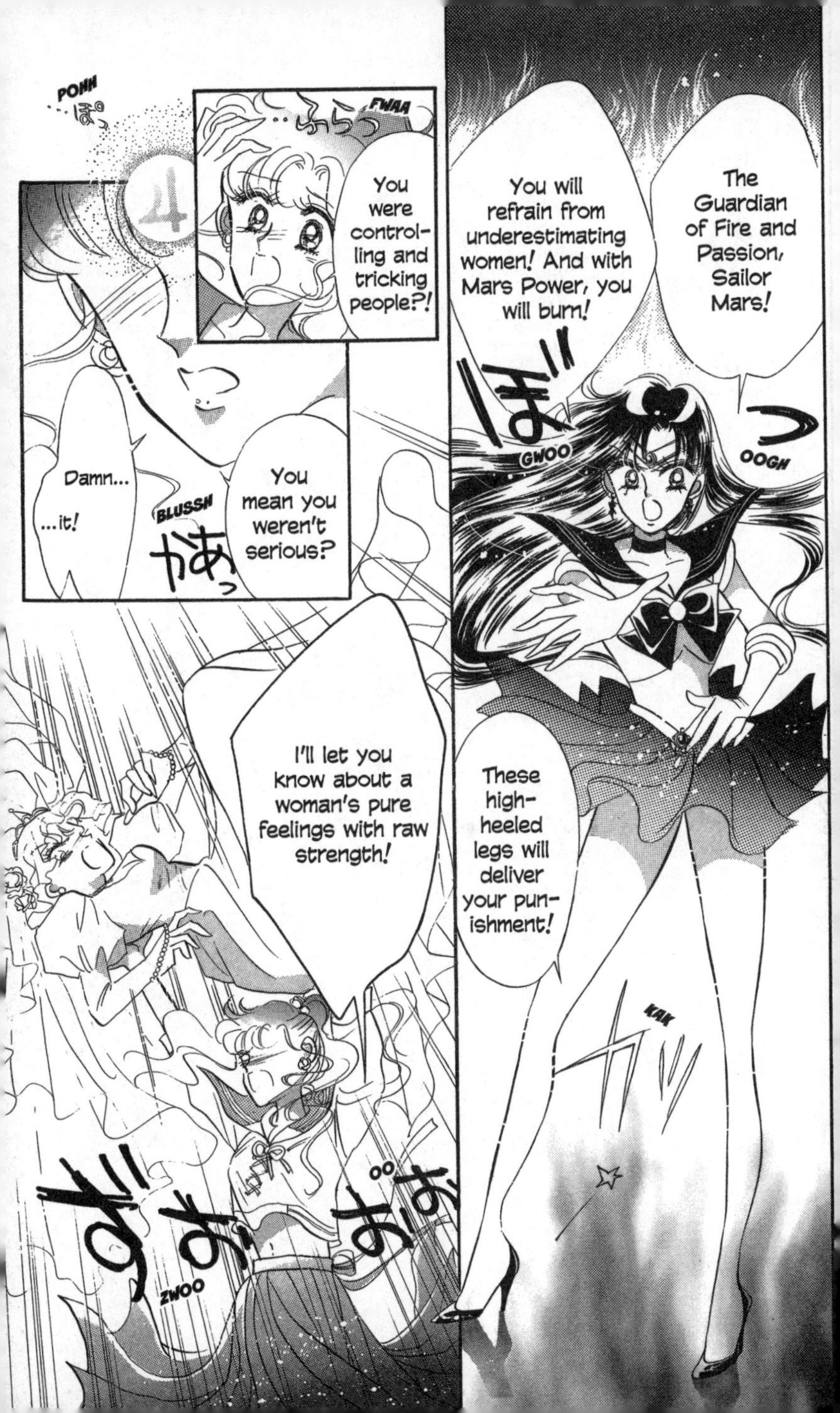

The Guardian of Fire and Passion, Sailor Mars!
OOGH
You will refrain from underestimating women! And with Mars Power, you will burn!
GWOO
These high-heeled legs will deliver your punishment!
KAK
FWAA
You were controlling and tricking people?!
POHH
You mean you weren't serious?
BLUSSH
Damn...
...it!
I'll let you know about a woman's pure feelings with raw strength!
OO
ZWOO

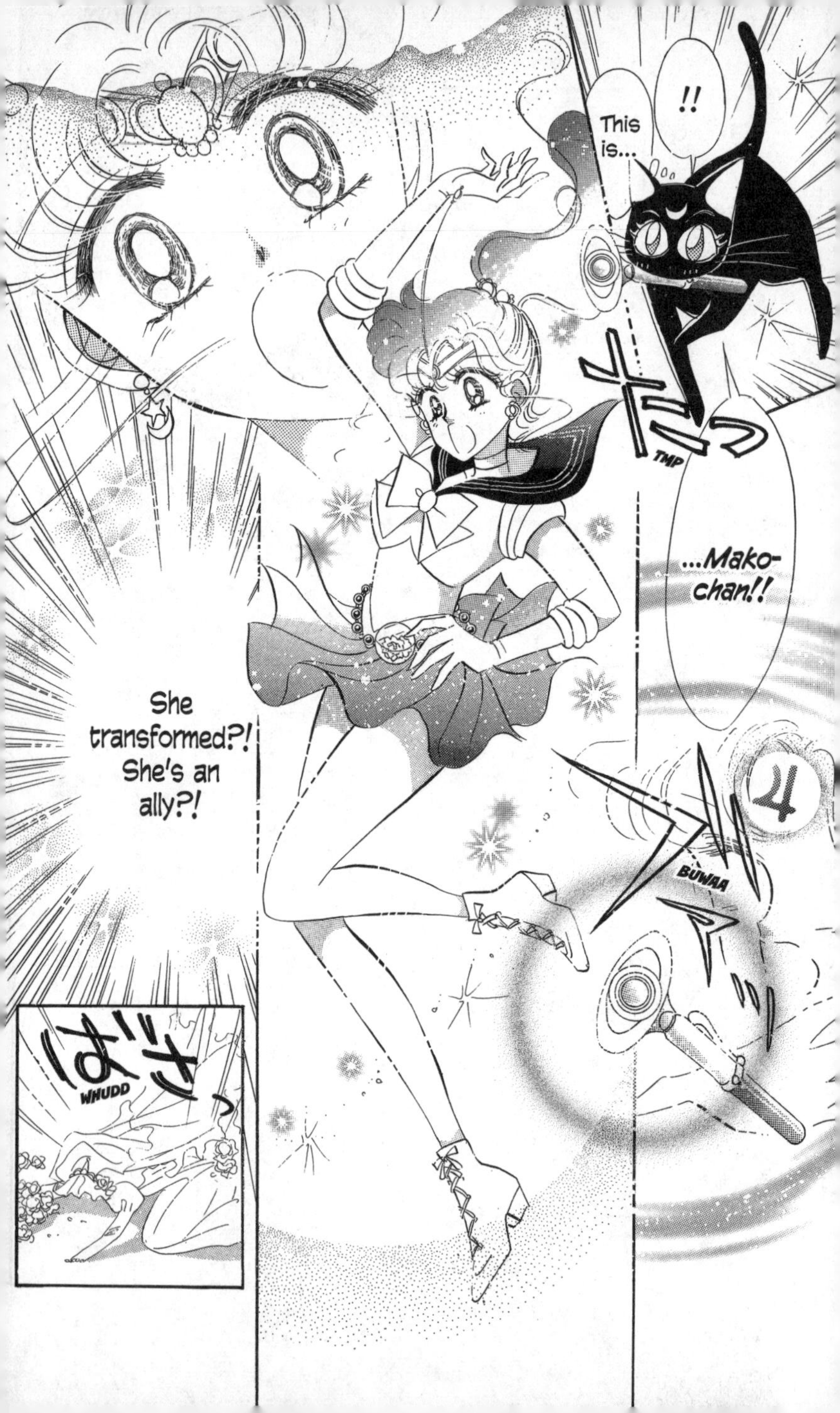
!!
This is...
TMP
...Mako-chan!!
BUWAA
She transformed?! She's an ally?!
WHUDD

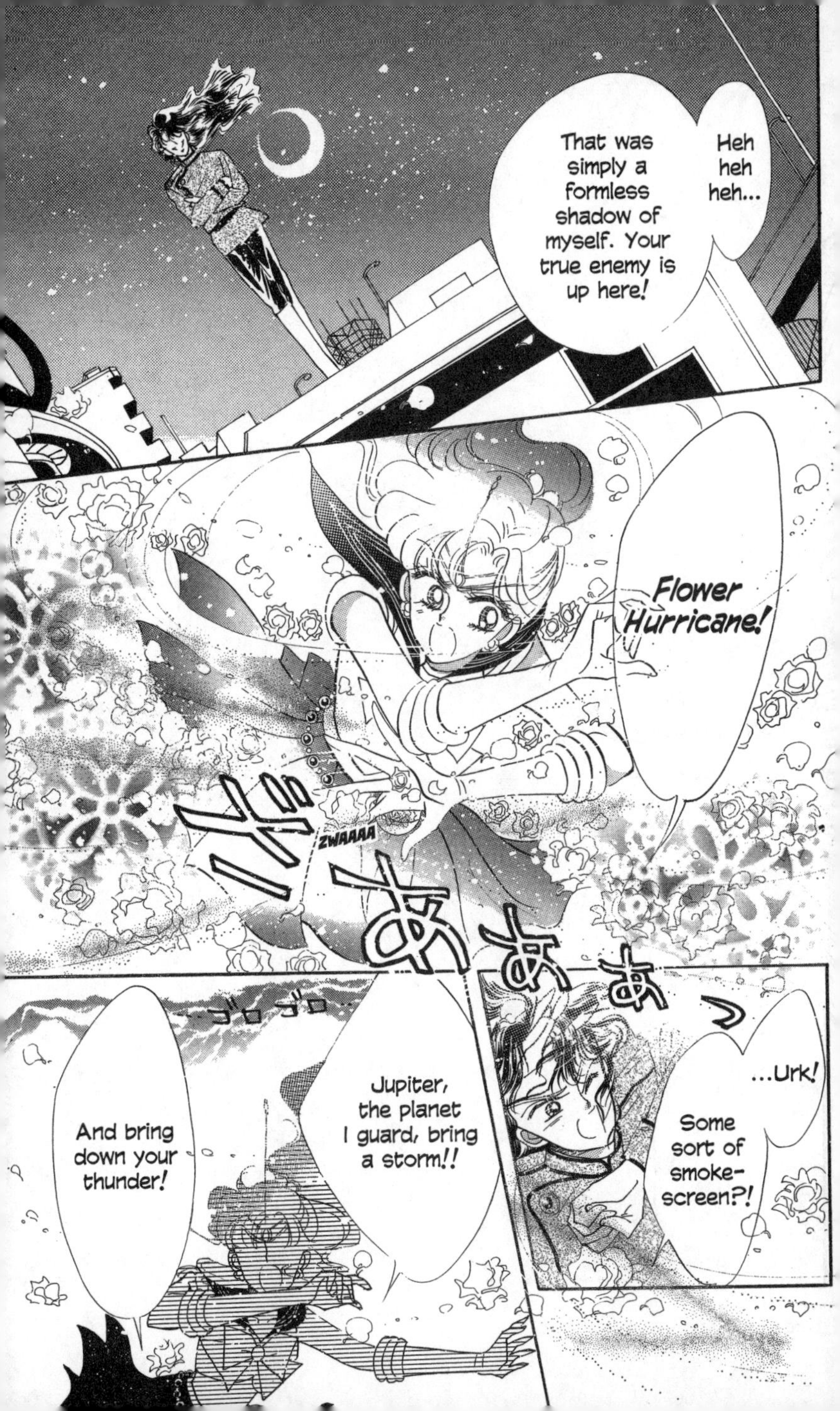

Heh heh heh...
That was simply a formless shadow of myself. Your true enemy is up here!
Flower Hurricane!
ZWAAAA
...Urk!
Some sort of smoke-screen?!
ゴロゴロ…
Jupiter, the planet I guard, bring a storm!!
And bring down your thunder!

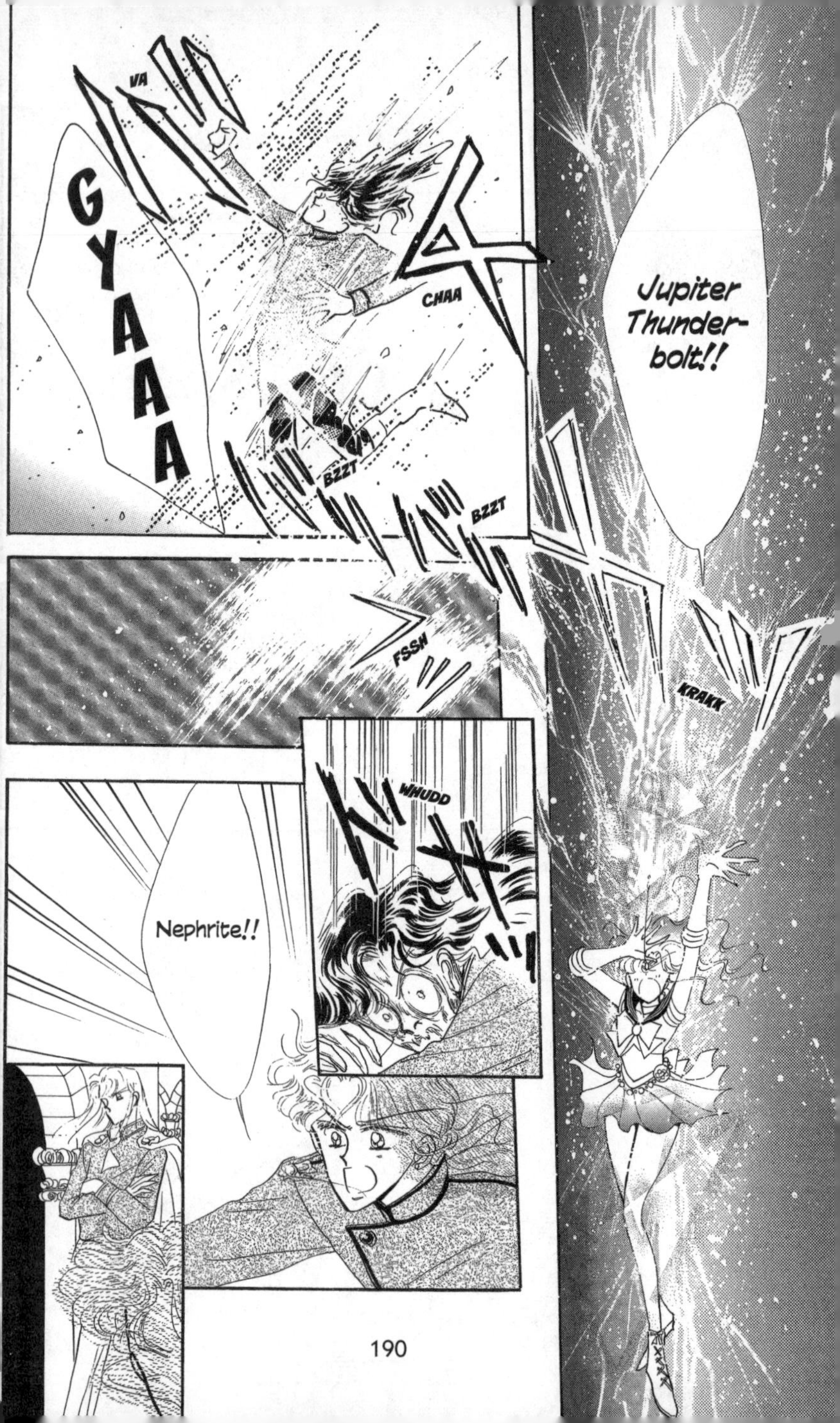
Jupiter Thunder-bolt!!
KRAKK
VA
GYAAA
CHAA
BZZT
BZZT
FSSH
WHUDD
Nephrite!!

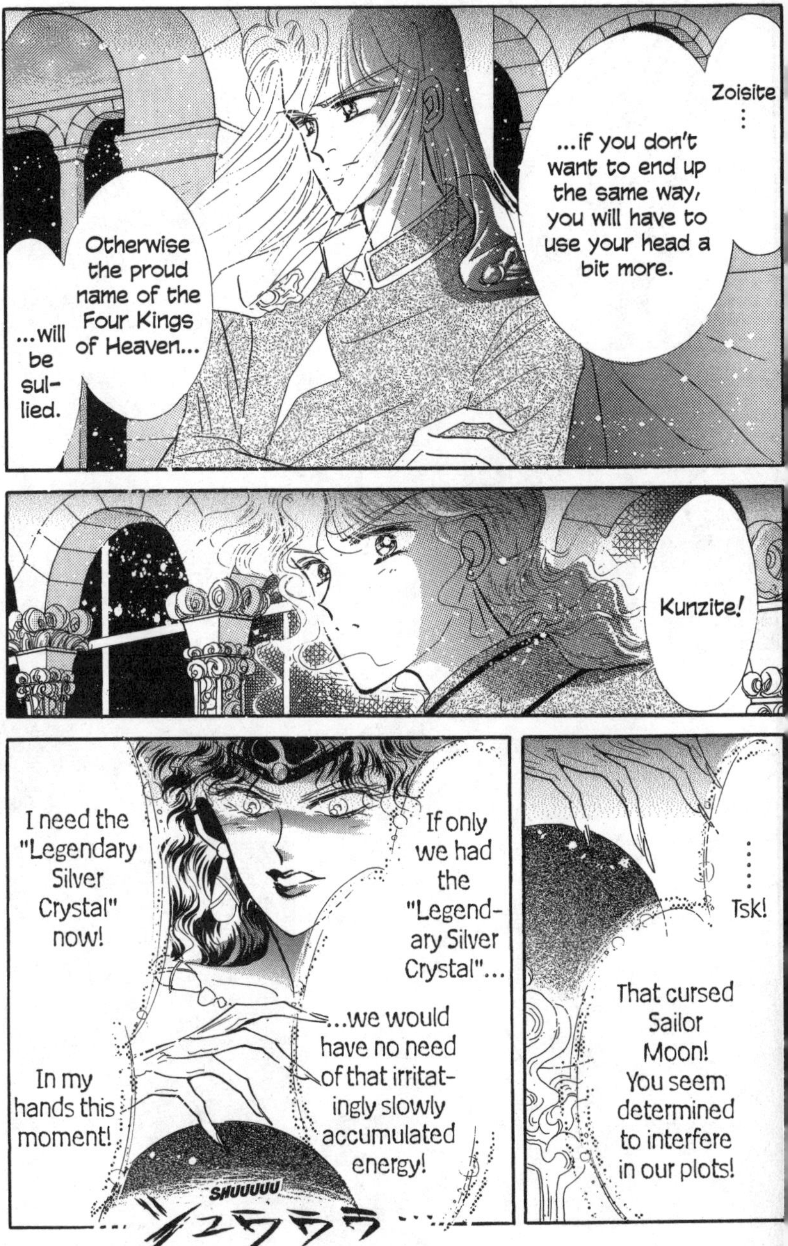
Zoisite…
…if you don't want to end up the same way, you will have to use your head a bit more.
Otherwise the proud name of the Four Kings of Heaven…
…will be sul-lied.
Kunzite!
……Tsk!
That cursed Sailor Moon! You seem determined to interfere in our plots!
If only we had the "Legend-ary Silver Crystal"…
…we would have no need of that irritat-ingly slowly accumulated energy!
I need the "Legendary Silver Crystal" now!
In my hands this moment!
SHUUUUU

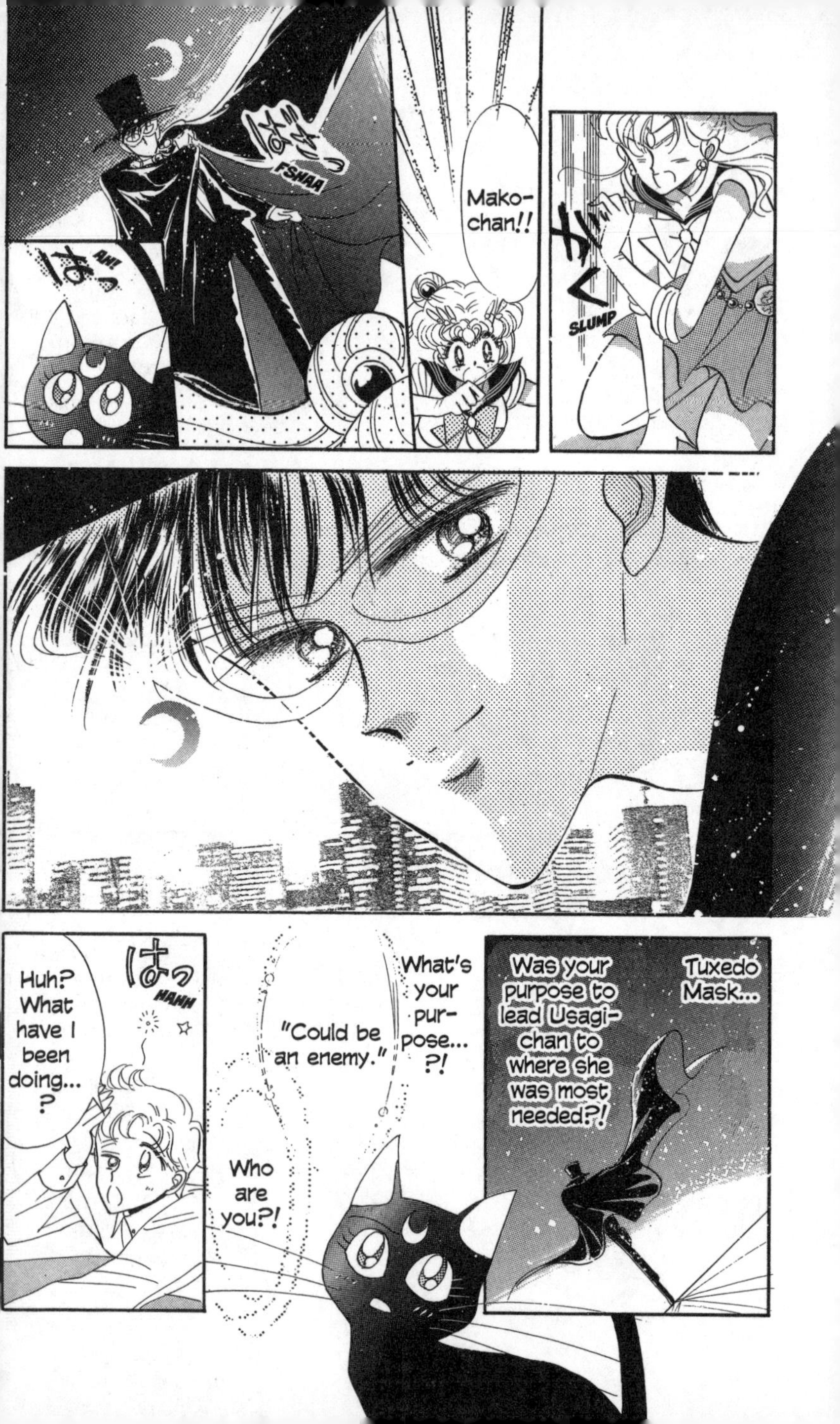
SLUMP
Mako-chan!!
FSHAA
AH!
Tuxedo Mask...
Was your purpose to lead Usagi-chan to where she was most needed?!
What's your purpose...?!
"Could be an enemy."
Who are you?!
はっ
HANH
Huh? What have I been doing...?

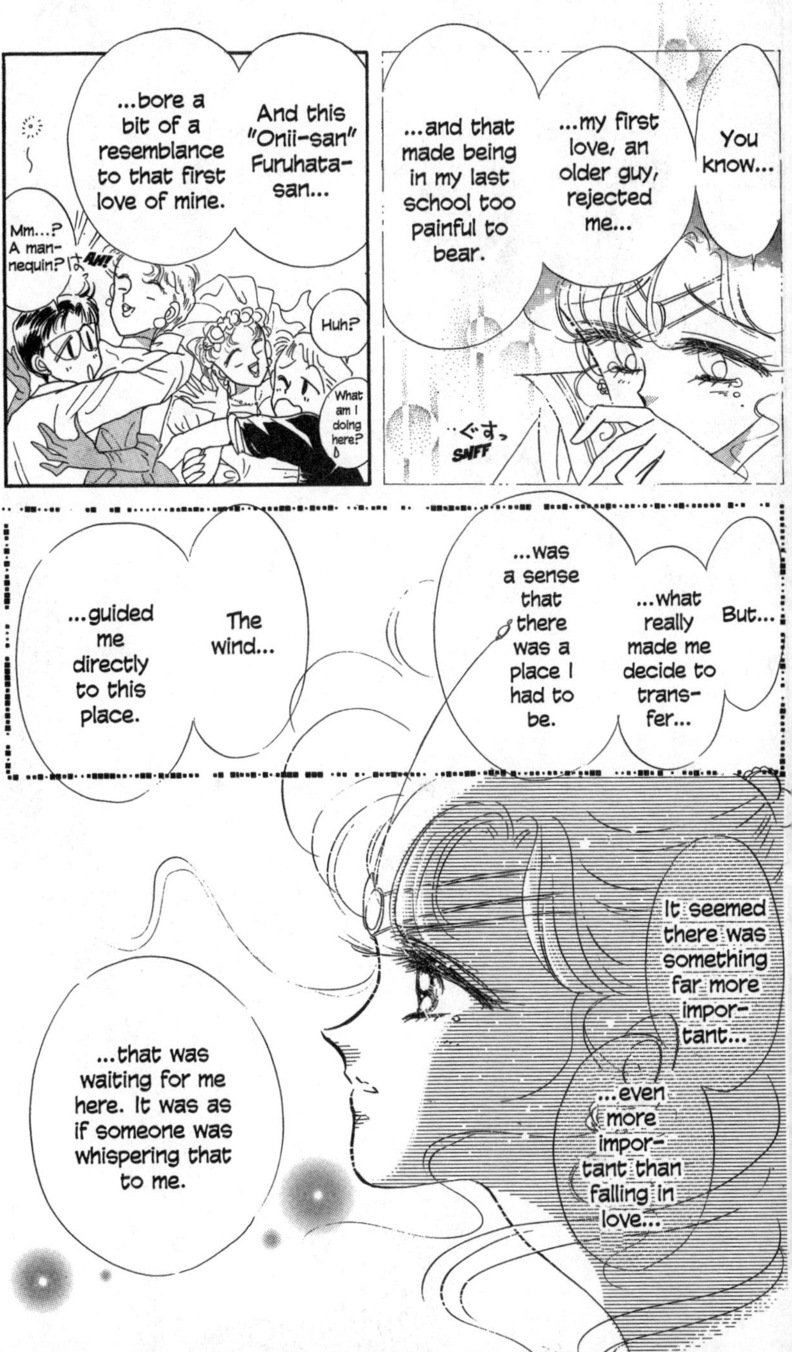
You know...
...my first love, an older guy, rejected me...
...and that made being in my last school too painful to bear.
...ぐすっ
SNFF
And this "Onii-san" Furuhata-san...
...bore a bit of a resemblence to that first love of mine.
Huh?
Mm...? A mannequin?
はAH!
What am I doing here?
But...
...what really made me decide to transfer...
...was a sense that there was a place I had to be.
The wind...
...guided me directly to this place.
It seemed there was something far more important...
...even more important than falling in love...
...that was waiting for me here. It was as if someone was whispering that to me.

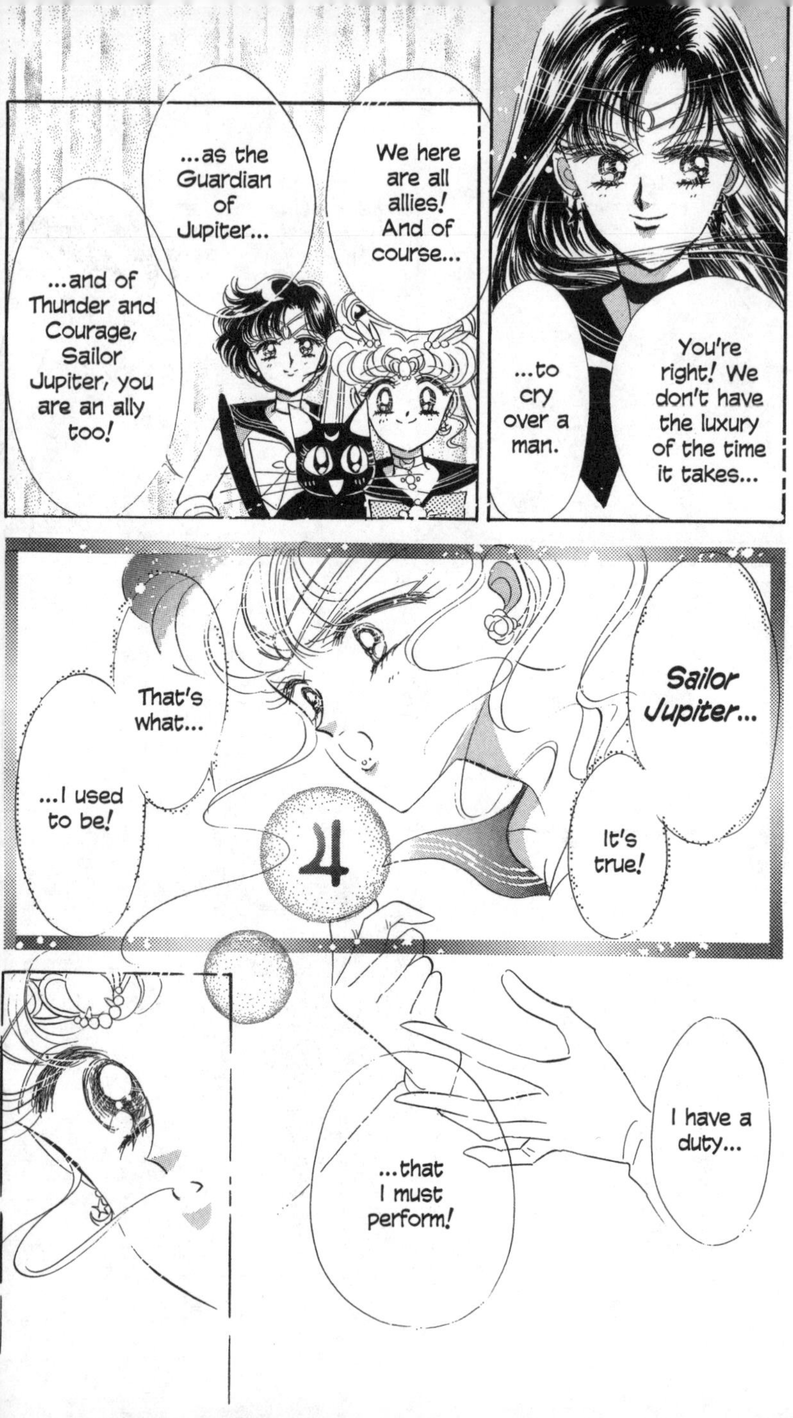
You're right! We don't have the luxury of the time it takes...
...to cry over a man.
We here are all allies! And of course...
...as the Guardian of Jupiter...
...and of Thunder and Courage, Sailor Jupiter, you are an ally too!
Sailor Jupiter...
It's true!
That's what...
...I used to be!
I have a duty...
...that I must perform!

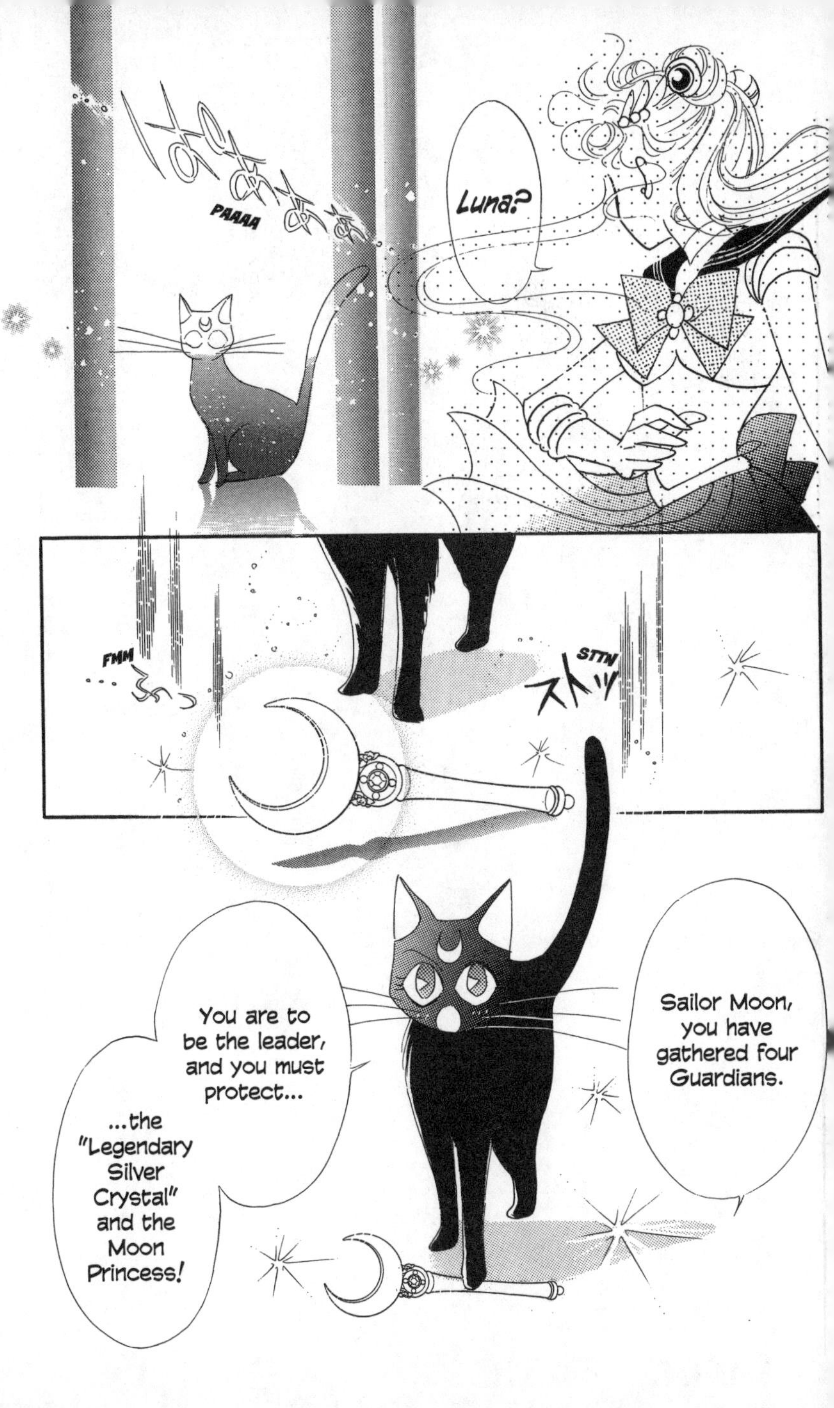

Luna?
PAAAA
STTN
FMM
Sailor Moon, you have gathered four Guardians.
You are to be the leader, and you must protect...
...the "Legendary Silver Crystal" and the Moon Princess!

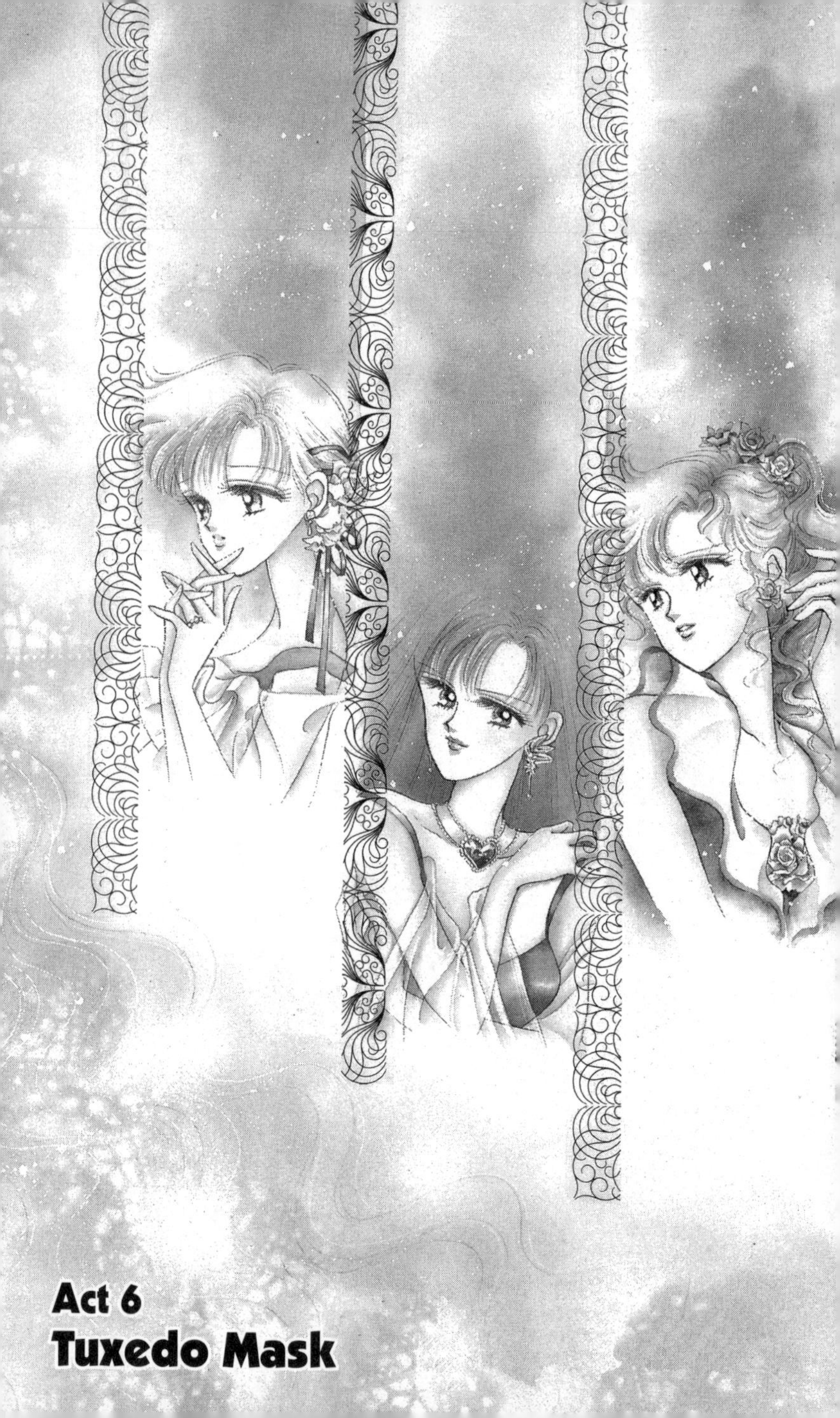

Act 6
Tuxedo Mask

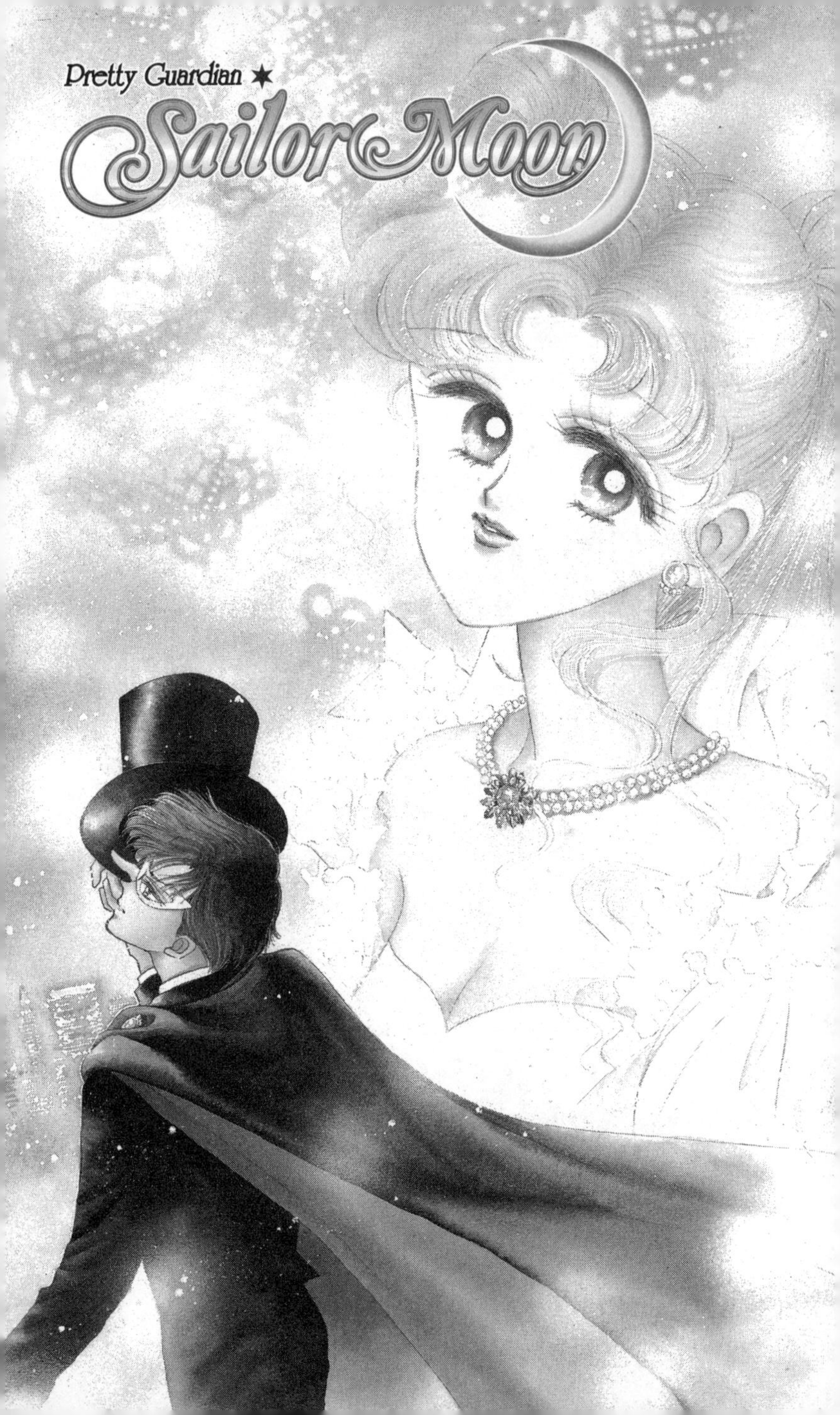
Pretty Guardian
Sailor Moon

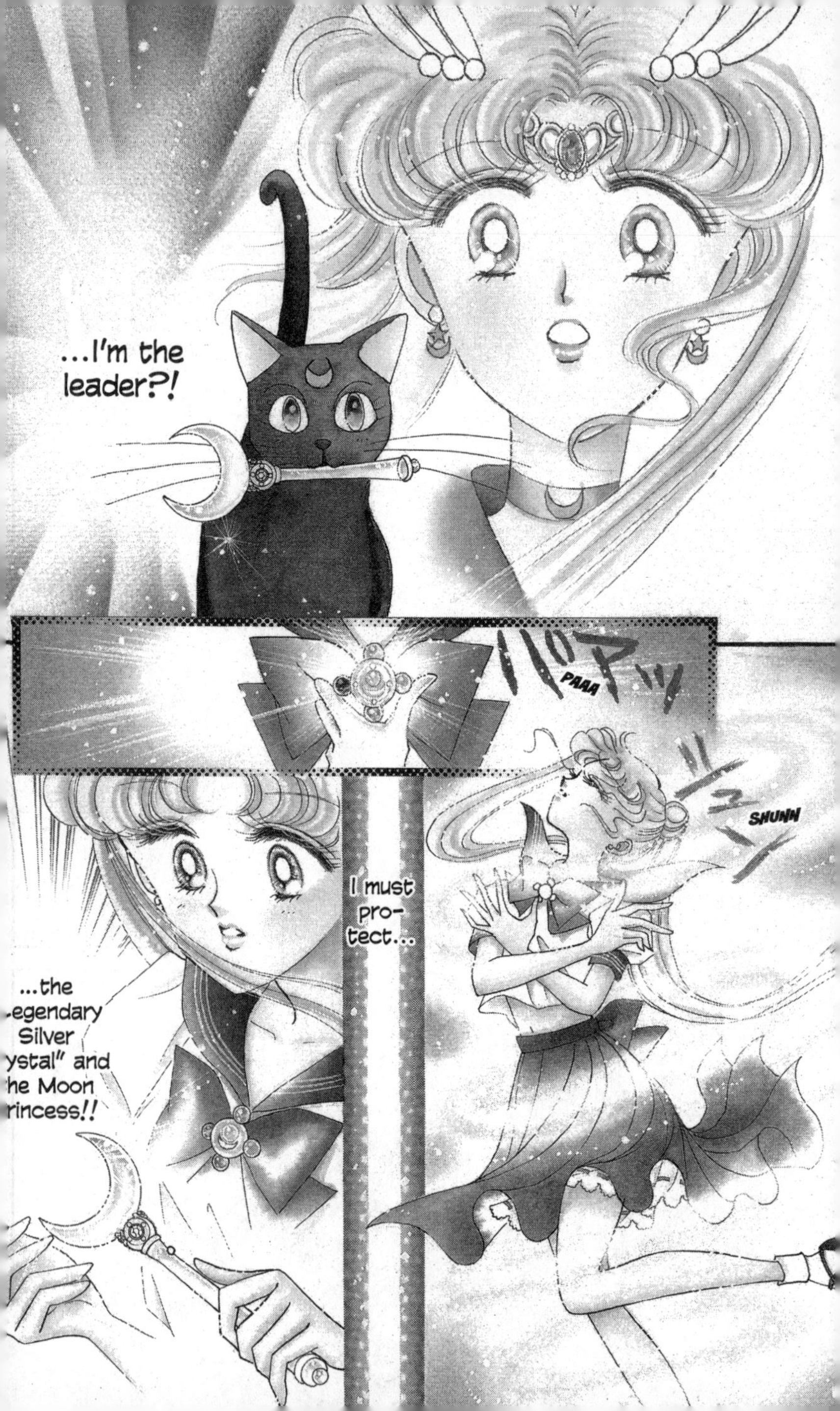
...I'm the leader?!
PAAA
SHUNN
I must pro-tect...
...the
egendary
Silver
ystal" and
he Moon
rincess!!

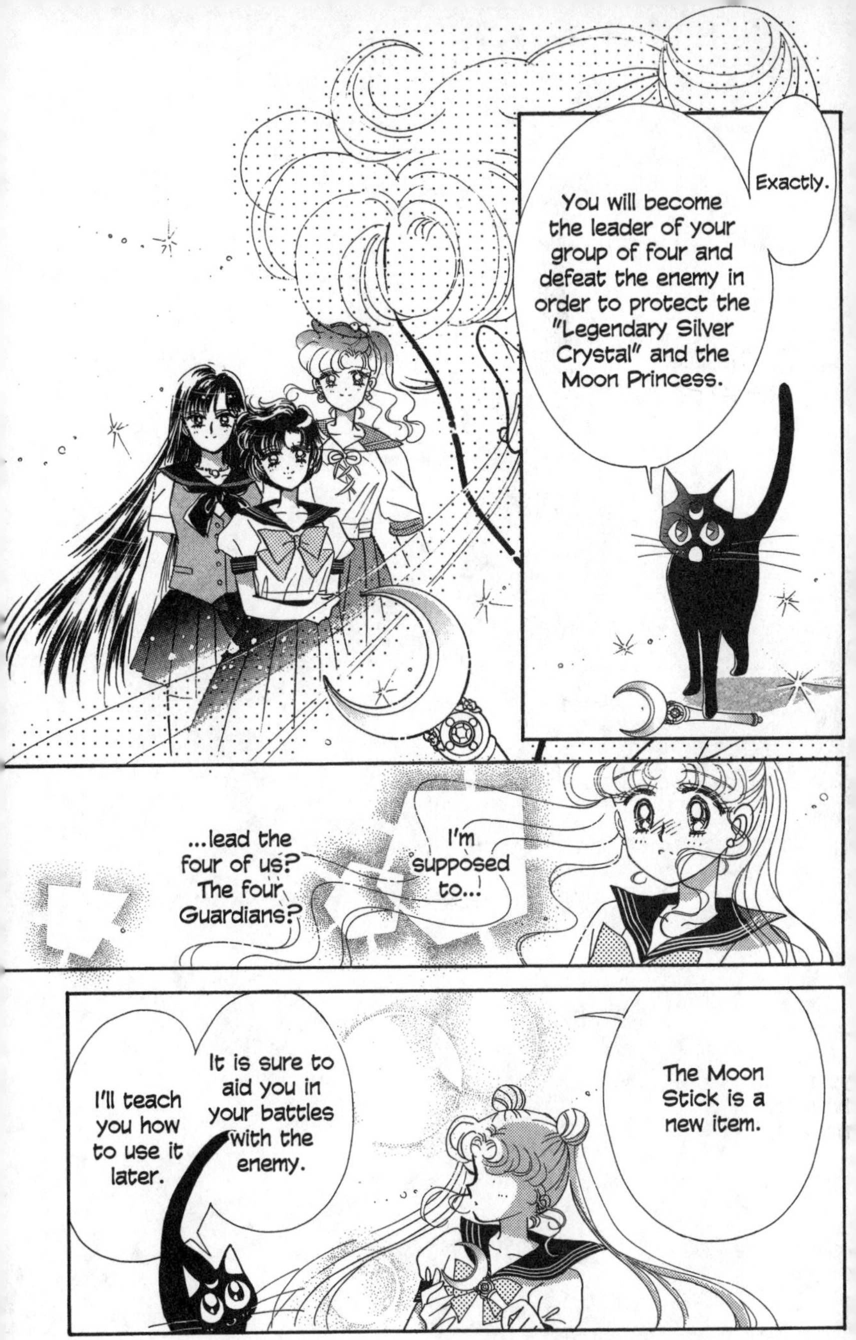
Exactly.
You will become the leader of your group of four and defeat the enemy in order to protect the "Legendary Silver Crystal" and the Moon Princess.
I'm supposed to...!
...lead the four of us? The four Guardians?
The Moon Stick is a new item.
It is sure to aid you in your battles with the enemy.
I'll teach you how to use it later.

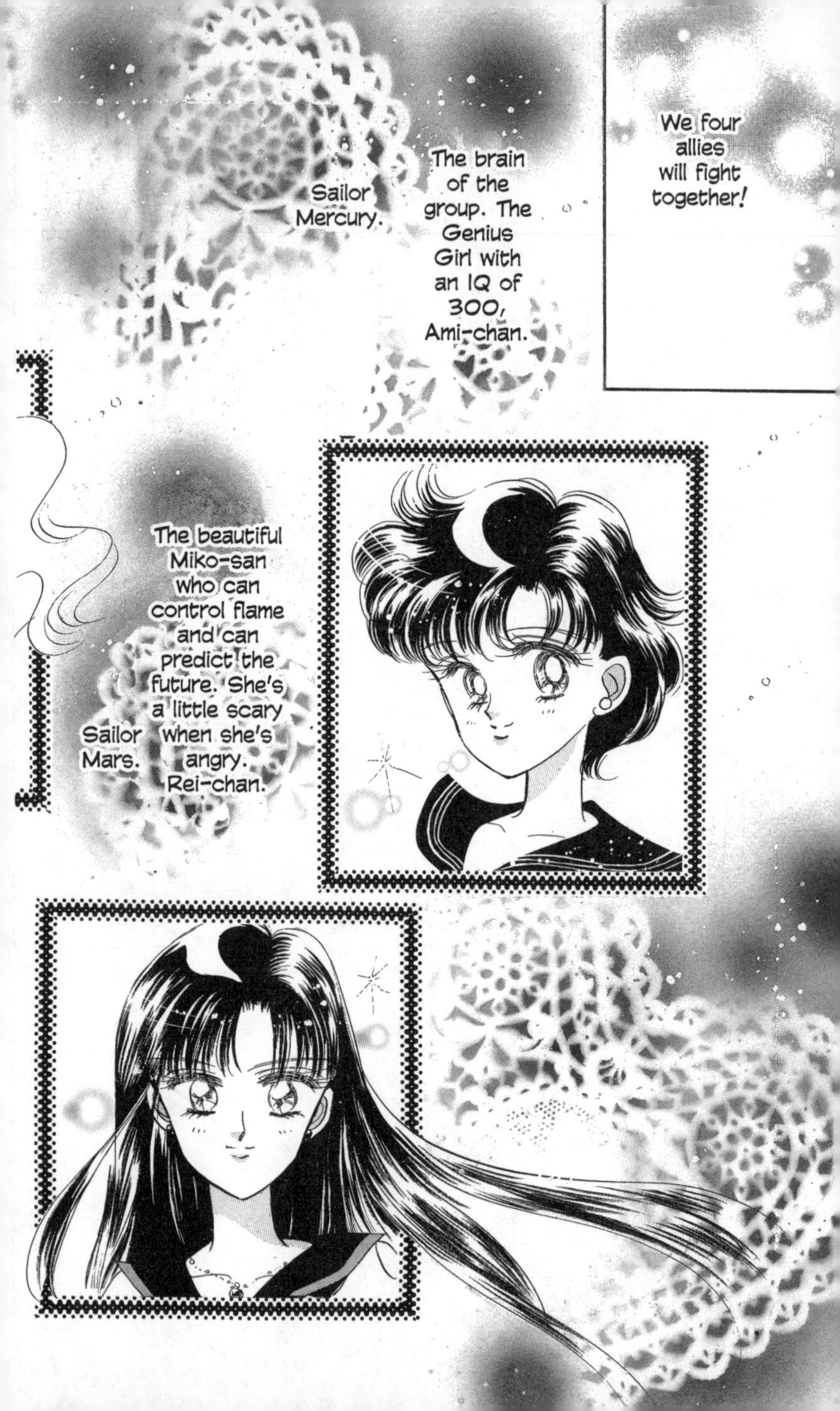
We four allies will fight together!
The brain of the group. The Genius Girl with an IQ of 300, Ami-chan.
Sailor Mercury.
The beautiful Miko-san who can control flame and can predict the future. She's a little scary when she's angry. Rei-chan.
Sailor Mars.

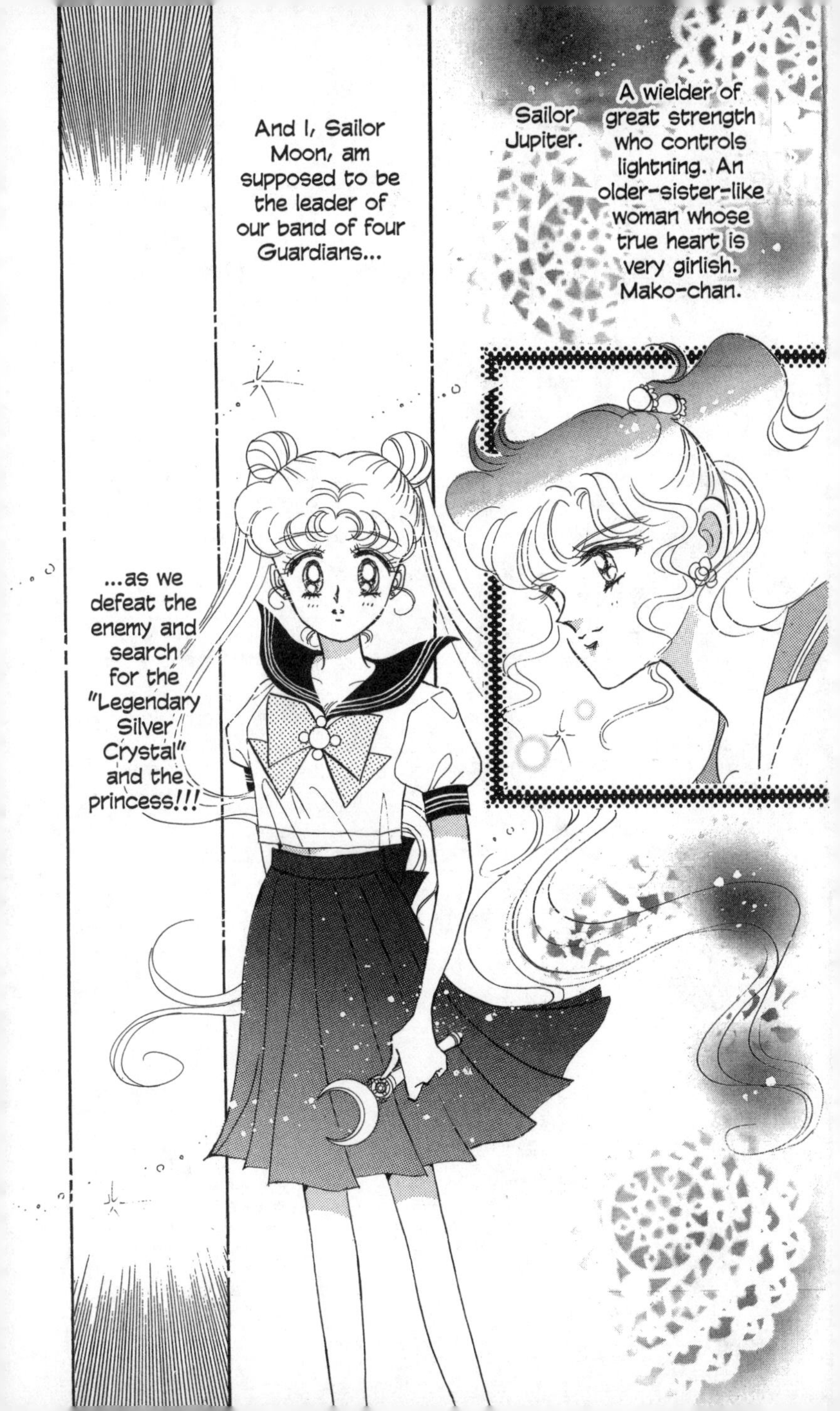
A wielder of great strength who controls lightning. An older-sister-like woman whose true heart is very girlish. Mako-chan.
Sailor Jupiter.
And I, Sailor Moon, am supposed to be the leader of our band of four Guardians...
...as we defeat the enemy and search for the "Legendary Silver Crystal" and the princess!!!

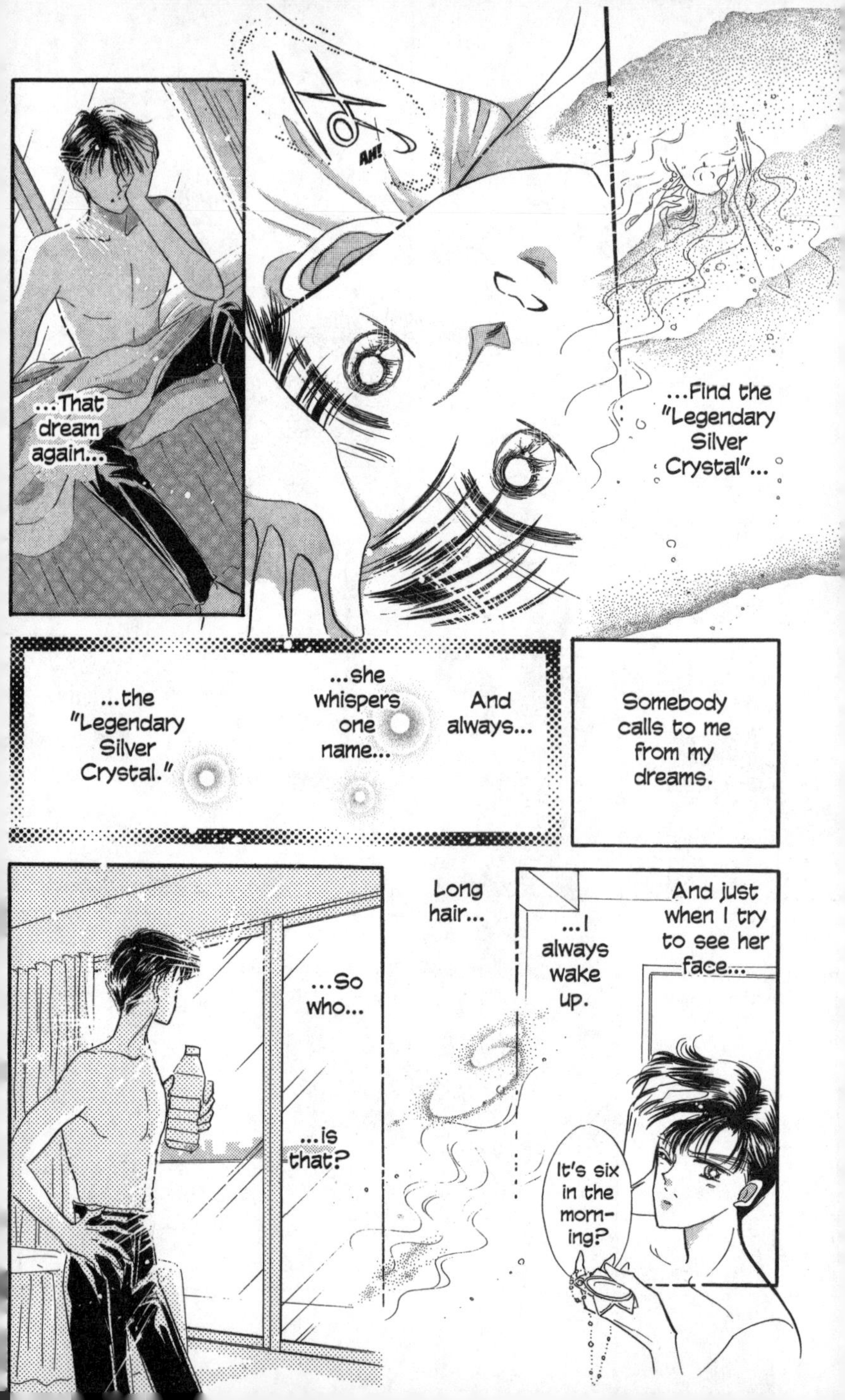
...Find the "Legendary Silver Crystal"...
AH!
...That dream again...
Somebody calls to me from my dreams.
And always...
...she whispers one name...
...the "Legendary Silver Crystal."
And just when I try to see her face...
...I always wake up.
It's six in the morning?
Long hair...
...So who...
...is that?

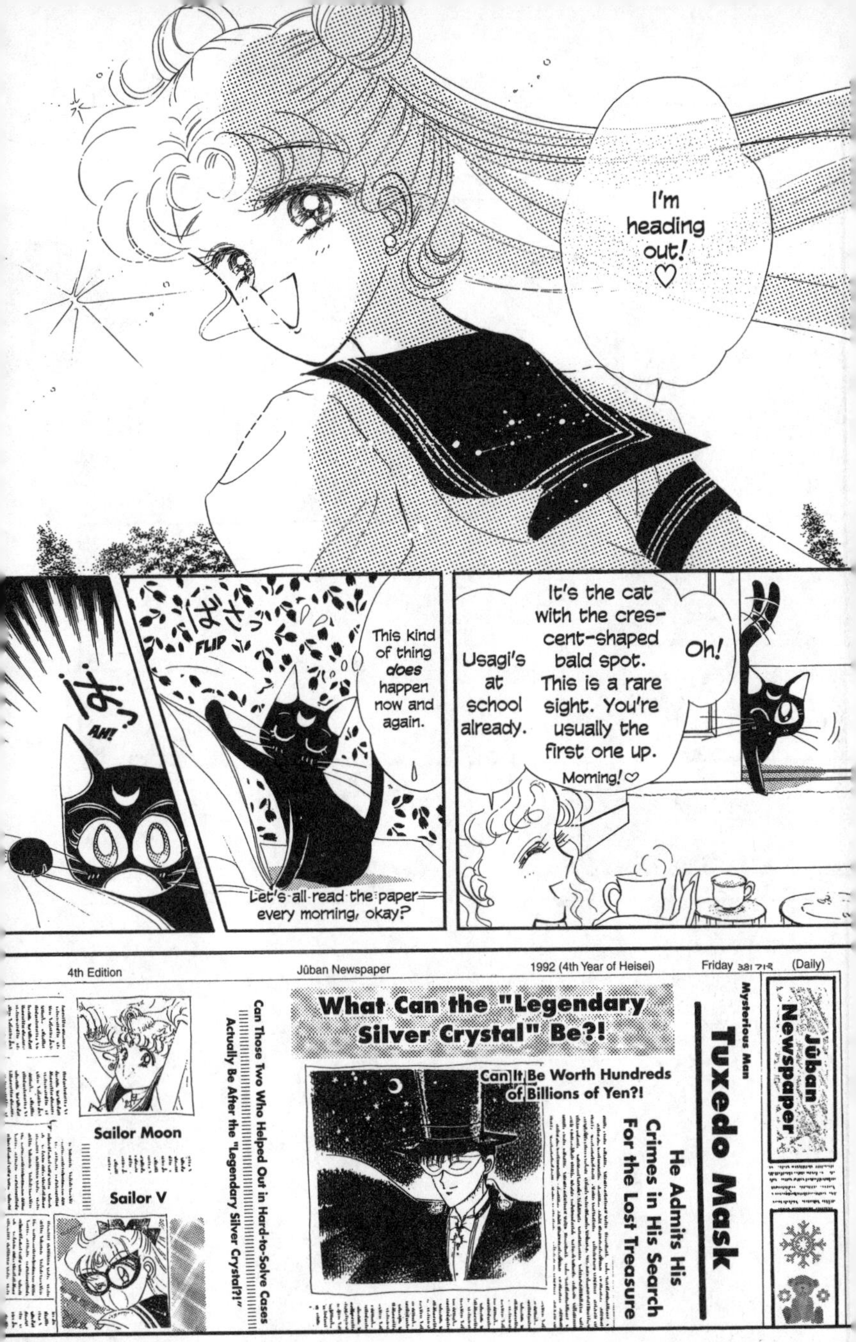
I'm heading out! ♡
Oh!
It's the cat with the cres-cent-shaped bald spot. This is a rare sight. You're usually the first one up.
Usagi's at school already.
Morning! ♡
This kind of thing *does* happen now and again.
ばさっ
FLIP
Let's all read the paper every morning, okay?
あっ
AH!
4th Edition
Jûban Newspaper
1992 (4th Year of Heisei)
Friday
(Daily)
Jûban Newspaper
Mysterious Man
Tuxedo Mask
He Admits His Crimes in His Search For the Lost Treasure
What Can the "Legendary Silver Crystal" Be?!
Can It Be Worth Hundreds of Billions of Yen?!
Can Those Two Who Helped Out in Hard-to-Solve Cases Actually Be After the "Legendary Silver Crystal?!"
Sailor Moon
Sailor V

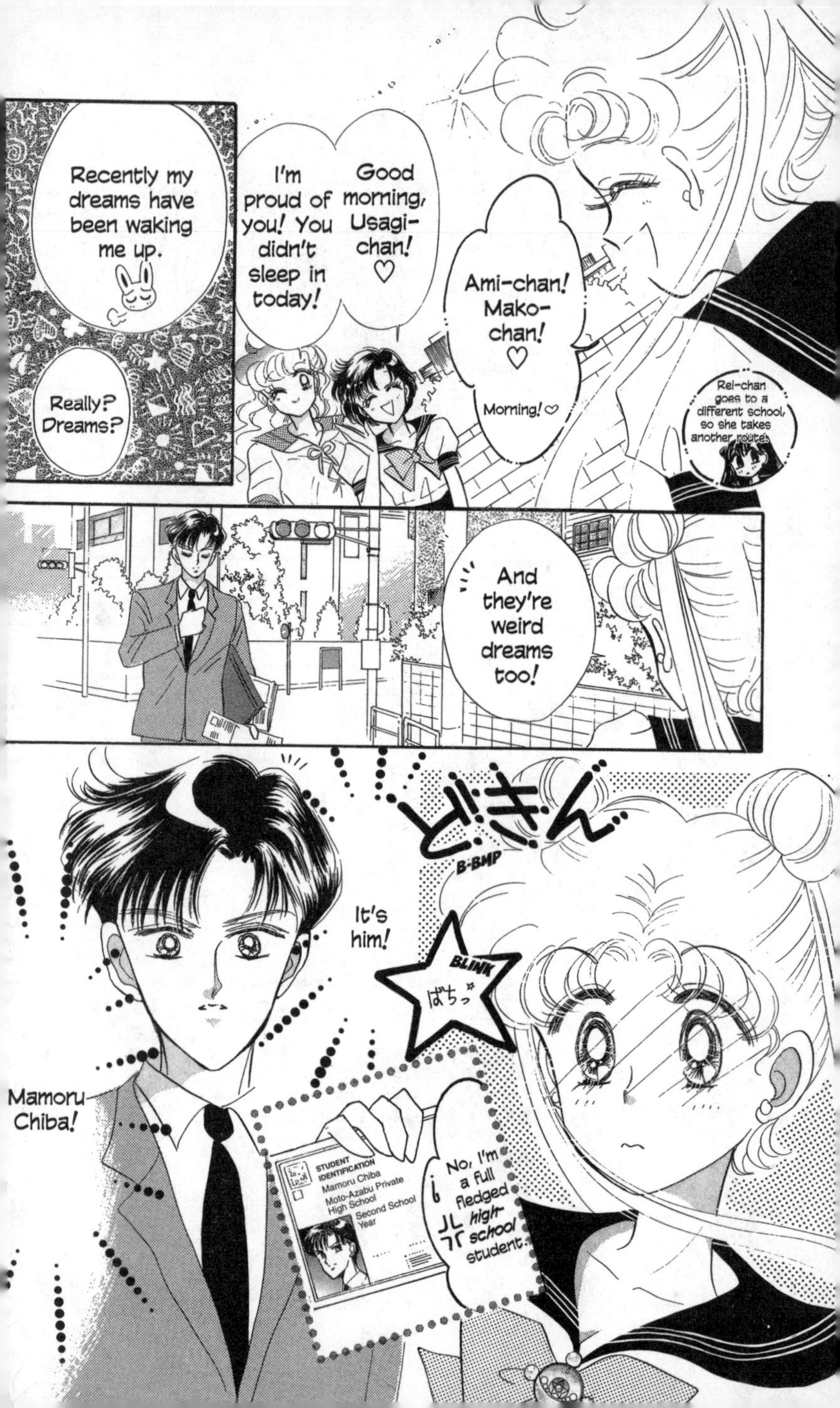
Ami-chan! Mako-chan! ♡
Morning! ♡
Rei-chan goes to a different school, so she takes another route.
Good morning, Usagi-chan! ♡
I'm proud of you! You didn't sleep in today!
Recently my dreams have been waking me up.
Really? Dreams?
And they're weird dreams too!
どきん
B-BMP
It's him!
BLINK
ばちっ
Mamoru Chiba!
No, I'm a full fledged *high school* student.
STUDENT IDENTIFICATION
Mamoru Chiba
Moto-Azabu Private High School
Second School Year

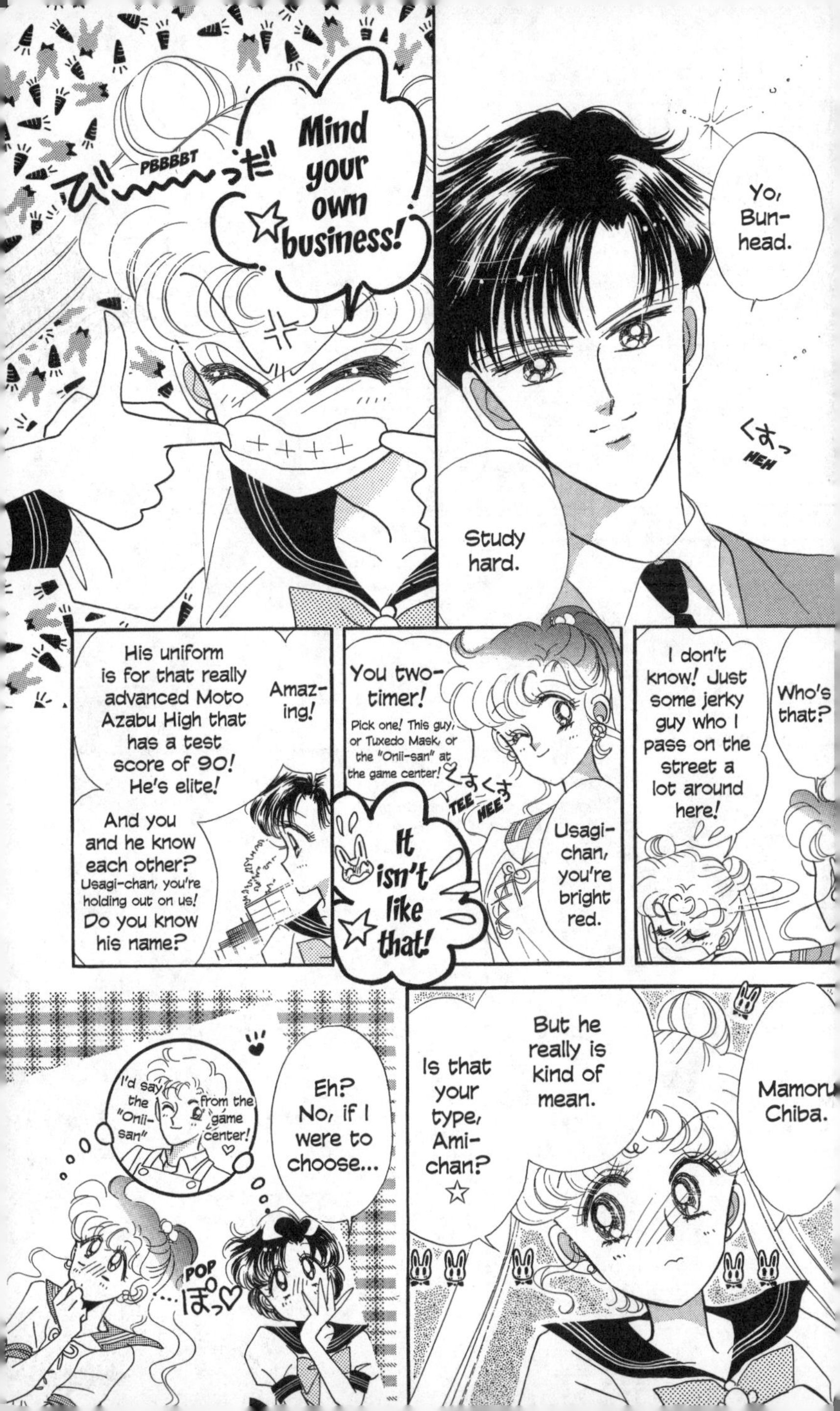

Yo, Bun-head.
くすっ
NEH
Study hard.
びーーーっだ
PBBBBT
Mind your own ☆ business!
Who's that?
I don't know! Just some jerky guy who I pass on the street a lot around here!
Usagi-chan, you're bright red.
You two-timer!
Pick one! This guy, or Tuxedo Mask, or the "Onii-san" at the game center! ♡
くすくす
TEE HEE
It isn't like ☆ that!
Amaz-ing!
His uniform is for that really advanced Moto Azabu High that has a test score of 90! He's elite!
And you and he know each other? Usagi-chan, you're holding out on us! Do you know his name?
Mamoru Chiba.
But he really is kind of mean.
Is that your type, Ami-chan? ☆
Eh? No, if I were to choose...
I'd say the "Onii-san" from the game center! ♡
POP
ぽっ♡

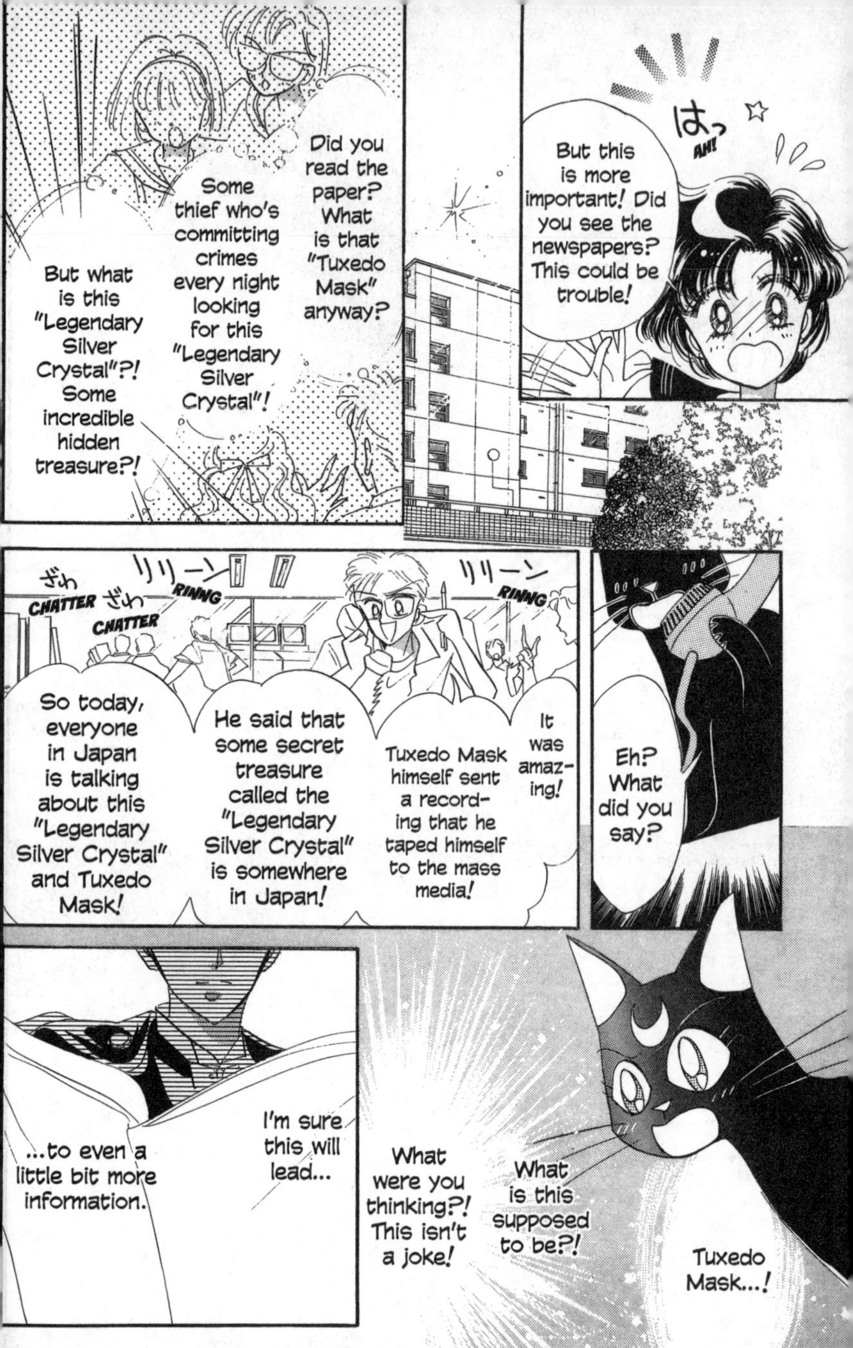
はっ
AH!
But this is more important! Did you see the newspapers? This could be trouble!
Did you read the paper? What is that "Tuxedo Mask" anyway?
Some thief who's committing crimes every night looking for this "Legendary Silver Crystal"!
But what is this "Legendary Silver Crystal"?! Some incredible hidden treasure?!
Eh? What did you say?
リリーン
RING
リリーン
RING
ざわ
CHATTER
ざわ
CHATTER
It was amazing!
Tuxedo Mask himself sent a recording that he taped himself to the mass media!
He said that some secret treasure called the "Legendary Silver Crystal" is somewhere in Japan!
So today, everyone in Japan is talking about this "Legendary Silver Crystal" and Tuxedo Mask!
Tuxedo Mask...!
What is this supposed to be?!
What were you thinking?! This isn't a joke!
I'm sure this will lead...
...to even a little bit more information.

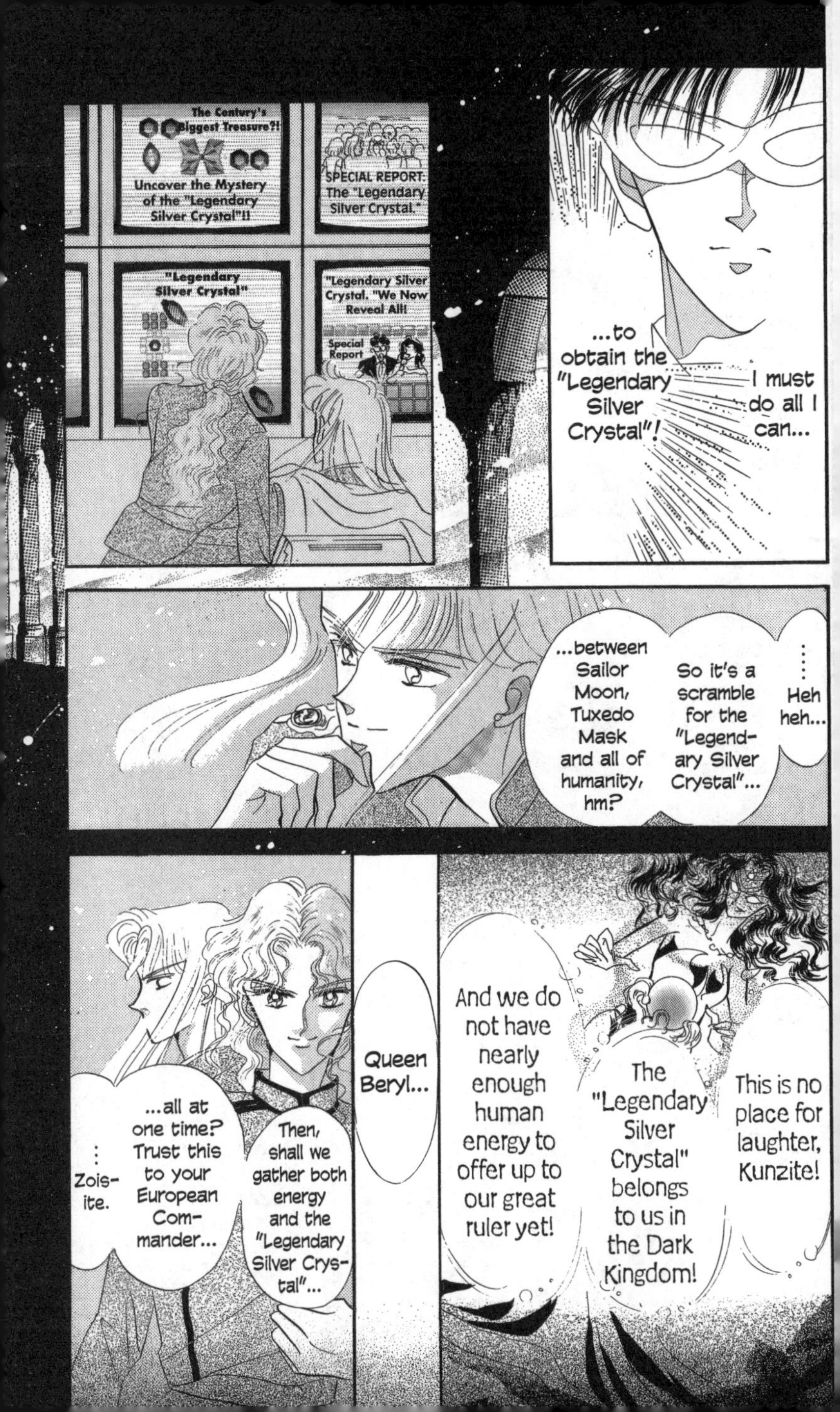
I must do all I can...
...to obtain the "Legendary Silver Crystal"!
SPECIAL REPORT: The "Legendary Silver Crystal."
The Century's Biggest Treasure?!
Uncover the Mystery of the "Legendary Silver Crystal"!!
"Legendary Silver Crystal. "We Now Reveal All!
Special Report
"Legendary Silver Crystal"
...... Heh heh...
So it's a scramble for the "Legend-ary Silver Crystal"...
...between Sailor Moon, Tuxedo Mask and all of humanity, hm?
This is no place for laughter, Kunzite!
The "Legendary Silver Crystal" belongs to us in the Dark Kingdom!
And we do not have nearly enough human energy to offer up to our great ruler yet!
Queen Beryl...
Then, shall we gather both energy and the "Legendary Silver Crys-tal"...
...all at one time? Trust this to your European Com-mander...
... Zois-ite.

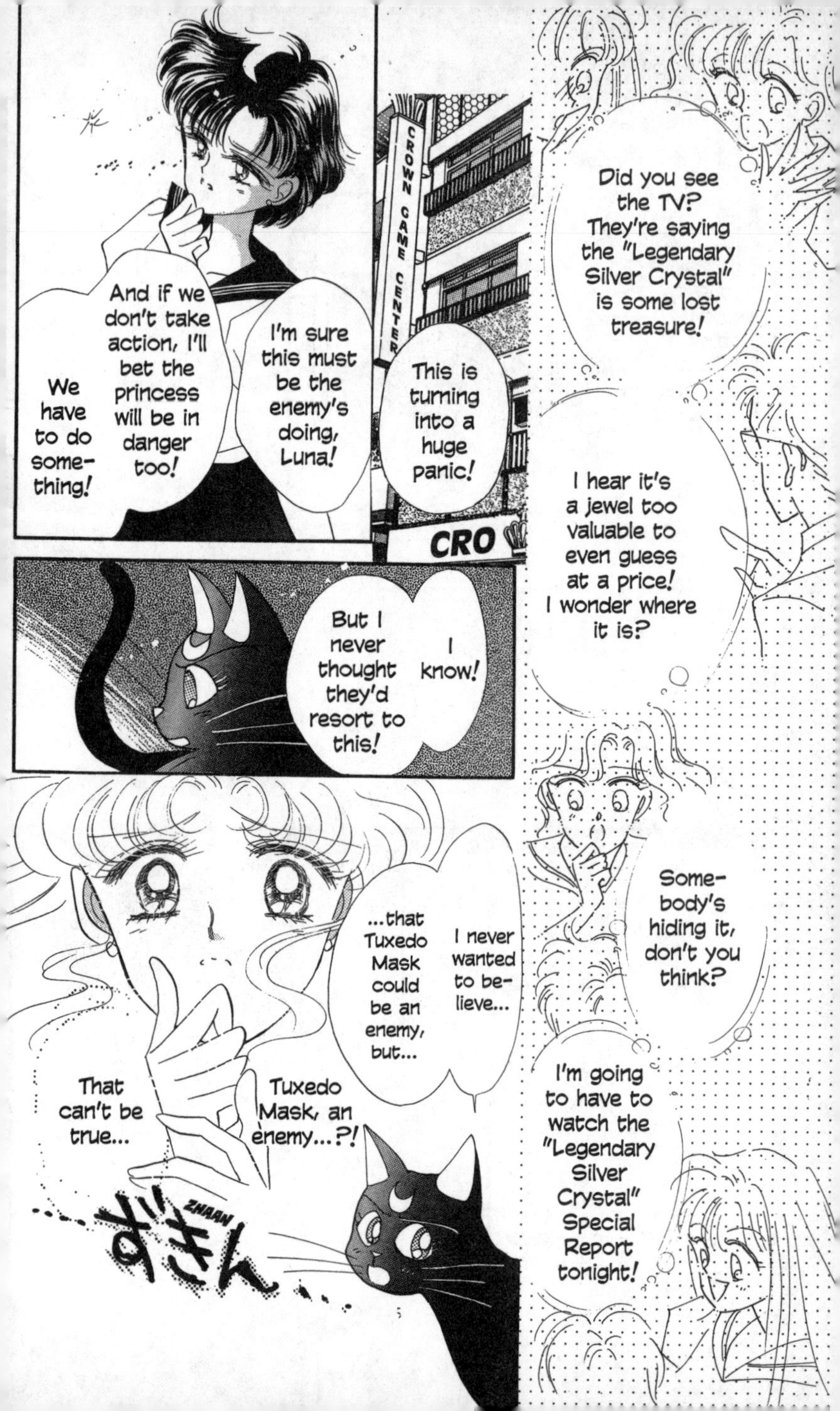
Did you see the TV? They're saying the "Legendary Silver Crystal" is some lost treasure!
I hear it's a jewel too valuable to even guess at a price! I wonder where it is?
Some-body's hiding it, don't you think?
I'm going to have to watch the "Legendary Silver Crystal" Special Report tonight!
CROWN GAME CENTER
CRO
This is turning into a huge panic!
I'm sure this must be the enemy's doing, Luna!
And if we don't take action, I'll bet the princess will be in danger too!
We have to do some-thing!
I know!
But I never thought they'd resort to this!
I never wanted to be-lieve...
...that Tuxedo Mask could be an enemy, but...
Tuxedo Mask, an enemy...?!
That can't be true...
ZHAAN

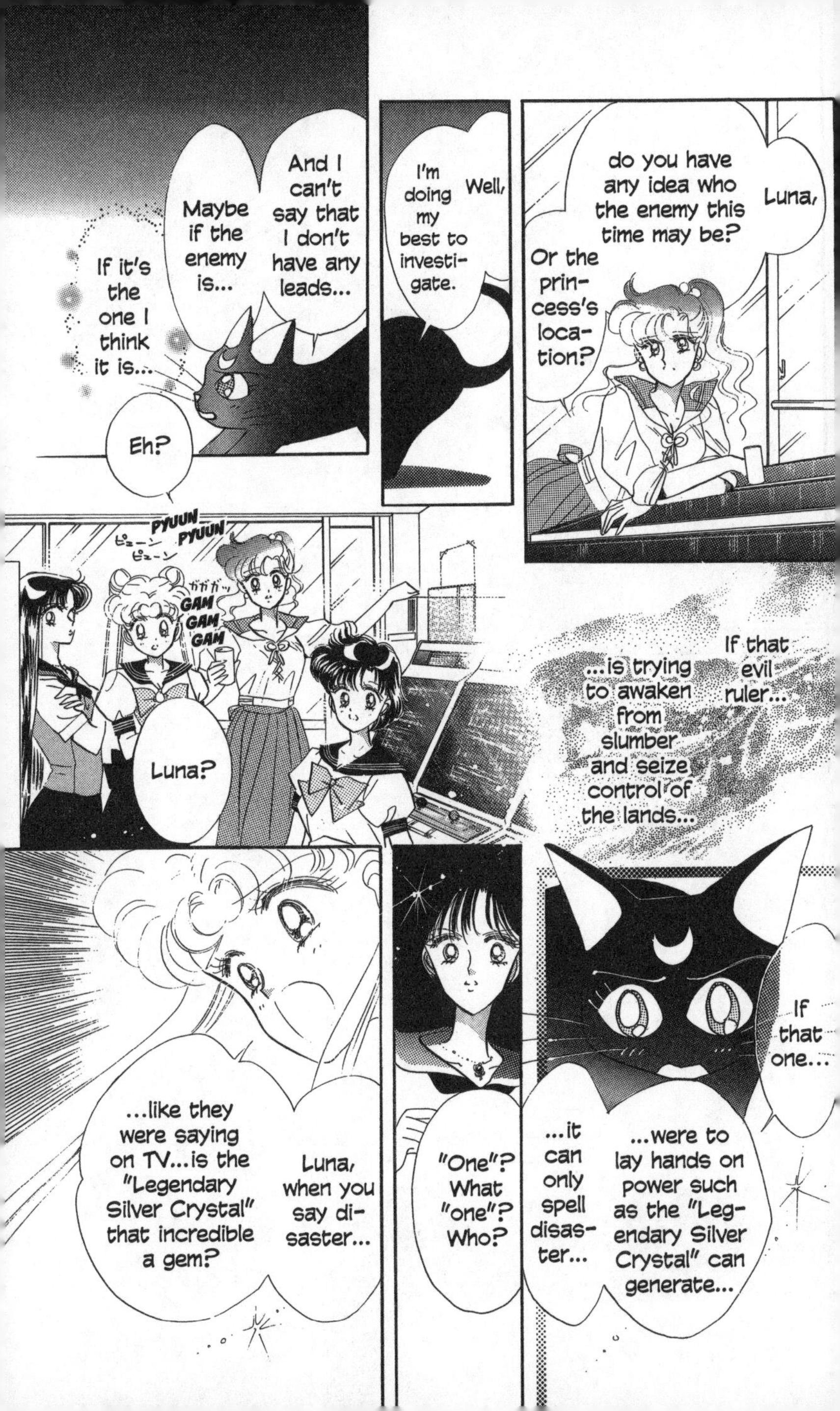
Luna,
do you have any idea who the enemy this time may be?
Or the princess's location?
Well,
I'm doing my best to investigate.
And I can't say that I don't have any leads...
Maybe if the enemy is...
If it's the one I think it is...
If that evil ruler...
...is trying to awaken from slumber and seize control of the lands...
Eh?
PYUUN ピューン
PYUUN ピューン
GAM GAM GAM ガガガッ
Luna?
If that one...
...were to lay hands on power such as the "Legendary Silver Crystal" can generate...
...it can only spell disaster...
"One"? What "one"? Who?
Luna, when you say disaster...
...like they were saying on TV...is the "Legendary Silver Crystal" that incredible a gem?

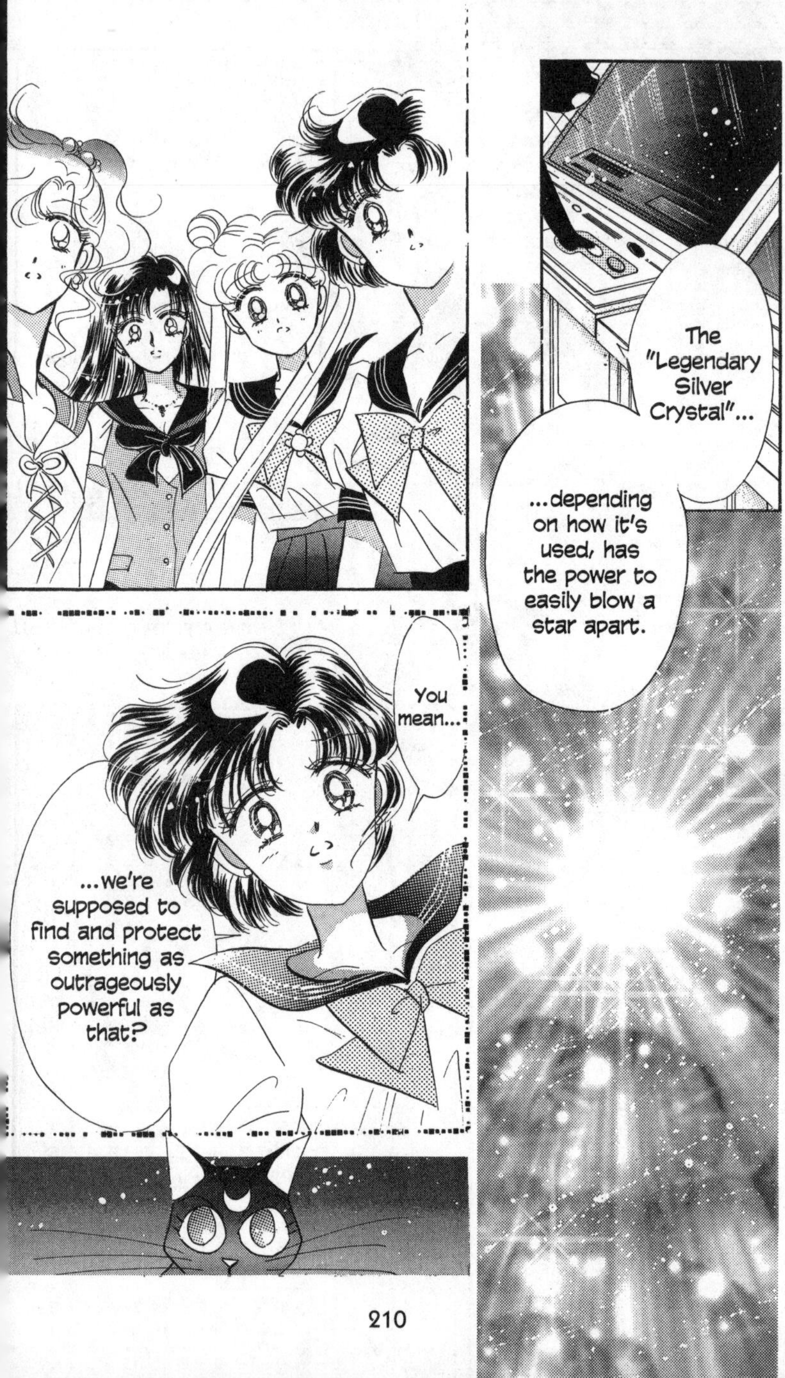
The "Legendary Silver Crystal"...
...depending on how it's used, has the power to easily blow a star apart.
You mean...
...we're supposed to find and protect something as outrageously powerful as that?

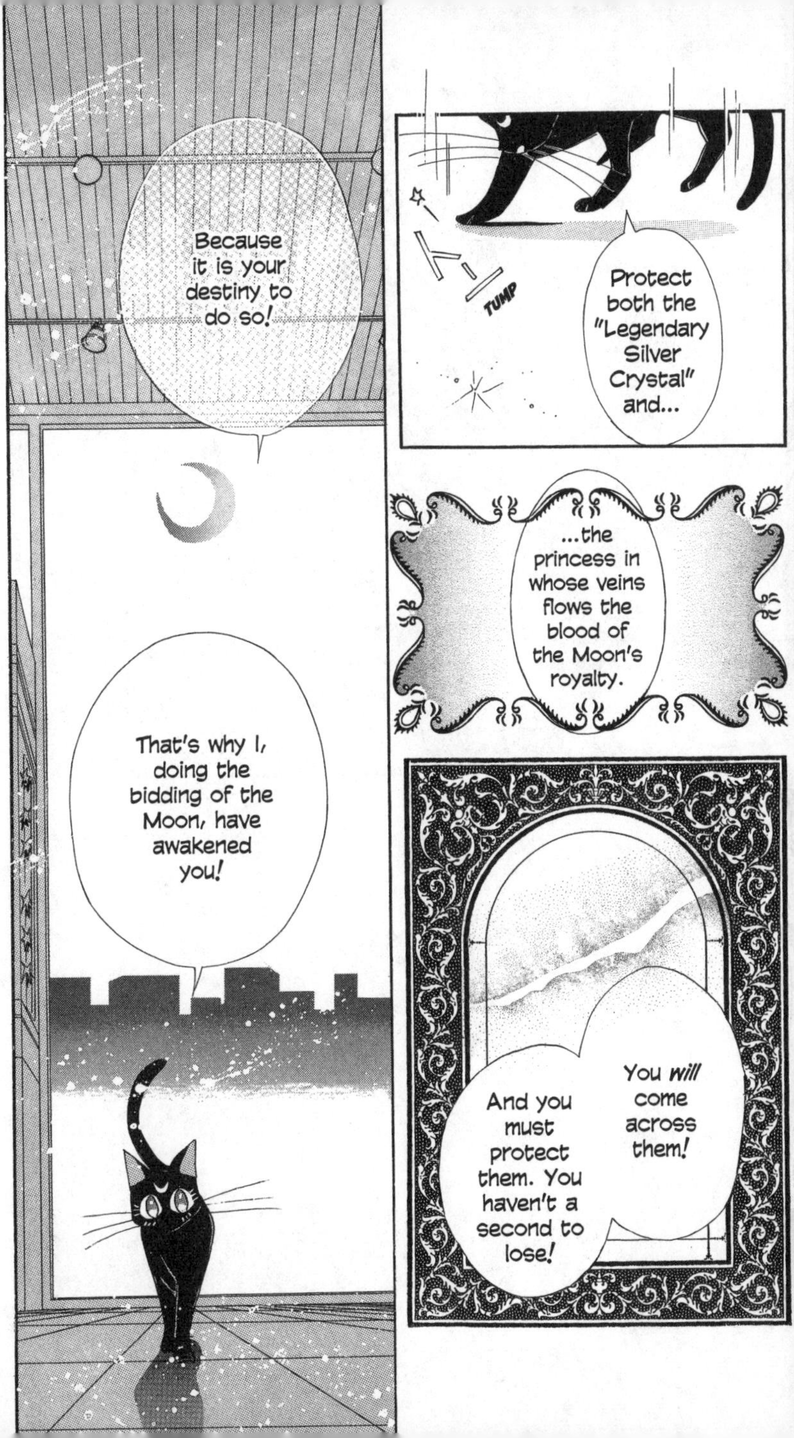
Protect both the "Legendary Silver Crystal" and...
TUMP
...the princess in whose veins flows the blood of the Moon's royalty.
You *will* come across them!
And you must protect them. You haven't a second to lose!
Because it is your destiny to do so!
That's why I, doing the bidding of the Moon, have awakened you!

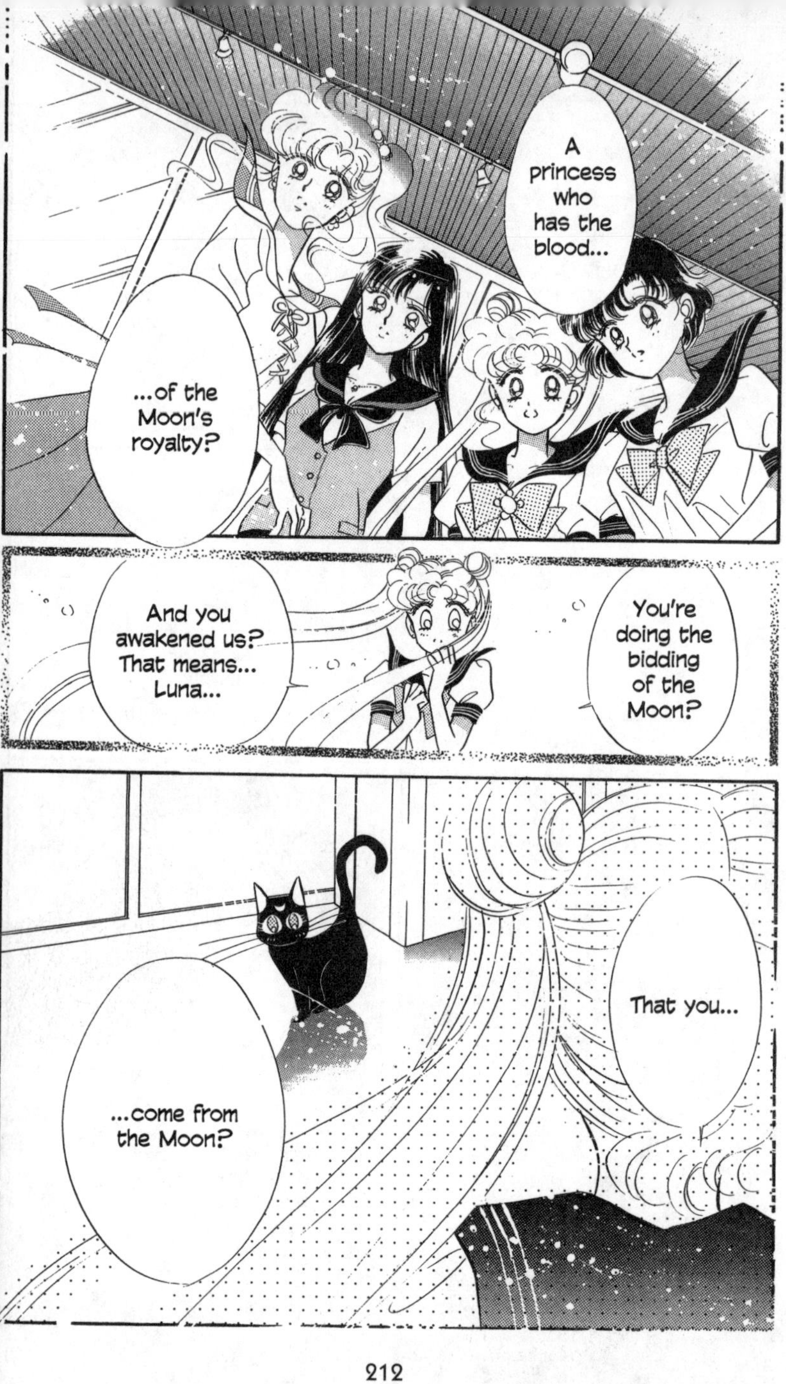
A princess who has the blood...
...of the Moon's royalty?
You're doing the bidding of the Moon?
And you awakened us? That means... Luna...
That you...
...come from the Moon?

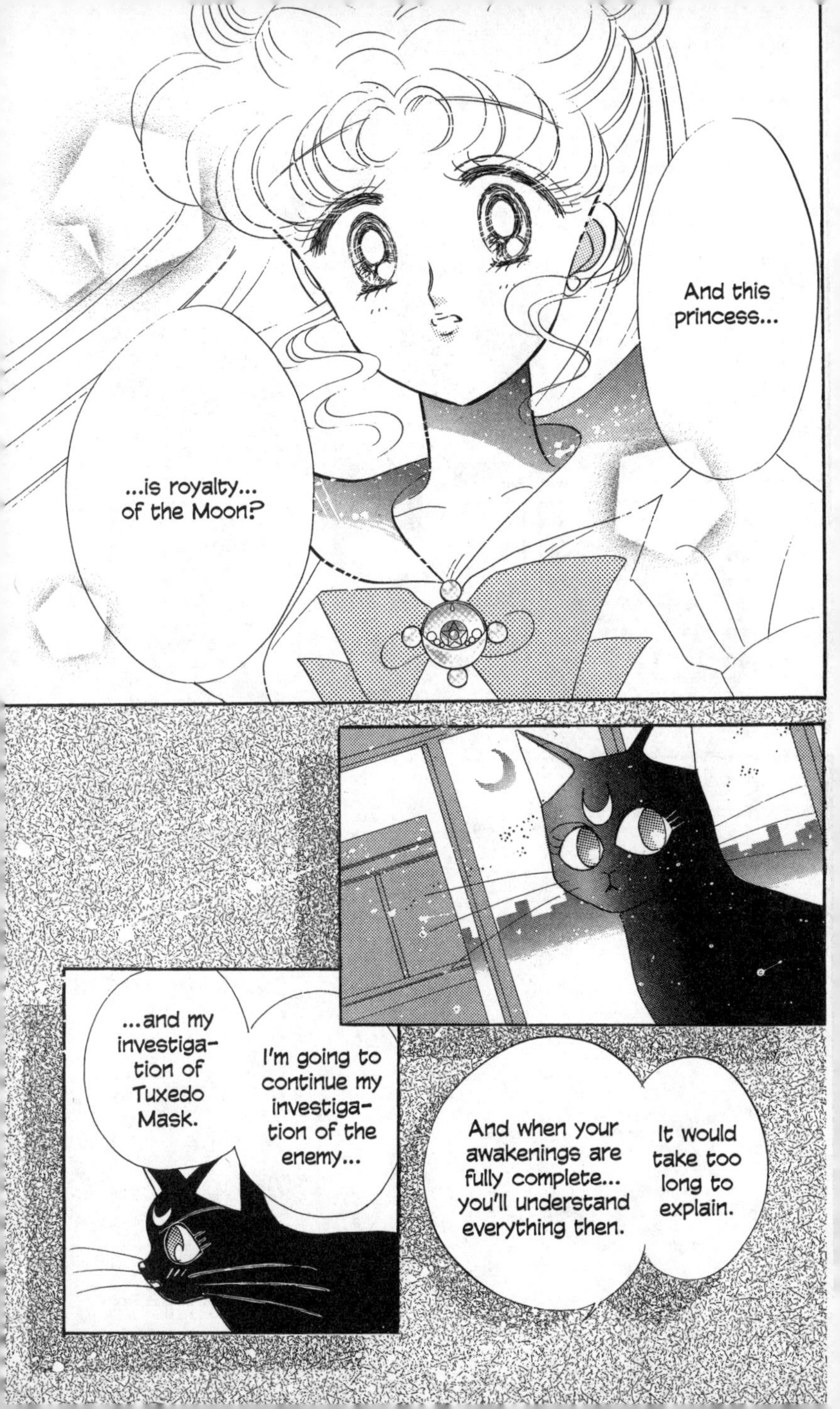

And this princess...
...is royalty... of the Moon?
It would take too long to explain.
And when your awakenings are fully complete... you'll understand everything then.
I'm going to continue my investigation of the enemy...
...and my investigation of Tuxedo Mask.

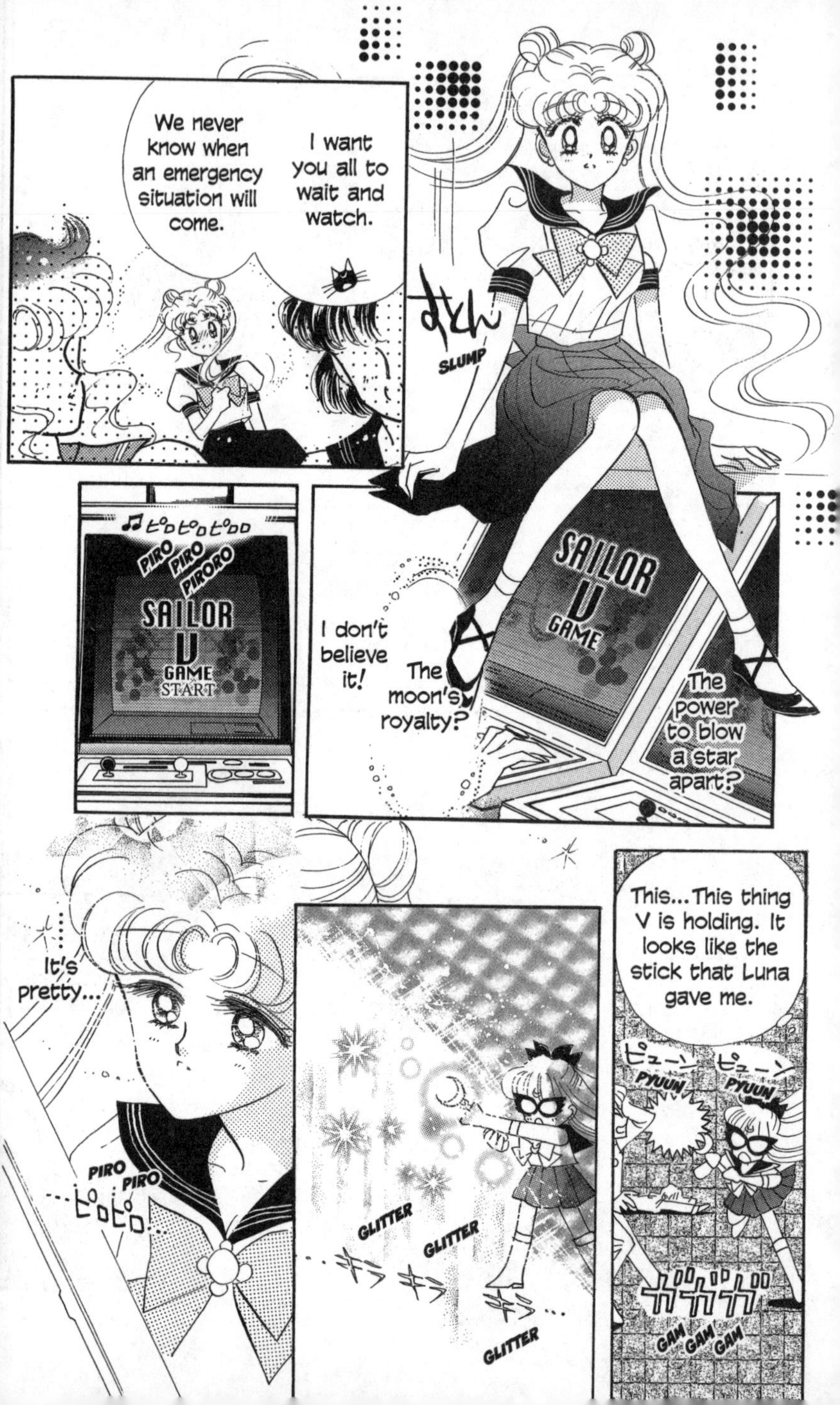
I want you all to wait and watch.
We never know when an emergency situation will come.
SLUMP
The power to blow a star apart?
The moon's royalty?
I don't believe it!
SAILOR V GAME
PIRO PIRO PIRORO
SAILOR V GAME START
This...This thing V is holding. It looks like the stick that Luna gave me.
PYUUN
PYUUN
GAM GAM GAM
GLITTER
GLITTER
GLITTER
It's pretty...
PIRO PIRO

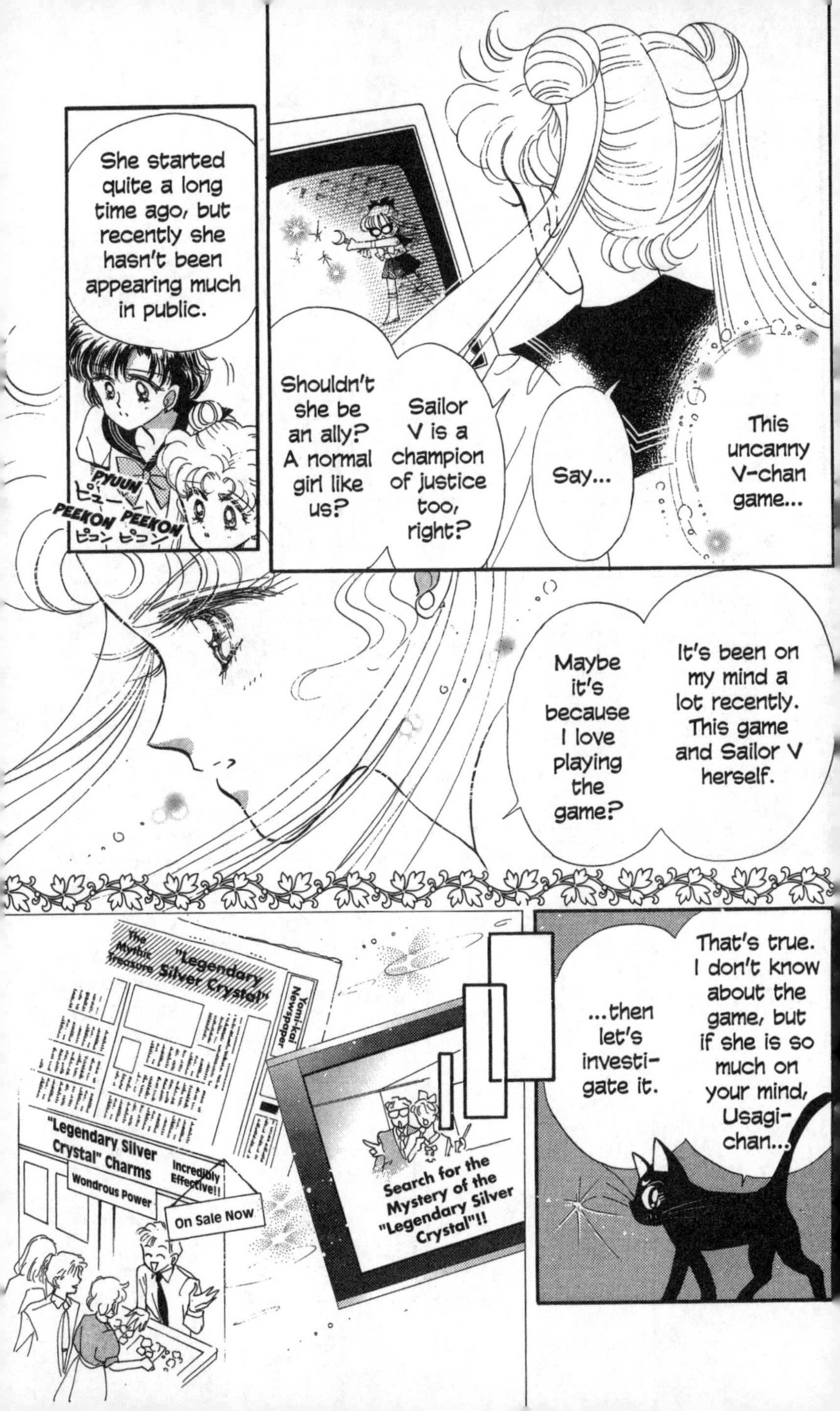
This uncanny V-chan game...
Say...
Sailor V is a champion of justice too, right?
Shouldn't she be an ally? A normal girl like us?
She started quite a long time ago, but recently she hasn't been appearing much in public.
PYUUN ピューー
PEEKON PEEKON ピコン ピコン
It's been on my mind a lot recently. This game and Sailor V herself.
Maybe it's because I love playing the game?
That's true. I don't know about the game, but if she is so much on your mind, Usagi-chan...
...then let's investigate it.
The Mythic Treasure "Legendary Silver Crystal"
Yomi-kai Newspaper
"Legendary Silver Crystal" Charms
Wondrous Power
Incredibly Effective!!
On Sale Now
Search for the Mystery of the "Legendary Silver Crystal"!!

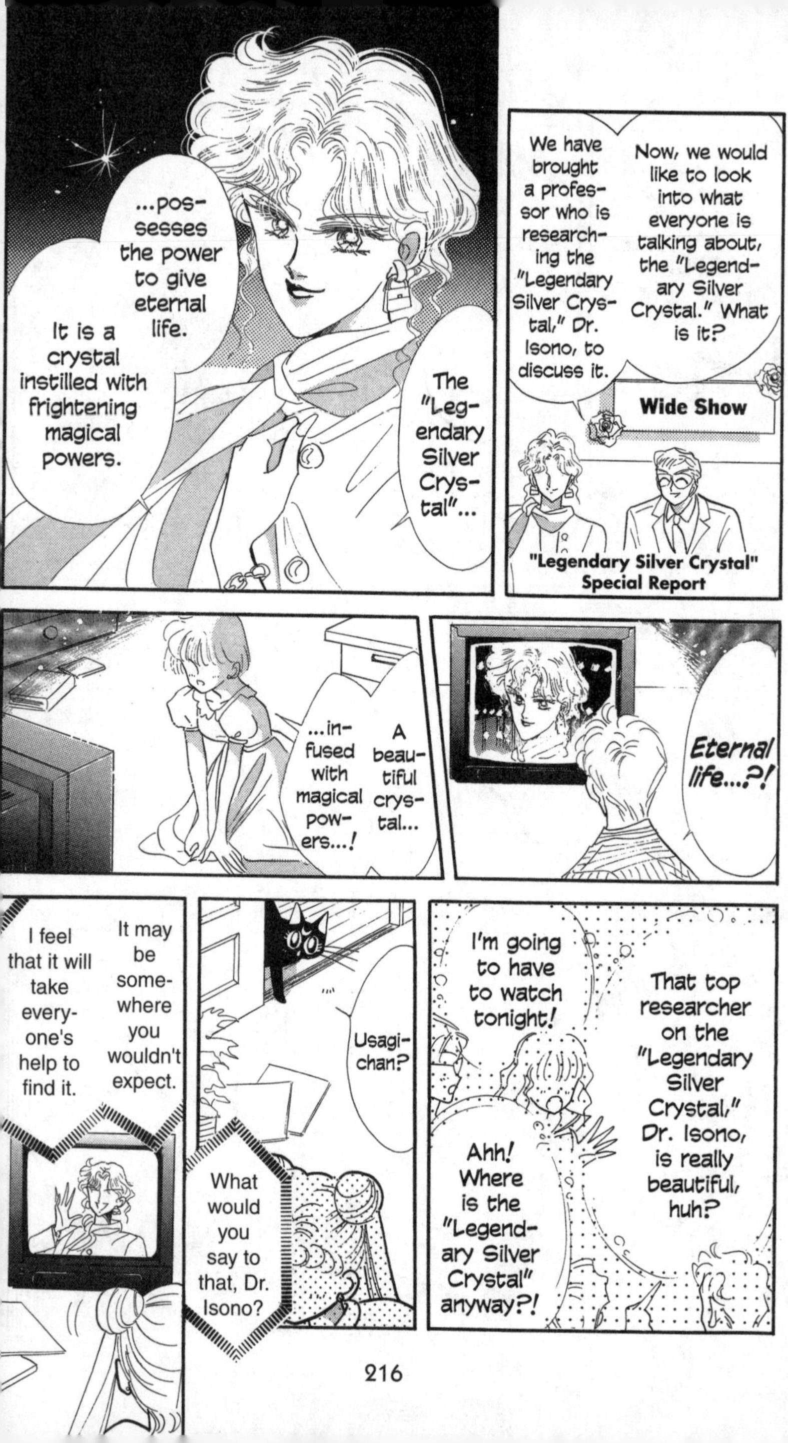

Now, we would like to look into what everyone is talking about, the "Legendary Silver Crystal." What is it?
We have brought a professor who is researching the "Legendary Silver Crystal," Dr. Isono, to discuss it.
Wide Show
"Legendary Silver Crystal" Special Report
The "Legendary Silver Crystal"...
...possesses the power to give eternal life.
It is a crystal instilled with frightening magical powers.
Eternal life...?!
A beautiful crystal...
...infused with magical powers...!
That top researcher on the "Legendary Silver Crystal," Dr. Isono, is really beautiful, huh?
I'm going to have to watch tonight!
Ahh! Where is the "Legendary Silver Crystal" anyway?!
Usagi-chan?
What would you say to that, Dr. Isono?
It may be somewhere you wouldn't expect.
I feel that it will take everyone's help to find it.

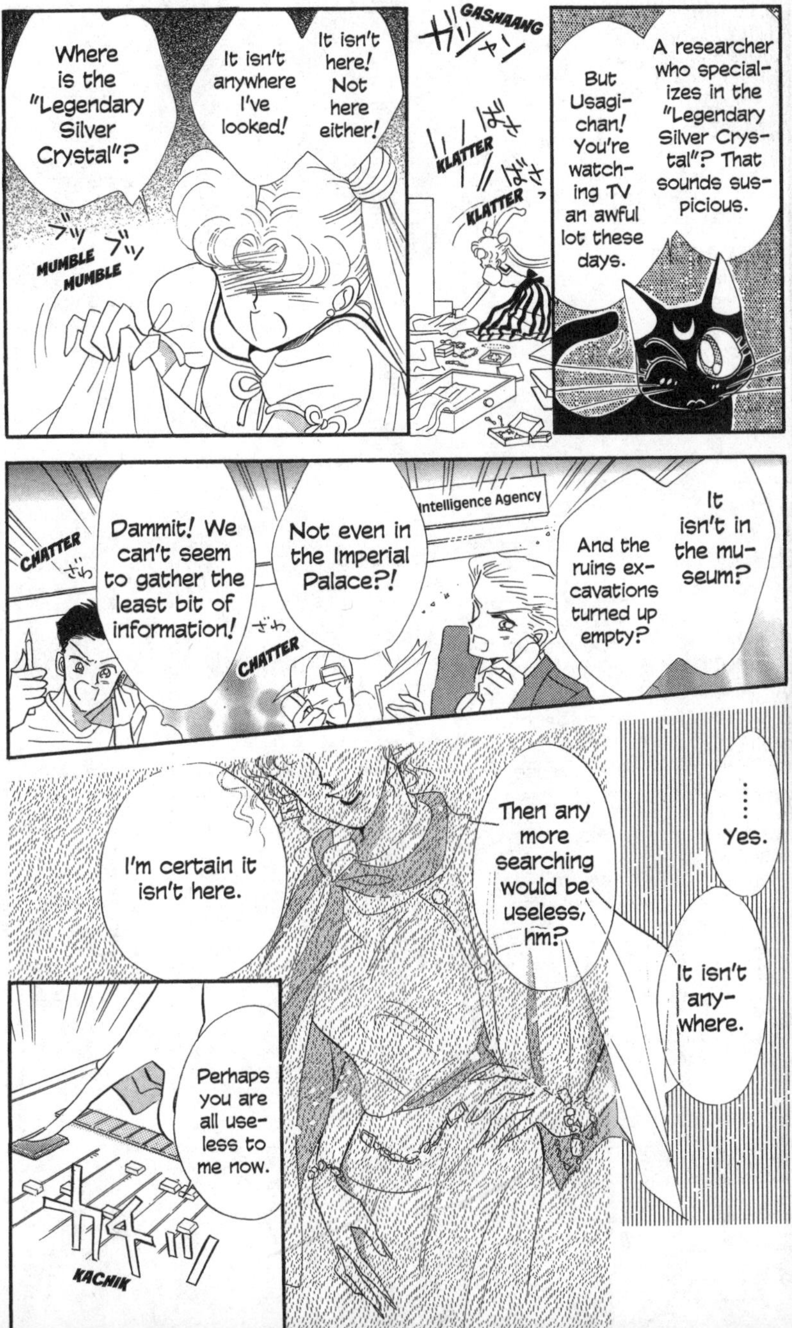

A researcher who specializes in the "Legendary Silver Crystal"? That sounds suspicious.
But Usagi-chan! You're watching TV an awful lot these days.
GASHAANG
KLATTER
KLATTER
It isn't here! Not here either!
It isn't anywhere I've looked!
Where is the "Legendary Silver Crystal"?
MUMBLE MUMBLE
It isn't in the museum?
And the ruins excavations turned up empty?
Intelligence Agency
Not even in the Imperial Palace?!
CHATTER
Dammit! We can't seem to gather the least bit of information!
CHATTER
...... Yes.
It isn't anywhere.
Then any more searching would be useless, hm?
I'm certain it isn't here.
Perhaps you are all useless to me now.
KACHIK

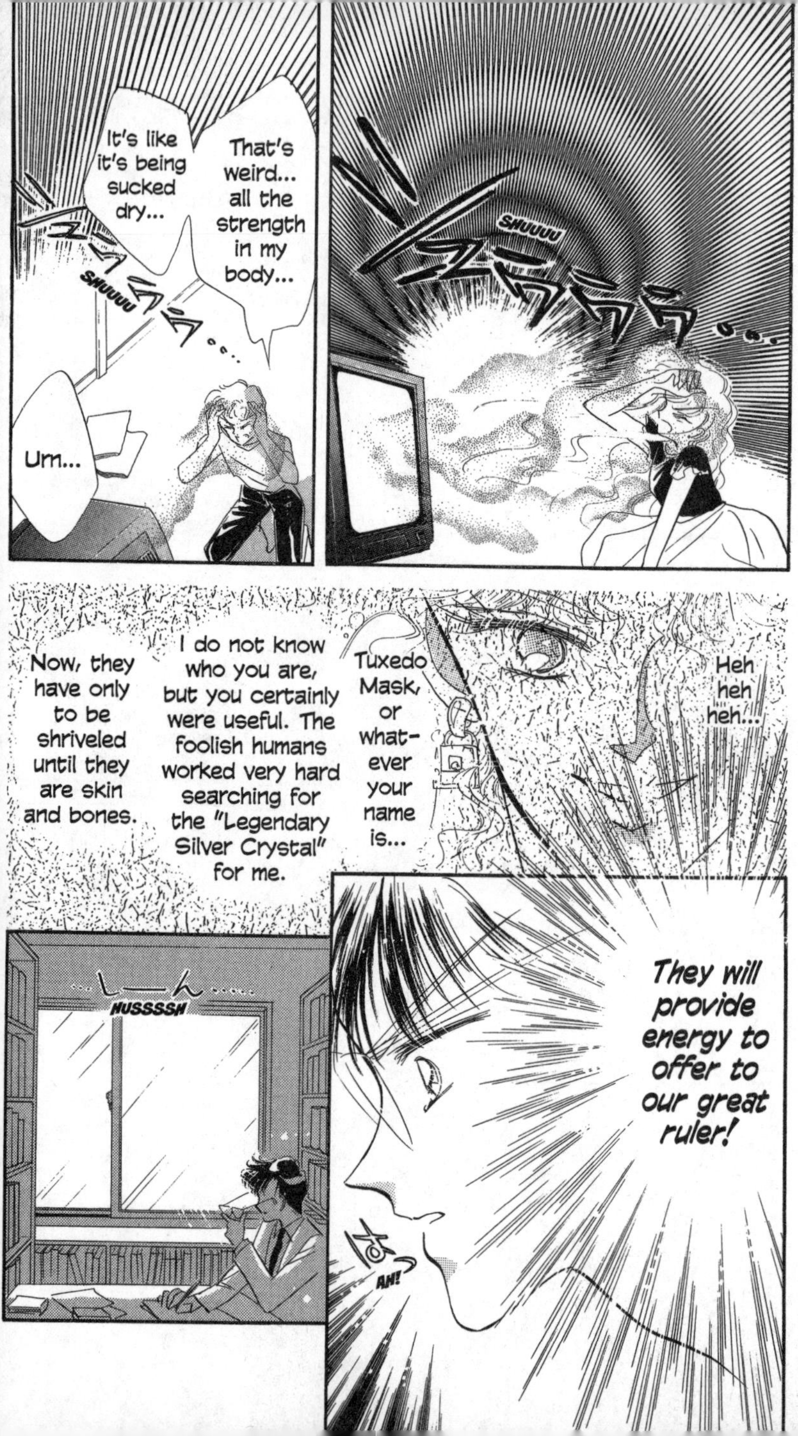
SHUUUU
That's weird... all the strength in my body...
It's like it's being sucked dry...
SHUUUU
Um...
Heh heh heh...
Tuxedo Mask, or whatever your name is...
I do not know who you are, but you certainly were useful. The foolish humans worked very hard searching for the "Legendary Silver Crystal" for me.
Now, they have only to be shriveled until they are skin and bones.
They will provide energy to offer to our great ruler!
AH!
HUSSSSH

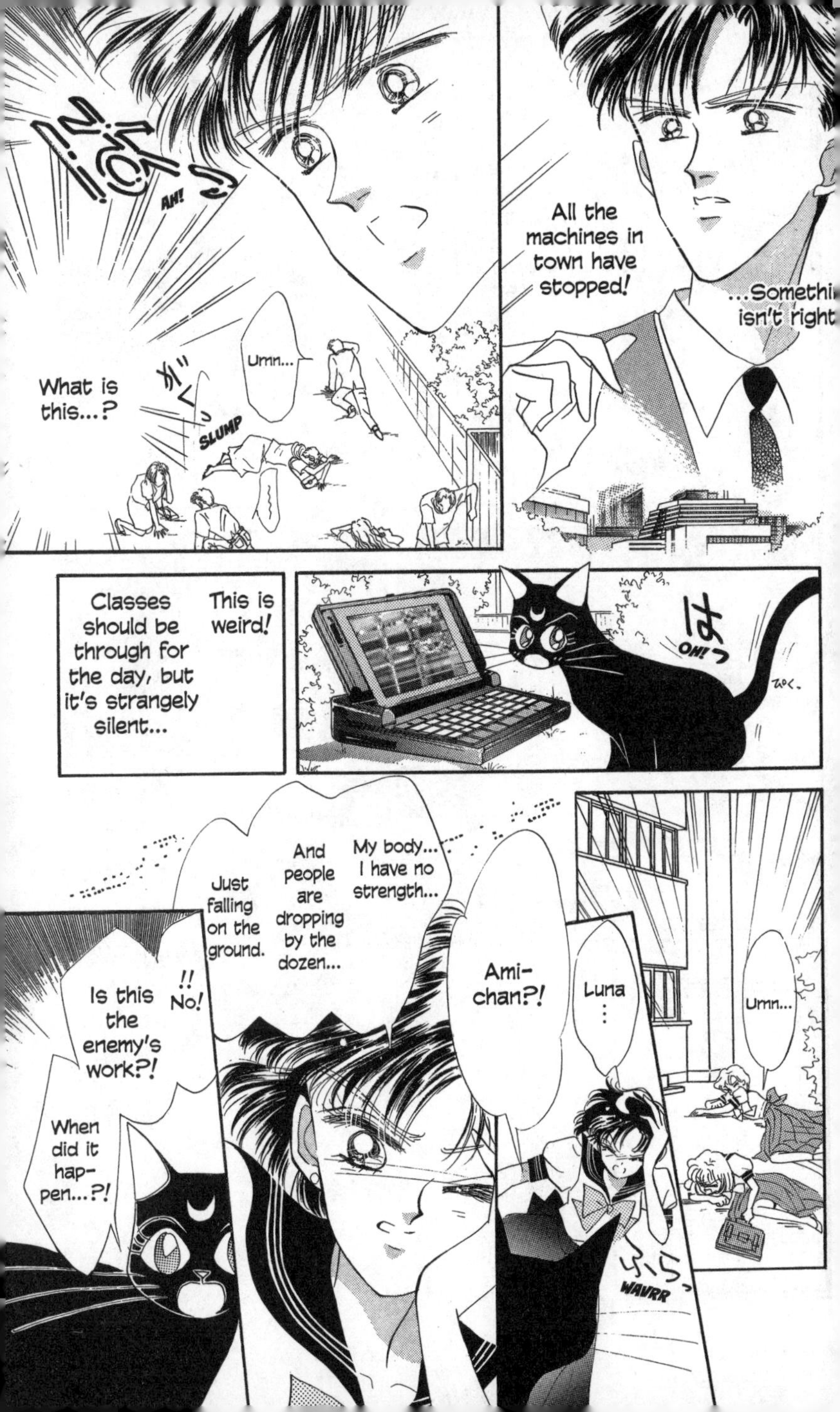

All the machines in town have stopped!
...Somethi isn't right
AH!
Umn...
What is this...?
SLUMP
OH!
This is weird!
Classes should be through for the day, but it's strangely silent...
Umn...
Luna ...
Ami-chan?!
WAVRR
My body... I have no strength...
And people are dropping by the dozen...
Just falling on the ground.
!! No!
Is this the enemy's work?!
When did it hap-pen...?!

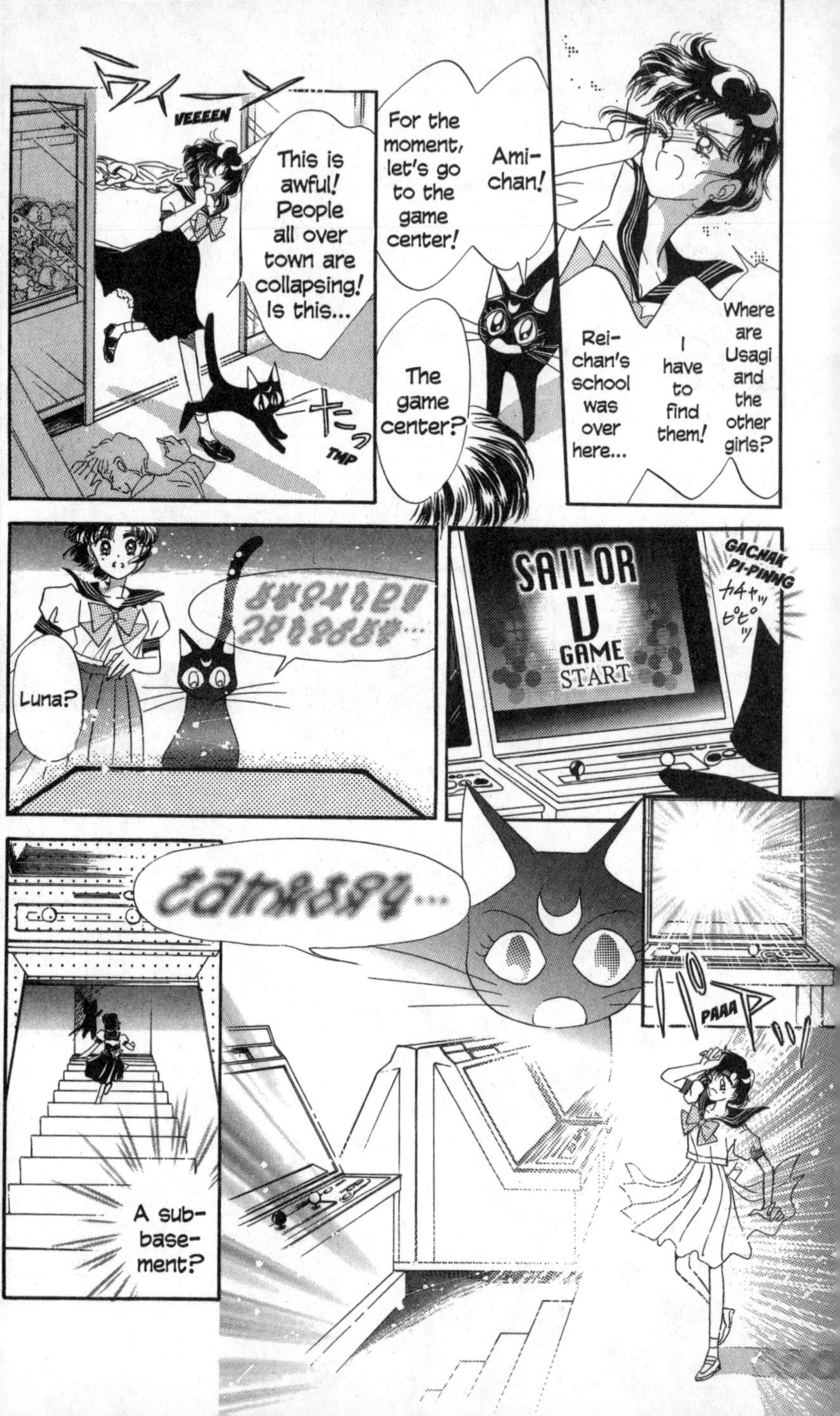
Where are Usagi and the other girls?
I have to find them!
Rei-chan's school was over here...
Ami-chan!
For the moment, let's go to the game center!
The game center?
VEEEEN
This is awful! People all over town are collapsing! Is this...
TMP
SAILOR V GAME START
GACHAK PI-PINNG
Luna?
PAAA
A sub-basement?

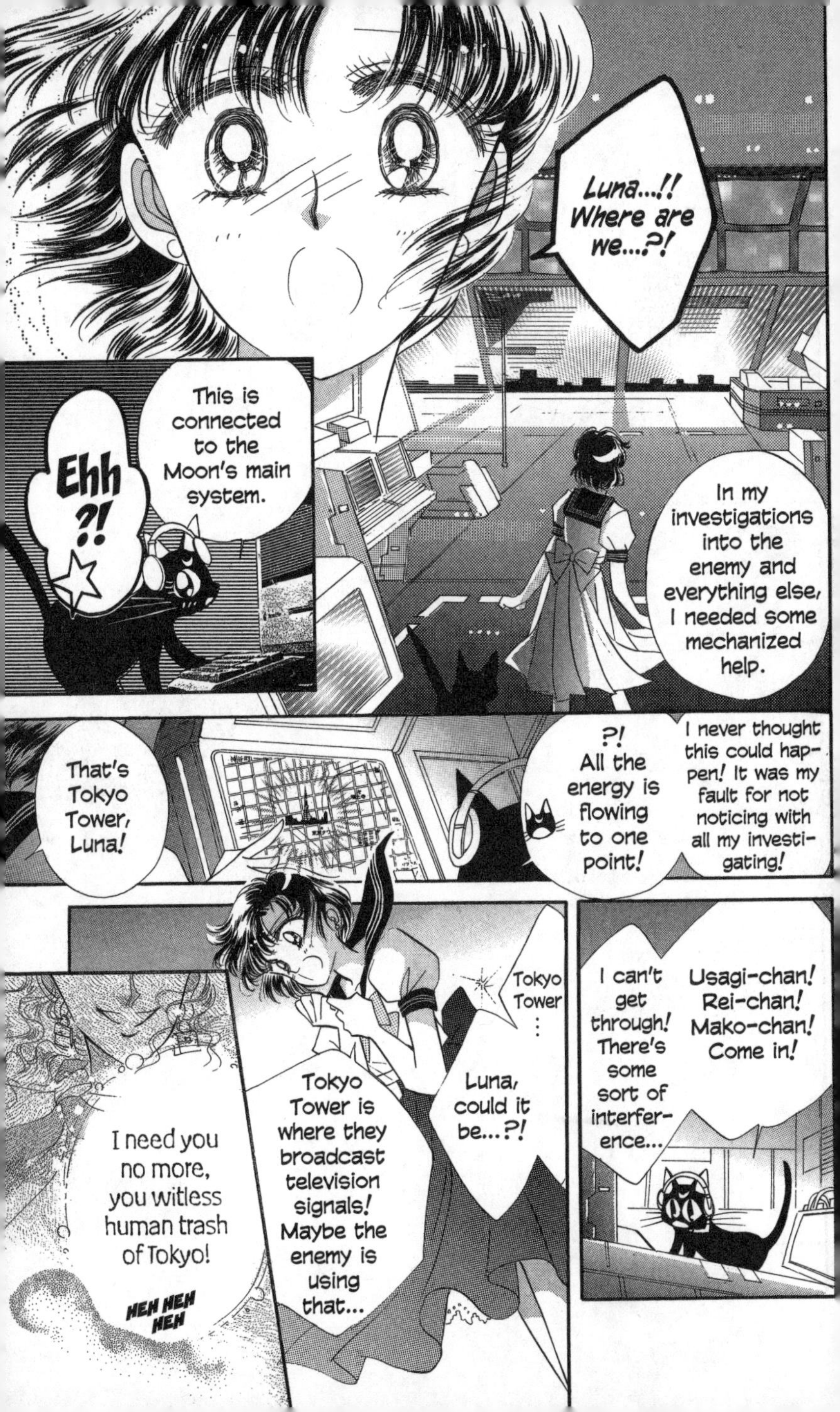
Luna...!! Where are we...?!
This is connected to the Moon's main system.
Ehh ?!
In my investigations into the enemy and everything else, I needed some mechanized help.
I never thought this could hap-pen! It was my fault for not noticing with all my investi-gating!
?! All the energy is flowing to one point!
That's Tokyo Tower, Luna!
Usagi-chan! Rei-chan! Mako-chan! Come in!
I can't get through! There's some sort of interfer-ence...
Tokyo Tower...
Luna, could it be...?!
Tokyo Tower is where they broadcast television signals! Maybe the enemy is using that...
I need you no more, you witless human trash of Tokyo!
HEH HEH HEH

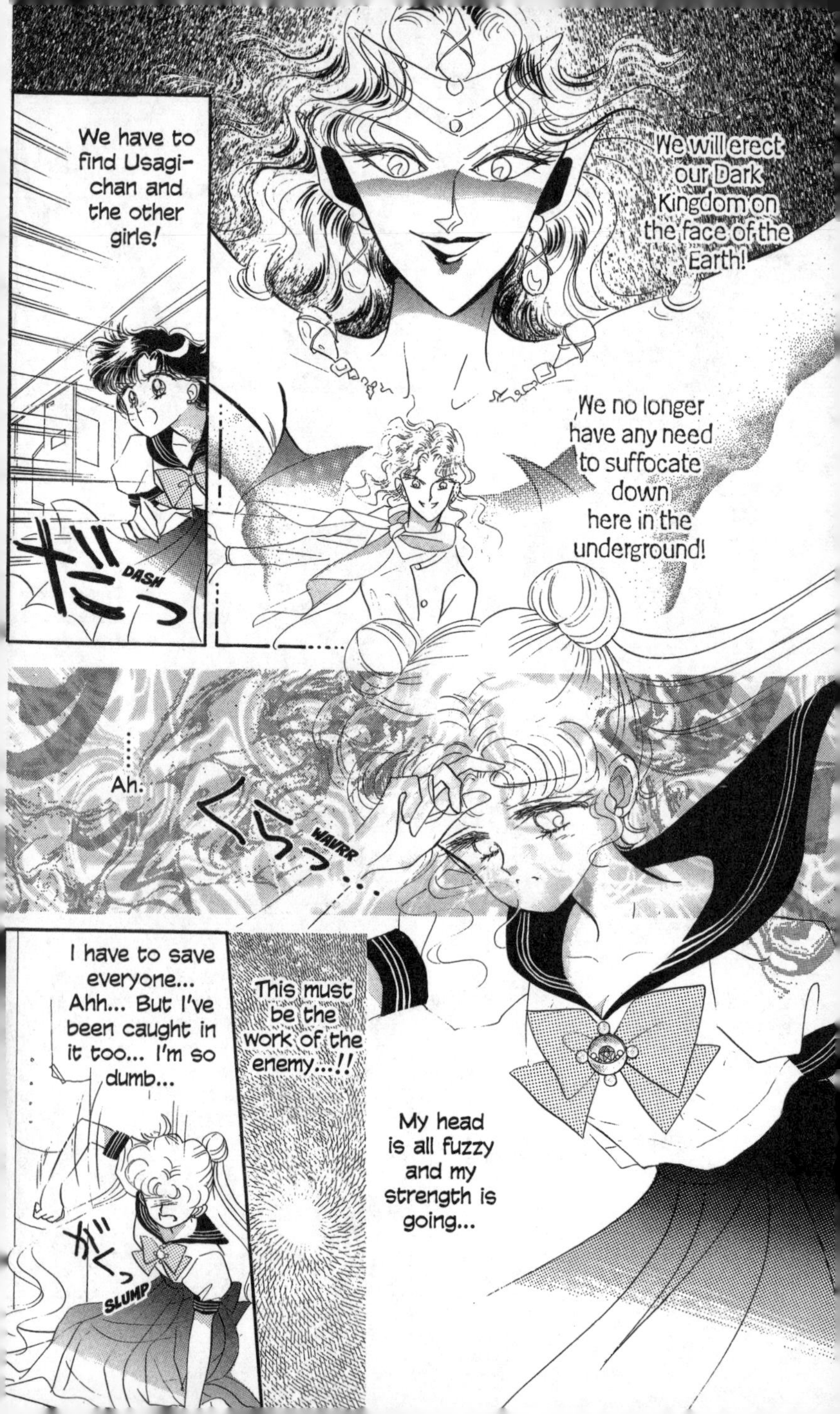

We will erect our Dark Kingdom on the face of the Earth!
We no longer have any need to suffocate down here in the underground!
We have to find Usagi-chan and the other girls!
だっ
DASH
Ah.
くらっ
WAVRR
My head is all fuzzy and my strength is going...
This must be the work of the enemy...!!
I have to save everyone... Ahh... But I've been caught in it too... I'm so dumb...
がくっ
SLUMP

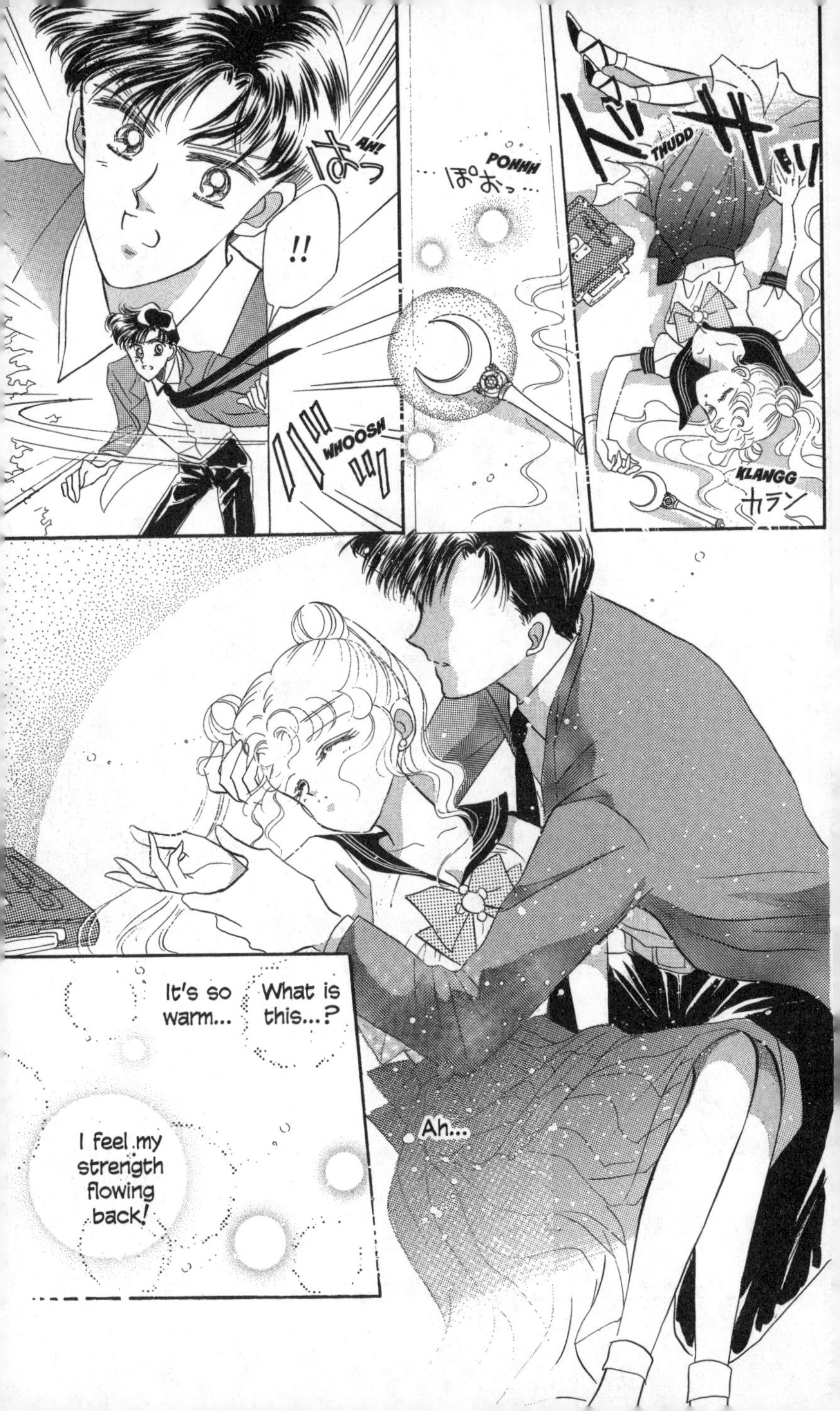
THUDD
KLANGG
カラン
POHHH
ぽおっ
AH!
はっ
!!
WHOOSH
What is this...?
It's so warm...
Ah...
I feel my strength flowing back!

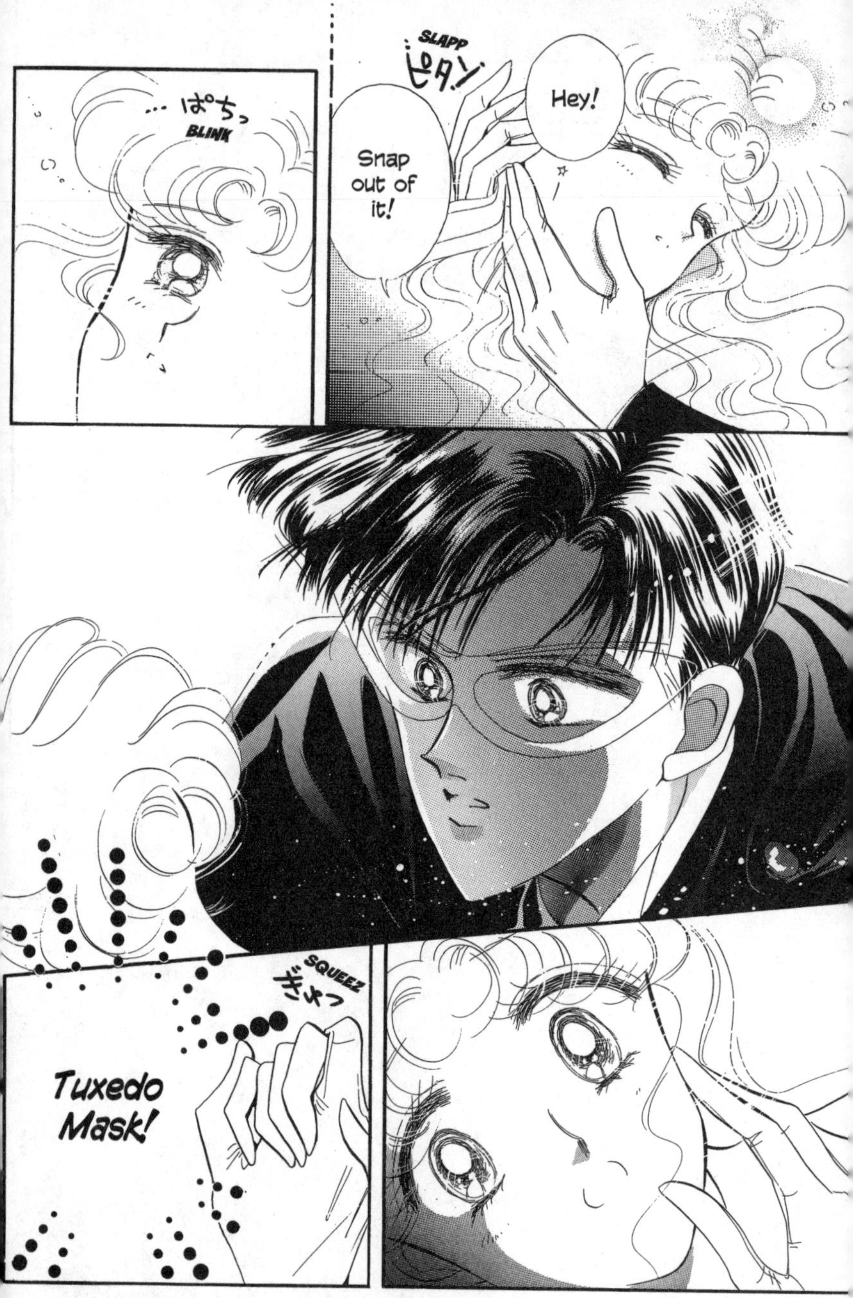
Hey!
SLAPP ピタン
Snap out of it!
… ぱちっ
BLINK
ぎゅっ
SQUEEZ
Tuxedo Mask!

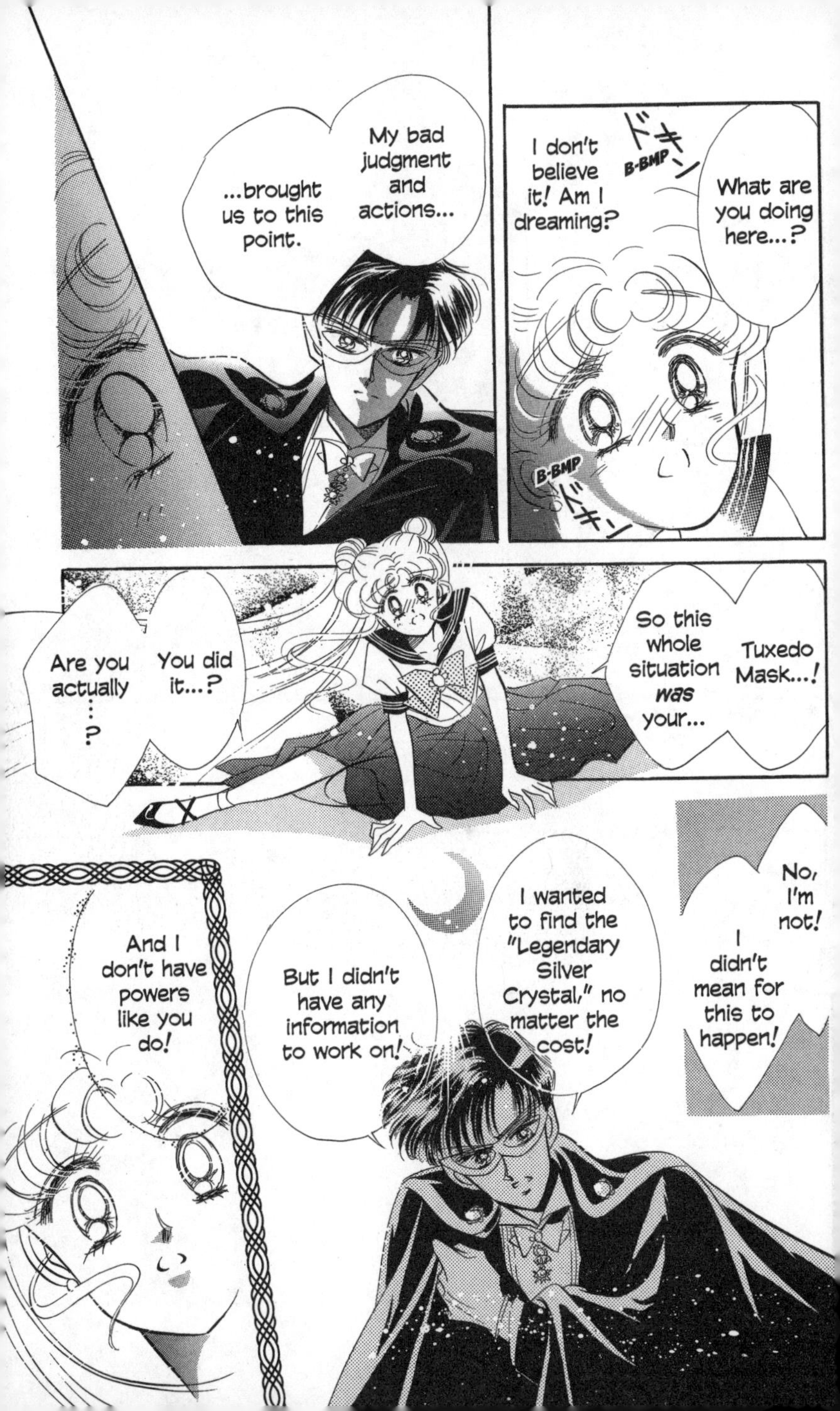
What are you doing here...?
ドキン
B-BMP
I don't believe it! Am I dreaming?
B-BMP
ドキン
My bad judgment and actions...
...brought us to this point.
Tuxedo Mask...!
So this whole situation *was* your...
You did it...?
Are you actually ...?
No, I'm not!
I didn't mean for this to happen!
I wanted to find the "Legendary Silver Crystal," no matter the cost!
But I didn't have any information to work on!
And I don't have powers like you do!

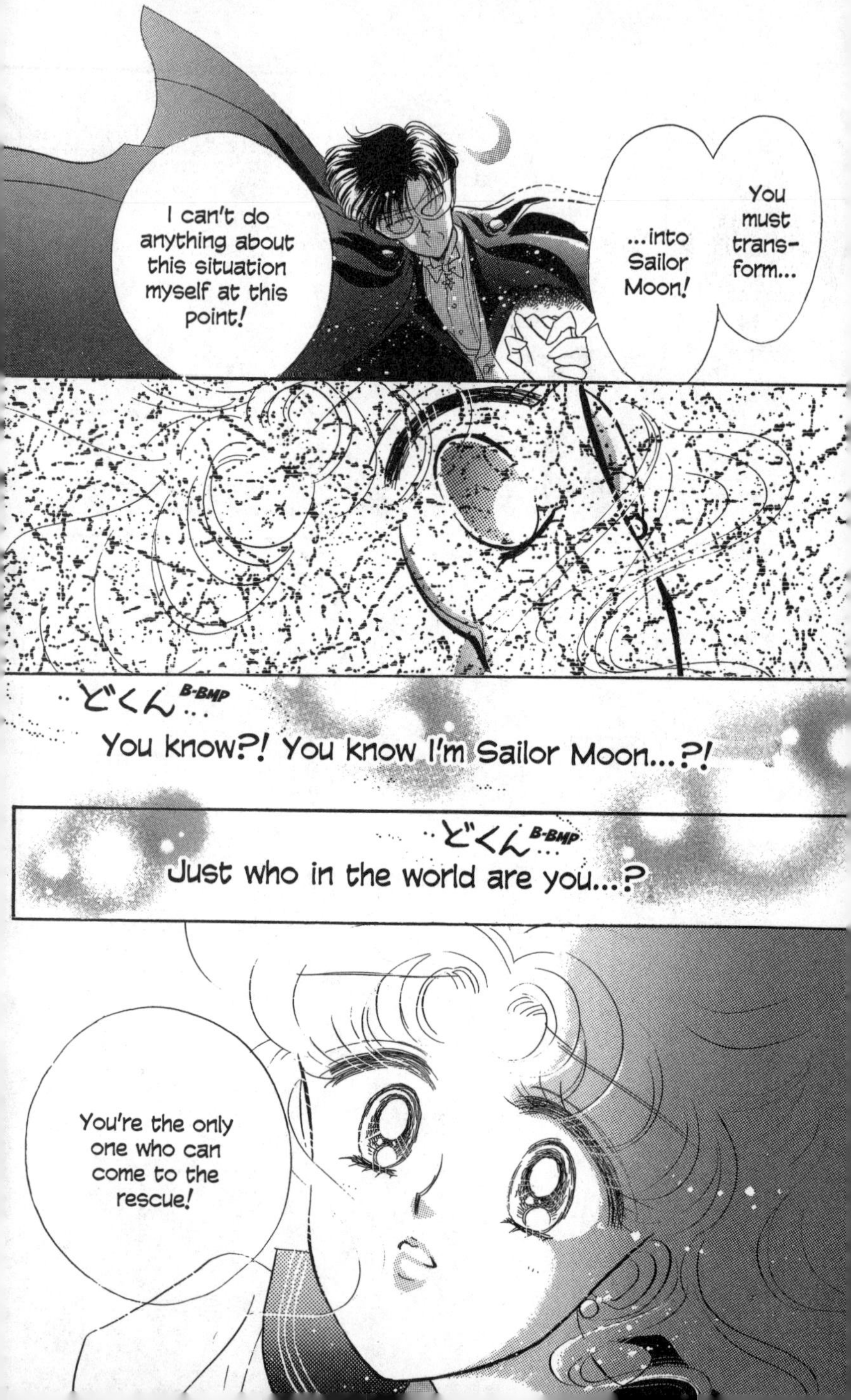
You must transform...
...into Sailor Moon!
I can't do anything about this situation myself at this point!
どくん B-BMP
You know?! You know I'm Sailor Moon...?!
どくん B-BMP
Just who in the world are you...?
You're the only one who can come to the rescue!

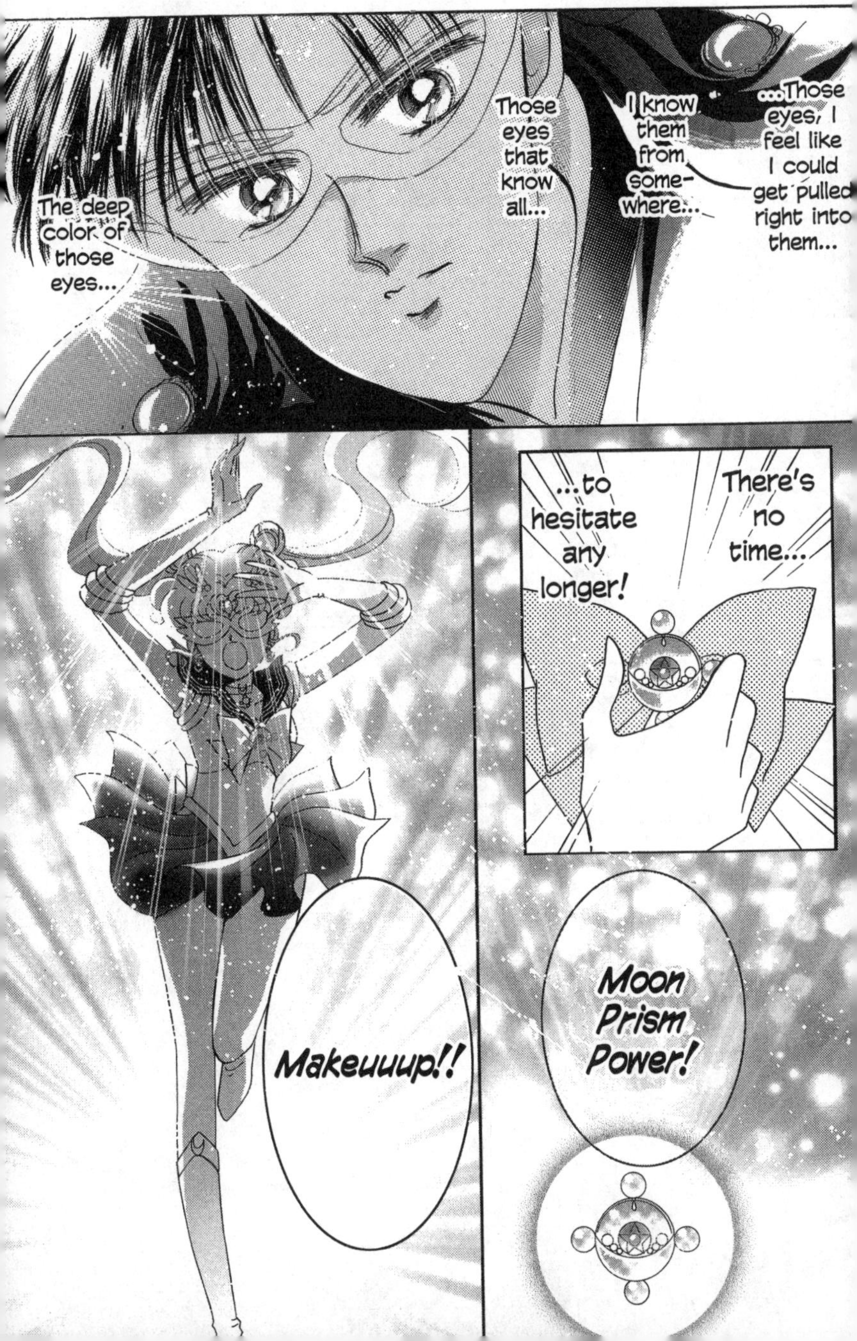
...Those eyes, I feel like I could get pulled right into them...
I know them from some-where...
Those eyes that know all...
The deep color of those eyes...
There's no time...
...to hesitate any longer!
Moon Prism Power!
Makeuuup!!

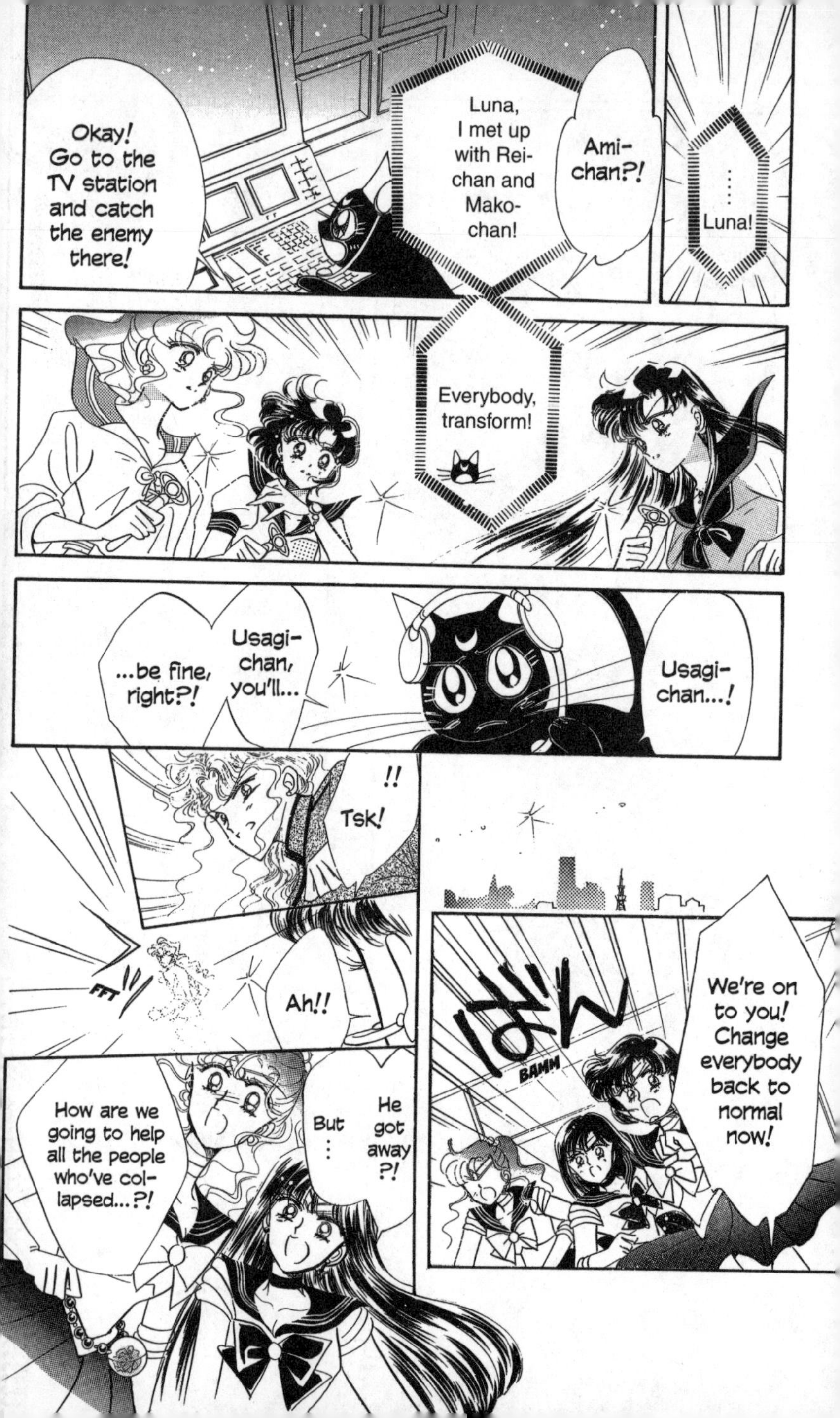

....Luna!
Ami-chan?!
Luna, I met up with Rei-chan and Mako-chan!
Okay! Go to the TV station and catch the enemy there!
Everybody, transform!
Usagi-chan...!
Usagi-chan, you'll...
...be fine, right?!
We're on to you! Change everybody back to normal now!
ばん
BAMM
!!
Tsk!
Ah!!
FFT
He got away?!
But...
How are we going to help all the people who've col-lapsed...?!

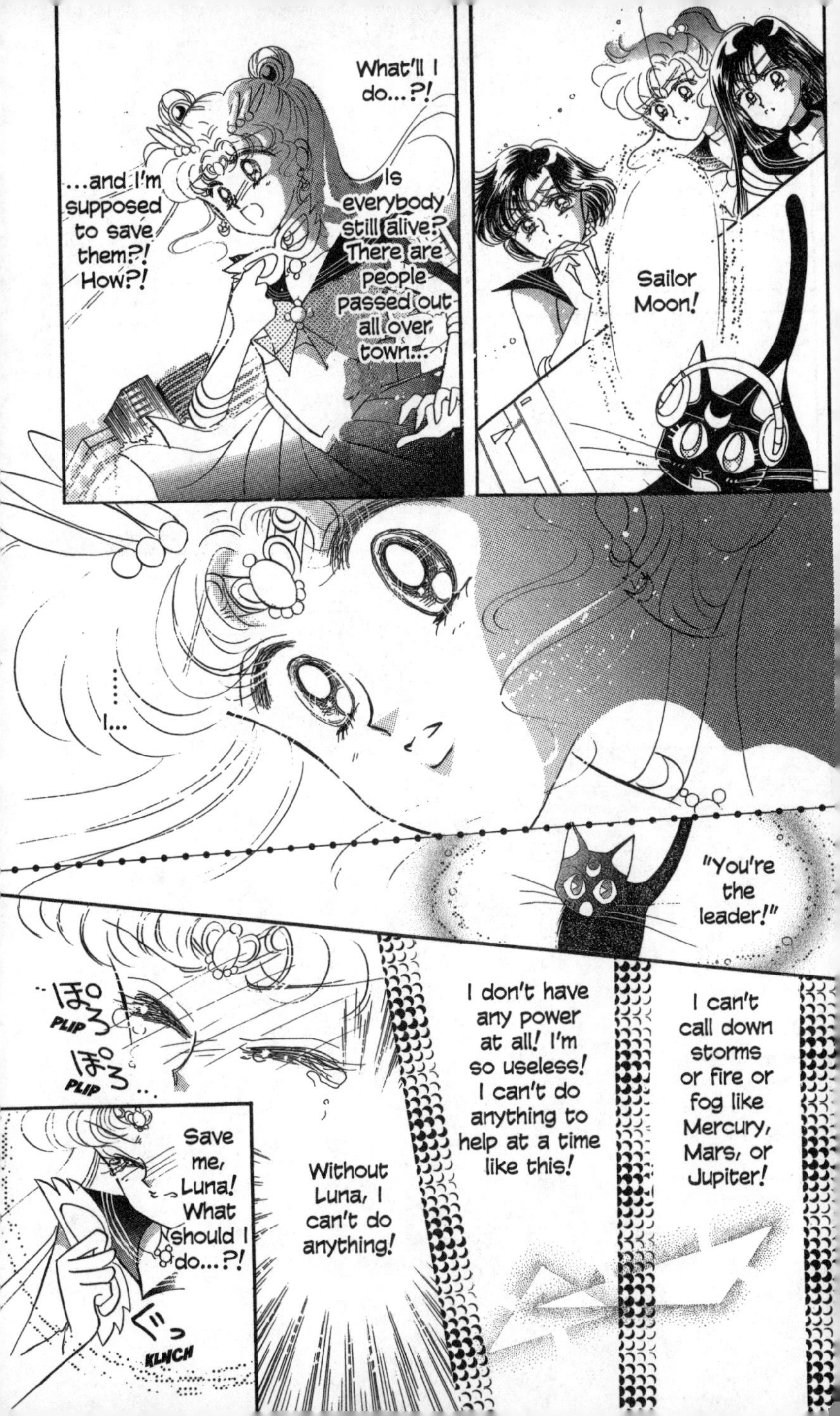
Sailor Moon!
What'll I do...?!
Is everybody still alive? There are people passed out all over town...
...and I'm supposed to save them?! How?!
I...
"You're the leader!"
I can't call down storms or fire or fog like Mercury, Mars, or Jupiter!
I don't have any power at all! I'm so useless! I can't do anything to help at a time like this!
Without Luna, I can't do anything!
ぽろ PLIP
ぽろ PLIP
Save me, Luna! What should I do...?!
ぐっ KLNCH

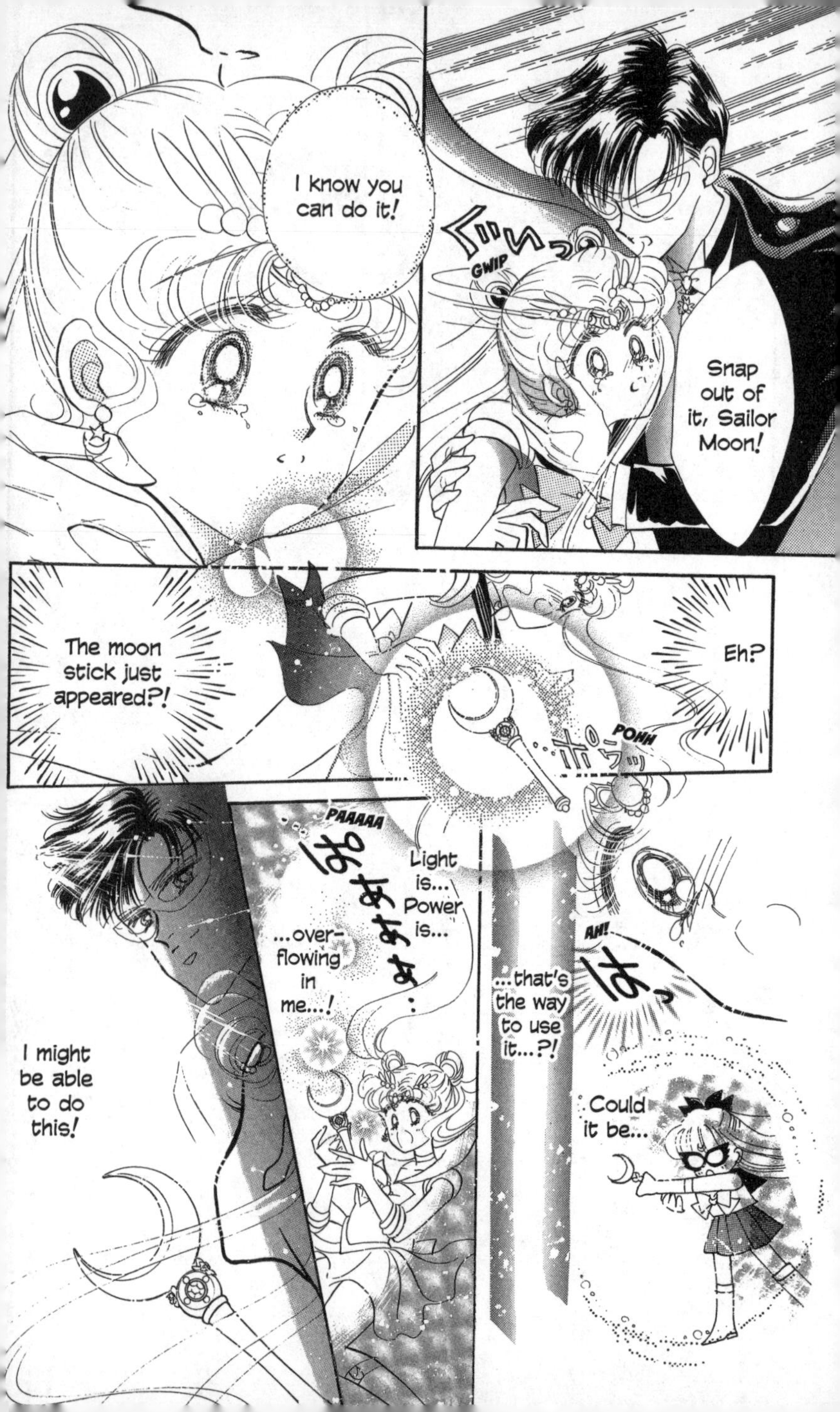
GWIP
Snap out of it, Sailor Moon!
I know you can do it!
Eh?
PONH
The moon stick just appeared?!
AH!
Could it be...
...that's the way to use it...?!
PAAAAA
Light is... Power is...
...over-flowing in me...!
I might be able to do this!

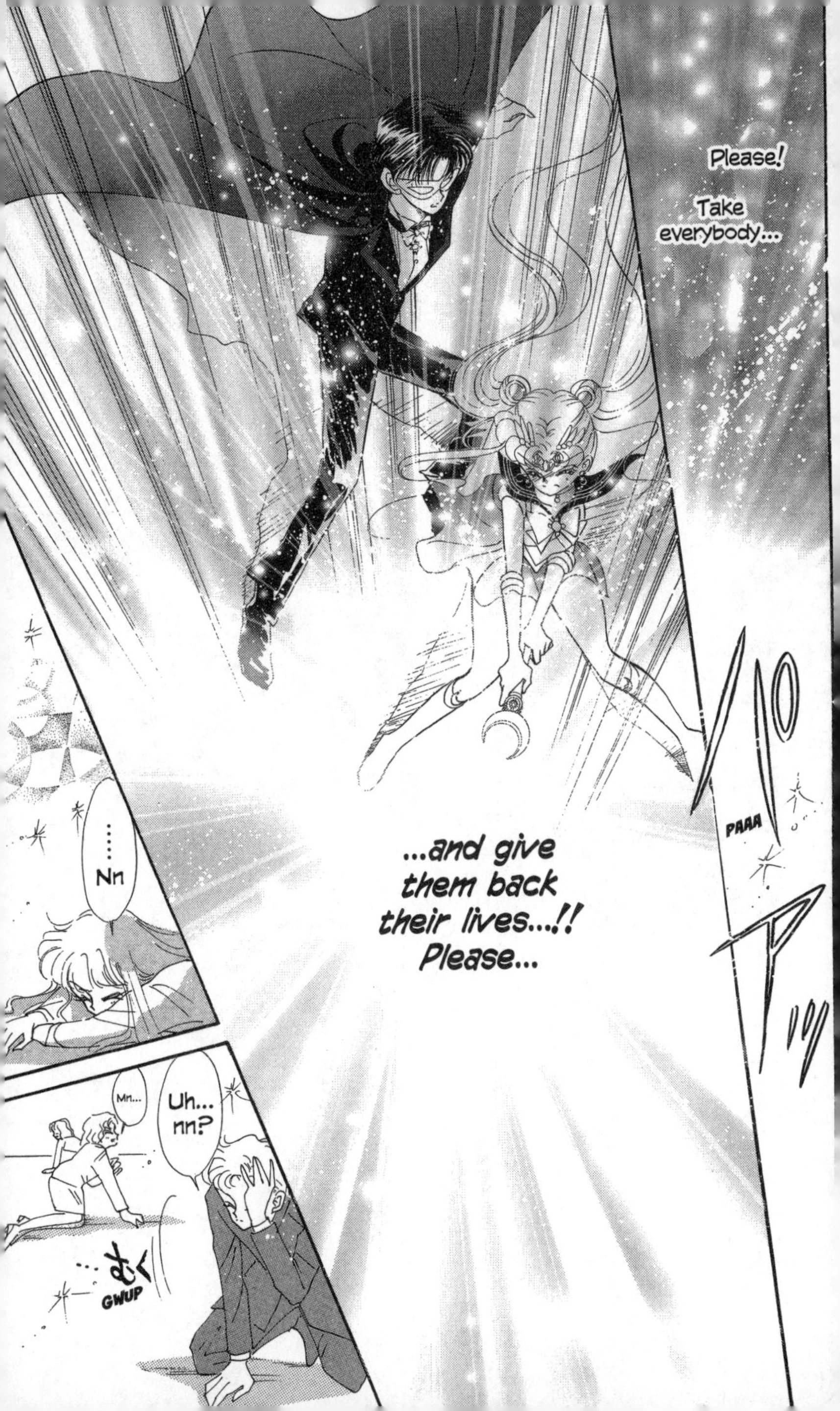
Please!
Take everybody...
...and give them back their lives...!! Please...
PAAA
Nn
Uh... nn?
Mn...
GWUP

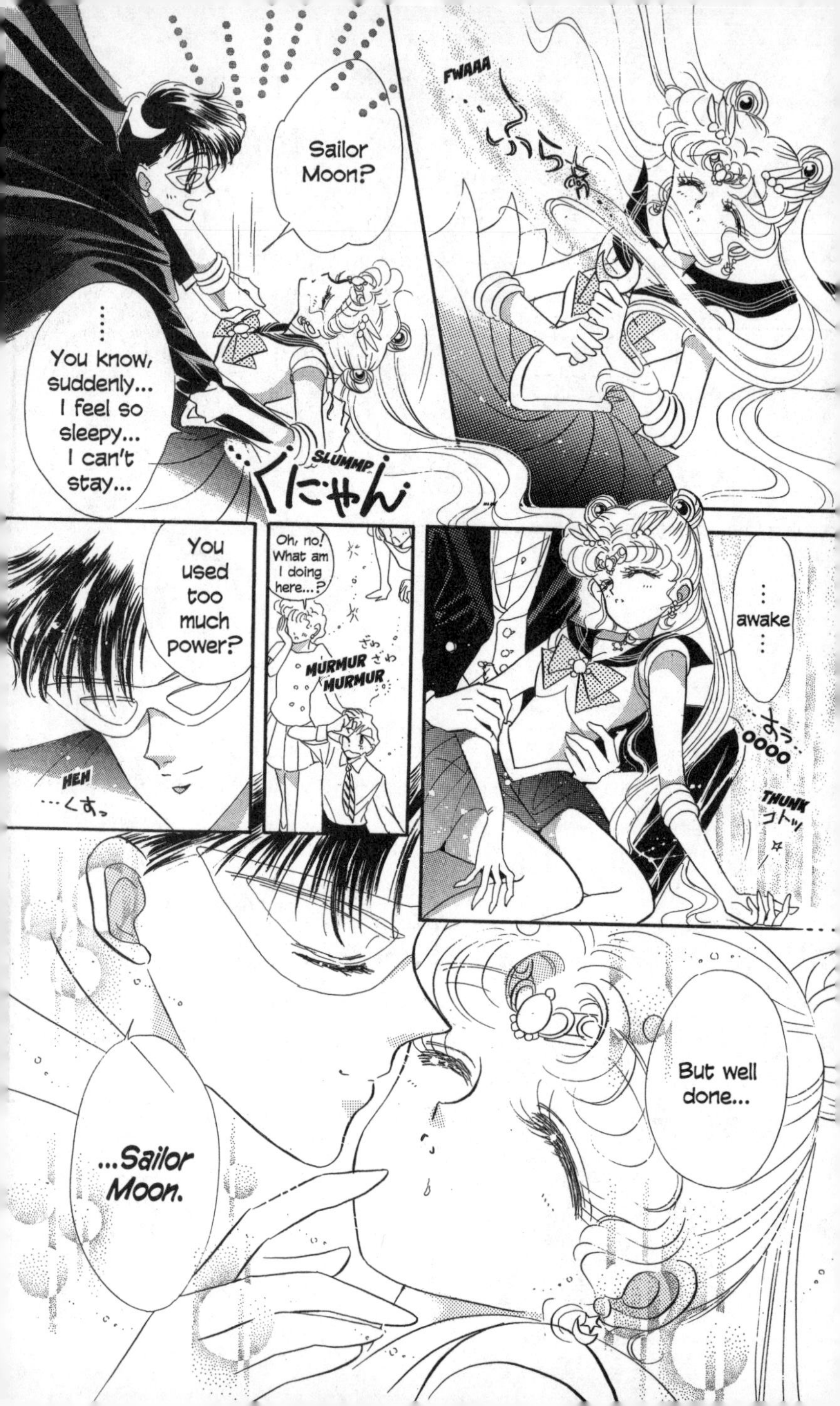
FWAAA
Sailor Moon?
...
You know, suddenly... I feel so sleepy... I can't stay...
SLUMMP
くにゃん
...
awake
...
OOOO
THUNK
コトッ
Oh, no! What am I doing here...?
MURMUR MURMUR
You used too much power?
HEH
…くすっ
But well done...
...Sailor Moon.

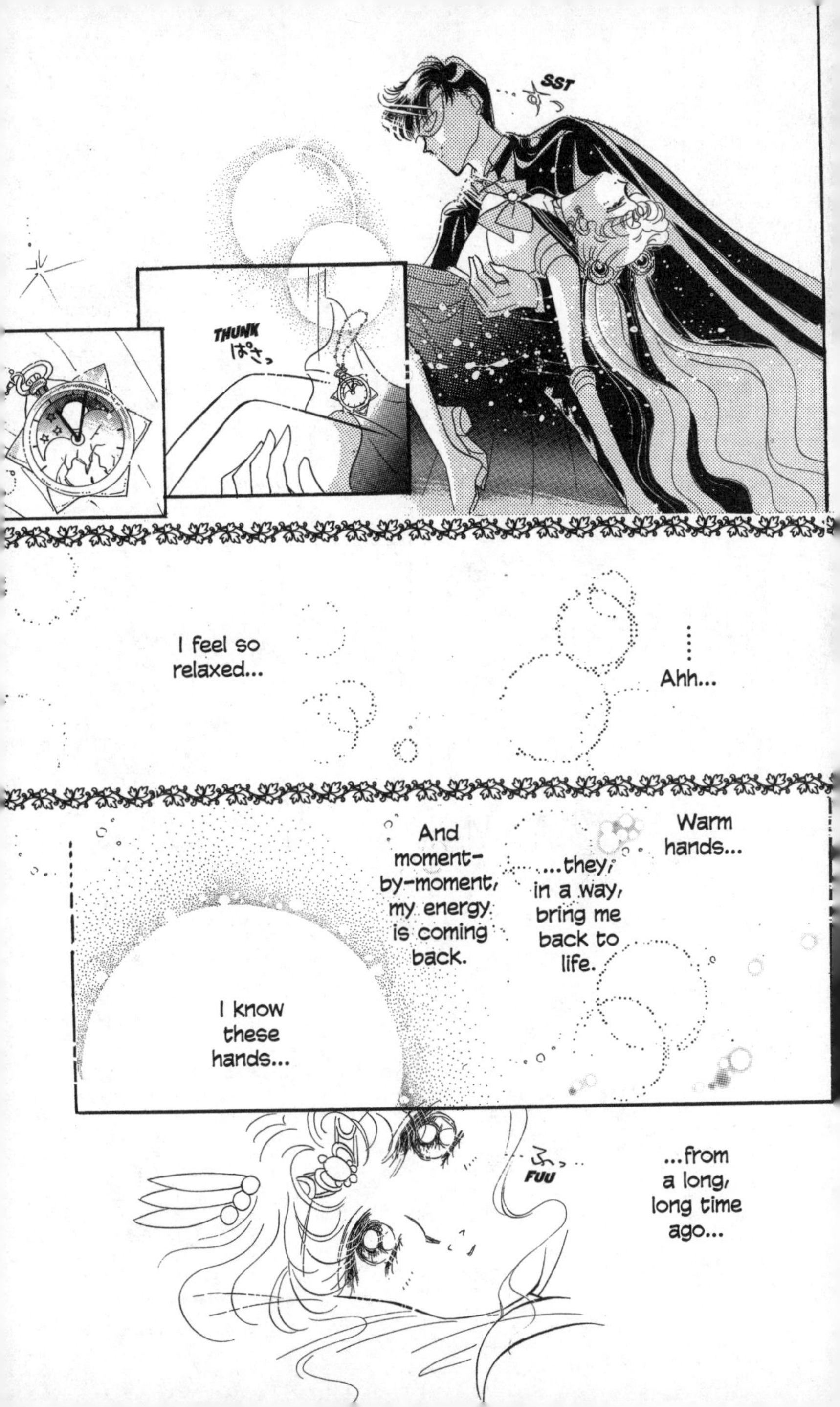
SST
THUNK
ぱさっ
Ahh...
I feel so relaxed...
Warm hands...
...they, in a way, bring me back to life.
And moment-by-moment, my energy is coming back.
I know these hands...
...from a long, long time ago...
ふっ
FUU

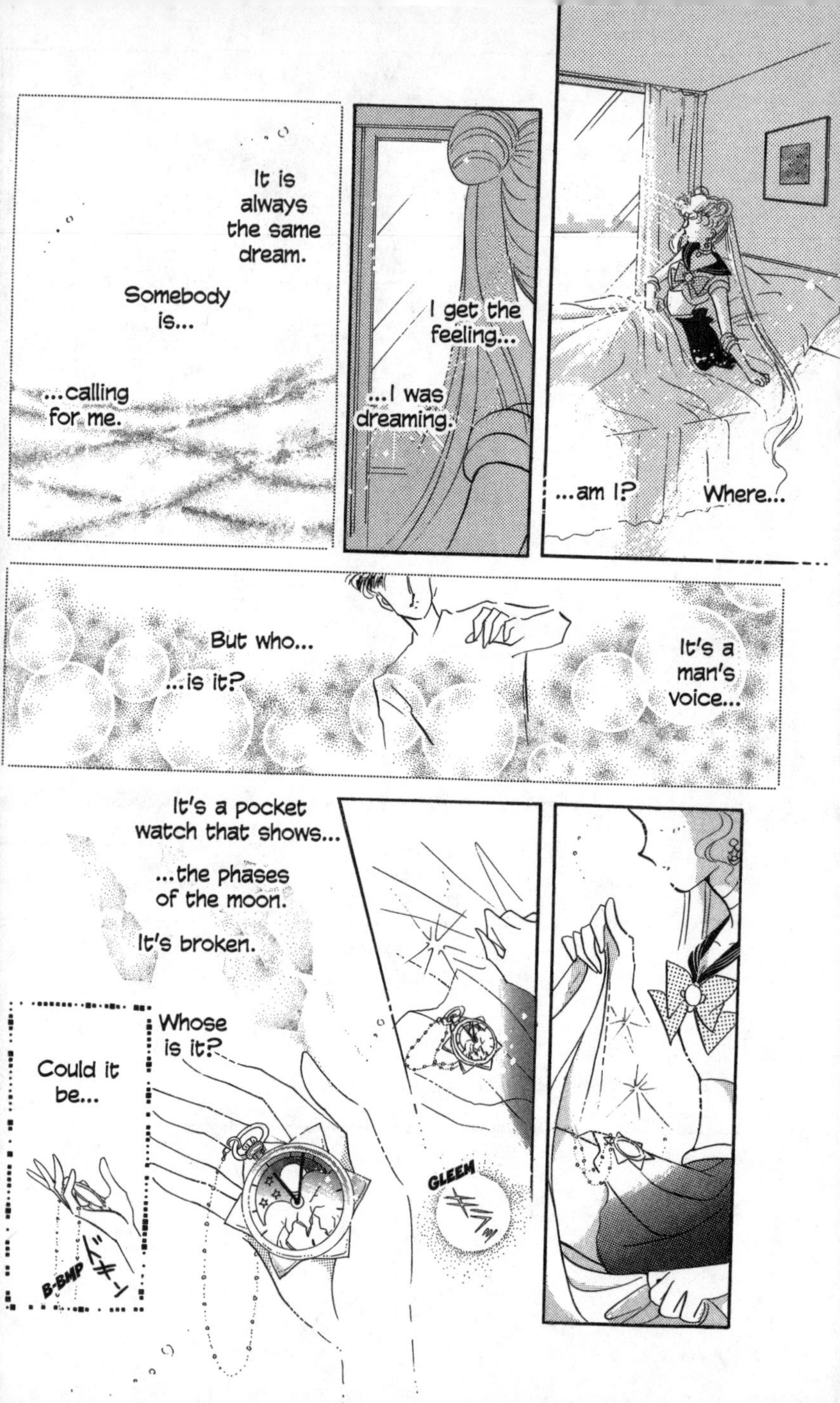
Where...
...am I?
I get the feeling...
...I was dreaming.
It is always the same dream.
Somebody is...
...calling for me.
It's a man's voice...
But who...
...is it?
GLEEM
It's a pocket watch that shows...
...the phases of the moon.
It's broken.
Whose is it?
Could it be...
B-BMP

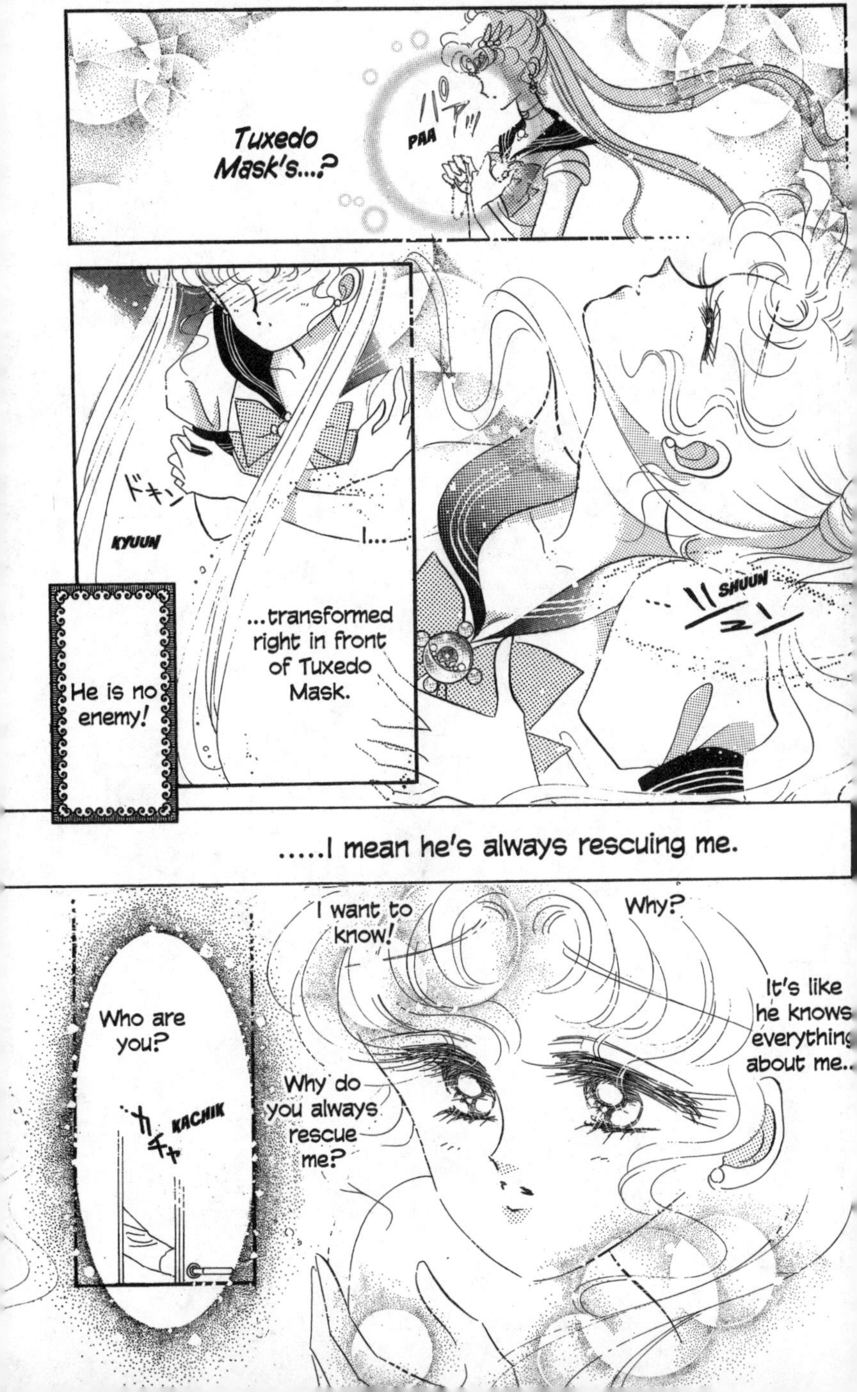
パァッ
PAA
Tuxedo Mask's...?
SHUUN
I...
...transformed right in front of Tuxedo Mask.
ドキン
KYUUN
He is no enemy!
.....I mean he's always rescuing me.
Why?
It's like he knows everythin about me..
I want to know!
Why do you always rescue me?
Who are you?
カチャ
KACHIK

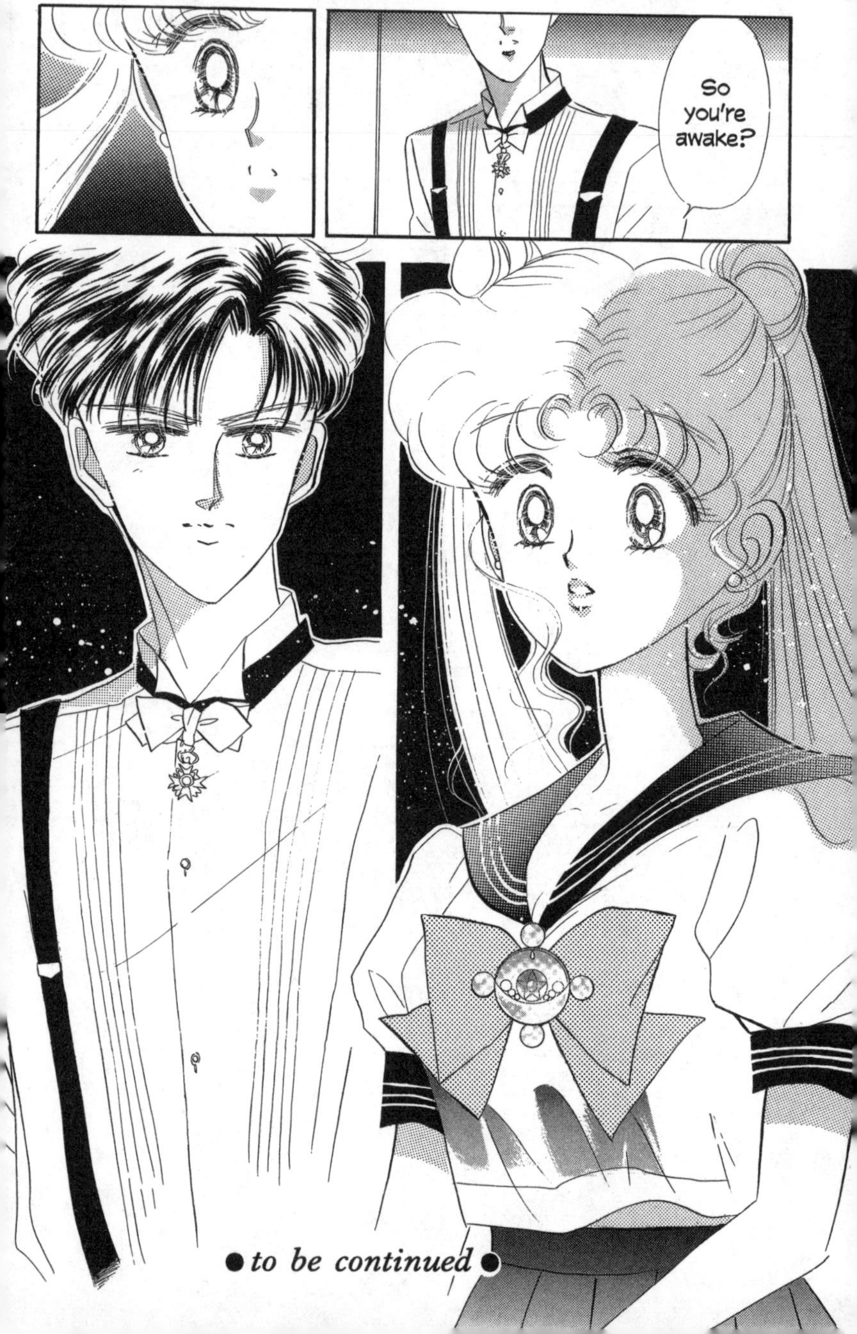
So you're awake?
●to be continued●

Translation Notes

Japanese is a tricky language for most Westerners, and translation is often more art than science. For your edification and reading pleasure, here are notes on some of the places where we could have gone in a different direction with our translation of the work, or where a Japanese cultural reference is used.

Sports, page 3

Some of the most popular tabloid-style newspapers in Japan are called "Sports" papers. They do cover the sports scene intensely, but they also cover news to a certain extent and a lot of celebrity gossip.

Usagi Tsukino, page 7

Usagi's name is a bit of a pun. Usagi means "Rabbit." Although the characters of her last name mean "Field of the Moon," the sound of *tsukino* would come out to mean, "of the Moon." So in Japanese name order, Tsukino Usagi would mean "The Rabbit of the Moon." To the Japanese, the dark and light spaces on the Moon look like a rabbit making mochi (where it looks like a face to western eyes giving rise to "The Man in the Moon" legends), and rabbits are as associated with the Moon in Japanese minds as green cheese is in American minds.

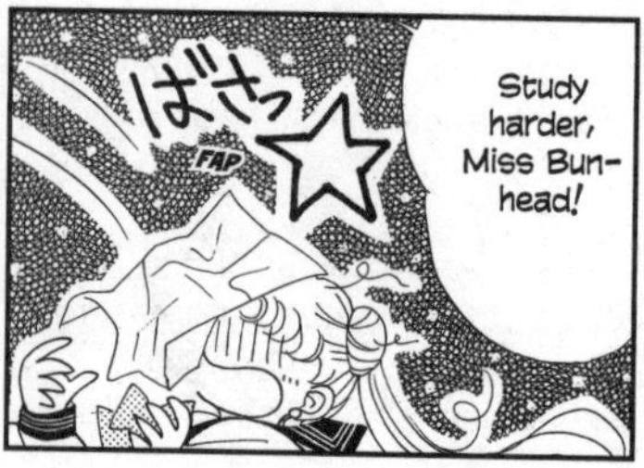
Study harder, Miss Bun-head!
ばさっ
FAP

Bun-Head, page 16

Usagi's hair style is called "dango," or "dumpling" style. However the Western word for such a hairstyle is "buns," so this translation has Mamoru Chiba chidingly referring to Usagi as "Bun-head."

Lupin, page 42

Most likely, she's referring to the manga hit by the artist Monkey Punch, *Lupin III*, but it's possible she is referring to the original French novels from which Monkey Punch drew his inspiration about a dashing thief in turn-of-the-20th-century France.

Princess, Royal Chocolate, page 51

The original pun played on how the word princess (pronounced "purinsesu" by the Japanese) sounds like the word "pudding" (pronounced "purin" by the Japanese). Unfortunately, they don't sound all that similar in English.

Seminar (Night School), page 53

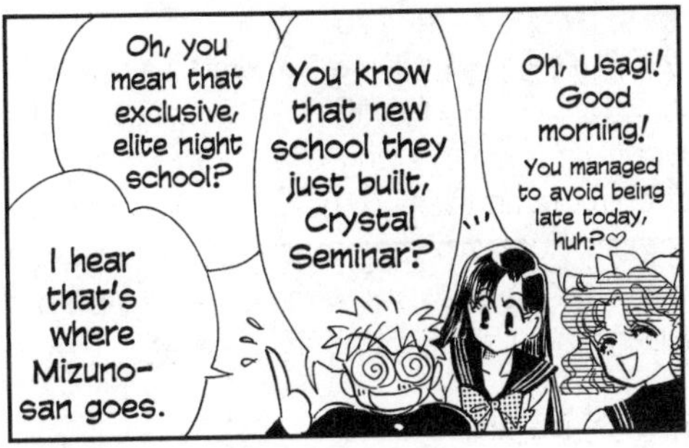
Oh, Usagi! Good morning!
You managed to avoid being late today, huh?♡
You know that new school they just built, Crystal Seminar?
Oh, you mean that exclusive, elite night school?
I hear that's where Mizuno-san goes.

Since one enters a new school, not by simply graduating the previous level, but by passing entrance exams to get into the new school, there is an industry of supplemental schools where students study specifically to pass these entrance exams. These are called *juku* or "seminars" (*zeminaaru*) in Japanese, and are usually translated with the pejorative term, "cram schools." The most popular are the evening or night-time schools meant to help prepare for college entrance exams, but since most people who get into elite colleges come from elite high schools, there are such schools that prepare for middle school and high school entrance exams as well.

Miko, page 95

These are young women, usually the daughters of Shinto priests, who assist with Shinto rites at the shrines and have certain rites that they perform themselves. Their red-and-white traditional garb has been fetishized by Japanese popular culture for centuries.

Clapping Twice at a Shrine, page 96

There are many rituals performed at Shinto shrines such as ritual purification at designated fountains and tossing a coin into a box at the shrine. And one of the rituals is clapping before making one's prayers. This ritual clapping is not universal for all Shinto shrines, but it is performed at a majority of shrines.

Glamorous, page 135

Although Furuhata was saying the English word "glamor," in this instance, it is one word where the Japanese use of the word and the English meaning has diverged slightly. Glamorous in English usually refers to an opulent lifestyle whereas in Japanese, it refers to a large bust size on women.

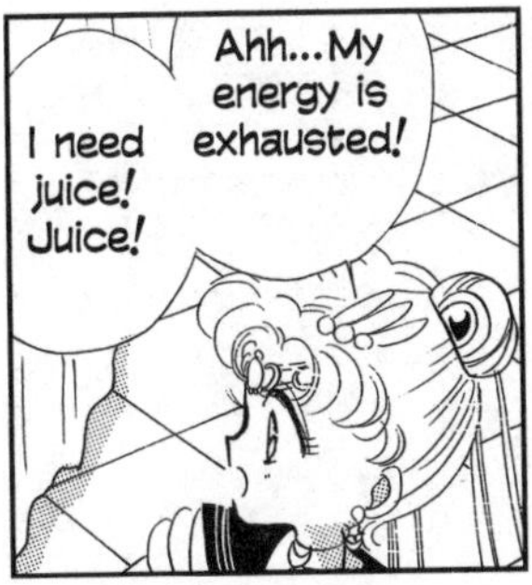
Ahh...My energy is exhausted!
I need juice! Juice!

Juice, page 158

Like "glamorous" above, the English word "juice," when used in Japan, doesn't simply refer to fruit or vegetable juices, but any sweet, non-alcoholic drink and can include sodas and bottled sweetened coffee or tea. Such sweet drinks are considered to be children's drinks (although they are probably mainly purchased by adults).

June Bride, page 170

This installment probably was published in June, but one reason why the Japanese would associate this installment with June is all the rain. June is traditionally the rainy season in Japan, with bouts of rain nearly everyday. Japanese readers would have seen the rain and assumed the season depicted was in or around June.

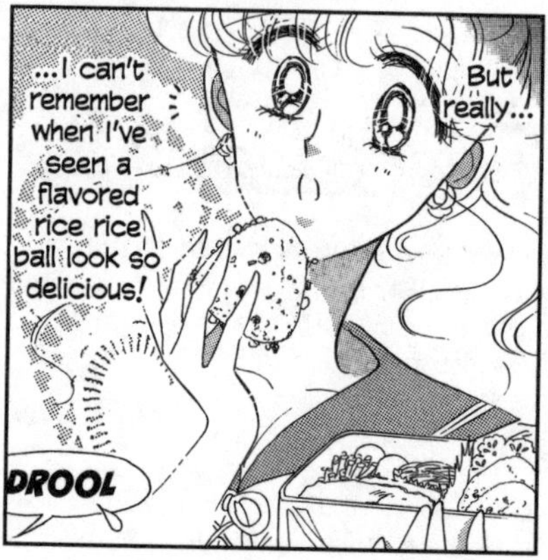

But really...
...I can't remember when I've seen a flavored rice rice ball look so delicious!
DROOL

Flavored Rice Rice Ball, page 173

What Makoto had brought for lunch was a rice ball made of rice cooked in broth along with vegetables (and sometimes meats) called *takigohan*. Most rice balls come with an *umeboshi* pickled apricot or other flavorings in the center, but *takigohan*, being flavored already, is usually just the rice formed into a ball.

Mizuno, Hino, and Kino, page 200

Just like Usagi's name is Tsukino, a name that can mean "of the Moon," the names of the other Guardians too have names representing their planets. In Japanese, Mercury is called Suisei (the water star), Mars is called Kasei (the fire star) and Jupiter is called Mokusei (the wood star). And appropriately, Mizuno means, "of water," Hino means, "of fire," and Kino means, "of wood."

Yomi-kai Newspaper, page 215

One of Japan's biggest newspapers is the Yomi-uri Newspaper (which would translate as "read-sell" newspaper). The newspaper in Usagi's world is the Yomi-kai Newspaper (which would translate out to "read-buy").

Tokyo Tower, page 221

Built in 1958, Tokyo Tower has been a central tourist attraction for the Tokyo area ever since. It was built as a broadcast tower, and continued to broadcast analog television signals until Japan ended its analog broadcasts in July of 2011. Because digital broadcasts rely to a great extent on line-of-sight angles, the Tokyo Tower proved to be too small to become Tokyo's digital broadcast tower, so the Tokyo Sky Tree tower was constructed to replace the Tokyo Tower's TV broadcast duties.

Preview of *Sailor Moon 2*

We're pleased to present you a preview from *Sailor Moon 2*. Please check our website (www.kodanshacomics.com) to see when this volume will be available in English. For now, you'll have to make do with Japanese!

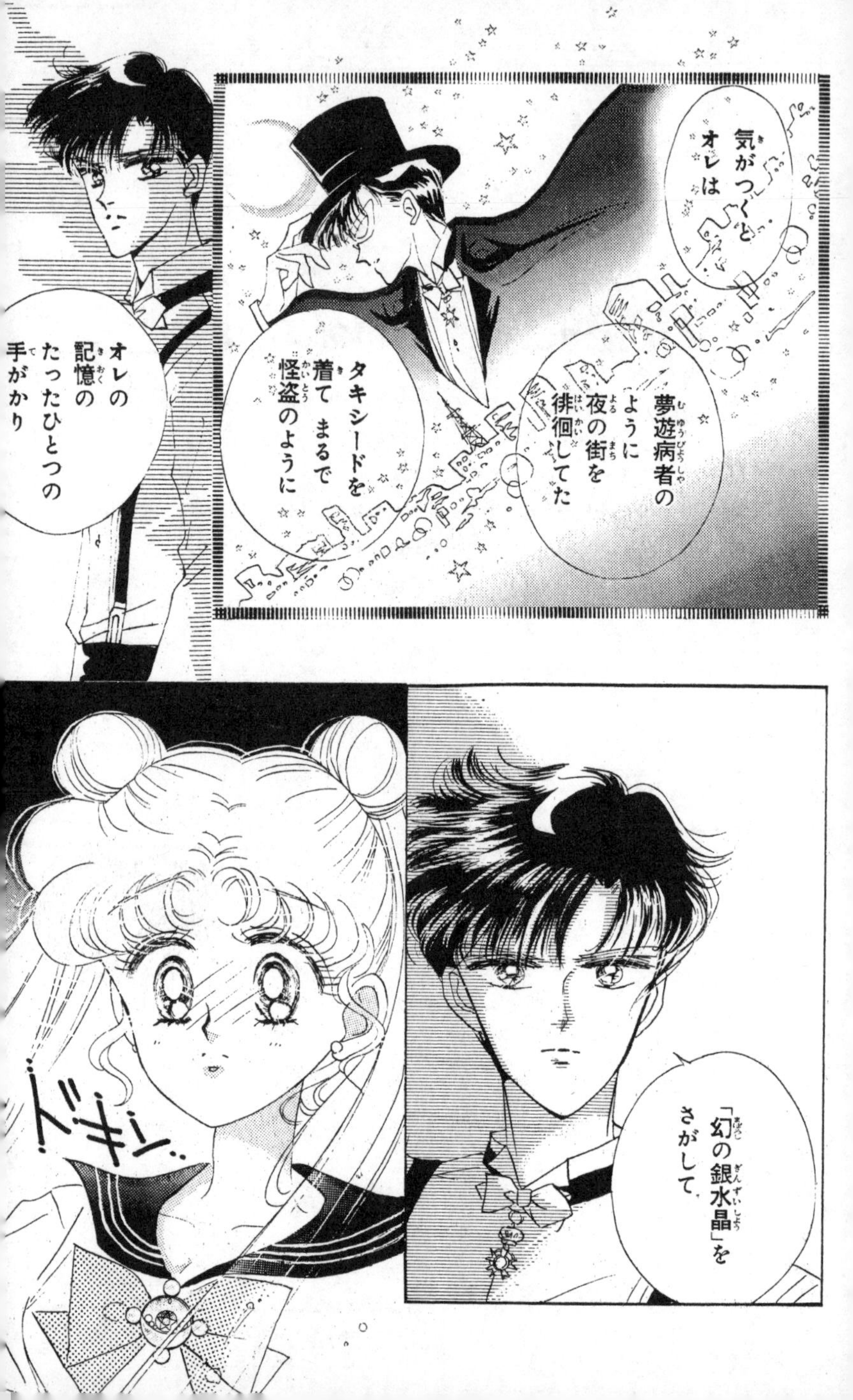
気がつくと オレは
夢遊病者のように 夜の街を徘徊してた
タキシードを着て まるで怪盗のように
オレの記憶の たったひとつの手がかり
「幻の銀水晶」を さがして
ドキン…

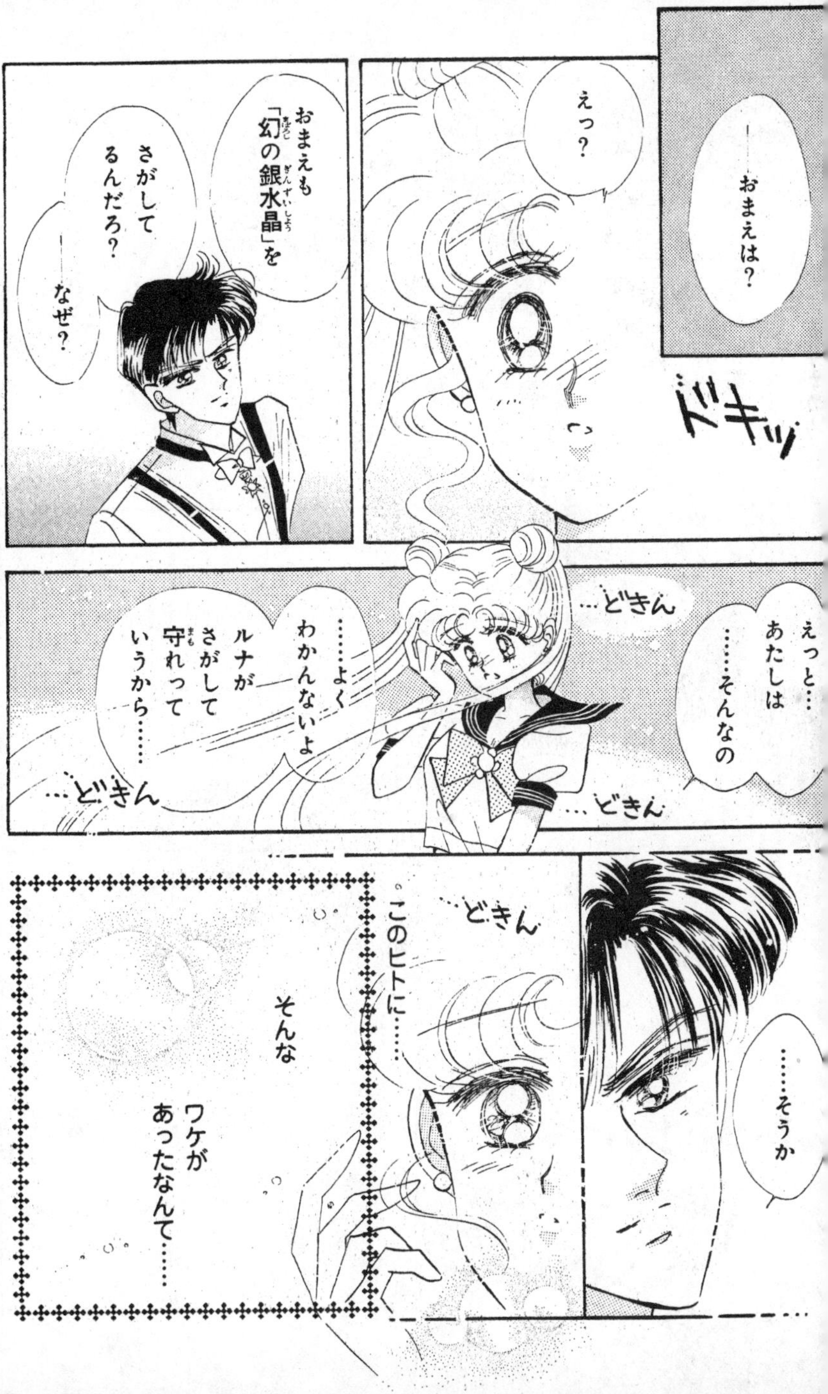
──おまえは？
ドキッ
えっ？
おまえも「幻の銀水晶」をさがしてるんだろ？
──なぜ？
えっと…あたしは……そんなの
…どきん
……よくわかんないよ ルナがさがして守れっていうから……
…どきん
…どきん
……そうか
…どきん
このヒトに……
そんな ワケがあったなんて……

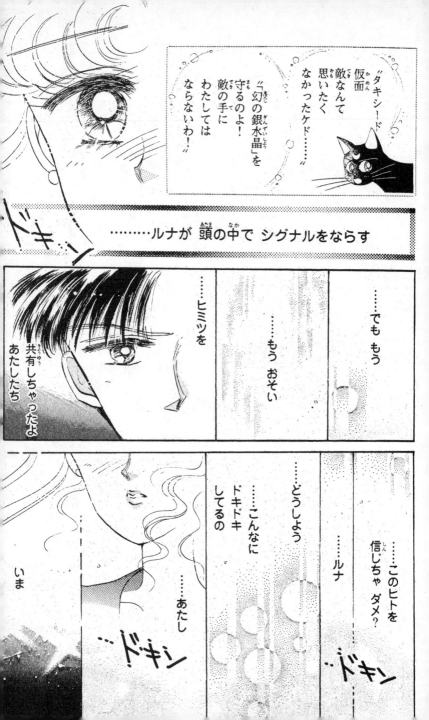

"タキシード仮面……"

敵なんて思いたくなかったケド……

"幻の銀水晶"を守るのよ！敵の手にわたしてはならないわ！"

………ルナが 頭の中で シグナルをならす

……ヒミツを共有しちゃったよ あたしたち

……もう おそい

……でも もう

……いま

……あたし

……こんなにドキドキしてるの

……どうしよう

……ルナ

……このヒトを信じちゃ ダメ？

ドキン

ドキン

ドキン

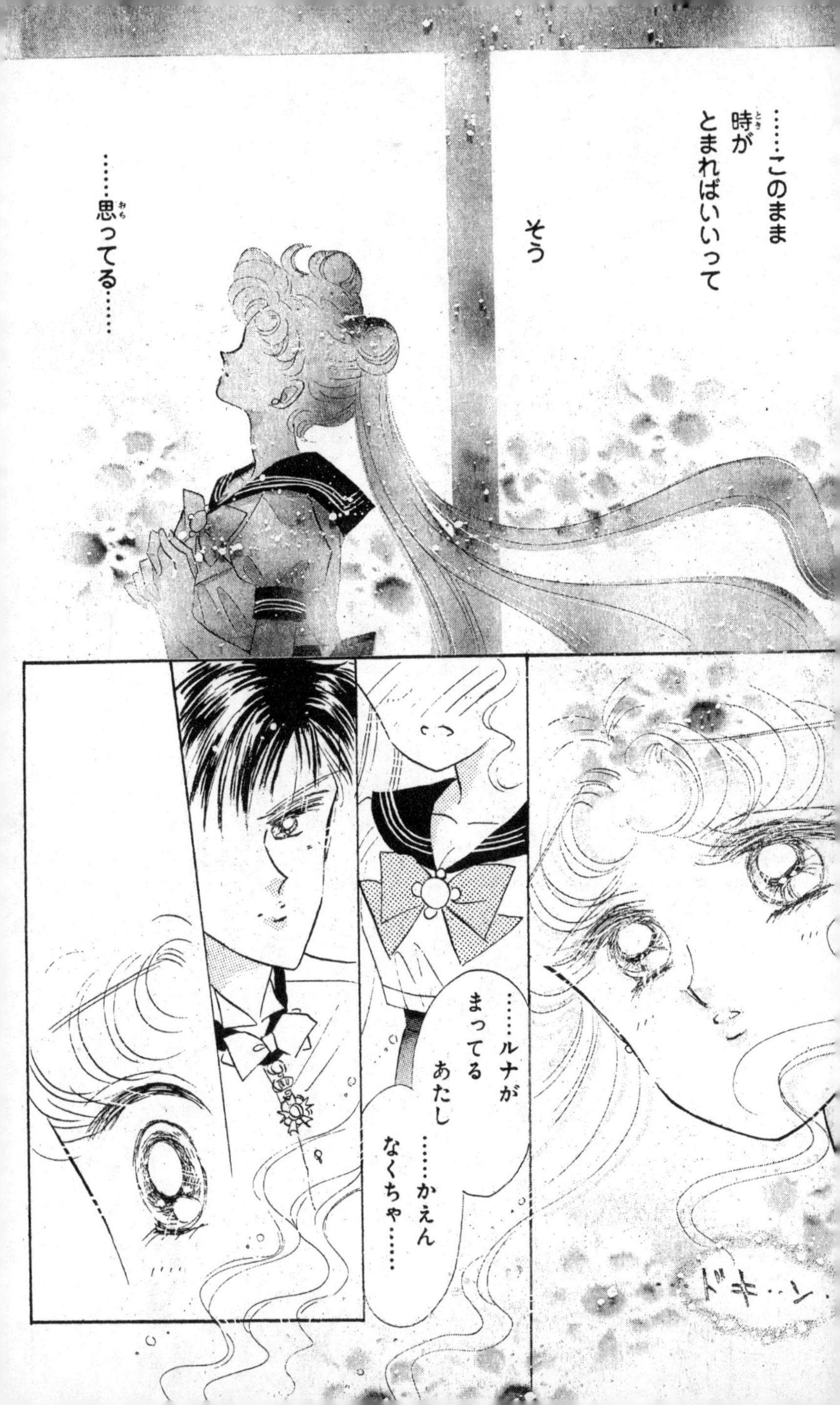
……このまま
時が
とまればいいって
そう
……思ってる……
ドキ…ン
……ルナが
まってる
あたし
……かえん
なくちゃ……

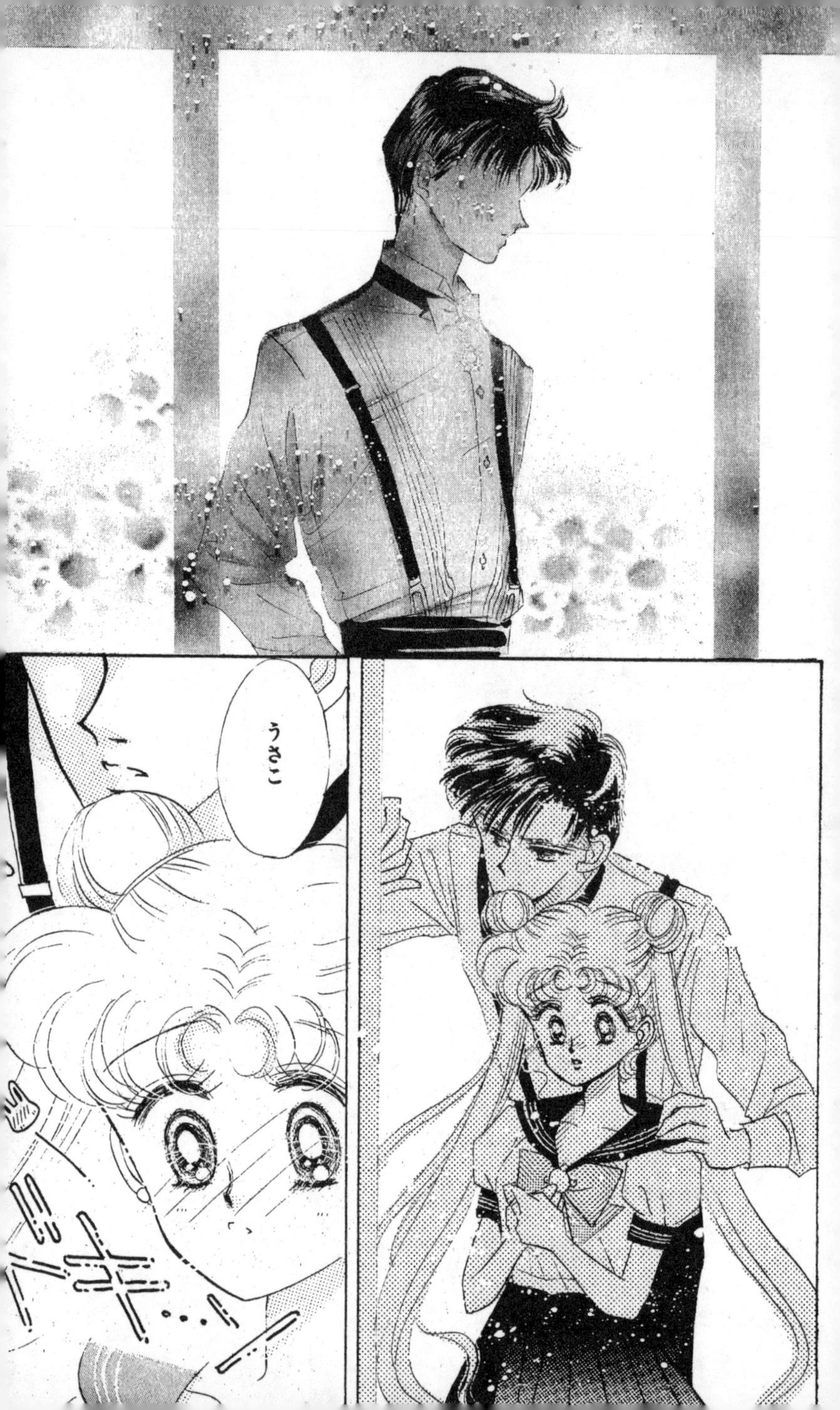
うさこ

Pretty Guardian Sailor Moon volume 1 is a work of fiction. Names, characters, places, and incidents are the products of the author's imagination or are used fictitiously. Any resemblance to actual events, locales, or persons, living or dead, is entirely coincidental.

A Kodansha Trade Paperback Original.

Published in the United States by Kodansha Comics, an imprint of Kodansha USA Publishing, LLC, New York.

Publication rights for this English edition arranged through Kodansha Ltd., Tokyo.

First published in Japan in 2003 by Kodansha Ltd., Tokyo, as *Bishoujosenshi Sailor Moon Shinsoban*, volume 1.

ISBN 978-1-93542-974-6

Printed in Canada.

www.kodanshacomics.com

12

Translator/Adapter: William Flanagan
Lettering: North Market Street Graphics

TOMARE!
STOP

You're going the wrong way!

Manga is a completely different type of reading experience.

To start at the beginning,
Go to the end!

That's right! Authentic manga is read the traditional Japanese way—from right to left, exactly the opposite of how American books are read. It's easy to follow: Just go to the other end of the book and read each page—and each panel—from right side to left side, starting at the top right. Now you're experiencing manga as it was meant to be!